A Companion to the
Early Printed Book in Britain
1476–1558

A Companion to the Early Printed Book in Britain 1476–1558

Edited by Vincent Gillespie and Susan Powell

D. S. BREWER

First published 2014
D. S. Brewer, Cambridge
Paperback edition 2019

ISBN 978 1 84384 363 4 hardback
ISBN 978 1 84384 536 2 paperback

D. S. Brewer is an imprint of Boydell & Brewer Ltd
PO Box 9, Woodbridge, Suffolk IP12 3DF, UK
and of Boydell & Brewer Inc.
668 Mt Hope Avenue, Rochester, NY 14620–2731, USA
website: www.boydellandbrewer.com

The publisher has no responsibility for the continued existence or accuracy
of URLs for external or third-party internet websites referred to in this book,
and does not guarantee that any content on such websites is,
or will remain, accurate or appropriate

A CIP catalogue record for this book is available
from the British Library

This publication is printed on acid-free paper

Contents

Illustrations

The Printed Book as Artefact
4: Materials: Paper and Type
PAMELA ROBINSON

5: Bookbinding and Early Printing in England
ALEXANDRA GILLESPIE

6: Woodcuts and Decorative Techniques
MARTHA W. DRIVER

**16: Catholicism, the Printed Book and the Marian Restoration
LUCY WOODING**

The editors, contributors and publishers are grateful to all the institutions and
persons listed for permission to reproduce the materials in which they hold
copyright. Every effort has been made to trace the copyright holders; apologies
are offered for any omission, and the publishers will be pleased to add any
necessary acknowledgement in subsequent editions.

List of Contributors

Tamara Atkin is Lecturer in Late Medieval and Early Renaissance Literature, Department of English, Queen Mary, University of London.

Alan Coates is an Assistant Librarian, Rare Books & Printed Ephemera, in the Department of Special Collections at the Bodleian Library, University of Oxford.

Thomas Betteridge is Professor of Theatre at Brunel University.

Julia Boffey is Professor of Medieval Studies in the Department of English at Queen Mary, University of London.

James Clark is Professor of History at the University of Exeter.

A.S.G. Edwards is Professor of Medieval Manuscripts at the University of Kent, Canterbury.

Martha W. Driver is Distinguished Professor of English and of Gender and Women's Studies at Pace University in New York City.

Mary Erler is Professor of English at Fordham University, New York.

Alexandra Gillespie is an Associate Professor of English and Medieval Studies at the University of Toronto.

Vincent Gillespie is J.R.R. Tolkien Professor of English Literature and Language at the University of Oxford and a Fellow of Lady Margaret Hall.

Andrew Hope has taught history at the Universities of Oxford and Reading and is a former editor of the journal *Reformation*.

Brenda Hosington is Professeure associée at the Université de Montréal and Research Associate at the Centre for the Study of the Renaissance at the University of Warwick.

Susan Powell is Professor Emeritus of Medieval Texts and Culture at the University of Salford and a Research Associate at the Centre for Medieval Studies, University of York.

Pamela Robinson is a Senior Research Fellow at the Institute of English Studies, University of London.

Anne F. Sutton is Archivist and Historian Emerita of the Mercers' Company of London.

Daniel Wakelin is Jeremy Griffiths Professor of Medieval English Palaeography in the University of Oxford and a Fellow of St Hilda's College.

James Willoughby is a Research Fellow of New College, Oxford.

Lucy Wooding is Senior Lecturer in Early Modern History at King's College London.

Preface

SUSAN POWELL

This volume had its origins in a paper I gave at a conference held at the University of Oxford in April 2009. 'After Arundel: Religious Writing in Fifteenth-Century England' was organised by a committee which included Vincent Gillespie, and it resulted in a volume of essays of the same name, edited by Vincent Gillespie and Kantik Ghosh, published by Brepols in 2011. At the conference I was approached by Caroline Palmer, Editorial Director at Boydell & Brewer Ltd, who suggested a 'Companion' to the early printed book, the history of which I had sketched in my paper. This book is the result.

The material culture of the book trade has burgeoned as an area of diverse as well as specific research over the last twenty-five years. Arguably this began at the University of York in the 1970s with the scholarship of Derek Pearsall and the late Elizabeth Salter, whose postgraduate students, several now distinguished scholars themselves (two represented in this volume), explored significant new areas in manuscript production and culture. 1981 marked the first of the continuing York Manuscript Conferences, 'Manuscripts and Readers in Fifteenth-Century England'. The link to the printed book was inevitable and was explored in sessions at the International Congress on Medieval Studies held annually at Western Michigan University, Kalamazoo. Organised by Martha Driver and the late Sarah Horrall, the Early Book Society (several of whose members are represented in this volume) emerged from these sessions in 1987 and held the first of its biennial conferences at the University of Durham in 1989. The *Journal of the Early Book Society for the Study of Manuscripts and Printing History* appeared in 1998 (for 1997) and has become a major forum for research into the material and social culture of both manuscripts and printed books.

In this context a Companion to the Early Printed Book might well seem overdue. Inevitably, interests and focus have shifted over the past quarter-century. The first York conference had as its sub-title 'The Literary Implications of Manuscript Study': those implications have arguably been side-lined in much current manuscript research (although less so in the field of the early printed book). As Vincent Gillespie suggests in his Introduction, the early emphasis on Caxton as the purveyor and producer of literary works, primarily romances, for and by the aristocracy and gentle classes, has given way, rightly, to a more comprehensive view of Caxton as the forerunner, whose initiative led to a customer-driven trade in vernacular printed books focused on a wide middle-class audience. In this, Caxton's successor, the formerly marginalised Wynkyn de Worde, was a major figure from Caxton's death, probably in the spring of

1492, until his own in 1535. In this context, the publications of the late Norman Blake on both Caxton and de Worde were seminal.

However, the vernacular books published by Caxton, let alone his successors, were focused rather more on religious and devotional works than used to be admitted. Arguably, thirty years ago religion had been air-brushed out of medieval studies in English departments. It was there but lurking in the background, and the pretence seemed to be that it was really no more important in late medieval England than in late twentieth-century England. That has changed dramatically, and religion, rightly or wrongly a major element in the life of every individual in medieval and early modern England, has come to the fore. This volume takes full account of this, and in doing so considers too the Latin output that reached England, or was, to a much lesser extent, printed in England in this period.

The marginalisation of Latin was not ideological, as arguably that of religion was. It has been contingent on the loss of Latin scholarship (at least outside Continental Europe), so that medieval scholars, especially those of the religious and academic culture of the period, work in a milieu where most secondary, and even many primary, sources are lost to them. Digitisation is starting to correct this for at least primary sources, but translation from Latin is not a focus for many university departments or scholars these days. One can, however, at least be aware of the primacy of Latin in the debates and scholarship of the medieval world, and later, until, at least for religion, the importance of providing propaganda to the masses introduced the vernacular into this previously forbidden field. As late as 1772, however, Edmund Waller could express general sentiments about Latin in relation to English: 'Poets that lasting marble seek, / Must carve in LATIN or in GREEK: /we write in sand . . .'.

Our choice of the time-period 1476 to 1558 allows our contributors to explore the development of the craft of printing and binding, the trade in books in England and from abroad, the different clientele of the early printed book, intellectual and social innovations, and, of course, the varying responses to the bewildering changes in religious orthodoxy from the safe reign of Edward IV through the tumultuous events of Henry VIII's reign to the brief oppositional reigns of Edward VI and Mary Tudor. This volume therefore illuminates the adapting and evolving role of print and the printed word in a 'long Middle Ages'. We trust that it will illuminate, as well as interest and instruct, its readers.

Acknowledgements

The Editors wish to acknowledge with gratitude the co-operation and scholarship of their contributors, the support and advice of Caroline Palmer, Editorial Director at Boydell & Brewer, and the expertise of Rohais Haughton, Production Editor. We are indebted to the News International Fund of the Faculty of English Language and Literature at the University of Oxford for funding which enabled us to employ Dr Ayoush Sarmada Lazikani to prepare the volume for submission to the press and generate the index and lists of printed books and manuscripts.

The publishers acknowledge the generous financial support of the
Marc Fitch Fund in the production of this volume

MARC FITCH FUND

Abbreviations and Short Titles

BL	British Library
BMC XI	*Catalogue of Books Printed in the XVth Century Now in the British Library. Part XI: England*, ed. Lotte Hellinga ('t Goy-Houten, The Netherlands, 2007)
Bod-inc.	Alan Coates et al., *A Catalogue of Books Printed in the Fifteenth Century Now in the Bodleian Library*, 6 vols (Oxford, 2005)
BodL	Bodleian Library
BRUC	A.B. Emden, *A Biographical Register of the University of Cambridge to 1500* (Cambridge, 1963)
BRUO	A.B. Emden, *A Biographical Register of the University of Oxford to A.D. 1500*, 3 vols (Oxford, 1957, 1958, 1959)
BRUO 1501–40	A.B. Emden, *A Biographical Register of the University of Oxford A.D. 1501 to 1540* (Oxford, 1974)
CBMLC	Corpus of British Medieval Library Catalogues
CHBB II	*The Cambridge History of the Book in Britain: Volume II 1100–1400*, ed. Nigel Morgan and Rodney M. Thomson (Cambridge, 2008)
CHBB III	*The Cambridge History of the Book in Britain: Volume III 1400–1557*, ed. Lotte Hellinga and J.B. Trapp (Cambridge, 1999)
Complete Works More	*The Yale Edition of the Complete Works of St Thomas More*, ed. Thomas M.C. Lawler, Germain Marc'hadour and Richard C. Marius, 15 vols (New Haven, CT and London, 1963–97)
CUL	Cambridge University Library
Directory of London Stationers	C. Paul Christianson, *A Directory of London Stationers and Book Artisans 1300–1500* (New York, 1990)
Duff	E. Gordon Duff, *A Century of the English Book Trade: Short Notices of all the Printers, Stationers, Bookbinders, and Others Connected with it from the Issue of the First Dated Book in 1457 to the Incorporation of the Stationers' Company in 1557* (London, 1905)
Duff rev.	E. Gordon Duff, *Printing in England in the Fifteenth Century: E. Gordon Duff's Bibliography with Supplementary Descriptions, Chronologies and a Census of Copies by Lotte Hellinga* (London, 2009)
EETS	Early English Text Society (OS: Original Series, ES: Extra Series)

'English Purchases'	Elizabeth Armstrong, 'English Purchases of Printed Books from the Continent 1465–1526', *English Historical Review* 94 (1979), 268–90
Goff	F.R. Goff, *Incunabula in American Libraries: A Third Census of Fifteenth-century Books Recorded in North American Collections* (New York, 1964)
HLQ	*Huntington Library Quarterly*
Humanism	Daniel Wakelin, *Humanism, Reading and English Literature, 1430–1530* (Oxford, 2007)
'Importation'	Margaret Lane Ford, 'Importation of printed books into England and Scotland', in *CHBB III*, pp. 179–201
Incunabula	*Incunabula: Studies in Fifteenth-century Printed Books Presented to Lotte Hellinga*, ed. Martin Davies (London, 1999)
King's Mother	Michael K. Jones and Malcolm G. Underwood, *The King's Mother: Lady Margaret Beaufort, Countess of Richmond and Derby* (Cambridge, 1992)
LP Henry VIII	J.S. Brewer *et al.*, eds, *Letters and Papers Foreign and Domestic . . . of Henry VIII*, 22 vols in 38 (London, 1864–1932)
'Marketing Printed Books'	A.S.G. Edwards and Carol M. Meale, 'The Marketing of Printed Books in Late Medieval England', *The Library*, 6th ser., 15 (1993), 96–124
MLGB (1)	*Medieval Libraries of Great Britain: a List of Surviving Books*, ed. N.R. Ker, Royal Historical Society Guides 15, 2nd edn (London, 1964)
MLGB (2)	*Medieval Libraries of Great Britain: a List of Surviving Books*, ed. N.R. Ker: Supplement to the Second Edition, ed. A.G. Watson (London, 1987)
Oates	J.C.T. Oates, *A Catalogue of the Fifteenth-century Printed Books in the University Library Cambridge* (Cambridge, 1954)
'Press, politics and religion'	Pamela Neville-Sington, 'Press, politics and religion', in *CHBB III*, pp. 576-607
Printer and Pardoner	Paul Needham, *The Printer and the Pardoner: An Unrecorded Indulgence Printed by William Caxton for the Hospital of St Mary Rounceval, Charing Cross* (Washington, DC, 1986)
'Private ownership'	Margaret Lane Ford, 'Private ownership of printed books', in *CHBB III*, pp. 205–28
PRO	Kew, Public Record Office, now part of The National Archives

Rhodes	Dennis E. Rhodes, *A Catalogue of Incunabula in all the Libraries of Oxford University outside the Bodleian* (Oxford, 1982)
STC	*A Short-Title Catalogue of Books Printed in England, Scotland & Ireland and of English Books Printed Abroad 1475–1640*, first compiled by A.W. Pollard and G.R. Redgrave, 2nd edn, rev. and enlarged, begun by W.A. Jackson and F.S. Ferguson, completed by Katharine F. Pantzer, 3 vols (London, 1976–91)
Stripping of the Altars	Eamon Duffy, *The Stripping of the Altars: Traditional Religion in England, c.1400–c.1580*, 2nd edn (New Haven, CT, 2005)
Syon Abbey and its Books	*Syon Abbey and its Books: Reading, Writing and Religion c. 1400–1700*, ed. E.A. Jones and Alexandra Walsham (Woodbridge, 2010)
TCBS	*Transactions of the Cambridge Bibliographical Society*
TRHS	*Transactions of the Royal Historical Society*
TRP	*Tudor Royal Proclamations*, ed. Paul L. Hughes and James F. Larkin, 3 vols (New Haven, CT and London, 1964–69)
William Caxton	Lotte Hellinga, *William Caxton and Early Printing in England* (London, 2010)
YML	York Minster Library

Websites

EEBO	*Early English Books Online* <http://eebo.chadwyck.com/home>
GW	*Gesamtkatalog der Wiegendrucke* (Leipzig, 1925–2009) <http://www.gesamtkatalogderwiegendrucke.de>
ISTC	*Incunabula Short Title Catalogue* <http://www.bl.uk/catalogues/istc/index.html>
ODNB	*Oxford Dictionary of National Biography* (Oxford, 2004) <http://www.oxforddnb.com>
TAMO	*The Unabridged Acts and Monuments Online*, HRI Online Publications (Sheffield, 2011) <http//www.johnfoxe.org>
USTC	*The Universal Short Title Catalogue*, hosted by the University of St Andrews <http://www.ustc.ac.uk/>

Chronology of the Period

1476   William Caxton sets up the first printing press in England, at Westminster.

1483   Edward IV dies and Richard III takes the throne.

1485   Henry VII defeats Richard III at the Battle of Bosworth Field.

1492   Caxton dies; his practice is taken over by Wynkyn de Worde (d. 1535).

1504   William Faques appointed King's Printer (d. c.1508).

1506   Richard Pynson appointed King's Printer (d. 1530).

1509   Henry VII dies; his son Henry VIII ascends to the throne.

1520   Leo X promulgates a ban on the writings of Martin Luther.

1529   Thomas Wolsey resigns as Lord Chancellor, unable to resolve the king's divorce petition; Thomas More takes the post (resigns 1532).

1530   Thomas Berthelet appointed King's Printer (d. 1555).

1533   Thomas Cranmer becomes Archbishop of Canterbury on the death of William Warham; Henry marries Anne Boleyn.

1534   Act of Succession, Act of Supremacy, and other major Acts passed by Parliament. Thomas Cromwell becomes chief minister to the Crown.

1535   Thomas More and John Fisher executed. Wynkyn de Worde dies.

1536   Anne Boleyn executed; Henry marries Jane Seymour.

1540   After the death of Jane Seymour in childbirth (1537), Henry marries Anne of Cleves, who is soon replaced by Catherine Howard. Cromwell is executed.

1542   Catherine Howard is executed.

1543   Henry marries Catherine Parr.

1547   Henry VIII dies. Edward VI, Henry's son by Jane Seymour, becomes king, with the Protestant Edward Seymour as Protector. Richard Grafton is appointed King's Printer, with Reyner Wolfe King's Printer in Latin, Greek and Hebrew.

1553   Edward dies. After an abortive attempt to put Lady Jane Grey on the throne, the Roman Catholic Mary Tudor becomes queen. John Cawood is appointed Queen's Printer.

1558   Mary dies.

Introduction

VINCENT GILLESPIE

For as the first decay and ruine of the Churche, before began of rude ignoraunce, and lacke of knowledge in teachers: so to restore the Church agayne by
doctrine and learning, it pleased God to open to man, the arte of Printyng, the
tyme whereof was shortely after the burnyng of Hus and Hierome. Printyng
beyng opened, incontinent ministred to the Church, the instrumentes and tooles
of learnyng and knowledge, whiche were good bookes and authors, whiche
before lay hyd and vnknowen. The science of Printyng beyng found, immediatly
folowed the grace of God, whiche styrred vp good wittes, aptely to conceaue the
light of knowledge and of iudgemēt: by which light, darkenes began to be espyed,
and ignoraunce to be detected, truth from errour, religion from superstition to bee
discerned.[1]

Like all totalising narratives, John Foxe's polemical narrative of the invention of printing as a providential preliminary to the wholesale reformation of
the Church can only work by omitting much that is inconvenient in the story.
But his ideologically biased analysis, mounted from the Protestant haven of
Elizabethan England, formed only a few years after the change of regime that
marks the terminal date for this volume, has the merit of reminding us that
there is much more to the history of printing in England than Caxton and his
chivalric and gentry romances that have occupied so much space in literary and
general histories of the period. Caxton's early secular publications were largely
translations from other languages, seemingly on the basis of a sound business
assessment of the size and taste of the market for such works in English as much
as (or as well as) out of any nationalistic desire to build up cultural or literary
capital by having these works available.[2] The prologue to his very first translation, Raoul Lefevre's *Recuyell of the Historyes of Troye* (1473, Bruges; STC 15375),
remarks that:

Hit shold be a good besynes to translate hyt into oure Englissh to thende that hyt
myght be had as well in the royame of Englond as in other landes.[3]

---

[1]   John Foxe's *Actes and monuments of these latter and perillous dayes, touching matters of the church* (STC 11223, 1570) (*TAMO*, 1570 edn, 7.1006).
[2]   On Caxton's career, see now *William Caxton*; William Kuskin, *Symbolic Caxton: Literary Culture and Print Capitalism* (Notre Dame, IN, 2008).
[3]   N.F. Blake, *Caxton's Own Prose* (London, 1973), p. 97, ll. 14–16.

But John Foxe's analysis emphasises that printing in the wider European context was very much a learned, scholarly and Latinate phenomenon, closely allied in the minds of sixteenth-century cultural analysts, polemicists and historians with the other great sea change in European life at the end of the fifteenth century, the rise of the New Learning and the emergence of new scholarly vectors in the analysis of scriptural texts, theological doctrines, liturgical studies and catechetic priorities. Foxe comments that soon after the invention of printing:

> after these wyttes styrred vp of God, folowed other moe, increasyng dayly more and more in science, in tongues, and perfection of knowledge: who now were able, not onely to discerne in matters of iudgement, but also were so armed and furnished with the helpe of good letters, that they did encounter also with the aduersarye, susteynyng the cause and defense of learnyng agaynst barbaritie: of veritie, agaynst errour: of true religion, agaynst superstition. In number of whom, amongest many other here vnnamed, were Picus & Franciscus Mirandula, Laur. Valla. Franc. Perarcha. Doct. VVesalianus, Reuclinus, Grocinus, Coletus, Rhenamus, Erasmus. &c.

So the 'Latin trade' inevitably looms large in any account of the early printed book in Britain. Several of the essays here note that the first printed book known to be purchased by an Englishman was a copy of the 1459 Mainz edition of Durandus printed by Fust and Schoeffer (GW 9101), bought in Hamburg in 1465 by James Goldwell, fellow of All Souls College Oxford and an early humanist (the book is still in the college library). The next documented purchase was made by John Russell, bishop of Lincoln and chancellor of England under Edward IV, who bought two copies of Fust and Schoeffer's 1466 edition of Cicero's De officiis (GW 6922) in Bruges in April 1467. Between July 1466 and March 1468, Gerhard von Wesel, the agent of the London Hanse in Cologne, sent two printed bibles to London for 'my lord Worchester', John Titptoft, earl of Worcester. So by the mid 1460s Englishmen were both buying printed books while abroad and ordering them for delivery from overseas.[4]

---

[4] The standard discussions of the English trade in continental printed books are: H.R. Plomer, 'The Importation of Books into England in the Fifteenth and Sixteenth Centuries', The Library, 4th ser., 4 (1924), 146–50; Nelly J.M. Kerling, 'Caxton and the Trade in Printed Books', The Book Collector 4 (1955), 190–99; Howard M. Nixon, 'Caxton, his Contemporaries and Successors in the Book Trade from Westminster Documents', The Library, 5th ser., 31 (1976), 305–26; Graham Pollard, 'The English Market for Printed Books', Printing History 4 (1978), 7–48; 'English Purchases', 268–90; Nicolas Barker, 'The Importation of Books into England 1460–1526', in Beiträge zur Geschichte des Buchwesens im konfessionellen Zeitalter, ed. Herbert G. Göpfert et al., Wolfenbüttler Schriften zur Geschichte des Buchwesens 11 (1985), pp. 251–66; Lotte Hellinga, 'Importation of Books Printed on the Continent into England before c. 1520', in Printing the Written Word: The Social History of Books circa 1450–1520, ed. Sandra Hindman (Ithaca, NY and London, 1991), pp. 205–24; 'Marketing Printed Books'; Anne F. Sutton and Livia Visser-Fuchs, 'Choosing a Book in Late Fifteenth-Century England and Burgundy', in England and the Low Countries in the Late Middle Ages, ed. Caroline Barron and Nigel Saul (Stroud, 1995), pp. 61–98. An invaluable biographical conspectus is provided by Directory of London Stationers. See also the important essays in CHBB III, especially, 'Importation'; C. Paul Christianson, 'The Rise of London's Book Trade', pp. 128–47; Paul Needham, 'The Customs Rolls as Documents for the Printed-Book Trade in England', pp. 148–63; Elisabeth Leedham-Green, 'University Libraries and Book Sellers', pp. 316–53; Kristen Jensen, 'Text Books in the Universities: The Evidence from the Books', pp. 354–79. The following discussion is greatly indebted to these pioneering studies.

Printed books were probably being imported into England as early as July 1466 (and perhaps even before then), unsurprisingly by a German, Gerhard von Wesel of (equally unsurprisingly) Cologne, who was alderman of the German community in London.[5] But it seems to have been only in the late 1470s that the customs rolls begin to record substantial imports of printed books into England, with Nelly Kerling misreporting the first extant reference in December 1477 (a date now corrected by modern scholarship to 10 January 1478) when the alien merchant Henry Frankenbergh and the Louvain printer John of Westfalia imported £6 worth of books (though the records for the preceding four years are missing).[6] It is, in fact, also from 1477 that the first record of a purchase of a printed book in England comes, when the newly-arrived papal collector Giovanni Gigli bought a copy of Diodorus Siculus, printed in that same year by Andreas de Paltasichis in Venice.[7]

From very soon after the invention of commercial printing, England had been a good market for the new commodity. This market included not only liturgical books (printed abroad in substantial numbers for the English market) and devotional books, but also Latin works of theology, philosophy, canon law, grammar and classical learning, aimed at and bought by the students or, more probably, the teachers at the great universities of Oxford and Cambridge and also by scholars and teachers in the great schools and monastic centres of learning with which fifteenth-century England was so richly endowed. Early continental printers seem to have sought trade agreements with stationers in such centres, or well connected to them. In Oxford, evidence survives from 1483 of books being supplied to Thomas Hunt by Peter Actors and John of Westfalia, apparently on a sale or return basis, and a similar list may describe books provided by the Parisian printer Pierre Levet in 1480.[8] Lotte Hellinga has noted that 'the first books printed at Mainz were aimed at a clearly defined market, a clientele largely confined to monastic houses', and there is no reason to doubt that continental printers were seeking to tap into a similar market when they began importing into England.[9]

The established trade route of the Rhine, Flanders and Antwerp happened to link together the major centres of the new technology – Basel, Mainz, Strasbourg, Cologne and the Low Countries – whose trade with England was dominated by the members of the Merchant Adventurers company: men like

[5] 'Importation', p. 197, on the authority of Graham Pollard and Albert Ehrman, *The Distribution of Books by Catalogue from the Invention of Printing to A.D. 1800*, Roxburghe Club (1965).

[6] Kerling, 'Caxton', p. 192; Christianson, 'Rise', p. 137; Needham, 'Customs Rolls', p. 151. See now Yvonne Rode, 'Importing Books to London in the Late Fifteenth and Early Sixteenth Centuries: Evidence from London Overseas Customs Accounts', *Journal of the Early Book Society* 15 (2012), 41–84.

[7] 'English Purchases', pp. 272–73. See the essays in *Incunabula and Their Readers: Printing, Selling and Using Books in the Fifteenth Century*, ed. Kristian Jensen (London, 2003).

[8] Paul Needham, 'Continental Printed Books Sold in Oxford, c. 1480–3', in *Incunabula*, pp. 243–70.

[9] Hellinga, 'Importation of Books Printed', p. 205. See also John L. Flood, '"Volentes Sibi Comparari Infrascriptos Libros Impressos ...": Printed Books as a Commercial Commodity in the Fifteenth Century', in *Incunabula and Their Readers*, ed. Jensen, pp. 139–51 (text), 255–62 (notes).

William Wilcocks, Roger Thorney and, of course, William Caxton, who also played a significant role in the 'Latin trade' in imported continental printed books.[10] As a Mercer and a Calais Stapler, Caxton's public identity was mercantile and commercial far more than it was literary: his application for a royal pardon in 1483 identifies him as 'civis et mercerus Londinie', 'mercator Stapule Calesie' and 'nuper Magister sive Gubernator mercatorum Anglie residencium in partibus Brabancie Falandrie Holandi et Zelandi'.[11] His book making and selling is subsumed within his broader commercial identity.

When Caxton returned to London in 1476, he brought with him experience of the book trade in Cologne and in Bruges, and it is likely that he imported books into England, using his mercantile networks of contact and influence, as well as printing them himself. Johann Veldener, who had supplied Caxton's types, was, by this date, printing on his own account in Louvain, and Nicolas Barker has argued that Veldener books in Caxton bindings 'suggest that this link provided an early source of import'.[12] The surviving evidence suggests that this market for imported books was dominated by foreign merchants. Frankenbergh, for example, in addition to importing other people's editions, commissioned the printing by William de Machlinia (another alien working in London, also known as William Ravenswalde) of the first English edition (*STC* 26012, of about 1484) of the pastoral manual *Speculum christiani*, 'ad instanciam necnon expensas Henrici Vrankenbergh mercatoris'. This looks like a good example of a collaborative and speculative printing venture by alien merchants targeted at the special needs of the English market.[13] Other significant alien importers of books included another 'docheman', John of Westfalia (otherwise known as John of Acon), who appears alongside Frankenbergh in customs rolls from early in 1478 through to 1491. Another initiative by alien merchants (in this case the innovative Cologne adventurers who sought to establish satellite presses across Europe to print and import Cologne materials) was the relatively short-lived Oxford press of Theodoricus Rood. This European and learnedly Latinate dimension in the early history of the printed book in Britain is important, reinforcing the need to look beyond the world of vernacular romances chronicles, and other secular materials, even beyond the culturally significant printing of the literary remains of Britain's 'three crowns', Chaucer, Gower and Lydgate, whose canonisation in print finally apotheosised them as this country's equivalent to the Italian 'tre coroni', Dante, Petrarch and Boccaccio.[14]

Before the religious dissensions of the 1520s and later, printing as a vehicle for

[10] See the brilliant overview of this commercial milieu in Anne F. Sutton, 'Caxton was a Mercer: His Social Milieu and Friends', in *England in the Fifteenth Century*, ed. Nicholas Rogers, Harlaxton Medieval Studies 4 (Stamford, 1994), pp. 118–48.

[11] The document is edited and discussed in Louise Gill, 'William Caxton and the Rebellion of 1483', *EHR* 112 (1997), 105–18.

[12] Barker, 'Importation', p. 255.

[13] Needham, 'Customs Rolls'; Christianson, 'Rise', pp. 136–38; Sutton, 'Caxton was a Mercer', pp. 134–38. The information on printers and merchants outlined in the following paragraphs is assembled from the studies listed in n.1.

[14] Alexandra Gillespie, *Print Culture and the Medieval Author: Chaucer, Lydgate, and Their Books, 1473–1557* (Oxford, 2006).

humanist learning was considered an unmitigated good. Anthony Woodville's translation of *The Dictes and Sayings of the Philosophers*, printed by Caxton in 1477 (*STC* 6826), praises Aristotle, saying:

> And therfore it is good to compose and make bookis by the whiche science shalbe lerned/ & whan our memorie shal fayle it shalbe recouered by mean of bookis. (unsigned, 41r–v)

A good illustration of the impact of the New Learning on English institutional libraries is found at Syon Abbey. It is striking to see a large monastic library like that of the brethren of Syon making a major shift from manuscripts to printed books in the years after 1471. Ease of navigation and legibility must have been among the physical attractions of the new printed books, and the gradual emergence of 'collected works' or cumulative editions of patristic authors would also have been a welcome development for institutional libraries with a desire to foster sound scholarship and orthodox teaching, fast supplanting hard to read and confusingly compiled manuscript miscellanies.

Such a collection, dominated by Latin printed books from the period 1470 to 1525, was de facto a Christian humanist collection.[15] Even after the emergence of Lutheranism and proto-Protestantism, the ideologies and academic horizons of both sides of the debates had many points of contiguity and symmetry: differences were often in nuance and lexis rather than in substance and radical divergence. In Foxe's eyes these humanists were the harbingers of the reformation. In the eyes of the brethren of Syon, and on the shelves of their library, these authors were the new tools with which they were furnishing their spiritual armoury. But any sense of a shared Christian humanism started to change in the 1520s with the emergence of the first printed vernacular bibles, and the divergence gathered pace in the years that followed.

From John Foxe's perspective in the second half of the sixteenth century, the success of the protestant reformations is indissolubly bound up with the new scholarly tools that humanists were able to access. He rehearses, for example, Pope Hadrian VI's lament to the princes of Germany about the growing influence of Martin Luther, who:

> dayly more & more forgetting & contemning all Christian charitie and godlynes, ceaseth not to disturbe and replenysh þᵉ world with new bookes fraught full of errours, heresies, contumelies, and seditiō (whether vpon his own head, or by the helpe of other) and to infecte the countrey of Germanie, and other regions aboute, with hys pestilence, and endeuoreth still to corrupt simple soules, and maners of men, with the poyson of his pestiferous tongue.[16]

In extending the coverage of this book to 1558, we try to capture some of that sense of the way that both sides used the press to tussle for intellectual control of the evolving argument and of the ideological high ground.

---

[15] *Syon Abbey*, ed. Vincent Gillespie, CBMLC 9 (London, 2001); 'Syon and the New Learning', in *The Religious Orders in Pre-Reformation England*, ed. James G. Clark, Studies in the History of Medieval Religion 18 (Woodbridge, 2002), pp. 75–95; 'Syon and the English Market for Continental Printed Books: The Incunable Phase', in *Syon Abbey and its Books*, pp. 104–28.
[16] *TAMO*, 1570 edn, 7.1006/7.

That access to books would bring about cultural and intellectual change was not a discovery made by sixteenth-century humanists, or indeed continental printers. The need for books to be made available cheaply and plentifully to supply the spiritual needs of lay people had already been recognised in the 1440s and 1450s by Bishop Reginald Pecock. Drawing on his experiences as Master of Whittington College in London, as a London Rector, and one of the founders of the All Angels Guild at Syon, and socially linked to the groups of London merchants who produced for their own shared use the so-called 'common-profit books', Pecock was seeking to provide instructive, edifying, well-corrected and authoritative vernacular books to a wide audience. In his *Book of Faith*, he urges prelates and 'othere myȝty men of good' to cause books 'to be writun in greet multitude, and to be wel correctid, and thanne aftir to be sende, and to be govun or lende abrood amonge the seid lay persoonys':

> it is not ynouȝ that the seid bokis be writen and made and leid up or rest in the hondis of clerkis, thouȝ fame and noise be made greet to the seid lay peple of suche bokis [. . .] but tho bokis musten be distributid and delid abrood to manye where that need is trowid that thei be delid.[17]

In the *Poor Man's Mirror*, Pecock describes how he made his *Donet* 'to be of litil quantite þat welniȝ ech poor persoon maye bi sum meene gete coost to haue it as his owne' and how, to assist the poorest, he has made an 'extract or outdrawȝt' from the *Donet* so that 'aftir sufficient pupplisching of þis book to hem' they may have no excuse for ignorance of the law of God.[18] As Boffey's essay here points out, Caxton, no doubt well aware of the commercial potential of his target audience in London and Westminster, made similar claims for printed books in his 1480 edition of *The Cronicles of England* (STC 9991):

> Also aboute this tyme the crafte of enprintinge was first founde in Magunce in Almayne / Whiche craft is multiplied thurgh the Worlde in many places and bookes bene had grete chepe and in grete nombre by cause of the same craft. (sig. y1v)

So Wynkyn de Worde's sales blurb for Richard Whitford's new translation of the *Rule of Augustine* was treading well-worn ground in emphasising the physical and financial benefits of the new medium, and advising all the disciples of this rule 'to bere alway one of these bokes upon them syth they ben so portatyue & may be had for so small a pryce' (1525, STC 922.3: title page).

Not that printed books were necessarily thought of as more durable than manuscripts: the bibliographer Johannes Trithemius, writing in the 1490s, commented that while handwriting on parchment would be able to endure for a thousand years, printing was an unknown quantity because it used paper: 'if in a paper volume it lasts for two hundred years, that is a long time'. But ease of

---

[17] *Reginald Pecock's Book of Faith: A Fifteenth Century Theological Tractate*, ed. John Lyle Morison (Glasgow, 1909), p. 116.
[18] London, BL, MS Additional 37758, fols 3r–4v.

mass reproduction, and (perhaps increasingly as the ideological skies darkened in the 1520s and 1530s) the ability to ensure relatively accurate reproduction meant that printing would be seen as having distinct advantages. Whitford, Syon Abbey's prolific author of orthodox defences and catechetic didacticism, stresses the advantages of mechanical reproduction for the writer. In his 1537 *A Dayly exercise and experience of dethe* (STC 25414) he explains the provenance of his text:

> This lytle tretie or draght of deth dyd I wryte more than .xx. yeres ago at the request of the reuerende Mother Dame Elizabeth Gybs whome Jesu perdon then Abbes of Syon. And by the oft calling vpon and remembraunce of certeyne of hyr deuout systers. And nowe of late I haue been compelled [. . .] to wryte it agayne and agayne. And bycause that wrytynge vnto me is very tedyouse I thought better to put it in print. (sig. ai^v–aii^r)

But, as Syon realised in its active engagement with printers as part of a sustained campaign of defence of orthodox catholic teaching in the face of Lutheran ideas spreading quickly on the fluttering wings of printed books, making translations of orthodox works available through the presses in affordable and portable formats was as important a part of the defence of Holy Church by Catholic apologists as access to the press was for the success of satires and arguments of the Protestant reformers.[19]

Indeed, the value of printing for ecclesiastical markets had been obvious from the outset, allowing the production of uniform service books, Books of Hours and other liturgical and para-liturgical materials. From the start of his career in Westminster, Caxton's 1477 *Advertisement* speaks to precisely this market:

> If it plese ony man spirituel or temporrel to bye ony pyse of two and thre comemoracions of salisburi use empryntid after the forme of this present lettre whiche ben wel and truly correct/ late hym come to westmonester in to the almonelrye at the reed pale and he shal haue them good chepe. Supplico stet cedula. (STC 4890)

It is doubtful if printing could have established itself as an economically viable medium without the financial underpinning provided by ecclesiastical texts and by jobbing work in the form of indulgences or special print runs for the larger monastic houses. So this book pays close attention to those ecclesiastical markets and makers. Indeed, the history of printing in England is shot through by a narrative of close encounters, commissions, donations and speculative ventures between printers and secular and monastic clergy. So we believe that the greater emphasis on religious printing in this book accurately reflects the reality of the market for printed books in England before 1558. Another feature of the essays in this book, however, is the recognition it gives to the many women who as translators, patrons, commissioners, donors and authors have received much less attention than they deserve. Just as our understanding of fifteenth-century vernacular theology has been enhanced by a fuller grasp of the roles of women

---

[19] See, most recently, Alexandra da Costa, *Reforming Printing: Syon Abbey's Defence of Orthodoxy 1525–1534* (Oxford, 2012).

as epicentres of domestic devotional culture, so too the history of printing needs to acknowledge the roles adopted and performed with distinction by women. Lady Margaret Beaufort, the mother and grandmother of sovereigns, has too often been used as a passing cipher for the role of women in the book trade in the era of printing, her character forever crystallised by John Fisher's funeral sermon:

> A redy wytte she had also to conceyue all thynges albeit they were ryght derke. Right studious she was in bookes whiche she had in grete nombre . . . and for her exercyse and for the prouffyte of other she dyde translate dyuers maters of deuocyon out of Frensshe into Englysshe.[20]

But the essays in this book show that the activity and agency of bookish women run in an unbroken and broadening line to a bookish and learned woman who was herself a sovereign, Elizabeth I.

The nascent technology of printing arrived in a country at first embroiled in, and then emerging painfully from, a period of debilitating civil war, adapting to the new Tudor dynasty and its austere and high-minded matriarch, Lady Margaret Beaufort, an early adopter and patron of the new technology, and then revelling in what began as the golden age of her grandson, Henry VIII, though within a decade of her death and his accession in 1509, it began its long descent into turmoil, contention and a tyrannical reign of terror. The essays in this book show that the introduction and development of printing in England was not a seamless story of Whiggish entrepreneurial success. The provincial presses in Oxford and St Albans failed to last for long, monastic institutional printing was crude and spasmodic, home-made paper making was a shaky and short-lived industry, and even Caxton himself seems to have had a hiatus in his printing career in the mid-1480s. The mixed economy of manuscript and print continued for many decades, with manuscript being the medium of choice for de-luxe and presentation copies and a matter of personal taste or economic necessity for many readers. The impact of the new technology on the producers of manuscript books has long been assumed to be significant. Philip Wrenne, a stationer of London, complaining against his imprisonment for debt sometime around 1487, lamented that, despite his years of work in 'lymnyng', 'the occupation ys almost destroyed by prynters of bokes'.[21] But evidence in this book challenges the assumption of a speedy or decisive paradigm shift from one medium to the other. The hybridised world of mixed and multi-media access to texts in which we operate today, where daily reports of the death of printed book remain greatly exaggerated, perhaps helps us to appreciate the complex, asymmetrical and uneven assimilation of printing in Britain after its first arrival. But the introduction of printing, with all its concomitant social, commercial, mercantile and intellectual impacts, was recognised within a very few generations as being an enormous vector of change. In 1530 John Rastall revised and extended Caxton's

---

[20] *The English Works of John Fisher*, ed. J.E.B. Mayor, EETS ES 27 (1876), pp. 291, ll. 34–292, l. 6 (punctuation altered).
[21] Early Chancery Proceedings, Bundle 74, no. 50. cit. C. Paul Christianson, 'An Early Tudor Stationer and the "prynters of bokes"', *The Library*, 6th ser., 9 (1987), 257–62.

note on the benefits of printing: 'Also in this same tyme the crafte of Printynge of bokes [. . .] hathe ben cause of great lernynge and knowelege / and hathe ben the cause of many thynges and great chaunges / & is lyke to be the cause of many straunge thynges here after to come.'[22] The intention of this book is to help explore why this was the case.

---

[22] *The pastyme of people* (STC 20724), sig. ²[E]6v.

THE PRINTED BOOK TRADE

1

From Manuscript to Print: Continuity and Change

JULIA BOFFEY

The introduction to Europe of 'the crafte of printyng' was noted with approbation in a short passage included in William Caxton's 1480 printed edition of *the
cronicles of england* (*STC* 9991):[1] 'Also a=//boute this tyme the crafte of enprint-
ing*e* was first founde in Ma=//gunce in Almayne / Whiche craft is multiplied
thurgh the World*e* // in many places / and bookes bene had grete chepe and
in grete nom//bre by cause of the same craft' (sig. y1v). Caxton composed the
passage himself, adapting it from a widely circulating compilation of European
history called the *Fasciculus Temporum*, which was probably available to him in
a Continental printed edition.[2] The passage was to have a long life, reappearing
in variant forms in other chronicles well into the sixteenth century.[3] As rendered
in John Rastell's *The pastyme of people* (*STC* 20724, 1530?) it was further elaborated: 'Also in this same tyme the crafte of Printynge of bokes began in the city
of Almayne / na=//med Magonce whiche is nowe meruaylously increasyd /
whiche hathe ben cause of great ler=//nynge and knowelege / and hathe ben
the cause of many thynges and great chaunges / & is lyke // to be the cause of
many strau*n*ge thynges here after to come' (sig. [2][E]6v).[4]

Both Caxton and Rastell noted the positive effects of printing. It made books
available more cheaply and in greater numbers; it enabled more efficient dissemination of knowledge, and thus had a dynamic role in processes of intellectual and cultural change. Given the investment of both writers in printing,
it is inevitable that their accounts should have stressed the benefits of this new
technology. But what of English manuscript books and their producers in the
decades following Caxton's move from the Low Countries to Westminster in

---

[1] Editions of works printed in England discussed in the text are identified by their numbers
in *STC*. Titles are given in the forms cited there, except in the case of well-known works like *The
Canterbury Tales*. Continental incunabula are identified by their numbers in *ISTC*.
[2] By Werner Rolewinck; see *ISTC* ir00253000, etc., and Lister Matheson, *The Prose Brut: The
Development of a Middle English Chronicle* (Tempe, AZ, 1998), pp. 165–66.
[3] Included in editions of the *Chronicles of England* by the St Albans printer, de Worde, Notary,
etc.; also, in the context of the 'Liber ultimus' added by Caxton to the *Polychronicon*, in his and
later printed editions of this work (*STC* 13438, etc.). Versions of this account of the beginnings
of printing continued into the seventeenth century: see Richard Atkyns and John Streater, *The
Original and Growth of Printing* (1664), sig. C1v, discussed by Douglas A. Brooks, '"This heav-
enly boke, more precious than golde": Legitimating Print in Early Tudor England', in *Tudor
Books and Readers: Materiality and the Construction of Meaning*, ed. John N. King (Cambridge,
2010), pp. 95–115.
[4] For a reproduction of this page, see *William Caxton*, p. 184.

1476? Contrary to the sporadic complaints apparently made by both scribes and readers – that printing put scribes out of work; that mass-produced printed books were cheap, distasteful attempts to replicate the uniqueness of valuable manuscripts – the new technology did not simply or quickly overtake the established one, whether in England or in Europe more generally.[5] The production of manuscripts continued, and many different kinds of overlap between the two technologies remain visible, offering support for Norman Blake's contention that 'there was no conflict between the two means of production, for they complemented each other'.[6] This discussion will explore some of the sites in which the two means of production came into contact, looking briefly also at the developing demarcations of territory between printers and scribes, and at the range of aesthetic, textual and functional implications of the differences between their products.

The prologues and epilogues which Caxton supplied to many of the books he printed contain illuminating information about his use of manuscripts. His allusion to the 'many diverse paunflettis and bookys' in his study (*Eneydos*, sig. A1r; *STC* 24796, not before 23 June 1490) suggests a jumble of works in many forms from which he selected items for translation and/or printing; and he also describes several encounters with individuals who brought him books – probably in both manuscript and print – likely to provide inspiration for new ventures. The first literary work he printed, *the recuyell of the histories of Troy* (*STC* 15375, 1473), reproduced a translation he produced from French by hand (written with 'penne and ynke', sig. [A]2v). His undertaking to circulate the completed work not just to Margaret of York, who had ordered it, but also to 'dyverce gentilmen and to my frendes', would have weighed heavily had he not had the option to reproduce it by other means: 'I have // practysed & lerned at my grete charge and dispense to // ordeyne this said book in prynte after the maner & forme // as ye may here see and / [it] is not wreton with penne and // ynke as other bokes ben / to thende that every man may // have them attones.' (sig. ³[K]9).

References elsewhere in Caxton's writings flesh out this depiction of the multiplying power of print, in the context of an evolutionary narrative in which single manuscripts were replaced by multiple printed copies. Anthony Woodville's translation of the *Cordiale quattuor novissimorum* was brought to

---

[5] On which see the examples cited in Curt F. Bühler, *The Fifteenth-Century Book: The Scribes, the Printers, The Decorators* (Philadelphia, PA, 1960), pp. 25–39. Further references include part of a petition by Philip Wrenne, stationer, some time before 1500 (Early Chancery Proceedings Bundle 74 No. 50): 'the occupation [of scribe?] ys almost destroyed by printers of bokes'; see C. Paul Christianson, 'An Early Tudor Stationer and the "Prynters of Bokes"', *The Library*, 6th ser., 9 (1987), 259–62, and *Directory of London Stationers*, p. 176; and a practice sentence in William Horman's *Vulgaria* of 1519 (*STC* 13811, sig. O2r): 'Pryntynge hathe almooste vndone scriueners crafte'.
[6] N.F. Blake, 'Manuscript to Print', in *Book Production and Publishing in Britain 1375–1475*, ed. Jeremy Griffiths and Derek Pearsall (Cambridge, 1989), pp. 403–19 (419). For an influential argument about the significance of printing, see Elizabeth L. Eisenstein, *The Printing Press as an Agent of Change: Communications and Cultural Transformations in Early-Modern Europe*, 2nd edn (Cambridge, 1991), and the more recent discussions in Alexandra Walsham and Julia Crick, 'Introduction: Script, Print and History', in *The Uses of Script and Print, 1300–1700*, ed. Crick and Walsham (Cambridge, 2004), pp. 1–26, and William Kuskin, 'Introduction: Following Caxton's Trace', in *Caxton's Trace: Studies in the History of English Printing*, ed. Kuskin (Notre Dame, IN, 2006), pp. 1–31.

Caxton, presumably in manuscript form, 'for to be enprinted / and so multi-plied // to goo abrood emonge the peple' (STC 5758, 1479, sig. [K]4v); the *dictes and sayengis of the philosopphres*, also translated by Woodville, was sent to Caxton 'in certayn // quayers to ouersee', before being set up for printing (STC 6826, before 18 November 1477, sig. [K]2r); a copy of the translation of Cicero's *De senectute* originally made for Sir John Fastolf, again presumably a manuscript, was sought out 'with grete instaunce labour // and coste' so that Caxton could 'put it in enprynte' (STC 5293, 1481, sigs [a]2v–[a]3r); and the preparation of the second edition of *The Canterbury Tales* famously involved consultation of a new and better manuscript than that used by Caxton for the first edition (STC 5083, [1483], sigs a2r–v).[7] The situations recorded in these anecdotes are ones in which Caxton would have had a manuscript text prepared for printing, probably by having a manuscript marked up in order to 'cast off' or divide up the copy into sections of text of an appropriate length to fill individual printed pages, and to provide any further necessary instructions for the compositor.[8]

The transference of manuscript to print in these ways is confirmed by the survival of a manuscript of Laurentius Traversanus's *Nova Rhetorica* (Rome, Biblioteca Apostolica Vaticana, MS lat. 1141, fols 1–88) apparently used by Caxton as setting copy for his edition of 1478 or 1479 (STC 24188.5).[9] It is one of a small number of surviving manuscripts to have been identified as setting copy for specific printed editions produced in the first fifty years of printing in England, all retaining material signs of some of the processes involved in preparing a text for printing.[10] But it is clear that Caxton, like later English printers, often also worked with texts already in printed form, certainly using printed books as sources for a number of his own translations,[11] and on some occasions using his own printed editions as setting copy when making reprints. Straightforward sequences of the transmission of text from manuscript to print might in practice have been rarer than we would suppose: the manuscript trans-lation of the *Cordiale* which Anthony Woodville must have given to Caxton for printing, for example, was itself based on a copy of the French *Cordiale* earlier printed for Caxton in Bruges.[12]

---

[7] See also N.F. Blake, ed., *Caxton's Own Prose* (London, 1973), pp. 61–63, 70, 73, 121.
[8] Terms commonly used for such manuscripts include 'setting copy', 'copy', 'copy-text', and 'exemplar'; for a detailed account of the processes involved, see *BMC XI*, pp. 20–24.
[9] See José Ruysschaert, 'Les manuscrits autographes des deux oeuvres de Lorenzo Guglielmo Traversagni imprimées chez Caxton', *Bulletin of the John Rylands Library* 36 (1953–4), 191–97; Lotte Hellinga, *Caxton in Focus* (London, 1982), pp. 44–47. See also the evidence that the Winchester manuscript of Malory's *Morte D'Arthur* (London, BL, MS Additional 59678) was at one stage in Caxton's printing house, even though it seems not to have served directly as his setting copy (for STC 801, 1485); Lotte Hellinga, 'The Malory Manuscript and Caxton', in *Aspects of Malory*, ed. Toshiyuki Takamiya and Derek Brewer (Cambridge, 1981), pp. 127–41; and *Caxton in Focus*, pp. 89–94.
[10] For useful lists, see Blake, 'Manuscript to Print', pp. 419–29, and J.K. Moore, *Primary Materials Relating to Copy and Print in English Books of the Sixteenth and Seventeenth Centuries*, Oxford Historical Society Occasional Publications 24 (Oxford, 1992); and see also Lotte Hellinga, 'Manuscripts in the Hands of Printers', in *Manuscripts in the Fifty Years after the Invention of Printing: Some Papers Read at a Colloquium at The Warburg Institute on 12–13 March 1982*, ed. J.B. Trapp (London, 1983), pp. 3–11.
[11] Listed in *BMC IX*, p. 21, n.1.
[12] *William Caxton*, pp. 51, 68.

Use of a mixture of manuscripts and printed books for the provision of copy seems to have become fairly standard practice. Printers in the decades after Caxton regularly reprinted works originally put in print by others, and in such circumstances it is clear that the exemplars used were more often than not printed books. When Wynkyn de Worde decided to make a new, enlarged edition of the *boke . . . of hawkinge & huntynge . . . And of the blasynge of armys* (STC 3309, 1496), first printed in or shortly after 1486 by the St Albans Printer (and hence often known as *The Book of St Albans*), he used a copy of the earlier printed text (*STC* 3308). The annotations made to this by his editor and compositors, some designed to modernise the language and make it more acceptable to a metropolitan readership, are still visible in the partial copy now in the British Library (IB. 55712).[13] The preparation of his 1498 edition of *The Canterbury Tales* (*STC* 5085) evidently involved consultation of both Caxton's printed version (the second edition, *STC* 5083, 1483, in a copy with existing annotations) and one or more manuscripts. A note at the end of the apparently incomplete 'Squire's Tale' reads 'There can be founde no more of this for=//sayd tale. whyche I have right diligently ser=//chyd in many dyvers copyes' (sig. [m]6r).[14]

Since in this instance there is no extant setting copy, de Worde's consultation of both printed and manuscript copies of *The Canterbury Tales* has had to be hypothesised from collation of his printed text with other printed and manuscript copies that have survived. Reverse situations, in which marks in extant manuscripts or printed books indicate that they were used as setting copy for printed books of which no copies now remain, have also been identified: part of London, BL, MS Cotton Faustina B III, for example, with a series of such marks, may have served as setting copy for a lost printed *Life of St Edith*; parts of Oxford, BodL, MS Bodley 638, with marginal evidence of marking-up, for recorded but now lost editions of the poems *The Chance of the Dice* and *Ragmans Roll*.[15] The case for de Worde's use of MS Bodley 638 is strengthened by the existence of editions of other works for which he used this manuscript, Lydgate's verse *complaynte of a louers lyfe* (STC 17014.7, 1531?) and Chaucer's *Parliament of Fowls* (*The assemble of foules*, STC 5092, 1530). Perhaps the manuscript remained in his hands for some years, or was somehow readily available for use and re-use. The manuscript which is now Warminster, Longleat House, MS 258 may have served an unidentified printer for a lost edition of the verse debate *The Eye and the Heart* before later becoming available for the collected edition of Chaucer's works put together by William Thynne and printed by Thomas Godfray in 1532 (*STC* 5068).[16]

---

[13] See *BMC XI*, pp. 203–05.

[14] See further *BMC IX*, pp. 214–16. Thomas Berthelet's 1532 edition of Gower's *Confessio Amantis* (STC 12143) begins with a note pointing out the differences between Caxton's printed edition of 1483 (STC 12142) and the manuscripts still in circulation: 'I thought it good to warne the // reder, that the writen copyes do not agre // with the prynted. Therefore syr I haue // printed here those same lynes, that I // fynde in the written copies' (sig. aa3r).

[15] J. Ayto, 'Marginalia in the Manuscript of *The Life of St Edith*: New Light on Early Printing', *Library*, 5th ser., 32 (1977), 28–36; Moore, *Primary Materials*, p. 16.

[16] James E. Blodgett, 'Some Printer's Copy for William Thynne's 1532 Edition of Chaucer', *The Library*, 6th ser., 1 (1979), 97–113 (101–04) and 'William Thynne', in *Editing Chaucer: The Great Tradition*, ed. Paul G. Ruggiers (Norman, OK, 1984), pp. 35–52 (39, 42–45). The marginal

The compilation of an extensive edition such as Thynne's Chaucer no doubt involved a variety of forms of setting copy. Thynne, for instance, used a manuscript of Chaucer's translation of *The Romance of the Rose* (now Glasgow, University Library, Hunterian MS V. 3. 7), but for Chaucer's *Boece* translation relied on a copy of Caxton's 1478 printed edition (*STC* 3199; the copy is now at Longleat House).[17] Twenty-five years later, the amalgam of sources used for preparing the collected edition of the works of Thomas More, edited by William Rastell (*STC* 18076), included an edition of *The supplycacyon of soulys* printed by Rastell himself in 1529 (*STC* 18092; now New Haven, Yale University, Beinecke Rare Book and Manuscript Library 1f.M.81).[18]

The business of preparing a new edition for print, especially when it involved consultation and marking up of multiple sources, was clearly complex. Scholarly shorthand often attributes this work directly to named printers – Caxton, de Worde, Pynson, Berthelet and others – but it was most likely the responsibility of foreman editors and/or compositors working under the master-printer. Naturally enough, the forms of marking-up and annotation visible in setting copy are sometimes consistent within a printing-house: the manuscripts used for Pynson's editions of *Dives and Pauper* (*STC* 19212, 1493) and Lydgate's *Fall of Princes* (*STC* 3175, 1494), respectively Oxford, BodL MS Eng. th. d. 36 and Manchester, John Rylands Library, MS English 2 (from fol. 140 onwards), display similar systems of marginal marks relating to the process of casting-off copy.[19] It is also possible that rough manuscript copies of some works were made especially for use in the printing house, so as not to damage the more valuable volumes that would otherwise have to have been borrowed from private or institutional owners. Nonetheless, some strikingly lavish manuscripts seem to have been in printers' hands. The Oxford printer of Rufinus used as setting copy for the first book printed in Oxford (*exposicio . . . in simbolum apostolorum*, *STC* 21443, 1478) a beautifully illuminated Florentine manuscript, now London, BL, MS Sloane 1579.[20]

In practice, printers must have spent a good deal of their time with manuscripts, whether undertaking preliminary research and preparation for prospective editions, or – as clearly happened in some printing houses – buying

---

marks in the Longleat MS of *The Eye and the Heart* do not correspond to the page divisions in de Worde's edition *a lytel treatyse called the dysputacyon or co[m]playnt of the herte thorughe perced with the lokynge of the eye* (*STC* 6915, 1516?), although the texts are almost identical.

[17] Blodgett, 'Printer's Copy' and 'Editing Chaucer'.

[18] Ralph Keen, 'Appendix F. The Printer's Copy for the *Supplication of Souls* in the 1557 *English Works*', in *Complete Works More*, 7, *Letter to Bugenhagen, Supplication of Souls, Letter against Frith*, ed. Frank Manley, Germain Marc'hadour, Richard Marius and Clarence H. Miller (New Haven, CT and London, 1990), pp. 457–81.

[19] See Marjery M. Morgan, 'Pynson's Manuscript of *Dives et Pauper*', *The Library*, 5th ser., 8 (1953), 217–28, and 'A Specimen of Early Printer's Copy: Rylands English 2', *Bulletin of the John Rylands Library* 33 (1950–51), 194–96. BodL MS Eng.th.d.36 is illustrated in Morgan, 'Pynson's Manuscript', and Rylands MS English 2 can be consulted in digital reproduction online at <http://www.library.manchester.ac.uk/inthebigynnyng/manuscript/ms2/>. Detailed discussion of the variety of practices involved in casting off text is in Blake, 'Manuscript to Print', pp. 409–12.

[20] A.C. de la Mare, 'The First Oxford Book', *TLS*, 24 March 1978, and A.C. de la Mare and Lotte Hellinga, 'The First Book Printed in Oxford: The *Expositio Symboli* of Rufinus', *TCBS* 7 (1978), 184–244; see the illustrations in *William Caxton*, p. 77; and online at <http://www.bl.uk/catalogues/illuminatedmanuscripts/results.asp>.

and selling manuscripts, and commissioning their copying, decoration and binding. Caxton's early experiments with printing in Flanders were undertaken within the circle of Margaret of York, duchess of Burgundy (the sister of Edward IV), where he also worked closely with scribes and manuscript producers; the copperplate engraving which survives in one copy of his *the recuyell of the histories of Troy* (STC 15375), for example, has been identified as the work of an artist associated with the Flemish scribe David Aubert.[21] Caxton's English translation of the French *Ovide moralisé* survives only in a high quality, two-volume illuminated manuscript (Cambridge, Magdalene College, Old Library, MS F.4.34), with copying and illustration completed in London, probably on commission for a patron, and it may be the case that this work was never destined for print.[22]

In England, Caxton and the later printers who established businesses certainly cultivated contacts with rubricators and artists, craftsmen whose skills remained in demand for the finishing of both manuscript and printed books. The apparently standardised forms of rubrication present in a number of Caxton volumes suggest that this work might have been added in-house, while the rubrication of early lawbooks printed by Machlinia seems likely to have been similarly systematic.[23] The material added to books after printing could range from simple coloured capitals and paraph signs to more complicated amalgams of border decoration, historiated initials and miniatures.[24] Although the presentation volumes produced by English printers were not as numerous or as lavish as those made by their Continental counterparts, decorated copies of English printed books survive in reasonable numbers, indicating that the provision of manuscript illumination and illustration (at the instigation of either printer or buyer) was a reasonably common practice. One copy of the first edition of Caxton's 1477 *Canterbury Tales* (STC 5082) has twenty-four full-page added illuminated borders, together with the arms of the Haberdashers' Company of London; one copy of de Worde's 1519 *the orcharde of Syon* (STC 4815), possibly destined for Richard Sutton, steward of the house and underwriter of the edition, is coloured and illuminated throughout.[25] The presentation copy of the translation of Vives's *De institutione foeminae Christianae*, which Richard Hyrde

---

[21] The copy is now in the Huntington Library, San Marino, CA (RB 62222). For a reproduction and further discussion, see *William Caxton*, pp. 37–40.
[22] See *The Metamorphoses of Ovid translated by William Caxton 1480*, 2 vols (New York, 1968); K. Scott, *The Caxton Master and his Patrons*, Cambridge Bibliographical Society Monographs 8 (Cambridge, 1976); and Blake, 'Manuscript to Print', pp. 414–16.
[23] A.S.G. Edwards, 'Decorated Caxtons', in *Incunabula*, pp. 493–506. On Machlinia, see plate 3.4 in *CHBB III*.
[24] Some of the most lavishly enhanced printed books in English hands during the late fifteenth and early sixteenth centuries were Continental ones. The Parisian printer Antoine Vérard presented to Henry VII a number of such volumes during the years between 1492 and 1507; see Mary Beth Winn, *Anthoine Vérard: Parisian Publisher 1485–1512: Prologues, Poems, and Presentations* (Geneva, 1997), pp. 138–45. One example is the copy of Vérard's edition of a prose version of Deguileville's *Le Pelerinage de vie humaine* now in the Huntington Library (RB 103394), which was printed on vellum, with red line ruling, Henry's arms on an inserted leaf at the start, and beautifully executed border illustration and miniatures which include Tudor badges; see Winn, *Vérard*, p. 145, for a reproduction of the illustration on fol. 4.
[25] Respectively Merton College, Oxford, Scr.P.2.1, described and illustrated in Edwards, 'Decorated Caxtons', pp. 499–501; and the former Longleat House copy, described and illustrated in Christie's Sale Catalogue, 13 June 2002, lot 17.

undertook at the request of Catherine of Aragon, printed by Berthelet as *A very frutefull and pleasant boke called the instruction of a christen woman* (*STC* 24856, 1529?), has a hand-coloured title-page;[26] and a vellum copy of the 1540 'Great Bible' (*STC* 2070), printed by Whitchurch and apparently presented to Henry VIII by 'Anthonye Marler of London, Haberdassher', is illuminated throughout, and has an entirely new hand-painted title-page replacing the original one with its printed woodcut.[27]

Products of both manuscript and printed book production are strikingly intermingled in a volume put together for the London mercer Roger Thorney. Apparently a bibliophile of some wealth and enthusiasm, Thorney is known to have underwritten de Worde's editions of John Trevisa's translation of the *Polychronicon* (*STC* 13439, 1495; previously printed by Caxton) and Bartholomaeus Anglicus's *De proprietatibus rerum* (*STC* 1536, 1495);[28] his support is acknowledged in verse added by de Worde to each of the editions. He owned copies of Caxton's editions of the romance *Godefrey of Boloyne* (*STC* 13175, 1481), and the *Quattuor sermones* (*STC* 17957, [1483]), and two Caxton Chaucers of about the same date: copies of *Troilus and Criseyde* (*STC* 5094, [1483]) and the second edition of *The Canterbury Tales* (*STC* 5083, [1483]).[29] But he also owned manuscripts, including a copy of John Lydgate's verse *Siege of Thebes* (Oxford, St John's College, MS 266) made by a scribe who collaborated with other London scribes in the production of at least one further anthology. At some point – perhaps in the early 1490s when his association with de Worde was intensifying – Thorney decided to amalgamate his printed Chaucers and the *Quattuor sermones* with his manuscript of the *Siege of Thebes*, and to arrange for decoration that would smooth over the differences between printed and manuscript pages: the text lines of the printed books were ruled, major initials supplied in gold on coloured backgrounds, the illustrations to *The Canterbury Tales* were coloured, and a hand-painted frontispiece illustrating *Troilus and Criseyde* was inserted.[30] Finally, in around 1494 the volume was evidently lent to de Worde to be marked up for a printed edition of *The Siege of Thebes* (*STC* 17031).[31]

[26] BodL Arch.B.e.30, illustrated in James P. Carley, *The Books of Henry VIII and his Wives* (London, 2004), p. 117 (Carley gives a date of 1524).

[27] BL C.18.D.10, illustrated at: <http://www.bl.uk/onlinegallery/onlineex/henryviii/muss powor/greatbible/index.html>. Thomas Cromwell's copy of the first edition (*STC* 2068), also on vellum, and with hand-colouring, is now St John's College, Cambridge Bb.8.30; see the reproductions at <http://www.joh.cam.ac.uk/library/special_collections/early_books/pix/ gbible.htm>.

[28] A book for which setting copy has survived in the form of Columbia University Library, Plimpton MS 263: see Robert W. Mitchner, 'Wynkyn de Worde's Use of the Plimpton Manuscript of *De Proprietatibus Rerum*', *The Library*, 5th ser., 6 (1951–52), 7–18 (see images on the Digital Scriptorium at: <http://scriptorium.columbia.edu/>).

[29] For his Caxton volumes, see Seymour de Ricci, *A Census of Caxtons* (Oxford, 1909). Thorney's name also appears in the copy of de Worde's *The Iustices of peas* (*STC* 14864.5, 1515) in the Huntington Library (RB 82448). Although Thorney's will was made in 1515 it was not proved until 1517, presumably the year of his death.

[30] For description and illustration, see Edwards, 'Decorated Caxtons', p. 500; Alexandra Gillespie, *Print Culture and the Medieval Author: Chaucer, Lydgate and their Books 1473–1557* (Oxford, 2006), pp. 77–86.

[31] Gavin Bone, 'Extant Manuscripts Printed from by W. De Worde with Notes on the Owner, Roger Thorney', *The Library*, 4th ser., 12 (1932), 284–306; see further the diverging views of Blake, 'Manuscript to Print', pp. 411–12, and Alexandra Gillespie, '"Folowynge the trace of

The striking diversity of Thorney's book-related activities means that he has often been cited in discussions of the impact of the arrival of print in England. It is tempting to see in the narrative of his patronage and book acquisition a move-ment from manuscript to print, and to read in his treatment of *The Siege of Thebes* an urge first to make his manuscript look like a printed book by attaching it to other printed volumes, then to activate its potential to spawn printed volumes by supplying it to a printer as setting copy. Certainly he seems to have moved in circles interested in new technology: the 'prohemium' attached to de Worde's edition of *De proprietatibus rerum* signals the contribution to knowledge made possible not just by Caxton and de Worde and de Worde's backer Thorney, but also by the mercer-papermaker John Tate, whose mill near Hertford, the first in England, was de Worde's source of supply.[32] But Thorney's activities took place in a larger cultural environment where forms of overlap and interpenetration between manuscript and print were relatively commonplace. Evident continui-ties in manuscript availability warn us against interpreting his promotion of the technology of print as a move to overwrite established patterns of manuscript production. Thorney's London contemporary Robert Fabyan, in instructive contrast, seems to have spent many years on the copying and enhancement of manuscript volumes of the two chronicles with which he can be associated.[33] A reader of considerable means, from a prosperous family of drapers, Fabyan demonstrably owned printed books and used them in a number of ways; but he seems to have understood the attractions of a manuscript book that could be a unique artefact somehow representative of one's own person and concerns. Fabyan's *new cronycles* were not printed until 1516 (by Pynson; *STC* 10659), three years after his death.

Like Fabyan, a surprising number of readers continued to commission or make for themselves copies of works they wished to read or own or present as gifts, even though those works were available for purchase in printed form. Any number of reasons might persuade someone to exercise this option: a simple preference for manuscript over print, perhaps associated with entrenched reading habits; inability to source a printed copy; economic factors which could in certain circumstances make a scribal copy cheaper than a printed book; special requirements, like the need for an especially *de luxe* volume for presentation purposes. One of the best known examples of such a volume is now London, Lambeth Palace Library, MS 265, a copy of the translation made for Caxton by Anthony Woodville of the *dictes and sayengis of the philosopphres*, designed for presentation to Edward IV, and prefaced with an appropriate miniature.[34] The work of a scribe who names himself as Haywarde, 'apud sanctum Jacobum in campis' (of St James in the Fields, Westminster?),[35] this copy reproduces the

mayster Caxton": Some Histories of Fifteenth-Century Printed Books', in Kuskin, *Caxton's Trace*, pp. 167–95. For the date, see *BMC XI*, p. 194.
[32] Sigs oo4v–oo5v; see further Anne F. Sutton, *A Merchant Family of Coventry, London and Calais: The Tates, c. 1450–1515* (London, 1998).
[33] Fabyan's handwritten copy of the *new cronycles*, which he calls the 'Concordance of storyes', survives in Holkham Hall MS 671 and London, BL MS Cotton Nero C XI.
[34] Reproduced in Carol M. Meale, 'Book Production and Social Status', in *Book Production and Publishing*, ed. Griffiths and Pearsall, pp. 201–38 (210, plate 18).
[35] As suggested by A.I. Doyle, 'English Books In and Out of Court', in *English Court Culture in*

text of Caxton's first edition, printed in 1477 (*STC* 6826–7), but seemingly from a modified version whose printing was completed on 18 November 1477.[36] Haywarde's own colophon made no attempt to conceal the reliance of his copy on a printed edition: 'Thus endeth the boke of the dictes and notable // wise sayenges of Philosophres. late translated // out of ffrenssh into Englissh by my forsaide // lorde. Therle of [Ryuers and lord Skales] and // by his comaundment sette in fourme & enprinted // in right substanciale maner. And this boke // was ffinisshed the xxiiij day of Decembre. the // xvij[th] yere of our liege lord. King Edward þe iiij[th]' (fols 105v–106).[37]

Why it should have been thought appropriate to make a *de luxe* manuscript of a work already in existence in printed form is not clear, unless the explanation is simply that Edward IV knew and admired the manuscript libraries of some of his Flemish acquaintances, and appreciated gifts that took the form of hand-produced books.[38] Caxton's editions of the *dictes and sayengis* were copied in manuscript in other contexts, suggesting that this was a popular work with a wide circulation. The first of the 1477 editions seems to lie behind an abbreviated version, in a northern dialect, which is now Chicago, Newberry Library MS F. 36 Ry 20, while an edition printed *c.*1480 (*STC* 6828; erroneously preserving a colophon which dates it to 1477) served the purposes of a scribe named Thomas Cokke who produced the copy which is now London, BL Add. MS 22718; further scribally copied extracts and summaries also survive.[39]

Imported Continental printed books were also copied by English scribes. In 1496 John Whetham of the London Charterhouse transcribed a Latin translation of Chrysostom's homilies on the Gospel of St John for the prior of the Charterhouse at Sheen, Ralph Tracy, using a copy printed in Rome in 1470 or in Cologne in 1486; in London or Westminster before 1492 an anonymous scribe made a copy of a book printed in Mainz in 1474, Henricus de Herpf, *Speculum aureum decem preceptorum dei*, for William Morland, prebend of St Paul's.[40] Examples from the sixteenth century seem to confirm that these forms of transcription were a regular practice rather than a short-lived phenomenon relating to the novelty of print. Among later instances are the copies of Pynson's 1521 edition of Henry Bradshaw's *holy lyfe and history of saynt Werburge* (*STC* 3506) in Oxford, Balliol College, MS 268; of John Rastell's 1530 edition of *A new boke of purgatory* (*STC* 20719) in Cambridge, Trinity College, MS O. 3. 26; and of

the *Later Middle Ages*, ed. V.J. Scattergood and J.W. Sherborne (London, 1983), pp. 163–81 (181, n.54).

[36] The modified version survives in a copy in the John Rylands Library, Manchester (Inc. 15542); see *BMC IX*, pp. 108–10, and the illustration in Hellinga, *Caxton in Focus*, plate I.

[37] See Hellinga, *Caxton in Focus*, figure 41 (and plate III for a further example of Haywarde's hand).

[38] For further discussion, see Blake, 'Manuscript to Print', pp. 413–14.

[39] See Blake, 'Manuscript to Print', pp. 421–22, and Curt F. Bühler, 'The Dictes and Sayings of the Philosophers', *The Library*, 4th ser., 15 (1934), 316–29.

[40] *Homiliae super Iohannem*, *ISTC* ij00286000 (1470) or ij00287000 (1486); *ISTC* ih00039000, and Blake, 'Manuscript to Print', pp. 428–29. For the larger European context, see Albert Derolez, 'The Copying of Printed Books for Humanistic Bibliophiles in the Fifteenth Century', in *From Script to Print: A Symposium*, ed. H. Bekker-Nielsen et al. (Odense, 1986), pp. 140–60, and M.D. Reeve, 'Manuscripts Copied from Printed Books', in Trapp, *Manuscripts in the Fifty Years after the Invention of Printing*, pp. 12–20.

Berthelet's 1534 edition of Thomas Lupset's *compendious . . . treatyse teachynge the waye of dyenge well* (*STC* 16934) in Oxford, BodL, MS Tanner 118.[41]

Some of these scribal transcriptions draw attention to their printed sources with copies of printers' colophons and reproductions of printed ornaments and woodcuts: such is the case in a scribal copy of Caxton's *Chronicles of England*, now London, Lambeth Palace Library, MS 264, the work of an individual called Rydyng.[42] But scribes did not consistently replicate features of any printed exemplars they used – indeed they sometimes made significant changes, for example adapting linguistic forms to their own usage[43] – and demonstration of their reliance on printed sources can become clear only after exhaustive textual analysis. The identification of transcriptions from print is especially challenging in compilations which draw together extracts from several sources. Such manuscripts include London, BL, Royal MS 18 D II, with scribal copies of some printed works of Lydgate; Manchester, Chetham's Library 6709, with copies of printed saints' lives and Marian material; Oxford, Balliol College, MS 354, with material taken from *Arnold's Chronicle* (*STC* 782) and some copies of printed verse; San Marino, Huntington Library, MS HM 144, with a compilation of extracts from Caxton's printed edition of the *Polychronicon*.[44] Manuscript miscellanies are especially hospitable environments for such extracts. Recent analysis of London, BL, Harley MS 494, a collection of prayers and devotional treatises made between 1532 and 1535 for a female reader, has revealed many instances of scribal dependence on printed exemplars, often simply for short portions of text.[45] As might be expected, the scribal transcription of excerpts from printed texts was especially common in relation to widely circulating works such as the *Polychronicon*, versions of the *Brut* chronicle, and the writings of Chaucer and Lydgate.[46] Some extracts from *The Golden Legend* surviving in manuscript copies were also clearly taken from printed editions.[47] No doubt many more such relationships remain to be identified.

Evidence from handwritten books compiled by readers for their own use, with all that it can suggest about the range of exemplars which an individual had to hand or was able to procure, seems to confirm that the practice of most literate people in the late fifteenth and early sixteenth centuries involved a mixture of manuscript and print. Instances of intersection between products of the two

[41] See Moore, *Materials*, pp. 9 and 8 respectively.

[42] Matheson, *The Prose 'Brut'*, p. 163. Some Continental instances are cited in Derolez, 'The Copying of Printed Books', pp. 142–43. A striking late example is the transcription of de Worde prints in the seventeenth-century manuscript miscellany BodL Eng. poet. e. 97, of which examples are reproduced in Crick and Walsham, *The Use of Script and Print*, pp. 13–14.

[43] See, for example, the practice of the Scottish scribe Adam Loutfut in copying Caxton's *Ordre of Chyvalry* (*STC* 3356.7) in London, BL MS Harley 6149. Loutfut's version was itself copied in other, later sixteenth-century Scottish manuscripts; see Blake, 'Manuscript to Print', p. 424.

[44] All listed in Blake, 'Manuscript to Print'; and on the last, see also Kate Harris, 'Unnoticed Extracts from Chaucer and Hoccleve: Huntington HM 144, Trinity College, Oxford D 29 and the *Canterbury Tales*', *Studies in the Age of Chaucer* 20 (1998), 167–99.

[45] Alexandra Barratt, *Anne Bulkeley and her Book: Fashioning Female Piety in Early Tudor England* (Turnhout, 2009).

[46] Matheson, *The Prose 'Brut'*, pp. 157–72; Harris, 'Unnoticed Extracts'.

[47] V.M. O'Mara, 'From Print to Manuscript: The *Golden Legend* and British Library Lansdowne 379', *Leeds Studies in English* n.s. 23 (1992), 81–104.

processes in the form of manuscript additions made to prints are illuminating in this regard, since they sometimes record active simultaneous engagement with scribal and printed copies.[48] Readers' marks sometimes correct obvious errors, or indicate attempts at textual collation, or supply indices or other finding aids. Larger-scale manuscript interventions occasionally represent attempts to make good absences or losses in printed works. A copy of Caxton's 1491 edition of Mirk's *Liber Festiualis* and *Quattuor sermons* (*STC* 17959, CUL Inc. 3.J.1.1) has been patched in this way with portions of hand-copied material.[49] In some cases manuscript additions were necessary additions to printed books and documents, and anticipated by printers who left appropriate spaces for them. Letters of confraternity and indulgences were printed with gaps for the names of the purchasers – individuals like the Simon and Emma Mountford whose names appear on an indulgence printed by Caxton before 31 March 1480 (*STC* 14077c.107; BL IA.55024).[50] Other forms, modelled on indulgences, were produced for use in connection with the payment of subsidies (for example by de Worde in 1513, *STC* 7764; and by Pynson in 1515, *STC* 7766 and 7767),[51] and blank certificates were also printed for completion after confession (for example, Pynson *c.*1517, *STC* 14077c.5). Missals printed abroad for use in England occasionally left blank spaces in the section devoted to the exchange of marriage vows, since those speaking them would make this exchange in the vernacular: in at least one case the necessary words have been copied in by hand.[52] The ingrained lawyers' habit of noting ownership in lawbooks seems to have persuaded Pynson to leave a gap for ownership inscriptions to be added in his yearbook for 5 Hen. VII (*STC* 9928.5, sig. k6).[53]

Interventions made in the other direction, from printed books into manuscripts, may have posed more practical challenges but certainly took place. The practice of embellishing manuscript books with images or portions of text excised from printed ones, for example, was not uncommon, especially in the context of devotional compilations. Surviving examples include pious roundels pasted into a manuscript copy of additions to the rule for the brethren of the Birgittine house of Syon (London, Guildhall Library, MS 25524), and pious woodcuts added to the sixteenth-century Scottish anthology of devotional verse which is now London, BL Arundel MS 285.[54] Robert Fabyan's autograph manuscripts are decorated with printed woodcuts and portions of border decoration excised

---

[48] For a survey of such practices, see William H. Sherman, *Used Books: Marking Readers in Renaissance England* (Philadelphia, PA, 2008).

[49] Oates 4114.

[50] Duff rev., number 204 (additions to other indulgences are listed under numbers 205–21). The Mountford in question may be Sir Simon Mountford of Coleshill, Warwickshire, executed in 1495 after the Perkin Warbeck rebellion: see R.A. Griffiths, 'The Hazards of Civil War: the Mountford Family and the Wars of the Roses', *Midland History* 5 (1979), 1–19.

[51] 'Press, Politics and Religion', p. 583.

[52] Duff rev., numbers 322, 324, 325.

[53] J.H. Baker, 'The Books of Common Law', in *CHBB III*, pp. 411–32 (414, n.23).

[54] See Bühler, *The Fifteenth-Century Book*, pp. 84–87, for general discussion, and, for English examples, Mary C. Erler, 'Pasted-In Embellishments in English Manuscripts and Printed Books c. 1480–1533', *The Library*, 6th ser., 14 (1992), 185–206. An instance from BL Arundel MS 285 is illustrated in J.A.W. Bennett, ed., *Devotional Pieces in Prose and Verse from MS. Arundel 285 and MS. Harleian 6919*, Scottish Text Society, 3rd ser., 23 (Edinburgh, 1955), facing p. 7.

from a range of Continental printed works.[55] It is occasionally possible to chart whole sequences of movement between manuscript and print, as in the manuscript copy of *The Canterbury Tales* which is now Oxford, BodL, Laud Misc. MS 739, into which a sixteenth-century reader wrote corrections taken from a copy of Caxton's first printed edition of the work.[56]

The ease with which contemporary readers adapted to the changing technology of book production is perhaps most strikingly visible in the form of early 'hybrid books': volumes mostly still in their early bindings in which portions of both manuscript and printed material were juxtaposed. Because such volumes are of necessity compilations of a number of independently produced books or pamphlets they are often subsumed in the bibliographical category of 'tract volumes' or *Sammelbände*, but, properly speaking, they are a specialised form of this type of assemblage. Roger Thorney's collection of Chaucer and Lydgate and the *Quattuor sermones*, described above, is one such hybrid book; others survive, sometimes identifiable in specialised catalogues of incunabula or of bindings, but mostly rather overlooked, if not actually troublesome for the libraries which possess them and need to apportion them either to a department of manuscripts or to one of printed books (a number have been disbound and can only be retrospectively reconstructed). Among surviving hybrid books are another volume in the library of St John's College, Oxford, in which a manuscript copy of Lydgate's *Kalendar* is bound with four Caxton prints (MS 340);[57] a volume from the Abbey of St Werburg in Chester which unites six thirteenth-century manuscript booklets with a Latin commentary on the Song of Songs printed in Paris in 1509 (now London, Gray's Inn MS 14);[58] and a volume now in the library of Peterhouse, Cambridge, uniting a manuscript copy of works by Virgil with a 1475 Louvain edition of the works of Juvenal and Persius (MS 159).[59]

That readers should have constructed hybrid books like these is entirely unsurprising in a context where many bound volumes would have been composites of one sort or another. Printers recognised that readers would want to keep certain works together, as much for practical convenience as for reasons to do with complementarity of contents, and they sometimes facilitated such practice by producing books in standard formats or serial editions.[60] De Worde's

[55] Erler, 'Pasted-In Embellishments'.
[56] J.M. Manly and Edith Rickert, *The Text of 'The Canterbury Tales'*, 8 vols (Chicago, IL, 1940), 1.319.
[57] See *Printer and Pardoner*, p. 77; and Ralph Hanna, *A Descriptive Catalogue of the Western Medieval Manuscripts of St John's College, Oxford* (Oxford, 2002), pp. 333–34.
[58] Gregorius, *Exposicio super cantica canticorum*, B. Rembolt et J. Waterloes (Paris, 1509); P.R. Robinson, *Catalogue of Dated and Datable Manuscripts c. 888–1600 in London Libraries* (London, 2004), p. 35.
[59] *ISTC* ij00636300; and M.R. James, *A Descriptive Catalogue of the Manuscripts in the Library of Peterhouse* (Cambridge, 1899), pp. 187–88. Peterhouse MS 250, described in James, pp. 305–07, and also mixing manuscript and printed materials, has a similar binding, and contains a note of ownership by '*magistri Thome deynman medici*'. On forms of hybridity more generally, see David McKitterick, *Print, Manuscript and the Search for Order 1450–1830* (Cambridge, 2003).
[60] For some examples, see Alexandra Gillespie, 'Caxton's Chaucer and Lydgate Quartos: Miscellanies from Manuscript to Print', *TCBS* 12 (2000), 1–26; E.A. Jones and Alexandra Walsham, 'Syon Abbey and its Books: Origins, Influences and Transitions', in *Syon Abbey and its*

introduction to his first quarto edition of the schoolbook called the *Promptuarium paruulorum* (*STC* 20435–9) drew attention to the features which made it suitable for binding with his edition of another schoolbook called the *Ortus vocabulorum* (*STC* 13830.7–37): 'we haue ordened thys libel in small volum for to byynde with Ortus vacabulorum [*sic*]' (*STC* 20435, 1508, sig. [n]4r).[61] Such incitement to compilation, gesturing at the 'booklet' forms of production already in use by scribes and stationers,[62] is just one instance of the many ways in which printers replicated established production habits and patterns.

While this and other links represent continuities between the worlds of printers and of scribes, there developed nonetheless some clearly demarcated areas of operation. The production of certain kinds of book in regular demand, such as schoolbooks and some lawbooks (especially statutes and year-books), was fairly quickly monopolised by printers.[63] The printing of propaganda, similarly, facilitated by the existence of the post of King's Printer after 1504, was to become a significant force, increasingly so in the face of the religious and political pressures of the 1520s and 1530s.[64] Contexts in which scribal production energetically continued were various, ranging from the administrative ones which generated minutes and records and business documents to diplomatic circles where secrecy was at a premium, or milieux in which heterodox views were expressed and exchanged. In some cases printing simply complemented scribal production. Perhaps surprisingly, indulgences and letters of confraternity still continued to be produced by hand, even though printers took over much business in these areas.[65] Handmade presentation volumes were produced alongside printed editions of some works, as with Whittinton's *Libellus epygrammaton* which survives in a manuscript made for presentation to Cardinal Wolsey (Oxford, BodL, MS Bodley 523) and also in an edition printed by de Worde in 1519 (*STC* 25540.5) for wider circulation.[66] The dissemination of propaganda sometimes necessitated both manuscript and print in order to cover all bases: Henry VIII's *Assertio septem sacramentorum* of 1521, directed against Luther, was printed by Pynson (*STC* 13078–9), with some copies on vellum for targeted distribution, and also prepared in a manuscript copy for presentation to the pope (Biblioteca Apostolica Vaticana, MS lat. 3731).[67]

Just as many individual bound volumes from this period contained both manuscript and print, so the libraries of individuals and institutions would have

---

Books, pp. 1–38 (31–34); Julie Smith, 'Woodcut Presentation Scenes in Books Printed by Caxton, de Worde and Pynson', *Gutenberg Jahrbuch* (1986), 322–43.

[61] Like printed lawbooks, printed schoolbooks often survive in tract volumes.

[62] Ralph Hanna, 'Booklets in Medieval Manuscripts: Further Considerations', in *Pursuing History: Middle English Manuscripts and their Texts* (Stanford, CA, 1996), pp. 21–34.

[63] See Baker, 'The Books of the Common Law', and Nicholas Orme, 'Schools and Schoolbooks', in *CHBB III*, pp. 449–69.

[64] 'Press, Politics and Religion'.

[65] R.N. Swanson, *Indulgences in Late Medieval England: Passports to Paradise?* (Cambridge, 2007), pp. 172–8.

[66] See David Carlson, *English Humanist Books. Writers and Patrons, Manuscript and Print, 1475–1525* (Toronto, 1993), pp. 109–22; and H.M. Nixon, 'The Gilt Binding of the Whittinton Epigrams, MS Bodley 523', *The Library*, 5th ser., 7 (1952), 120–21.

[67] *William Caxton*, pp. 118–19.

probably contained a mixture of books produced by both methods.[68] Authors also adapted their practices to both modes of production. Some, like Alexander Barclay, who evidently forged a partnership with Pynson, seem to have exercised a determined preference to publish their works in printed editions;[69] others, such as Thomas More in the 1530s, were restricted by force of circumstance to scribal publication. Richard Whitford of Syon explored both possibilities, recounting in the preface to his *dayly exercice and experience of dethe* (*STC* 25413.7, 1534?, etc.) that he had first composed and copied the work twenty years before, and that in the face of renewed requests to 'wryte // it agayne & agayne ... bycause // that wrytynge vnto me is very te=//dyouse: I thought better to put it // in print' (sig. A[1]v). The options for originators of texts and documents, as for readers, continued to remain flexible, shaped by individual combinations of factors relating to intended readership, circumstance, means and available technology.

Further Reading

Bühler, Curt F., *The Fifteenth-Century Book. The Scribes, the Printers, The Decorators* (Philadelphia, PA, 1960).
Blake, N.F., 'Manuscript to Print', in *Book Production and Publishing in Britain 1375–1475*, ed. Jeremy Griffiths and Derek Pearsall (Cambridge, 1989), pp. 403–19.
Carlson, David, *English Humanist Books. Writers and Patrons, Manuscript and Print, 1475–1525* (Toronto, 1993).
Edwards, A.S.G., 'Decorated Caxtons', in *Incunabula: Studies in Fifteenth-Century Printed Books Presented to Lotte Hellinga*, ed. Martin Davies (London, 1999), pp. 493–506.
Erler, Mary C., 'Pasted-In Embellishments in English Manuscripts and Printed Books c. 1480–1533', *The Library*, 6th ser., 14 (1992), 185–206.
Hellinga, Lotte, *William Caxton and Early Printing in England* (London, 2010).
Kuskin, William, ed., *Caxton's Trace: Studies in the History of English Printing* (Notre Dame, IN, 2006).
McKitterick, David, *Print, Manuscript and the Search for Order 1450–1830* (Cambridge, 2003).
Scott, K., *The Caxton Master and his Patrons*, Cambridge Bibliographical Society Monographs 8 (Cambridge, 1976).
Trapp, J.B., ed., *Manuscripts in the Fifty Years after the Invention of Printing. Some Papers Read at a Colloquium at the Warburg Institute on 12–13 March 1982* (London, 1983).
Walsham, Alexandra, and Julia Crick, eds, *The Uses of Script and Print, 1300–1700* (Cambridge, 2004).

[68] See the published volumes of the Corpus of British Medieval Library Catalogues, and *The Cambridge History of Libraries in Britain and Ireland. Volume I, To 1640*, ed. Elisabeth Leedham-Green and Teresa Webber (Cambridge, 2006).
[69] David Carlson, 'Alexander Barclay and Richard Pynson: A Tudor Printer and his Writer', *Anglia* 113 (1995), 283–302.

2

Printers, Publishers and Promoters to 1558[1]

TAMARA ATKIN AND A.S.G. EDWARDS

The Printers: 1476–91

Printing did not begin in England until around 1476, when William Caxton set up a shop in Westminster, within the precincts of the Abbey there. The earliest work he printed there seems to have been John Russell's *Propositio* (*STC* 21458), completed before September of that year.[2] But he already had considerable experience of the new technology of moveable type on the Continent before he returned to his native land; in 1472 he had been involved in the printing of several books at Cologne, including an edition of a very large medieval encyclopaedia, Bartholomaeus Anglicus's *De proprietatibus rerum*. Subsequently, he was involved in the printing of a number of books in Bruges and very probably in Ghent, including the earliest book printed in English, his translation of Raoul le Fèvre, *The Recuyell of the History of Troy* (1473–74, *STC* 15375), which was printed alongside the French original, *Le recueil des histoire de Troie* (c.1474), and *The Game and Play of Chess* (1474, *STC* 4920). The translations of both texts from the French were Caxton's own work.[3]

England was the first country where printing was introduced by a native. Caxton (c.1420–92) was born in Kent and began a mercantile career in London before spending much of his commercial life in the Low Countries.[4] When he returned to England to set up its first printing press, he brought to the country of his birth the Continental expertise he had acquired, as well as more tangible debts to Europe reflected most directly in his use of type cast from matrices made by his former Cologne collaborator, Johannes Veldener.[5]

Caxton's books, like those of his earliest followers, lagged behind Continental

---

[1] In this chapter we have relied for information on some resources that are not specifically cited here: for all dates for persons on *ODNB*; for all dates for books, on *STC*; for all information about printers' outputs on the information in Volume 3 of *STC*; for other information about printers and others connected with the book trade, on Duff. In spite of these resources biographical information about many early printers is very scanty and for a number of figures mentioned here no useful information survives apart from their books.

[2] On the chronology of Caxton's publications, see *Printer and Pardoner*, pp. 83–91.

[3] For the most recent and most authoritative discussion of Caxton's Continental printing, see *William Caxton*, especially pp. 26–51.

[4] There are numerous biographies of Caxton; the most recent and most useful is George Painter, *William Caxton: A Quincentenary Biography of England's First Printer* (London, 1976).

[5] On the introduction of Continental type into England, see Nicolas Barker, 'Caxton's Typography', *Journal of the Printing Historical Society* 11 (1976/7), 114–33.

developments in a number of technical respects. His own earliest books lacked pagination or quire signatures, were undated, and never had title pages (these did not become standard in England until the 1490s). Book illustration did not begin there until Caxton's first edition of *The Mirror of the World* in 1481 (*STC* 24762) and, although it became a fairly common feature thereafter, wood-cuts were often borrowed from Continental models and frequently recycled, sometimes with limited contextual appropriateness.[6] Type was also imported from the Continent; this seems generally to have continued to be the case until well after the incorporation of the Stationers' Company in 1557.[7] Unlike the Continent, where roman or italic types became the norm for general use as early as the 1490s, England continued to work with black-letter and some bastarda types until well into the sixteenth century. When a roman fount was eventually introduced, by Richard Pynson in 1509, it was used for texts that had obvious classical associations. Paper, the most common material used for printed books (vellum was only occasionally employed), was only produced in England for a brief period in the 1490s.[8] Otherwise it came primarily from Italy. At the same time, English books did not receive the sometimes lavish hand decoration and illumination often enjoyed by Continental incunables.[9] Similarly, there was little printing in colour or in gold in England.[10]

There is, however, in one crucial respect, a level of national distinctiveness in English printing from its beginnings. From the outset, the majority of the printed books were in the vernacular. Overall, some 59 per cent of all books printed in England before 1501 were English; the comparable figure for other European vernaculars is under 30 per cent.[11] In the case of Caxton himself this figure was higher: of the hundred and ten books he printed at Westminster from 1476 to 1491, seventy-one were either wholly or significantly in English; often these were substantial books. It is clear that he brought to his new role as publisher an evident sense that the native tongue was the crucial factor in creating markets for printed books.

The range of Caxton's English publications is considerable. There was a substantial amount of Middle English verse: Chaucer, including the *Canterbury Tales* twice, *Troilus and Criseyde*, and the *Parliament of Fowls*; Lydgate, several of his shorter poems and his *Life of Our Lady*; and Gower's *Confessio Amantis*. There were also a number of substantial works in Middle English prose, some

---

[6]   On English woodcuts in this period, see E. Hodnett, *English Woodcuts 1480–1535*, revised edn (Oxford, 1973).

[7]   Two early exceptions to this general pattern are the presses established at Oxford by Theodoric Rood, who deployed types that may have been cut in Oxford, and at St Albans, where it seems that three of the four types used there between 1479 and 1486 were cut locally. On the first Oxford press, see Nicolas Barker, *The Oxford University Press and the Spread of Learning: An Illustrated History, 1478–1978* (Oxford, 1978), pp. 2–4. On the press at St Albans, see Nicolas Barker, 'The St. Albans Press: The First Punch-Cutter in England and the First Native Typefounder?', *TCBS* 7 (1979), 257–70.

[8]   By John Tate, in Hertfordshire. The books involved were all printed for de Worde; see Allan Stevenson, 'Tudor Roses from John Tate', *Studies in Bibliography* 20 (1967), 15–34.

[9]   See A.S.G. Edwards, 'Decorated Caxtons', in *Incunabula*, pp. 491–503.

[10]   See further, V. Carter, Lotte Hellinga and T. Parker, 'Printing with Gold in the Fifteenth Century', *British Library Journal* 9 (1983), 1–13.

[11]   See Lotte Hellinga and J.B. Trapp, 'Introduction', in *CHBB III*, p. 19.

historical, like John Trevisa's translation of Higden's *Polychronicon* and the *Brut* (the latter reprinted), some devotional, like Nicholas Love's *Mirror of the Life of Christ* (again reprinted), some more broadly religious, like his several editions of John Mirk's sermons generally issued together with the *Quattuor sermones*, or the *Golden Legend*. To these works were added secular romances, for example, Thomas Malory's *Morte Darthur* and Caxton's own translations from the French, of prose romances, like *Charles the Great*, the *History of Jason* and the *Four Sons of Aymon* and other of his translations, including the *Mirror of the World*, the *Royal Book* and *Reynard the Fox*, and a further edition of the *Game of Chess*. Caxton's own literary agenda as translator seems to have been a factor in the output of his press.

Caxton was also the first early English printer to establish his press on a stable economic footing. There were other early printers who were briefly active in the 1480s, both within the metropolitan area and elsewhere during the period from around 1476 to around 1491 when Caxton was operating his press. Almost all of these printers came from Europe.[12] William de Machlinia (*fl.* 1482–90), from Belgium, printed about twenty-five books in London between *c.*1481 and *c.*1486; seven of these, between 1481 and 1483, were collaborative works with John Lettou (*fl.* 1475–83), who probably came from Lithuania. Outside London, Theodoric Rood, from Cologne, printed seventeen surviving books in Oxford between around 1478 and 1486, seven of them in collaboration with the Oxford stationer, Thomas Hunt. They were all seemingly primarily intended to meet the demands of the university market. A few books were also printed at St Albans, chiefly in the late 1470s and early 1480s by an unknown printer or printers. In addition, a small number of other Continental printers served the early English market for printed books from abroad: Gerard Leeu, who printed in Gouda and in Antwerp between 1477 and 1484, produced seven books for the English market; Martin Morin printed about twenty books for it in Rouen between 1492 and 1519; and Wolfgang Hopyl, in Paris, produced nearly thirty books between 1494 and 1520.

The Printers: 1491–1534

Caxton differed from all these other printers because he was able to create a substantial business in the metropolis that was sufficiently economically viable to be handed on to his successor, Wynkyn de Worde (d. 1534/5).[13] That he was able to do so served to create market conditions in which, after his death, for the first time, there was real competition in book production in England. In 1492, the

---

[12] For a general overview of the debt of early English printing to the Continent, see A.S.G. Edwards, 'Continental Influences on London Printing and Reading in the Fifteenth and Early Sixteenth Centuries', in *London and Europe in the Fifteenth Century*, ed. Julia Boffey and Pamela King (London, 1995), pp. 229–56.

[13] For an overview of de Worde's career and a list of his publications, see James Moran, *Wynkyn de Worde, Father of Fleet Street, with a Chronological Bibliography of Works on de Worde Compiled by Lotte Hellinga and Mary Erler and a Preface by John Dreyfus*, 3rd revised edn (London, 2003); N.F. Blake, 'Wynkyn de Worde: The Early Years', *Gutenberg Jahrbuch* (1971), 62–69 and 'Wynkyn de Worde: The Later Years', *Gutenberg Jahrbuch* (1972), 128–38.

year Caxton died, Richard Pynson (c.1449–1529/30) established his own press in London. For the next thirty years de Worde, who came from Holland, and Pynson, a Frenchman, were to dominate English publishing and to shape its future by their extension of large and stable markets. During this period de Worde printed about 850 separate editions and Pynson about 600; for both printers the bulk of their output was works in English. To put these figures into some sort of perspective, 477 incunable printings are recorded of books either printed in England or for the English market; de Worde printed 120 and Pynson about 125.[14] This means that in less than a decade, de Worde and Pynson printed about half of all surviving books printed for English markets before 1501.

The kinds of books they printed suggest something of the pragmatic apportioning of markets that seems likely to have taken place between them, and points to other factors that probably shaped their outputs.[15] Pynson, for example, became King's Printer in 1506/7. And though he was not the first to hold the title – in 1504, William Faques gives his title as 'ye King Printer' (STC 9357) – he was the first systematically to develop the role. Yearbooks, statutes and proclamations amount to more than a sixth of his overall output, a figure that no doubt reflects the growing control the King's Printer had over such official publications. Pynson also seems, by virtue of this role, to have enjoyed privilege in printing indulgences, of which he also published more than a hundred (out of the 154 that survive); de Worde printed just fifteen. Pynson's increasing responsibility for the printing of political and religious propaganda further highlights some of the ways that he developed the office to reflect government policy, first during the 1512–13 war with France, through such works as *The gardyners passetaunce* (1512, STC 11562.5) and later against Lutheran heresy. It was his printing of the *Assertio septem sacramentorum aduersus M. Lutherum* in 1521 (STC 13078), written in part by Henry VIII himself, which directly resulted in a papal bull conferring upon the king the title 'Fidei Defensor'.

In such circumstances, the pressure of establishing new markets fell considerably more heavily on de Worde than on Pynson. De Worde was the most prolific and wide-ranging of the early printers. He seems to have sought to develop markets, particularly for smaller, hence cheaper books, that required less capital investment and could be produced more quickly. His regular use of woodcuts, both on title pages and elsewhere, sometimes integrated with considerable adroitness into the text itself, seems to suggest a desire to make his books as attractive, and hence as marketable, as possible.[16] Over half de Worde's surviving books have illustrations compared to less than a third of Pynson's.

The economic bases of the early book trade in general and de Worde's in particular are not easy to determine.[17] To what extent was de Worde's output

---

[14] We derive these figures from Duff rev.

[15] For some analysis of the creation and shaping of markets, see 'Marketing Printed Books', pp. 96–124.

[16] See, for example, A.S.G. Edwards, 'Poet and Printer in Sixteenth Century England: Stephen Hawes and Wynkyn de Worde', *Gutenberg Jahrbuch* (1980), 82–88 and William Marx, 'Julian Notary, Wynkyn de Worde, and the Earliest Printed Texts of the Middle English Gospel of Nicodemus', *Neuphilologische Mitteilugen* 96 (1995), 389–98, especially 306.

[17] For brief and necessarily inconclusive discussion, see James Raven, *The Business of Books* (New Haven, CT, 2007), pp. 15–17.

speculative, significantly or wholly determined by the perceived demand of the market? It seems possible (but by no means certain) that in some instances de Worde may have been able to secure some form of economic support for various books he published. But it is hard to determine what such support amounted to. Lady Margaret Beaufort (1443–1509), the mother of Henry VII, provides a case in point. She was associated with Caxton, Pynson and de Worde, all of whom invoke her name in connection with various of their publications. But her most extended support (of whatever kind) seems to have been for de Worde, who was named as her printer just before her death in 1509. She may have provided some assistance of a material kind, involving some form of subvention, or guaranteed purchases of numbers of copies, though there is no hard evidence to suggest this was the case. Or it might have been that her name alone was enough to guarantee a boost to sales.[18]

Lady Margaret herself may have had some role in de Worde's involvement with the Birgittine house of Syon in Middlesex with which she had her own connections.[19] He printed a number of works by its religious and other residents, including Simon Winter's *Life of St Jerome* ([1499?], STC 14508), Thomas Betson's *Ryght profitable treatyse* (1500, STC 1978), William Bonde's *Pilgrimage of perfection* (1531, STC 3278), Richard Whitford's *Pomander of prayer* (1532, STC 25421.6), and editions of his *Werke for housholders* (1530, STC 25422; 1533, STC 25423).[20] He also printed, at the 'greate coste' of Richard Sutton, steward of Syon, an edition of *The Orchard of Syon* (1519, STC 4815). In at least one instance he provided Syon with sixty copies of one of his books, *The Image of Love* (1525, STC 21471.5).[21]

Such indications of a close economic relationship with a particular institution are rare for de Worde, but they do point to the possibility that, for at least some of his publications, he had some form of financial support. For example, in 1495, he printed two very big books, both translations by John Trevisa. One was of Bartholomaeus Anglicus's *De proprietatibus rerum* (STC 1536), the largest English incunable (478 leaves), the other (398 leaves) of Ranulf Higden's *Polychronicon* (STC 13440b). The first of these was printed 'at prayer and desire // Of Roger Thorney mercer' according to its colophon. The second was a book 'whiche Roger Thorney Mercer hath exhorted // Wynkyn de Worde of virtuous entent . . . // This specyall boke to make and sette in prent' (sig. A1v). Roger Thorney, a London mercer who also had had connections with Caxton, was evidently a man of some wealth; he owned both printed books and manuscripts and provided de Worde with the copy-text for his edition of Lydgate's *Siege of Thebes*

[18] For a discussion of Lady Margaret's relationship with de Worde and other printers, see Susan Powell, 'Lady Margaret Beaufort and her Books', *The Library*, 6th ser., 20 (1998), 197–240, especially 211–19.

[19] See further, George Keiser, 'Patronage and Piety in Fifteenth-Century England: Margaret, Duchess of Clarence, Symon Wynter and Beinecke MS 317', *Yale University Library Gazette* 50 (1985), 32–46, especially 44–46; 'Marketing Printed Books', pp. 99–103, 115–16; Powell, 'Lady Margaret Beaufort', pp. 220–21, 223–24.

[20] See further, J.T. Rhodes, 'Syon Abbey and its Religious Publications in the Sixteenth Century', *Journal of Ecclesiastical History* 44 (1993), 11–25; Susan Powell, 'Syon Abbey as a Centre for Text Production', in *Saint Birgitta, Syon and Vadstena: Papers from a Symposium in Stockholm 4–6 October 2007*, ed. Claes Gejrot, Sara Risberg and Mia Akestam, Konferenser 73 (Stockholm, 2010), pp. 50–67.

[21] On this book, see A.W. Reed, *Early Tudor Drama* (London, 1926), pp. 166–69.

(*STC* 17031) in 1498.[22] Whether de Worde published his large books in 1495 with financial support of some kind from Thorney cannot be established, but, given the capital risk involved in printing two such books of this size in quick succession and the emphasis given to his name and commercial identity, it seems generally probable that Thorney provided some financial cushion, even if we cannot establish of what kind.

However, by and large de Worde seems to have had to create his own markets with varying degrees of speculativeness, some of which may have been riskier than others. Education was one safe area: the proliferation of editions of the various grammars of John Stanbridge (1463–1510) and Robert Whittinton (*c*.1480–1553) were an obvious manifestation of such a demand for basic educational tools, particularly in the early sixteenth century.[23] De Worde seems to have dominated this market; over eighty editions of Stanbridge's works and nearly 150 of Whittinton's survive from his press, about 30 per cent of his entire output.

In developing other markets de Worde sometimes seems to have built on ones first perceived by Caxton, as with his printing of Middle English devotional works, like those by Nicholas Love and John Mirk, and of secular literature, like Chaucer and Malory, both of whom he also reprinted.[24] But in both these fields he widened patterns of publication from the outset. In the 1490s, for example, he added new English devotional works to his list, like *The Abbey of the Holy Ghost* (1496 and 1500, *STC* 13609–10), *The Chastising of God's Children* (1493, *STC* 5065), *St Bernard's Meditations* (1496, *STC* 1916), and *The tretyse of love* (1493, *STC* 24234). He also printed other current religious writings from early in his career, including for the first time sermons by contemporary divines. In the 1490s these included seven editions (*STC* 278–79, 281–87) of those of John Alcock (1430–1500), bishop of Ely, and one ([1495?], *STC* 11024) by Richard Fitzjames (d. 1522), bishop of Rochester and later London. He enlarged the print corpus of Middle English verse to include Middle English metrical romances, and he was also the first printer to seek to develop a market for contemporary verse, printing the full corpus of Stephen Hawes (*c*.1474–*c*.1529) and William Walter (*fl. c*.1525–33), as well as other poems by Thomas Feylde, Christopher Goodwyn (*fl.* 1520–42), and William Neville (b. 1497, d. in or before 1545).[25] Over eighty-five separate editions of verse texts survive from his press.

De Worde's role in developing printing in London and beyond is also an

[22] See Gavin Bone, 'Extant Manuscripts Printed from by W. de Worde with Notes on the Owner, Roger Thorney', *The Library*, 4th ser., 12 (1931–32), 284–309.
[23] For further consideration of the printing of educational texts, see Daniel Wakelin's chapter in this volume.
[24] On the sequence of Love's early editions, see Lotte Hellinga, 'Nicholas Love in Print', in *Nicholas Love at Waseda*, ed. S. Ogura, R. Beadle and M.G. Sargent (Cambridge, 1997), pp. 143–62. On his edition of Chaucer, see Satoko Tokunaga, 'The Sources of Wynkyn de Worde's Version of "The Monk's Tale"', *The Library*, 7th ser., 2 (2001), 223–35; on Malory, see Tsuyoshi Mukai, 'De Worde's 1498 *Morte Darthur* and Caxton's Copy-Text', *Review of English Studies* n.s., 51 (2000), 24–40.
[25] On his printing of these, see Carol M. Meale, 'Caxton, de Worde and the Publication of Romance in Late Medieval England', *The Library*, 6th ser., 14 (1992), 281–98. On his printing of contemporary verse, see A.S.G. Edwards, 'Wynkyn de Worde and Contemporary Poetry', *Gutenberg Jahrbuch* (1991), 143–48.

important one. He seems to have retained commercial and personal links with a circle of native print artisans. They include figures who became established printers in their own right, men like Robert Copland (*fl.* 1505–47), John Butler, John Byddell (*fl.* 1543–45?) and James Gaver (d. 1545), all of whom are mentioned in de Worde's will, as well as John Gough, also a bookseller (d. 1543/4), Henry Pepwell (d. 1539/40), John Skot (*fl.* 1521–37) and Henry Watson, who all had commercial and/or other links to him. For example, Byddell, who inherited de Worde's establishment at the sign of The Sun, is identified in his will as a former servant. His business later passed to another printer, Edward Whitchurch (d. 1562).[26] Copland too seems to have started his printing career in de Worde's shop, and their working relationship extended through to de Worde's death in 1535. To put it another way, he seems to have retained close economic links to his former master. Copland is named as printer in a number of editions bearing de Worde's colophon or device, and it is quite possible that at least some of the thirty-five editions in which he was identified as publisher were in fact printed for de Worde.

Pynson seems to have followed de Worde into some of the markets he developed, publishing the various works in verse and prose of Alexander Barclay (*c.*1484–1552) and, in the 1520s, the sermons of Bishop John Longlond (1473–1547).[27] However, he seems to have developed fewer connections with other printers, perhaps because his role as King's Printer made alliances unnecessary. John Haukyns (*fl.* 1530), who married Pynson's daughter, Margaret, seems to have had links to the trade, albeit of a negligible kind. Pynson's relationship with Robert Redman (d. 1540), who would eventually take over his establishment, is hard to define. During the last five years of his life, Pynson's monopoly in the field of legal printing was challenged by Redman. In 1525 he began printing and selling books from Pynson's old premises at St Clement Danes, outside Temple Bar, adopting both his sign of The George and an 'RR' monogram clearly designed to resemble Pynson's 'RP'. In 1527, Redman moved to his own shop on Fleet Street, just 100 yards from Pynson, and on Pynson's death in 1530 he purchased his business and moved into his old shop.

Pynson was clearly unimpressed by Redman's mimicry, and in his 1528 edition of Thomas Littleton's *Tenures* (*STC* 15728) he described him as 'Rob. Redman, sed verius Rudeman' ('Robert Redman, but more correctly called "rude man"'). Still, by adopting Pynson's signs, and on his death, his premises and devices, Redman was able to compete in a field of the book market that was dominated by the King's Printer. After Pynson's death Redman continued to compete with his successor to the office of King's Printer, Thomas Berthelet (d. 1555), by issuing legal books for which the King's Printer had specific privileges.[28] Berthelet himself seems to have worked for Pynson (and also possibly

---

[26] On Copland, see F.C. Francis, *Robert Copland, Sixteenth Century Printer and Translator* (Glasgow, 1961) and Mary C. Erler, ed., *Robert Copland, Poems* (Toronto, 1993). For de Worde's will, see Mary C. Erler, 'Wynkyn de Worde's Will: Legatees and Bequests', *The Library*, 6th ser., 10 (1988), 107–21. Whitchurch is treated more extensively below.

[27] See David Carlson, 'Alexander Barclay and Richard Pynson: A Tudor Printer and his Writer', *Anglia* 113 (1995), 283–302.

[28] A more extensive discussion of the legal book trade can be found in J.H. Baker 'The Books of Common Law', in *CHBB III*, pp. 411–32.

for John Rastell) before establishing his own business. The emergence of such aggressive competition is perhaps another sign of the economic pressures such sixteenth-century printers faced and the strategies they employed to resolve them. After Redman's death, his widow, working under her maiden name, Elisabeth Pickering (c.1510–62), became the first English woman to print books, in 1540–41, the majority of them law books first printed by her husband.[29]

There were other London printers who seem to have operated outside such networks and in some instances formed their own dynasties. John Rastell (c.1465–1536) printed from c.1509 to 1533; his son William (1508–65) also printed from 1529 to 1534. William Faques, printer from 1504 to 1507, was possibly the father of Richard Faques who seems to have succeeded him and printed from 1507 to 1531. It is also appropriate to mention in this context William Copland (d. 1569), probably Robert Copland's son, who took over the former's press and operated from 1545 to 1567.

However, it would be simplistic to isolate family relationships from other patterns of trade activity. Pragmatic collaboration seem to have been possible in ad hoc ways: de Worde and Pynson occasionally seem to have jointly printed large books, such as the *Royal Book* and *Golden Legend*, both in 1507, doubtless in the face of shared commercial pressures. Later, Redman used Rastell's types, a fact which suggests that there were connections between the two printers.[30] Similarly, de Worde seems to have had links to various Continental and provincial printers and stationers. Such collaboration seems to have expressed itself in other practical ways, as in the loaning or bequest of materials. De Worde appears to have given a set of his types to Hugo Goes in York, and Goes was later in partnership with Henry Watson in London.

The ramifications of such alliances beyond London point to a series of further attempts to establish printing houses in provincial towns in the earlier years of the sixteenth century. These attempts were often made by printers who seem to have been of foreign extraction: in Oxford by George Chastelain (1503–08) and Henry Jacobi (1512–14), both apparently French; in Exeter in 1505 by Martin Coffyn, from Normandy; in York by a series of printers: Hugo Goes (1506–09), possibly from Antwerp, who subsequently printed in London, Gerard Wandsforth (1507) from the Low Countries, Ursyn Mylner (c.1513–19), whose origins are unclear but probably not English, and John Gaschet (1509–17), a Frenchman who also printed in Hereford in 1517; in Cambridge by the German bookseller, John Siberch (1520–23/4). Only a few natives took to provincial printing, and then with only intermittent success. Thomas Richard printed in Tavistock in 1525 and 1534, and John Mychell (d. 1556), who seems to have moved to Canterbury in 1533 from London where he had printed a few books, returned to London in 1547 after producing no more than sixteen books from his

---

[29] On the inheritance of stock, patents, equipment by wives and widows, see Susan Lenkey, 'Printers' Wives in the Age of Humanism', *Gutenberg Jahrbuch* (1975), 331–37. For the early history of women and book production more generally, see Helen Smith, '"Print[ing] your royal father off": Early Modern Female Stationers and the Gendering of the British Book Trades', *TEXT* 15 (2003), 163–86, and her monograph, *'Grossly Material Things': Women and Book Production in Early Modern England* (Oxford, 2012).
[30] See Baker, 'The Books of Common Law', p. 426.

provincial press. In short, none of these early, non-metropolitan presses lasted very long.[31]

In other regions the impact of printing varied between the non-existent and the fragmented. There was no printing in Ireland recorded before 1551 or in Wales before 1585.[32] In Scotland, there is scattered evidence of some activity from the middle of the first decade of the sixteenth century in the publication of an edition of William Dunbar's *Twa mariit wemen and the wedo* (1507, *STC* 7350). At around the same time, but from a different unidentified press, there appeared a Scottish version of Donatus's *Ars Minor* (*c*.1507, *STC* 7018). Before that, in 1505, Andrew Myllar (*fl*. 1503–08) had commissioned in Rouen another grammar, John of Garland's *Equivoca* (*STC* 11604.5) for the Edinburgh market. Several years later, in collaboration with Walter Chepman (1471?–1528), he began printing in Edinburgh. In 1508 they published eleven books in English, which, with one exception, *The porteous of noblesse* (*STC* 5060.5), were all in verse: *The book of good counsel* (*STC* 3307); several poems of Dunbar (*STC* 7347–9); poems by other Scots poets (one by Robert Henryson (*STC* 13166), one by Richard Holland (*STC* 13594) and Harry's *Wallace* (*STC* 13148)); Lydgate's *Complaint of the Black Knight* (*STC* 17014.3); and the romances *Eglamour of Artois* (*STC* 7542) and *Golagros and Gawane* (*STC* 11984). This spurt of activity was not sustained, presumably because of the lack of secure markets for such a narrowly focused output, and henceforward there were only isolated attempts at publication in Scotland down to the 1550s.[33]

However, in England markets began to change and to expand. A factor here was probably changes in trade conditions. If the early history of printing there was dominated by alien printers, by the middle of the sixteenth century the trade was the preserve of English craftsmen.[34] The gradual preferment of

---

[31]   On the early history of provincial presses, see E.G. Duff, *The English Provincial Printers, Stations and Bookbinders to 1557* (Cambridge, 1912); and Paul Morgan, *English Provincial Printing* (Birmingham, 1959).

[32]   The first Dublin press was established by Humphrey Powell, who may have been related to the London printers William and Thomas Powell. The only surviving book to emerge from his press is a reprint of the first Book of Common Prayer (1551, *STC* 16277). He may also have been responsible for the 1558 publication of a verse history of the fall of Troy ([*c*.1558?], *STC* 7481.7) of which only a few sheets survive. Other extant publications include a number of broadsides and a theological tract. The first book printed in Welsh was John Price's *Yny lhyvyr hwnn y tra-ethir* in 1546 by Edward Whitchurch (*STC* 20310). The first book to be printed on Welsh soil was *Y Drych Cristianogawl* (*c*.1585, *STC* 21077), a Catholic book which was printed in secret by Roger Thackwell and given a false imprint to mislead the authorities. On the early history of print-ing in Ireland, see Raymond Gillespie, *Reading Ireland: Print, Reading and Social Change in Early Modern Ireland* (Manchester, 2005); and *The Oxford History of the Irish Book*, 5 vols (Oxford, 2006), III: *The Irish Book in English, 1550–1800*, ed. Raymond Gillespie and Andrew Hadfield, esp. chap-ters 2, 4, 5 and 8. For Wales, see E. Rees, 'Welsh Publishing before 1717', in *Essays in Honour of Victor Scholderer*, ed. Dennis E. Rhodes (Mainz, 1970), pp. 323–36; and Rheinallt Llwyd, 'Printing and Publishing in the Seventeenth-Century', in *A Nation and its Books: A History of the Book in Wales*, ed. Philip Henry Jones and Eiluned Rees (Aberystwyth, 1998), pp. 93–107.

[33]   All the Chepman and Myllar publications are now available as *The Chepman and Myllar Prints: Digitised Facsimiles with Introduction, Headnotes, and Transcription* (Edinburgh: Scottish Text Society and National Library of Scotland, 2008). For a general overview of early Scottish printing, see Robert Dickson, *Annals of Scottish Printing* (Cambridge, 1890).

[34]   Aliens connected with the British book-trade account for two-thirds of books produced in Britain between 1476 and 1535. See Duff, *The English Provincial Printers*, p. 189. For a list of aliens connected with the book-trade during the period, see Ernest James Worman, *Alien Members of the Book-Trade during the Tudor Period* (London, 1906).

English printers was largely the result of legislation passed between 1515 and 1534, which made it increasingly difficult for foreign printers to practise their craft on British soil. While the Act of 1484, which regulated the conditions under which aliens might practise their trade, undoubtedly recognised the extent to which the English book trade relied on Continental expertise (its restrictions 'in no wise extende [. . .] to any Artificer or merchaunt straungier of what Nacion or Countrey he be or shalbe of, for bryngyng into this Realme, or sellyng by retaill or otherwise, of any maner bokes wrytten or imprynted, or for the inhabitynge within the said Realme for the same intent'), a series of later laws leading to the incorporation of the Stationers' Company in 1557 eventually made it legally impossible for foreign printers to reside and work in England.[35] An Act of 1523 prevented alien printers, denizen or otherwise, from employing foreign apprentices and limited the number of foreign journeyman that an alien printer could keep to two. A supplementary Act was passed in 1529, which prohibited further aliens from setting up print shops in England; its restrictions did not yet apply to those foreign printers who were already active. Finally, in 1534, the 1484 Act was repealed and replaced by a new Act, which not only proscribed the importation of bound books from the Continent, but also prevented non-denizened aliens from retailing foreign-printed books. Banned from employing foreign apprentices, limited to keeping two foreign journeymen, and eventually barred from selling directly to the general reading public, it is perhaps no surprise that Pynson and de Worde's establishments passed to native hands. But legislation probably only strengthened natural tendencies within the book trade, as de Worde's circle of artisan printers seems to suggest.

By the time of the deaths of Pynson and de Worde, in the mid-1530s, printing in England was the business of Englishmen. Up to this time it had become a secure but relatively unadventurous business exemplified by the activities of one of their lesser contemporaries, Peter Treveris (fl. 1525–32). Treveris published for less than a decade, between 1525 and 1532/33, during which time he issued about seventy books from his house in Southwark. Nearly half of his output comprised new editions of grammars by Lily, Stanbridge and Whittinton, drawing on a market carefully nurtured by Pynson and (particularly) de Worde. Almost all his other books were also reprints, usually of works by these two printers. His most ambitious book was his folio edition of The Great Herball in 1525 (STC 13176), which was sufficiently successful to be reprinted (STC 13177, 13177.5). He did produce a number of other folio editions either independently – for example, Trevisa's Polychronicon translation (STC 13440) and Lucian (STC 16895) – or for, or in, collaboration with John Rastell, such as The act agayns the kyllyng of calues (1529, STC 7773) and A, C, mery talys (1526, STC 23664). However, the general conservatism of his output suggests both the limited ambition and narrow scope of a moderately successful printer in a period dominated by de Worde and Pynson.

---

[35] Statutes of the Realm, ed. A. Luders, 11 vols (London, 1810–28), 2.493.

The Printers: 1534–58

Thomas Berthelet (*fl.* 1524–55) succeeded Pynson as King's Printer by February 1530 and perforce became involved in the increased politicisation of the role. Like Pynson, Berthelet contributed to a propaganda campaign, this time against Rome, orchestrated by the Chancellor, Thomas Cromwell.[36] Among those books issued from his press that supported Cromwell's project to promote reformed faith were the ten *Articles* (1536, *STC* 10033) and the *Bishop's Book* (1537, *STC* 5163). After Cromwell's fall in 1540 and the king's retreat to a more conservative position, the ten *Articles* and the *Bishop's Book* were radically revised as the six *Articles* (1539, *STC* 9397, 9397.5, 9398) and the *King's Book* (1543, *STC* 5170). The fact that both of these revised texts were also printed by Berthelet indicates the extent to which the King's Printer was required to promulgate the king's agenda.

Up to 1550 Berthelet published over 550 books, the great majority of these after he assumed his official role. To a substantial degree this output reflects the responsibilities of that role. Charged with representing the king as he wanted others to see him, the King's Printer was responsible for the publication of all texts which communicated the king's mind and desired image. For Pynson, who held the position from 1508 until his death in 1530, this meant that, in addition to printing new statutes and proclamations as they were issued by parliament and the court, he was also responsible for printing court records and law texts, as well as new imprints of older statutes. For as long as Pynson occupied the post its business remained unprotected by the law, a fact which goes some way to explain Redman's success in the field of legal publishing, an area more obviously associated with the role of the King's Printer. Though Berthelet inherited Pynson's old rivalry with Redman when he assumed the post in 1530, he distinguished himself from his competitor by ensuring the superior quality of his publications. Working with newly purchased type (Redman had inherited Pynson's old type), and binding his editions with expensive calf or deerskin as opposed to the more workaday sheep or goat, Berthelet was quick to establish the prestige (and privilege) of his press in material terms. At the same time, he was able to deploy the force of law against his competitors when his royal privilege was challenged. In what is believed to be the first recorded penalty for the infringement of privilege, Berthelet successfully petitioned against Redman for pirating Christopher St German's *Treatise concernynge the diusion betwen the spirtualtie and temporaltie* ([1532?], *STC* 21586), a text which he had himself printed twice (*STC* 21587, 21587.5) and for which he held special privileges.[37]

The activities of other contemporary printers were on a much smaller scale and suggest some jockeying to find niche markets. John Rastell, for example, seems to have had some sort of privileged access to the publication of law for a period, perhaps in part through the influence of Thomas More, whose daughter

---

[36] Cromwell's use of the press is discussed in Geoffrey Elton's *Policy and Police: The Enforcement of the Reformation in the Age of Thomas Cromwell* (Cambridge, 1972), pp. 171–216. See also Susan Powell's and Thomas Betteridge's chapters in this volume.

[37] See E.G. Duff, *The Printers, Stationers and Bookbinders of Westminster and London from 1476–1535* (Cambridge, 1906), p. 171. Privileges are treated more extensively below.

Elizabeth he had married in 1497. Law books constitute about a third of the sixty-odd books he published between 1509 and 1533.[38] The other distinctive aspect of his publications is the emphasis on verse texts, both Middle English and modern. The former include Chaucer's *Parliament of Fowls* ([1525?], STC 5091.5), the romance *Eglamour of Artois* ([1528?], STC 7542.5) and various saints' lives, of St Margaret (*c*.1530, STC 17324.5) and St Thomas (*c*.1520, STC 23954.3). His interest in modern literature included various interludes including Medwall's *Fulgens and Lucrece* (1512–16, STC 17778) and several of Skelton's works including his play *Magnifycence* ([1530?], STC 22607).[39]

But by the 1530s the shape of contemporary printing was beginning to be crucially affected by political and religious controversy in ways that drew printers into new relationships and new kinds of publishing ventures. For example, while most of John Byddell's books were of a theological character, the successor to his house at the sign of The Sun in 1544, Edward Whitchurch (d. 1562), had already begun to take such printing in different directions and with new alliances. Whitchurch had earlier, in 1537, become involved in Thomas Cromwell's project to produce an official English translation of the Bible. Working under Cromwell's authority, he and fellow-printer and business associate Richard Grafton acted as publishers, at their own expense, for an edition of the Bible printed in Antwerp by Matthias Crom. Though the so-called Matthew Bible (STC 2066) had appeared 'with the Kinges most gracious lyce[n]ce', it was this revised version, printed without marginal notes as the Great Bible (STC 2068), that was to become the official version, ordered by Cromwell's 1538 Injunctions (STC 10086) to be 'set up in sum convenient place' within every church in the land. The printing of the Great Bible was begun in Paris by François Regnault, with Whitchurch and Grafton again acting as publishers. However, when publication stalled after the University of Paris deemed the work heretical, the two publishers, working with equipment secured by Edmund Bonner, bishop of London, were forced to act as printers. Working 'cum priuilegio ad imprimendum solum' ('with privilege for the sole or exclusive printing'), their first edition of the Great Bible appeared in April 1539.[40] However, despite the royal privilege, later that year Byddell and Berthelet produced an edition of Richard Taverner's translation of the Bible (STC 2067) claiming similar privilege, and a year later Thomas Petit (1494–1565/6), Redman, and Berthelet jointly issued their own edition of the Great Bible (STC 2069), again 'cum priuilegio' ('with privilege').

According to one recent estimate, for the 2233 extant titles printed during the reign of Henry VIII, 302 were printed 'cum privilegio regia majestate' (with the privilege of the king's majesty'), 'cum privilegio regis' ('with the privilege

---

[38] For a fuller treatment of all aspects of Rastell's career as a printer, including his role as a leading figure in the development of law books, see E.J. Devereux, *A Bibliography of John Rastell* (Montreal, 1999).

[39] Skelton was unusual among living poets in the number of printers he employed over more than thirty years; they included, apart from Rastell, de Worde, Faques and Pynson; see further A.S.G. Edwards, 'Skelton's English Poems in Print and Manuscript', in *John Skelton and Early Modern Culture: Papers Honoring Robert S. Kinsman*, ed. David R. Carlson (Tempe, AZ, 1998), pp. 85–98.

[40] On this term and its implications, see W.W. Greg, '*Ad imprimendum solum*', in *The Collected Papers of W. W. Greg*, ed. J.C. Maxwell (Oxford, 1966), pp. 406–12.

of the king'), or simply 'cum privilegio' ('with privilege'), a number that reflects both Henry's break with Rome and Thomas Cromwell's rise to power.[41] However, while the conferment of privilege was a purely commercial agreement – the exclusive right to copy – there is evidence to suggest that at least some readers took it to indicate official approbation.[42] Perhaps in an effort to resolve this confusion of privilege for licence, a proclamation was printed in 1538 (*STC* 7790) directing printers 'not to put these words *cum privilegio regali* ("with royal privilege") without adding *ad imprimendum solum* ("for the sole or exclusive printing")'. It was a move that troubled Grafton who, like other printers, had clearly seen the appropriation suggested by privilege as an advantage when marketing his books. Writing to Cromwell in 1538 he complains that the additional words 'would give occasion to the enemies to say it is not the King's mind to set it forth, but only to license printers to sell what are put forth'.[43]

Though their fortunes suffered somewhat in the aftermath of Cromwell's downfall in 1540 – Grafton was imprisoned three times between 1540 and 1542 – the Whitchurch and Grafton association was a long and productive one.[44] They were granted joint patents for printing service books in 1541, 1543, 1546, and again in 1547 on the accession of Edward VI, and were given exclusive rights to the official English Primer of 1545 (*STC* 16034). In the same year they became attached to the household of the young Prince Edward, though the description of Grafton in the colophon to the Primer as 'Printer to the Prince's grace' suggests that it was not long before he was acting as sole printer to the future king. Grafton would subsequently strengthen his relationship to the crown when he took over the duties of King's Printer from Berthelet on Edward's accession.

If Grafton's reformed convictions helped secure his position as King's Printer, they also led to his loss of office for printing a proclamation declaring Lady Jane Grey queen on the death of Edward VI in 1553 (*STC* 7846). The position then passed to John Cawood, whose own religious leanings made him particularly suitable for the role under the Catholic Mary I.[45] In addition to publishing all statute books, acts, proclamations and injunctions in English, he also took over Reginald Wolfe's privilege to print and sell books in Latin, Greek and Hebrew. Just as Berthelet and Grafton had turned their presses to promulgate the reformed cause, so Cawood (1513/14–72), as Queen's Printer, was responsible for printing key texts of the Marian Counter-Reformation, among them Edmund Bonner's *Homilies* (1555, *STC* 3285.1, 3285.2, 3285.3, 3285.4, 3285.5, 3285.6, 3285.7, 3285.8, 3285.9, 3285.10), Thomas Watson's *Twoo notable sermons*

[41] Cyndia Susan Clegg, *Press Censorship in Elizabethan England* (Cambridge, 1997), p. 9.

[42] A.W. Reed, 'The Regulation of the Book Trade before the Proclamation of 1538', *Transactions of the Bibliographical Society* 15 (1920), 157–84.

[43] *LP Henry VIII*, 13/2.409–26.

[44] Whitchurch and Grafton also seem to have had close ties with John Day (1522–84) with whom they shared staff and stock, particularly woodcuts. Day is perhaps best known as the printer of John Foxe's *Acts and Monuments* (*STC* 11222, 11223, 11224, 11225). See Stephen Alford, *Kingship and Politics in the Reign of Edward VI* (Cambridge, 2002), pp. 116–22; and Elizabeth Evenden, *Patents, Pictures and Patronage: John Day and the Tudor Book Trade* (Farnham, 2008), pp. 10–11, 22.

[45] He received the grant for this office on 29 December 1553. See *Calendar of Patent Rolls Preserved in the Public record Office: Philip and Mary*, 4 vols (London, 1936–39), 1.53.

(1554, *STC* 25115.3, 25115, 25115.5), and *The vvorkes of Sir Thomas More* (with John Walley and Richard Tottel, 1557, *STC* 18076).[46] Although pivotal in the circulation of Marian propaganda, he was perhaps less close to the crown than has previously been assumed; unlike his predecessor he survived the fall of Mary's regime, and with Richard Jugge (*c*.1513/14–77) held the office of Queen's Printer under Elizabeth until his death in 1572.

Printers other than those with the title of Royal Printer were also pressed into service in the 1530s. The career of Thomas Godfray lasted only six years, from 1531 to 1536, during which period he printed about forty books from at least two different addresses. However, very early in his career, in 1532, he showed himself capable of producing very large books when he printed the first edition of the complete *Workes* of Chaucer (*STC* 5068), a work that must have involved considerable resources, both economic and textual. The availability of such resources suggests that Godfray had access to patrons of wealth and prominence, as does the editorship of this book by William Thynne (d. 1546) and the Preface by Brian Tuke (d. 1545), both members of the royal household. Godfray's use of some types that seem to have been acquired from Pynson, the late King's Printer, may also indicate his links to influential printing circles.[47] Probably in the following year, 1533, he printed Giles Duwes's French grammar dedicated to Henry VIII, Anne Boleyn and their daughter Elizabeth (*STC* 7377), perhaps taking over publication from de Worde after his death, and in 1536–37 he printed a work in praise of the king (*STC* 13089a). Much of the rest of his output is broadly concerned either with religious works or with works of current religious controversy, including works concerned with the interpretation of scripture (*c*.1532, *STC* 12731.6), a primer ([1533?], *STC* 15988a) and a Paternoster (*c*.1535, *STC* 16816), treatises concerning the power of the clergy ([1535?], *STC* 21588) and on ecclesiastical institutions (*c*.1535, *STC* 24236), and an anti-Catholic tract on images (1535, *STC* 24238, 24239). He also printed works by the radical controversialist William Marshall, including his *Forme and maner of subuention or helping for pore people* (1535, *STC* 26119). The general scope of his activities suggests that he was actively involved in the politicisation of print in the 1530s. Marshall, for example, had close connections to Thomas Cromwell, and it is possible that the seemingly abrupt cessation of Godfray's contemporary political publications may be connected to the gradual political decline of Cromwell.

Not all printers were so directly involved in the political and religious controversy of the times. Some devoted their energies to very different markets, with degrees of success that are not easy to assess. The careers of John Skot (*fl.*

---

[46] On the role of the printing press in the dissemination of Marian propaganda, see Jennifer Loach, 'The Marian Establishment and the Printing Press', *EHR* 101 (1986), 135–48, in which the author challenges the earlier prevailing view that the 'regime did not sufficiently understand how the new technology could be used for influencing public attitudes'. See J.W. Martin, 'The Marian Regime's Failure to Understand the Importance of Printing', *HLQ* 44 (1981), 231–47 (at 231).

[47] While some of the types may have been acquired from Pynson, the woodcuts were first cut for Caxton's second edition of the *Canterbury Tales* (1483, *STC* 5083) and then reused in Wynkyn de Worde's 1498 *Tales* (*STC* 5085). See David R. Carlson, 'Woodcut Illustrations of the *Canterbury Tales*, 1483–1602', *The Library*, 6th ser., 19 (1997), 25–67.

1521–37) and Richard Lant are of some interest in the insight they afford into the activities of the lower level of commercial printers. John Skot printed in London for a considerable period between 1521 and 1537;[48] about forty books survive with his imprint, issued from a number of different addresses, and it is probable that more may have once existed. He is known, for example, to have printed a book about Elizabeth Barton (c.1506–34), a Benedictine nun and so-called Holy Maid of Kent, of which no copy survives. The record of what does survive from his press suggests a quite small but relatively steady output, primarily of books in English. He seems to have begun his career by printing for de Worde, for whom he printed editions of *A boke of a ghostly fader* (STC 3288) and *A treatise of a galaunte* (STC 24242), both around 1521, and of Lady Margaret Beaufort's translation of Dionysius the Carthusian, *The mirroure of golde for the synfull soule* (STC 6895), in 1522. He also printed a Stanbridge grammar (STC 23162) for John Toy, a short-lived printer in 1531.

What is particularly striking about Skot's activities is the way they mirror de Worde's own. He primarily focused on markets de Worde had developed. He printed for John Butler, an associate of de Worde's, several grammars ([1528?], STC 23172, [1530?], 23182.8) as well as some under his own name ([1521?], STC 15580.5, [1529?], 23199, and [1530?], 23150.5).[49] He also published vernacular religious texts, apart from those for de Worde, including two editions of *The Gospel of Nichodemus* (1529, STC 18569; [1537?], STC 18570a), *The rosary* (1537, STC 17545.5) and Christine de Pisan's *Body of Polycye* (1521, STC 7270).[50] And, perhaps most interestingly, he steadily published English verse. Apart from *A treatise of a galaunte* for de Worde and Stephen Hawes's *Conversyon of swerers* for Butler ([1531?], STC 12944), he printed *Thystory of Jacob and his .xii. sones* (1522–3, STC 14324), *Maide Emeleye* (1525, STC 7681), two editions of *Everyman* ([1528?], STC 10606) and ([1535?], STC 10606.5), *the Jest of Sir Gawaine* ([1528?], STC 11691a.3), *A dialogue between the comen secretary and jelowsy* ([1530?], STC 6807), the *Nutbrowne mayde* (1535, STC 14553.7), and the *Batyll of Egeyncourte* (1536, STC 198). None of these was a large book and the capital risk was consequently small. But such modest, if fairly regular, ventures seem to have provided a basis for Skot to sustain a quite long career, built significantly on markets already established by his more successful predecessor de Worde.

The career of Richard Lant followed a rather similar pattern. He too had at least five different addresses, and while he printed over a longer period, from 1539 to 1561, there are gaps of years where no publications survive and a number in which there is only one. In all, only thirty-four books survive from this twenty-two-year period. A number are printed for other publishers, several for Richard Bankes (1540, STC 12206a.3, 1545, 14126.5, 1545, 20197.3), others for a de Worde associate, John Gough (1540, STC 1323.5), others for Richard Grafton (1544, STC 523), T. Gybson ([1539?], STC 21307a.7), Henry Tab ([1545?], STC

---

[48] For an overview of Skot's career, see H.R. Plomer, *Wynkyn de Worde & his Contemporaries from the Death of Caxton to 1535* (London, 1925), pp. 213–15.

[49] De Worde had also printed such works for Butler; see, for example, STC 23150 [1530?] and STC 23150.3 [1530?].

[50] In 1525 he was also briefly able to enter the market for legal books; see STC 7709.7, 7713.7 and 7726.7.

22598), and Thomas Purfoot (1546, STC 17764.5). And even more than with Skot, there is a heavy commitment to verse publication, which amounts to nearly 50 per cent of his surviving output (STC 1323.5, 1419, 1656, 4999.5, 5225.5, 5252, 5258, 10615, 11186, 12206a.3, 17559, 20197.3, 22880.4, 22598, 23251.5 and 23292) and included verse by Thomas Churchyard, William Forrest, John Skelton and Thomas Smyth. In addition, he produced a smattering of prose religious books (STC 19465.3, 22249.5 and 26098.7). Once again, such modest achievements seem to reflect an inability, conceptual and/or economic, to move beyond earlier trade paradigms.

Other printers were more long-lived and ambitious to a greater degree. One such was Robert Wyer (fl. 1524–56), who printed in London from 1528 to 1556 and produced about 170 surviving books. If these books provide an accurate picture of his output, what is immediately striking is the highly erratic patterns of publication. For example, between 1536 and 1538/9 only a single book survives from each year, and there are similar instances of attenuated publication in the 1540s and 1550s.[51] One may surmise that Wyer represents the predicament of a printer with capital investment in the materials of his trade of sufficient size to make him reluctant to abandon it, but without access to secure and stable markets. He seems to have compensated for this by pragmatism. Few of Wyer's books are large and most suggest rather low production values. The range of his production, much of it reprints, suggests the likelihood of, at least at some points in his career, a hand-to-mouth existence that may reflect the wider economic precariousness in this period. While he published little that was new, he did consolidate certain markets, like those for popular medicine (see STC 3378.5, 3379, 3382.5, 18214a, 18225.6, 20060.5, 20061, 22153b and 24725.3) and other popular science (see STC 3188a, 11930.5, 11930.7, 20480a and 20481), other forms of advice (see STC 1967.5), prognostications and almanacs (see STC 392.2, 399.7, 406.3, 439.3, 439.5, 439.9, 470.10, 517.10, 769 and 13522), various practical works on such subjects as how to measure land (STC 1874) or build a house (STC 3373), as well as cheap editions of vernacular religious (STC 788.5, 1914, 13608.4 and 14041), historical works (STC 9984) and a few contemporary poems, The complaynt of a dolorous louer (STC 5608) and Christopher Goodwin's The maydens dreme (STC 12047).[52] In its range and diversity Wyer's output points towards the emergence of a new kind of commercially pragmatic publisher, producing cheap books for a variety of mass audiences.

Such activity is a far cry from the situation facing Caxton when he returned to England in the late 1470s to establish his press. The development of printing in England from its beginnings to the 1550s does not present a clear evolutionary form. The early imperatives were the tentative identification of commercial markets for printed books and the ensuing establishment of such markets on a commercially viable basis. Though early printed English books may have lagged

[51] An even more striking example of extended and attenuated output is provided by John Reynes who, between 1527 and 1544, produced eight surviving books.
[52] For discussion of Wyer's output and a partial chronology, see P.B. Tracy, 'Robert Wyer: A Brief Analysis of his Types and a Suggested Chronology for the Output of his Press', The Library, 6th ser., 2 (1980), 293–303. For a succinct and valuable assessment of him, see the article by N.F. Blake in ODNB.

behind their Continental cousins in terms of their technical expertise, and, in many instances, their overall quality of production, the early history of print in England is nonetheless a story of survival by adaptation to swiftly changing economic and political circumstances. By the middle of the sixteenth century, the English book trade was populated by a number of printers who in different ways and with varying degrees of success either sustained established markets or created new ones for their publications. For some, like those who occupied the role of Royal Printer, this meant organising the publication of all books related to, and in support of, royal policy, thereby acting to represent the established political order. For others, this meant producing books for specific audiences, and in some instances creating new ones. The early attempts to establish presses at Oxford and St Albans offer clear evidence of printers seeking to print books designed for local audiences. These initial experiments were short-lived, and regional printing seems to have been generally limited throughout this period. London remained the primary site of production, and its printers seem to have had the capacity to both consolidate their markets within the metropolitan area and extend them regionally.[53]

By 1558 print was established as the primary means of written communication throughout mainland Britain. Such an achievement was a Darwinian one; few printers had lengthy careers and many had ones that were so brief as to demonstrate commercial failure. Those who prospered are testimony to the tenacity and enterprise that first established print culture in England.

Further Reading

Barker, Nicolas, 'Caxton's Typography', *Journal of the Printing Historical Society* 11 (1976/7), 114–33.

Blake, N.F., 'Wynkyn de Worde: The Early Years', *Gutenberg Jahrbuch* (1971), 62–69.

_____, 'Wynkyn de Worde: The Later Years', *Gutenberg Jahrbuch* (1972), 128–38.

Carlson, David, 'Alexander Barclay and Richard Pynson: A Tudor Printer and his Writer', *Anglia* 113 (1995), 283–302.

Clegg, Cyndia Susan, *Press Censorship in Elizabethan England* (Cambridge, 1997).

Duff, E.G., *The Printers, Stationers and Bookbinders of Westminster and London from 1476–1535* (Cambridge, 1906).

Edwards, A.S.G., 'Continental Influences on London Printing and Reading in the Fifteenth and Early Sixteenth Centuries', in *London and Europe in the Fifteenth Century*, ed. Julia Boffey and Pamela King (London, 1995), pp. 229–56.

_____, 'Wynkyn de Worde and Contemporary Poetry', *Gutenberg Jahrbuch* (1991), 143–48.

_____ and Carol Meale, 'The Marketing of Early Printed Books in Late Medieval England', *The Library*, 6th series, 15 (1993), 96–124.

Evenden, Elizabeth, *Patents, Pictures and Patronage: John Day and the Tudor Book Trade* (Farnham, 2008).

Hellinga, Lotte, *William Caxton and Early Printing in England* (London, 2010).

---

[53] As early as the 1490s copies of Caxton's books were evidently available in some numbers in northern England, for example; see J. McN. Dodgson, 'A Library at Pott Chapel, Pott Shrigley, Cheshire, c. 1493', *The Library*, 5th ser., 15 (1960), 47–53.

Hodnett, E., *English Woodcuts 1480–1535*, revised edn (Oxford, 1973).

Loach, Jennifer, 'The Marian Establishment and the Printing Press', *English Historical Review* 101 (1986), 135–48.

Martin, J.W., 'The Marian Regime's Failure to Understand the Importance of Printing', *Huntington Library Quarterly* 44 (1981), 231–47.

Meale, Carole M., 'Caxton, de Worde and the Publication of Romance in Late Medieval England', *The Library*, 6th series, 14 (1992), 281–98.

Moran, James, *Wynkyn de Worde, Father of Fleet Street, with a Chronological Bibliography of Works on de Worde Compiled by Lotte Hellinga and Mary Erler and a Preface by John Dreyfus*, 3rd revised edn (London, 2003).

Needham, Paul, *The Printer and the Pardoner* (Washington, DC, 1986).

Painter, George, *William Caxton: A Quincentenary Biography of England's First Printer* (London, 1976).

Plomer, H.R., *Wynkyn de Worde & his Contemporaries from the Death of Caxton to 1535* (London, 1925).

Reed, A.W., 'The Regulation of the Book Trade before the Proclamation of 1538', *Transactions of the Bibliographical Society* 15 (1920), 157–84.

3

The Latin Trade in England and Abroad

ALAN COATES

Although William Caxton brought printing with moveable type to England in 1476, it was to be about another century and a half before England was 'self-sufficient' in its printing needs. In the meanwhile it became a good market for Latin printed books of all sorts. Liturgical and devotional works and also Latin works of theology and canon law would have been crucial to members of the clergy in their dealings with each other, the laity, the church and state. Works of philosophy, classics and grammar would have been aimed at the academic and student bodies in the universities.[1] This chapter will examine the kind of books which were being brought in, who was bringing them in, and who was buying or being given them.

Before Caxton's arrival in England, demand for books was met solely from abroad; the position in Scotland was the same up till the early part of the sixteenth century. Once started, the importation of printed books into both England and Scotland continued even after printing presses had been established in both countries.[2] The trade in printed books took off in earnest in the 1470s, with a marked increase in the 1480s into the 1490s. Lotte Hellinga has noted that 'for the whole of this period the scale of dependence on provision from overseas is an exceptional characteristic of the use of books in the British Isles. It not only shaped the nature of printing in England and Scotland, it also had a profound influence on the Continental book-trade, in the Netherlands, in particular on that of Antwerp and Louvain.'[3]

A detailed statistical study of the import of books into England and Scotland has been undertaken by Meg Ford. Building on the work of Lotte Hellinga, Ford has shown that the marked increase in imports in the 1480s through into the 1490s began with books from German-speaking countries. They were then replaced by those from Italy (especially Venice, based round the supply of canon and civil law books, and also classical and philosophical texts). French imports (particularly from Parisian presses, but also those in Lyons) increased rapidly in number towards the end of the century.

---

[1]   Vincent Gillespie, 'Syon and the English Market for Continental Printed Books: The Incunable Phase', in *Syon Abbey and its Books*, pp. 104–28 (105).
[2]   'Importation', pp. 179, 182.
[3]   Lotte Hellinga, 'The Bookshop of the World: Books and their Makers as Agents of Cultural Exchange', in *The Bookshop of the World: the Role of the Low Countries in the Book-trade 1473–1941*, ed. Lotte Hellinga et al. ('t Goy-Houten, 2001), pp. 11–29 (16).

Moving into the sixteenth century, Ford suggests that there is an increase in the numbers of imports from German-speaking areas again. This no doubt reflects the dominance of Basel, a centre of humanist printing, but also a supplier of increasing numbers of patristic texts, between the 1520s and 1540s. Ford rightly stresses the fact that the picture is affected by the problems of the surviving evidence. For example, no liturgical books of Sarum Use (the modification of the Roman rite used by Salisbury Cathedral and, increasingly, throughout England by the later Middle Ages) occur during the 1520s and 1530s, nor prohibited books from the same period. These had, presumably, been suppressed and destroyed. In Scotland, the picture is slightly different from that in England. Before 1500 there were few imports, with no printing centre being predominant. After 1500, there is a sharp then steady rise in imports from France and the German-speaking areas. Up until the later 1550s, most of the imports come from France. The dominance of Paris is not surprising, given the strength of the 'Auld Alliance'.[4]

From a business point of view, Caxton and his successors, and early printers in Scotland as well, realised that they would be in a better position if they chose to print the sort of books which could not be obtained elsewhere. This included books in the vernacular, English common law texts and books for use in English and Scottish schools.[5]

There were some books which were too complex for new printing presses to contemplate printing. In this category came liturgical books, which involved complicated layouts, printing in two colours (red and black), and, in some cases, the printing of musical staves and notation. The printing of service books and devotional texts was a distinct part of the book trade. Until the Reformation, Sarum breviaries (containing the daily round of prayers for church services) and hours would be printed in Venice, Paris, Rouen and in the Low Countries, and imported into England. The first printed Sarum Breviary was produced in the Low Countries in c.1475. The second was printed in Venice by the Dutchman Reynaldus de Novimagio in 1483. The first Sarum Missal (containing the priest's texts for the Mass) followed in 1487, printed by de Maynyal for Caxton (see below). The second came from the press of Michael Wenssler in Basel, probably in 1489.[6]

One publisher much involved in the importation of liturgical books was Frederick Egmondt, active in the Low Countries from the 1490s until his death in 1511. Egmondt financed the publication of a York Breviary in Venice in 1493. In the following two years he published a book of hours, two missals and two breviaries, all of the Sarum rite, and all for importation into England. It is clear that Egmondt must have been investing large sums of money into this exclusively English undertaking. The York stationer, Gerard Freez (Wandsworth), had, at

[4]   'Importation', pp. 182–91, 194–95.
[5]   Hellinga, 'Bookshop of the World', p. 16; Antony Kamm, *Scottish Printed Books 1508–2008* (Dingwall, 2008), pp. 8–11.
[6]   Nicolas Barker, 'The Importation of Books into England 1460–1526', in *Beiträge zur Geschichte des Buchwesens im konfessionellen Zeitalter*, ed. Herbert G. Göpfert et al., Wolfenbüttler Schriften zur Geschichte des Buchwesens 11 (Wiesbaden, 1985), pp. 251–66 (256); 'English Purchases', pp. 272, 279–80. The breviaries are *STC* 15794, 15795; missals *STC* 16164, 16165.

his death in 1510, an enormous number of liturgical books in stock in his house in York.[7] These included 252 missals, 399 breviaries and 570 ordinals. Armstrong has suggested that the large number of chantry chapels may account for so many printed service books being held by a bookseller.[8] Roberts notes the evidence of the 'Day Book' of John Dorne, the Low Countries-born stationer, in which Dorne recorded his sales for most of 1520. Of these books, only one breviary was English, the rest being Continental imports, many presumably from Rouen.[9]

Julian Roberts has noted that, during this period, the learned press in England was weaker because the two universities and the religious centres were separated from the commercial ones. The learned presses which did try to establish themselves in Oxford and Cambridge did not last. Printing in Oxford (the press of Theodoric Rood) was overwhelmed by the volume of the 'Latin Trade' (the process of importing Latin books into England) during the 1480s. And, in Cambridge, John Siberch, the printer and stationer who arrived in the city in 1519, is known only to have produced ten books and an indulgence before his departure in 1523. Roberts suggests that Siberch was '. . . thwarted by the sudden deflection of academic interest from humanism into theological dispute'.[10]

Academic books were the principal part of the Latin imported trade into England, for reasons noted earlier. An early and well-documented example of this importation is provided by the survival of a document in an incunable in the Bodleian Library.[11] The document shows the dealings between the Savoyard bookseller, Peter Actors, Johannes de Westfalia, the Louvain printer, and the Oxford stationer, Thomas Hunt, in 1483. It consists of a priced list of some sixty-six titles, the majority of which are works for the academic market in Oxford. Of these, some twenty-five were in two or more copies, giving an overall total of 105 copies. Most of the books were either printed in Cologne or in Louvain, with a significant number from other towns in the Low Countries. Ten books on the list came from Venice. They may have been imported from Venice via Cologne, through trade connections of Johannes de Colonia (who was the publisher of five of the Venetian titles). Or they may have arrived through the agency of Ludovicus de Ravescot, a Louvain bookseller, who would have been known to Westfalia, and seems to have been responsible for trade in books from Venice. The heading of the document states that Hunt promised to return to Actors and Westfalia either the prices mentioned in the document or the books themselves, if any were not sold. If all of these books had been sold, then Actors

[7]   See Andrew Hope's chapter in this volume.
[8]   Hellinga, 'Bookshop of the World', p. 13; 'English Purchases', pp. 272, 281; the York breviary is *STC* 15856.
[9]   Julian Roberts, 'Importing Books for Oxford, 1500–1640', in *Books and Collectors 1200–1700: Essays Presented to Andrew Watson*, ed. James P. Carley and Colin G.C. Tite (London, 1997), 317–33 (319); the day-book was edited by Falconer Madan, 'The Day-book of John Dorne', *Oxford Historical Society* 5 (*Collectanea*, 1st series, part III; Oxford, 1885), 73–177; and 'Supplementary Notes', *Oxford Historical Society* 16 (*Collectanea*, 2nd series; Oxford, 1890), 453–78.
[10]   Roberts, 'Importing Books for Oxford', pp. 317–18; S.H. Steinberg, *Five Hundred Years of Printing*, new edn, revised John Trevitt (London, 1996), p. 51.
[11]   Auct. R sup. 1 (Livius, *Historiae* (Paris: [Antoine Caillaut & Jean du Pré], 1486); Bod-inc. L-126); Paul Needham, 'Continental Printed Books Sold in Oxford, *c*.1480–3: Two Trade Records', in *Incunabula*, pp. 243–70 (260); Barker, 'Importation of Books', pp. 255–6.

and Westfalia would have received £27 7s. 11d. However, the annotations to the list suggest that nine books remained unsold and were returned. This would clearly have had cost implications for Actors and Westfalia, who had bought (in Westfalia's case, printed) the books initially, and had paid to ship the books to England. Perhaps it also indicated that the demand in the book market for these particular works was not as strong as Hunt believed.[12]

Hunt was University Stationer at Oxford from 1473 until his death in 1492. University stationers were, traditionally, privileged servants of the university, elected by Convocation. Their original role had been both to act as valuers of effects, especially books, which were pledged in return for money (an elevated form of pawn-broking), and to keep the master copies of texts in manuscript for hire by scribes. By Hunt's time the University Stationer still retained these roles, but clearly also dealt with a wider range of book-related matters in the university. In addition to acting as an entrepreneurial importer and retailer, Hunt was also associated with the German printer, Theodoric Rood, in the publication of the latter's edition of Phalaris, *Letters* in 1485 (he is named with Rood in the colophon). As Daniel Wakelin notes in his chapter in this volume, the colophon (in verse) includes a rousing challenge to the printers of Venice, announcing that printing was established in England (although, within a few years, Rood was gone from Oxford). Finally, it should be noted that there are no grounds for associating Thomas Hunt with any of Rood's other books.[13] Peter Actors became Royal Stationer to King Henry VII in 1485. His name appears on at least fifteen occasions in the customs rolls for the port of London as an importer of books between 1478 and 1491, with an additional mention in the 1497 customs rolls of Winchelsea (where the Parisian Michael Morin also received shipments of books in 1498 and 1500). Actors imported thirty-two volumes of books in 1480,[14] and four cargoes of books, with a total value of £27, into London during the period April to July 1483. By 1491 it is estimated that he had brought more than 1300 books into England, valued in excess of £140.[15] His family seems to have continued the involvement with books. Peter's son, Sebastian, was an Oxford stationer. Another relative, Anthony, imported two cargoes of books into London in 1478. Johannes de Westfalia, in addition to being a printer in Louvain, also imported two cargoes of books into London. The first, of twenty-one books in January 1478, was worth £6 13s. 4d., and the second, in July 1481, £9 6s. 8d. Johannes de Westfalia continued to appear in customs rolls until 1491.[16]

---

[12] Hellinga, 'Bookshop of the World', p. 16; Needham, 'Continental Printed Books', pp. 244, 260–61.

[13] Harry Carter, *A History of the Oxford University Press: Vol. 1 to the Year 1780* (Oxford, 1975), pp. 2–3; M.B. Parkes, 'The Provision of Books', in *The History of the University of Oxford: Vol. II: Later Medieval Oxford*, ed. J.I. Catto and Ralph Evans (Oxford, 1992), pp. 407–83 (420–21); *BMC XI*, p. 14; the edition of Phalaris is *STC* 19827.

[14] Paul Needham, 'The Customs Rolls as Documents for the Printed-book Trade in England', in *CHBB III*, pp. 148–63 (151–52). For Morin, see C. Paul Christianson, 'The Rise of London's Book-trade', in *CHBB III*, pp. 128–47 (141) (Morin also received shipments in London in 1503 and 1506); Elisabeth Leedham-Green, 'University Libraries and Book-sellers', *CHBB III*, pp. 316–53 (347–48).

[15] Christianson, 'Rise of London's Book-trade', p. 137.

[16] Needham, 'Continental Printed Books', pp. 249–50; Gillespie, 'Syon and English Market', p. 117.

The Bodleian incunable of Livy also contains a second inventory. This records books delivered by the French printer, Pierre Levet, to Peter Actors in about 1480. The list includes some thirty-three titles, with twenty-one printed in Paris by Ulrich Gering. These books were presumably intended for sale in Oxford.[17]

Imports of editions of canon law, especially of William Lyndwood's *Provincial constitutions* (a digest of the constitutions of the Province of Canterbury), are noteworthy. Although Rood, Caxton, de Worde and Pynson all printed the text, it was the edition published by Badius Ascensius in Paris in 1501 that was the text (plus Lyndwood's commentary) most popular for the English market, along with the 1504 edition containing the commentary of Johannes de Athon. Hopyl reprinted the 1501 edition for William Bretton, the London grocer and merchant in 1505, for it to be sold by Jacobi and Pelgrim at their shop in St Paul's Churchyard (see below). Later still, in 1525, Franz Birckmann published an edition, which was printed in Antwerp, for sale at his London shop.[18]

The Latin imports were, however, not exclusively liturgical or academic. Gheraert Leeu printed Latin books for schools, including Aesop's *Fables*, which have been found in early English ownership.[19] But Leeu was intent on going further. After Caxton died, Leeu printed four editions in English at Antwerp. Three were reprints of Caxton's publications, including Raoul Lefèvre's *History of Jason* in 1492, and a *Chronicles of England* in 1493. Although this may seem to challenge the position of printers in England, it has been suggested that these may have been commissions from Caxton's executors or from de Worde, with the intention of filling a gap in printing, till de Worde was in production on his own.[20]

The earliest imports of printed books into England came not only from booksellers or printers, but from members of the nobility or clergy, who purchased books abroad, and brought them back to England. The earliest known of these seems to have been James Goldwell. Goldwell was dean of Salisbury, and later bishop of Norwich. Whilst on an embassy in Hamburg for King Edward IV in September and October 1465, he acquired a copy of Durandus, *Rationale divinorum officiorum* (*the Reasoned Exposition of Divine Duties*, a compendium of liturgy with allegorical interpretation), printed in Mainz in 1459 by Johann Fust and Peter Schoeffer. He subsequently bought editions of classical texts in Rome when there between 1467 and 1472. Goldwell left thirty printed books to All Souls College, Oxford in 1499, all of them printed before 1484, and most before 1475. They included classical texts, theological works, canon and civil law, and the works of contemporaries, such as Cardinal Bessarion, the distinguished churchman and classical scholar. More than half of these were printed in Italy, with the rest from Mainz, Nuremberg, Paris and Utrecht.[21]

Another cleric, John Russell, archdeacon of Berkshire, and later bishop of

[17] Needham, 'Continental Printed Books', pp. 264–69.
[18] 'English Purchases', p. 281; *STC* 17107, 17108, 17109.
[19] Daniel Wakelin considers schoolbooks in more detail in his chapter in this volume.
[20] Hellinga, 'Bookshop of the World', pp. 18-22; Barker, 'Importation of Books', p. 256; 'English Purchases', p. 288; Lowry, 'Arrival and Use', pp. 453–54. The *History of Jason* is *STC* 15384, the *Chronicles STC* 9994.
[21] Barker, 'Importation of Books', p. 253; 'English Purchases', pp. 268, 282; the Durandus is Rhodes 722.

Lincoln and chancellor of England, purchased copies of works by Cicero (printed
in Mainz by Fust and Schoeffer in 1466), whilst on an embassy to Charles the
Bold in Bruges in 1467. Russell gave some printed books to New College, Oxford,
including a copy of Plutarch's *Lives* (printed in Venice by Nicolaus Jenson in
1478), and acquired in England.[22] An interesting acquisition made by Russell in
1482 was his copy of the five-volume edition of Baldus de Ubaldis's commentary
on the Codex (or Corpus Iuris Civilis, the great collection of works of civil law
issued by order of the Emperor Justinian). The printer, Johannes Herbort, finished it for his Venetian publishers in February 1481. Given that Venetian galleys
are known to have sailed from Venice to Flanders and England in the later
summer, Lowry has suggested that this provides a good example of the direct
link established between the printers of Venice and their English customers.[23]

John Shirwood, bishop of Durham, is known to have bought a copy of Cicero's
Orations, printed in Rome in 1471 by Sweynheym and Pannartz, during a visit to
the city in 1474. Lowry notes that Shirwood was 'the first serious English collector
to visit Italy after printing had taken hold there'. Shirwood's acquisitions were
principally Latin humanist works, with his initial purchases including, in addition
to the Cicero, works by Livy and Aulus Gellius. Further purchases followed on
later visits included Lactantius, Martial and Terence. Shirwood's Latin collection
was later to be transferred to Corpus Christi College, Oxford on its foundation as
a centre for the new humanist learning.[24] Hellinga has observed, of the acquisition
of books in Rome by both Shirwood and Goldwell, that 'these great men account
for most of the books printed in Rome, and they give the impression that Roman
printers, certainly at that time (and I think also later), did not depend on trade
channels: they did not export books but catered to the international clientele that
would gravitate sooner or later toward the centre of the ecclesiastical world'.[25]

Another senior cleric who acquired early printed books and then passed them
on to an institution was Thomas Rotherham, archbishop of York and chancellor
of England. He gave thirty-five to Cambridge University Library (he was the
chancellor of the university).[26]

---

[22] Martin Lowry, 'The Arrival and Use of Continental Printed Books in Yorkist England', in
*Le Livre dans l'Europe de la Renaissance. Actes du xxviiie Colloque international d'Etudes human-
istes de Tours*, ed. P. Aquillon and H-J. Martin (Paris, 1988), pp. 449–59 (450–51); the Cicero is
Oates 28; the Plutarch is Rhodes 1451c; 'Importation', p. 181; Barker, 'Importation of Books', p.
254; Gillespie, 'Syon and English Market', p. 116; 'English Purchases', pp. 269, 282–83; Lowry,
'Arrival and Use', p. 453.
[23] Lowry, 'Arrival and Use', p. 453 and n.16, with references; the Baldus is Rhodes 1757.
[24] Daniel Wakelin's chapter in this volume contains a more wide-ranging examination of
humanism and printing, in terms both of imports and of works printed in England.
[25] Barker, 'Importation of Books', p. 254; Gillespie, 'Syon and English Market', p. 116; 'English
Purchases', pp. 270–71; Lowry, 'Arrival and Use', pp. 452–53; Lotte Hellinga, 'Importation
of Books Printed on the Continent into England and Scotland before *c*.1520', in *Printing the
Written Word: the Social History of Books, circa 1450–1520*, ed. Sandra Hindman (Ithaca, NY,
1991), pp. 205–24 (215); the Cicero is Rhodes 555a. On Corpus Christi College and its humanist-
inspired curriculum, see James McConica, 'The Rise of the Undergraduate College', in *The
History of the University of Oxford: Vol. III: The Collegiate University*, ed. James McConica (Oxford,
1986), pp. 1–68 (17–29).
[26] 'English Purchases', p. 283. One of Rotherham's incunables which 'escaped' is now contained in Oxford, BodL, BB 19 Art. Seld., as item 3; this is a composite volume, put together by a
later owner, the seventeenth-century lawyer and politician, John Selden (Bod-inc. F-064).

Agents also supplied aristocratic patrons. Gerhard von Wesel was the agent for the London Hanse (the alliance of trading guilds) in Cologne. He sent two printed Bibles to London for John Tiptoft, earl of Worcester between July 1466 and March 1468. However, it is not clear whether this was an unsolicited gift from the merchants, or whether Tiptoft actually ordered it. If there is some doubt about whether or not this was a presentation copy, then that does not exist with the copy of Bessarion's *Letters and Orations*, printed at the Sorbonne in 1471, which was presented to Edward IV in the following year. It came with a specially printed letter of dedication, and has been claimed as the first French book to reach England.[27]

The earliest English acquisition of an Italian printed book (if not the Cicero bought by Shirwood, above) would seem to have been a copy of Chrysostom's *Homilies on John*, printed by Lauer in Rome in 1470. It was being used in 1474 by the German scribe, Theodoric Werken, in the library at Christ Church, Canterbury. The text is known not to have been readily available in England before it was printed.[28]

Printed books imported from the Continent by a bookseller were also sold on. The first fully documented purchase of a printed book in England took place in 1477, when Giovanni Gigli, the newly-arrived Papal Collector, acquired a copy of Diodorus Siculus (the Greek historian and author of a world history), in the Latin translation of the Italian humanist, Poggio Bracciolini, printed by Andreas de Paltasichis in Venice in the same year.[29]

John Gunthorpe, dean of Wells, bought a copy of the commentary on Valerius Maximus by Dionysius de Burgo Sancti Sepulcri (Strasbourg: R-Printer, not after 1475) in 1475. This purchase *may* have taken place in England. The acquisition, probably in the early 1480s, of his copy of Pliny's *Natural History*, printed by Nicolaus Jenson, however, must have been made in England, because Gunthorpe is not known to have left England at that time. Another surviving book which belonged to Gunthorpe was a composite volume containing seven editions, five of which were printed by John of Westphalia in Louvain, and the two others from Venetian presses. According to the list of contents in Gunthorpe's own hand, it was a gift from one Jacopo Maletta and already consisted of this collection when he acquired it.[30]

It was not simply members of the secular clergy who were acquiring printed books. Vincent Gillespie has shown that several members of the community of Syon Abbey obtained printed books, including two Confessors General of

[27] Gillespie, 'Syon and English Market', p. 116; 'English Purchases', p. 269; Barker, 'Importation of Books', p. 254; the Bessarion is now Vatican, Cod. Vat. lat. 3586.

[28] Barker, 'Importation of Books', p. 254; 'English Purchases', p. 270; the Chrysostom is Goff, J-286.

[29] Gillespie, 'Syon and English Market', p. 117; Barker, 'Importation of Books', pp. 256–57; 'English Purchases', pp. 272–73. The Diodorus is Yale University, Beinecke Library, Zi +4421 (Thomas E. Marston, 'A Book Owned by Giovanni Gigli', *The Yale University Library Gazette* 34 (1960), 48).

[30] The Valerius Maximus does survive, as Oxford, BodL, Auct. N 4.4 (Bod-inc. D-091); see 'English Purchases', pp. 271, 283; Lowry, 'Arrival and Use', pp. 451–53 (who suggests at p. 451 that the book 'cannot have been acquired until the end of the decade'); Barker, 'Importation of Books', p. 254, who suggests the purchase took place in London. The book containing seven editions is now Oxford, BodL, Auct. N 5.3 (Bod-inc. A-605, etc.).

the Birgittine Order, Thomas Westhaw and Stephen Saunder. Westhaw had ten printed books from Germany and the Low Countries, and Saunder more than a dozen.[31] Brother John Grene, a Franciscan from Bedford, is known from an inscription in the book to have bought a volume containing three incunable editions in Oxford in 1483.[32] On some occasions the normal trade routes did not work as they should have done. The prior of the London Carthusians had to write directly to his opposite number in Cologne, to place a bulk order for the works of Dionysius Carthusiensis (the medieval theologian and mystic), which had been printed in the city in 1531, but which had somehow not found their way to London.[33]

An interesting incident in 1475 highlights another group who were importing books, namely foreign nationals resident in England, in this case the Florentine community. The latter had appealed to one of the Strozzi family (the famous Florentine bankers) to send them copies of the Italian translation of Pliny's *Natural History* and other works. The printer Nicolaus Jenson duly arranged for these to be sent by galley via Flanders in 1476.[34]

In addition to the market for new books, the market for second-hand books developed quickly. An early documented example of this is a purchase by Fernando Colon, Christopher Columbus's son, on a visit to London in June 1522. He bought a copy of Albertus de Padua's *Commentary on the Evangelists* (Venice, 1476) from the bookseller John Taverner for 4s. 5d.[35] A good example of a book changing hands in England is provided by a copy of a work by Johannes de Imola, printed in Venice in 1475. It was probably bound in London by the 'Indulgence Binder', and bears an inscription showing that it was bought by Peter Potkin from Master Starkey. Potkin, who died in 1520, has been identified by Dennis Rhodes as a benefactor of New College, Oxford, where the book now is.[36]

It is interesting to note how books were brought into England, and from where they were acquired on the Continent by booksellers. The River Rhine linked the major Continental centres of printing, from cities such as Basel, past Mainz, Strasbourg and Cologne, then through Flanders to the ports of which Antwerp was the main one. It has been suggested that books arrived directly from the city where they were published. For example, books printed in Venice would be sent along with cargoes of luxury goods on Venetian galleys, which would come to England twice a year. It is known from the evidence of the port books that galleys called regularly at Southampton from Bruges. In 1478–79 seven cases of books were landed from the galley of Jerome Contaryn. Other ships seem to have come from the Low Countries. In 1488 one Richard Brent

[31] Gillespie, 'Syon and English Market', pp. 122–23.
[32] The book is now Oxford, BodL, Arch. G e.5 (Bod-inc. A-021(3), etc., Terence, *Vulgaria* ([Oxford: Theodoricus Rood, not after 1483]), Petrus Paulus Vergerius, *De ingenuis moribus* . . . ([Louvain]: Johannes de Westfalia, [1476–77]), Adelard Bathonensis, *Quaestiones naturales* ([Louvain: Johannes de Westfalia, 1476–77]).
[33] Barker, 'Importation of Books', p. 262.
[34] Lowry, 'Arrival and Use', pp. 453–54; the Pliny is Goff P-801.
[35] Christianson, 'Rise of London's Book-trade', p. 144; Hellinga, 'Importation of Books', p. 220; the Albertus is Goff A-339.
[36] Hellinga, 'Importation of Books', p. 220 and n.19; Johannes de Imola, *Lectura super prima parte Infortiati* (Venice: J. de Colonia & J. Manthen, 1475), Rhodes 1021.

landed at Southampton various commodities, including ginger and malmsey, along with five chests of books, probably for William Caxton, the whole worth £300. A further consignment, in 1495, of seven chests, included books 'some printed and some written by hand'.[37]

In what form did books arrive in England? In the fifteenth century and early sixteenth centuries, it was conventional practice to bring books into England in sheets and have them bound on arrival in London, Oxford, or elsewhere. It is recorded that a book was bound up in York 'soon after 1480 [which] contained 10 separate pieces, 5 printed at Paris, between 1473 and 1477, 1 from Cologne, 1 printed by John of Westphalia and 2 Caxtons, compact evidence of the extent of the book trade in the provinces'. Jean Biennayse, from Paris, is known to have imported a pipe, which was the largest form of barrel available, in 1503. It was normal at that time to pack books in barrels in sheets. Some books, however, were imported in finished form, bound up, in spite of the extra weight. Material brought in by Arnold Birckmann and Conrad Mollar, from Cologne, may suggest that there was a difference in the way bound books and unbound sheets were imported, since a distinction was made in this case between five barrels and two baskets.[38] Stationers no doubt welcomed unbound imports, because, along with those books requiring decoration and rubrication (such as the two Gutenberg Bibles which were sent to London to be illuminated not long after they were printed), they would have created extra business, in these instances for binders and illuminators.[39]

Quantification and valuation of books and the units in which they are listed is extremely difficult to analyse. Needham has noted that early rolls refer only to the containers in which the books are carried (chests, vats and the like), although by the 1480s some sort of counting is tried, only to be dropped after the 1490s. Books of Rates for commodities, including books, were introduced, which detailed the fixed rate values for imported items. The earliest surviving one for printed books dates from 1545, showing books valued at £4 unbound per basket, and 40 shillings unbound the half basket.[40]

Caxton and other early printers in England were all involved in the importation and retail of books. Caxton published the first book printed in English, the *Recuyell of the Histories of Troy*, in Bruges in 1475, with the intention of importing it into England. Later, Caxton is known to have both exported and imported books through London during 1487–88. A chest of 140 books in French, valued at £6, left England in December 1487, whilst a fardel of 112 books was imported in February 1488, with a value of £13. Caxton then imported more books during April 1488, with a combined value of nearly £30.[41]

[37] Gillespie, 'Syon and English Market', pp. 104–05; Barker, 'Importation of Books', pp. 255–56; Christianson, 'Rise of London's Book-trade', p. 141, with the assertion that the books were for Caxton; 'English Purchases', p. 275, with further examples of the shipping used at p. 277.
[38] Barker, 'Importation of Books', p. 257, with the quotation on the same page.
[39] Christianson, 'Rise of London's Book-trade', p. 136. On the two Gutenbergs, see Eberhard König, 'New Perspectives on the History of Mainz Printing: A Fresh Look at Illuminated Imprints', in *Printing the Written Word*, pp. 143–73 (145 and n.7).
[40] Needham, 'Customs Rolls', pp. 156–60. For Bretton, see Anne Sutton's chapter in this volume.
[41] 'English Purchases', pp. 272, 277; Needham, 'Customs Rolls', p. 154. There must have been many other such consignments, but there is very little surviving evidence: Caxton's import and

Caxton also established strong links with Johann Veldener in Cologne. The latter supplied Caxton's types, whilst Caxton perhaps managed the sale of Veldener's books in England. Caxton had connections with Guillaume de Maynyal in Paris. De Maynyal printed editions of a Missal and a *Sarum Legenda* (containing extracts from saints' lives for readings) for Caxton in 1487 and 1488. He was an expert at printing in red and black, whereas Caxton was not. Caxton's successor, Wynkyn de Worde, was himself a major importer of printed books, as already noted above. He also collaborated with Continental printers, including Michael Morin in Paris, and others, to import service books.[42]

The Mercers' Company (of which Caxton was a member) played a considerable role in the importation of books into England, as is shown by the records for the period. Members of other guilds played a more minor part. These included the London haberdasher, Henry Somer, and the skinner William Danyell, who imported books with other shipments in 1494 and 1495. The grocer and merchant of the Staple, William Bretton, was the publisher of six liturgical and religious books, printed in Paris between 1506 and 1510. He imported them and had them sold in St Paul's Churchyard by Joyce Pelgrim and Henry Jacobi.[43]

However, the biggest importers of all were the alien merchants, men such as Henry Frankenberg, Frederick Egmondt, Franz Birckmann, Michael Morin and Joyce Pelgrim. Henry Frankenberg imported £6 worth of books in December 1477. Along with Barnard van Stando (from Utrecht), he brought in forty-four volumes, plus 'some small books' and thirty-six red skins, perhaps to be used for binding, in October 1480. Frankenberg continued to import books until 1485, and, given the number of servants he and van Stando employed, it has been suggested that they acted as agents at book fairs as well.[44]

Andrew Rue, from Frankfurt, imported 177 volumes in 1480. He is presumably the Andrew Rue, who, with his brother John Rue, owned a bookshop in St Paul's Churchyard. He must also be identified with 'Andreas Ruwe', who, in a letter of 8 August 1495 written from London to Johann Amerbach, made what was probably the earliest reference to the Frankfurt Book Fair and its importance to the book trade with London. He asked Amerbach to supply fifty copies each of half a dozen editions printed by Amerbach, including works by Augustine, Ambrose, Bernard and Holkot.[45]

export during 1487–88 appears in the one London subsidy roll to survive from the 1470s until 1491; the *Recuyell* is *STC* 15375.
[42] Barker, 'Importation of Books', p. 255; Lotte Hellinga, *Caxton in Focus: The Beginnings of Printing in England* (London, 1982), pp. 49–51; *BMC XI*, pp. 335–40; 'English Purchases', pp. 274, 277; 'Marketing Printed Books', pp. 120–22; Gillespie, 'Syon and English Market', pp. 120–21; the *Sarum Legenda* is *STC* 16136.
[43] Christianson, 'Rise of London's Book-trade', pp. 141–42.
[44] Peter W.M. Blayney, *The Stationers' Company before the Charter, 1403–1557* (London, 2003), p. 35, note †; 'English Purchases', pp. 273, 278. Christianson, 'Rise of London's Book-trade', pp. 136–37.
[45] Barker, 'Importation of Books', p. 255; Christianson, 'Rise of London's Book-trade', p. 138; John died in 1492, Andrew in 1517. John Flood, '"Omnium totius orbis emporiorum compendium": The Frankfurt Fair in the Early Modern Period', in *Fairs, Markets, and the Itinerant Book Trade*, ed. Robin Myers, Michael Harris and Giles Mandelbrote (New Castle, DE, 2007), pp. 1–42, repr. in *The History of the Book in the West, II: 1455–1700*, ed. Ian Gadd (Farnham, 2010), pp. 11–13; the works were Augustine, *Super Johannem, De civitate Dei, De trinitate*; Ambrose, *Opera*; Holkot, *Super librum Sapientiae*; Bernard, *Liber meditationum*. Flood identifies Ruwe as

Between 1492 and 1535 no fewer than ninety-eight aliens appear on the Customs rolls paying duty on the importation of books. Wynkyn de Worde headed the list, importing twenty-nine shipments between 1503 and 1531 at a total value of £147 10s (with one shipment alone in 1503 worth £10). Another important figure who appeared regularly in the customs rolls of that period was Franz Birckmann, from Cologne.[46] He sold books there, and also in both Antwerp and London, appearing twenty-nine times on the London customs rolls between 1503 and 1521. When he died in about 1530, his importing business was continued by his son, Franz, and his nephew, John. They, like the Rue brothers, established a shop in St Paul's Churchyard. Joyce Pelgrim also sold books imported by Frederick Egmondt. It is unfortunate that the survival rate of the customs rolls of the principal ports of England, including London, only provides somewhat patchy evidence.[47]

The importance of aliens, whether printers or merchants, was clear. It was obvious that England had much to gain from the output of Continental printing houses. When an Act of Parliament was passed in 1484 to limit the activities of foreign merchants in England, a Proviso was added which specifically exempted those involved in the book trade. Alien booksellers were valued in Cambridge. In 1528/9 the university petitioned Cardinal Wolsey to permit them to have three alien booksellers, on the grounds that they were especially skilled at purchasing books from abroad. This request was duly granted under a charter of 1534.[48]

The 1520s indeed saw an increase in the amount of imports made by native Englishmen, who were probably selling books with other items. Among these was the mercer, John Coleyns, who recorded in 1520 that his trade involved selling printed books, and what he called 'other small tryffylles'.[49] However, views changed, clearly reflecting the resentment of the English members of the book trade, and during the 1520s and 1530s, a series of laws were passed against aliens. In 1523 aliens were forbidden to have more than two foreign journeymen, and were obliged to take on English apprentices. This was followed in 1529 by an act which forbade aliens to set up business unless they had obtained a licence to live and trade in England.

The importation of books in the vernacular but printed on the Continent was seen as a threat to local, English trade. An act was passed in 1534 whereby

being a merchant from Cologne, but it seems more likely that he was actually Andrew Rue, the bookseller (from Germany, now resident in London, and selling books in St Paul's Churchyard, see above); Andrew Pettegree, *The Book in the Renaissance* (New Haven, CT, 2010), p. 77.

[46] For further discussion of the role of the Birckmanns, see the chapter by Andrew Hope in this volume.

[47] Christianson, 'Rise of London's Book-trade', pp. 140–41; 'English Purchases', p. 278. On the nature of the evidence of the customs rolls, see Needham, 'Customs Rolls as Documents', pp. 148–63.

[48] 'English Purchases', pp. 276–77; Roberts, 'Importing Books for Oxford', p. 320; by contrast, Oxford did not receive such assistance, and was duly regulated by the Act of 1534.

[49] Christianson, 'Rise of London's Book-trade', p. 142; on Coleyns, see Carol M. Meale, 'Wynkyn de Worde's Setting-copy for "Ipomydon"', *Studies in Bibliography* 35 (1982), 156–71 (157, 169–71); also Carol M. Meale, 'The Compiler at Work: John Colyns and BL, MS. Harley 2252', in *Manuscripts and Readers in Fifteenth-Century England: The Literary Implications of Manuscript Study*, ed. Derek Pearsall (Cambridge, 1983), pp. 82–103.

aliens were forbidden to sell in England (except by wholesale) books which had been printed or bound abroad.[50] This act would obviously have hit, for example, smaller, retail booksellers selling to academic customers in Oxford, whilst not really affecting the larger, Continental wholesale importers of books, such as the Birckmanns of Cologne, who were based in London. The result of this was that alien booksellers were obliged to become naturalised Englishmen, or they would be put out of business.

Whilst this has been seen as part of an attempt by the Livery Companies of London (especially the Stationers' Company) to take as much control over all book-related activities as possible, there were some advantages to naturalisation. These included access to the royal court, and being allowed to make a will.[51] Roberts has noted that the documentary evidence may have distorted the number of alien booksellers, as against native Englishmen. The former would be liable to more and heavier taxes than the latter, and would, therefore, appear in a greater number of records.

The Customs rolls show that those buying academic books in Oxford and Cambridge up to 1557 did not have to depend wholly on the London book trade. They still seem to have been catered for by booksellers who imported their own books. These included Nicholas Spierinck, trading in Cambridge, who is listed in Customs rolls for London for 1503 and 1520, and Hermann Evans, from Oxford, in rolls between 1536/7 and 1555/6. Indeed, in the roll for 1555/6, Evans imported a barrel of unbound books (perhaps as many as 600) valued at £4. John Dorne, who is known from his 'Day Book' to have been abroad, presumably buying books, during the summer of 1520, does not appear on any surviving customs rolls. He may, however, have been importing books through a smaller port than London. Books destined for Cambridge seem also to have been imported through the East Anglian ports.[52]

Not all books followed the conventional paths of importation into England taken particularly by academic books in Latin, and discussed above. Some printers in the Low Countries (especially in Antwerp) and in Germany smuggled across the Channel books which were prohibited in England, particularly works by Luther and his associates, and also works of scripture printed in the vernacular, including copies of William Tyndale's translation of the *New Testament*.[53] The authorities were hugely concerned about the arrival of Tyndale's *New Testament* in England. Among those involved in this smuggling were Franz Birckmann and Christoffel van Ruremond. The former was brought before the royal council in 1527, becoming the first person to be interrogated in person over importing scripture in the vernacular into England. Van Ruremond printed Tyndale's *New Testament*, and, when he came to England to sell books, he was thrown into prison (where he died in 1531). Richard Bayfield was burnt in the same year for importing works of Luther, Zwingli and others. For obvious reasons, a considerable amount of subversive material of this sort simply disappeared. So, it seems,

[50] 'English Purchases', p. 276; Barker, 'Importation of Books, pp. 262–63.
[51] Roberts, 'Importing Books for Oxford', pp. 320–21.
[52] Roberts, 'Importing Books for Oxford', pp. 322–24; Leedham-Green, 'University Libraries and Book-sellers', p. 348.
[53] This is discussed in detail in Andrew Hope's chapter in this volume.

have copies of what may have been the first list of prohibited books to appear in England, which probably appeared in a proclamation of 1529, in a clear attempt to clamp down on the importation of heretical material. In subsequent reigns, efforts by the government to stop books being imported were equally unsuccessful.[54] The works of John Bale, for example, were secretly brought into England, while Bale was in exile in the mid to late 1540s.[55]

During the late fifteenth and the first half of the sixteenth centuries the British Isles depended heavily on the importation of Latin printed books, especially for academic and liturgical needs. The early printers simply could not produce the amount and types of material required. In this chapter a picture has been given of the kind of books which were imported, who was bringing them in and how they were doing this, showing the great variety in all these aspects of the importation process, and the significance of its role in the history of the book in early modern Britain.

Further Reading

Armstrong, Elizabeth, 'English Purchases of Printed Books from the Continent', *English Historical Review* 94 (1979), 268–90.

Barker, Nicolas, 'The Importation of Books into England 1460–1526', in *Beiträge zur Geschichte des Buchwesens im konfessionellen Zeitalter*, ed. Herbert G. Göpfert et al., Wolfenbüttler Schriften zur Geschichte des Buchwesens 11 (Wiesbaden, 1985), pp. 251–66.

Christianson, C. Paul, 'The Rise of London's Book-trade', in *CHBB III*, pp. 128–47.

Ford, Margaret Lane, 'Importation of Printed Books into England and Scotland', in *CHBB III*, pp. 179–201.

Gillespie, Vincent, 'Syon and the English Market for Continental Printed Books: The Incunable Phase', in *Syon Abbey and its Books: Reading, Writing and Religion c.1400–1700*, ed. E.A. Jones and Alexandra Walsham (Woodbridge, 2010), pp. 104–28.

Hellinga, Lotte, 'The Bookshop of the World: Books and their Makers as Agents of Cultural Exchange', in *The Bookshop of the World: the Role of the Low Countries in the Book-trade 1473–1941*, ed. Lotte Hellinga et al. ('t Goy-Houten, 2001), pp. 11–29.

Hellinga, Lotte, 'Importation of Books Printed on the Continent into England and Scotland before c.1520', in *Printing the Written Word: the Social History of Books, circa 1450–1520*, ed. Sandra Hindman (Ithaca, NY, 1991), pp. 205–24.

Lowry, Martin, 'The Arrival and Use of Continental Printed Books in Yorkist England', in *Le Livre dans l'Europe de la Renaissance. Actes du xxviiie Colloque international d'Etudes humanistes de Tours*, ed. P. Aquillon and H.-J. Martin (Paris, 1988), pp. 449–59.

Needham, Paul, 'Continental Printed Books Sold in Oxford, c.1480–3: Two Trade Records', in *Incunabula: Studies in Fifteenth-century Printed Books Presented to Lotte Hellinga*, ed. Martin Davies (London, 1999), pp. 243–70.

---

[54] For a discussion of these measures, see Susan Powell's chapter in this volume.
[55] Hellinga, 'Bookshop of the World', p. 24; John N. King, 'The Book-trade under Edward VI and Mary I', in *CHBB III*, pp. 164–78 (168); on the list of prohibited books, see 'Press, Politics and Religion', p. 588.

Needham, Paul, 'The Customs Rolls as Documents for the Printed-book Trade in England', in *CHBB III*, pp. 148–63.

Roberts, Julian, 'Importing Books for Oxford, 1500–1640', in *Books and Collectors 1200-1700: Essays Presented to Andrew Watson*, ed. James P. Carley and Colin G.C. Tite (London, 1997), pp. 317–33.

THE PRINTED BOOK AS ARTEFACT

4

Materials: Paper and Type

PAMELA ROBINSON

Paper was first made by the Chinese from a variety of materials including mulberry and bamboo bark. The technique of paper making was first introduced into the Islamic world by Chinese artisans taken prisoner after the battle of Atlakh, Kazakhstan, in 751. Knowledge of the craft then spread from Central Asia to Damascus, Cairo, and the Maghreb by the tenth century. From North Africa the Moors introduced the technique to Europe, where a mill at Játiva, Valencia, had become famous for its paper by the mid-twelfth century. As the knowledge spread, further mills were established elsewhere in the West. By 1283 a mill at Fabriano, Italy, had become one of the earliest in Europe to make paper on a large scale.

Early European paper was made from linen rags, which were washed, steeped in water, and then reduced to a pulp before being transferred to a large vat full of water. Sheets of paper were formed by the vatman dipping his mould into the vat to scoop up the pulp. This mould or sieve consisted of a rectangular wooden frame across which was stretched wire, with a removable frame or 'deckle' around the edges in order to retain the pulp on the mould's surface when the water drained through. The sheet of matted fibres left behind was dried to become paper.

Although the English must have become acquainted with paper quite soon (a letter datable 1216–22 from Raymond of Toulouse to Henry III, preserved in the National Archives at Kew, is written on paper), its earliest known use in this country is almost a century later, in the Register of the Hustings Court of [King's] Lynn, begun in 1307.[1] At first paper was used only for archival material, but by the late fourteenth century it had begun to be used for manuscript books. In the fifteenth century the population's increasing literacy led to a greater demand for books, a demand that could partly be met by the increased use of paper, since paper was cheaper than parchment and its use thus meant cheaper books.[2] Paper was almost invariably used by the printers; only a few *de luxe* copies were ever printed on vellum. The anonymous scribe who gave among the causes of sore eyes 'to study moche on whyte boks and namely

---

[1] PRO, SC 1/4/98a, and King's Lynn, Borough Muniments, C/10/1, the 'Red Register'; for the latter, see New Palaeographical Society, ser. 2, pl. 90.

[2] Erik Kwakkel, 'A New Type of Book for a New Type of Reader: The Emergence of Paper in Vernacular Book Production', *The Library*, 7th series, 4 (2003), 219–48, and P.R. Robinson, 'The Format of Books – Books, Booklets and Rolls', in *CHBB II*, p. 48.

pryntyd book' certainly associated white (as opposed to brown) paper with printed editions.[3]

The paper used in English books, whether manuscript or printed, was chiefly imported from Italy or France. The first English paper mill was only founded in the late fifteenth century near Hertford by the merchant, John Tate (d. 1508). Tate's paper was used by Wynkyn de Worde in several books printed by him: *The Canterbury Tales* (1498, STC 5085), *The Assembly of Gods* (1498, STC 17005), and *The Golden Legend* (1498/9, STC 24876), as well as in his edition of John Trevisa's translation of Bartholomaeus Anglicus, *De proprietatibus rerum* (c.1496, STC 1536), a fact he famously advertised in the versified colophon:

> And John Tate the yonger, Ioye mote he broke
> Which late hathe in Englond' doo make this paper thynne
> That now in our englyssh this boke is prynted inne.

For whatever reason, Tate's mill did not long survive him. His will directed that it should be sold – 'doo sell my paper mill with all the goodes, woodes, pastures, medes with all the commodities concernyng the said mill to the moost avauntage'.[4] Possibly he had had difficulty competing with foreign imports, as was suggested in 1549 by the author of *A Discourse of the Common Weal of this Realm of England*:

> ... there was paper made a while within the realm. At the last the man perceaued that made it that he could not fourde his paper as good cheape as that came beyonde the seaze, and so he was forced to lay downe the makinge of paper ... for men would geve never the more for his paper because it was made heare.

The writer goes on to say he wished its import was banned or else so taxed that 'oure men might afford their paper better cheape then straungers might doe theirs, the custome considered'.[5] The printer and bookseller, Richard Tottell (c.1528–93), attempted to get an embargo on the export of rags and to set up a paper mill, but it was John Spilman, a German entrepreneur and jeweller to Elizabeth I, who was granted the monopoly of the collection of rags and who established the first successful paper mill in England on the River Darenth, in Kent, 1588.

Tate's paper can be recognised by its watermark, described as a 'wheel ... of eight spokes or a rayed star within a double circle'.[6] The watermark, which served as an individual manufacturer's trade mark, already appeared in paper made at Fabriano in the 1280s. A design fashioned in wire was sewn with knots of fine wire to the wire screen of the mould and left its traces on the paper. At first, the watermark was placed anywhere in the mould but by the fifteenth century it was usually placed in the centre of one half of it. Popular designs such

---

[3] Berkeley Castle, Special Book 89, fol. lxxxiij. I owe this reference to Professor Linda Voigts.
[4] Anne F. Sutton, *A Merchant Family of Coventry, London and Calais: The Tates, c. 1450–1515* (London, 1998), pp. 24–25.
[5] *A Discourse of the Common Weal of this Realm of England*, ed. Elizabeth Lamond (Cambridge, 1954), pp. 65–66.
[6] Paul Needham, 'The Paper of English Incunabula', in *BMC XI*, p. 311 and fig.

as a bull's head, hand or glove, were common, but the detailed study of water-marks has led to the creation of repertories of them which can help the scholar to identify one mill's use from another's of a particular pattern.[7]

Paper could be made in four different sizes: Imperial (c.490 x 740 mm), Royal (c.430 x 620 mm), Median (c.350 x 510 mm) and Chancery (c.310 x 450 mm). Most early English books were printed on Chancery paper, Imperial was not used, and Median or Royal were only preferred in a few instances. William Caxton's edition of Gower's *Confessio Amantis* (1483, STC 12142) and Richard Pynson's edition of Lydgate's *Fall of Princes* (1494, STC 3175) were both printed on Median; this may have been because it enabled the stanzas of lengthy poems to be printed in double columns.[8] However, the format of a book was deter-mined not by the size of a sheet of paper but by the number of times the sheet was folded. The watermark can tell us, for instance, whether a sheet was simply folded in half (as in a folio) since the watermark will then appear in the centre of one half of the bifolium, or four times (as in quarto) when the watermark will appear in the central gutter.[9] When the latter happens or if a book is heavily printed, it can be impossible to examine the watermark.

Although the wear and tear of a mould in continuous use could cause a watermark to become distorted, perhaps leading to a badly sewn repair or even loss altogether within as little as six months,[10] the watermark nevertheless has a number of evidential uses. The use of different watermarks in a single volume is evidence of the use of different paper stocks within a printing house, a common situation in English incunables. A notable example is Caxton's *Royal book* (1485–86, STC 21429), his translation of Laurent d'Orléans's *Somme le Roi,* where twenty-six different paperstocks are used. The preliminaries of a book are often of a different stock to the rest of it, as they were printed separately from the rest of the job. In a substantial work two or more compositors may have worked concurrently on different sections and used different stocks, sending their type-pages independently to one or more presses. Bibliographical analysis may also reveal that the same paper stock was used in two different books, suggesting they were printed more or less at the same time.

Early English printers, like their predecessors the scribes, show little concern as to whether or not they dated their work. If a watermark is known to appear in books or documents that are firmly dated or datable within a limited time span, it is reasonable to assume an undated book using the same paper stock was produced within the same few years. This assumption is reinforced when two or more stocks, both or all of which are closely datable, are used together, as study has shown that on average paper stock was used within three or four years of manufacture. Dating by the watermark is considered more reliable than typographic evidence since a casting of type can continue to be used until it is

---

[7] C.M. Briquet, *Les filigranes: dictionnaire historique des marques du papier dès leur apparition vers 1282 jusqu'en 1600,* ed. Allan Stevenson (Amsterdam, 1968); Gerhard Piccard, *Wasserzeichen Dreiberg* (Stuttgart, 1996). See also <www.gravell.org> for a digital archive of watermarks.

[8] Needham, 'The Paper', p. 315.

[9] As illustrated by Jean Irigoin, 'La datation par les filigranes du papier', *Codicologica,* 5 vols (Leiden, 1976–1980), 5.10, fig. 1.

[10] Philip Gaskell, *A New Introduction to Bibliography* (Oxford, 1979), p. 63.

too worn out to employ. Thus, a chronological list of all Caxton's printing has been established as a result of an investigation into the sequence of paper stocks he used.[11]

The early English printers depended on Continental supplies not only for paper but also for all their other materials. While customs records reveal the importation of paper, there are no such records for the trade in typographical materials. None of the equipment of England's first printer, William Caxton (d. 1492), has survived and there are no contemporary descriptions of it. While representations of the printing press occur from as early as 1499 on the Continent, the first such illustration to appear in an English book occurs in *The Ordenarye for all faythfull Chrystians* (1548, STC 5199.7), a translation by Anthony Scoloker of a Dutch work printed by the Ghent typefounder and printer, Joos Lambrecht, from whom the woodcut was obtained.[12] The 'earliest trustworthy account of the making of type' only occurs in 1567 with the publication of the anonymous *Dialogues francois pour les ieunes enfans* by the Antwerp printer Christophe Plantin (c.1520–89).[13] Hence bibliographers must rely on the evidence of later practice and on what they can deduce from a careful study of incunabula as to the earlier process of casting type.

The technique demanded great skill, and was a long and costly process. A letter was first cut in relief on one end of a long rectangular piece of steel known as a punch. The punch was then struck into copper to form a matrix or mould in which to cast type. Each resulting piece of type formed a small piece of metal made of an alloy of lead, tin and antimony, with a letter on one end. Since the earliest types were modelled on handwriting in order to reproduce the appearance of manuscript books, a complete set or fount of type consisted not only of variant forms of the letters of the alphabet but also of a large number of ligatures (tied letters) and abbreviations commonly used, such as the 'titulus' or stroke placed above letters to indicate a contraction. Caxton's Type 2 had some 250 different sorts. Over time the number of sorts was gradually reduced as founts were simplified in the interests of efficiency.

Founts of type were not made to standard sizes as they are today (for example, 10 or 12 point). In an age when printers cast their own type and type was modelled on contemporary scripts, there was no question of uniformity until type foundries that designed and distributed type faces were established. As typographical differences can hence be slight, determining the body-size of a type can help to distinguish between different specimens. Body-size is established by determining the average measurement of twenty lines of type from the foot of the letter **m** to the foot of the letter **m** on the twenty-first line above. Thus bibliographers have designated the different founts used by Caxton and his

---

[11] *Printer and Pardoner.*

[12] Falconer Madan, 'Early Representations of the Printing Press', *Bibliographica*, 3 vols (London, 1895–97), 1.233–48 and 499–502; Janet Ing Freeman, 'Anthony Scoloker, the "*Just Reckoning Printer*", and the Earliest Ipswich Printing', *TCBS* 9 (1990), 476–96.

[13] Harry Carter, *A View of Early Typography Up to about 1600*, repr. with an Introduction by James Mosley (London, 1969), pp. 5–6; see further, *An Account of Calligraphy and Printing in the Sixteenth Century from dialogues attributed to Christophe Plantin. Printed and Published by him at Antwerp, in 1567*, facsimile edn, English transl. and notes by Ray Nash; foreword by Stanley Morison (Cambridge, MA, 1940).

successors by a number signifying the chronological order in which they were used followed by a measurement expressed as, for example, 'Type 4: 95'. This tells us that a printer's fourth type had a body-size of 95 mm. The classification of types in this way has led to the identification of the work of different printers and printing houses.

Caxton's first and principal punchcutter was Johann Veldener with whom he had become acquainted during his time in Cologne from July 1471 to December 1472.[14] The types Caxton used were influential among his immediate successors and were modelled on two different scripts, a calligraphic script used in France and Burgundy in *de luxe* manuscripts and known as *lettre bâtarde* and textura. *Lettre bâtarde* was characterised by the letter forms single compartment **a**, single compartment **g**, short **r**, small loops on ascenders, tapering descenders and angular broken strokes instead of curved ones, giving the script a prickly appearance. Textura was an upright and angular narrow 'Gothic' script with alternating thick and thin strokes, a heavy black appearance, used north of the Alps to copy liturgical texts.[15] Roman type, to which we are accustomed today, although first used by Richard Pynson in 1509, was not widely used until the middle of the sixteenth century.

William Blades (1829–90), himself a printer, first examined the types used by Caxton in over 400 copies of his books.[16] He identified eight separate founts, six of which are cursive types known as bastarda and two more formal types based on textura. He believed Caxton's first types were modelled on the *lettre bâtarde* of the scribe and printer Colard Mansion (*c.*1425–84) who worked in Bruges where Caxton was based. Today a more nuanced picture has emerged, and it is argued that Caxton returned to Bruges from Cologne via Ghent where he formed an association with the scribe David Aubert (*fl.* 1449–79) who produced manuscripts for the court of Burgundy. Caxton's Type 1: 120, found in four editions (the *Recuyell of the histories of Troy* (1473, STC 15375), the *Game of Chess* (1474, STC 4920), and two books in French also published in 1474) is seen as a close approximation to Aubert's wide, slanting handwriting.[17] As a type, it was not very practical since it had too many ligatures. Back in Bruges by 1475 when he published two books, including an edition of the Sarum Hours (the prayer book of the laity), Caxton had commissioned another fount, Type 2: 135, based on a more common Flemish style of *bâtarde* favoured by Mansion.[18]

On Caxton's return to England to set up a press in 1476 in the precincts of Westminster Abbey, he brought with him Type 2, a more upright and rounded fount than Type 1 with larger body size. Since it was modelled on Burgundian

[14] Severin Corsten, 'Caxton in Cologne', *Journal of the Printing Historical Society* 11/12 (1976/7), 1–18.

[15] Albert Derolez, *The Palaeography of Gothic Manuscript Books From the Twelfth to the Sixteenth Century* (Cambridge, 2003), pp. 72–101 (on textura) and pp. 157–60 (on *lettre batârde*). See also Stanley Morison, '"Black-Letter" Text', in his *Selected Essays on the History of Letter-Forms in Manuscript and Print*, ed. David McKitterick (Cambridge, 1981), pp. 177–205 (first publ. 1942).

[16] William Blades, *The Biography and Typography of William Caxton, England's First Printer* (London, 1897).

[17] See *Les manuscrits de David Aubert 'escripvain' bourguignon*, ed. Danielle Quéruel (Paris, 1999) and plates.

[18] *William Caxton*, pp. 33–51 and figs.

script, it must at first have appeared foreign-looking to English readers accustomed to manuscripts written in Anglicana (the national hand with two-compartment **a**, eight-shaped two-compartment **g**, and long **r**) or the native interpretation of Secretary, a script introduced in the later fourteenth century from France. Unlike printing in the vernacular elsewhere, it took a long time before typefaces were created here that gave printing in England 'a style of its own'.[19] However, from the start, the special sorts **w**, **k**, and **y** (a debased version of the runic letter 'thorn' used to represent 'th') had to be cut for the English language, and a limited number of characteristic English letter forms, such as the use of two-compartment **a** or **d** with a looped ascender (found in Anglicana) and otiose terminal strokes on final **d** and **g**, were provided. Caxton used Type 2 until 1484 (having had it recast with added sorts for ligatures of **wa**, **we** and **wo** in 1479, Type 2*) for all his work except liturgical printing where he used types designed upon textura. In 1480 Caxton adopted as his principal text type a scaled down version of his Type 2, Type 4: 95. With a smaller body size, Type 4 was more economical, omitting some ligatures, and no longer used the two-compartment **a** or the **d** with looped ascender. This proved to be the most successful of his types, as seen in his edition of the *Cronicles of Englond* (1480, *STC* 9991; Figure 4.1). Later it was inexpertly recast in 1482 or early 1483 on a larger body, Type 4*: 95 (100). A yet further bastarda type employed by Caxton from 1489 is Type 6: 120, a crude copy of his Type 2, smaller in body size with fewer ligatures.[20]

Caxton's textura-based types were used by him for headings, display purposes and in printing liturgical works. Type 3: 135, of similar body size to Type 2, was probably commissioned at the same time as Type 2 and was used in conjunction with it. His Type 5: 115, probably used as early as 1484, is basically a scaled-down version of Type 3 but with fewer ligatures, and was used in both English and Latin editions. His smallest type, Type 7: 84 resembling Type 5, was introduced *c*.1487, and his final type, Type 8: 114, consisting of only eighty sorts, was used towards the end of his life and may have been cut by the Parisian printer, Guillaume Maynyal, from whom Caxton had commissioned a Sarum Missal (*STC* 16164) and a Legenda (*STC* 16136).

Caxton found it necessary to seek Maynyal's expertise to print liturgical books since early English printers had not yet mastered the technique of printing in two colours. This was felt to be required as it was customary for liturgical manuscripts to be rubricated, that is, to have headings in red and to mark the beginning of texts with coloured initials. However, supplying colour by hand in multiple printed copies was laborious, a problem that the printer could overcome by the use of a 'frisket'. Two such early French friskets are known to survive, sheets of paper and parchment held in a frame. Holes or windows were specially cut into these sheets so that when the frisket was lowered down over type set for a page of text and locked up in a chase ready for printing, only those

[19] Lotte Hellinga, 'Printing Types and Other Typographical Material', in *BMC XI*, p. 335.
[20] The subtle variations between all these different founts are best exemplified by the illustrations and accompanying drawings of distinctive sorts provided in *BMC XI*, pp. 351–60 and plates 1–9.

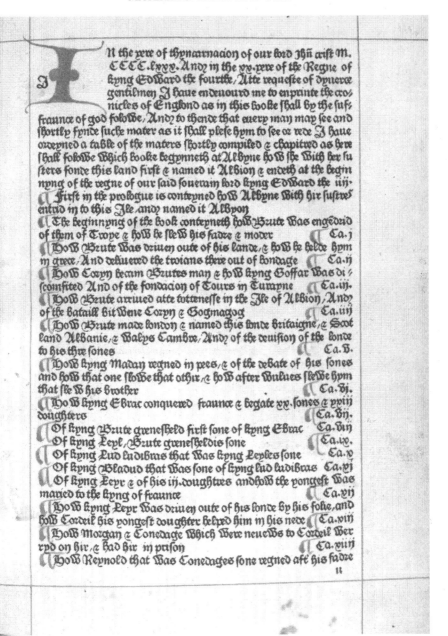

Figure 4.1 *The cronicles of Englond* (Westminster: William Caxton, 1480; *STC* 9991). University of London, Senate House Library, Special Collections, Incunabula 131 (SFL).

types intended to be in a specific colour (red) were inked by the first impression.[21] The rest of the page could then be inked in black on a second impression.

Caxton is typical of the early printers who all employed several sets of types. While his Type 5 was not used by any other printer, other types were taken over or copied by some of his contemporaries. His Type 4 was adopted by two immigrants, Johannes Lettou and William de Machlinia, who printed legal works in the 1480s. As their Type 3: 102 it can be distinguished from Caxton's Type 4 by the use of two-compartment **a** and the shorter descender of the letter **y**. Lettou had already adopted Caxton's Type 3 as his Type 2: 140. In addition, the pair employed a rotunda type to print an edition of the Statutes of the Realm, the *Nova Statuta* (*STC* 9264).[22] Rotunda, as the name implies, had rounded curved letter forms instead of angular ones and was modelled after the Italian version of textura.

Besides Lettou's and de Machlinia's press, a few other printing houses briefly flourished in London, Oxford and at St Albans in the later fifteenth century. However, Caxton's principal successors were two aliens, Richard Pynson (c.1449–1529/30) and Wynkyn de Worde (d. 1534/5), whose publishing houses began in the 1490s and remained dominant until 1535. Books issued from their presses were radically different in typographical appearance to Caxton's, since they imported their types from Rouen and Paris rather than Flanders.

De Worde had been Caxton's apprentice and took over his master's premises at Westminster as well as his tools. Whereas Caxton's output has been dated by his use of paper stocks, the chronology of de Worde's productions is based on recent study of the state of his types. The traditional numeration of them as established by E. Gordon Duff is preserved in *BMC XI*, but it no longer necessarily indicates the order in which they were first used (see further below).[23] Before moving to Fleet Street in late 1500, de Worde used Caxton's types. Thus *The Life of St Catherine* (1492–93, *STC* 24766), one of the first books he printed after taking over the business, was printed in a recast version of Caxton's smaller and worn-out Type 4, de Worde's Type 1: 99, while in *The Chastising of God's Children* (1492–93, *STC* 5065) he used Caxton's Type 6, de Worde Type 3: 120. He also continued to use Caxton's Type 3, de Worde Type 6: 135, both in *The Canterbury Tales* (where he used Tate's paper) and as a display type, while Caxton's smallest type, Type 7: 84, was taken over as de Worde Type 5: 84 for marginalia. Caxton's Type 8 which he had scarcely used also became part of de Worde's equipment, his Type 2: 114. It was first used in early editions of the Sarum Hours but later is found as a heading or for display in conjunction with his new main text type.

This new text type, de Worde Type 4: 96, acquired after the completion of *The Golden Legend* (1493, *STC* 24875) came from Paris where it was used also by local printers. It became known as 'English black letter', and remained de Worde's

---

[21] Margaret M. Smith and Alan May, 'Early Two-colour Printing', *Printing Historical Society Bulletin* 44 (1997), 1–4; Margaret M. Smith, 'Fragments Used for "Servile" Purposes: The St Bride Library Frisket for Early Red Printing', in *Interpreting and Collecting Fragments of Medieval Books*, ed. Linda L. Brownrigg and Margaret M. Smith (London, 2000), pp. 177–88. See also Martha Driver below, p. 98 and n.12.

[22] *BMC XI*, pp. 393–95 and plate 31.

[23] Duff rev.

main type for printing both Latin and English, being recast on a slightly smaller body $c.1497$, his Type 4: 94. It was the standard style for English printing until roman type began to take over in the mid-sixteenth century. At first this new type lacked the capitals **W**, **K** and **Y** as well as the English contractions y^e y^t w^t (for 'the', 'that' and 'with'). These were gradually introduced as well as other characters. The 'almost constant internal development' of this type has led to recent changes in the hitherto accepted dating of de Worde's undated editions. For example, his edition of *Vita et Transitus S. Hieronymi* (*STC* 14508) is now dated 1493 rather than $c.1499$ as previously thought.[24] In the case of lengthy texts, such as the *Cronycles of England* (1497, *STC* 9996) and Malory's *Le morte d'Arthur* (1498, *STC* 802), where copy was divided between compositors, distinct type-cases show that new characters were not introduced simultaneously.

De Worde also had a Dutch text type, Type 7: 103, recast and adapted for English-language printing. This was used only in his edition of Dame Juliana Berners's *Book of Hawking, hunting, and blasing of arms* (1496, *STC* 3309), reprinted from a version originally printed at St Albans in 1486. This may be because he thought its 'rather archaic and rustic appearance' to be more appropriate for a book destined for the countryman than his Parisian type. The fount was used by Govert van Ghemen, an itinerant printer who moved between Gouda and Leiden in Holland, and Copenhagen, and who is believed to have been the punchcutter. In 1499 he acquired two further types from Paris, a text type, Type 8: 93, and a rotunda, Type 9: 53, which he used until his death. Both type faces are employed in his edition of *Catho cum commento* (1512, *STC* 4839.7), textura for the main text and rotunda for the commentary (Figure 4.2).[25]

Wynkyn de Worde's competitor Richard Pynson, King's Printer from 1506, acquired the exclusive rights to print statutes of the realm and royal proclamations from 1513 and specialised in printing legal works. It is not known where he learned to print, but $c.1490$ he commissioned two legal works, an anonymous abridgement or digest of case-law known as 'Statham' (*STC* 23238), from Guillaume le Talleur of Rouen (from whom Pynson probably also obtained type) and Sir Thomas Littleton's *Tenores novelli* (*STC* 15721), a treatise in law French that rapidly became an authoritative text, earlier printed by Lettou and Machlinia in 1481, as the first law book to be printed in England (*STC* 15719).

When Pynson printed his edition of the *Canterbury Tales* (1491–92, *STC* 5084), he used a heavy bastarda type, his Type 1: 120, for the verse and a second, more elegant version, Type 2: 101, for the prose sections. Type 2 is found in four different states: 2^A distinguished by **k** composed of the letter **l** and the two-shaped **r** scribes had used after bow strokes; 2^B distinguished by **k**, the long **r** used when printing Law French, and the introduction of the contraction y^t (for 'that') in printing in English; 2^C where the type was recast on a slightly smaller body (there is only a difference of about 1 mm per twenty lines); and 2^D with an

---

[24] Lotte Hellinga, 'Tradition and Renewal: Establishing the Chronology of Wynkyn de Worde's Early Work', in *Incunabula and their Readers: Printing, Selling and Using Books in the Fifteenth Century*, ed. Kristian Jensen (London, 2003), pp. 27–30; see also *BMC XI*, pp. 367–80 and plates 10–19.
[25] Frank Isaac, 'Types Used by Wynkyn de Worde, 1501–34', *The Library*, 4th ser., 9 (1928), 395–410 and plates.

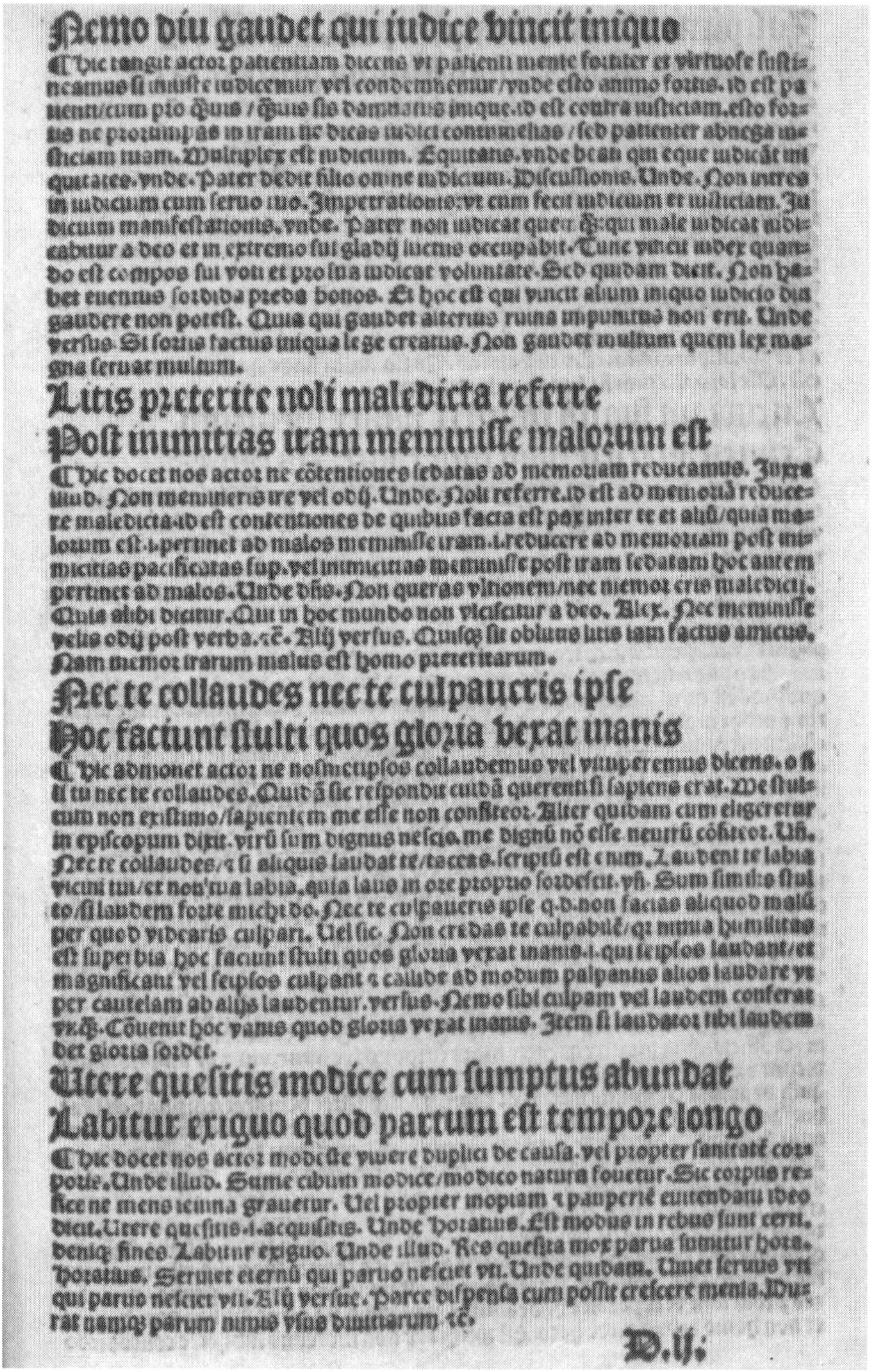

Nemo diu gaudet qui iudice vincit iniquo

Hic tangit actor patientiam dicens vt patienti mente fortiter et virtuose sustineamus si iniuste iudicemur vel condemnemur, vnde esto animo fortis. id est patiens/cum pio quis / quis sic damnatus inique.id est contra iusticiam. esto fortis ne proruinpas in iram nec dicas iudici contumelias / sed patienter abnega iudiciam tuam. Multiplex est iudicium. Equitatis. vnde beati qui eque iudicat iniquitates. vnde. pater dedit filio omne iudicium. Discussionis. Unde. Non intres in iudicium cum seruo tuo. Imperationis: vt eum fecit iudicium et iusticiam. Iudicium manifestationis. vnde. Pater non iudicat quem. Et qui male iudicat iudicabitur a deo et in extremo sui gladij luctus occupabit. Tunc vincit iudex quando est compos sui voti et pro sua iudicat voluntate. Sed quidam dicit. Non habet euentus sordida preda bonos. Et hoc est qui vincit alium iniquo iudicio diu gaudere non potest. Quia qui gaudet alterius ruina impunitus non erit. Unde versus. Si fortis factus inique lege creatus. Non gaudet multum quem lex magna seruat multum.

Litis preterite noli maledicta referre
Post inimicitias iram meminisse malorum est

Hic docet nos actor ne contentiones sedatas ad memoriam reducamus. Iuxta illud. Non memineris ire vel obij. Unde. Noli referre. id est ad memoriam reducere maledicta. id est contentiones de quibus facta est pax inter te et alij/quia malorum est. i. pertinet ad malos meminisse iram. i. reducere ad memoriam post inimicitias pacificatas sup. vel inimicitias meminisse post iram sedatam hoc autem pertinet ad malos. Unde dns. Non queras vltionem nec memor eris maledictj. Quia alibi dicitur. Qui in hoc mundo non vicisitur a deo. Alex. Nec meminisse velis obij post verba. &c. Alij versus. Quisqz sit oblitus litis iam factus amicus. Nam memor irarum malus est homo preteritarum.

Nec te collaudes nec te culpaueris ipse
Hoc faciunt stulti quos gloria vexat inanis

Hic admonet actor ne nosmetipsos collaudemus vel viituperemus dicens. o si si tu nec te collaudes. Quidam sic respondit cuidam querenti si sapiens erat. Me stultum non existimo/sapientem me esse non confiteor. Alter quidam cum eligeretur in episcopum dixit. virum sum dignus nescio. me dignum non esse neutrum confiteor. Un. Nec te collaudes. i. si aliquis laudat te/ta ces s. scriptum est enim. Laudent te labia vicini tui: et non tua labia. quia laus in ore proprio sordescit. vel. Sum simile stulto /si laudem forte michi do. Nec te culpaueris ipse q. d. non facias aliquod malu per quod videaris culpari. Uel sic. Non credas te culpabile/qi nimia humilitas est superbia hoc faciunt stulti quos gloria vexat inanis. i. qui se ipsos laudant/et magnificant vel seipsos culpant s. callide ad modum palpantis alios laudere vt per cautelam ab alijs laudentur. versus. Nemo sibi culpam vel laudem conferat vis. &c. Conuenit hoc vanis quod gloria vexat inanis. Item si laudator tibi laudem det gloria sordet.

Utere quesitis modice cum sumptus abundat
Labitur exiguo quod partum est tempore longo

Hic docet nos actor modice viuere duplici de causa. vel propter sanitatem corporis. Unde illud. Sume cibum modice/modico natura fouetur. Sic corpus re ficere ne meno ieiunia grauetur. Uel propter inopiam s. pauperie euitendam ideo dicit. Utere quesitis .i. acquisitis. Unde Horatius. Est modus in rebus sunt certi. deniqz fines. Labitur exiguo. Unde illud. Res quesita mox parua sumitur hora. Horatius. Seruiet eternum qui paruo nesciet vti. Unde quidam. Quiet seruus vis qui paruo nesciet vti. Alij versus. Parce dispensa cum possit crescere menia. Dum erat nemiqz parum nimis visus diuitiarum &c.

D.ij.

Figure 4.2 *Catho cum commento*, (London: Wynkyn de Worde, 1512; *STC* 4839.7). University of London, Senate House Library, Special Collections [S.L] I [Cato – 1512].

admixture of capitals from Pynson's Type 7: 95. The last remained his main text type until well into the sixteenth century and can only be distinguished from de Worde's Type 8: 93 by its size, the letters s and w, and Pynson's use of a double hyphen. Two further of Pynson's types, Type 3, a small commentary type used for interlinear glosses and marginal notes, and Type 4 also exist in different states.[26]

In addition to these bastarda types, Pynson also acquired a roman type, the use of which 'emphasized his identity as a printer of modern learning'.[27] Roman type was based on humanist minuscule, a script itself derived by the Italian humanists from the neat rounded letter forms of Caroline minuscule which eschewed ligatures and variant graphs. He first used it to print a Latin oration addressed to Henry VII by Pietro Griffo (Gryphus), the papal collector, in 1509 (*STC* 12413). He used it again for Henry VIII's tract *Assertio septem sacramentorum adversus M. Lutherum* (1521, *STC* 13078), and for the first arithmetic printed in England, Cuthbert Tunstall's *De arte supputandi* (1522, *STC* 24319; Figure 4.3). Pynson further had an italic fount, an informal version of roman type with letter forms sloping to the right and many ligatures, first used by Aldus Manutius (1449–1515) for cheap editions of the classics, and even obtained a Greek fount to print words in Thomas Linacre's *De emendata structura Latini sermonis* (1524, *STC* 15634). De Worde also acquired roman and italic founts. His edition of Lucian's *Complures dialogi* (1528, *STC* 16891) was printed in italic, and that of Robert Wakefield's *Oratio de laudibus trium linguarum* (1528–29, *STC* 24944) in roman type with woodcut letters for Arabic, Aramaic and Hebrew words.[28] Metal type for these alphabets was not available in England until much later. Although Reginald Wolfe was appointed King's Printer for Latin, Greek and Hebrew to Edward VI in 1547, he never owned a Hebrew fount, and the first book printed in England in which 'any quantity' of Hebrew type was used was *Cambrobryttanicae cymraecaeue linguae institutiones* (1592, *STC* 20966), while there was no printing in Arabic until the mid-seventeenth century.[29] However, Wolfe did acquire a Greek fount from Basel and was the first to print a complete book in Greek in England, an edition of Chrysostom's homilies (1543, *STC* 14634).

The earliest stage of printing in England was dominated by foreign trades-men, but by 1534 when the Act for Printers and Bynders of Bokes was passed, repealing an earlier statute of Richard III in 1484 which had specifically exempted foreign printers from the restrictions applying to other foreign traders, we find several native-born English printers such as Henry Pepwell (d. 1539/40), Robert Copland (*fl.* 1505–47) and John Rastell, lawyer and printer (*c.*1475–1536). One of the first books Rastell printed was *The Lyfe of Johan Picus* ([1510?], *STC* 19897.7) in a Parisian textura. He specialised in producing law books for which a bastard type was employed; roman type occurs in only one of his books, Lucian's

[26] *BMC XI*, pp. 399–407 and plates 36–47.
[27] *William Caxton*, p. 120.
[28] Richard Rex, 'The Earliest Use of Hebrew in Books Printed in England: Dating Some Works of Richard Pace and Robert Wakefield', *TCBS* 9 (1990), 517–25; Isaac, 'Types Used by Wynkyn de Worde', plates 11 and 12.
[29] Talbot Baines Reed, *A History of the Old English Letter Foundries*, new edition revised and enlarged by A.F. Johnson (London, 1952), pp. 57, 59.

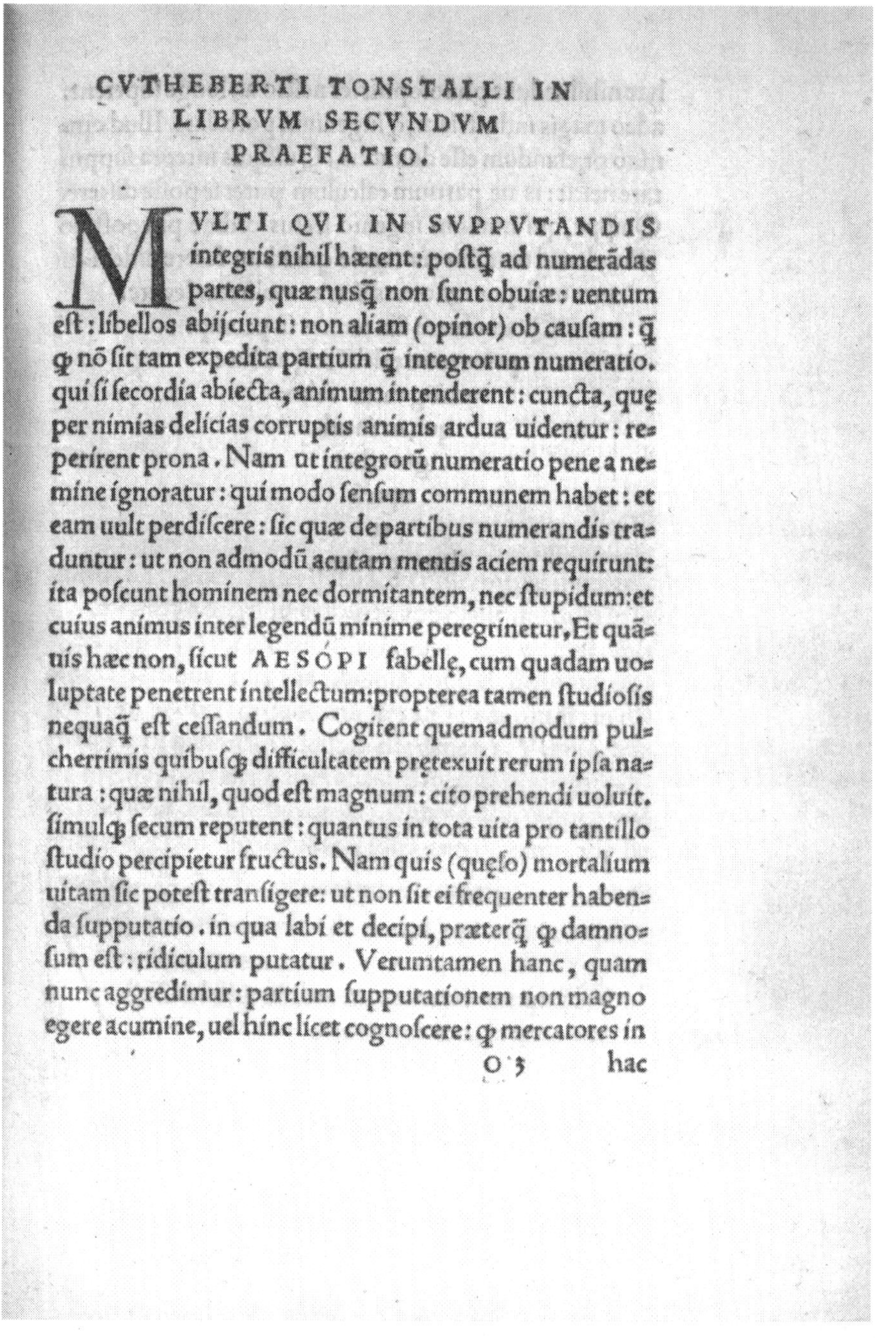

CVTHEBERTI TONSTALLI IN
LIBRVM SECVNDVM
PRAEFATIO.

MVLTI QVI IN SVPPVTANDIS
integris nihil hærent: poftǭ ad numerãdas
partes, quæ nusǭ non funt obuiæ: uentum
eft: libellos abijciunt: non aliam (opinor) ob caufam: ǭ
ǫp nõ fit tam expedita partium ǭ integrorum numeratio.
qui fi fecordia abiecta, animum intenderent: cuncta, quę
per nimias delicias corruptis animis ardua uidentur: re=
perirent prona. Nam ut integrorũ numeratio pene a ne=
mine ignoratur: qui modo fenfum communem habet: et
eam uult perdifcere: fic quæ de partibus numerandis tra=
duntur: ut non admodũ acutam mentis aciem requirunt:
ita pofcunt hominem nec dormitantem, nec ftupidum:et
cuius animus inter legendũ minime peregrinetur,Et quã=
tis hæc non, ficut AESÓPI fabellę, cum quadam uo=
luptate penetrent intellectum:propterea tamen ftudiofis
nequaǭ eft ceffandum. Cogitent quemadmodum pul=
cherrimis quibufǫp difficultatem prętexuit rerum ipfa na=
tura :quæ nihil, quod eft magnum: cito prehendi uoluit.
fimulǫp fecum reputent: quantus in tota uita pro tantillo
ftudio percipietur fructus. Nam quis (quęfo) mortalium
uitam fic poteft tranfigere: ut non fit ei frequenter haben=
da fupputatio. in qua labi et decipi, præterǭ ǫp damno=
fum eft: ridiculum putatur. Verumtamen hanc, quam
nunc aggredimur: partium fupputationem non magno
egere acumine, uel hinc licet cognofcere: ǫp mercatores in

O 3   hac

Figure 4.3 Cuthbert Tunstall, *De arte supputandi libri quattuor* (London: Richard Pynson, 1522; *STC* 24319). University of London, Senate House Library, Special Collections [DeM] L.1 [Tunstall].

Necromantia (*STC* 16895), a translation from the Greek into Latin by his brother-in-law Sir Thomas More with English verse by Rastell. This was printed for him by Peter Treveris (perhaps a Frenchman) in parallel columns with the English in textura and the Latin in roman. The textura of the two men can be distinguished by Rastell's use of a capital **T** with a diamond-centred flourish, and their use of different sorts for **s** and **w**.[30] Rastell also pioneered a music fount that enabled him to print staves, notes and text together in a single impression.[31] The type was taken over by the bookseller John Gough (*fl.* 1520s–40s) in printing Miles Coverdale's *Goostly psalmes and spirituall songs* ([1535?], *STC* 5892).

While there was no further need to seek protection for printers in England from 'merchant strangers', since the expertise of alien craftsmen was no longer required to teach the locals, printing in this country was old-fashioned compared with Continental typography. Following the example set by Caxton, printers here long continued to employ bastarda and textura founts, when roman and italic ones had become the norm on the Continent for printing books in both Latin and the vernacular. Thus Robert Wyer (*fl.* 1524–56), a printer of popular literature, had five bastard and five textura typefaces, distinguishable by size from one another.[32] Pages in such types appear heavy and pompous contrasted with the lightness and airiness of a page in roman type. A widespread shift to it for all kinds of books did not take place until the end of the sixteenth century, and many English bibles continued to be printed in black letter even after *c.*1590.[33]

This short account has focused on printers in London and Westminster, as central to early printing in England, although presses were briefly established at both universities (Oxford 1468/1478–87 and 1517–20; Cambridge 1521–24), and elsewhere at Abingdon, St Albans, Bristol, Canterbury, Ipswich, Tavistock, Worcester and York.[34] Even the Carthusians of Mount Grace, Yorkshire, seem to have attempted some printing.[35] London's pre-eminence was consolidated by the terms of the charter of Incorporation of the Stationers' Company in 1557. This ruled that no-one in England who was not a member of the Company should print anything for sale, either himself or through an agent, unless he were a freeman of the Company or had royal permission to do so; moreover, it gave the Master and Wardens of the Company the right to search in any place or building owned by a printer, bookbinder and bookseller for printed matter, and to seize any book printed contrary to the statute and imprison anyone who

[30] E.J. Devereux, *A Bibliography of John Rastell* (Montreal and Kingston, 1999), p. 64.
[31] A. Hyatt King, 'The Significance of John Rastell in Early Music Printing', *The Library*, 5th ser., 26 (1971), 197–214; John Milson, 'Rastell, John', in *The New Grove Dictionary of Music and Musicians*, 29 vols, 2nd edn (London, 2001), 20.842.
[32] P.B. Tracy, 'Robert Wyer: A Brief Analysis of his Types and a Suggested Chronology for the Output of his Press', *The Library*, 6th ser., 2 (1980), 293–303.
[33] John N. King, 'Early Modern English Print Culture', in *A Companion to the History of the English Language*, ed. Haruko Momma and Michael Matto (Chichester, 2008), p. 290.
[34] William K. Sessions, *A Printer's Dozen. The First British Printing Centres to 1557 after Westminster and London* (York, 1983); E. Gordon Duff, *The English Provincial Printers, Stationers and Bookbinders to 1557* (Cambridge, 1912).
[35] Glyn Coppack, '"Make straight in the desert a highway for our God": Carthusians and Community in Late Medieval England', in *Monasteries and Society in the British Isles in the Later Middle Ages*, ed. Janet E. Burton and Karen Stöber (Woodbridge, 2008), pp. 175–76.

printed without the proper qualification or who resisted arrest.[36] The Company
was further empowered to make by-laws regulating the trade. Such provisions
did not mean printing outside the capital became impossible but they ensured
that the Company and London controlled the trade for the foreseeable future.

Further Reading

Blayney, Peter W.M., *The Stationers' Company before the Charter, 1403–1557* (London,
    2003).
Glaister, Geoffrey Ashall, *Encyclopedia of the Book,* 2nd edn, with a new Introduction
    by Donald Farren (London, 1996).
Isaac, Frank, *English and Scottish Printing Types, 1501–58,* 2 vols (Oxford, 1930, 1932).
_____, *English Printers' Types of the Sixteenth Century* (Oxford and London, 1936).
Moran, James, *Wynkyn de Worde: Father of Fleet Street; with a Chronological Bibliography
    of his Works,* compiled by Lotte Hellinga and Mary Erler (London, 2003).
Plomer, Henry R., *Wynkyn de Worde and his Contemporaries from the Death of Caxton to
    1535* (London, 1925).

---

[36]   *A Transcript of the Registers of the Company of Stationers of London; 1554–1640 AD,* ed. Edward
Arber, 5 vols (London, 1875), 1.xxviii–xxxii.

5

Bookbinding and Early Printing in England

ALEXANDRA GILLESPIE*

From the time of the arrival of the first printed books up to the Reformation many different kinds of bindings were used on early English books. To a greater extent than has been previously suggested, the story of the early printed English book is a story about these bindings: about the men and women who bound them and continuity in their craft and business practice before and after print-ing; and about the changes wrought by print upon the structure of the English codex and the uses to which it was put.

This discussion begins with some examples: bindings on three of the earli-est surviving English printed books. Several copies of William Caxton's 1478 edition of Chaucer's *Boece* (*STC* 3199) survive in their earliest bindings.[1] One of these is now in the library at Magdalen College, Oxford. It is a *Sammelband*: soon after it was acquired it was bound together with an incomplete copy of the Latin text of Boethius's *Consolatio philosophiae* printed by Johann Koelhoff in Cologne in 1481 (Boethius's text is intact, but gatherings containing a com-mentary by pseudo-Aquinas are missing).[2] The two books have been bound together between two bevelled and cushioned oak boards; these have been covered in a dyed and whittawed sheepskin which is now very faded, so that the original green colour of the cover is visible only on the turn-ins. The sewing supports are laced into straight channels and secured with wooden pegs. The book bears the remains of two fastenings: hook clasps on short red leather straps that closed to the lower board. It has endbands of leather (see Figures 5.1, 5.2 and 5.3).

Some glossing of terms may be necessary here. 'Whittawing' or tawing involves treating skins with the chemical alum. Bevelling describes the shaping of edges of boards and cushioning the rounding of the outer face of boards. Turn-ins are pieces of the cover glued to the inner face of these boards. Supports,

* The following discussion owes a great deal to Peter Blayney, who generously allowed me to read *The Stationers' Company and the Printers of London 1501–1557*, 2 vols (Cambridge, 2013) in advance of publication, and who directed me to most of the archival records I cite. Thanks also to Nicholas Pickwood for generous help, and to Devani Singh for assistance. Any errors here are, of course, my own.

[1] Brian Donaghey, 'Caxton's Printing of Chaucer's *Boece*', in *Chaucer in Perspective: Middle English Essays in Honour of Norman Blake*, ed. Geoffrey Lester (Sheffield, 1999), pp. 73–99, nos 5, 6, 9, 16.

[2] B.III.2.12. See Alexandra Gillespie, *Print Culture and the Medieval Author: Chaucer, Lydgate, and their Books, 1473–1557* (Oxford, 2006), p. 68.

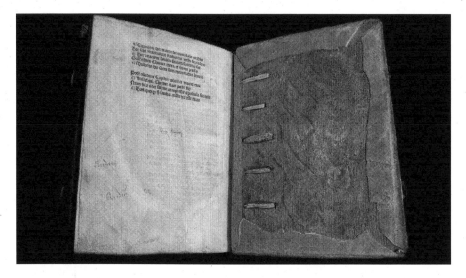

Figure 5.1 Oxford, Magdalen College, B.III.2.12, showing the turn-ins of the tawed cover on the lower board and the pattern of the lacing in of the whittawed sewing supports.

Figure 5.2 Oxford, Magdalen College, B.III.2.12, showing an endband.

onto which gatherings were sewn, were made from tawed or tanned leather or cord. Hook clasps attached to a short leather strap nailed directly to the boards came into fashion in England in the fifteenth century, replacing longer straps with metal catches that attached to pins on the centre lower cover of books.

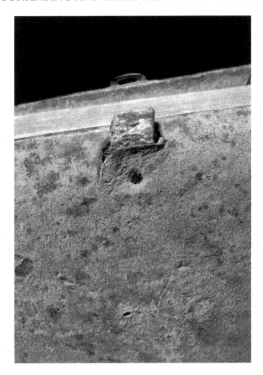

Figure 5.3 Oxford, Magdalen College, B.III.2.12, showing remains of the hook-clasp fastening (the strap on the upper board, the catch on the lower).

Endbands were constructed from cores of skin or cord that were usually laced into the boards and sewn into the text-block.[3]

Two other copies of *Boece*, one in Colchester Public Library, another in St Bride's Printing Library in London, are in a different sort of binding.[4] The cover of the copy in St Bride's Printing Library has become detached, revealing fragments of cancelled leaves of an edition of Lygdate's *Life of Our Lady* that was printed by Caxton in 1483 (*STC* 17024). The binder's association with Caxton is discussed further below. Here, it is of note that the basic technique that he or she employed was similar to that used by the binder of Magdalen B.III.2.12: four sewing supports were laced into boards which were covered in skin. But the tanning, blind stamping and blind ruling of the books' brown leather covers make for a striking contrast with the soft green cover on the Magdalen copy.[5]

---

[3] For all these terms, see J.A. Szirmai, *The Archaeology of Medieval Bookbinding* (Aldershot, 1999); on tawing, Ronald Reed, *Ancient Skins, Parchments and Leathers* (London, 1972), pp. 62–64; Eike Barbara Dürrfeld, 'Terra Incognita: Toward a Historiography of Book Fastenings and Book Furniture', *Book History* 3 (2000), 305–13; Monica Gast, 'A History of Endbands Based on a Study by Karl Jäckel', *New Bookbinder* 3 (1983), 42–58.

[4] Howard M. Nixon, 'William Caxton and Bookbinding', *Journal of the Printing Historical Society* 11 (1976–77), 91–113 (94, 106–07). St Bride's Printing Library closed recently; Colchester Public Library was unable to locate its copy of *Boece* at the time of writing.

[5] On tanning, see Reed, *Ancient Skins, Parchments and Leathers*, ch. 3; on blind tooling, Szirmai, *Archaeology*, pp. 243–47 and J. Basil Oldham, *English Blind-Stamped Bindings* (Cambridge, 1952).

Of these examples it is the 'blind-stamped' bindings that are more familiar to students of early printed English books ('blind' here means that no gold has been pressed into the patterns made by metal stamps, tools and rules). There are three intersecting reasons for this. First, binding historians have traditionally been interested in decorated bindings, because the study of bookbinding was originally conceived as an aspect of the study of the 'decorative arts'.[6] Second, because of scholarly interest in them, conservators have been more inclined to preserve 'decorated' bindings like that on the Colchester *Boece*. Many students of early printing will have seen a book, for example, Cambridge University Library's copy of Caxton's edition of John Gower's *Confessio Amantis* (*STC* 12142), that has had part of its blind-stamped cover mounted on a twentieth-century binding.[7]

Third, not only have more blind-stamped bindings survived, they have proven of greater interest to scholars as the history of bookbinding has been drawn into a broader history of the book.[8] The technique of blind stamping came into fashion at about the same time that printers first set to work in Europe, and, like pieces of metal type, the metal stamps that were used to impress leather covers on books were distinctive: they can be traced to certain locales, to periods of time, and even to particular workshops. As a result many of the important discussions of bookbindings in England in this period – those of G.D. Hobson, J. Basil Oldham, Graham Pollard, Howard M. Nixon and Mirjam Foot, for example – are more interested in blind-stamped than other sorts of books, and in what these books can tell us about the operations of the commercial book trade in the early decades of printing.[9]

This essay addresses some questions that these studies of English blind-stamped bindings have left unanswered. The first section considers the Continental origins of the technique of blind stamping. The arrival (or rather revival) of the technique serves to introduce a discussion of the economic and regulatory conditions for binding as an aspect of the fifteenth-century English book trade, before and after the advent of printing. The second section raises a new question about blind stamping. In 1400, 90 per cent of English books whose bindings are extant were covered in plain or dyed whittawed covers, like that on Magdalen's Boethius *Sammelband*. By 1500, 90 per cent of surviving book covers were tanned and stamped.[10] Even considering that the latter were more likely to be preserved, this represents an extraordinary reversal of practice. What was it that changed? If the answer is not *simply* 'printing', in what way did

---

[6]   Szirmai, *Archaeology*, p. x; Mirjam M. Foot, *Bookbinders at Work: Their Roles and Methods* (London, 2006), ch. 1.
[7]   CUL Inc.3.J.1.1 [3508] (Oates 4086).
[8]   See Mirjam M. Foot, 'Bookbinding and the History of Books', in *A Potencie of Life: Books in Society: The Clark Lectures, 1986–1987*, ed. N.J. Barker (London, 1993), pp. 113–26.
[9]   G.D. Hobson, *English Binding before 1500* (Cambridge, 1929); Oldham, *English Blind-Stamped Bindings*; Graham Pollard, 'The Names of Some English Fifteenth-Century Binders', *The Library*, 5th ser., 25 (1970), 193–218; Nixon, 'William Caxton and Bookbinding' (among others); Foot, 'Bookbinding 1400–1557', in *CHBB III*, pp. 109–27 and 'English Decorated Bookbindings of the Fifteenth Century' (1989), in *Studies in the History of Bookbinding* (Aldershot, 1993), pp. 98–120 (among others).
[10] From the survey by Nicholas Hadgraft, 'English Fifteenth-Century Bookbinding Structures' (unpublished PhD thesis, University College, London, 1998), p. 245.

printing nevertheless create some of the conditions for this new fashion in book-binding? The final section of the essay deals with a variety of other medieval binding technologies that were employed by the English artisans who bound early printed books.

Bookbinding and the Book Trade

Blind tooling of some sort can be traced to much earlier surviving English bindings than those of concern in a study of printing. A handful of 'Romanesque' blind-stamped bindings from twelfth and early thirteenth-century England survive. Many can be associated with binderies in religious houses or cathedrals. The Romanesque style may nevertheless have had lay, commercial origins: Christopher de Hamel observes that a significant proportion of extant bindings of this sort – 139 at the last census – are found on Bible texts that were 'mass produced' by lay craftsmen and women in Paris. Such books were distributed all over Europe and they influenced local book producers including binders.[11]

In the fourteenth century some Continental binders continued to stamp their books, but with less frequency. No English blind-tooled bindings that I know of survive from between 1300 and 1450. The 'revival' of blind stamping in England followed Continental trends. In Germany and Austria, for example, the Melk reform of religious houses led to the restocking and refurbishment of libraries, and the binders of books for those renovated libraries – some of whom worked in-house, some of whom were from commercial shops in local towns – often used blind tools.[12] The earliest fifteenth-century English binder to use stamped and tanned leather covers worked from the 1450s until the 1480s. He is known as the 'Scales' binder after an ornament that appears on many of his books. He was probably not a native but, like the style of the bindings he produced, a traveller. He was the only English binder of the fifteenth century who created 'cut' leather or *cuir cisclé* bindings as well as the first who stamped his covers. The cut leather technique involved cutting outlines of objects into the surface of tanned skins and texturing the background using a matting punch. It was commonly used by binders and leatherworkers in Germany, Austria and Bohemia in this period.[13] It seems likely that the Scales binder came to England from one of these regions. Once in England, he bound a variety of books. His distinctive stamps appear on manuscripts as well as printed books, books from the Continent or made by other foreign artisans, and books produced closer to his new home. He bound Cambridge, St John's College, MS D.23, a manuscript of Orosius's *Historia* copied by an Italian scribe, and the English law book, London, Guildhall Library MS 208. One of his bindings unites a manuscript of Ambrose's

---

[11] *Glossed Books of the Bible and the Origins of the Paris Booktrade* (Woodbridge, 1984), pp. 64–86; the latest census is in Freidrich Adolf Schmidt-Künsemüller, *Die abendländischen romanischen Blindstempeleinbände* (Stuttgart, 1985).
[12] Ernst von Kyriss, *Verzierte gäotische Einbände im alten deutschen Sprachgebiet* (Stuttgart, 1951–58).
[13] Szirmai, *Archaeology*, pp. 241–42.

Figure 5.4 Cambridge, St John's College, MS F.19, showing 'Scales' binder's stamps and William Langton's rebus on the cover on the upper board.

De Officiis, Cambridge, St John's, MS F.19 with a copy of an edition of Cicero's *De Officiis, Paradoxa, & c* (on which Ambrose modelled his text) that was printed in Mainz by Johannes Fust in 1466 (see Figure 5.4). (The discussion will return to the technique of blind stamping and the role of Continental book producers in England in more detail below.)

The work of the Scales binder is useful here because it suggests that medieval manuscript culture has something to teach us about the way that books were produced and distributed in England after the arrival of printing, and about the importance of bookbinding to the book trade. The Scales binder bound books for all manner of people: among them, a member of an armigerous family, a precentor from York, and a lawyer from one of the London Inns of Chancery. Such broad-based custom argues for a location for his business in a major commercial centre for book production, probably London.[14] As it was on the Continent, the lay, commercial book trade was a vitally important context for the new style of binding. Blind-stamped bindings were being made for the wide range of customers who were already involved in that trade when printed books first entered the market.[15]

[14] Nicolas J. Barker, 'A Register of Writs and the Scales Binder: II The Scales Binder', *Book Collector* 21 (1972), 356–79; see also Foot, 'English Decorated Bookbindings', pp. 100–01.
[15] For owners' social status, see Kate Harris, 'Patrons, Buyers and Owners: The Evidence for Ownership and the Role of Book Owners in Book Production and the Book Trade' and Carol M. Meale, 'Patrons, Buyers and Owners: Book Production and Social Status', both in

The metropolitan book trade in England can be traced back to thirteenth-century Oxford, when *stationarii* first established themselves as suppliers of books to the university and its students. Many of the early Oxford bookmen are identified in records as binders.[16] More formal organisation of binding as a craft began not in Oxford but in London in 1403, when the previously separate London Companies of the Limners and Text-Writers petitioned the City for recognition of a joint mistery that they wished to form with other 'good people, citizens of London, who use to sell and bind books'. As Graham Pollard notes, the petition goes on to describe the new mistery's members slightly differently: the Text-Writers and Limners, it says, '*also* use to bind and sell books' (my emphasis).[17] C. Paul Christianson's meticulous work on archival records of members of the resulting 'Stationers' Company' (as it came to be called in the latter part of the fifteenth century) confirms what the petition's wording suggests: the commercial makers of manuscripts in London were very often occupied by more than one trade. Those who sold books often also limned them; those who wrote them were also trained as binders – and so on. Christianson describes the career of John Pye in these terms: a London Stationer who was active in the 1440s, Pye located and sold second-hand books, was employed as a binder, and served as executor for a will that mentions another bookman, based in Oxford, who worked as a binder-illuminator.[18] Binding manuscripts was integral to the process of copying or illustrating or selling them; given that so much of the retail trade in books before and after printing was second-hand, and that older products might be usefully rebound for the market, English booksellers who did not practise binding themselves probably made sure they had at least one binder in service or near to hand.

All these observations are useful to the student of early printing, and they help to account for the bound forms of both the blind-stamped and whittawed copies of *Boece* described above. First, the history of bookbinding as an aspect of the commercial metropolitan English book trade explains how certain bindings come to be associated with particular printers. Just as manuscript producers had before them, England's early printers had multiple occupations and among these was bookbinding. Caxton was a Mercer and a Merchant Adventurer, a translator and author. He had taken the trouble to learn how to work a printing press (so he says in his *Recuyell of Troy*, STC 15375), and customs records show that he was an importer of books. Commercial logic dictates that he must have moved some of his own books wholesale to London-based and provincial booksellers.[19] But Caxton was also a retailer. He ran his

---

Book Production and Publishing in Britain 1375–1475, ed. Jeremy Griffiths and Derek Pearsall (Cambridge, 1998), pp. 163–200 and 201–38.

[16]   Graham Pollard, 'The University and the Book Trade in Mediaeval Oxford', in *Beiträge zum Berufsbewusstsein des mittelalterlichen Menschen*, ed. P. Wilpert and W. Eckert (Berlin, 1964), p. 337; see also M.A. Michael, 'Urban Production of Manuscript Books and the Role of University Towns', in *CHBB II*, pp. 168–94.

[17]   Graham Pollard, 'The Company of Stationers before 1557', *The Library*, 4th ser., 18 (1937), 4. See also discussion in Blayney, *The Stationers' Company*, p. 5, from which this translation is quoted.

[18]   *Directory of London Stationers*, pp. 145–48 for Pye.

[19]   Blayney, *The Stationers' Company*, pp. 28–33, covers many earlier accounts of Caxton's career.

press out of the almonery in the precinct of Westminster Abbey but also had a shop adjoining the chapter house.[20] In 1482 a William Purde purchased a Caxton *Polychronicon* (*STC* 13438, 1482) and he noted the name of the vendor: 'Willelmo Caxton'.[21]

Many copies of Caxton's own editions and other books – manuscripts and English and Continental printed editions – exist in bindings so similar that they have been ascribed to a single 'Caxton' binder. The Colchester and St Bride's copies of Caxton's *Boece* are examples of this binder's work. Not all of the books that he or she covered were copies from Caxton's own editions, however. The Caxton binder's stamps appear on books printed on the Continent, such as BL IB37262a, a 1481 vocabulary of Johannes Reuchlin printed in Basel (see Figure 5.5). They also appear on some manuscripts – for example, London, British Library, MS Additional 10106, a chronicle copied by the scribe William Ebesham who, like Caxton, was based at Westminster.[22] Such books testify to the wide variety of trade practices in which Caxton and his binder were involved. For example, the blind-stamped copies of Caxton's *Boece* could have been produced in one of two ways: either part of the 1478 *Boece* edition was pre-bound for wholesale or for retail at Caxton's Westminster shop (after 1483, the date of the fragments in the St Bride's binding); or the printer had a binder close to hand, who produced identical bindings for two purchasers of the *Boece* at their request. Either way, Caxton, printer-publisher, author-translator, importer-wholesaler and retailer, was also involved in binding books. He probably never stitched a quire or glued a cover in place, but after he reached England he most likely never set up a forme or stood at a shop counter either. These were tasks for the men Caxton paid to work for him. So inasmuch as we call Caxton a 'printer', we can also say that he was a binder.[23]

These conclusions are bolstered by evidence from the careers of the printers and artisans who followed where Caxton ventured. After Caxton's death the Caxton binder's stamps were frequently used on books associated with his foreman Wynkyn de Worde. De Worde like Caxton was an importer of books, and also of materials for bindings. In May 1507, the London port rolls customs show that he imported 300 'parui boordes pro bokes', small, perhaps paste, boards which he probably used as cheap covers for wholesale books.[24] We know that de Worde employed binders directly: in his will (proved 1534/5) he made bequests to 'Alard, book-binder my servant'. But we also know that he had dealings with some independent bookbinders. 'Nowell [Havy] the binder in shoo lane' received another bequest from him and there was a Dionysius 'Ducheman' and binder who may have been working for de Worde

[20] Howard M. Nixon, 'Caxton, His Contemporaries, and Successors in the Book Trade from Westminster Documents', *The Library*, 5th ser., 31 (1976), 305–26.
[21] Anne F. Sutton and Livia Visser-Fuchs, *Richard III's Books: Ideals and Reality in the Life and Library of a Medieval Prince* (Stroud, 1997), p. 255.
[22] On Ebesham, see A.I. Doyle, 'The Work of a Late Fifteenth-Century English Scribe, William Ebesham', *Bulletin of the John Rylands Library* 39 (1957), 298–325 and Linne R. Mooney, 'Vernacular Literary Manuscripts and Their Scribes', in *The Production of Books in England, 1350–1500*, ed. Alexandra Gillespie and Daniel Wakelin (Cambridge, 2011), pp. 192–211 (201).
[23] Nixon, 'William Caxton and Bookbinding'.
[24] PRO, E 122/80/4, m. 10v.

Figure 5.5 London, British Library, IB37262a, showing the stamps and ruling of the 'Caxton' binder on the cover on the upper board.

in Westminster (and perhaps even de Worde's master, Caxton) before he leased a tenement of his own there.[25]

The case of Richard Pynson is also telling. He is sometimes described as a binder in records and his editions are associated with some distinctive stamped and panel bindings.[26] Two of Pynson's many documented legal cases involve

[25] Nixon, 'William Caxton and Bookbinding', 92.
[26] G.D. Hobson, *Blind-Stamped Panels in the English Book-Trade c.1485–1555* (London, 1944), p. 14; Oldham, *English Blind-Stamped Bindings*, pp. 28, 57 and *Blind Panels of English Binders* (Cambridge, 1958), *passim*.

bindings, and they prove that his wholesale business, like de Worde's, involved ready-bound books. In 1507 or so, he claimed that in the mid-1490s he had printed half of his editions of John Lydgate's *Fall of Princes* (1494, STC 3175) and other books for a gentleman business partner, John Rushe. He supplied Rushe with the books bound and clasped as requested. (The later dispute was with Rushe's widow and concerns a debt Pynson is said to have owed when Rushe died.) In 1506, Pynson was also in court, this time over the 1499 *Abbreviamentum statutorum* (STC 9514). Pynson's bill says that he delivered 144 bound copies of the edition and another 265 bound *and* clasped copies to the Middle Temple lawyers, Robert Bowring, Robert Fermour and Christopher St German who failed to pay Pynson all of the agreed sum for the books.[27]

Other printers and stationers who had books published in the pre-Reformation period are associated with bookbinding. For example, Theodoric Rood appears to have employed or been a binder of copies of the books he printed in Oxford between 1481 and 1486.[28] In 1529 the printer-stationer Thomas Berthelet took on the role of King's Printer from Pynson, which meant he was required to produce editions at the king's behest. He responded to other royal needs. A surviving account from 1541–43 shows payment to him for books bound for the king.[29] This led some early commentators to describe him as a binder. Following the logic above, he was, in that he had books bound. But unlike Caxton, de Worde or Pynson, Berthelet does not seem to have worked with the same artisan repeatedly, to have had books bound at his own premises, or to have supplied any binder with tools that might identify him with certain books. One of the books he had bound has been identified as YML, VIII I. 32 (a copy of Smaragdus of Saint-Mihiel's *Summaria in epistolas et evangelia* from 1536) and assigned by Nixon and Foot to a 'Greenwich' bindery. Others are linked to the 'King Edward and Queen Mary' binder (who also worked during Henry's reign).[30] Here is an example of a stationer who was acting less as a binder than as a middle man between his royal patron and a variety of artisans.[31]

This evidence of the involvement of early printers (and in Berthelet's case, publishers) in bookbinding corrects the opinion of many scholars that early printed books were usually sold unbound. In fact, books could be bound at several stages of their production and distribution – at the place of their printing or abroad; in a printer's house or in his shop; before moving from printer to retailer or in a retailer's own bindery; or, following a printer-publisher's

---

[27] Henry R. Plomer, 'Two Lawsuits of Richard Pynson', *The Library*, 2nd ser., 10 (1909), 115–33; updated by Blayney, *The Stationers' Company*, pp. 78–81.

[28] Oldham, *English Blind-Stamped Bindings*, p. 20.

[29] The first to draw attention to Berthelet's work was Cyril Davenport, *Thomas Berthelet, Royal Printer and Bookbinder to Henry VIII* (Chicago, IL, 1901); his assumptions have been corrected by several scholars; see James Carley, *The Libraries of King Henry VIII*, CBMLC 7 (London, 2000), H3.

[30] Howard M. Nixon and Mirjam M. Foot, *The History of Decorated Bookbinding in England* (Oxford, 1992), p. 31 (Greenwich), p. 29 (King Edward and Queen Mary). See Foot, 'Bookbinding 1400–1557', p. 118.

[31] On the stationer as 'middle man', see Erik Kwakkel, 'Commercial Organization and Economic Innovation', in *The Production of Books in England, 1350–1500*, ed. Gillespie and Wakelin, pp. 180–81.

instructions, in the specialised workshop of an artisan such as Nowell Havy or the 'King Edward and Queen Mary' binder.[32]

But other evidence suggests the opposite: that some of the printed books left the place of their production or sale, wholesale or retail, unbound. Caxton seems to have sold part of his edition of *Boece* unbound. This is the best explanation for the unique forms of Magdalen B.III.2.12. There, Caxton's book is bound with a Latin version of the text and covered – unusually in this period – in a tawed rather than stamped cover. Caxton clearly left the decision about binding this copy of his *Boece* in the hands of others – other retailers or binders and their customers, whose idiosyncratic decisions about how the sheets that came of his press should be collated and covered made for a distinctive book.

The variety inherent to the practice of bookbinding in this period suggests continuities between the book trade before and after printing. The activities of book 'shops' (artisans' workshops and wholesale and retail outfits) were complex in both eras. The producers of books could parcel out tasks, do work themselves, or have work done by employees in-house. So long as they conformed to certain civic and national regulations, booksellers could sell books bound or unbound, and they could sell them to customers or to other book sellers.

The regulation of such activities turns the discussion back to its starting point: that is, to the influence of Continental artisans and their techniques on the English book trade and to the newly imported technique of blind stamping. The importance of foreign binders to the book trade in England was recognised in 1484, when Richard III gave his assent to 'An Act touchinge the Merchant*es* of Italy' (1 Ric III, c. 9). Its provisions were aimed at Italian middle men profiteering from the wool trade; one section prevented newly arrived alien merchants from living and working for other aliens, or practising their trade unless as a servant to one of the king's subjects (so a native or someone who had purchased letters of denization). Binders were included among those whom Richard singled out from this act by a proviso that states that the act is not intended to 'hurte or impediment' any importer, retailer, 'lympner bynder or imprynter' of books.[33]

The result of this proviso was that the regulations controlling the book trade stayed the same: anyone was free to sell or make books – including their bindings – anywhere in England (if local regulations allowed). In London, the Stationers presumably kept a watchful eye on those in the book business. If a freeman of the City considered that his interests were put at risk by the commercial activities of an alien or 'foreigner' (an Englishman who was not free of the City) he might ask his guild to step in. But the book trade in the metropolis was still dominated by outsiders. Some sought guild protection themselves. De Worde was a denized alien and Pynson a Norman; both obtained the freedom of the Stationers' Company by redemption in the early fifteenth century. The publisher and binder John Reynes was originally from Gueldres in the Low Countries; he took out letters of denization in 1510 and soon after that he too became free

---

[32] See Oldham, *English Blind-Stamped Bindings*, p. 3.
[33] PRO, C 65/114 m.20, cited in Blayney, *The Stationers' Company*, pp. 38–45.

of the Stationers' Company.[34] But many of the binders these men employed in house or by subcontracting were from abroad and were never freed: think of Dionysius the Dutch binder in Westminster, or de Worde's servant 'Alard'.

Outside London and its environs, the work of alien craftsmen is sometimes evident from books themselves. The Greyhound binder – who worked in the 1490s and who bound several manuscripts and a printed book that were gifted by Bishop Richard Fox to Corpus Christi College, Oxford – used braided leather endbands.[35] Like the Scales binder's cut leather technique, braided endbands were a Continental fashion; English endbands were more typically decorated using coloured thread.[36] Meanwhile, blind-stamped books from all over England continued to be influenced by foreign trends. Hundreds of different stamps were being used on English bindings by the late fifteenth century, and those on books from Salisbury and Canterbury Cathedral or from the university towns, no less than those from London, were based on German, French and Low Countries models.[37]

Blind Stamping and the Impact of Print

So far the discussion has treated the complex arrangements of the English book trade, before and after printing, and the importance to that trade of binders, many of whom, like the Scales binder, probably arrived in England from the Continent. To understand how the technique of blind stamping that the Scales binder brought with him took hold in England (as it did elsewhere in Europe), we need to think further about the international trade in goods and materials that sustained English book production, and to do so against the backdrop of printing.

For binders the most momentous change of the 1450s may not have been Gutenberg's invention of movable type, but the fall of Constantinople. The chemical used to make 'whittawed' skins like that on the Magdalen *Boece* was alum – hydrated potassium aluminium sulphate. In the Middle Ages much of it came from an island called Foça near Turkey and in 1453, trade routes between Europe and such Middle Eastern sites were cut off by the Turks. By the sixteenth century the alum trade had been assumed by the Papal States, but for a period of time Europe suffered an 'alum famine'.[38] In that context, tanned skins may have

---

[34]   E.G. Duff, 'Reynes, John (d. 1545)', rev. Anita McConnell, *ODNB*: <http://www.oxforddnb. com.myaccess.library.utoronto.ca/view/article/23404>, accessed 9 June 2011. On Pynson, de Worde, and Reynes's freedom, see Blayney, *The Stationers' Company*, pp. 68–69, 158, 460.

[35]   Oldham, *English Blind-Stamped Bindings*, p. 27, n.3: see Rodney M. Thomson, *A Descriptive Catalogue of the Medieval Manuscripts of Corpus Christi College Oxford* (Cambridge, 2011), MSS 16, 31, 49, 58, 82 and printed book θ.F.5.4.

[36]   Szirmai, *Archaeology*, pp. 211–14.

[37]   See Oldham, *English Blind-Stamped Bindings* and Foot, 'Influences from the Netherlands on Bookbinding in England during the Late Fifteenth and Early Sixteenth Centuries' (1979), in *Studies in the History of Bookbinding*, pp. 146–63; on the Salisbury bindings, see Foot, 'English Decorated Bookbindings', pp. 101–02; on the link between the Germanic style of surviving stamped bindings from Canterbury and those of the Scales binder, see Oldham, *English Blind-Stamped Bindings*, p. 25.

[38]   J. Cherry, 'Leather', in *English Medieval Industries: Craftsmen, Techniques, Products*, ed. J. Blair and N. Ramsay (London, 1991), p. 299.

been cheaper and easier to obtain and work with, especially for binders in far-off England. Stamping them, following an older medieval practice, must have seemed expedient. Skin was darkened and browned by the vegetable tannins used in place of alum. One of the few aesthetic advantages that a hide tanned in this way had over a soft white or brightly dyed tawed one was that it looked better stamped.[39]

If the interruption to the alum trade in 1453 was (perhaps) one context for change, the spread of printed books was obviously another. By 1476, when William Caxton arrived in England with his printing press, at least eleven different English binders were using stamps on books they bound. (They are, from London, the Scales, Sheen, and one other binder; two binders associated with Salisbury books; Oldham's L and K binders, perhaps associated with Tavistock and St Albans abbeys, respectively; an Oxford 'quasi-Romanesque' binder and the Oxford Fishtail binder; the Cambridge Demon binder; and the Winchester Virgin and Child binder.)[40] Most of their work survives on printed books that had been carried or imported to England.[41] As noted above, in the fifteenth century a great many of the printed books available to English readers were Continental, imported by wholesalers, many of whom were trying their hand at printing as well: for example, Julian Notary and William Faques as well as Caxton and de Worde. The importers named in the London Customs rolls had responsibility for fifty-eight cargoes of printed books before 1492, each containing tens or hundreds of books.[42]

In the context of this movement of books to England from the Continent, the shift to blind stamping makes a particular kind of sense. At least some imported books arrived in England ready-bound. Primers or *horae*, for example, were imported not by the sheet and in barrels as were most printed books, but bound and in chests with other dry goods (probably following an established custom of the manuscript trade).[43] In 1534 a series of protectionist legal measures that had been taken in the 1520s and that had narrowed the rights of alien book men in England culminated in an 'Acte for prynters & bynders of bok*es*' (25 Hen. VIII c. 15). The act forbade the importation of books '[r]edy bounden in bourd*es* lether or p*ar*chement'. By the time of the Reformation this was apparently a common enough practice to warrant local binders' successful agitation against it.[44] Blind tooled and tanned skins were the stock of the Continental book trade by this time, so English readers may have become accustomed to seeing foreign-printed books dressed up in the new sort of binding.

If stamps first appealed to a growing, pan-European community of

[39] Gillespie, 'Bookbinding', in *The Production of Books in England, 1350–1500*, ed. Gillespie and Wakelin, p. 171; on the tanned skins preferred for stamping, see Szirmai, *Archaeology*, p. 162.
[40] Foot, 'English Decorated Bookbindings', pp. 101–05.
[41] Scott Husby's census, 'Bookbindings on Incunables in American Library Collections', had ninety-seven early English bindings when he generously shared it with me. Of these, eighty were on books printed on the Continent. See also Andrew Hope's chapter in this volume.
[42] Paul Needham, 'The Customs Rolls as Documents for the Printed-Book Trade in England', in *CHBB III*, p. 153.
[43] Needham, 'The Customs Rolls', p. 159 (on the separate treatment of these 'primers' by the rolls); Blayney, *The Stationers' Company*, p. 95.
[44] Cited from Blayney, *The Stationers' Company*, pp. 332–33.

urban-based, commercial binders because they were a way to dress up tanned skins, they ultimately proved useful in other ways. The value of blind tooling to a commercial binder working within the printing industry was twofold. First, in the context of mass production, stamps could potentially become distinctive commercial marks, rather like printers' devices and other early trademarks. This is why they interest binding historians, who can link the scales stamp, the fish-tail, the greyhound and so on, to particular binders' 'shops'. It is important to note, however, that binders appear to have purchased one another's stamps (as printers did their type and woodcuts); and that the decorations used on a par-ticular binding may have served to advertise the work of that book's wholesaler or retailer, rather than its binder.[45] John Reynes may be a useful example here. In 1952 J. Basil Oldham had seen 473 English bindings bearing stamps, rolls and panels signed by or otherwise connected to him (and estimated that many thousands did not survive). He may have bound such large numbers of books in his own premises: he had a very large number of apprentices. It is possible that he also subcontracted other binders (as Berthelet and de Worde did) and distributed his tools to those who bound books on his behalf.[46]

Reynes's rolls and panels suggest the second commercial advantage of blind stamping in the context of printing. Stamping was a relatively labour-intensive technique. It did not help binders much as printing increased the volume of their work. But by 1500, two more efficient tools had been added to the binder's col-lection. One was the panel, which was in effect a very large stamp, big enough to decorate a large section of a cover. The other was the roll, which could be used in place of smaller and more finicky single stamps to create tidy borders around a tooled area.[47] In California's Huntington Library, for example, is a *Sammelband* containing some early printed editions of poems by John Lydgate and others and some reformist tracts (RB 69017). Its black calf binding is decorated simply by a panel of 'columns and wheels' that Oldham identifies in a book he dates 1550–56; he places the binder in London.[48] Both rolls and panels sped up the process of decorating a book binding, just as print was making speed a virtue.

Printing did not bring about the post-1450 shift to blind stamping in England or elsewhere. As the work of the Scales binder proves, blind-stamped bindings were used on manuscript books before they decorated printed ones; the earliest practitioners of the new technique probably arrived in England in advance of the printing press and its products. Other factors – such as the supply of alum – may have come into play. But as printing gradually transformed the English scene, the commercial advantages and Continental associations of blind tooling secured it an important new place in the history of English book decoration.

[45]   Foot, 'Bookbinding 1400–1557', p. 119.
[46]   *English Blind-Stamped Bindings*, p. 38 and Plate XXVIII for examples of Reynes's rolls and stamps. See also Hobson, *Blind-Stamped Panels*, pp. 32–38 and Oldham, *Blind Panels of English Binders, passim*. On his apprentices, see Blayney, *The Stationers' Company*, p. 526.
[47]   See Szirmai, *Archaeology*, pp. 243–46.
[48]   Gillespie, 'Poets, Printers, and Early English *Sammelbände*', *HLQ* 67 (2004), 189–91; Oldham, *English Blind-Stamped Bindings*, RP. *e* 1 (56).

Medieval Binding Technologies in the Context of Printing

The story of blind stamping is the story of a medieval technique given new life in the new conditions of print. Like other aspects of book production in this period, bookbinding merged the old and the new. The biggest difference between book selling before and after printing was that after the arrival of the press, a great many books were produced speculatively rather than to custom-ers' orders. But bookbinders continued to depend on traditional ways of doing business. Binding involved bespoke practices familiar from the manuscript trade – Berthelet's commissions from the king, for example – *and* speculative work, as when Pynson bound up half of his editions of texts and sent them with his partner Rushe 'into the countre to sell'.[49]

Examples of the bespoke trade in bookbindings after the advent of printing constitute further evidence of both tradition and innovation in the period of early printing. Bindings that are extant on books known to have belonged to the great libraries of Syon Abbey are a useful example. At the Huntington is a manuscript that was gifted to Syon by Robert Elyot in 1490.[50] It was rebound either before or after it reached its new home. It is in whittawed sheepskin; it has been supplied with one of the brass and horn book labels and brass fastenings that were added to many Syon books during the last quarter of the fifteenth and early sixteenth centuries, perhaps by the lay binder sometimes hired at Syon to deal with liturgical books, Thomas Baillie. Under the horn label, the Huntington book shows evidence of the remains of a chemise. Chemises were a kind of secondary cover, attached to the primary cover of a book by pockets, glue and stitching, with flaps of skin that extended over the edges of the book and around the text block.[51] They were commonly used for the binding of institutional books in the later Middle Ages: many bindings at Bury St Edmunds were supplied with chemises in the early fifteenth century, for example.[52] When Syon started to acquire printed books, those who cared for its collections made little distinc-tion between the old and the new. Cambridge, Emmanuel College, 32.6.49 is a *Sammelband* containing four printed books (1501–23) that belonged to Syon. Its cover is stamped calf, but it was supplied with metal fittings that match those on Elyot's manuscript closely: a label and fastenings (and perhaps a chemise, though no trace of it now remains).[53]

Some bindings can be shown to have been made to order according to an individual patron's particular interests in an innovative binding technique. In the early 1500s, the originally Arabic and then Italian technique of gold tooling made it to Paris: the bookbinder Simon Vostre began gold tooling books in

---

[49]   Plomer, 'Two Lawsuits of Richard Pynson', p. 126.

[50]   MS 35300. Neil R. Ker, 'Robert Elyot's Books and Annotations', *The Library*, 5th ser., 30 (1975), 233–37.

[51]   Frederick Bearman, 'The Origins and Significance of Two Late Medieval Textile Chemise Bookbindings in the Walters Art Gallery', *Journal of the Walters Art Gallery* 54 (1996), 167–78.

[52]   Gillespie, 'Bookbinding', pp. 153–55.

[53]   See Vincent Gillespie and A.I. Doyle, *Syon Abbey with the Libraries of the Carthusians*, CBMLC 9 (London, 2001), pp. xlvi–xlvii for care of the books; li–lvi on post-print acquisitions; Appendix 2, no. 1 for the *Sammelband*.

about 1503 using rolls and Italian-inspired tools. By 1519, the humanist Thomas Linacre, physician to Henry VIII, had developed a taste for the style. He had Vostre bind presentation copies of his translations of Galen's *Methodus medendi* (Paris, 1519) and *De sanitate tuenda* (Paris, 1517) for Cardinal Wolsey (now BL C.19.e.15 and C.19.e.17 – see Figure 5.6).[54] He also had an English binder try out the technique. The copy of Paulus de Middelburgo's *De recta Paschae celebratione* (Fossombrone, 1513) that Linacre presented to the king in the early 1520s was bound by John Reynes in calf. Reynes's Tudor Rose and royal arms panels were applied with gold leaf.[55]

Plainer tanned and stamped bindings could be individualised for bespoke customers. The *Sammelband* containing manuscript and printed copies of Ambrose's and Cicero's *De Officiis* that was assembled by the Scales binder and is now Cambridge, St John's College, MS F.19 (described above) was bound for William Langton, Chancellor, and later Precentor, of York (d. 1496). In the central panel of the binding is a rebus with the letters 'Lang' and a picture of a barrel or 'tun' imposed over the L (see Figure 5.4).[56]

The new pressures introduced by printing left marks on bookbindings, just as individuals' whims did. Binders were sometimes faced with the need to cover several hundred books at once for edition or part-edition bindings. There was simply more work in this period, as books arrived from Europe and from local presses in increasing numbers. These new conditions of book production are evident in some 'abbreviations' of the bookbinding process that became common in the sixteenth century. Nicholas Pickwoad argues persuasively for such techniques as evidence of the way that the practice of bookbinding moved 'onwards and downwards' during the era of print. Abbreviated sixteenth-century bindings proved to be harbingers of the flimsy structures of modern bindings.[57]

It would be wrong to suppose, however, that methods for making bindings simpler, faster to produce, and cheaper were new to the print era. As Pickwoad notes, binders used old techniques to bind the new printed books. Consider the paste boards that may have been imported to England by the likes of de Worde early in the fifteenth century. They were used for retail as well as wholesale bindings: in 1541, for instance, Berthelet delivered copies of Smaragdus of Saint-Mihiel's *Summaria in epistolas et evangelia* (printed in 1536) to Henry VIII. Two of these are described as being 'in paper bordes at vii d. the pece'. Paste boards were an earlier medieval invention. They were used on medieval Islamic books; and Italian binders were imitating them before the advent of printing. For later binders dealing with the rising volume of printed books they were a lightweight alternative to wooden boards; both the boards themselves and the books they

[54] Foot, 'The Earliest-Known European Gold-Tooled Bookbindings', *The New Bookbinder* 20 (2000), 16–17; Foot and Nixon, *The History of Decorated Bookbinding*, p. 25.
[55] Howard M. Nixon, *Five Centuries of English Bookbinding* (London, 1978), no. 5. The Reynes binding is now in Paris, Bibliothèque Sainte-Geneviève.
[56] Barker, 'A Register of Writs and the Scales Binder', pp. 356–79 (binding no. 9).
[57] Nicholas Pickwoad, 'Onward and Downward: How Bookbinders Coped with the Printing Press 1500–1800', in *A Millennium of the Book: Production, Design and Illustration in Manuscript and Print, 900–1900*, ed. R. Myers and M. Harris (Winchester, 1994), pp. 61–106.

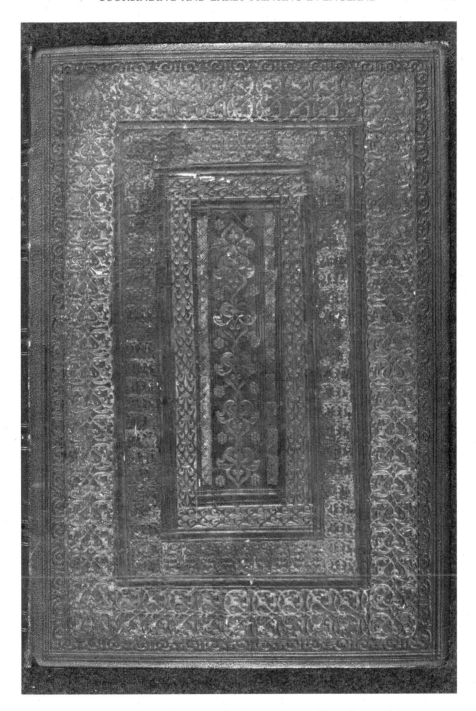

Figure 5.6 London, British Library, C.19.e.15, showing gold tooling and decoration by the Paris binder Simon Vostre on the cover on the upper board.

bound were more 'movable' and they may also have been cheaper.[58] Cheap, light boards had other medieval antecedents. The same entry in Berthelet's royal account book describes ten copies of the *Collectiones* 'in forrelles' which are even cheaper than the paste board-bound ones, 'at vi d. the pece'.[59] The word 'forrel' may describe boardless parchment covers; it first appears in English to describe the binding of little pamphlets in the poem *Mum and the Sothsegger*, c.1410, and it refers to a common way of covering medieval books.[60]

Leaving books unbound was another medieval habit adapted to facilitate the transportation of books between printers, wholesalers and retailers.[61] So was stab stitching, in which books were sewn not through the centre of quires but horizontally, through stab holes made from the top to bottom of the textblock, near the quire fold. In England, the 'stitched' book has often been associated with the 1580s. In 1586 several London Stationers asked the Lord Mayor and Court of Aldermen to regulate the practice of stab stitching. They presumably did so because it posed a threat to the binders who were members of their company. Printers and booksellers were sometimes stitching their own books and selling them in that condition, rather than employing binders in house, or passing unbound sheets to retailer-binders, or at least selling unbound books in some form that demanded the binder's craft. The wording of the London Aldermen's decree implies that the practice was a new one: books of a certain size may only be sold if they have been 'sowed uppon a sewing presse as heretofore hathe bene accustomed'.[62] But the reference to custom is a little misleading. Stab stitching subsisted alongside more elaborate customs for binding books in the Middle Ages: for example, a fifteenth-century copy of Chaucer's *Treatise of the Astrolabe* in Cambridge, St John's College, MS E.2 has been stab stitched (at or near the time of its production). In the 1580s, it seems that some printers and booksellers realised, as scribes had before them, that stab stitching was an excellent way to bypass the binder's specialised 'presse' (the frame on which quires were sewn onto bands) while still providing customers with books that hung together. Another example of a similar medieval technique adopted in the era of printing is tacketing – the use of loops of thread or skin to attach quires to covers.[63]

The binding of composite volumes represents a final expeditious measure taken in the context of both printing and manuscript production. I have argued

---

[58] G.D. Hobson, *Humanists and Bookbinders: The Origins and Diffusion of the Humanistic Bookbinding 1459–1559* (Cambridge, 1989), Appendix I; Pickwoad, 'Onward and Downward', pp. 79–80.

[59] Carley, *The Libraries of King Henry VIII*, H3.15.

[60] Alexandra Gillespie, 'Books', in *Twenty-First-Century Approaches to Literature: Middle English*, ed. Paul Strohm (Oxford, 2007), pp. 95–96; on French 'forels', see Reed, *Ancient Skins, Parchments, and Leathers*, p. 125.

[61] Pamela Robinson, 'The Format of Books: Books, Booklets and Rolls', in *CHBB II*, ed. Morgan and Thomson (41–42 for books kept 'in quaterno').

[62] David Foxon, 'Stitched Books', *The Book Collector* 24 (1975), 111–24, the decree quoted 111.

[63] Pickwoad describes tacketed bindings on printed books in 'Onward and Downward', pp. 66–67 and 'Tacketed Bindings: A Hundred Years of European Bookbinding', in *'For the love of the binding': Studies in Bookbinding History Presented to Mirjam Foot*, ed. David Pearson (London, 2000), pp. 119–67; for uses of tackets in the pre-print era, see Gillespie, 'Bookbinding', pp. 166–69.

elsewhere that early printed books were brought together in *Sammelbände* in two circumstances. In the first, *Sammelbände* were bound at the request of an owner: this seems to be the case for the Huntington *Sammelband* in the 1550–56 panel binding described above and for the Magdalen Boethius *Sammelband* with which the discussion began. Binding multiple small books together was a practical way to protect them; it was less fiddly and less expensive than providing each small item with its own cover. *Sammelbände* were also produced at the instigation of retailers, who hoped to encourage customers to buy more than one copy of one edition. This was a 'trade binding' practice and there are surviving examples of it from the first few decades of printing in England (though these are over-looked by scholars of later trade bindings).[64] For example, all but two of the eight known copies of Pynson's 1526 edition of *The Canterbury Tales* (STC 5086) survive in *Sammelbände* with copies of his 1526 *Troilus and Criseyde* (STC 5096) and *The House of Fame* (with other Chaucerian pieces, STC 5088).[65]

The model for the binder of printed *Sammelbände* was medieval: the pro-duction of medieval manuscript miscellanies often involved binding together manuscript 'booklets'. Sometimes these booklets were produced with a view to their compilation as a single book. A direct comparison can be made, for example, between the Pynson *Sammelbände* just described and a manuscript such as CUL, MS Gg. 4. 27, a collection of Chaucer's *Tales*, *Troilus*, and some other Chaucerian poems. Although the contents of this manuscript were designed by the manuscript's two scribes as the components of a single volume, in that their layout and content is carefully matched, they were also produced in booklets. The first quire of minor poems and the quires containing *Troilus* are discrete production units.[66] In other cases, very disparate items – parts of older books, quires of material that had been lying around unbound for some time – were bound up into medieval miscellanies. When printers planned trade *Sammelbände* or booksellers dealt in them, or when owners commissioned binders to create *Sammelbände* out of a variety of early printed items, they were reinventing entirely traditional kinds of books.[67]

Bookbindings often seem to be the very last thing of interest to book historians – at the furthest remove from scholars' often textual preoccupations. They never-theless have a great deal to teach anyone interested in the advent of printing; the manuscript book trade that preceded it; and the techniques both new and old that made books so widely useful and widely available in this period. Archival and bibliographical evidence together argue that the bookbinder's craft was inte-gral to the manufacture, importation and sale of books in England. Many of the men and women who established a successful, lay, commercial trade in books in the later Middle Ages were binders. Their activities and their customers pro-vided the conditions for the introduction of printing. Their methods served as

[64] Stuart Bennett, *Trade Bookbinding in the British Isles, 1660–1800* (New Castle, DE, 2004).
[65] On *Sammelbände*, see Gillespie, 'Poets, Printers, and Early English *Sammelbände*'; and on the Pynson books, *Print Culture and the Medieval Author*, pp. 126–34.
[66] *The Poetical Works of Geoffrey Chaucer: A Facsimile* of *C.U.L. MS Gg. 4. 27*, ed. M.B. Parkes and R. Beadle, 3 vols (Cambridge, 1979–80).
[67] See Alexandra Gillespie, 'Medieval Books, Their Booklets, and Booklet Theory', *English Manuscript Studies* 16 (2011), 1–29.

models for the binders who had to adapt the form of the book to accommodate changes wrought by the transformative new technology of print.

Further Reading

Bearman, Frederick, 'The Origins and Significance of Two Late Medieval Textile Chemise Bookbindings in the Walters Art Gallery', *Journal of the Walters Art Gallery* 54 (1996), 167–78.

Blayney, Peter W.M., *The Stationers' Company and the Printers of London 1501–1557*, 2 vols (Cambridge, 2013).

Foot, Mirjam M., 'Bookbinding and the History of Books', in *A Potencie of Life: Books in Society: The Clark Lectures, 1986–1987*, ed. N.J. Barker (London, 1993), pp. 113–26.

Foot, Mirjam M., *Studies in the History of Bookbinding* (Aldershot, 1993).

Gillespie, Alexandra, 'Bookbinding', in *The Production of Books in England, 1350–1500*, ed. Alexandra Gillespie and Daniel Wakelin (Cambridge, 2011), pp. 150–72.

Hadgraft, Nicholas, 'English Fifteenth-Century Bookbinding Structures' (unpublished PhD thesis, University College, London, 1998).

Nixon, Howard M., 'William Caxton and Bookbinding', *Journal of the Printing Historical Society* 11 (1976–77), 91–113.

Oldham, J. Basil, *English Blind-Stamped Bindings* (Cambridge, 1952).

Oldham, J. Basil, *Blind Panels of English Binders* (Cambridge, 1958).

Pickwoad, Nicholas, 'Onward and Downward: How Bookbinders Coped with the Printing Press 1500–1800', in *A Millennium of the Book: Production, Design and Illustration in Manuscript and Print, 900–1900*, ed. R. Myers and M. Harris (Winchester, 1994), pp. 61–106.

Pickwoad, Nicholas, 'Tacketed Bindings: A Hundred Years of European Bookbinding', in *'For the love of the binding': Studies in Bookbinding History Presented to Mirjam Foot*, ed. David Pearson (London, 2000), pp. 119–67.

Szirmai, J.A., *The Archaeology of Medieval Bookbinding* (Aldershot, 1999).

6

Woodcuts and Decorative Techniques

MARTHA W. DRIVER

In his discussion of London, BL Additional, MS 36985, the 'Founders' Book' of Tewkesbury Abbey, which was purposely made in the late sixteenth century to look like a printed book and was 'designed for a readership accustomed to the organization and appearance of printed books rather than manuscripts', Julian Luxford concludes that 'logic of organization and appearance made printed books more generally comprehensible than handwritten ones'.[1] Contributing to their clarity of meaning were woodcuts, metal prints and even ornaments, decorations that accompanied printed images. While woodcuts functioned in some cases very like manuscript miniatures, and their purposes were as various, they also expanded visual vocabulary, introducing and labelling texts for a mass-market audience. Further, printing allows an emphasis on visual continuity, which can occur within one book or across collections of books, creating networks of meaning for fledgling readers. As I argue elsewhere, with print the development of visual literacy is connected with rising verbal literacy, while organisation of content is most particularly seen with the introduction of the title page.[2] This survey considers briefly some changes that occurred in illustration from manuscript to print, sources for English woodcuts (mainly French), and the ways in which images were used to introduce and sometimes to link portions of texts or texts together in *Sammelbände*.

While every manuscript miniature is to some extent unique (even when copied from exemplars, sketches or model books), woodcuts were mechanically produced and were not usually in colour unless they had been painted by hand. A few editions printed by William Caxton are adorned with hand-decorated initials and borders. For example, Caxton's second edition of *The Canterbury Tales* in St John's College, Oxford (*STC* 5083) has carefully painted woodcuts of the pilgrims.[3] In addition, there is a copy of Caxton's *Golden Legend* (*STC* 24873) in a private collection with woodcuts painted in watercolour; in this edition, red

---

[1]   Julian M. Luxford, '"*Secundum originale examinatum*": The Refashioning of a Benedictine Historical Manuscript', in *Design and Distribution of Late Medieval Manuscripts in England*, ed. Margaret Connolly and Linne R. Mooney (York, 2008), pp. 162, 178.
[2]   Martha Driver, 'Ideas of Order: Wynkyn de Worde and the Title Page', in *Texts and Their Contexts: Papers from the Early Book Society*, ed. John Scattergood and Julia Boffey (Dublin, 1997), pp. 87–149. *STC* numbers are cited in the notes that follow for books examined at first hand in the order they are mentioned in the text.
[3]   A.S.G. Edwards, 'Decorated Caxtons', in *Incunabula*, pp. 493–506, (497–500).

initials were provided by the printing house for purposes of decoration (and clarification), and the colouring of the woodcuts is thought to be contemporary.[4] Among other English examples are watercolour additions to woodcuts in a Sarum Hours printed in London by de Worde in 1502 (*STC* 15898), and painting in gouache of the woodcuts in *The Orchard of Syon* (*STC* 4815) printed on vellum by de Worde in 1519; illuminated borders have been added to the woodcut illustrations and also to the opening page of text.[5] The painting in both volumes again looks to be roughly contemporary.

Another painted example is the endleaf of a copy of *Dives et Pauper* (*STC* 19213) in the Morgan Library, a woodcut of the two eponymous debaters hand-coloured in blue, yellow, green and brown watercolour with a xylographic title (Figure 6.1). In this case, the illustration along with the text has been cut with a knife from the wood block and printed only on one side of the page (also called xylography), the same process used to create text and image in contemporary blockbooks. The book features printed initials highlighted in yellow wash throughout and another woodcut of a monk kneeling before the Virgin suckling the Christ Child. This is an indulgence image with a prayer that celebrates the Holy Name. Like the title in the *Dives et Pauper* woodcut, this text is also xylographic and begins, 'Sic dolce nomen domini nostri.' The same woodcut appears in Walter Hilton's *Scala perfectionis* (*STC* 14042), commissioned in 1494 by Lady Margaret Beaufort. In the Morgan *Dives et Pauper*, the Marian woodcut is painted in the same colours as the scene of the two debaters, and Mary's crown and the halo of the Christ Child are filled in with gold gouache. In this case, again, the colouring, though faded, is most likely professional and contemporary.[6]

On the Continent, the painting of prints may have been trade-organised, but the paucity of surviving English examples suggests that printed pictures

---

[4] Lotte Hellinga, 'The Golden Legend', in Susan Foister, 'Private Devotion', in *Gothic: Art for England 1400–1547*, ed. Richard Marks and Paul Williamson (London, 2003), item 226, pp. 346–47, described as the edition printed by Caxton in Westminster *c*.1483. One of its previous owners was Beriah Botfield (1807–63), a member of the Roxburghe Club, whose edition of *The Orchard of Syon* was also hand-coloured (see n.5).
[5] *Horae ad usum Sarum* (London, 1502), Oxford, BodL Arch. G.e.39. A page is reproduced in Martha Driver, *The Image in Print* (London, 2004), p. 195, fig. 7. *The Orchard of Syon* (*STC* 4815) in the collection of Beriah Botfield was auctioned at Christie's on 13 June 2002: 'Although the Botfield copy contains no contemporary inscription of ownership, it was clearly intended for presentation, perhaps to [Sir Richard] Sutton as publisher, or more likely, to [Syon] abbey itself' (*Printed Books & Manuscripts from Longleat* (London, 2002), item 17, pp. 70–71). Sutton, steward of Syon Abbey, commissioned the translation into Middle English.
[6] Henry Parker (attrib.), *Dives et Pauper* (Westminster: de Worde, 3 December 1496), PML 734 ChL f1809. This copy lacks its title page. Lotte Hellinga discusses Hilton's *Scala perfectionis* in 'Prologue', in *Tudor Books and Readers*, ed. John N. King (Cambridge, 2010), pp. 15–22, 21. It is possible that the image of the Virgin was a marker for publications connected with the Birgittine House of Syon Abbey, and the woodblock may have originated there (it is illustrated in Martha Driver, 'The Illustrated de Worde', *Studies in Iconography* 17 (1996), 349–403, fig. 13). Lady Margaret Beaufort was the patron of several of de Worde's publications, both religious and secular, including Sebastian Brant's *Ship of Fools*, the first English edition, translated by Henry Watson and published in July 1509 (*STC* 3547). De Worde's edition derived many of its pictures from Jehan Droyn's prose edition issued by Guillaume Balsarin (*fl.* 1487–1525) in Lyons on 17 November 1499. Balsarin's edition essentially follows the woodcuts in the original Basel and subsequent Paris editions (Edward Hodnett, *English Woodcuts 1480–1535* (Oxford, 1973), pp. 25–26, 293).

Figure 6.1 Two debaters (end-leaf). Henry Parker (attrib.), *Diues & Pauper*
(Westminster: Wynkyn de Worde, 3 Dec. 1496; *STC* 19213), fol. 195v. PML 734, ChL
f1809.

were painted to appeal to a specific patron or at a particular owner's behest.[7]
Most woodcut illustrations survive *sans* painting and were printed in black and
white like the fonts used for the text, creating one form of visual continuity that
connects image and text in the printed book.

[7] David McKitterick, *Print, Manuscript and the Search for Order 1450–1830* (Cambridge, 2003),
p. 63. The gorgeous volumes published by Antoine Vérard in Paris for Henry VII, in which each
woodcut is painted with gouache, form an exception, but these are French books intended for a
very specific royal market. See Mary Beth Winn, *Anthoine Vérard: Parisian Publisher, 1485–1512:
Prologues, Poems and Presentations* (Geneva, 1997), who comments: 'The uniqueness expected of
manuscripts characterises Vérard's printed copies, especially those on vellum, but even those
on paper. No two vellum copies are identical, each being prepared for a different patron' (11).

Another sort of transition is indicated by surviving examples of printed images that were added to English books. The best-known English example of an illustration added to a printed book is the frontispiece engraving of the *Recuyell of the Histories of Troy* (STC 15375), the first book printed by William Caxton and dedicated by him to Margaret of York, found in the copy that was formerly owned by Elizabeth Woodville, queen of Edward IV, which is now in the Huntington Library.[8] Inserted prints were, however, more often indulgences originating as single-leaf woodcuts. These circulated widely in the fifteenth and sixteenth centuries, and some are preserved in the books they came to illustrate. London, BL, MS Egerton 1821, a late-fifteenth-century manuscript compilation of devotional texts, incorporates four indulgence prints, some of which were painted by hand. The last woodcut in the volume, an Image of Pity with a kneeling Carthusian monk, is hand-painted with 'streams of blood; even the monk's head and white habit are spotted with small drops'.[9] A vellum Book of Hours (STC 15875) printed by de Worde in 1494 and now housed in Lambeth Library 'at one time included no less than eighteen inserted woodcuts and copper engravings'.[10] Oxford, Bodleian Library, MS Rawlinson D. 403, a fifteenth-century paper manuscript probably produced in the Birgittine convent of Syon, includes three single-leaf prints as illustrations. One of these, a *Pietà*, was later copied by de Worde and used as a woodcut illustration in the *Imytacion of Cryst* (STC 23956) printed around 1518. This example suggests the continued iconographic influence of single-leaf prints originally intended as pious ephemera upon later illustration in printed books.[11]

There were also some attempts early on at colour printing, usually in black and red (examples include *The Orchard of Syon* (STC 4815) and a *Manuale ad usum insignis ecclesie Sarum* (STC 16140) printed by Richard Pynson), along with stunning examples of coloured coats of arms in the St Albans printer's *Bokys of haukyng and hunting and blasyng of armys* of 1486 (STC 3308), which were copied by de Worde in his *Book of Hawking* (STC 3309) printed at Westminster in 1496.[12] Further, just as there are manuscripts copied from printed books, there

---

[8]   For more on the artist of this copper engraving, see Lotte Hellinga-Querido, 'Reading an Engraving: William Caxton's Dedication to Margaret of York, Duchess of Burgundy', in *Across the Narrow Seas: Studies in the History and Bibliography of Britain and the Low Countries Presented to Anna E. C. Simoni*, ed. Susan Roach (London, 1991), pp. 1–15 (2); and Martha W. Driver, 'Printing the *Confessio Amantis*', in *Re-Visioning Gower*, ed. R.F. Yeager (Asheville, NC, 1998), pp. 269–303, 275–76, 275, n 14, 276, n 15.

[9]   David S. Areford, *The Viewer and the Printed Image in Late Medieval Europe* (Burlington, VT, 2010), pp. 77, 78, fig. 28. The image is captioned: 'The greatest comfort in al temptacyon. Is the remembraunce of crystes passion.' For further description of this and other insertions, see Mary C. Erler, 'Devotional Literature', in *CHBB III*, pp. 495–525, (499–500, 506, 511–14).

[10]   McKitterick, *Print, Manuscript*, p. 62. Mary C. Erler, 'Pasted-in Embellishments in English Manuscripts and Printed Books, c. 1480–1533', *The Library*, 6th ser., 14 (1992), 185–206.

[11]   Martha W. Driver, 'Nuns as Patrons, Artists, Readers: Bridgettine Woodcuts in Printed Books Produced for the English Market', in *Art into Life: Collected Papers from the Kresge Art Museum Medieval Symposia*, ed. Carol Garrett Fisher and Kathleen L. Scott (East Lansing, MI, 1995), pp. 237–67, (239–41, 240, fig. 1).

[12]   A page from the Stonyhurst College copy of *Manuale ad usum insignis ecclesie Sarum* (London, Richard Pynson, 1506) is reproduced (plate 310) in *Gothic: Art for England 1400–1547*, ed. Richard Marks and Paul Williamson (London, 2003), p. 418. For the St Albans edition, see

are extant examples of miniatures copied from woodcuts.[13] But in the main, the great innovation allowed by printing was the use of illustration to organise and sometimes to link texts thematically. Pictures were used to introduce texts and to separate texts in collected volumes, and sometimes created associations or networks of meaning between texts.

Though we do not know for certain, it is thought that the early printers oversaw the illustration of their books rather like the medieval stationers who oversaw various stages of book production.[14] Other printers seem to have worked like Antoine Vérard, who describes himself consistently as a publisher and who produced books for both French and English readers by jobbing out various aspects of book production, including their illustration.[15] Vérard's publications were frequently used as exemplars for their illustration and layout by the early English printers, especially Richard Pynson and Wynkyn de Worde, though woodcuts in books published by other French printers were also copied; the use of French woodcuts as models or the use of French woodblocks themselves is no doubt connected to the vigorous import trade, whereby books were printed in France for English printers.

Perhaps the most deft (and possibly the cheapest) use of pictures occurs with factotums, separate woodcuts used in various combinations to form different illustrations within a text or across a number of texts. Developed initially to represent scenes from drama, these separate figures could be combined in a number of ways. Vérard used this method of illustration in his French translation of the plays of Terence, *Therence en françois*, printed in 1499 (Figure 6.2), and again in *Le jardin de plaisance et fleur de rhetorique* of 1501 (Figure 6.3), an anthology of several hundred miscellaneous French lyrics spoken by young men and women. This volume is illustrated with a series of woodblocks that represent 'some thirty-one characters, male or female, young or old, of different social classes, with different and often representative expressions and hand-gestures, five architectures (two different castles, a city, a tower, a gateway), a set of four trees of different shapes and configurations'.[16] The illustrations guide the reader

Edwards, 'Decorated Caxtons', p. 495. There is a copy of the de Worde imprint of 1496 in the Morgan Library (ChL 1808, PML 732). The difficulty of colour printing is discussed by Thomas Primeau, 'The Materials and Technology of Renaissance and Baroque Hand-Colored Prints', in *Painted Prints: The Revelation of Color*, ed. Susan Dackerman (University Park, PA, 2002), pp. 49–75, who comments that colours were more difficult to make than black ink, dried more quickly, and had 'a shorter working time and storage life' (68–69).

[13] Luxford, '"*Secundum originale examinatum*"', p. 172, fig. 3, p. 174, fig. 4. Martha W. Driver, 'When is a Miscellany Not Miscellaneous? Making Sense of the *Kalender of Shepherds'*, *Yearbook of English Studies* 33 (2003), 199–214 (206–10).

[14] A.I. Doyle, 'The English Provincial Book Trade', in *Six Centuries of the Provincial Book Trade in Britain*, ed. Peter Isaac (Winchester, 1990), pp. 13–29 (18). Peter Beal, 'Stationers' Company, Stationers' Register', in *A Dictionary of English Manuscript Terminology, 1450–2000* (Oxford, 2008), describes the petition in 1403 of the Writers of the Text Letter and manuscript limners and illuminators sent to the Lord Mayor of London to form a guild with 'suitable wardens to oversee the affairs of each craft' (397). *Directory of London Stationers*, pp. 24–25.

[15] See Winn, *Anthoine Vérard*, for essays and a catalogue of Vérard's publications; his most deluxe illustrated publications with painted woodcuts were made for Charles VIII and Henry VII, among other royal patrons.

[16] Jane H.M. Taylor, *The Making of Poetry: Late-Medieval French Poetic Anthologies* (Turnhout, 2007), p. 239. See also Driver, *Image in Print*, pp. 50–55.

Figure 6.2 Symon, Chremes, Pamphile. *Le fable de andre*. Terence, *Therence en francois* (Paris: Antoine Vérard, 1499), sig. i2r. PML 547, ChL1545.

through miscellaneous texts while imposing a visually dramatic narrative frame on the whole. Among these figures are several that reappear in books printed by de Worde and Pynson (and then by later English printers), who were quick to adopt this economical method of illustration.

Figure 6.3 Lacteur and Lamant with two ladies. *Le Jardin de Plaisance et Fleur de Rhetorique* (Paris: Antoine Vérard, 1501), sig. f5v.

For example, figures that illustrate scenes in Vérard's books recur in *Nychodemus Gospell* (*STC* 18567, Figure 6.4), published by de Worde in 1511.[17]

---

[17]   PML 20360. See also C. William Marx, 'Julian Notary, Wynkyn de Worde, and the Earliest Printed Texts of the Middle English Gospel of Nicodemus', *Neuphilologische Mitteilungen* 96 (1996 for 1995), 389–98.

Figure 6. 4 Joseph of Arimathea, Pilate, and Nicodemus. *Nychodemus Gospell* (London: Wynkyn de Worde, 1511; *STC* 18567), sig. D4v. W16A, PML 20360.

This prose text is dramatised visually in print by illustrations and rubrics that divide up the text. First described in the New Testament as a 'leader of the Jews' who seeks out Jesus in private, Nicodemus later prepares Christ's body for burial with Joseph of Arimathea (John 3:1–17, 19:39–42). The apocryphal

Gospel of Nicodemus circulated in England from the eleventh century, and parts of the story were dramatised in the English mystery plays, notably in the York and Towneley cycles. The printed text was independent of English manuscript sources and was probably translated from a French version of the story. Between 1507 and 1537, this text was emended and printed at least eight times by three publishers. De Worde's 1511 publication 'established the format for all subsequent printings down to 1537'.[18]

Many of the pictures in de Worde's twenty-two-page episodic text are clearly drawn from Vérard's Terence; it is tempting to surmise that de Worde's memory of Nicodemus as played in later medieval drama influenced his choice of picture format. De Worde's illustrations highlight either the main speakers or the themes of each chapter. The action of the conclusion (sig. D4v), which describes eyewitness testimony to the divinity of Jesus (and the conversion of Pilate), is introduced by a descriptive title with figures of the three principals, Joseph of Arimathea, Pilate and Nicodemus, beneath, their names neatly inset into the scrolls above their heads. The illustration is filled out with metal-cut borders.

The figure identified as Pilate appears fairly consistently in that role in the *Nicodemus* text (more often than not) and was used by both Vérard and de Worde to represent older characters. De Worde employed him earlier to represent an old man married to a young, unfaithful wife in the *Fyftene Joyes of Maryage* (1509, STC 15257.5), a satirical look at marriage from the perspective of a put-upon husband, attributed to Antoine de la Sale and composed and edited by an anonymous English translator.[19] Like the story of Nicodemus, the *Fyftene Joyes* is episodic, with illustrations made up of factotums to introduce the main characters in each part of the story. In the 'Fifth Joy', for example (Figure 6.5), this bearded male figure represents the husband, who has become old before his time after marrying a young wife of higher lineage. The other man is her admirer (and his rival). As in the *Nychodemus Gospell*, the illustrations provide a dramatic frame separating each chapter and usually introduce main characters or speakers who appear over several episodes.[20] Many of the woodcut figures are also repeated, and 'the idea of having two identical woodcuts when the interlocutors are the same likewise serves to signal continuity in sameness'.[21]

[18] C. William Marx, 'The Gospel of Nicodemus in Old English and Middle English', in *The Medieval Gospel of Nicodemus: Texts, Intertexts, and Contexts in Western Europe*, ed. Zbigniew Izydorczyk, Medieval and Renaissance Texts and Studies 158 (Tempe, AZ, 1997), pp. 207–59 (255).
[19] Antoine de la Sale, *Fyftene Joyes of Maryage* (London, de Worde, 1509), Morgan W 16A, PML 21589. There are several illustrations of children in this volume, pertinent, of course, to the subjects of home and family, which the work treats satirically (see Driver, *Image in Print*, p. 62). Other examples of these factotum figures are reproduced and discussed in Anne E.B. Coldiron, *English Printing, Verse Translation, and the Battle of the Sexes 1476–1557* (Burlington, VT, 2009), figs 3.1, 3.2, 3.3, 3.4 (English), 3.7, 3.8, 5.1 (French), pp. 70–85.
[20] Coldiron, *English Printing*, pp. 113–40, notes that while the English version of this text published by Adam Islip was proscribed, the translation published by de Worde was emended from the originally racy French text.
[21] Michael Camille, 'Reading the Printed Image: Illuminations and Woodcuts of the *Pèlerinage de la vie humaine* in the Fifteenth Century', in *Printing the Written Word: The Social History of Books circa 1450–1520*, ed. Sandra L. Hindman (Ithaca, NY, 1991), pp. 259–91 (269).

Figure 6.5 'Fifth Joy'. Antoine de la Sale (attrib.), *Fyftene Joyes of Maryage* (London: Wynkyn de Worde, 1509; *STC* 15258), sig E3r. W 16A, PML 21589.

Each of these figures also has a descriptive banderole or scroll above, which is sometimes filled in to identify the character.

Scrolls in printed images derive from those found in medieval manuscript illumination, paintings, tapestries, and Tudor wall hangings. For example, the remarkable Buxton Achievement, a painted linen cloth made in England about 1470, features scrolls with inspirational texts ('Whatever you undertake, do it as well as you can') accompanying allegorical figures of day, night and the three Fates, among others. This is an inexpensive yet instructive wall decoration that 'was not made to last', rather like single-leaf prints and printed paper pamphlets. Similar wall hangings with speech scrolls or captions were apparently devised by the young Thomas More:

> More in his youth devised in hys fathers house in London, a goodly hangyng of fyne paynted clothe, with nyne pageauntes: which verses expressed and declared, what the ymages in those pageauntes represented: and also in those pageauntes were paynted, the thynges that the verses over them dyd (in effecte) declare.[22]

In printed books, banderoles might identify characters in the story, as we have seen, or they might represent speech, whether or not the scroll has been filled in.[23] These and other techniques to indicate speech were also apparently drawn from Vérard's and other French publications. Vérard's *L'Art de bien vivre et de bien mourir* and *The book intytulyd the art of good Lywyng & good deyng* (with a xylographic title page, *STC* 791), a peculiar English translation of the former published by Vérard in Paris in 1503, furnished models to English printers for a woodcut of Christ preaching to the Apostles. A copy of this woodcut was one of many illustrations in *The Crafte to Lyue Well and Die Well* (1505, *STC* 792), published by de Worde, to accompany a vernacular exposition of the Lord's Prayer. The same woodcut then appeared in de Worde's *Floure of the Commaundements* (1510, *STC* 23876) (Figure 6.6). The text of the prayer was inset into the scroll above the Apostles' heads by inserting metal type into a space left in the woodblock. Study of the ink patterns suggests that metal type was inserted into a groove cut into the opening and was held in place by bits of malleable metal, probably lead. In this case, the slightly abbreviated text represents Jesus teaching his followers (and the readers of this book) – one way in which print allows speech to be visualised within an illustration. A related method of indicating speech can be found in de Worde's later edition of the *Floure of the Commaundements* (*STC* 23877), published on 8 October 1521, near the end

---

[22] Described by Susan Foister, *Gothic: Art for England*, item 155, pp. 291–92 (292). The Beauchamp Pageants (BL, Cotton MS Julius E IV, art. 6), made in England about a decade later, have captions over narrative images. Thomas More, 'Pageant Verses', in *English Sixteenth-Century Verse: An Anthology*, ed. Richard S. Sylvester (New York, 1984), pp. 119–28 (119). The whole notion of cheap paper quartos is called into question in Joseph Dane and Alexandra Gillespie, 'The Myth of the Cheap Quarto', in *Tudor Books and Readers: Materiality and the Construction of Meaning*, ed. John N. King (Cambridge, 2010), pp. 25–45.
[23] See John N. King, 'Reading the Woodcuts in John Foxe's *Book of Martyrs*', in *Tudor Books and Readers: Materiality and the Construction of Meaning*, ed. John N. King (Cambridge, 2010), pp. 196–210.

Figure 6.6 Christ Teaching the Lord's Prayer. *Floure of the Commaundements of God* (London: Wynkyn de Worde, 1510; *STC* 23876), fol. Xxxvir (sig. F6r). BL Huth 30.

of his career. The title page (Figure 6.7) was directly copied from Vérard's *La Fleur de commandemens de Dieu*, published in March 1500 or 1501 (Figure 6.8). In both the French and English examples, the text of the Ten Commandments is bracketed by woodcut illustrations. The woodcuts function as narrative borders that highlight the central spoken text. Moses is shown at left literally holding up the text and dramatically displaying the Ten Commandments to the Israelites (the foremost of whom anachronistically wears a bishop's mitre).[24] Representation of the text within an image is similar in the scene below of the pope explaining the five commandments of Holy Church. This woodcut was used repeatedly by de Worde to illustrate a range of appropriate scenes for some twenty years.

Wynkyn de Worde and Richard Pynson also used banderoles on their title pages as labels, often surrounded by metal ornaments of various kinds. These descriptive labels might range from a simple scroll to an ornate winding banner, and their simplicity or complexity of design is not a reliable clue to date. The title page of *The Way to the Holy Lande* (1515, *STC* 14082), published by de Worde, features an ornate scroll with the book's title (Figure 6.9). The moveable type has been fitted neatly into the woodcut scroll. Beneath is the central image, a narrative woodcut of the pilgrim with his staff and rosary, setting forth barefoot on his journey. There is a border beneath featuring a bird, flowers, a thistle and

[24] There are several French models that may have been used in this case, for example, Guy Marchant's *Kalendrier des bergeres*, Antoine Vérard's *L'Art de bien vivre* and perhaps most directly, *The book intytulyd the art of good Lywyng & good deyng*.

Figure 6.7 Title page. Moses Displaying the Ten Commandments / Pope Teaching the Five Commandments. *Floure of the Commaundements of God* (London: Wynkyn de Worde, Oct 8, 1521; *STC* 23877). W16B, PML 748.

Figure 6.8 Title page. Moses Displaying the Ten Commandments / Pope Teaching the Five Commandments. *La Fleur des commandemens de Dieu* (Paris: Antoine Vérard, 7 March 1501). PML 42037, ChL 1543A.

Figure 6.9 Title page. The Pilgrim Departs. *The way to the holy lande* (London: Wynkyn de Worde, 16 May 1515; *STC* 14082). PML 20898.

acanthus leaves that looks to be related to the set of borders used by Caxton in the *Fifteen Oes* (*STC* 20195) in about 1491 and is perhaps even more closely derived from a border series used by Richard Pynson. One example of this border appears upside down surrounding Pynson's device at the end of his 1496 edition of *The Boke of John Maunduyle* (*STC* 17246), the first edition of this book in English and the first printed in England.[25]

Other sorts of illustrative ornaments, used to adorn the page and to fill out the printer's forme, included the fleuron, or floral ornament, seemingly made of metal. The ornament was used either by itself in repetition or along with other abstract border pieces. One simple scene introduces the comic *Mery Iest of the Mylner of Abyngton* (*STC* 78, Figure 6.10), printed by de Worde in 1532, and includes fleurons above and below a woodcut of a building perhaps intended to represent Cambridge. (The plot of this bawdy story resembles Chaucer's 'Reeve's Tale' of the duping of a miller by two Cambridge students.) Both de Worde and Pynson seem to have had ample sets of fleurons, which closely resemble each other. On the title page of de Worde's 1508 *Remedy against the Troubles of Temptations* (*STC* 20875.5), fleurons set off a woodcut of the badge of Margaret Beaufort; curiously, the top set of fleurons has been cut off to accommodate the central image.[26] De Worde's *Mirror of Sinners* (*STC* 954.5), printed about 1509, features fleurons on its title page; on the verso, around an Image of Pity, are fleurons and metal-cut rope borders.[27]

Pynson used similar fleurons and rope borders in his 1508 *Carmen* (*STC* 4659) by Petrus Carmelianus to adorn the title-page woodcut of the royal badge, indicating his status as Printer to the King. Among many further examples, fleurons appear on the title page of Erasmus (*STC* 10450.7), printed by de Worde in 1520, flanking a woodcut of de Worde's device, and on the title page of de Worde's *The Complaynt of a Louers Lyfe* (17014.7), printed about 1531, where fleurons are used both vertically and horizontally.[28] Fleurons were also employed by later printers. Richard Fawkes used a multitude of fleurons to form borders around woodcuts in *The Myrroure of our lady* (*STC* 17542), printed in London in 1530. Fawkes also used this format to decorate his printer's mark in John Skelton's *A right delectable tratyse vpon a goodly garlande* (*STC* 22610), his device surrounded by printers' ornaments composed of fleurons.[29] These ornaments were used to set off the title and the title illustration to decorate the page and appeal to potential buyers.

[25] PML 20898. See A.M. Hind, *An Introduction to a History of Woodcut*, 2 vols (New York, 1963), 2.716–7. See also Henry R. Plomer, *English Printers' Ornaments* (1924, repr. New York, , n.d.), pp. 17–24, 151, fig. 2, 153, fig. 4, 155, fig. 5, 159, fig. 7, 161, fig. 8, 163, fig. 9. Pynson's device with up-ended border is reproduced from Mandeville in William Kuskin, *Symbolic Caxton: Literary Culture and Print Capitalism* (Notre Dame, IN, 2008), p. 292, fig. E.2. For a description of this volume, see Stanley Howard Johnston, 'A Study of the Career and Literary Productions of Richard Pynson' (PhD dissertation, University of Western Ontario, 1977), p. 254, item 20.

[26] PML 20896.1. The latter is reproduced in Driver, *Image in Print*, p. 85, fig. 7. See other examples in Plomer, *English Printers*, pp. 159, fig. 7, 163, fig. 9, 169, fig. 12.

[27] Jeremy Griffiths, intro. and trans., *Speculum peccatorum, 'The Mirror of Sinners' Printed in London by Wynkyn de Worde, c. 1509–10* (Cambridge, 1992).

[28] Plomer, *English Printers*, p. 155, fig. 5, Driver, *Image in Print*, p. 80, fig. 3, p. 63, fig. 42.

[29] Driver, *Image in Print*, p. 196, fig. 8; Plomer, *English Printers*, p. 169, fig. 12. A survey of ornaments in English books has been undertaken by Joseph Gwara.

Figure 6.10 Title Page with Fleurons. *Miller of Abingdon* (London: Wynkyn de Worde, *c.* 1532; *STC* 78). W 16A, PML 20896.1.

The title page was a new idea that came along with printing and was used simultaneously to label, market and identify the title, the maker and sometimes the author of the text. In some cases, for example *The Orchard of Syon*, *Dives et Pauper* and *ThOrdynary of Crysten Men* (*STC* 5199), the book has a title page at

both the start and the end of the text, in effect encapsulating the text.[30] This
occasionally obsessive-seeming labelling of early printed texts is related to the
technical requirements of the binding process. Howard Nixon comments that
a printer would keep 'some bound copies in stock, if only as patterns for the
customer to choose from', but the customer would purchase an unbound copy,
taking the sheets 'to a bookbinder of his choice, or more frequently would probably ask the bookseller to arrange for the binding'.[31] In *The Printer & the Pardoner*,
Paul Needham says that early printed books were sold in sheets, 'and binding
would be an extra expense for the customer', so it would make sense for a customer to opt for several of his books to be bound together in one binding, 'rather
than pay the labor and materials for three or four separate bindings'.[32]

Books bound together, called *Sammelbände*, are (usually) thematically related
texts that were intended to be sold, and presumably read, as single editions
by their publishers. Such collections represent late-medieval and early modern
ideas about anthologies and sometimes are derived from, or related to, medieval
manuscript anthologies.[33] Pictures may help to determine how such books were
considered or thought of, whether as separate entities or bound to be sold (and
read) together, even in cases where the original binding no longer exists or the
volumes have been separated. In some cases, the placement of pictures seems to
indicate a shrewd marketing sense. Some books were apparently designed for
sale as a bound set of two or more separate but related works, with the buyer
given the option of purchasing each work separately. Woodcuts in *Sammelbände*
can create unity between disparate texts yet can also serve as visual markers
separating texts.

For example, the *Boke of St Albans*, or the *Book of Hawking, Hunting and Heraldry*
(*STC* 3309), printed by de Worde in 1496, contains several treatises. De Worde
based his edition on the previous printed edition, produced in three colours
by the St Albans printer in 1486, which is 'a four-part manual of instruction
in hawking, hunting, coat-armour, and blazing of arms'.[34] As in the previous
edition, the treatises included by de Worde were intended to be bound together

[30] *ThOrdynary of Crysten Men*, a vernacular prose handbook printed in 1506 by de Worde, and
Dives et Pauper, printed by de Worde on 3 December 1496, both have xylographic title pages
and end leaves.
[31] Howard M. Nixon, 'William Caxton and Bookbinding', *Journal of the Printing Historical
Society* 11 (1976–77), 92–113.
[32] *Printer and Pardoner*, p. 17.
[33] See Pamela Robinson, '"The Booklet": A Self-Contained Unit in Composite Manuscripts',
Codicologica 3 (1980), 46–69; Linne R. Mooney, 'Scribes and Booklets of Trinity College,
Cambridge, MSS R.3.19 and R.3.21', in *Middle English Poetry: Texts and Traditions: Essays in
Honour of Derek Pearsall*, ed. Alistair Minnis (York, 2001), pp. 241–66. Joel Fredell points to
a trend in the production of literary manuscripts in England after 1450, 'when commercial
stationers seem to have been producing standardised booklets which were bound together in
Sammelbände-like codices' ('"Go litel quaier": Lydgate's Pamphlet Poetry', *Journal of the Early
Book Society* 9 (2006), 51–73 (52)).
[34] Rachel Hands, *English Hawking and Hunting in 'The Boke of St Albans'* (Oxford, 1975), p. xiii.
Joseph A. Dane describes the complexities of multi-coloured printing and the possibility that
'the elaborate printing procedures for each page' might not have been perfectly repeated in the
Book of Hawking, and he cites the problems such books pose 'for anyone wishing to quantify evidence, or even to use the evidence that seems to be available' (*The Myth of Print Culture: Essays
on Evidence, Textuality and Bibliographical Method* (Toronto, 2003), p. 75).

as one book, though some parts are found bound as separate items, while other parts are dropped. After sig. i4v in de Worde's edition of 1496, the printer started over with his numbering of signatures, beginning again on sig. a1r with the title 'Here begynnyth the blasynge of armes'. In addition to the title, the page is illustrated by an initial in red and two shields (Figure 6.11). This text appears to continue from the previous treatise and begins, 'I have shewed to you in this book afore how gentylmen began & how the lawe of armes was fyrst ordeyned', though the tract that precedes it is actually about fishing and ends with a caveat about its practice by idle persons.[35] The *Blazing of Arms* ends on sig. d7v with a colophon that ties the four main treatises together:

> Here in this boke afore ben shewed the treatyses perteynynge to hawkynge & huntynge with other dyuers playsaunt materes belongynge vnto noblesse: and also a ryght noble treatise of Cotarmours as in this present boke it may appere. And here we ende this laste treatyse whyche specyfyeth of blasynge of armys Enprynted at Westmestre by Wynkyn de Worde the yere of thyncarnacion of our lorde. M.CCCC.lxxxxvi.

Caxton's device (used later by de Worde) follows, printed in red.[36] In de Worde's quarto edition of this work, printed about 1518, the heraldic tract is not included, and in 1533, despite his apparent earlier misgivings about whether the fishing treatise should be published by itself, de Worde issued the fishing treatise separately. In the *Book of St Albans*, then, the illustrations of arms and Caxton's device separate and introduce texts while also linking them, but single texts also circulate. Of the four tracts that form the one book, the *Treatise of Hunting* and the *Treatise of Fishing* were also printed later separately.[37]

The case of de Worde's 1498 edition of Chaucer's *Canterbury Tales* (*STC* 5085) is also interesting in terms of both its woodcuts and its pairing with *The Assembly of Gods* (*STC* 17005), one of several works spuriously attributed to John Lydgate. The same woodcut used to introduce the Canterbury Pilgrims at the Tabard Inn is reused to illustrate the gods on Olympus in the latter work (Figure 6.12). The catalogue of printed books in the Morgan Library compiled by Richard Bennett in 1907 comments on *The Assembly of Gods*:

---

[35] The *Treatise of Fishing with an Angle* is brief (sigs a3v–i4v). 'The propretees of a good hors', a text reprinted in the *Boke of St Albans* (Hands, *English Hawking*, p. 81), lists many of the same properties as appear in a manuscript described in Curt F. Bühler, 'A South German "Sammelband" of the Fifteenth Century', in *Early Books and Manuscripts: Forty Years of Research* (New York, 1973), pp. 598–602 (610, n.25).

[36] 'Marketing Printed Books', 95–124, describes de Worde's employment of a woodcut used earlier by Pynson which appears as well in de Worde's 1496 edition of *The Book of St Albans* in the position usually reserved for a printer's mark. This 'complex cut of an angel surmounting the shields of France and England, surrounded by the Tudor badges of the rose and Beaufort portcullis, and royal supporters' may have 'provided a visual accompaniment to texts with a nationalistic bias' (112).

[37] George R. Keiser, 'Practical Books for the Gentleman', in *CHBB III*, pp. 470–94 (470–72). Eloise Pafort lists separately bound copies of the *Treatise of Hunting* and the *Treatise of Fishing* printed later; see Eloise Pafort, 'Notes on the Wynkyn de Worde Editions of the *Boke of St. Albans* and Its Separates', in *Studies in Bibliography*, ed. Fredson Bowers, Papers of the Bibliographical Society of the University of Virginia 5 (1952–53), pp. 43–52.

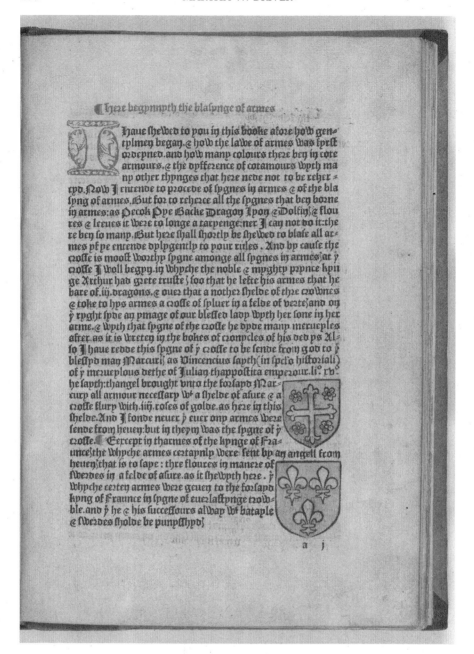

Figure 6.11 'Here begynnyth the blasynge of armes'. Dame Juliana Berners, attrib., *Book of Hawking, Hunting and Heraldry* with *Treatise on Fishing with an Angle* (Westminster: Wynkyn de Worde, 1496; *STC* 3309), sig. Air. ChL 1808, PML 732.

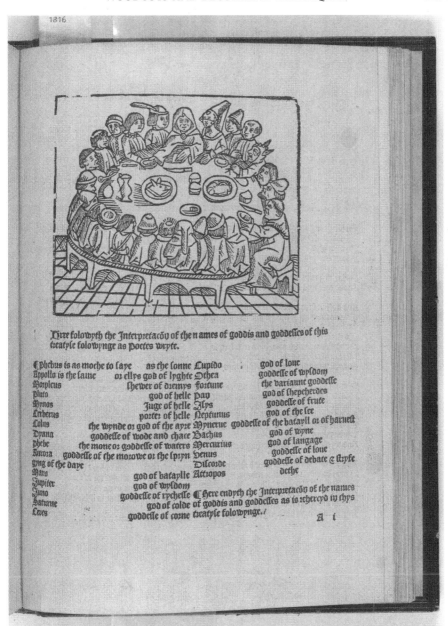

Here folowyth the Interpretacōn of the names of goddis and goddesses of this treatyse folowynge as poetes wryte.

¶Phebus is as moche to saye as the sonne Cupido god of loue
Appollo is the same or ellys god of lyghte Othea goddesse of wysdom
Sorpicus shewer of dremys the variaunt goddesse
Pluto god of helle Fortune
Mynos Juge of helle Pan god of shepherdes
Cerberus porter of helle Alys goddesse of frute
Eolus the wynde or god of the ayre Neptunus god of the see
Dyana goddesse of wode and chace Mynerue goddesse of the batayll or of harnest
Phebe the mone or goddesse of waters Bachus god of wyne
Aurora goddesse of the morowe or the spryng Mercurius god of langage
of the daye Venus goddesse of loue
Mars Discorde goddesse of debate & stryfe
Jupiter god of batayile Attropos dethe
Juno god of wysdom
Saturne goddesse of rychesse ¶Here endyth the Interpretacōn of the names
Ceres god of colde of goddis and goddesses as is rehercyd in thys
 goddesse of corne treatyse folowynge./ A i

Figure 6.12 The Gods at Table. John Lydgate, attrib., *The Assembly of Gods* (Westminster: Wynkyn de Worde, 1498; *STC* 17005), sig. Air. ChL 1815, PML 737.2.

On the first page is the woodcut intended originally for the Canterbury Pilgrims, but here used for the assembly of gods. The book was printed in the same form and at the same time as the Chaucer of 1498, and was apparently intended, as is the case with both the known copies, to be bound up with it.[38]

The other copy to which Bennett refers is that in the British Library, in which the 1498 *Canterbury Tales* (G.11587.(1.)) again was bound at an early date with the *Assembly of Gods* (G.11587.(2.)), printed the same year.[39]

De Worde's 1498 edition of *Canterbury Tales* has a separate title page and includes Caxton's preface (adding at the end, 'By Wyllyam Caxton, His soule in heuen won'), illustrated by a woodcut used later to introduce 'The Merchant's Tale' (perhaps a fitting association, as Caxton, too, was a merchant). The text of 'The Parson's Tale' ends on fol. 152r with an illustration that represents Chaucer the narrator (used previously to mark Chaucer's 'Tale of Sir Thopas'), which is here captioned: 'Here takyth the maker of this boke his leue.'[40] Fol. 152v contains Chaucer's Retraction following 'The Parson's Tale' and then de Worde's colophon. The last leaf (fol. 153r) of the *Canterbury Tales* has the woodcut of the Pilgrims at Supper, and on its verso is Caxton's device. The text of *The Canterbury Tales* is thus enclosed by a separate title page and an illustrated ending leaf which encapsulate and clearly identify this text as distinct from the next.

The *Assembly of Gods* begins on a new signature, A1r, and is introduced by the same woodcut of the Pilgrims at the Tabard Inn, now presumably translated to Mount Olympus. This text first provides its readers with etymologies and explanations of the names of classical gods and goddesses (for example, 'Phebus is as moche to saye as the sonne / Appollo is the same or ellys god of lyghte').[41] The instructive list of the gods and their attributes that opens the *Assembly* might be helpful as a reference when confronted with Chaucer's classical allusions in *Canterbury Tales*, one possible explanation for their being bound together.

The *Assembly* is a dream vision in which the Olympian gods are vividly drawn; some seem similar in character to Chaucer's pilgrims, perhaps a reason for the appropriation of the Pilgrims at Supper woodcut, though this repetition could be readily explained by simple economy. However, as D.F. McKenzie reminds us, though the decisions made by printers and booksellers may be primarily commercial, they are 'unlikely to be arbitrary'.[42] The *Assembly* text closes

---

[38] Alfred William Pollard, *Catalogue of Manuscripts and Early Printed Books from the Libraries of William Morris, Richard Bennett, Bertram, Fourth Earl of Ashburnham, and Other Sources, Now Forming a Portion of the Library of J. Pierpont Morgan*, 4 vols (London, 1906–07), 3: item 738, p. 211.

[39] Interestingly, both works are cited separately in the BL online catalogue under their authors, Geoffrey Chaucer and John Lydgate (this is misattributed), with the notation: '[Single Works].'

[40] For a survey of Chaucer portraits from manuscript to print, see Derek Pearsall, 'Appendix I: The Chaucer Portraits', in *The Life of Geoffrey Chaucer: A Critical Biography* (Cambridge, MA, 1992), pp. 285–305.

[41] Among the Olympian gods cited in *The Assembly of Gods* are 'Fortune the variant goddesse', 'Pan god of shepeherdes' and Othea, who is described as 'goddess of wysdom' (sig. A1r). For a teaching edition, see Jane Chance, ed., *The Assembly of Gods* (Kalamazoo, MI, 1999).

[42] D.F. McKenzie, 'Typography and Meaning', in *Making Meaning: 'Printers of the Mind' and Other Essays*, ed. Peter D. McDonald and Michael F. Suarez (Amherst, MA, 2002), pp. 196–236 (220).

with an ekphrastic description of the 'pastime of pilgrimage', and pilgrimage, of course, is another metaphor shared by this text and *Canterbury Tales*. The *Assembly* text, too, is enclosed by images, by the picture on its opening leaf and by the woodcut of Caxton's device at the end of the volume supplied after the colophon. Alexandra Gillespie has noticed that:

> The ending of [the *Assembly*] text matches the ending of the text with which it is bound: 'Here endyth the boke of the tales of Caunterbury Compiled by Geffray Chaucer / of whoos soule Criste haue mercy.' The medieval author buttresses the connection posited between the two works, asserts the devotional value of the single book made from them, and distinguishes it from any other copy, bought or bequeathed, of Chaucer's *Canterbury Tales*.[43]

In this case, images both separate yet tie the two works together. But there are at least four separately bound copies of these 1498 editions still extant, of which Bennett was unaware a hundred years ago when he wrote his entry for the Morgan Library catalogue, and there are further fragments. One fragmentary stand-alone copy of de Worde's 1498 *Canterbury Tales* is housed in the collections of the University of Illinois Library at Urbana-Champaign; this copy is described as lacking the fourteen leaves on which the woodcuts appear, along with the printer's device and other leaves, and as being bound 'in English roll-stamped calf over oak boards', which suggests that the binding dates from an early period.[44] Another apparently separate copy is in the Folger Library in a nineteenth-century binding.[45] And according to the *STC*, separate editions of de Worde's 1498 *Canterbury Tales* may also be found in fragmentary form in Cambridge University Library, which preserves one leaf; in Worcester Cathedral Library, two leaves; and in the State University Library of Victoria, Melbourne, one leaf. Except for the case of the Urbana copy, which seems to be in its original binding, it is impossible to ascertain whether these copies circulated separately or were once bound with the *Assembly*.

In addition, a separately bound edition of de Worde's 1498 *Assembly of Gods*

[43] Alexandra Gillespie, *Print Culture and the Medieval Author: Chaucer, Lydgate, and Their Books, 1473–1557* (New York, 2007), p. 100.

[44] Marian Harman, *Incunabula in the University of Illinois Library at Urbana-Champaign*, Robert B. Downs Publication Fund 5 (Urbana, IL, 1979), item 252, p. 45. No separate *STC* number is cited. HC 4924, GW 6588, Pr 9710, Goff. third census, C-434. (These references are the same as those for the Morgan copy.) The Urbana book is described as containing 113 leaves, with the rest supplied in facsimile 'by handwritten text and tracings made from the British Museum (Grenville) copy'. Further, the volume '[c]ontains a receipted bill by D. C. Baxter to Major C. H. Fisher, dated Jan. 27, 1886, for supplying the missing text and illus.'

[45] The Folger *Canterbury Tales* may be a rare instance of a de Worde edition circulating on its own, though its binding is nineteenth-century (by the specialist binder J. Leighton of Brewer Street, who was responsible for binding many late-medieval and Tudor books now in the Huntington and Folger collections). Georgianna Ziegler, Head of Reference, Folger Shakespeare Library, confirms that the Folger copy of the 1498 *Canterbury Tales* printed by de Worde is not currently bound with any other text (private communication, 7 March 2006). See also *Hamnet*, the Folger Library online catalog, available at <http://shakespeare.folger.edu>. For more on J. Leighton, the binder of the Folger copy, see Edmund M.B. King, 'The Binding Designs of John Leighton', in *Aspects of the Victorian Book*, available at <http://www.bl.uk/collections/early/victorian/pr_leigh.html>.

is held in the collections of the Huntington Library.[46] Like the fishing treatise included in the *Book of St Albans*, the *Assembly of Gods* also had a later life
on its own: there are two quarto editions printed by de Worde around 1500
(*STC* 17006, *STC* 17007), at least one copy of which finds its way into another
Sammelband now in the British Library. So again, in some cases one might buy
two books bound together as a thematically related collection, a *Sammelband*. Or
a purchaser who wished to own only the *Canterbury Tales* or the *Assembly of Gods*
could acquire the work as a stand-alone copy. Illustrations both separate yet
visually tie the two works together.

As a final example, Richard Pynson's 1526 compilation of works by Chaucer
and related texts is sometimes described as the earliest collection or edition
of the works of Chaucer. Julia Boffey and Tsuyoshi Mukai have investigated
specific texts contained within this volume and argue that Pynson's edition
(*STC* 5086), and not William Thynne's edition of Chaucer's *Works* of 1532 (*STC*
5069), represents the first edition as well as 'the first attempt to establish the
text from different sources', including manuscript exemplars.[47] Pynson's literary compilation comprises several volumes introduced by woodcuts and bound
together, which were probably intended to be 'issued as a ready-made (trade)
Sammelband'.[48]

The volume in the British Library contains what seem to be three distinct
units, each set off by its own title page and a closing page. The first text in this
volume is *Troilus and Criseyde* (*STC* 5096), which has its own title page, on which
the lovers are shown with a child (representing Criseyde's niece, Antigone?) as
the central image. The page is set off by floral borders, fleurons and metal ornaments. *Troilus* ends on sig. K6v with Pynson's device. Next the reader encounters the title page of *The boke of Fame* (*STC* 5088, Figure 6.13), which begins a
new signature. On this title page is a figure of Fame. The illustration is adorned
with floral borders and fleurons, as well as a border beneath with images of
the pelican, cross and the dove of the Holy Spirit. This text ends on sig. C3r,
the verso of which is blank. On the next page begins *The assemble of Foules*, its
text introduced and set off by a woodcut. Other short texts included here are
La bele Dame Sauns mercy, Chaucer's *Truth*, the *Morall proverbes of Christine*, *The*

---

[46] Herman Ralph Mead, *Incunabula in the Huntington Library* (San Marino, CA, 1937), p. 241,
item 5264, *The Assembly of Gods* (incomplete), printed by de Worde in 1498 (call number 9735.9).
According to Mead's catalogue, the Huntington does not own de Worde's 1498 edition of
The Canterbury Tales, but the later copy of de Worde's *Assembly of Gods* (1500?), item 5265, is
included in the library's collections.
[47] Julia Boffey, 'Richard Pynson's Book of Fame and The Letter of Dido', *Viator: Medieval and
Renaissance Studies* 19 (1988), 339–53; Tsuyoshi Mukai, 'Richard Pynson's 1526 Edition of *The
Parliament of Fowls*: Textual Editing from Multiple Sources', *Poetica* 49 (1998), 49–62 (50). See
also Kathleen Forni, 'Richard Pynson and the Stigma of the Chaucerian Apocrypha', *Chaucer
Review* 34, no. 4 (2000), 428–36. Jack White, 'Ricardus Pynson de Parochia Sancti Clementis
Danorum', *Fifteenth Century Studies* (1983), 275–90 (283), says Pynson's second edition of
The Canterbury Tales (1526) 'was the first attempt of a printer to collect Chaucer's complete
works'. Derek S. Brewer, *Geoffrey Chaucer: The Workes 1532 with Supplementary Material from the
Editions of 1542, 1561, 1598, and 1602* (Menston, 1969), on the other hand, describes Pynson's
1526 edition as 'an apparently tripartite volume' and 'a half-hearted approach to a "complete
works"', n.p. (1).
[48] *STC* 5096, 5088, 5086. Alexandra Gillespie, 'Poets, Printers, and Early English *Sammelbände*',
HLQ 67, no. 2 (2004), 189–214 (205); Gillespie, *Print Culture*, pp. 126–27.

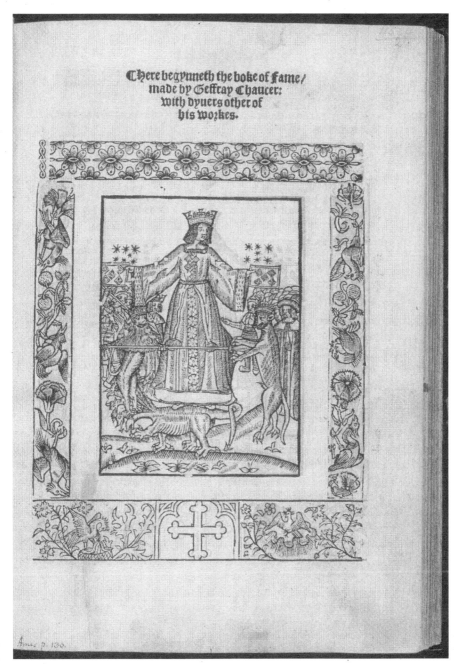

Figure 6.13 Title Page. Geoffrey Chaucer, *The Boke of Fame* (London: Richard Pynson, 1526?; *STC* 5088). BL G. 11584. (2.).

complaynt of Mary Magdaleyne, The letter of Dydo to Eneas and the *Proverbs of Lydgate*. Several of these shorter texts also appeared together earlier in fifteenth-century manuscript compilations. This section ends with Pynson's colophon on sig. F6r, the verso of which is also blank. The title page with the blank verso suggests a separation of these texts into a second complete unit that is distinct from the rest of the volume. Turning the page, the reader again begins a new signature, introduced by the title page that announces the text of the *Canterbury Tales* (STC 5086, Figure 6.14). The fleuron border and the border with pelican, cross and the dove from the title page of the *Boke of Fame* recur, this time decorating a woodcut of the Squire. The fleuron borders are repeated on all four title pages. The repetition of borders may indicate conscious linking of the texts together as a volume while the title pages themselves simultaneously serve to separate them. Pynson's edition then ends with the colophon on sig. Y3v.

There are six extant copies of this edition, and all six retain all the texts bound together, even though they seem to comprise separate booklets, which are marked by woodcuts. In some cases, these are bound in a different order. For example, Stanley Johnston in his catalogue of Pynson's editions describes the texts in this order: *Canterbury Tales* first, then the *Book of Fame*, and then the *Troilus*; and he notes further that 'the *Book of Fame* and the *Canterbury Tales* appear to be linked through the use of the same top and bottom border-pieces on their respective title-pages'. Johnston explains that the placement of *Canterbury Tales* third in the British Library copy 'may suggest that this was the last book of the trilogy printed, but may equally reflect a whim of the bookbinder to put the only dated section of the works last'.[49]

There is also at least one stand-alone copy of this edition of Pynson's *Canterbury Tales* that has been bound separately and is now housed in the Hunterian collection of Glasgow University Library. As Robert Foley suggests, there are probably others that remain untraced.[50] In this example, as well as in the earlier examples we have seen, it seems the customer could purchase either a comprehensive volume or a smaller unit with just one or two texts, set off by a title page and the printer's device on the verso of the last leaf. In each case, pictures function to organise and introduce texts, both creating visual unity and serving as visual markers between texts. By packaging each section of the compilation with a separate title page and illustration, Pynson is creating, in effect, several products that could be bought together or singly as dictated by the tastes and purse of the purchaser. While the primary reason to produce and bind several titles together may always be economic, such collections also raise questions about thematic relationships between texts and about literary tastes of fifteenth- and sixteenth-century readers.

---

[49] Johnston, 'Study of the Career', calls Pynson's collection 'a three volume set comprised of the *Canterbury Tales*, the *Book of Fame* and *Troilus and Creseyde* all composed in two columns of 95 textura with 144 textura used for the headings', with *Troilus* as the least uniform of the three' (195–96). See also Johnston, 'Descriptions', in 'Study of the Career', p. 444.

[50] Robert A. Foley, 'Richard Pynson's *Boke of Fame* and Its Non-Chaucerian Poems: A Study and an Edition' (PhD dissertation, Jesus College Oxford, 1987), p. 41. Johnston further suggests that Pynson put out this edition of the *Canterbury Tales* first and 'that the idea of issuing companion volumes did not occur until later' (cited in 'Study of the Career', p. 19).

Figure 6.14 Title Page. Geoffrey Chaucer, *The boke of Caunterbury tales* (London: Richard Pynson, 1526; *STC* 5086). BL G. 11584. (3.).

This brief survey of illustration cites several innovations brought to the book form by print. Though sometimes hand-coloured, woodcuts were printed from the same ink as the text, which creates visual continuity not found in illuminated manuscripts; like type fonts, images are repeatable and through repetition, images introduce and connect ideas within texts and between texts. Single-leaf prints that either predate or coexist with printing with moveable type were bound into books and in some cases, influenced later woodcut iconography. Representations of speakers and speech are common in printed illustration, the texts converted, visually at least, into dramatic performance peopled by readily recognisable actors. By observing the figures in printed books, one can see the play of Nicodemus unfold or, along with the Apostles, learn the Lord's Prayer as spoken by Jesus. Scrolls similar to those used to denote speech also appear on title pages; these literal labels identify the text and are often accompanied by narrative or iconic illustration that suggests the action to come or by a royal badge or printer's device that indicates the intended patron or that markets the maker of the book. Title pages are sometimes further ornamented with fleurons, rope borders and other abstract images that can be repeated in a variety of decorative combinations. Finally, the study of pictures in anthologies raises larger questions about the production and binding of Tudor books, about selling and circulation, and about the expectations of Tudor readers. Illustration provides one key to understanding how designers, printers and publishers of English printed books used a range of visual resources 'to help direct their readers' responses to the verbal language of the text'.[51]

Further Reading

Brewer, Derek S., *Geoffrey Chaucer: The Workes 1532 with Supplementary Material from the Editions of 1542, 1561, 1598, and 1602* (Menston, 1969).

Christianson, C. Paul, *A Directory of London Stationers and Book Artisans, 1300–1500* (New York, 1990).

Coldiron, Anne E.B., *English Printing, Verse Translation, and the Battle of the Sexes 1476–1557* (Burlington, VT, 2009).

Driver, Martha W., *The Image in Print* (London, 2004).

Foley, Robert A., 'Richard Pynson's Boke of Fame and Its Non-Chaucerian Poems: A Study and an Edition' (unpublished PhD dissertation, Jesus College Oxford, 1987).

Gillespie, Alexandra, *Print Culture and the Medieval Author: Chaucer, Lydgate, and Their Books, 1473–1557* (New York, 2007).

Harman, Marian, *Incunabula in the University of Illinois Library at Urbana-Champaign*, Robert B. Downs Publication Fund 5 (Urbana, IL, 1979).

Hind, A.M., *An Introduction to a History of Woodcut*, 2 vols, II (New York, 1963).

Hodnett, Edward, *English Woodcuts 1480–1535* (Oxford, 1973).

Johnston, Stanley Howard, 'A Study of the Career and Literary Productions of Richard Pynson' (unpublished PhD dissertation, University of Western Ontario, 1977).

---

[51] McKenzie, 'Typography', p. 223.

Marks, Richard, and Paul Williamson, eds, *Gothic: Art for England 1400–1547* (London, 2003).

McKitterick, David, *Print, Manuscript and the Search for Order 1450–1830* (Cambridge, 2003).

Mead, Herman Ralph, *Incunabula in the Huntington Library* (San Marino, CA, 1937).

Needham, Paul, *The Printer and the Pardoner* (Washington, DC, 1986).

Plomer, Henry R., *English Printers' Ornaments* (London, 1924, repr. New York, n.d.).

Pollard, Alfred William, *Catalogue of Manuscripts and Early Printed Books from the Libraries of William Morris, Richard Bennett, Bertram, Fourth Earl of Ashburnam, and Other Sources, Now Forming a Portion of the Library of J. Pierpont Morgan*, 4 vols (London, 1906–07).

Taylor, Jane H.M., *The Making of Poetry: Late-Medieval French Poetic Anthologies* (Turnhout, 2007).

Winn, Mary Beth, *Anthoine Vérard: Parisian Publisher, 1485–1512: Prologues, Poems and Presentations* (Geneva, 1997).

PATRONS, PURCHASERS AND PRODUCTS

7

Merchants

ANNE F. SUTTON

It was a merchant, William Caxton, past-governor of the Merchant Adventurers of England in the Low Countries, who introduced printing in the English language to England, in the 1470s, operating first from Bruges and then from Westminster Sanctuary, free from the interference of the city of London where he belonged to the Mercers' Company. A merchant may be defined as a man who traded overseas, the only way to make serious profits; lesser men retailed and distributed goods in England.[1] Caxton's mercantile expertise told him there was little point in competing in the saturated market of Latin or French books, except as a retailer of other printers' goods. The English language would not excite competition from overseas, English competitors would take time to establish themselves, and migrant, alien printers would always be at a disadvantage. He made a business decision to supply books in bulk to those who read English: 'hit shold be a good besynes to translate hyt into oure Englissh to thende that hyt myght be had as well in the royame of Englond as in other landes'.[2] As he found a shortage of English texts, he had to work on his own translations, drawing on the languages he had learnt in the cross-Channel trade (French and Dutch). His industry in translation was phenomenal and continued literally to the day he died.[3]

By this date any wealthy scholar could obtain almost any existing book he wanted in Europe. Printed books had become so essential to the well-being of the clerical and educated ranks of English society that when an act of parliament of 1484 threatened to limit alien workers and products in England, books and those who made or traded in them were specifically excluded.[4] By 1483 it is known that London had a number of alien printers supplying its needs from the

---

[1]   There remains a tendency to underrate Caxton as a merchant, the fortune that enabled him to start a new trade and his efficiency in that trade, and to present him, for example, as an employee of Margaret of York (he does not inform us of the nature of that service), and always dependent on the largesse of patrons, e.g. *William Caxton*, p. 49, and *BMC XI*, pp. 6–7. Compare the excellent summary of the changes brought by printing which reduced patronage to 'talismanic', 'Marketing Printed Books', pp. 95–103.

[2]   Prologue to his first translation, the *Recuyell of the Historyes of Troye*: N.F. Blake, *Caxton's Own Prose* (London, 1973), p. 97.

[3]   The most recent list of his publications with the most up-to-date dating, *BMC XI*, pp. 86–88.

[4]   1 Richard III, cap. 9, for which see further, Anne F. Sutton and Livia Visser-Fuchs, *Richard III's Books* (Stroud, 1997), ch. 10; 'Importation', pp. 179–80, for the bias of the origins of imported books and bias of the ownership of surviving copies towards university-men.

jobbing printing of indulgences for clerical institutions, devotional images, proclamations of civic and royal origin, or advertisements for any shopkeeper, such as Caxton himself. The alien printers aimed first at the Latin market of church and university, or the Anglo-French market of the common lawyers; the fact that they were drawn to the city shows that they were well aware of a mercantile market as well. The compiler of the 1483 poll tax on aliens – one of the assessors was William Pratte, Caxton's lifelong friend – carefully added 'bokprynter' to each of the following names: John Lettou, John Hawkes, Henry Frankenberg and Bernard van Stando his partner; Lettou had four workers including William Ravenswalde, presumably to be identified as William de Machlinia (from Malines). Frankenburg was one of several major alien importers of printed books into England in the 1470s and 1480s.[5] Caxton knew the Low Countries intimately, as past governor of the Merchant Adventurers of England, and quite as well as any of these men, and he too had an alien workforce.[6] The longevity of Caxton's press shows the advantage of his broader mercantile background, judicious judgement of profit margins and knowledge of what readers of the English language wanted.

Book printing was expensive and the returns could be unreliable and slow. Few English merchants developed a passion for the new art like Caxton; others invested as businessmen looking for a profit: William Wilcocks, a draper and common councilman of London with a Dutch wife, paid for two productions of John Lettou in 1480–81, commentaries on Aristotle's *Metaphysics* and the Psalms, neither designed for the reading of his own class. Wilcocks may have been investing in works aimed at readers in the universities and monastic houses on the recommendation of the Austin friar Thomas Penketh, the editor of the Aristotle commentaries, who had taught in Italy and had books published there, and was now well known in higher clerical circles. It is even possible Wilcocks encouraged Lettou to come to London (possibly from Rome where again Penketh might have been the catalyst), but if he did, he seems to have taken no further interest in the printer.[7] William Pratte urged his life-long friend, Caxton, to translate and print the *Book of Good Manners* for the improvement of morals and piety, but it was the printer who paid for the edition and recorded in the prologue his grief at his friend's death. The goldsmith of London, Hugh Brice, in contrast, could afford to commission Caxton to print the *Mirror of the World* in order to be able to present a copy to William Lord Hastings, his superior at the Mint, in 1481.[8]

All printers' bread and butter were commissions of such items as indulgences

---

[5]   Anne F. Sutton, 'Caxton was a Mercer', in *England in the Fifteenth Century*, ed. N. Rogers (Stamford, 1994), pp. 118–48 (133–37).
[6]   Sutton, 'Caxton was a Mercer', pp. 125–31 (office of governor). Anne F. Sutton and Livia Visser-Fuchs, *The Book of Privileges of the Merchant Adventurers of England 1296–1483* (London, 2009), pp. 177–84 (the background to Caxton's election 1462), pp. 361–72 (office of governor), Plate 2 (Caxton's commission of the company seal).
[7]   Sutton, 'Caxton was a Mercer', pp. 133–35. Sutton and Visser-Fuchs, *Richard III's Books*, pp. 253–54, 262–63. Vincent Gillespie, 'Syon and the English Market for Continental Printed Books: the Incunable Phase', in *Syon Abbey and its Books*, pp. 104–28 (118–19). For Lettou's possible Roman career, see *BMC XI*, pp. 16, 245.
[8]   Sutton, 'Caxton was a Mercer', pp. 140–45 (Pratte). Blake, *Caxton's Own Prose*, pp. 114–19 (*Mirror*).

for clerical institutions, of which the issue might run to many hundreds of copies on vellum or paper to be transported round the country,[9] compared to the small and speculative print runs of books. The royal administration was certainly taking advantage of the new medium by the beginning of 1483 when the *Promise of Matrimony* (STC 9176) publicised Louis XI's reneging on his treaty with Edward IV, and was clearly designed to advertise the anger of the English monarch to his parliament and the realm. Sessional printing of the acts of parliament probably began with this parliament, the last of Edward's reign. Meanwhile the royal use of Caxton's press had already been recorded by his fellow mercer, William Purde, who inscribed his copy of Trevisa's translation of Higden's *Polychronicon* as having been bought from Caxton, 'printer of the king', on 20 November 1482.[10] The printing of the *Promise* and the statutes for Edward IV (as they survive in the *Nova statuta*) and for the only parliament of Richard III is usually attributed to the aliens John Lettou in partnership with William Machlinia, and then Machlinia alone, rather than Caxton. However, the English past governor of the Merchant Adventurers, well-known to the Yorkist kings and their councillors, better suits the role of King's Printer who commissioned these alien printers to do the jobbing work – carefully having the work proof-read by appropriate experts – while he used his own presses to print his new translations and reprints of his more successful ventures such as the *Canterbury Tales*. Caxton was the only printer operating in England in 1491 when it was finally decided to print the first statutes for the reign of Henry VII.[11]

Caxton remained the inspiration of mercantile investors in the business of his successor, Wynkyn de Worde. Roger Thorney not only owned several Caxtons, he supplied some copy-texts, such as the *Siege of Thebes*, to de Worde, and in 1495 paid for new editions of his master's first book, the great encyclopaedia of Bartholomew the Englishman, and the *Polycronicon*.[12] Thereafter, de Worde had few investors as opposed to patrons. Another mercer, John Tate III, spent his and his wife's considerable inheritances on setting up the first paper mill in England which just managed to survive his death in 1508. This was an attempt to lower the cost of the most expensive component of the printed book, but in the long term an English mill could not compete with foreign imports.[13] Pynson appears to have found a merchant-investor for his business, the mysterious John Russhe, with whom he proceeded to fall out.[14] Another hopeful investor or col-laborator was John Colyns, a mercer who sold 'prynted bokes and other small tryfylles' and who supplied de Worde with some copy-texts, such as the verse

[9] R.N. Swanson, 'Caxton's Indulgence for Rhodes, 1480–81', *The Library*, 7th ser., 5 (2004), 195–201; 'A Rounceval Pardon of 1482', *Archives* 30 (2005), 51–54. On indulgences, see Mary Erler's essay in this volume.

[10] Illustrated in *Richard III's Books*, p. 255; *BMC XI*, p. 128.

[11] *BMC XI*, pp. 250–51, 324–25, 260 respectively (Machlinia); pp. 177–78 (Caxton 1491 statutes). *Richard III's Books*, p. 254 n.62 (summary); Anne F. Sutton, 'William Caxton, Merchant and King's Printer', in *The Medieval Merchant*, Harlaxton Studies 24 (forthcoming).

[12] G. Bone, 'Extant Manuscripts Printed from by W. de Worde with Notes on the Owner, Roger Thorney', *The Library*, 4th ser., 12 (1932), 284–306.

[13] Anne F. Sutton, *A Merchant Family of Coventry, London and Calais: The Tates, c. 1450–1515* (London, 1998), pp. 22–27; P. Needham, *BMC XI*, p. 315.

[14] H.R. Plomer, *Wynkyn de Worde and His Contemporaries* (London, 1925), pp. 113–14; 'English Purchases', pp. 280–81.

romance, *Ipomydon*.[15] In 1507 the twenty-one-year-old William Brettoñ invested his patrimony in some of the finest books ever produced by the Parisian printers, providing opulent and discriminating clerics in England with Lyndwood's *Constitutions* and de Burgh's *Pupilla Oculi*, as well as the more reliable market for Books of Hours. He came of a wealthy mercantile family (and was a blood relation of John Tate III's wife) with wide clerical contacts, notably with John Yonge, rector of All Hallows Honey Lane and later master of St Thomas of Acre, and with Humphrey Hawarden, dean of Arches. Yonge was a friend of Dean John Colet and his circle, while Hawarden's knowledge of the books needed by church lawyers would have been exemplary. Bretton seems to have intended to make the retail of books for wealthy clerics his business: he found himself alien partners: Joyce Pelgrim of Antwerp and Henry Jacobi, a Frenchman, from whom Yonge is known to have bought a Savonarola. They had regular outlets in Paternoster Row, London, and Oxford. The death of Jacobi, by far the most experienced and interesting of his partners, in 1514 probably brought Bretton's involvement to an end, long before he himself died in 1526.[16] The Stationers' Company of London soon made the control and retail of printed texts their particular business, secured the repeal of the act favouring aliens in 1534, and progressed to their registration of all printed books in 1557, thereby also partly solving the government's need for censorship.[17] The merchant-investor and the merchant-printer were no longer needed.

On the whole merchants were far more likely to import foreign publications by the barrel, a phenomenon noticeable by about 1479.[18] Alien importers appear to have been the most important in the early years, but a study of the sparse customs records 1460–1558 has only produced 150 merchant-importers and about 600 cargoes of books through London and the provincial ports; printed primers and church service books were the staple of this trade.[19] There was also always the possibility that the well placed buyer, such as a religious house, could circumvent the mercantile channels and ask a related house to find them copies.[20] Mercantile investment in printing was probably far less important than their role as unthinking importers of book, everything done in bulk, with the importer acting solely as an agent for better informed stationers and other retailers; some printers undoubtedly did their own importing, such as Caxton or de Worde, with primers and service books being favourite basic stock. Caxton

---

[15]   Carol M. Meale, 'Wynkyn de Worde's Setting-copy for *Ipomydon*', *Studies in Bibliography* 35 (1982), 156–71; 'The Compiler at Work: John Colyns and BL MS Harley 2252', in *Manuscripts and Readers in Fifteenth-Century England: The Literary Implications of Manuscript Study*, ed. D. Pearsall (Cambridge, 1983), pp. 82–103; 'London, British Library, Harley MS 2252, John Colyns' Boke: Structure and Content', *English Manuscript Studies 1100–1700* 15 (2010), 65–122.

[16]   Anne F. Sutton, 'William Bretton, Publisher of Fine Books, 1506–10: His Life and Inspiration', *The Library*, 7th ser., 14 (2013), 1–17, and 'English Purchases', p. 281. For general size of book-runs and expected sales in European countries, see 'English Purchases', p. 289.

[17]   Graham Pollard, 'The Company of Stationers before 1557', *The Library*, 4th ser., 18 (1937), 1–38 (20–36).

[18]   'English Purchases', p. 290; 'Importation', pp. 179–201, for the rise and fall in the popularity of cities as suppliers based on a survey of 4300 surviving books.

[19]   Paul Needham, 'The Customs Rolls as Documents for the Printed-book Trade in England', in *CHBB III*, pp. 148–63 and plate 6.1, esp. p. 153.

[20]   'English Purchases', p. 286.

imported to keep his shop stocked and, in the ancient traditions of mercers, probably distributed to markets throughout the country via chapmen who came to London to buy; he also might take a stall in Westminster Abbey's precinct when parliament was sitting.[21]

Actual ownership and readership of the printed book by the merchant class is not easy to establish: few inventories survive, few surviving books were inscribed by their owners, and few books were mentioned by title or specified as printed in wills. Yet it must be assumed that friends and admirers of Caxton, for example, like William Pratte (d. end July 1486) and certainly Thorney (d. 1517) owned many of his books. John Skirwith, leatherseller of London (d. 1486) had a copy of Caxton's 'Policronycan in paper prynttid' in his parlour and an English 'Legend Auria' [sic] printed on paper in his shop.[22] William Tenacre, apprentice of William Pratte, who would have known Caxton as a visitor to his master's house, left a mass book 'prynted of the use of Sarum with all the new festys' to Herne Hill parish church, Kent, in 1498. Richard Wright, draper of Chester, also owned Caxton's Polychronicon in the 1550s.[23] After 1500 it might perhaps be assumed that any book mentioned in a will was printed, but a survey of a total of approximately 280 wills of London mercers and their widows between 1500 and 1558, proved in the Prerogative Court of Canterbury, and therefore all wealthy enough to have bought books easily, finds no book specified as printed after that of Tenacre until 1520 when Richard Fielding left a printed mass book to St Laurence Jewry. Of the 280, only thirteen persons referred to books. Religious handbooks remained the most likely bequests before 1546, several of which were probably manuscripts. It is an anecdote which informs us that the mercer George Robinson owned Simon Fish's Supplication for the Beggars which he showed to Henry VIII in 1529. Books had to be valuable and uncontroversial to be mentioned in wills, or of exceptional interest like the mercer John Skinner's books of physic and surgery left to a merchant tailor. Data accumulated systematically from surviving books has been found to be heavily biased towards clerical and academic owners and to endorse the conclusion that Caxton had captured the English readers among merchants and gentlemen.[24]

Men and women, such as mercers of London, were as devotionally literate in the age of the printed book as they had been in the heyday of manuscript: everyone owned a primer, and worn-out manuscript service books had to be replaced. As the wealthiest mercantile households often had their own chapels, they needed a large complement of such books, not just personal books

---

[21] 'English Purchases', pp. 273–81; Gervase Rosser, Medieval Westminster (Oxford, 1989), p. 39.
[22] Anne F. Sutton, 'John Skirwith, King's Pointsmaker, 1461–(?)86 and Leatherseller of London', The Ricardian 11 (1997–99), 54–93 (64, 67, 73, 75).
[23] Sutton, 'Caxton was a Mercer', p. 146 (Tenacres); 'Private ownership', p. 217 (Richard Wright).
[24] The survey of mercers' wills up to 1558 in this paragraph extends that of the author in 'The Acquisition and Disposal of Books for Worship and Pleasure by Mercers of London in the Later Middle Ages', in Manuscripts and Printed Books in Europe 1350–1550: Packaging, Presentation and Consumption, ed. Emma Cayley and Susan Powell (Liverpool, 2013), pp. 95–114. Will of Fielding: PRO, PROB 11/19, f. 242. Anne F. Sutton, The Mercery of London: Trade, Goods and People, 1130–1578 (Aldershot, 2005), p. 385 (Robinson). Will of Skinner, PRO, PROB 11/27, f. 261v. 'Private ownership', passim, esp. p. 227.

of hours. William Bromwell, a pillar of the Jesus Guild in St Paul's Cathedral, had the *Vitas patrum* in English to bequeath in 1536, which has to be identified as Caxton's last translation (as well as a Froissart left to a gentleman), and the pious Sir John Alen, by no means an enemy of the religious reforms, nevertheless left a psalter with a heavy gilt cover to the same guild in 1546.[25]

Merchant adventurers of London and England were among the main conduits of the reformed religion into England: the young men spent their last years of apprenticeship in the Low Countries and imbibed the new ideas, the English House in Antwerp acting as a centre – Thomas Cromwell was said to have worked for adventurers in Antwerp – and they were the importers of the new texts, notable examples being William Lock (d. 1550), Robert and Augustine Packington, and Humphrey Monmouth (d. 1537), the last two actively promoting Tyndale's translation of the Bible.[26] Some contributed to the polemics, such as the mercer, Henry Brinklow (d. 1546), author of the *Complaint of Roderick Mors* (1543) and the *Lamentation of the City of London* (1545).[27] The general encouragement by their menfolk that women concentrate on works of piety may have made them especially open to the influence of the reformed religion, even when that activity became highly dangerous. They might keep their husband's accounts, manage his business while he was away, and not infrequently have a personal business as a silkwoman which took them into the households of great ladies, including queens of England. The mercer William Lock supplied a French translation of the New Testament to Anne Boleyn, and his daughter, Rose Lock-Hickman, wrote a memoir of her religious struggle; his daughter-in-law, Anne Vaughan-Lock, was an admired friend of John Knox; and Anne's step-mother, Marjory Brinklow-Vaughan supplied silkwork to Anne Boleyn and Catherine Parr. Other women of this evangelist circle received letters from the martyrs of the new religion which were passed in due course to John Foxe to be printed in his *Book of Martyrs*. Among these were a letter from Cranmer to Joan Wilkinson, silkwoman and widow of the mercer William Wilkinson (d. 1543), urging her to leave England, and another of farewell from Hugh Latimer. She had visited Cranmer, Hooper, Latimer and Ridley while they were in prison, and she died in exile during Mary's reign. In her will Joan left all her books, of which John Hooper (burnt 1555) had had the use in his life, to Richard Chamber 'to the profit of Christ's church', one small aspect of her concern for the exiled protestant communities in Germany and Switzerland.[28] This bequest alone provides ample proof of the value mercantile men and women placed on books, although printing had made them such a common commodity that only a special consideration secured them a mention in the last document of their lives, and few of them thought it financially profitable to invest in printing.

[25] Sutton, *Mercery*, pp. 381–82.
[26] Sutton, *Mercery*, pp. 384–94.
[27] Sutton, *Mercery*, pp. 388–89. *Henry Brinklow's Complaynt of Roderyck Mors ... and the Lamentacyon ... agaynst the Cytye of London*, ed. J.M. Cowper, EETS ES 22 (1874).
[28] Sutton, *Mercery*, pp. 389–93. Patrick Collinson, 'The Role of Women in the English Reformation Illustrated by the Life and Friendships of Anne Locke', in *Studies in Church History* 2, ed. G.J. Cumming (1965), 258–72, and his *Godly People: Essays on English Protestantism and Puritanism* (London, 1983), *passim*.

Further Reading

Elton, G.R., 'The Sessional Printing of Statutes, 1484–1547', in *Wealth and Power in Tudor England: Essays Presented to S.J. Bindoff*, ed. E.W. Ives, R.J. Knecht and J.J. Scarisbrick (London, 1978), pp. 68–86.

Hirsch, R., *Printing, Selling and Reading 1450–1550* (Wiesbaden, 1967).

Pantzer, K.F., 'Printing the English Statutes, 1484–1640: Some Historical Implications', in *Books and Society in History*, ed. K.E. Carpenter (New York, 1983), pp. 69–102.

Sutton, A.F., 'Caxton was a Mercer', in *England in the 15th Century*, ed. N. Rogers, Harlaxton Medieval Studies IV (Stamford, 1994).

_____, 'William Caxton, Merchant and King's Printer', in *The Medieval Merchant*, ed. C.M. Barron and A.F. Sutton, Harlaxton Studies 24 (forthcoming).

_____, *The Mercery of London: Trade, Goods and People, 1130–1578* (Aldershot, 2005).

_____, 'The Acquisition and Disposal of Books for Worship and Pleasure by Mercers of London in the Later Middle Ages', in *Manuscripts and Printed Books in Europe 1350–1550: Packaging, Presentation and Consumption*, ed. Emma Cayley and Susan Powell (Liverpool, 2013), pp. 95–114.

_____, 'William Bretton, Publisher of Fine Books, 1506–10: His Life and Inspiration', *The Library*, 7th ser., 14 (2013), 1–17.

_____, and L. Visser-Fuchs, *Richard III's Books* (Stroud, 1997), ch. 10.

8

The Laity

MARY C. ERLER*

Although we tend to see the demand for private reading as fuelling the work of early printers, it may be more correct to imagine printing's beginnings as spurred by what James Raven has called 'a demand for objects viewed as worthy of possession'.[1] These printed objects may not have been books, or if they were, may not have been books intended primarily for private reading. Three categories of early printing, in their great popularity, can illustrate what products of the press were early seen as valuable by a lay audience: indulgences, almanacs/calendars, Books of Hours. Patterns of publication show their widespread appeal and in the first part of this chapter we will examine these desirable kinds of early printing. Later and more conventionally, we will turn to books intended for private reading, focusing on the surviving volumes that belonged to a small group in the first thirty years after printing came to England, between 1476 and 1509. This is Margaret Beaufort's circle – a mixed company of aristocrats and gentry, male and female readers, who were connected to the king's mother by ties of blood or friendship or employment, and whose books give a collective sense of printing's first English lay readership.

Indulgences, produced very early in printing's history and distributed very widely, seem to have been recognised at once as fitting printing's capacity to produce multiples by the thousands.[2] Books, by contrast, in these early years were characteristically produced by the hundreds. We might think, too, that the wide distribution of printed indulgences meant, for many people, that ownership of an indulgence would have preceded ownership of a printed book or, more inclusively, that familiarity with printing might have come more naturally and earlier through printed ephemera like indulgences, rather than through books. Both clerics and lay people owned these spiritual documents, whose charitable focus was two-fold: religious building projects and crusades.

* I am grateful to Lotte Hellinga for generous help with this essay.

[1] James Raven, 'Selling Books around Europe, c. 1450–1500: An Overview', *Publishing History* 34 (1993), 5–19 (15).

[2] For recent consideration of the importance of job printing, in which indulgences were the largest component, see David Carlson, 'A Theory of the Early English Printing Firm: Jobbing, Book Publishing, and the Problem of Productive Capacity in Caxton's Work', in *Caxton's Trace: Studies in the History of English Printing*, ed. Wiliam Kuskin (Notre Dame, IN, 2006), p. 35, and Peter Stallybrass, '"Little Jobs": Broadsides and the Printing Revolution', in *Agent of Change: Print Culture Studies after Elizabeth L. Eisenstein*, ed. S.A. Baron, E.N. Lindquist and E.F. Shevlin (Amherst, MA, 2007), pp. 315–41.

By the time William Caxton produced the first English example in 1476, printed indulgences had been available on the Continent for around twenty years. The earliest of these had been printed in Mainz in 1454/5 (two editions).[3] The Continental success of indulgence printing was probably familiar both to those who printed the early English indulgences – Caxton or John Lettou – and to those who administered them – for instance, John Sant or Giovanni Gigli. These highly placed ecclesiastical diplomats, career civil servants, were the men who took the opportunity that printing afforded to increase both the accessibility of indulgences' spiritual benefits and the revenue that they understood indulgences could generate.

What might be called the first period of English indulgence printing from 1476 to about the end of the century, when sponsors like this dominated, followed the model of European indulgence printing in being largely papally inspired and crusade-directed. In fact, the first English printed indulgence extended the rewards for the previous jubilee year, 1475, and collected money for arms and a fleet against the Turks. Its administrator was John Sant, abbot of Abingdon, who was appointed as papal nuncio and collector for England. Pope Sixtus IV also appointed Giovanni Gigli to the same offices. Gigli's relation to Sant is unclear, but later the pope revoked Sant's commission on the grounds that large sums of money were unaccounted for, and in 1476 he appointed Gigli to collect the remaining money and to inspect the accounts.[4] Almost immediately on his arrival in London, in 1477, Gigli had purchased a copy of Diodorus Siculus printed earlier that year in Venice and Elizabeth Armstrong calls this 'the first fully documented purchase in England of a printed book'.[5] Gigli's familiarity with the new technology at such an early point suggests the possibility of his influence in producing the printed indulgences he commissioned from Caxton in 1481 and 1488/9.

Alternatively, Caxton's opportunity to print the first English indulgence may have come as a result of the friendship between two Benedictine abbots, Sant and John Eastney of Westminster.[6] Eastney's interests probably profited in a collateral way from Sant's indulgence. Westminster Abbey at this time was engaged in building a new nave, a project strongly forwarded by Eastney during his tenure as abbot, and the abbey accounts for 1477 show income of sixty pounds in 'offerings made to the work [i.e. the nave] at the stations in the time of the abbot of Abingdon's indulgence'.[7] Chests to receive the papal indulgence money had been placed in several churches and Westminster Abbey may have been one such

---

[3]   Janet Ing, 'The Mainz Indulgences of 1454/5: A Review of Recent Scholarship', *British Library Journal* 9 (1983), 14–31.

[4]   Sant was abbot of Abingdon from 1468, and before and after his 1476 appointment as papal collector he served on various international diplomatic missions. See *BRUO* 3.1641. For Gigli, *BRUO* 1.764–65 and J.B. Trapp, 'Gigli, Giovanni (1434–1498)', *ODNB* at: <http://www.oxforddnb.com/view/article/10670>.

[5]   'English Purchases', p. 272.

[6]   George D. Painter, *William Caxton: A Quincentenary Biography of England's First Printer* (London, 1976), p. 84.

[7]   Gervase Rosser, 'A Note on the Caxton Indulgence of 1476', *The Library*, 6th ser., 7 (1985), 256–58 (256), drawing on A.W. Pollard, 'The New Caxton Indulgence', *The Library*, 4th ser., 9 (1928), 86–89 (89).

site at which visitors contributed both to the papal jubilee indulgence and the abbey's building campaign. In addition, Caxton's shop in Westminster would have been convenient not only to Abbot Eastney but to Abbot Sant who had a house nearby, in Westminster's King Street. Caxton certainly knew Eastney, since in his preface to the *Boke yf Eneydos* (1490, *STC* 24796), he recounts how, in a discussion of language change, the abbot showed him various examples in Old English.[8] Indeed, both this indulgence and Caxton's later similar work for the hospital of St Mary Rounceval (whose guild was attached to Caxton's parish of St Margaret's Westminster) can be seen as partly a function of the printer's Westminster location and of his personal contacts.

Alternatively, the printed indulgence may have been Sant's idea. He was familiar both with the manuscript forms for confraternity membership and with the process of collection. Certainly one of these men, whether it was Gigli, Eastney or Sant, understood that in the easy multiplication of printed copies lay the possibility of increased revenue from this traditional source. A similar realisation would have been borne upon the printer, as he saw that the potential for generating relatively large sums in the re-sale of these papers would make their printed production extremely desirable to the institutional clients who were so important in developing a wholesale printed enterprise, rather than an exclusively retail one. When producing the first printed indulgence, then, Caxton drew upon his available resources of acquaintances and locale, but apparently did not attempt to go much beyond them.

In what might be called the second period of English indulgence printing, the picture changes. From roughly the turn of the century to around 1530, although several printers were active, including Wynkyn de Worde, by far the most successful printer of indulgences was Richard Pynson. Caxton printed twenty indulgences; Pynson produced over one hundred editions. Of the surviving sixty-eight indulgences sponsored by a religious house or guild or hospital, Pynson printed forty, de Worde only ten.[9]

Sponsorship in this period changed substantially. The first English indulgences were products of the world of international diplomacy, of Anglo-papal relations (though crusade indulgences continued to be produced as late as the 1530s). Now the principal sponsors of indulgences were English. Guilds issued about half of the surviving local indulgences, while a quarter came from religious houses and the rest from churches or hospitals (Figure 8.1). Their highest popularity came in the second decade of the sixteenth century, a period when local guilds were increasingly seeking a wider, often national, membership. Writing about York guilds David Crouch says, 'By the turn of the century [1500], entries [to the York Corpus Christ guild] from outside York had overtaken those within the city' and he speaks of 'a new interest in gilds further afield, and particularly, perhaps, those with a national reputation that offered indulgences consequent on membership'.[10] These local institutions, scattered all over the

---

[8]   *BMC XI*, p. 174.

[9]   Indulgences counted here are *STC* 14077c.1-.154, plus nine more entries in *STC* vol. 3: *Additions and Corrections*.

[10] David J.F. Crouch, *Piety, Fraternity and Power: Religious Gilds in Late Medieval Yorkshire 1389–1547* (York, 2000), p. 183.

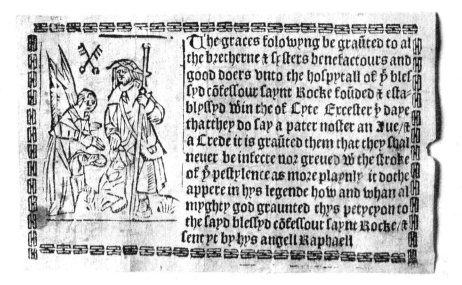

The graces folowyng be grauted to al the brecherne & fysters benefactours and good doers vnto the hofpytall of þ blef fyd cófeffour faynt Rocke foused & efta blyffyd witn the of Cryte Excefter þ dave thattheý do fay a pater noffer an Aue/& a Crede it is grauted them that they ſhal neuer be infecte nor greued wt the ſtroke of þ peftylence as more playnly it dothe appere in hys legende how and whan al myghty god graunted thys petycyon to the fayd bleffyd cófeffour faynt Rocke/& fent pt by hys angell Raphaell

Figure 8.1 Letter of confraternity for the hospital of St Rock, Exeter, c.1510 (R. Faques, c.1510); *STC* 14077c.41.

country, by 1500 had became Pynson's clients. The largest and most remarkable was the guild of Our Lady in Boston and the alliance between Pynson and the guild's alderman, or head, John Robynson, made it possible for the Lincolnshire guild to build a national indulgence empire. Between 1504 and 1522 eight Boston indulgence editions survive, plus a 1523 letter from Robynson ordering 4000 letters (membership forms) and 4000 briefs (advertising material).[11] For the fledgling industry, printers' regional travel and sales must have played a part in such growth: Pynson, the London printer, was a member of the Corpus Christi guild of Coventry, while his son, Richard Pynson junior, belonged to that city's Trinity Guild.

At its start, then, English indulgence printing was probably initiated by top-level clerical administrators who were familiar with similar European uses of the press. Subsequently, the expansion of guilds across the country at the end of the fifteenth and beginning of the sixteenth centuries met the parallel expansion of commercial printing. The effect was reciprocal, as printing supported the growth of local institutions, while the expansion of such institutions accelerated printing's economic possibilities. The agency of printers in stimulating a market for their product through a widely cast network of contacts should also be recognised, since it gives a limited glimpse of the stratagems by which printing was naturalised in England. Indulgences were the first products of the press to be commercially profitable. An old form in a new dress, they lasted only about fifty years, yet they did much to familiarise a new audience with the possibilities of printing.

Similarly significant is the first appearance in print of books of useful

[11] *LP Henry VIII*, 3/1.3015.

information, which subsequently evolved in various ways from their original form as 'almanacs, prognostications or kalendars', the collective title given them by the *STC*. Like indulgences, in their printed form both almanacs and prognostications emerged first on the Continent and were solidly established there by the 1470s, about thirty years before the first examples appeared in England.[12] Two prognostications, one issued by de Worde (*STC* 385.3), the other by Pynson (*STC* 385.7), were printed in or around 1498. From that time until 1558 – sixty years – *STC* lists about a hundred almanacs, prognostications and calendar editions, roughly one and a half editions per year. Then, starting about the middle of the sixteenth century and extending well beyond the end of our period, a surge in printed almanacs made them the most popular printed books in England by the end of the seventeenth century.[13]

The earliest English format for the almanac, in 1498, had been the single sheet, but by 1508 Wynkyn de Worde had produced an almanac in booklet form (*STC* 387), and though this particular example was tiny, the booklet offered the multiple margins that were to prove so attractive later in the seventeenth century for the personal jottings that often distinguish these books and that make this form important in the development of what has been called 'life-writing'. Not only its format but its contents changed, offering a continuously expanding body of information. In 1525, for instance, Richard Faques printed an almanac in booklet form (*STC* 390) with a paragraph at the bottom of each page giving for every year the length of time between Christmas and Shrovetide, the dates of eclipses, the dates of important feasts, the golden number, and the dominical letter. Bernard Capp describes the inclusion of other kinds of material: in 1546 Achilles Gasser supplied in his almanac 'a detailed breakdown of likely price levels for various cereals, fruit, dairy products, and metals' (*STC* 447.5),[14] and in 1549 Kaspar Vopell offered an almanac with epistles and gospels (*STC* 522.20) – a clever fusion of secular and religious material. Useful calendar-related information found other printed homes as well, some of them quite distant from the calendar's original appeal to an ecclesiastical clientele. In 1546 Thomas Phaer's *A newe boke of presidents*, a collection of legal forms such as leases, deeds of sale, and warrants, added a table that printed in columns from left to right the year, the date of Easter, the golden number, the dominical letter, and whether or not it was a leap year (*STC* 3328.5).

Printers were aware of differing markets for this product. Linne Mooney has traced two strands in early printed almanac/calendars.[15] The first derived from a manuscript tradition historically associated with clerical ownership and interested in knowledge of the physical world (natural science). In this tradition, the mathematical and scientific work of two writers was paramount. Between 1548 and 1557, fourteen almanac editions appeared compiled by Anthony Askham

---

[12]   Bernard Capp, *English Almanacs 1500–1800, Astrology and the Popular Press* (Ithaca, NY, 1979), pp. 25–26.

[13]   Adam Smyth, 'Almanacs, Annotators and Life-Writing in Early Modern England', *English Literary Renaissance* 38 (2008), 200–44 (202).

[14]   Capp, *English Almanacs*, p. 28.

[15]   Linne Mooney, 'English Almanacs from Script to Print', in *Texts and Their Contexts: Papers from the Early Book Society*, ed. John Scattergood and Julia Boffey (Dublin, 1997), pp. 11–25.

(*STC* 410-410.12) whose joint emphasis was on popular science and traditional Catholicism, while the long series of books written by mathematician Leonard Digges included explanations and instructions for predicting weather, times for planting, grafting, and bloodletting, tide tables, diagrams of the heavens, and much more. First published in 1553 and extending into the seventeenth century, Digges's 'scientific' books created the fullest paradigm for later manuals (*STC* 435.35–435.63).

The second kind of almanac evolved toward a wider general market, perhaps as a result of printing's reduced costs, and featured helps for daily life (lists, dates, travel information). It is this type that Anne Lawrence-Mathers has in mind when she suggests that the real cultural significance of the almanac was not its astrological information, but its transformation, via printing, into 'a highly portable annual calendar' and eventually, into a compendium of other useful information – what she calls 'a disposable object of consumer choice'.[16] From the 1540s on, a wealth of such printed information appeared, variously formatted and contextualised, testifying to a long-sustained desire for a small, easily portable book to assist with daily tasks. Relevant here is another form of personal-use book, the writing table and/or table book, which was likewise associated with the presentation of useful information in the early years of printing. The *STC* lists nineteen editions of such miscellanies between 1577 and 1628, which, besides their inclusion of tables of weights and measures, dates of fairs and terms, and illustrated tables of English and foreign coins, most importantly provided blank leaves (the 'tables') for personal memos.[17] In fact the addition of blank pages in books of information probably occurred somewhat earlier, at least by 1565 or 1566.[18] This innovation thus falls slightly outside our period, but nonetheless the early years of printing allow us to see the origins of printed guides to everyday life, and indeed, the origins of the personal diary.

A third class of printing that claimed an enormous response was the Book of Hours. As with manuscript primers, the popularity of printed Books of Hours transcended that of any other category of book,[19] perhaps partly because the inclusion of a calendar and other useful information gave these books both secular and religious relevance. Like that other popular printed form, indulgences, Books of Hours had a long previous history in manuscript. Realising their historic appeal, printing immediately seized upon both these items and presented them successfully in new incarnations – only to find this initial commercial success of printed indulgences and Books of Hours truncated by religious change.

Caxton printed the first Sarum Book of Hours probably in 1475 before leaving

[16] Anne Lawrence-Mathers, 'Domesticating the Calendar: The Hours and the Almanac in Tudor England', in *Women and Writing c. 1340–c.1650, The Domestication of Print Culture*, ed. Anne Lawrence-Mathers and Phillipa Hardman (York, 2010), p. 36.
[17] H.R. Woudhuysen, 'Writing Tables and Table-Books', *Electronic British Library Journal (eBLJ)* (2004), article 3 at: <http://www.bl.uk/eblj/2004articles/article3.html>.
[18] Mooney, 'English Almanacs', p. 20, says the earliest example is Joachim Hubrigh's almanac in 1565 (*STC* 462.5), while Smyth, 'Almanacs', p. 204, cites Thomas Purfoote's *A blanke and perpetuall Almanacke* in 1566 (*STC* 401).
[19] Mary C. Erler, 'Devotional Literature', in *CHBB III*, pp. 495–525.

Bruges for England (*STC* 15867). Almost simultaneously with his book, other primers appeared elsewhere in Europe, witnessing to the immediate, widespread understanding of the audience for this spiritual classic's printed versions: Rome 1473, Venice 1474 and 1475, Ferrara 1475. For England, this promise was fulfilled by the first quarter of the sixteenth century when, between 1486 and 1525, each decade produced an average of twenty Sarum primer editions, or about two editions annually.[20] In the next decade, 1526 to 1535, primer production more than doubled (fifty-three editions), and it reached its high point in the following ten years between 1535 and 1545: sixty editions.

Within the decade that saw the first sharp increase in primers, the accounts of the Cambridge bookseller Garrett Godfrey (1527–33) give us a good idea of what these books cost as they approached the height of their popularity. Godfrey's accounts give prices for thirteen primers (although he listed others without giving their cost). The most popular price was fourpence (five appearances). In addition, Godfrey sold primers at twopence, threepence, fivepence (two), eightpence, tenpence, and two copies, called 'premarium magnum' at fourteen pence each.[21] These large primers fall into the same price range as, for instance, Pynson's 1502 edition of Aesop, price twelve pence (*STC* 168), while the small primers cost about the same as Caxton's small 1483 edition of Chaucer's *House of Fame* (fourpence) (*STC* 5087) or *The chastysing of goddes chyldern* (eightpence) (*STC* 5065).[22] Godfrey's stock suggests that there was a considerable sale for Books of Hours at the bottom end of the market.

1534 was a watershed year which saw the publication of the first English Sarum Book of Hours, *A prymer in Englyshe* (*STC* 15986). A stunning assortment of primers followed, representing a variety of different religious positions. The primers' indulgenced devotions were attacked by the reformers as superstitious, but because of the book's extreme popularity, strenuous efforts were made to allow it a continuing place in spiritual life in various new shapes. Reforming additions to the primer included, for instance, *The prymer with the pystles and gospels in Englysshe* (1537?, *STC* 15997.5) or Savonarola's exposition on Psalm

---

[20] These tabulations are based on *STC* listings, hence they record only copies from surviving editions and do not reveal the number of editions actually produced. For incunable printing the tabulations include corrections provided in Duff rev.

1475–85: 3 editions
1486–95: 17 editions
1496–1505: 21 editions
1506–15: 18 editions
1516–25: 23 editions
1526–35: 53 editions
1536–45: 60 editions
1546–55: 43 editions
1556–75: 23 editions
1576–99: 0 editions

Primer production in France was ten times as large, between twenty and thirty editions per year before 1516, then nine to seventeen editions annually from 1516 to 1535. Virginia Reinburg, 'Books of Hours', in *The Sixteenth-Century French Religious Book*, ed. Andrew Pettegree et al. (Aldershot, 2001), p. 74.

[21] *Garrett Godfrey's Accounts c.1527–1533*, ed. Elisabeth Leedham-Greene et al., Cambridge Bibliographical Society monograph 12 (Cambridge, 1992), p. 147.

[22] A.I. Doyle, 'Books Belonging to R. Johnson', *Notes and Queries* 5 (July 1952), 293–94.

51, which prays for purification of the church and which had been previously edited and published by Martin Luther: *A goodly prymer in Englysshe, newely corrected* (1538? *STC* 15998).

Royal supervision of this extremely popular book was consistent: in 1545 appeared *The primer set foorth by the kynges maiestie*, the first primer authorised by Henry VIII and prepared under his supervision (*STC* 16034), while ten years later, Mary's reign produced *An vniforme and catholyke prymer in Latin and Englishe . . . to be only vsed* (*STC* 16060). Thirty-two primer editions were printed in the next three years, from 1555, but after Mary's death in 1558, with the decline of prospects for a revival of Catholicism the book lost its cultural centrality. Only five editions appeared from 1558 until 1575, then none at all until 1599, when the primer resurfaced as a recusant devotion. To summarise: for about the first half century of printing in England, printed Sarum Books of Hours were the central vehicle of lay devotion, produced both at home and abroad at the rate of about two editions a year. Then the decade between 1525 and 1535 saw a doubling of production to over five editions yearly, and in the next ten years, 1535–45, the period of most intense religious upheaval, production increased to six editions yearly. This was the high point both of primer publication and of a new, religiously driven variety in primer content, but this popularity was not sustained and by 1575 the English printing of primers had effectively ceased. Like printed indulgences which lasted only about fifty years, English Books of Hours' early success as a printed product directed mainly at a lay audience was short-lived, lasting only about seventy-five years.

During this short span of time, however, it is possible to see in the production of this early mass-market success, as with almanacs, the printers' recognition of the necessity to reach multiple audiences. The diversification of English printed Books of Hours has been documented in the years between 1526 and 1535, when the French printer François Regnault issued a flood of primers for the English market. These were effectively divided into a larger quarto series, mainly in Latin, and a smaller octavo series featuring considerably more English.[23] The implication, though there is no direct evidence, is that Regnault intended a higher and a lower priced line. Probably the books' different dominant languages, Latin and English, also suggest his intention to reach both a religious and a lay readership.

Earlier than this, however, printed Books of Hours had been differentiated in another way – by their material, either vellum or paper.[24] The large number of primer survivals allows us to see market differentiation via vellum/paper more sharply than in other sorts of books less widely produced. Multiple copies from a 1497 Paris-printed primer (*STC* 15885; Duff 191) show two production levels, and hence presumably two prices and two intended audiences. The British Library, Pierpont Morgan Library and Folger Library copies of this book are printed on vellum, with full-page cuts coloured in red, blue, brown and pale

[23] Mary C. Erler, '*The Maner to Lyue Well* and the Coming of English in François Regnault's Primers of the 1520s and 1530s', *The Library*, 6th ser., 6 (1984), 229–43.
[24] Lotte Hellinga offers an overview of the kinds of books printed on vellum in *CHBB III*, pp. 92–95.

green. Initial letters are picked out in gold against a red or blue ground. In two paper copies, however, at Oxford and Cambridge, the ground colour is considerably less sumptuous: no doubt intended for red and blue, it might better be described as brown and aqua. The similarity of the decoration across copies, however, shows that it was workshop-done, both in the vellum and the paper copies, and hence that from the start two audiences were intended.

So far I have asked what printed products might have appealed most broadly to a lay audience, through looking at the publication of early printed material that falls outside the category of private reading. The popularity of these three items – indulgences, almanacs/calendars and Books of Hours – suggests that the provision of traditionally defined reading material was only one of the services for which printing was initially valued, although it has received the largest share of attention. Nonetheless, investigation of audiences for early printing must necessarily look also at the book choices made by individuals, as well as at trends. In the first quarter century of English printing, those selections might well be identified with England's first printer, and might rightly be thought to represent what has recently been called 'Caxton's taste'. Who were the readers whose interests and desires meshed with Caxton's taste? This early lay audience might be represented by a group of readers linked by blood or service or interests. A social circle or a household is able to provide such points of contact, and to set out the taste of a particular social element. As household accounts have much to show about daily life and practice, so the reading and exchange of books in a particular setting can also reveal the preferences of a particular social group comprised of connected individuals.

English printing's great patron before 1500 was Margaret Beaufort. The king's mother's interests were shared, however, by a group of friends and relatives and employees, most of whom lived in close proximity to her, often at Collyweston (Northamptonshire), four miles west of Stamford, which has been called 'the greatest household in England',[25] or at her London mansion at Coldharbour. The record of these men and women's reading, found in surviving printed books, encompasses the first thirty-three years of English printing, from 1476 to Margaret Beaufort's death in 1509. Caxton was the major printer of the first sixteen years (d. 1492), while Wynkyn de Worde was the dominant figure later. The persons who were attached to Collyweston, who worked or visited there, included the king's mother's friends and her employees, and, since printing was so recent, they owned both manuscripts and printed books. Several of their remarkable manuscripts are visible as bequests in Margaret Beaufort's will.[26] It is their printed books, however, that will be the focus here, and these books' capacity to illustrate current taste, rather than to display inherited treasures.

Relatives of the king's mother regularly found places in her household, and this was the case with her nephew Alexander Frogenhall, the son of Margaret's half-sister Mary St John Frogenhall. This member of the younger generation had been bequeathed a printed copy in French of the Magna Carta by Lady

[25] *King's Mother*, p. 165.
[26] C.H. Cooper, *The Lady Margaret: A Memoir of Margaret, Countess of Richmond and Derby* (Cambridge, 1874).

Margaret,[27] but his ownership inscription appears also in a copy of Caxton's *Myrrour of the world* [28] where 'Thys boke his Alexander Frognall' written on sig. I 7v is deleted and 'Constat Roberto Ford de Borham' (vicar of Boreham, Essex, d. 1555) is written below (1490, *STC* 24763). A scientific work on cosmography with diagrams of the earth's place in the universe, it had been Caxton's first illustrated book, in 1481. Frogenhall's name is also found in another informative book, de Worde's *De proprietatibus rerum* in John Trevisa's English translation (*c.*1495, *STC* 1536). This classic medieval encyclopaedia was an important reference work, and these books owned by Frogenhall demonstrate the press's power to inform. It is possible that Frogenhall acquired them as an adolescent, as suggested by his jottings in a contemporary Paris-printed primer: 'xiij ffurlonggys makythe one myle & xl roddys to one ffurlonge, and xviij fete to one rodd quod Alysander thrognall' on sig. C4v (1495, *STC* 15880, Douce 24).[29]

Another relative, Mary Rivers, was the daughter of Margaret Beaufort's first cousin, Elizabeth Beaufort Fitzlewis, and the wife of Anthony, Earl Rivers. As with other female relatives, a room was appointed for her at Collyweston. A message from her is written in the same remarkable printed primer that bears Frogenhall's note. It reads: 'good my peter remember me/ your awn with all my hert mary revers' (sig. I 6v). The Christian name is somewhat unusual and the addressee might have been Peter Baldwyn, a scribe and illuminator, binder and dresser of books, who worked at Coldharbour.[30] Frogenhall's and Rivers's inscriptions indicate that the primer was sometime in the Beaufort household; this suggestion is strengthened by the many detailed royal events entered in its calendar margins in an exquisite small hand – perhaps Baldwyn's. These include Henry VII's 1485 landing at Milford Haven, his coronation at Westminster, his 1487 victory at Stoke Newark, the births of his children Arthur, Mary and Margaret (though not Henry), and Catherine of Aragon's 1501 voyage to England to marry Prince Arthur. The book has been owned, as well, by Anne, the wife of merchant adventurer Paul Withypoll, and it contains two sewn-in holy cards from the Carthusian house of Sheen, making its provenance richly complicated. Such printed images were an element in popular devotion and Margaret Beaufort herself purchased examples. The accounts of her cofferer show that on 28 July 1502 the 'hardware man' was paid a penny each for two 'papers of imagery' and he received four shillings for three 'images in parchment': one of the pity of Our Lord, one of St Anne and one of St Ursula (Cambridge, St John's College MS D.91.20, p. 35). St Anne was the subject of local piety (Lincoln had a guild devoted to her) and Lady Margaret commissioned a verse *Lyf of Saynt Vrsula* around 1509 (*STC* 24541.3).

Primers such as this were often the common currency of friendship exchange, but in the Beaufort household devotional books filled this niche as well. Mary Roos, who had served both Margaret Beaufort and Elizabeth of York, received

---

[27] Susan Powell, 'Lady Margaret Beaufort and her Books', *The Library*, 6th ser., 20, no. 3 (1998), 197–240 (202).
[28] *BMC XI*, pp. 170–71.
[29] Bod-inc. 3: 1393 (H-188) gives a full description.
[30] Jones and Underwood in *King's Mother* identify him, calling him also 'Peter of Coldharbour', p. 268.

from her two mistresses a copy of de Worde's 1494 edition of the *Scala perfectionis* (*STC* 14042), and it might be argued that Walter Hilton's instructions on the spiritual life had achieved almost the same classic status as Books of Hours.[31] Also popular are two other early printed devotional texts owned by members of the Beaufort circle: Eleanor Massey, a member of the household, wrote her name in Nicholas Love's translation of the Bonaventurean *Vita Christi*, the *Mirrour of the Blessed Life of Jesus Christ*, while Eleanor Verney, Margaret Beaufort's niece, daughter of her half-sister Edith St John Pole, entered a gift inscription in the hagiographic collection *Vitas patrum* (1495, *STC* 14507, Lambeth Palace),[32] a book purchased by Margaret Beaufort herself on 16 November 1504 for five shillings.[33] The *Scale*, Love's *Mirrour* and the *Vitas patrum* are among the most popular of early printed devotional works and though they were owned by both sexes, the female names found in these copies from the Beaufort circle suggest a very substantial women's readership. If it is possible to identify the most characteristic female choices from Caxton's and de Worde's products, these might be the books.

The volumes owned by another member of Margaret Beaufort's circle, Henry Parker, Lord Morley, have been investigated earlier.[34] Morley was in Lady Margaret's service in various capacities from 1491 until her death in January 1509, and her biographers speak of her affection for him.[35] Morley and his relatives' book holdings, however, are rather surprisingly concentrated on manuscripts. An exception, which changed hands in the Beaufort circle, is a Lyons-printed copy of Boccaccio's *De la ruine des nobles hommes et femmes* (1483, PML 600), an excerpt from his nine-volume *De casibus virorum illustrium* on the vanity of human affairs. It bears on its first leaf, the inscription 'Cest lyuere partient a moy Hery Parker'. Near the volume's end, the book's change of ownership has been recorded in a fluent and able hand: 'Thys boke ys myne Margaret yon gevyn by master parkar' (sig. 174v) and again on the leaf after the colophon 'mastres margrett yon'.

This woman, previously unidentified, was in service both to Elizabeth of York and Margaret Beaufort and like Parker was still in her service at the latter's death. In the single surviving year of Elizabeth of York's accounts, one of the queen's gentlewomen Eleanor Verney (mentioned above) was repaid on 4 November 1502 'for money by here payed for thexpenses of the hors of Margret Yone' from 13 June to 25 October, or 135 days at fourpence a day. The payment

---

[31] P.J. Croft, *Lady Margaret Beaufort, Countess of Richmond, Elizabeth of York and Wynkyn de Worde* (London, 1958).

[32] Mary C. Erler, *Women, Reading and Piety in Late Medieval England* (Cambridge, 2002), pp. 124–26. Verney received a royal annuity of £20 in 1520–21.

[33] Powell, 'Lady Margaret Beaufort', p. 233, who points out that a copy at Lincoln Cathedral carries a binding with Beaufort shields 'although the differencing of the coat is not that of Lady Margaret'.

[34] Julia Boffey and A.S.G. Edwards, 'Books Connected with Henry Parker, Lord Morley, and His Family', in *'Triumphs of English', Henry Parker, Lord Morley, Translator to the Tudor Court*, ed. Marie Axton and James P. Carley (London, 2000), pp. x–75. Boffey and Edwards print a list of twenty-two book titles found in Oxford, Balliol College, MS 329, concluding that 'at least the majority of these books are manuscripts'.

[35] *King's Mother*, p. 280.

totalled twenty-five shillings.[36] After Lady Margaret's death her gentlewoman appears twice in the settlement of her estate. She received ten pounds 'payd to Maistres Yan at her departing by the commaundemente of thexecutours'. Sometime in the first ten years of Henry VIII's reign 'Maister Metcalff', chaplain to Bishop John Fisher, received ten shillings for copying 'a lettre by the kyng writton in the ffavor of Maistrez Yane'.[37] Both these payments seem designed to help a courtier, temporarily at least without employment.

That two of Margaret Beaufort's dependents, a man and a woman, shared the reading of Boccaccio testifies to the English interest in courtly Continental works – and of course Lydgate's translation of Boccaccio's *De casibus*, the *Fall of Princes*, was extremely popular, its printed version surviving in between thirty and forty copies.[38] This interest was continuous from the manuscript period,[39] though in this turn-of-the-century instance it was fuelled not by English printing but by French. (The book also indicates Parker's early reading of Boccaccio; he would later translate part of the latter's work on exemplary women, *De claris mulieribus*, as a gift for Henry VIII.)

The most substantial information about readership in the Beaufort circle, however, comes from another connection of Lady Margaret's. In 1508 her clerk of the works James Morice wrote the names of twenty-three books he owned on the first leaf of Caxton's 1481 edition of Cicero's *De senectute* (*STC* 5293).[40] It has been called 'the earliest surviving list of exclusively English books'. Morice had kept Lady Margaret's accounts for her Croydon estate in 1504/5 as well as the building accounts for Christ's College, Cambridge, and was involved in the settlement of her estate after her death. He went on to a significant administrative career, as J.C.T. Oates established in some detail, including a position as comptroller of the customs at Boston and a friendship with Thomas Cromwell. He died between March 1555 and November 1557. Oates's brisk assessment says Morice 'united ambition and a not overscrupulous regard for the main chance to a decent respect for letters and a willingness to suffer . . . for a point of principle'. Like him, all three of Morice's sons enjoyed important administrative careers and their evangelical sympathies may well have been shared with Morice also, as Diarmaid MacCulloch suggests. Change of religious position would lie in the future, however, and in 1508, MacCulloch says Morice 'shared Lady Margaret's cultivated piety' and refers to 'his significant devotional library'.[41]

---

[36] N.H. Nicolas, ed., *Privy Purse Expenses of Elizabeth of York* (London, 1830), p. 55.

[37] Cooper, *Memoir*, p. 190.

[38] *BMC XI*, p. 37.

[39] Edward IV owned a manuscript of the 'widely popular *Cas des nobles homes et femmes mal-heureux*'; see Janet Backhouse, 'The Royal Library from Edward IV to Henry VII', in *CHBB III*, p. 267.

[40] J.C.T. Oates, 'English Bokes Concernyng to James Morice', *TCBS* 3 (1959–63), 124–32. The books were (spelling modernised): 1) *Vita Christi*, 2) *Ordinary of Christian Men*, 3) *The Book named the Royal*, 4) *Book of Good Manners*, 5) *Calendar of Shepherds*, 6) Gower, 7) *Prologue* of Cato, 8) *Dives and Pauper*, 9) *Sayings of Philosophers*, 10) *The Story of the Seven Wise Masters of Rome*, 11) Richard Rolle, 12) *Stans Puer ad Mensam*, 13) *Little John*, 14) *Book of Carving*, 15) *Book of Cookery*, 16) *Temple of Glass*, 17) *Order of Knighthood*, 18) *Mars and Venus*, 19) chronicles, 20) *Reynard the Fox*, 21) Aesop, 22) *Canterbury Tales*, 23) Tully *De Senectute*. Oates identified the editions and provided *STC* numbers.

[41] Diarmaid MacCulloch, *Thomas Cranmer, A Life* (New Haven, CT, 1996), p. 18.

Morice's books and Lady Margaret's did indeed overlap slightly. The list's 1508 dating, established by Oates, means that Morice collected the books during his period of employment with the king's mother and his choices may have been influenced by exposure to her own or her circle's reading. Particularly noticeable is the similarity in literary taste: Morice's list includes the traditional literary triumvirate of Chaucer-Gower-Lydgate; like him, Lady Margaret owned a printed copy of the *Canterbury Tales*, purchased in late January 1508 (1477, STC 5082).[42] Morice's list just has the name 'Gower', while Lady Margaret bequeathed to Alice Parker, neé St John, the wife of Henry Parker, what might be either a manuscript or, less likely, a print, described as a vellum book of Gower in English.[43] Lydgate appears on Morice's list with *Stans puer ad mensam* (1477?, STC 17030) and *Temple of glas* (1477?, STC 17032), while Lady Margaret's will left to her son a manuscript copy of the *Siege of Troy*.[44] The books of the two thus demonstrate how this important literary interest was shared by aristocratic and gentry readers. One more book of Morice's was likewise owned by his patron (in fact, Lady Margaret bought two copies from different editions): the *Kalender of shepeherdes* (1506, STC 22408 and 1508, STC 22409), a compendium of useful information, virtually certain to appeal widely.

The independent fascination of Morice's list, however, lies in classifying its selections, and indeed, the number of devotional books is not high. Nicholas Love's English *Mirrour*, of course, with its affective meditations on the life of Christ, deserves that title, and so does the *Contemplacyons of the drede and love of God* (1506, STC 21259, not by Rolle), a late fourteenth-century work on the four degrees of love. But if the traditional category of lay devotion or 'devotional reading' were defined more precisely, several of Morice's books would not fall under that rubric. The *Boke ... named Ryal* (1488? STC 21429) and the *Thordinary of crysten men* (1506, STC 5199) might more accurately be called catechetical, while *Dives and Pauper* (1493, STC 19212) is a dialogue of theological instruction. Rather than 'sharing Lady Margaret's cultivated piety', these books deploy an approach to the spiritual life that is less interior, more instructive.

Indeed, the whole list is strongly behavioural. Morice lists twenty-three titles, but eight of these are bracketed, with the notation 'in j book'. We do not know whether Morice put these small books together himself or whether this represents a marketing strategy favoured by many early printers: producing small books that could be assembled into a larger volume by printer or buyer. Of the eight short works, five are educational, including Ramon Lull's *Book of the ordre of chyualry* (1484, STC 3356.7), directed to 'young lords, knights, and gentlemen', as well as *Stans puer ad mensam*, the *Book of curtesye* or *Little John* (1477–78, STC 3303), the *Boke of keruynge* (1508, STC 3289), and the *Boke of cokery* (1500, STC 3297). Elsewhere, this interest is sustained: Morice's list included Cicero on old age and on friendship, the *Book of good maners* (1487, STC 15394), a conduct manual for estates, and the *Dictes or sayengis of the philosophhers* (1477, STC 6826), an anthology of wise sayings, which though it has often been classified as a

[42] Powell, 'Lady Margaret Beaufort', p. 234.
[43] Cooper, *Memoir*, p. 134.
[44] Powell, 'Lady Margaret Beaufort', p. 202.

school text, in its fourth edition is called 'a short and profitable treatise for all maner of people' – that is, for a general readership.[45] (A copy of this book, which Caxton translated in 1477 for presentation to the Prince of Wales, was owned by Oliver St John, Margaret Beaufort's half-brother.)[46] Finally, Morice also owned the immensely popular *Book callid Caton* (*STC* 4853) which, like *Dictes*, attracted both a school readership and an adult one. For the most part these titles are what Nicholas Orme calls 'household texts', appealing to adults and children both. He suggests that though their focus is educational, their particular audience was found in noble households rather than schoolrooms, and that their readership had historically been an elevated one.[47]

These ten treatises on behaviour comprise the largest group in Morice's list, nearly half the total. If Orme's categorisation is accepted, they too, like Morice's literary texts, might be seen as participating in traditional aristocratic reading taste. Diversion likewise has a considerable place on the list: *Seven Wise Masters of Rome* (1493, *STC* 21297), *Reynart the foxe* (1481, *STC* 20919) and *Aesop* (1502, *STC* 168) were all entertaining pastimes, while printed chronicles, which survive in substantial numbers, were a widespread reading choice, mostly owned by men.

What can this investigation of book ownership show, narrowly focused as it is on the reading choices of a small but importantly situated group of loosely connected readers? To a substantial extent, Margaret Beaufort's circle was reading books that have endured physically. Frogenhall's Bartholomeus, Verney's (and Lady Margaret's) *Vitas patrum*, Morice's *Dives and Pauper*, all are notable for their high rate of survival, between thirty and forty copies each. Morice's Cicero too, the book in which he wrote his list, remains in twenty to thirty copies, as does Pynson's *Canterbury Tales*.[48] These reading choices were not marginal ones. Although survival rate does not correlate either with edition size (about which we have little early information) or sales, it is hard to escape the impression – particularly when we see early signatures in these and other copies of these books – that this reading was widely shared.

From the assortment of texts presented for the buyer's choice by Caxton and de Worde, several directions preferred by these readers are visible, though individual taste still remains somewhat elusive. Frogenhall's acquisitions – history, cosmography, an encyclopaedia – show clearly that the early decision to print works of information was perceptive, though perhaps the general audience for such works would have been smaller than for the devotional texts owned by Roos, Massey and Verney. Possession of Love's *Mirrour* (owned both by Massey and Morice) seems not to be correlated with gender, or even, perhaps, with individual piety. Rather, its expansion of the scriptural account of Christ's life was perhaps the cultural equivalent of bible ownership in later centuries. In Verney's choice of the *Vitas patrum* and Parker and Yan's choice of Boccaccio we might see a continuing interest in moralised biography,

[45] *BMC XI*, p. 115.
[46] 'Private ownership, p. 215 (BL C.10. b.2).
[47] Nicholas Orme, 'Schools and School-books', in *CHBB III*, pp. 449–69 (451).
[48] *BMC XI*, p. 37.

whether religious or secular. Finally, Morice's list presents traditional aristo-cratic reading taste in both literature and behaviour, with an overwhelming interest in the latter. Its strong investment in secular self-improvement might be considered to represent the reading preferences of an emerging professional class. Morice's list lets us see one function of printing around 1500 – to widen the audience for these traditional reading choices, long popular in their earlier manuscript forms.

About fifty years later, on 20 August 1556, another Englishman made a list of his books.[49] William More, later Sir William, belonged to the generation after Morice and was in some ways a comparable figure. Morice was a highly placed administrator, working first for Margaret Beaufort and later for Cromwell and Henry VIII. More was Queen Elizabeth's man in Surrey and Sussex, an MP and a country gentleman. The continuities in the reading of these two men, since they shared approximately the same social level, should perhaps not surprise us. Like Morice, More owned copies of the literary triumvirate: a 'chausore', Lydgate's *Fall of Princes* and *Destruction of Troy* and Gower's *Confessio Amantis*. Like Morice, he had a book of Cato's precepts (and like Alexander Frogenhall, he owned the Magna Carta – in his case, three copies). Surprisingly, since More was a religious reformer, he owned the *Scala perfectionis*, and he had both a book of fables and an old book of fables, perhaps Aesop, as Morice did. Finally, although indulgences and Books of Hours were now in decline, the third cate-gory of popular printing discussed above, prognostications, was on the rise and More owned two, plus a perpetual almanac. Thus about seventy-five years after the introduction of printing, certain continuities in lay reading choice were sus-tained. The great difference between Morice's and More's collections, however, is size. Both lists were made by men at an early stage in life, in their twenties or thirties: Morice wrote down twenty-one printed titles while More listed about 140 (only about five of them manuscripts). Comparison of these two collections shows the power of printing, which had now made possible substantial private libraries at a level below the aristocratic.

Further Reading

Capp, Bernard, *English Almanacs 1500–1800, Astrology and the Popular Press* (Ithaca, NY, 1979).

Erler, Mary C., 'Devotional Literature', in *CHBB III*, pp. 490–525.

_____, *'The Maner to Lyue Well* and the Coming of English in Francois Regnault's Primers of the 1520s and 1530s', *The Library*, 6th ser., 6 (1984), 229–43.

_____, *Women, Reading and Piety in Late Medieval England* (Cambridge, 2002).

Hellinga, Lotte, *William Caxton and Early Printing in England* (London, 2010).

_____ and J.B. Trapp, eds, *The Cambridge History of the Book in Britain, Volume III, 1400–1557* (Cambridge, 1999).

Jones, Michael K. and Malcolm G. Underwood, *The King's Mother, Lady Margaret Beaufort Countess of Richmond and Derby* (Cambridge, 1992).

---

[49] John Evans, 'Extracts from the Private Account Book of Sir William More of Loseley, in Surrey, in the time of Queen Mary and Queen Elizabeth', *Archaeologia* 36 (1855), 284–310.

Kuskin, William, ed., *Caxton's Trace: Studies in the History of English Printing* (Notre Dame, IN, 2006).

Lawrence-Mathers, Anne and Phillipa Hardman, eds, *Women and Writing c. 1340–c.1650: The Domestication of Print Culture* (York, 2010).

Painter, George D., *William Caxton: A Quincentenary Biography of England's First Printer* (London, 1976).

Swanson, R.W., *Indulgences in Late Medieval England: Passports to Paradise?* (Cambridge, 2007).

9

The Secular Clergy

SUSAN POWELL

The secular clergy might well be assumed to be a major supporter of print.[1] After all, from the time of the Fourth Lateran Council (1215), their duty had been both to preach and to teach: to preach regular sermons to their parishioners and to teach them, at least quarterly, the basic tenets of the Church, as well as to prepare them for confirmation, marriage and death, and to confess them, even if only at Easter. If these duties could be supported by the written word, it could only be advantageous to all. Moreover, not all clergy were themselves prepared for these duties, and needed to be instructed, again, most easily, through the written word.

For the numbers of clergy with a duty of care to a parish the singly produced manuscript could achieve little.[2] However, the opportunity of multiple copies of a printed text made feasible the education of many. Printed books were also much cheaper than manuscripts, and so available to a wider audience of the literate than in the pre-print era. Certainly, there is plenty of evidence that, in those institutions where mass education was required, the value of print became evident very quickly.[3]

However, in her analysis of the market of English printers in the incunable period, Lotte Hellinga puts the clergy well below laymen as clients of, respectively, Caxton, de Worde/Notary and Pynson. As a group, their use of the printers was, however, normally higher than that of other interest groups: scholars and the universities, schools, lawyers and official publications. Only with Pynson do schools and lawyers overtake the clergy as clients of print, and it is notable that Caxton's (ultimately, less successful) competitors in the early

---

[1] This chapter will seek to focus, not on fellows of university colleges or canons of secular colleges, but on those secular priests (including pluralists) who held cures of souls and appear to have served their parishes, dioceses or provinces to some extent. The distinction is not a strong one, but the intention has been to avoid, as far as possible, overlap with James Willoughby's chapter in this volume.

[2] For the Latin manual of John Mirk (extant in thirteen fifteenth-century manuscripts), see Susan Powell, 'John to John: the *Manuale Sacerdotis* and the Daily Life of a Parish Priest', in *Recording Medieval Lives: Proceedings of the 2005 Harlaxton Symposium*, ed. Julia Boffey and Virginia Davis (Donington, 2009), pp. 112–29.

[3] For example, Syon Abbey soon replaced its manuscripts by printed books, and the libraries of Christ's College and St John's College Cambridge were furnished with printed books from their foundations (1505, 1511). For Syon, see n.11 below; for the colleges, see *The University and College Libraries of Cambridge*, ed. Peter D. Clarke, CBMLC 10 (London, 2002), pp. 107–18 (Christ's), 604–33 (St John's).

days of print (1478–86) focused their attentions (perhaps perforce) on the clergy (and other interest groups) more than layfolk.[4]

Caveats are necessary. Hellinga does not disaggregate regular and secular clergy, and her survey is only pre-1501. Caxton was anomalous in his early dependence on lay patronage. For the vast majority of editions after Caxton, no sponsor or support is known, and there may be a bias towards those who announce themselves and those who prefer not to. There is also the matter of English or Latin as the language of print. As the language of scholarship and the Church, which differentiated the parish priest (perhaps less so his curate) from his parishioners, and which certainly marked out the senior clergy, the Latin market was exclusive, whereas the English market could embrace both lay and clerical readerships (although an English publication could not cater solely for the unLatined cleric *qua* cleric for fear of allowing the lay reader into the mysteries of the profession).

Luther and the English Reformation, however, put the mysteries of the profession into a different relationship with the Church and the laity (not to mention the king). Broadly speaking, an attempt to consider the relationship of the secular clergy to print before 1520 is a simple matter (although there is relatively little evidence, assumptions are likely to be correct), whereas after 1520 the situation is much more volatile and complex. This essay will deal first with the early period of print and then tackle the period from 1520 to the death of Edward VI in 1553; the return to Roman Catholicism under Mary Tudor (1553–58) will form a codicil.

Owners of Incunables

The earliest evidence to link the secular clergy with printed books pre-dates the introduction of print into England by William Caxton. It is clear that the earliest printed books in England had been acquired by individuals abroad, such as James Goldwell, then dean of Salisbury, later bishop of Norwich (d. 1499), who bought a *Rationale divinorum officiorum* in Hamburg as early as 1465 while on diplomatic service there.[5] The same printers, Fust and Schoeffer of Mainz, were responsible for the two copies of a Cicero (*De officiis et paradoxa*) bought in Bruges in 1467 by John Russell (d. 1494), later bishop of Lincoln and for a short time Lord Chancellor.[6] Within ten years the trade in importing books printed in Germany, the Netherlands and Italy had started in earnest, while, after the incunable

---

[4]   Ratio of laymen to clergy: Caxton 91:6%, de Worde/Notary 86:9%, Pynson 40:15%. Ratio of clergy to scholars, etc.: clergy 6%: scholars/university 2% (Caxton); clergy 9%: schools 7%, official publications 2% (de Worde and Notary); clergy 15%, scholars/university 1.5%, schools 17%, lawyers 18%, official publications 8.5% (Pynson). Other printers: laymen 19%, clergy 19%, scholars/university 36%, schools 6%, lawyers 12%, official publications 8%. For these statistics, see *BMC XI*, Table 8 (46).
[5]   'Importation', p. 197. For Goldwell and Russell, and for others in this section, see further in the chapters by Alan Coates and James Willoughby in this volume.
[6]   'Importation', pp. 181–82, 197, citing Graham Pollard and 'English Purchases', pp. 268–90.

period, France and Basel rose to prominence.[7] One book, however, the Aldine edition of Aristotle, published in Venice in five volumes in 1498, stands out as the property of no fewer than eight notable English scholars, including, amongst the senior clergy, Richard Fox (d. 1528), bishop of Durham and later Winchester, and Cuthbert Tunstall (d. 1559), bishop of London and later Durham.[8]

Scholar-priests were able at an early stage to accumulate libraries of printed books. The booklists printed by Emden fully illustrate the foreign incunables brought or imported into England by men such as James Goldwell, who may even have been instrumental in the setting up of the first Oxford press,[9] and John Russell.[10] Similarly, the *registrum* of the brothers' library at Syon Abbey (a library dominated by Latin printed books from 1470 to 1525) can be mined for books owned by those Birgittine brothers who had served as vicars and rectors before taking the Birgittine habit. One such was Richard Terenden, who had served several parishes and was a canon at St Paul's when he entered Syon, perhaps in 1488. Several of his printed donations might have been brought with him to Syon.[11] Thomas Rotherham (or Scot), archbishop of York (d. 1500), gave 107 books to his foundation of Jesus College Rotherham, many of them printed books of the 1470s and 1480s. Similarly, the books given to the college at Bishop Auckland by Richard Fox while still bishop of Durham (1494–1501) contained a large number of printed books, the latest being the 1494 Paris edition of Augustine's *De sermonē Domini in monte*.[12] Fox, later bishop of Winchester, was a bibliophile from an early age – he may have bought his copy of Lorenzo Valla's *Elegantiae linguae Latinae*, printed at Louvain in 1475–76, when he matriculated at the university in 1479, and when he was appointed to Durham he bought the large library of nearly forty books (thirty of them printed), largely by Roman authors, which his predecessor, John Shirwood (d. 1493), had built up over many years in Rome and elsewhere. It was this library that Fox donated to his foundation of Corpus Christi College Oxford.[13]

---

[7] For full details, based on a pilot study by Lotte Hellinga, see 'Importation', pp. 179–201.

[8] For details, see 'Private ownership', pp. 225–27.

[9] *BMC XI*, p. 234.

[10] Goldwell's *Rationale* is still in the library of his college, All Souls Oxford, to which he gave ten manuscripts and thirty printed books (*BRUO* 2.783–6 (785–86)). In 1482 Russell gave New College Oxford eight printed books and six manuscripts (and Lincoln College one printed book and one manuscript) (*BRUO* 3.1609–11 (1610–11)). Emden (who also lists three printed books and three manuscripts owned by Russell) frequently provides useful details of inscriptions (see p. 1611). For lists of books owned by priests mentioned in this chapter, see *BRUO passim*, and for a list of books owned by Oxford graduates (some of whom were secular priests) see *BRUO 1501–40*, Appendix B (714–42).

[11] For the *registrum*, see *Syon Abbey*, ed. Vincent Gillespie, CBMLC 9 (London, 2001) (li–lxv for its printed books, pp. liii, 588–89 for Terenden/Terynden). See too Vincent Gillespie, 'Syon and the English Market for Continental Printed Books: The Incunable Phase', in *Syon Abbey and its Books*, pp. 104–28.

[12] See further in James Willoughby's chapter in this volume and in James Willoughby, 'The Provision of Books in the English Secular College', in *The Late Medieval English College and its Context*, ed. Clive Burgess and Martin Heale (York, 2008), pp. 154–79. For the inventory, see M.R. James, *A Descriptive Catalogue of the Manuscripts in the Library of Sidney Sussex College, Cambridge*, pp. 3–8 (MS 2.Δ.1.2, fols 10r–13r).

[13] *BRUO* 3.1692–93. In all, he donated 111 books to Corpus Christi and forty-one to Bishop Auckland College, Durham (*BRUO* 2.715–19 (717–19), which cites two articles on Fox's library). For Fox and Shirwood, see further *ODNB*.

The library of John Fisher, bishop of Rochester, was destined for St John's Cambridge but never reached it, being carted away in twenty-three 'great pypes' before his execution in 1535.[14]

As a case-study, I have focused on the evidence provided by the BodL incunables catalogue (Bod-inc.), occasionally supplemented by the similar catalogue for the British Library (*BMC XI*).[15] While owner inscriptions are rare and sometimes ambiguous, the evidence confirms the early ownership of Latin printed books by those destined for church service. Thomas Rotherham (mentioned above) was a high-ranking official in the court of Edward IV and enjoyed various preferments, culminating in the archbishopric of York in 1480. Thirty-five incunables are recorded for him, one of which (Bod-inc. F-064) was a presentation copy of the *Lucubratiunculae Tiburtinae* (Rome, 1477).[16] Several early Continental editions are contained in a single *Sammelband* belonging to John Gunthorpe, dean of Wells 1472–98 (Bod-inc. A-605), which contains eight Latin editions, mostly printed in Louvain (but also Venice and Strasbourg), which date from his appointment as dean of Wells in 1472 to, at the latest, 1483. Another edition (Strasbourg) appears from an inscription to have been bought new in 1474/5 (Bod-inc. D-091). Gunthorpe had spent time in Ferrara and Rome in 1460–65 and had returned to England with an inherited library which he then augmented and annotated; besides these nine incunables, twenty-three of his manuscripts are recorded.[17] A younger friend of his was William Atwater (d. 1521), appointed dean of Henry VII's Chapel Royal in 1508 (a post Gunthorpe had held 1478–83) and bishop of Lincoln in 1514–21 (a post Rotherham had held 1472–80), who had a library which included a *Sammelband* (Bod-inc. A-478) with editions of 1488 (Toulouse) and 1500 and 1509 (Paris).[18]

Very few Latin works printed in England (of those now in the Bodleian Library) can be associated with senior or lesser clergy (very few such works existed). Richard Rawlins, bishop of St Davids (d. 1536), owned a copy (Bod-inc. C-196 (3)) of the 1485 *Chronicles* of the Schoolmaster Printer of St Albans (*STC* 9995), although when he acquired it is not known.[19] Two copies (Bod-inc. L-043 (3) and Oxford, All Souls L.R.3.g.15) of John Lathbury's *Liber moralium* (*STC* 15297), printed in 1482 by the equally short-lived Oxford printer Theodoric Rood, appear to have been used by John Hawkins (d. 1494), a pluralist Fellow of All Souls College Oxford, and Pynson's 1500 Sarum missal (*STC* 16173) was owned by Richard Nykke, bishop of Norwich, as early as 1507 (Bod-inc. M-276(1)).[20] The missal had been sponsored by John Morton, archbishop of Canterbury and Lord Chancellor (d. 1500), and the extant copies are mostly on vellum, richly

---

[14] Quoted Richard Rex, *The Theology of John Fisher* (Cambridge, 1991), p. 192, in an Appendix (192–203) which attempts to catalogue his library on the basis of his cited books.
[15] For details of authors and owners of BodL incunables, see Bod-inc., Indexes, 6:2749-2831, 2833-2935; for brief information on BL incunables, see *BMC XI*, Indexes, pp. 447–54, 457–72.
[16] *ODNB*; Oates, p. 825; 'English Purchases', p. 283.
[17] *ODNB*. *BRUC*, pp. 275–77, cites two manuscripts given to Jesus College Cambridge and two incunables and eight manuscripts owned by Gunthorpe.
[18] *ODNB*. Emden cites ownership of six printed books and two manuscripts; Atwater gave one manuscript to Magdalen College Oxford (*BRUO* 1.73–74).
[19] *ODNB*.
[20] See too *BMC XI*, p. 70.

decorated with Morton's monogram and rebus.[21] Another work one might expect to find in clerical ownership is Lyndewode's *Constituciones prouinciales*, published (with a useful commentary) by Rood c.1483–84 (*STC* 17102). One of the BL copies (IC.55322) may have been owned by Thomas Chaundler, dean of Hereford (d. 1490), although the ascription can be dated to 1595 and is other-wise suspect too.[22] While he was still archdeacon of Essex and not yet bishop of Norwich (1499), Thomas Jane owned the London edition of a work on clerical privilege, the *De libertate ecclesiastica* (*STC* 13922), printed c.1482–83 by Lettou and Machlinia.[23]

Amongst lesser clergy who are recorded only as vicars and rectors there is less evidence of the ownership of BodL incunables unless the editions are old and obtained second-hand, such as the Louvain (1477–83) and Gouda (1482) editions bound together in a volume owned (*via* a Benedictine of Thorney Abbey) by William Powell, rector of St Peter's, Sandwich by 1551; the 1494 Nuremberg edition owned by Christopher Assheton (d. 1555), vicar of All Saints North Street in York; the 1495 Rouen edition owned by Thomas Burr (d. 1561), rector of Little Massingham, Norfolk; the 1496 Venice edition owned (possi-bly) by the Robert Jones who became rector of Eaton Bishop, Herefordshire in 1527; the 1497 Paris edition of the *Destructorium viciorum* acquired from Master Edward Feld by Richard Taylor, vicar of churches in Middlesex and Essex in the first quarter of the fifteenth century.[24] The BL copy (IA.55178) of Clement Maydestone's *Directorium sacerdotum*, de Worde's 1495 edition (*STC* 17723), was owned in the sixteenth century by 'Syr Roger Yrelond prest'.[25] Like the *Festial* (discussed below), it must have been owned by many priests, who would have made great use of this Sarum ordinal produced by an English Birgittine. In all, it ran through eleven editions between 1487 and 1508, two by Caxton, three by de Worde, five by Pynson, and one published in Antwerp (*STC* 17720–28.5).[26]

Printed editions such as this were valuable reference tools and were clearly passed from priest to priest.[27] Thomas Dalley, vicar of Marcham, bequeathed his *Legenda aurea* (Lyons, 1494) to Robert Field (d. c.1521), rector of Chilton, both in Berkshire.[28] John Moreman (d. 1554), chaplain to Mary Tudor and 'the most distinguished parish priest of his time in Cornwall', borrowed James Horswell's 1486 Mainz edition of the *Peregrinatio in terram sanctam*, which is inscribed (in English): 'Lent to Master Doctor Mooreman to be restored at Crystmas next

[21] Sigs a1v (Morton's rebus), kk6v (colophon and Nykke's inscription). See *BMC XI*, pp. 29, 52, 56, 61; Duff rev., p. 92 (item 329).

[22] See *BMC XI*, p. 240.

[23] *BMC XI*, pp. 52, 69. The book passed into the ownership of Syon Abbey, but only fragments remain.

[24] Bod-inc. A-301(2) and B-613; A-225; A-291; J-161(1); A-167.

[25] *BMC XI*, p. 199.

[26] For the importance of Antwerp in the English book trade, see further below (with particular reference to the publication of William Tyndale's New Testament) and in Andrew Hope's chapter in this volume. For images and descriptions of relevant printed works, see *Tyndale's Testament* (hereafter *TT*), ed. Paul Arblaster, Gergely Juhász and Guido Latré (Turnhout, 2002), *passim*, esp. pp. 3–9, 12–15, 39–54, 115.

[27] See further on books owned by and gifted to the lesser clergy in 'Private ownership', pp. 211–13.

[28] Bod-inc. J-063; for another incunable, see Dalley, Thomas (2858).

commyng after the date hereof', with the date 1 February 1531/2.[29] Amongst
the BL incunables, John Arundel (perhaps the bishop of Coventry and Lichfield,
later Exeter, who died in 1504) was given a copy of the Lathbury mentioned
above (IB.55317a) by a fellow-priest, Roger Rawlins.[30] Others might band
together to purchase printed editions, as appears to have been the case with
the 1496 Venice incunable mentioned above, which is inscribed (in Latin) as
'the book of Robert Jones and his friends'. A specific arrangement was made
between the Hartwell brothers, all three Fellows of King's College Cambridge.
Thomas (d. 1545) became vicar of Wootton Wawen, Warwickshire, William was
the holder of several livings, and John became a Carthusian at Sheen. Their 1486
Brescia edition of Lucan's *Pharsalia* records (in Latin) that 'Thomas Hartwell or
John is the owner of this book but William can choose who he wants to give it to'
(Bod-inc. L-159).

There is no clear evidence of clerical provenance amongst the English-
language BodL incunables, although the publication of religious and devotional
works in the vernacular grew fast after the incunable period.[31] The emphasis in
the earliest days of printing was on the production of literary and secular works
rather than works of lay devotion. In her analysis of the *genres* of English works
produced by the three main printers of the incunable period, Hellinga estimates
Caxton's English works of lay devotion and saints' lives at an output of 35 per
cent (out of a total production of 91 per cent), de Worde's at 47 per cent (out of
82 per cent), and Pynson's at 17 per cent (out of 39 per cent).[32] It was de Worde
who was to corner the market in English devotional works until his death in
1535.

Nevertheless, English works were published during the incunable period
which must have been owned by the secular clergy amongst others. The late-
fourteenth-century collection of English sermons known as the *Festial* is an
example. Originally compiled by the Austin canon, John Mirk, as a crib for
ill-educated curates,[33] it was first printed by Caxton in 1483 (*STC* 17957). In 1486
a different edition (*STC* 17958) was produced by Theodoric Rood, Rood's only
publication in English.[34] In 1491 Caxton produced another edition (*STC* 17959),
based on Rood's rather than his own previous edition. From then until 1532,
editions (all based on Caxton's second edition) were brought out by Pynson,
de Worde, Ravynell, Hopyl, Morin and Julian Notary, twenty in all, printed in
London, Westminster, Rouen and Paris (*STC* 17960–75). By 1491 the *Festial* was
normally issued together with another (originally separately produced) publication, the *Quattuor sermones*, pastoral and penitential basics which could be

[29] *ODNB*; Bod-inc. B-552(2).
[30] *BMC XI*, p. 238.
[31] Priests did not only own devotional works: in 1540 Robert Yomanson of Streeton-en-le-
Field, Derbyshire, owned a copy of the St Albans incunable (*c*.1486), *The Book of hawking, hunting
and blasing of Arms* (*STC* 3308).
[32] *BMC XI*, p. 45.
[33] *John Mirk's Festial Edited from British Library MS Cotton Claudius A.II.*, ed. Susan Powell, 2
vols, EETS OS 334 (Oxford, 2009, 2011).
[34] The printer is queried in *BMC XI* (243–44), but see *Three Sermons for Nova Festa, together with
the Hamus Caritatis*, ed. Susan Powell, Middle English Texts 37 (Heidelberg, 2007), pp. xii–xiii,
discussed below.

preached as sermons or read as tracts.[35] In 1491 Caxton added three sermons for recently promulgated new feasts (the Visitation of the Virgin, Transfiguration of our Lord, and the Holy Name of Jesus), together with a tract, *Hamus Caritatis*, directed at the male householder with family and servant responsibilities, but with a clerical emphasis in its title, 'A shorte exhortacyon ofte to be shewed to the peple'.

Such a publication must have reached parish priests and their curates. By 1491 the *Festial* itself had been updated and upgraded (by the Latin quotations which had been the new feature of Rood's edition), while the *Quattuor sermones* fulfilled Arundel's 1409 requirement that the basic tenets of the Church should be taught four times a year.[36] Here the clergy were provided with instant preaching and teaching material, and it may be that its monopoly of the sermon market can be explained by (un)official endorsement of the senior clergy. Certainly, although it must have fallen out of favour by 1532, no other English sermon collection was published in England between the first *Festial* of 1483 and Cranmer's *Book of Homilies* in 1547.[37]

Although evidence of clerical ownership is not clear in the extant BodL incunables,[38] Mirk's target audience is represented by an early sixteenth-century (Latin) inscription in the BL copy of de Worde's 1496 second edition of the *Quattuor sermones* (STC 17965 part 2): 'This book belongs to Conandus Fysher, chaplain of Kingston-upon-Hull.'[39] An edition of the following decade belonged to a 'John Leythlay', otherwise identified as a priest.[40] A further owner was Richard Bovy, who in 1497 recorded his ownership of a Pynson *Festial*.[41] These are the only examples of provenance in any *Festial* print known to me to date, although copies usually bear evidence of having been well used, even before the days of censorship and Protestant commentary.[42] Also in the British Library is a copy of de Worde's massive *Golden Legend* of 1493 (STC 24875), based, like the

---

[35] *Quattuor Sermones Printed by William Caxton*, ed. N.F. Blake, Middle English Texts 2 (Heidelberg, 1975). See Susan Powell, 'Why *Quattuor Sermones*?', in *Texts and their Contexts: Papers from the Early Book Society*, ed. John Scattergood and Julia Boffey (Dublin, 1997), pp. 181–95. The argument of Alexandra da Costa, 'From Manuscript into Print: the *Festial*, the Four Sermons, and the *Quattuor Sermones*', *Medium Ævum* 79 (2010), 47–67, inadequately addresses the parochial context of the work. From 1495 and Wolfgang Hopyl's edition (STC 17964), the two works were printed as one continuous volume.

[36] Susan Powell, 'After Arundel but before Luther: The First Half-Century of Print', in *After Arundel: Religious Writing in Fifteenth-Century England*, ed. Vincent Gillespie and Kantik Ghosh (Turnhout, 2011), pp. 523–41 (533).

[37] The Lollard sermon cycle was not, of course, printed, and it remained underground throughout the *Festial*'s life-span. See *English Wycliffite Sermons*, ed. Anne Hudson (vols 4 and 5 with Pamela Gradon), 5 vols (Oxford, 1983–96).

[38] For BodL *Festial* incunables, see Bod-inc. M-232-41.

[39] *BMC XI*, p. 208. The *Festial* and *Quattuor sermones* are bound together in this volume (IA.55188, 55189).

[40] 'Dominus Johanne Leythley' (see Roger Lovatt, 'The *Imitation of Christ* in Late Medieval England', *TRHS*, 5th ser., 18 (1968), 97–121 (119)).

[41] A.I. Doyle, 'A Survey of the Origins and Circulation of Theological Writings in English in the 14th, 15th and early 16th Centuries, with Special Consideration of the Part of the Clergy Therein' (unpublished PhD thesis, Cambridge, 1954), 2 vols, 1.36 (n.11).

[42] On the scarcity of extant printed copies, which he attributes to 'hard practical employment', see Doyle, 'A Survey', 1.36. Dunstan Roberts (private communication) has studied six BL, three BodL, and four CUL copies; only three of the thirteen are unmarked, and most of the marks indicate practical usage, such as underlinings. See n.100 below.

Festial, on Jacobus de Voragine's *Legenda aurea* but much fuller and more faithful to the original. This records in a contemporary hand that it was the property of Robert Howssun of Newport, Lincolnshire, 'presbiteri canterali in ecclesia cathedrali beate marie lincolnensi' ('cantor-priest in the cathedral church of the Blessed Mary at Lincoln').[43]

Sponsors

For English devotional books, even at the earliest period, the sponsor (if there was one) might as easily be a layman as a cleric, although the reader would more likely be lay. Perhaps surprisingly, this is true of Latin devotional books as well, although circumstances explain much. Both points may be illustrated by the case of the merchant, John Russhe, with whom Pynson made a contract to print several texts in the 1490s: the *Festial* (*STC* 17960 part I or 17961 part I) and *Diues and pauper* (*STC* 19213), as well as John Lydgate's *Falle of princis* (*STC* 3175), and various service books (some of the latter perhaps printed abroad). The details were only brought to light by the fact that Pynson challenged Russhe's heirs on the grounds that Russhe had broken his agreement to bear half the cost of printing and other charges.[44] Although we cannot read any particular interests of Russhe himself into this contract, since the books were for him to sell on, the mix of works is nevertheless instructive – an ultra-orthodox sermon collection, a dialogue between a friar and merchant considered at times to veer towards Lollardy, an English verse compendium, and Latin service books for the clergy. Moreover, the schedule attached to Pynson's lawsuit lists the price of the books, for example, *Diues and pauper* was printed and bound and sold at 4s. each, the *Falle of princis* at 4s., and the *Festial* at only 20d.[45]

Amongst clerical sponsors of print, the status is always senior clergy and the language almost always Latin. (Archbishop Morton's sponsorship of the *Liber moralium* has already been mentioned above.) What was perhaps Caxton's first work printed in England, John Russell's 1470 oration to Charles, duke of Burgundy (*STC* 21458), may have been commissioned by its author, who became bishop of Rochester in 1476, the year of its publication.[46] The first book printed in Oxford, Rufinus's *Expositio in symbolum apostolorum* (*STC* 21443), must have been sponsored by James Goldwell, bishop of Norwich, whose

---

[43] *BMC XI*, p. 186. Caxton's 1491 English *Ars moriendi* (*STC* 786) and 1489 Latin *Directorium sacerdotum* (*STC* 17722), which may have belonged contemporaneously to a church of St Francis (a friary?) in Newport, may relate to another (untraced) Newport (Bod-inc. A-450, D-107).

[44] *BMC XI*, pp. 18, 60–61. See Henry R. Plomer, 'Two Lawsuits of Richard Pynson', *The Library*, 2nd ser., 10 (1909), 115–33. Plomer assumes (as I do) that 'bokys called ffestivalls' (126) are *Festials*.

[45] By 1520 bound copies of de Worde's *Festial* sold for only 1s. 2d. (14d.), as recorded in John Dorne's day book (four were sold that year). See *The Day-Book of John Dorne, Bookseller in Oxford, A.D. 1520*, ed. F. Madan, in *Collectanea*, 1st ser., ed. C.R.L. Fletcher, Oxford Historical Society 5 (Oxford, 1855), pp. 71–177.

[46] The work was not a religious one, and the appointment (and publication) were political, as was that of John Alcock (see further below), who moved from Rochester to Worcester at the same time. See *BMC XI*, pp. 103, 328.

manuscript of the text survives.[47] Perhaps Richard Fox is the nearest to what one might consider a clerical sponsor at this period. In 1499, as bishop of Durham, he promoted the printing by Wynkyn de Worde of the *Contemplacyon of synners* (STC 5643), Latin scriptural passages with English meditations;[48] in 1501 (recently translated to Winchester) he edited the first printed Sarum processional (STC 16232.6), printed by Pynson;[49] finally, in January 1517 and still with Pynson, he made the first English translation of the Rule of St Benedict (STC 1859) at the request of Benedictine abbesses and a Cistercian prioress of his diocese.[50]

Authors

During this early period there is little evidence that the clergy ventured into print. An exception must be made, however, for the period 1496–99 when de Worde published five English and one Latin editions of single sermons.[51] All but one were by John Alcock, bishop of Ely (d. 1500), a man with an illustrious ecclesiastical and political career behind him who by this stage was fairly permanently settled in Cambridge, where he had just (in 1496) established Jesus College. The sixth (an English sermon) was by a younger man, Richard Fitzjames, later bishop of London, but in 1496 chaplain to Henry VII and treasurer of St Paul's (in the following year he became bishop of Rochester).[52]

The English sermons had all been preached, but in different contexts. *Mons perfeccionis* (STC 278) was delivered at the Coventry charterhouse[53] and *Desponsacio virginis Christo* (STC 286) at the consecration ceremony of a female religious in Alcock's diocese;[54] *Sermo Iohannis Alcok episcopi Eliensis* (STC 284) was preached before the usual audience of the mayor, aldermen and sheriffs, men of the legal profession, temporal and spiritual leaders, as well as the mass of the people, at Paul's Cross,[55] which was also the venue for *In die Innocencium sermo pro episcopo puerorum* (STC 282), written by Alcock for preaching by the boy bishop at the feast of Holy Innocents, that is, the last day of the period from St Nicholas's Day (6 December) during which a chorister replaced the bishop in all ceremonies except the celebration of mass.[56] Fitzjames's *Sermo die lune in ebdomada Pasche*

[47] *BMC XI*, p. 234. See A.C. de la Mare and Lotte Hellinga, 'The First Book Printed in Oxford: the *Expositio Symboli* of Rufinus', *TCBS* 7 (1978), 184–244.

[48] *Contemplacion of Synners*, fol. 2r.

[49] See *Lambeth Palace Library: Treasures from the Collection of the Archbishop of Canterbury*, ed. Richard Palmer and Michelle P. Brown (London, undated), pp. 84–85.

[50] *Rule of seynt Benet*, fol. 2r-v.

[51] For datings, see Lotte Hellinga, 'Tradition and Renewal: Establishing the Chronology of Wynkyn de Worde's Early Work', in *Incunabula and their Readers: Printing, Selling and Using Books in the Fifteenth Century*, ed. Kristian Jensen (London, 2003), pp. 13–30 (Appendix, pp. 27–30).

[52] For Alcock and Fitzjames, see *ODNB*.

[53] *BMC XI*, p. 210 (the second edition, STC 279).

[54] See Veronica O'Mara, 'Preaching to Nuns in Late Medieval England', in *Medieval Monastic Preaching*, ed. Carolyn Muessig (Leiden, 1998), pp. 93–119 (104–07).

[55] Luke 8: 8 (from the Gospel for Sexagesima Sunday).

[56] Not 'addressed to a boy bishop' (*BMC XI*, p. 208) but preached by a boy bishop. Not ascribed to Alcock but undoubtedly by him (compare similar complaints about fashions in *STC*

(*STC* 11024) was probably delivered as a Spital sermon, that is, as one of the Easter series of four sermons preached first to the public at St Mary's Hospital without Bishopsgate and then again on Low Sunday at Paul's Cross.[57] Whether Alcock and Fitzjames were the effective sponsors of these publications is likely but cannot be established. Ostensibly, at least, the *Mons perfeccionis* was printed, according to the colophon, 'at the Instaunce of the ryght reuerende relygyous fader Thomas, Pryour of þe house of saynt Anne the ordre of the Chartrouse'. However, the issues addressed by the sermons *ad populum* (beyond the explication of text) are heresy, a defence of the authority and liberties of the Church, false counsellors of the king, the sacraments (especially the sacrament of the altar), and the uncontrolled London youth. All three were published in 1496, which suggests that they were issued (as a group by the same printer, de Worde) as an assertion of church authority at a time when the city was unsettled. The merchant elite had been provoked by the burnings in 1494 of the widow of a former mayor and her eighty-year-old mother, and there had been abjurations and book-burnings at Paul's Cross in 1495–96.[58] The suspicion of a concerted programme to raise the Church's profile amongst the laity is perhaps confirmed by the fact that the two sermons delivered to monks and nuns respectively were adulatory of the enclosed life. (Alcock's sermon *Gallicantus* (*STC* 277), delivered to secular clergy at the synod at Barnwell, was printed by Pynson in 1498 and was less laudatory, but that was in Latin and so not accessible by the laity.)

The use of print for the dissemination of specific religious viewpoints was to come to the forefront after 1520, but before that date most of the material printed for the secular clergy took the form of utilitarian service books and standard works of theology and law, all in Latin, and intended for university students and fellows, secular and regular canons, monks and friars, as well as parish priests and higher clergy. In the English language the focus was primarily the lay bourgeois market, although priests, as indicated above, must also have owned, read, or been acquainted with, some of the sermons, devotional treatises, and saints' legends favoured by the laity.[59] Priests and the higher clergy did not normally rush into print before the Lutheran threat.

One who did (impelled at first by a powerful patron) was John Fisher (executed 1535), bishop of Rochester and life-chancellor of Cambridge from 1504, and close ally of Lady Margaret Beaufort, the mother of Henry VII, in her establishment of preacherships, readerships, and the two Cambridge colleges, Christ's and St John's.[60] I will take Fisher as a case-study to span the periods before and after the Lutheran crisis. For Lady Margaret (before and after her death) de Worde printed in 1508–09 Fisher's sermons on the penitential psalms, *The fruytfull saynges of Dauyd* (*STC* 10902); his funeral sermon for Henry VII, *This sermon folowynge* (*STC*

---

284). For the most recent edition, see *Ecclesiastical London*, ed. Mary C. Erler, Records of Early English Drama (Toronto, 2008), Appendix 3 (234–47).
[57]   Luke 24: 13–35 (the Gospel for the Monday in Easter Week). See *BMC XI*, pp. 199–200.
[58]   John A.F. Thomson, *The Later Lollards 1414–1520* (Oxford, 1965), pp. 156–57.
[59]   For the reading of religious and devotional texts in the first fifty years of printing, see Powell, 'After Arundel'.
[60]   On Lady Margaret Beaufort and print, see Powell, 'Lady Margaret Beaufort and her Books', *The Library*, 6th ser., 20 (1998), 197–240; on Fisher, see Rex, *Theology*.

10900); and his month's mind sermon for Lady Margaret herself, *A mornynge remembraunce* (*STC* 10891). That she was the impetus in Fisher's publications is clear from the fact that he published no more after Lady Margaret's death in 1509 until 1521, when he was prompted by another royal, her grandson, Henry VIII.

Luther and the 1520s

In June 1520 Leo X published the papal bull *Exsurge Domine*, requiring Martin Luther to retract 41 sentences of what are known as his Ninety-Five Theses (*Disputatio pro declaratione virtutis indulgentiarum*); in December 1520 Luther burned the bull; in January 1521 Leo issued the papal bull of excommunication *Decet Romanum Pontificem*. In May of the same year Luther was declared a heretic at Paul's Cross, his works burnt, and a sermon preached by Fisher. The sermon, delivered in English, was translated into Latin by Richard Pace and printed in Cambridge the same year (*STC* 10898); it was also printed in English by Wynkyn de Worde in 1521–22 (*STC* 10894, 10894.5).[61] In February 1526 Fisher preached at the recantation of the friar Robert Barnes, again at St Paul's (the venue for all public proclamations). Again, the work was printed at once, but now only in English. It was the public that needed convincing, and English was the essential medium. Fisher's later Latin publications were all to be printed abroad, polemical, pan-European, and for the priesthood.

Three editions of the second Paul's Cross sermon survive from 1526–27, all printed by Thomas Berthelet (*STC* 10892, 10892.4, 10892.7). Its publication created a problem, the discussion of which will serve to introduce the issue of censorship. In March 1526 Berthelet was summoned before Cuthbert Tunstall, bishop of London, charged with printing four English works without approval.[62] This was just the latest in a series of meetings, beginning in October 1524, in which the bishop attempted to control the London printers, not just in their importing but also in their printing of potentially heretical books. Three of Berthelet's books were by Erasmus, but the fourth was Fisher's Paul's Cross sermon, preached just a month earlier. It was asserted that one of Fisher's chaplains had rushed it to the printer after its delivery, and Berthelet was told to acquire Fisher's permission by Easter. That was obtained: at any rate, no edition now survives without an explanatory preface by Fisher.[63]

Fisher's sermon was, of course, far from heretical, and indeed Fisher had been named in 1524 as one of those from whom approval to print was to be obtained.[64] All four works were subsequently re-issued,[65] but the episode serves

[61]   Later English publications came in 1527, 1554 and 1556 (*STC* 10895–97).
[62]   For the following details, see A.W. Reed, 'The Regulation of the Book Trade before the Proclamation of 1538', *Transactions of the Bibliographical Society* 15 (1920), 157–84. See too 'Press, Politics and Religion' and index to *CHBB III sub* 'CONTROL of the press and booktrade'.
[63]   The chaplain may have been John Addison who took at least some of Fisher's works through the press (Rex, *Theology*, p. 81).
[64]   The others were Wolsey (Lord Chancellor) and Warham (archbishop of Canterbury).
[65]   The others were *A deuoute treatise vpon the Pater noster* (*STC* 10477), translated by Margaret Roper, Thomas More's daughter; *De immensa Dei misericordia* (*STC* 10474), translated for

to illustrate the preliminary attempts by the English Church to control print.[66] On 25 October of the same year the printers received a further warning that nothing was to be printed unless shown to Wolsey, Warham or Tunstall and nothing was to be imported. By 1529 the king had issued a proclamation (one of Pynson's last publications) with the first English list of prohibited books, perhaps prepared by Fisher and Tunstall;[67] another in 1530 names five works, condemns books 'imprinted beyond the sea' (whether in English, French or German), and warns printers to record in their publications that they have been examined for heresy.[68] 1538 saw a major proclamation, in which the king was directly involved, the first attempt to establish a regular censorship and licensing over all sorts of printing, and an Act of Parliament passed 12 May 1543 ('An Acte for thadvauncement of true Religion and for the abbolisshment of the contrarie') forbade all English translations with annotations or preambles, together with the reading of the English bible by the labouring classes or women other than noble or gentle women.[69] It was preceded (25 April) by the appearance before the Privy Council of twenty-five booksellers, who were required to return the following week with a list of English books bought and sold over the previous two years and which books had been brought into the country and by whom.[70] Under both Edward and Mary similar restrictions (but against different types of book) were imposed (1549, 1551, 1555).[71]

This digression from Fisher has been necessary to illustrate how dramatically the events of the 1520s were to change the relaxed world of the printers, the nature of their production, and the relationship of the secular clergy (as well as others) to print. As Pamela Neville-Sington has said, 'Although the press had served royal interests well since Edward IV, it was only in reaction to the religious heresies of the 1520s – when the printed word was ammunition and printers were partisans – that the Crown first fully exploited this powerful new medium.'[72] One might add that not only the printers were partisan, but also the clergy and, of course, the people. Not all those who published on one side or the other were priests, but many were, albeit some more used to serving the king

---

Margaret Pole, countess of Salisbury; a schoolbook, *The sayenges of the wyse*, which survives only in a 1527 edition (*STC* 10478.7).

[66] For an excellent account (particularly of the role of the universities in this period), see R.A.W. Rex, 'The English Campaign against Luther in the 1520s', *TRHS*, 5th ser., 39 (1989), 85–106.

[67] 'Press, Politics and Religion', p. 588 and n.75; *TRP* 1.181–86 (no. 122) (185–86). The only extant copy (*STC* 7772) is imperfect, but the list was printed in John Foxe's *Actes and monuments of these latter and perillous dayes, touching matters of the church* (*STC* 11222, 1563) (hereafter *A&M*). See *TAMO*, 1563 edn, 3.501–04.

[68] *TRP* 1.193–97 (no. 129).

[69] *TRP* 1.270–76 (no. 186); *The Statutes of the Realm printed by command of his Majesty King George the Third*, 9 vols (London: Eyre and Strahan, 1810–28), 3.894–97. For an overview of these and several such proclamations, see G.R. Elton, *Policy and Police* (Cambridge, 1972), pp. 218–21, 255–59; Frederick Seaton Siebert, *Freedom of the Press in England 1476–1776: The Rise and Decline of Government Control* (Urbana, IL, 1965), pp. 42–56.

[70] *Acts of the Privy Council of England: New Series [1542–1631]*, ed. John Roche Dasent, 46 vols (London, 1890–1964), 1.120. For other action against translators and printers in April and May 1543, see pp. 115, 117, 121, 126, 128, 129.

[71] *TRP* 1.485–86 (no. 353), 514–18 (no. 371), 2.57–60 (no. 422).

[72] 'Press, Politics and Religion', p. 607.

than the Church. That was not an issue until the king demanded loyalty, which he did in the Acts of Succession and Supremacy of 1534, on the second of which Fisher and More were to fall.

Meanwhile, to return to the 1520s, Fisher himself took up the Catholic cause with several publications, the flow of print having been initiated by the king himself (most likely with help) in his *Assertio septem sacramentorum* against Luther, printed by Pynson in 1521 (*STC* 13078).[73] In 1523 Fisher published his *Assertionis Lutheranae confutatio*, in 1525 his *Defensio regiae assertionis* and *Sacri sacerdotii defensio*, and in 1527 his *De veritate corporis et sanguinis Christi in eucharistia*.[74] In 1530, in *De causa matrimonii*, he made public his views as a theologian on the king's Great Matter, Henry's determination to have his marriage to Catherine of Aragon declared invalid. He also published purely theological works (although generally having been moved to write in response to the stance of a previous publication). The details of Fisher's publications are not relevant here, other than that, apart from the English material of the 1500s and the two Paul's Cross sermons, they were all in Latin, all printed in Europe, and all addressed to Europe as much, or more, than to England. They were the responses of a Catholic within Catholic Europe.

Until the king's Great Matter, England had been part of that response. After Pynson's first edition, Henry's *Assertio* had been immediately reprinted in Rome (1521, 1522), Strasburg (1522) and Antwerp (1522). Fisher's *Assertionis Lutheranae confutatio* had been published in Antwerp, his *Defensio*, *Sacri sacerdotii* and *De veritate* in Cologne, and the *De causa matrimonii* at Alcalá in Spain. King, pope, and Roman Catholic Europe could approve of Fisher's publications against Luther; what the king could not accept was his publication against the king. Amongst the many proclamations of censorship issued by Cromwell on behalf of the king in the 1530s, one of January 1536 was directed at works published 'in derogation and diminution of the dignity and authority royal of the King's majesty and his imperial crown'.[75] In fact, as John Stokesely, bishop of London, was aware, the proclamation was directed largely at Fisher (now dead), particularly his 1521 sermon against Luther (with its formerly innocuous defence of papal primacy).[76]

An English Bible

The issue of a vernacular bible was a pressing one. Print may be said to have started with the bible: the Gutenberg Bible, the Latin Vulgate printed at Mainz

[73] In speedy response to Luther's 1521 *Assertio omnium articulorum*. For the title-page, see *CHBB III*, Plate 28.2.
[74] For the *Assertio* and the *Assertionis*, see *TT*, pp. 73–75 (cat. 18–19). For a comprehensive account of Fisher's publications, see Rex, *Theology, passim*, and, for a list, p. 273. Neville-Sington suggests that he was probably subsidising his own independent campaign ('Press, Politics and Religion', p. 588).
[75] Quoted Elton, *Policy and Police*, p. 220 from *TRP* 1.235-7 (no. 161) (235).
[76] Elton, *Policy and Police*, pp. 220–21; see p. 237 for William Norton, who had a copy of the forbidden book. For a similar response to Stokesely's from Thomas Elyot, see Thomas Betteridge's chapter in this volume.

1452–55, was the first major publication using moveable type. In England Erasmus's *Novum instrumentum*, a new Latin translation of the New Testament with the original Greek *en face* (Basel, 1516), aroused tremendous interest in the intellectual circles where he was a friend of John Colet, Thomas More and others; he had collated Greek manuscripts in England in 1512–13 before moving to Basel. Latin, not to mention Greek, was not accessible to the mass of the literate English people. When Tyndale's New Testament appeared in 1526, it was not only in English, but it was also cheap.[77]

Before 1517 there were approximately 70,000 bibles, 120,000 psalters and 100,000 New Testaments printed in Europe. The first vernacular (German) bible to be printed was that of Luther, the New Testament in 1522 and the complete bible (with the Old Testament) in 1534. 'There was probably no other country in Europe where the Bible was more easily accessible to the people than in Germany at the dawn of the Reformation.'[78] Luther's New Testament made a profound impact on William Tyndale, whose own translation of the New Testament into English began printing in Cologne in 1525 (*STC* 2823) but was thwarted; it was finally published in very different format in Worms the following year (*STC* 2824).[79] The stemming of the flow of New Testaments to England immediately became the main concern of Cuthbert Tunstall, bishop of London, who sent out a prohibition in October 1526 ('in the english tongue that pestiferous and moste pernicious poyson dispersed throughout all our dioces of London in great number')[80] and preached at Paul's Cross the same month, when all the copies he could obtain were burnt. In 1520 Luther's works had been available only in Latin for the clergy to read;[81] now an English translation of the Bible was available in an England that had prohibited translations in any shape or form since Arundel's Constitutions of 1409. Tunstall preached at its burning in 1526,[82] and serious attempts were made to buy up 'all the bokes of the newe testamente translated into Englisshe and prynted beyond the see' in order to burn them.[83] Thomas More organised raids on the Hanseatic merchants

---

[77] In the 1420s a Wycliffite New Testament might cost £2 16*s* 8*d*; in the 1520s a Tyndale New Testament might cost 2*s*. 8*d*. ready bound (David Daniell, *Preface to The New Testament Translated by William Tyndale: The Text of the Worms Edition of 1526 in Original Spelling*, ed. W.R. Cooper (London, 2000), pp. xiv–xv).

[78] *TT*, pp. 27, 116–17 (cat. 57).

[79] For Tyndale, see *ODNB*; David Daniell, *William Tyndale: A Biography* (New Haven, CT, 1994) (esp. pp. 100–07, 'Printing in England in the 1520s'), 'William Tyndale, the English Bible, and the English Language', in *The Bible as Book: The Reformation*, ed. Orlaith O'Sullivan (London, 2000), pp. 39–50. See too Andrew Hope's chapter in this volume. For the New Testament and events surrounding its publication, see *TT*, pp. 148–49 (cat. 92), 151, and *passim* for valuable material on Tyndale and his peers. The source for much of our knowledge of Tyndale is Foxe (*A&M*).

[80] Quoted from A.W. Pollard in *ODNB*, 'Tyndale, William'.

[81] Rex notes that only fifteen sales of Luther's works were recorded in Dorne's Day-book in comparison with 150-plus of Erasmus's (*Theology*, p. 79). One might suggest, however, that this was not a small number for 1520, and two were the whole works (Madan, *Day-Book of John Dorne*, pp. 71–177 (164)).

[82] Rex, *Theology*, p. 83.

[83] *ODNB*, 'Rawlins, Richard', where it is suggested that the bishop who congratulated Archbishop Warham on this campaign and subscribed ten marks was Richard Nykke of Norwich.

at the London Steelyard in the winter of 1525–26,[84] and the following winter the Antwerp authorities were pressed to destroy heretical books to prevent their being shipped to England.[85] Although Antwerp was not wholehearted in this campaign, its general effectiveness may be judged by the fact that only three copies of the original print-run of (perhaps) 6000 survive.[86] (Within not much more than a decade, Antwerp was having to cope with Catholic material being shipped out of England.)[87]

Tyndale was working on the Old Testament when he was captured in Antwerp (where he had lived since being refused patronage in England by Tunstall) and garrotted and burnt at the stake in 1536. Ironically, the king of England was by then prepared to countenance an English bible: indeed, a few months after Tyndale's execution, the so-called Matthew's Bible (*STC* 2066), printed in Antwerp, received Henry's official licence – it was substantially Tyndale's translation (although this was not acknowledged), with additional work by Miles Coverdale.[88] In 1538 Thomas Cromwell (the king's 'minister for propaganda')[89] published Injunctions ordering that every parish priest should set up a large bible in his church for the people to peruse,[90] and in 1539 Coverdale's revision, the Great Bible (*STC* 2068), was published. Ironically, too, just as Tyndale had encountered problems with his first printing of the New Testament, so too did Cromwell, who masterminded the printing. Begun in Paris, it had to be completed in London (by Richard Grafton and Edward Whitchurch).[91] The title-page is famous: the king hands bibles to Cromwell and Cranmer who distribute them to the eager people.[92] Altogether, the Great Bible went through seven revised editions (*STC* 2068–76), but Henry very soon came to see problems in the open approach.[93] Already in 1539 he had limited the

---

[84] John Guy, *Thomas More* (London, 2000), pp. 118–19; *TT*, p. 168 (cat. 111). Fisher's second Paul's Cross sermon had been preached at the public penance (with Robert Barnes) of four of these merchants (Guy, *Thomas More*, p. 118).

[85] *TT*, pp. 151–52 (cat. 94).

[86] Lotte Hellinga and J.B. Trapp, 'Introduction', in *CHBB III*, pp. 1–30 (26), who also note that only a fragment of the Cologne print (*STC* 2823) survives. For a facsimile of one page from the only complete copy of the Worms print (*STC* 2824), see Daniell, *William Tyndale*, Plate 1.

[87] John Bale lamented that books from monastic libraries were 'sent over see to ye boke-bynders, not in small nombre, but at tymes whole shyppes full, to the wonderynge of the foren nacyons' (quoted by Margaret Aston, 'English Ruins and English History: The Dissolution and a Sense of the Past', in *Lollards and Reformers* (London, 1984), pp. 313–37 (327)).

[88] *TT*, p. 11. Coverdale's Bible (also largely based on Tyndale's) had been printed in Antwerp in 1535 (*pace STC* 2063 which has 'Cologne?') and was reprinted by James Nicolson of Southwark (*STC* 2063.3). It was dedicated to the king but not licensed by him. Its title-page foreshadowed that of the Great Bible. See *TT*, pp. 143–45 (cat. 91).

[89] 'Press, Politics and Religion', p. 594. Neville-Sington acknowledges the excellent work of Geoffrey Elton in establishing Cromwell's role (with Berthelet as the King's Printer) but argues that Wolsey and Pynson had fulfilled a similar role (589). One might suggest that they had less to cope with at that stage.

[90] 'Press, Politics and Religion', p. 592; Elton, *Policy and Police*, p. 254; *STC* 10085, 10086.

[91] 'Press, Politics and Religion', p. 592 (and see further pp. 592–94).

[92] Illustrated in R.B. McKerrow and F.S. Ferguson, *Title-page Borders used in England and Scotland 1485–1640* (London, 1932 for 1931), p. 26. For details of the passage of approval for the bible in English, see G.W. Bernard, *The King's Reformation: Henry VIII and the Remaking of the English Church* (New Haven, CT and London, 2005), pp. 521–27.

[93] The problems of *vox populi* had been foreseen from an early stage, as Bernard notes (*The King's Reformation*, pp. 526–27).

printing of bibles, and in 1543, as noted above, the perversely titled 'Acte for thadvauncement of true Religion' forbade the bible to the labouring classes and all women below the status of noble and gentle women.[94]

The printing of Tyndale's New Testament arguably provoked the most seismic change in English cultural life in the early Modern period, a change he is said to have envisaged thus, when addressing an unnamed scholar: 'if God spare my lyfe ere many yeares, I wyl cause a boye that dryueth ye plough, shall knowe more of the scripture then thou doest'.[95] Tyndale was a priest: he had been ordained just before incepting as an MA at Oxford in 1515. He had never practised as a cler-gyman, but had been a tutor and preacher in his native Gloucestershire before embarking on his biblical translation and other works. He was, therefore, very different from the average ordained priest and, in his scholarship and range of publications, an equal to his Oxford peers, Grocyn, Linacre and Colet.[96] How did the average ordained priest react to the years of contention in the Church?

It will be clear, even from the potted history supplied above, that, during the last years of Henry VIII, Injunctions, Proclamations, Acts, and other means of enforcement were so frequent (and sometimes so contradictory or short-lived) that it was hard for the ordinary vicar or rector, let alone his curate, to keep pace (not to mention the difficulties of communication, even in an age of print).[97] One matter which affected all and was clear-cut was the requirement in proclama-tions of 1535 and 1538 that all references to the pope and to Thomas Becket must be erased.[98] Again, one might use the example of the *Festial*, with the caveat that it was popular in lay circles and not by any means the sole province of the clergy. Most printed copies (like manuscripts) indicate their continued use by the excision of the sermons for Thomas Becket (the feast-days of his martyrdom and his translation), as well as the erasure of his name, that of the pope, and often of words such as *purgatory* or *pardon*.[99] Of the thirteen *Festial* incunables in Bod L (Bod-inc. M-232-41), seven are largely intact, but material has been cen-sored in two of these seven.[100] Very soon the datedness of so orthodox a collec-tion becomes apparent, and the *Festial* is defaced with secular and/or scurrilous

---

[94] See n.69 above (*Statutes of the Realm*).
[95] *A&M* (*TAMO*, 1563 edn, 3.570).
[96] For his range of publications, including translations, such as his earliest (Erasmus's *Enchiridion militis Christiani* into English, not extant) and other works, such as his most influ-ential original work, *The obedience of a Christen man* (*STC* 24446, Antwerp, 1528), which was proscribed in the 1529 list of prohibited books (see n.67 above), see *STC* 24436–71 and *ODNB* 'Tyndale', *passim*.
[97] Elton writes tellingly, and amusingly, on the problem (*Policy and Police*, pp. 258–62).
[98] *TRP* 1.229–32 (no. 158) (the pope, p. 231), 270–76 (no. 186) (Becket, p. 276). Discussed *Stripping of the Altars*, pp. 410–21.
[99] The latest reference to preaching of the *Festial* is the 1589 case of John Minet (Veronica M. O'Mara, 'A Middle English Sermon Preached by a Sixteenth-Century "Athiest": A Preliminary Account', *Notes and Queries* 323 (1987), 183–85).
[100] The two copies with censorship are M-237(2), 241. This compares well with Roberts's study of thirteen printed copies from London, Oxford and Cambridge (see n.42 above), in seven of which he noted censorship, compared to 64 per cent censorship of private prayer books and 80 per cent of service books (Dunstan Roberts, 'The Expurgation of Traditional Prayer Books (c.1535–1600)', *Reformation* 15 (2010), 23–49, p. 32). See too Dunstan C.D. Roberts, 'Readers' Annotations in Sixteenth-Century Religious Books' (unpublished PhD thesis, Cambridge, 2012), Chapter 4.

verses (Bod-inc. M-233, 234, 238). The 1496 de Worde edition once owned by Francis Douce (Bod-inc. M-238) has the word *festialis* altered to *bestialis* on the title-page: 'Incipit liber qui festialis appellatur'; the same hand has added 27 lines of anti-*Festial* verse to the back end-leaf. Not all comments, however, are hostile: 'I John Powell a member of the tru cathholick (*sic*) church' (Bod-inc. M-232).

Clerical Reactions

These two interventions illustrate a partisanship typical of the secular clergy after 1520. Whereas the senior clergy tended to support the status quo (mostly changing their opinions as and when the status quo changed),[101] there was less of a vested interest for the lesser clergy who variably favoured a Lutheran/ Reformed/Protestant or traditional Catholic stance. Although it was impossible to avoid printed polemic (even if one chose not to read it oneself), Catholic publications continued to be printed throughout the sixteenth century, even though de Worde's death in 1535 coincided with the ascendancy of Protestant printers.[102] For those clergy who favoured a Protestant stance, print offered numerous resources. The situation after the 1520s might be compared to the internet revolution of recent decades – a vast outpouring of pluralistic viewpoints and variably exact information, offering new liberties as well as new dangers.

Amongst those who first attempted to tap these possibilities were the influential London merchants, who not only had printers on their doorsteps but had connections with, and visited, the English House of the Merchant Adventurers in Antwerp: they were therefore in a position to develop an informed, as well as a commercial, interest in both printed books and reform.[103] The link between merchants and heterodoxy has been suggested above in relation to the shipping of Tyndale's New Testament from Antwerp to London. Tyndale (who came from a family of wool merchants) spent time in England in 1523 with both merchants and clergymen, and he was funded (after his rejection by Tunstall) by Humphrey Monmouth of the Drapers' Company.[104] Indeed, as A.G. Dickens

---

[101] As John Bale noted of Gardiner in the Preface and endnote to his translation of Stephen Gardiner's *De vera obedientia* (*STC* 11586, sigs a2v–b4v, i6v–k3v). The work was proscribed in the 1529 list of prohibited books (see n.67 above).

[102] For a comprehensive overview of Catholic publication in this period, see J.T. Rhodes, 'Private Devotion in England on the Eve of the Reformation' (unpublished PhD thesis, University of Durham, 1974). For the persistent publication programme of Richard Whitford, former brother of the abbey of Syon, see Susan Powell, 'Syon Abbey as a Centre for Text Production', and Ann M. Hutchison, 'Richard Whitford's *The Pype, or Tonne, of the Lyfe of Perfection*: Pastoral Care, or Political Manifesto?', in *Saint Birgitta, Syon and Vadstena: Papers from a Symposium in Stockholm 4–6 October 2007*, ed. Claes Gejrot, Sara Risberg and Mia Åkestam, Konferenser 73 (Stockholm, 2010), pp. 50–70 (60–67), pp. 89–103. For an argument emphasising evolution rather than stagnation in Catholic publication, see Lucy Wooding, 'The Marian Restoration and the Mass', in *The Church of Mary Tudor*, ed. Eamon Duffy and David Loades (Aldershot and Burlington, VT, 2006), pp. 227–57, and her chapter in this volume.

[103] On merchants in relation to religious change, see Anne F. Sutton, *The Mercery of London: Trade, Goods and People, 1130–1578* (Aldershot and Burlington, VT, 2005), pp. 379–407 (384–94 on the import of heretical books). See too her chapter in this volume.

[104] For full details, see *A&M* (*TAMO*, 1563 edn, 5.1822–23).

pointed out, 'Tyndale's subsequent publishing work can scarcely be explained except upon a basis of large-scale subsidisation by English merchants.'[105] It was from the English House that Tyndale was eventually lured and betrayed by the perfidious Henry Phillips, and it was John Rogers, chaplain to the English merchants of the English House, who prepared Tyndale's bible for publication as Matthew's Bible.[106]

The parishes of the London clergymen housed both merchants and print-ers. Some were orthodox; others were not. Tyndale's connection with reformist clerics and merchants had been with St Dunstan-in-the-West, off Fleet Street, in the City of London;[107] St Stephen, Coleman Street was also a parish noted for heresy.[108] As a case-study I will take All Hallows, Honey Lane, just off Cheapside in the City and in the heart of the merchant quarter. By 1526 and Tyndale's New Testament, the rector was a charismatic Lutheran, Robert Forman (d. 1528), president of Queens College, Cambridge, and well known for his sermons.[109] His curate was Thomas Garrard, or Garrett (1498–1540), who was engaged in the distribution of illicit books from the London booksellers to the universities and elsewhere.[110] Garrard was captured, escaped and cap-tured again. Having recanted, he went on to serve as chaplain to Sir Francis Bigod, then Hugh Latimer, and finally Cranmer. In 1537 Cromwell appointed him (now an Oxford BTh) rector of All Hallows. His preaching at Paul's Cross with Robert Barnes and William Jerome at Lent 1540 led to the burning of all three as heretics at Smithfield in July (soon after Cromwell), in the infamous even-handed executions, when three Catholic priests were hanged, drawn and quartered as traitors. In 1543 the rector and curate were also charged with heterodoxy.[111]

It is not known whether the incumbents of All Hallows had always held advanced opinions, and Sheila Lindenbaum has argued for the orthodoxy of the graduates who were sent into London parishes in the 1430s.[112] Little is known of the opinions of the All Hallows rector of this period, Robert Oppy

[105] A.G. Dickens, *The English Reformation*, 2nd edn (London, 1989), p. 93, who writes interest-ingly on the situation.
[106] *TT*, pp. 11, 147, 164; for Phillips and Rogers, see Daniell, *William Tyndale*, pp. 361–84, 335–38 respectively.
[107] Daniell suggests that St Dunstan's was 'a church moving to some reformed ideas about the gospel, and possibly one of the London Lollard communities' (*William Tyndale*, p. 104).
[108] Andrew Hope, 'Conformed and Reformed: John Colet and his Reformation Reputation', in *Image, Text and Church, 1380–1600: Essays for Margaret Aston*, ed. Linda Clark, Maureen Jurkowski and Colin Richmond (Toronto, 2009), pp. 214–38 (219).
[109] J.A. and J. Venn, *Alumni Cantabrigienses: a Biographical List of All Known Students, Graduates and Holders of Office at the University of Cambridge from the Earliest Times to 1900*, Part I (to 1751), 4 vols (Cambridge, 1922–27), 2.158 (but 'Thomas' Forman or Farman). Not in *BRUC*.
[110] *BRUO 1501–40*, pp. 228–29. For Foxe's narrative, see *A&M* (*TAMO*, 1563 edn, 3.492, 532, 660–69). See too *ODNB*, 'Garrard, Thomas'.
[111] Here and below, D.J. Keene and Vanessa Harding, 'All Hallows Honey Lane 11/0', pp. 3–9, *Historical Gazetteer of London before the Great Fire*, British History Online (1987) at: <http:// www.british-history.ac.uk/report.aspx?compid=8466&strquery=henry%20hoddys>, accessed 2 November 2011.
[112] Sheila Lindenbaum, 'London after Arundel: Learned Rectors and the Strategies of Orthodox Reform', in *After Arundel*, pp. 187–208. On this milieu, see Anne Hudson, 'Wyclif Texts in Fifteenth-century London', in *Studies in the Transmission of Wyclif's Writings* (Aldershot and Burlington, VT, 2008), pp. 1–18 (item XV).

(1429–64),[113] but from 1446 the Grocers' Company were patrons of the church, strengthening the link between the merchants and their scholarly priests (the Grocers seem to have had a custom of appointing learned incumbents from Oxford and Cambridge alternately).[114] An unusual publication in 1509 may testify to this link. This was a sermon for the eve of the Nativity of Christ, first preached by Savonarola and printed in Italian in Florence (cf. Bod-inc. S-096A), but translated into Latin and printed by Pynson (STC 21800) as the delayed fulfilment of a request by John Yonge (1462/3–1526), rector of All Hallows 1503–10, and Stephen Douce, master of Whittington College 1496–1509.[115] An interest in Savonarola would have been advanced in 1509,[116] but it was not the first work of his printed in England, since a Latin commentary on Psalm 30, prepared as he awaited death, had been printed by de Worde around 1500 (STC 21798), soon after its publication in Milan. The English edition (Bod-inc. S-076) bears no details of its publication circumstances but might also have been the same translator and the same patrons. Whether the case or not, merchants may have been involved in bringing to England these Italian texts, written by a charismatic anti-clerical friar burnt for heresy as recently as 1498. Indeed, as early as 1496, 'certain English merchants' (not otherwise identified) offered 200 ducats to have Savonarola's series of 48 sermons on the Book of Amos translated into Latin.[117]

Yonge was clearly an excellent preacher: he is recorded as having been summoned to preach before Lady Margaret Beaufort, mother of Henry VII, on four separate occasions in 1506–08.[118] He would regularly have preached to the mercer inhabitants of the All Hallows parish, and in 1510 they chose him as master of St Thomas of Acre, of which, unusually, they were the patrons.[119] As master of Whittington College, a secular college of five canons and a master, which provided training for London priests, Douce would have had an active interest in up-to-the-minute preaching and scholarship.[120] An earlier master (1431–44) had been Reginald Pecock, who wrote most of his works there, inevitably stimulated in his writing and preaching by living amongst clever and opinionated mercers. His dedicated attempts to deal with their needs and concerns were to lead to incarceration after his removal from the bishopric of St

[113] For Oppy, see BRUO 2.1399, which records no books for him, nor for Henry Hoddys (rector 1471–76, BRUC, p. 308), despite Keene and Harding's statement that they left the church 'money and books'.

[114] Emden records books owned by rectors John Chapman (1479–94), Simon Foderby, alias Grene (1494–1503), William Lambert (1517–22) (BRUC, p. 131; BRUO 2.702–03; BRUC, p. 347), but BRUO 1.427 records Robert Claydon as rector 1511–22.

[115] It had been translated by the priest Bartholomeus Gallus of Milan, with a final dedication to his friends, Thomas Scrow and John Yonge. For Yonge, see ODNB; Sutton, Mercery, pp. 360–64.

[116] Of the numerous copies of Savonarola in BodL (Bod-inc. S-065-101), none is of early date.

[117] John B. Gleason, John Colet (Berkeley, CA, 1989), p. 57.

[118] St John's College Cambridge Archives D91.21, pp. 102, 143; D91.19, pp. 42, 91.

[119] The Savonorola interest was perhaps encouraged by local Lucchese merchants, who had had a chapel in St Thomas of Acre since 1365 (Sutton, Mercery, p. 73). On the earlier history of St Thomas of Acre, see Anne F. Sutton, 'The Hospital of St Thomas of Acre in London: The Search for Patronage, Liturgical Improvement, and a School, under Master John Neel, 1420–63', in The Late Medieval English College, ed. Burgess and Heale, pp. 199–229.

[120] For Whittington College, see Victoria County History I: The Victoria History of London including London within the Bars, Westminster and Southwark, ed. William Page (London, 1909), pp. 578–80.

Asaph.[121] There was a close relationship between All Hallows and the College (whose masters were also rectors of St Michael Paternoster Royal): Pecock's successor and opponent, Thomas Eborall, served as master 1444–64 and then became rector of All Hallows 1464–71; Edward Lupton (master 1479–82) had previously served at All Hallows (1476–79).[122] Eborall and his succeeding master William Ive (1464–70) were the doctors of divinity who apparently licensed the possession of a Wycliffite New Testament.[123]

Heresy appears to have lingered in the Honey Lane parish after Garrard's curacy, since in 1543 'Reede, late curate off Honnye Lane' and 'Sir Wylliam of Honny Lane' were examined 'for abuses and enormities of religion'.[124] However, while, both before and after the 1520s, the London clergy were exposed to diverse opinions in a highly charged intellectual and cultural environment, not all held advanced views. Simon Appulby, an ordained priest and anchorite at All Hallows London Wall (perhaps from as early as 1513) until his death in 1537, was a conservative in a conservative church and parish. In 1514 de Worde published *The fruyte of redempcion* (STC 22557), thirty-one chapters of devotional prayers and meditations with woodcuts as visual aids. Appulby's book set forth the scriptural life of Christ and as such strictly required diocesan approval, which was given him by Richard Fitzjames, 'vnworthy bysshop of London' (colophon). About a quarter of the text is Birgittine material, and the Syon brothers William Bonde and Richard Whitford recommended the book in separate publications, the supreme endorsement of Catholic orthodoxy.[125]

At around the same time Pynson published a sermon (STC 5545) delivered by John Colet (1467–1519), dean of St Paul's, to Convocation 6 February 1512.[126] Colet was part of the intellectual circle of Erasmus, Fisher and More, and, perhaps significantly, he came from a wealthy mercer background, his father having twice served as mayor of London.[127] His relationship with his bishop, Fitzjames, was not an easy one, and this notoriously anti-clerical sermon (although delivered and printed in Latin) caused immense trouble, as did Colet's sermons at St Paul's. Indeed, although it is useless to guess Colet's affiliations had he lived longer, and although he clearly argued in 1512 for 'a Catholic not a Protestant reformation', his sermons, including (according to Erasmus) ones on the gospel of Matthew, the Creed and the Lord's Prayer, certainly attracted reformed interest.[128]

---

[121] On Pecock, see *ODNB*; Wendy Scase, *Reginald Pecock*, Authors of the Middle Ages, 8 (Aldershot, 1996); Sutton, *Mercery*, pp. 161–67.

[122] On Lupton, see Gillespie, *Syon Abbey*, p. 583.

[123] Manchester, John Rylands Library, MS Eng. 77 (Hudson, 'Wyclif texts in Fifteenth-Century London', pp. 3–4). On Ive, see *ODNB*.

[124] Keene and Harding, 'All Hallows Honey Lane'. See Dasent, ed., *Acts of the Privy Council*, 1.126, 128.

[125] *ODNB*; M.C. Erler, 'A London Anchorite, Simon Appulby: his *Fruyte of redempcyon* and its Milieu', *Viator* 29 (1998), 227–39.

[126] *ODNB*; Gleason, *John Colet*; Hope, 'Conformed and Reformed' (for the date, pp. 215–16, n.8).

[127] Instead of clerics, he chose the Mercers as the trustees of the school he founded with his father's money, St Paul's School.

[128] For details, see Hope, 'Conformed and Reformed' (for the statements here, pp. 217, 218).

Colet's sermon was not to appear in English until Berthelet printed it around 1530 (*STC* 5550), and indeed nothing of his appeared in print before 1527 (*STC* 5542). As late as 1566 it could be said: 'As for John Colet, he hath neuer a worde to shew, for he left no works.'[129] This was untrue (see *STC* 5542–5550.5), but nothing substantial survived Colet's early death, as he himself realised towards the end. However, the fact that the sermon was printed in the vernacular nearly two decades after its delivery, and that the range of print focuses on the 1530s and goes as far as 1641, demonstrates his appeal to Lutherans, Protestants, and even Puritans.[130] Comparison may be made with Fisher (executed in 1535), two of whose works appeared after his death, one (*A godlie treatisse*) translated from the Latin and published from *c.*1563 to 1640 (*STC* 10888–90) and the other (*A spirituall consolation*) written in English to his sister as he awaited death and published as late as *c.*1578 (*STC* 10899).[131]

This phenomenon is worth investigating briefly because it shows how, once the floodgates of printing were opened, religious works previously neglected or suppressed came to the fore. Of thirty prohibited books named at a sermon preached at Paul's Cross on 3 December 1531 most were by Tyndale and the like, but two dated back to the Lollard period, *A proper dyaloge, bytwene a gentillman and an husbandman* (*STC* 1462.3) and *The examinacion of master William Thorpe preste accused of heresye* . . . (*STC* 24045).[132] Both were printed in Antwerp in 1529–30 and were the forerunners of several Lollard works (long read secretly in manuscript) which were resurrected after 1520, such as *The dore of holy scripture*, attributed to Purvey (printed John Gough 1540, *STC* 25587.5), *The Lanterne of lyght* (Redman, 1535?, *STC* 15225), and *Wyclyffes wycket* (printed perhaps by John Day 1546, *STC* 25590).[133] Sometimes it was necessary to fudge the place of publication, so that no printer was named in *Wyclyffes wycket* and it was said to have been printed in 'Norenburch' (actually London).[134]

Diues and pauper was mentioned earlier as having been sponsored by a merchant, John Russhe. Dubiously orthodox (unlike the resolutely orthodox *Festial*, which Russhe also sponsored), it had appeared in Lollard investigations in the fifteenth century but was published, not only by Pynson in 1493 (*STC* 19212) but then by de Worde in 1496 (*STC* 19213).[135] The large number of thirty-one copies are extant. The 1493 edition was owned by 'John Adeson', perhaps Fisher's chaplain, John Addison; the second edition was given to 'Richarde Sodan' by

---

[129] Quoted in Gleason, *John Colet*, p. 3.

[130] In 1529 Tyndale recorded that Colet's English version of the Paternoster had aroused Fitzjames's anger; Colet's treatise on the Paternoster was eventually published in a Sarum primer of 1532 (*STC* 15978). See entry to *STC* 15992.

[131] No author was given for the *Godlie treatisse*, although it was noted that it had been 'written in Latin . . . more than fourtie yeres past' (*STC* 10888, sig.A4v).

[132] See Margaret Aston, 'Lollardy and the Reformation: Survival or Revival?', in *Lollards and Reformers*, pp. 219–42 (220–21).

[133] For these and further details, see Aston, 'Lollardy and the Reformation', *passim*, and Anne Hudson, *The Premature Reformation: Wycliffite Texts and Lollard History* (Oxford, 1988), pp. 483–94 ('Heretical Books in the Early Sixteenth Century') within the important chapter 10, 'The Re-emergence of Reform' (446–507).

[134] On the problems of dating heretical works, see Hudson, *Premature Reformation*, pp. 11–18.

[135] Hudson, *Premature Reformation*, pp. 417–20 and index (*Dives and Pauper*).

'Jno Fillde servaunte with Jesper allyn merchaunt'.[136] Its unorthodox status was confirmed by Berthelet's printing it in 1536 (STC 19214).

An original work of the 1520s published in Antwerp, perhaps around 1529, was Simon Fish's *Supplicacyon for the beggers* (STC 10883).[137] Fiercely anti-clerical but supporting the king in his fight against Rome, the *Supplicacyon* is of interest because of its size and means of distribution: a single quire of eight folios, according to Foxe it was 'thrown and scattered at the procession in Westminster' at the opening of Parliament in 1529.[138] The book was answered (at greater length) by Thomas More in *The supplycacyon of soulys . . . Agaynst the supplycacyon of beggars* (STC 18092), but the innovation of printed pamphlet polemics meant that it had already achieved wide circulation, perhaps even approved by the king himself.[139] Together with another 1529 work of Fish, *The summe of the holye scripture* (STC 3036), it was not to be published again until 1546 (STC 10884).

Thomas Cranmer

The thirty-eight-year reign of Henry VIII has inevitably occupied much of this chapter. His father, Henry VII, reigned twenty-four years (1485–1509), his son and daughter, Edward VI and Mary Tudor, for not much more than a decade between them (1547–53, 1553–58). The reigns of Henry VIII and his children will be considered in relation to Thomas Cranmer, who spanned all three reigns. As noted above, Cranmer had appeared with Henry and Cromwell on the title-page of the Great Bible in 1539, which Cromwell had masterminded and for which Cranmer had written the Preface. Within a year Cromwell was dead, executed in 1540 by his friend, the king; Cranmer had a fine career in front of him but was to be burnt in 1556 by the king's daughter, Mary Tudor.

After a university career, Cranmer had followed Warham as archbishop of Canterbury in 1533. A brief view of the publications for which he was responsible (and which he wrote, or wrote for) is important, both to link with the Great Bible and to demonstrate the development of an official, and officially enforced, English publication programme of the Reformed Church, approached hesitantly in the last years of Henry VIII but implemented in the reign of his son, Edward VI, and overturned (briefly) in Mary Tudor's reign. In 1543 Cranmer offered the Book of Homilies to Convocation at Canterbury (it was rejected); in the same year the conservative 'King's Book' (*A necessary doctrine and erudition for any christen man*, STC 5168) was published to replace the 'Bishops' Book' (*The institution of a christen man*, STC 5163) produced from Cranmer's office in 1537;[140] in 1544 a Litany was published (STC 10620);[141] in 1545 the King's Primer (STC

---

[136] *BMC XI*, pp. 67, 209.
[137] It was proscribed in the 1529 list of prohibited books (see n.67 above). For Fish, see *ODNB*.
[138] *A&M* (*TAMO*, 1563 edn, 3.497).
[139] For printed 'clamour writing' in this period, see Wendy Scase, *Literature and Complaint in England 1272–1553* (Oxford, 2007), pp. 147–69.
[140] The King's Book appeared in Latin in the following year (STC 5178).
[141] In 1543 Whitchurch and Grafton had been given a seven-year privilege to print a number of Latin and English service books ('Press, Politics and Religion', p. 595).

16034) was issued to replace earlier primers, the successors of the Books of Hours.[142] In January 1547 the king died and Edward, schooled as a Protestant from the start, came to the throne; the Protestant Richard Grafton became King's Printer.[143] The Book of Homilies (*STC* 13638.5) was published the same year,[144] the Order of the Communion (*STC* 16456.5) and the Catechism (*STC* 5992.5) in 1548, and the Book of Common Prayer in 1549 (*STC* 16267–77), revised in 1552 (*STC* 16279–90.5).

It was not until 1550 that Cranmer was cited as author, and this was of a controversial work, *A defence of the true and catholike doctrine of the sacrament of the body and bloud of Christ* (*STC* 6000–02), which defended the Protestant view of the Mass.[145] The work went through three editions in 1550, was translated into French and published in London in 1552 (*STC* 6003.5) and into Latin by John Cheke in 1553 (*STC* 6004). It was answered almost at once (in Paris (*STC* 22819) and Rouen (*STC* 11592) respectively) by Richard Smith, the leading Oxford conservative, and by the (now deprived) bishop of Winchester, Stephen Gardiner,[146] to whom Cranmer responded in 1551 with *An answere against the false calumniacions of D. Richarde Smyth* and *An answere . . . vnto a crafty cauillation by S. Gardiner* (*STC* 5990.5, 5991).[147] The First Act of Uniformity (1549) was now followed by the Second Act (1552), in which Roman Catholic doctrine, practices and rituals were abolished. Issued to enforce the use of the Book of Common Prayer, they effected the demise of Latin and the rise of English as the language of the Church in England and the language of print. Roman Catholicism was at an end.

Or so it seemed. However, in July 1553 the king died, and, after the brief attempt to install Jane Grey on the throne, Mary Tudor became queen. Smith became vice-chancellor of Oxford, and Gardiner was restored to Winchester and appointed Lord Chancellor (but died in 1555). When Gardiner's (carefully worded) Latin defence of the royal supremacy, *De vera obedientia* (1535, *STC* 11584), appeared in English translation in 1553 (*STC* 11585), it had been translated and published in Rouen by the Protestant bishop of Ossory, John Bale, in condemnation of its author as a turncoat.[148] In 1556 the press was called into play to print Cranmer's six recantations and his final speech, all of which he spectacularly rejected in the pulpit and then in the flames.[149]

---

[142] For the first reformed primers in English, see Mary C. Erler, 'Devotional Literature', in *CHBB III*, pp. 495–525 (504–05).

[143] To be succeeded by John Cawood as Queen's Printer in 1553. Printers had become entirely partisan by this date.

[144] All other sermons were banned by a proclamation of September 1548 (*STC* 7818); *TRP* 1.432–33 (no. 313).

[145] It was the evangelical printers who supported his family after his execution (*ODNB*).

[146] In 1537 Smith had been appointed master of Whittington College and rector of St Michael Paternoster Royal; on Edward's accession he had recanted twice, his earlier books burnt and his recantations published (*STC* 222822, 222824); a turncoat careerist, he ended his life vice-chancellor of the University of Douai publishing from the new Douai printing press (*ODNB*). Unlike Smith, Gardiner was a Catholic (and when necessary a crypto-Catholic) all his life; at the fall of Cromwell he became chancellor of Cambridge but was imprisoned for most of Edward's reign.

[147] John Foxe translated the latter into Latin but could not find a publisher, despite his relationship with the Basel printshops at the time (*ODNB*).

[148] On Bale, a great friend of, and influence on, John Foxe, see *ODNB*.

[149] For a graphic description, see Jasper Ridley, *Thomas Cranmer* (Oxford, 1962), pp. 405–11.

The End

It will have been clear that many of the publications of the years after 1520 were polemical, whether written by comparatively minor figures like Fish or Bale, or major figures like Fisher and Gardiner.[150] The sheer range and speed of writings coming from the press were remarkable. In contrast, however, Mary's reign has traditionally been seen as one which did not make effective use of the press – perhaps her preferred emphasis was on instructing the laity 'not through self-education but through the two pillars of the Catholic church, the clergy and ritual'.[151] The Protestant printers Grafton and Whitchurch were put out of business and replaced by the Catholic printers Robert Caly and John Wayland respectively. John Cawood became Queen's Printer. A manifesto of the Catholic faith was published by the bishop of London, Edmund Bonner, in 1555:[152] *A profitable and necessarye doctryne* (*STC* 3281.5), a re-working of the *King's Book* of 1543, together with *Certaine homelyes* (*STC* 3285.1), with some sermons from the Book of Homilies of 1547.[153] Both were to go through numerous issues and editions, all in 1555. The intention was to replace these with the comprehensive catechism of the Dominican Bartolomé Carranza de Miranda (to be translated from the Spanish) and a set of model sermons by Gardiner's former chaplain, Thomas Watson, bishop of Lincoln. Only the latter reached print, in June 1558: *Holsome and catholyke doctryne concerninge the seuen sacramentes ... set forth in maner of shorte sermons* (*STC* 25112). Mary died in November.

Martin Luther had indeed stirred a hornet's nest. The gentle first half-century of print, when (it seemed) the secular clergy read their Latin service books and scholarly works and the laity read their English devotional works, was followed by religious turbulence on a scale not known since, under three monarchs, Henry, Edward and Mary (not to mention the fourth, Elizabeth I, who is beyond the scope of this volume). Print had become a speedy medium to disseminate a range of opinions, variously orthodox or heretical, mannered or vitriolic, depending on the reign, the occasion, and the author. Latin had been largely usurped by English, thanks to a powerful and opinionated literate public. The printing presses had flourished, largely replacing the early reliance on Antwerp and the Continent for Protestant publishing. Censorship had become increasingly effective, by draconian means: in Mary's reign (1557) the Stationers' Company was given a charter of incorporation, turning it into 'a self-regulating closed shop' with powers of search and seizure of prohibited books.[154]

---

[150] For details and discussion of Gardiner's Latin polemical writings, see *ODNB*.

[151] 'Press, Politics and Religion', p. 605. For a detailed argument against this long-standing thesis, see Eamon Duffy, *Fires of Faith: Catholic England under Mary Tudor* (New Haven, CT and London, 2009), pp. 57–78. Duffy points out that the presses were heavily involved with printing service books for the restored Latin mass (59). For an assessment of the publishing performance of Mary's bishops, see David Loades, 'The Marian Episcopate', in *The Church of Mary Tudor*, ed. Duffy and Loades, pp. 33–56 (48–50).

[152] Under Henry, Bonner had been Wolsey's chaplain and then bishop of Hereford and London in quick succession until imprisoned during Edward's reign; he was to die in the Marshalsea in Elizabeth's reign (*ODNB*). He had written the vitriolic Preface to Bale's translation of *De vera obedentia*.

[153] For a comparison of the earlier and later publications, see Duffy, *Fires*, pp. 64–67.

[154] The term is Neville-Sington's ('Press, Politics and Religion', p. 606).

Much of the circumstantial evidence for the religious upheavals and tragedies of the 1520s–50s comes from John Foxe, whose *Acts and Monuments* was published in Elizabeth's reign (*STC* 11222, 1563).[155] Foxe had only been ordained three years earlier; indeed, in 1545 he had resigned his fellowship at Magdalen College, Oxford rather than enter holy orders and had spent much of the intervening years working for the Basel printers and composing, amongst other works, the Latin forerunner of *Acts and Monuments*, *Commentarii rerum in ecclesia gestarum* (Strasbourg 1554, Basel 1559).[156] His life had spanned the whole period of upheaval, and he was able to identify the value of the printing press to the religious awakening of the ordinary man. With the caveat that his positive view of the press would have been hotly contended by many in the period since 1476, his statement on the art of printing may serve as conclusion to this chapter on the secular clergy and print:

This art and science, how profitable it hath beene vnto all the whole worlde, theese oure dayes doo suffyciently declare, if that we dilygentlye waye and consyder, howe that thereby ignoraunce is vtterly banyshed, and truthe manifested and declared, and finally the poope and Antichriste there by vtterlye subuerted, whiche coulde neuer haue come to passe, if this mooste worthye science hadde not beene founde oute. For so much as otherwise, bokes were so skarse, and there wyth all of suche excessyue price, that fewe menne coulde there by attayne to knowledge or vnderstandynge, whiche now by this meanes, is made easy vnto all men.[157]

Further Reading

Primary Sources

Foxe, John, *Commentarii rerum in ecclesia gestarum* (Strasbourg 1554, Basel 1559).
_____, *Actes and monuments of these latter and perillous dayes, touching matters of the church* ('Acts and Monuments'), John Day (1563, *STC* 11222).

Secondary Sources

Arblaster, Paul, Gergely Juhász and Guido Latré, eds, *Tyndale's Testament* (Turnhout, 2002).
Aston, Margaret, *Lollards and Reformers* (London, 1984).
Elton, G.R., *Policy and Police* (Cambridge, 1972).
Erler, M.C., 'A London Anchorite, Simon Appulby: His *Fruyte of redempcyon* and its Milieu', *Viator* 29 (1998), 227–39.
Gillespie, Vincent, 'Syon and the English Market for Continental Printed Books: The Incunable Phase', in *Syon Abbey and its Books. Reading, Writing and Religion c. 1400–1700*, ed. E.A. Jones and Alexandra Walsham (Woodbridge, 2010), pp. 129–54.
Hope, Andrew, 'Conformed and Reformed: John Colet and his Reformation Reputation', in *Image, Text and Church, 1380–1600: Essays for Margaret Aston*,

---

[155] Foxe's research and concern for accuracy were remarkable for the day. Despite problems, 'the importance of *Acts and Monuments* is currently uncontested' (*ODNB*, 'Foxe, John').
[156] *A&M* brought him a prebend at Salisbury Cathedral (which he never visited, spending most of his life acting as sage and guru in the parish of St Giles Cripplegate).
[157] *A&M* (*TAMO*, 1563 edn, 3.414).

ed. Linda Clark, Maureen Jurkowski and Colin Richmond (Toronto, 2009), pp. 214–38.

Hudson, Anne, *The Premature Reformation: Wycliffite Texts and Lollard History* (Oxford, 1988).

Loades, David, 'The Marian episcopate', in *The Church of Mary Tudor*, ed. Eamon Duffy and David Loades (Aldershot and Burlington, VT, 2006), pp. 33–56.

Neville-Sington, Pamela, 'Press, Politics and Religion', in *CHBB III*, pp. 576–607.

Powell, Susan, 'After Arundel but before Luther: The First Half-Century of Print', in *After Arundel: Religious Writing in Fifteenth-Century England*, ed. Vincent Gillespie and Kantik Ghosh (Turnhout, 2011), pp. 523–541.

Reed, Arthur W., 'The Regulation of the Book Trade before the Proclamation of 1538', *Transactions of the Bibliographical Society* 15 (1920 for 1917–19), 157–84.

Rex, R.A.W., 'The English Campaign against Luther in the 1520s', *TRHS*, 5th ser., 39 (1989), 85–106.

Siebert, Frederick Seaton, *Freedom of the Press in England 1476–1776: The Rise and Decline of Government Control* (Urbana, IL, 1965).

10

The Regular Clergy

JAMES G. CLARK

The regular clergy were patrons of the printing revolution, converts to radical change at the cornerstone of the establishment. From the faint, fragmented testimony of the first, pioneering workshops, modern research has succeeded in focusing the critical contribution of the religious orders, mendicant and (perhaps especially) monastic: we now know that from Mainz, outward, through the Rhineland (Augsburg, Freiburg, Marienthal, Speyer and Basel), north and westward into the Netherlands (Brussels, Gouda, Hem, Rostock) and south of the Alps as far as Rome (Subiaco), the regulars represented more than the buyers, and occasional, benign sponsors, of the early printed book; they may also be counted among the early entrepreneurs of the press, exploiting, and perhaps, to a degree, directing the diaspora of German craftsmen, and even the practitioners – male and female religious alike – of what its first audience celebrated as the 'magical art'.[1]

This is, or has become, a story of Continental Europe. The large and culturally influential constituency of regular clergy has been left at the margins of accounts of the reception of printing in England. At first, of course, there was no compulsion for scholars to look for the traces of print culture in the English cloisters given the prevailing view that their traditions of book-learning had been forgotten long before the 42-line Bible was first seen at Frankfurt. Recently, the view

---

[1] For the role of the religious in the emergence of the press in Europe, see especially M. Davies, *The Gutenberg Bible* (London, 1996), p. 41; R.R. Post, *The Modern Devotion: Confrontations with Reformation and Humanism* (Leiden, 1968), pp. 551–53; K. Jensen, 'Printing the Bible in the Fifteenth Century: Devotion, Philology, Commerce', in *Incunabula and their Readers: Reading, Selling and Using Books in the Fifteenth Century*, ed. K. Jensen (London, 2003), pp. 115–38 (131–33); C. Beier, 'Producing, Buying and Decorating Books in the Age of Gutenberg', in *Early Printed Books as Material Objects: Proceedings of the Conference Organised by the Ifla Rare Books and Manuscripts Section, Munich, 19–21 August, 2009*, ed. B. Wagner and M. Reed (Munich, 2010) pp. 68–69, 75. For particular presses and productions, see R. Proctor, 'Ulrich von Ellenbog and the Press of S. Ulrich at Augsburg', *The Library*, n.s., 14 (1903), 163–79; H. Roelvink, 'The Missal of 1504 of the Nordic Franciscans', in *Franciscans in Sweden: Medieval Remnants of Franciscan Activities*, ed. H. Roelvink (Assen, 1998), pp. 152–71 (161–62). For monastic patronage of a master printer, see B.C. Halporn, ed., *Correspondence of John Amerbach. Early Printing in its Social Context* (Ann Arbor, MI, 2000), p. 75 (Letter 37: Brother Wilhelm Weldicus, canon regular priest of Dirmstein to Amerbach, 31 August 1497). For the contribution of women religious, see M. Conway, *The Diario of the Printing Press of San Jacopo di Ripoli* (Florence, 1999); Elissa Weaver, *Convent Theatre in Early Modern Italy: Spiritual Fun and Learning for Women* (Cambridge, 2002), p. 27 & n. For women religious and the art of woodblock printing, see W. Scheepsma, *Medieval Religious Women in the Low Countries: The 'Modern Devotion', the Canonesses of Windesheim, and their Writings* (Woodbridge, 2004), pp. 167–68.

has been revised. Now there is an emerging consensus that the seventy-five years after 1445 saw a (final) flowering of learning in monastic England: the academic capacity of the monasteries achieved its zenith in the years around 1500; their libraries (conventual and collegiate) were reorganised, yielding some of the best examples of the bibliographical art of any period, such as William Charyte's catalogue (1477x1494) of the (Augustinian) canons' library at Leicester, one of the largest to survive from medieval England, and Thomas Betson's remarkable *Registrum* (*c*.1500) of the books of which he was custodian at Birgittine Syon; and at a number of houses both of canons and monks books were made once more, not on a large scale, certainly, but still with a degree of scribal and artistic skill that can connect them with earlier centuries.[2] Yet the place, if any, of print among the pre-Reformation regulars remains for the most part unresolved. Only Syon Abbey has emerged from the shadows with any clarity – largely by means of Betson – as a place possessed not only of a general learned culture but also of a particular engagement with print.[3] Print came late (comparatively speaking) even to Syon: the reception, transmission and production (i.e. preparation for publication) of printed books by the Birgittine men and women took off only at the turn of the fifteenth century and was a dynamic feature of its public and pastoral life for little more than a decade and a half, at its most intense perhaps in the years from 1519 to 1534.[4]

The continuing obscurity of the scene beyond Syon, both monastic and mendicant, male and female, rests squarely on the state of the evidence. Scarcely more than 100 surviving printed books can be connected with any certainty to regulars in England before the Henrician suppressions (under Wolsey, 1524–28, and Cromwell, 1536–40) had been completed. Of course, the true extent of their institutional and individual holdings of incunabula and later imprints before 1540 can never be known, but as the remains of a constituency of more than 600 houses and a somewhat resurgent population of 10–12,000 inhabitants (the majority of whom in 1536 were too young themselves to remember a world before print), the number seems disproportionately small.[5] Overall, the survival

---

[2]   For the revised portrait of monastic learning in the pre-Reformation period see, for example, P. Lee, *Nunneries, Learning and Spirituality in Late Medieval England. The Dominican Priory of Dartford* (York, 2001); A. Barrett, *Anne Bulkeley and Her Book. Fashioning Female Piety in Early Tudor England. A Study of London, British Library, Harley MS 494*, Texts and Transitions 2 (Turnhout, 2009); *Syon Abbey and its Books*. For the academic presence of the monks, see P. Cunich, 'Benedictine Monks at the University of Oxford and the Dissolution of the Monasteries', in *The Benedictines at Oxford*, ed. H. Wansborough and A. Marrett-Crosby (London, 1997), pp. 155–84. For the catalogue of Leicester Abbey, see *Libraries of the Augustinian Canons*, ed. A.G. Watson and M.T. Webber, CBMLC 3 (1995), pp. 105–399 (A20). For Thomas Betson's Syon *registrum*, see *Syon Abbey*. On the making of manuscripts in this period, see n.36 below.
[3]   For Syon, see especially, V. Gillespie, 'The Book and the Brotherhood: Reflections on the Lost Library of Syon Abbey', in *The English Medieval Book: Studies in Memory of Jeremy Griffiths*, ed. A.S.G. Edwards, Vincent Gillespie and Ralph Hanna, British Library Studies in the History of the Book (London, 2000), pp. 185–208, and 'Syon and the English Market for Continental Printed Books: The Incunable Phase', in *Syon Abbey*, pp. 104–28.
[4]   This period of productive, printed publication is elaborated in 'Syon Abbey and its Religious Publications'. See also now S. Powell, 'Syon Abbey as a Centre for Text Production', in *Saint Birgitta, Syon and Vadstena. Papers from a Symposium in Stockholm, 6–9 October 2007*, ed. C. Gejrot (Stockholm, 2010), pp. 50–67.
[5]   For the recovery and rise in the population of regular religious, see S.H. Rigby, *English Society in the later Middle Ages. Class, Gender, Status* (London, 1995), p. 215. For examples of

rate of manuscript books is significantly higher for this period: the ratio of script to print rises to between 20:1 and as many as 50:1 in several well-preserved monastic collections.[6] There are chains of convents, including some of the largest (Augustinian) canon houses (Merton, Oseney, Waltham), the southern Cistercian settlements (Cleeve in Somerset, Forde in Dorset, Robertsbridge in Sussex), and the four Oxford *studia* of the friars, for which there is virtually no physical trace of print (from either side of 1500) at all.[7] The preservation appears particularly meagre in comparison with monastic mainland Europe: there are 798 surviving volumes printed before 1500 bearing the provenance of the Austrian (Benedictine) abbey of Melk; for the (Benedictine) abbey of Augsburg of SS Ulrich and Afra the figure is 1040; it has been shown that roughly 50 per cent of the 20,000 incunabula held at the Munich Bayerische Staatsbibliothek are of monastic provenance.[8]

The evidence from England, of course, could be regarded as final proof of the torpid book culture of pre-Reformation religious, of their disengagement from, if not active disdain for, the new medium of print. Yet it may be more accurate to see it as a sign of the particular status of print in a regular clerical context. By definition, these were books not formed exclusively from their own resources (or those of the corporate network) as many manuscript compilations still were, even in the second quarter of the sixteenth century. They were secured from a variety of sources beyond the convent walls, generally ad hoc and ad hominem to serve a specific purpose; as such, it seems that many of them were prone to pass into a parallel collection, perhaps somewhat ephemeral, certainly eclectic, a penumbra of print surrounding the core of the convent's books. Their currency surely also cast them in a different light at the dispersal of conventual libraries after 1536: their market value could scarcely match that of many manuscripts, which were secured without delay by eager antiquarians, sometimes almost in their original self-sequence.[9] In fact, it appears printed books were of comparatively little interest to the officers of Augmentations and surrendered religious were able to retain them, a concession which, ironically, may have curtailed their

growth among the monastic and canons orders between the early fifteenth and early sixteenth centuries, see D. Knowles and R.N. Hadcock, *Medieval Religious Houses England and Wales* (London, 1953), pp. 61, 65, 114, 152 (Bury, Evesham, St Osyth, Rievaulx).

[6] See, for example, the record of surviving provenanced books from a number of the Benedictine cathedral priories, such as Canterbury, Norwich, Rochester, Winchester and Worcester, from the Cistercian abbey of Fountains, and notable canon houses, such as Llanthony secunda and Waltham, in *MLGB* (1), pp. 29–47, 88–89, 108–112,135–39, 160–64, 192–93, 199–201, 205–15; and *MLGB* (2), pp. 10–12, 37, 41–43, 50–51, 58–59, 66, 68–69.

[7] The first reference-point for the printed books of the regulars in England remains *MLGB* (1) and *MLGB* (2). Now the evidence, especially in respect of provenance, is elaborated by Bod-inc. Fresh insights into provenance are also offered in the continuing revision of the catalogue of incunabula at Cambridge University Library, at: <http://www.lib.cam.ac.uk/deptserv/rarebooks/inc.html> (accessed 11 September 2013).

[8] Beier, 'Producing, Buying and Decorating Books', pp. 70, 74; B. Wagner, 'The Incunable Collection of the Bayerische Staatsbibliothek München and its Provenances', in *Books and their Owners: Provenance Information and the European Cultural Heritage*, ed. D. Shaw (London, 2005), pp. 55–60.

[9] Perhaps the most notable examples are the 120 manuscripts of glossed scripture and theological commentaries from the Benedictine abbey at Bury St Edmunds which passed into the library of Pembroke College, Cambridge: *MLGB* (1), pp. 17–19; *MLGB* (2), p. 5.

chances of preservation.[10] There is at least a hint that prints were transferred from the conventual collection at the eleventh hour, perhaps to provide for the brethren as they confronted secularisation.[11] Of course, the commercial value of manuscripts has continued to eclipse early printed books and while over time valuable monastic codices have been recovered from private ownership, printed books of monastic or mendicant provenance glimpsed fleetingly at auction too often have been reabsorbed into the closed world of the collector: printed books known to survive from (Benedictine) Colchester, Crowland, the convent of the Marlborough Carmelites, and the Augustinian priory at Walsingham, whose canons rose against Henry VIII, have not been seen for more than a generation.[12]

Recent re-cataloguing of the major collections at Cambridge and Oxford has increased slightly the tally of survivors, subjected the whole to modern methods of physical analysis, and also provided many of the raw data – indices of printer, press and provenance, etc. – essential for the study of transmission and reception.[13] The recent re-focus on female religious has also brought a handful of hitherto unnoticed survivors to wider attention.[14] At the same time an expanding corpus of edited catalogues and inventories of institutional and personal libraries has begun to describe a context – bibliographical, certainly, but also more broadly intellectual – in which these scant survivals may best be viewed.[15]

Print came to the attention of the regular clergy as early as any constituency of English society. The first documented presence of a printed book within the precinct walls of a convent can be dated to within twenty years of the Gutenberg Bible: it has been suggested that the manuscript copy of Chrysostom's *Homilies* made at the cathedral priory of Christ Church, Canterbury, in 1474 by the

---

[10] For an instance of religious dispensed from their vows at the Dissolution securing permission to retain their books, see the letter of Abbot John Stonywell of Pershore addressed to Thomas Cromwell: PRO, SP 1/143/1467 (*LP Henry VIII*, 14/1.349). See also J. Youings, *The Dissolution of the Monasteries* (London, 1971), pp. 174–75 (175).

[11] There is a suggestive memorandum preserved in a Bible (Venice, 1478: Oxford, Keble College, A 62) from Newark Priory in Nottinghamshire in which the prior provides the book to one of the canons barely days before the surrender in the winter of 1538.

[12] See Alexander Barclay, *Ship of Fools* (London, 1509) (1959 Kraus catalogue) [Colchester]; Erasmus, *Moriae Encomium* (Basel, 1521) (1950 Wilson catalogue) [Crowland]; Bartholomeus Anglicus, *De proprietatibus rerum* (no place, 1488) (Kerslake catalogue) [Marlborough]; Rodericus Zamorensis, *Speculum vitae humanae* (Paris, 1510), signed by Prior Richard Vowell [Walsingham]. See also *MLGB* (1), pp. 129, 281; *MLGB* (2), pp. 14–15, 66, 111.

[13] For the revision of the catalogue at Cambridge, see n.7 above. For the Oxford catalogue, see Bod-inc. For additions to and refinements of the information in the British Library's *Catalogue of Books Printed in the XVth Century now in the British Museum Library*, 13 parts (London, 1907–63), see <http://www.bl.uk/reshelp/findhelprestype/incanab/incunabulacoll/index.html> (accessed 11 September 2013).

[14] Mary Erler records a number of new identifications, of which six are printed in her *Women, Reading and Piety in Late Medieval England* (Cambridge, 2003), pp. 139–46. E.A. Jones and Alexandra Walsham have brought into focus a clutch of Syon books recently deposited at Exeter University Library: *Syon Abbey and its Books*, p. 252.

[15] In particular, the volumes of CBMLC, in which the records of the regulars are dominant: *The Libraries of the Cistercians*, ed. D.N. Bell, CBMLC 3 (1992); *English Benedictine Libraries: The Shorter Catalogues*, ed. R. Sharpe, J.P. Carley, K. Friis-Jensen and A.G. Watson, CBMLC 4 (1996) (hereafter *EBL*); *Dover Priory*, ed. W.P. Stoneman, CBMLC 5 (1999); *The Libraries of the Augustinian Canons*, ed. M.T. Webber and A.G. Watson, CBMLC 6 (1998); *Peterborough Abbey*, ed. K. Friis-Jensen and J. Willoughby, CBMLC 8 (2001); B.C. Barker-Benfield, ed., *St Augustine's Abbey*, 3 vols, CBMLC 14 (2008).

hired scribe Theodoricus Werken was reproduced from the printed edition of 1470 (Georgius Lauer: Rome) prepared by Francesco Griffolini.[16] It would be mistaken to conclude from the Canterbury example that the early reception of print was in some way stratified, passing in the first instance through religious houses of greatest corporate wealth and cultural reputation. Prior John Herbert of (Augustinian) Thremhall in Essex, a tiny cell whose total value was set at £60 p.a. in 1535, purchased at least two printed books during his priorate (1474–89), a copy of the writings of Thomas of Cantimpré (Cologne, no date) and of Johannes Junior's *Scala coeli* (Louvain, 1485).[17] Three monks of the Cistercian abbey of Stratford Langthorne in Essex, a convent of second rank, collaborated in the purchase of a printed bible (Strasbourg, no date) in four volumes as early as 1480.[18] Print appears to have been in the hands of William Spynk of Norwich before he became prior of the (Benedictine) cathedral monastery in 1488.[19] It may be more than coincidence that each of these early witnesses was located in south-east England, within radial reach of the principal points-of-entry for German, Flemish and French imports.[20] It was opportunity, in this instance, proximity, and not status that secured an early encounter with print.

If the canons and monks of the Home Counties were in advance of their northern and western brethren, it was not by a wide margin. Print may have reached (Benedictine) Durham Cathedral Priory as early as the mid-1470s. Two printed books, copies of Scotus (Strasbourg, 1474) and a two-volume set of homilies (Cologne, c.1475) bear inscriptions naming John Aukland, prior of the Durham *studium* at Stamford before 1475 and warden of Durham College, Oxford, from c.1481; the homiliary also holds an inscription naming William Law, scholar of college from 1460 to 1473 and Aukland's immediate predecessor as warden (1475–c.1481): these books may have reached Durham before the prints of its bishop, John Shirwood, who was an early connoisseur of the press but remained in Italy until 1477.[21] Before the end of the same decade, John Manbe may have returned from Oxford with the earliest of three surviving printed books to bear his *ex libris*;[22] Manbe's confrère and Oxford contemporary, William Law, certainly purchased a four-volume edition of Nicholas of

[16] 'English Purchases', pp. 268–90 (270). See also R.A.B. Mynors, 'A Fifteenth-Century Scribe: T. Werken', *TCBS* 1, no.2 (1950), 97–104.
[17] These volumes survive respectively as Gloucester Cathedral, D. 3. 18, and London, Dr Williams's Library, 4010 Q.10. See also *MLGB* (1), p. 311.
[18] Now, CUL Inc. 124 (shelf-mark BSS.120.A81.5). An inscription reads 'constat S[tratford Langthorne] quem fratres Robertus Serle, Thomas Lamborn et Thomas London emerunt AD 1480'. See also *MLGB* (1), pp. 183, 307.
[19] See Manchester, John Rylands Library, R32528 (copies of Antonius de Rampegollis (Cologne 1487) bound together with Theobaldus Anguilbertus). See also *MLGB* (1), pp. 138, 286.
[20] It is worth noting, for example, that the annual fair at the monastic town of Bury St Edmunds was recognised as a cross-current of Continental traders: M. Bailey, *Medieval Suffolk. An Economic and Social History, 1200–1500*, History of Suffolk (Woodbridge, 2011), pp. 119–20.
[21] The books are now Durham Cathedral Library Inc. 4a, 13 a-b. For John Aukland and William Law, see *MLGB* (2), pp. 85, 92; *BRUO* 1.76–77, 2.1111–12. See also A.I. Doyle, 'The Printed Books of the Last Monks of Durham', *The Library*, 6th ser., 10 (1988), 203–19 (206). For the printed books of Bishop John Shirwood, see 'English Purchases', pp. 270–71.
[22] John Manbe's *ex libris* appears in Durham Cathedral, Inc. 1f (Nicholas of Lyra: Nuremberg, 1481); Inc. 11a (Gregory, *Moralia*: Cologne, c.1476); Inc. 12 (Alexander Carpenter: Cologne, 1480). See also *MLGB* (2), pp. 93–94; *BRUO* 3.1212–13.

Lyra's Biblical postils in 1480, perhaps also at Oxford.[23] We do not know how early a 1474 printing of *Speculum discipulorum Christi* which bore the *ex libris* of Mount Grace entered that house; perhaps it was at the time of printing.[24] It may have been scarcely more than a year before print had also reached the regulars of the West: a print of Bartholomew the Englishman's *De proprietatibus rerum* (Strasbourg, 1480) bearing the *ex libris* of a Tewkesbury monk may also have been an early acquisition.[25] It has been suggested that scenes depicted in the misericords of the choir of St Augustine's Abbey, Bristol (Augustinian canons; now Bristol Cathedral), were modelled on Caxton's *Historye of reynart the foxe* printed at Westminster in 1481 (*STC* 20919).[26]

In fact, there are sufficient survivors bearing dated, or datable, inscriptions to suggest that at the turn of the decade, 1479x1480, print was no longer an absolute novelty for many canons and monks, even in the provinces. Now print entered their precincts at regular intervals, although it may not have been until close to the turn of the century itself (i.e. 1500) that it could be said to have become a commonplace. Whether the same pace of change was witnessed in the mendicant network, and in the nunneries, can scarcely even be speculated given the paucity of survivors. It seems a variety of incunabula were in circulation in the provincial convents of the largest orders, of Dominicans and Franciscans (respectively, Blackfriars and Greyfriars), by the early years of the sixteenth century, but there are neither the dated inscriptions nor the biographical data to pinpoint the moment of their first appearance.[27] If print was not only familiar to, but also readily available among, the convents of Black and Grey Friars as much as a decade before 1500, this may not have been true of the minor mendicant orders. Certainly there are no early provenances for the Augustinian, Carmelite, Crutched, Trinitarian or Observant convents amongst the survivors. The London Augustinians invested in a new library before 1467, perhaps the very last new collection for regular clergy to be stocked before the Reformation; the venture attracted early donations but the survivors are exclusively manuscripts.[28] Although almost one-third (six out of nineteen) of

---

[23] For William Law's set of Nicholas of Lyra, see Durham Cathedral, Inc. 1a–d. See also *MLGB* (2), p. 92; *BRUO*, 2.1111–12.

[24] The book has been untraced since the sales of Thomas Rawlinson's library which ended in March 1734: *MLGB* (1), p. 132.

[25] An identical *ex libris*, of John Evesham, also appears in a twelfth-century manuscript of Jerome, now Hereford Cathedral, MS P. iv. 6.

[26] J. Rogan, 'Monuments of the Cathedral' in *Bristol Cathedral. History and Architecture*, ed. J. Rogan (Stroud, 2000), pp. 113–31 (120).

[27] For example, a copy of William of Ockham's commentary on the first book of the Lombard's Sentences ([Urach], 1483), now London, Lambeth Palace, 1483.5, provenanced to the Canterbury Greyfriars; a copy of the works of Bernard of Clairvaux's sermons on the Song of Songs (Paris, 1494), now London, Lambeth Palace, 1494.2 provenanced to the Greenwich Observants; a copy of Antonius Andreae (Venice, 1496), now Oxford, Merton College, B. 8. G. 17, connected to the Newcastle and Coventry Carmelites, bearing only a partial personal inscription: MLGB (1), pp. 48, 93, 134, 283.

[28] Bishop John Lowe of St Asaph (d. 1467) gave at least two manuscript books to the London Augustinians 'pro novo librario': BL, Additional MS 34652 (Sidonius Appollinaris, *Epistulae*) and Dublin, Trinity College, MS 486 (Higden's *Polychronicon*). A single surviving printed book, a bible (Venice, 1484), now Glasgow, University Library, Dp. E. 6, is connected to the convent by two inscriptions naming friars, one with the year 1521. See *MLGB* (1), pp. 125, 280.

the surviving printed books connected to nuns or nunneries are incunabula, the earliest of them an edition of 1483 (a French translation of Boccaccio's *De casibus*, from Lyons), none of them appears to have been in the possession of a professed woman before 1499x1500. This first dateable provenance, preserved on a copy of Caxton's 1494 print of Walter Hilton's *Ladder of Perfecc[i]on* (*STC* 14042), was a profession gift made by James Greenhalgh to Joan Sewell of Syon Abbey. Of course, the giving of profession gifts was common practice in houses of women and it may be only the contingency of preservation which has left Sewell's book as the earliest printed example.[29]

It remains very difficult to assess the scale and scope of the printed books that passed into monastic and mendicant precincts, patchily at first but then with greater frequency as the century turned. Perhaps the only secure assertion can be that print never entirely displaced, or replaced, the collections of manuscripts which had accrued in these houses throughout their history. The largest regular libraries of the last century before the Reformation may have held collections of between 2500 and 5000 books: the largest library lists compiled in this period run to around 2000 entries, and so far as can be known they capture only the principal, conventual collection; subordinate holdings, including the personal libraries collected by many individual religious are likely to have raised the overall total.[30] Beyond Syon, none of these documents can be taken as a complete record of books held at the time of compilation. The proportions vary, rarely rising above 5 per cent of the total; only the Dissolution inventories surviving from the Lincolnshire circuit indicate instances where print was a dominant presence: of thirty-five institutional libraries investigated, eleven monasteries and four mendicant convents were found to hold such a quantity of printed books that manuscript holdings were deemed to be marginal.[31] Generally, there is nothing to suggest that accessions of print ever matched the number of manuscripts book-for-book. Betson's Syon catalogue bears witness to the substitution of manuscript copies of certain texts with printed editions.[32]

There is the suggestion of the same, sporadic substitution of manuscript for printed editions in the succession of inventories of books assigned by (Benedictine) Canterbury Cathedral Priory to its *studium* at Oxford, Canterbury College, between 1459 and 1534. The first of two inventories of 1501 records

[29] For Greenhalgh's gift to Sewell, see Erler, *Women, Reading and Piety*, p. 121. For the custom in general, see p. 44, and N.B. Warren, *Spiritual Economies: Female Monasticism in Later Medieval England* (Philadelphia, PA, 2001), pp. 60, 186 and references cited there.

[30] The largest library lists of this period are those from Leicester, St Augustine's, Canterbury and Syon. See *Libraries of the Augustinian Canons*, ed. Watson and Webber, pp. 105–399 (A20); *St Augustine's Abbey*, ed. Barker-Benfield, *passim*; *Syon Abbey*.

[31] The inventories, which are preserved in BL, Royal Appendix 69, fols 2r–9v, were compiled to record only manuscript copies of works of historical and devotional interest, as the heading on the first leaf underlines. Where no such works were to be found and there was a profusion of printed material, the compiler entered only a bald statement to this effect; neither numbers, nor titles, are specified. The monasteries recorded as holding print in quantity were Elsham, Kyme, Newstead, Thornholm, Wellow (Augustinian), Humberston (Benedictine: Tiron), Hotton [?Hough] (Carthusian), Louth Park (Cistercian), Haverholme, Ormsby (Gilbertine) and Newhouse (Premonstratensian). The mendicant convents found with such collections were the Augustinians of Grimsby and Lincoln, the Boston Carmelites, and the Franciscans of Grimsby.

[32] *Syon Abbey*, pp. li–lvi at lv.

the first accession of three, perhaps four, printed texts to the college collection, an eclectic mix, of Plutarch's *De liberis educandis*, bound together with a papal letter pronouncing the papal jubilee, Denys the Carthusian's *De celebratione*, John Lathbury's commentary on Lamentations (perhaps the most widely disseminated imprints of the early Oxford press) and, perhaps, the popular *Fortalicium fidei contra Iudeos* of Alfonso de Spina.[33] Twenty years on, a fresh inventory shows another mix of printed acquisitions, Nicholas de Orbellis, Willelmus Durandus's *De jurisdictione ecclesiastica*, Stephanus Brulefer, *Reportata in opus Bonventurae super sententias*, a *Breviloquium* (either that of Bonaventure or Reuchlin), Cicero's Tusculan disputations, an unidentified work of Philip Beroaldus, Pomponius's *De situ orbis*, Robert Duval's *Compendium memorandorum Plinii* and (it would appear) the humanist translation of Aristotle's *Ethica*.[34] A number of the purchases noted in the personal accounts of Prior William More of (Benedictine) Worcester point to the deliberate provision of printed versions of standard authorities readily accessible in manuscript; why else might the prior send to a distant bookseller for a copy of Lyndwood's *Provinciale*?[35] Yet there are too few instances of the kind to conclude that any house (of any order) undertook systematically to re-stock their holdings. Even the texts in greatest demand, the prescribed authorities of the academic syllabus, and the most popular pastoral manuals, were provided in an ad hoc mix of script and print. Moreover, there were still new accessions of manuscripts; indeed the years down to the Dissolution witnessed something of a resurgence of the monastic taste for the deluxe, decorated codex; as in mainland Europe, it may have been coupled with a renewed interest in the scribal art as a tool of observant reform.[36] If it was a question of securing new or rare authorities for conventual readers, at least before 1500 manuscript remained the necessary medium.[37] Even at the end (i.e. 1536x1540) it may have been rare for print to have risen above 10 per cent of the total of the conventual collection. The abundance of print at Premonstratensian Newhouse drew comment from the anonymous auditor at the Dissolution

---

[33] The inventory identifies only the first three as 'impressus' or 'pressuris in papiro': *Canterbury College, Oxford*, ed. W.A. Pantin, 4 vols, Oxford Historical Society, New Series, 6, 7, 8, (1946–85), i, 18–33 (20–21, 23).

[34] *Canterbury College, Oxford*, ed. Pantin, i, 55–65 (61–62).

[35] For the list of accessions (purchases) made during the priorate of William More, see *EBL*, pp. 662–74 (B117).

[36] For instances of late manuscript production at the hands of regulars themselves, see the copy of John of Glastonbury's chronicle made by William Wych, monk of Glastonbury, for Abbot Richard Beere, now Princeton University Library, Garrett MS 153; an historical and literary miscellany and an English *Brut*, both of which bear the signature of John Newton, cellarer and subsequently abbot of Battle: San Marino, CA, Huntington Library, HM 3039; Illinois, University of Chicago Joseph Regenstein Library, MS 259. For writing as reform, see Bishop Redman's visitation at Sulby in 1491: J.A. Gribbin, *The Premonstratensian Order in Late Medieval England*, Studies in the History of Medieval Religion 16 (Woodbridge, 2001), p. 164. The renewed commitment to scribal practice was not unique to England, and in the European mainland was a feature of female as well as male communities: *Saint Birgitta, Syon and Vadstena*, ed. Gejrot, pp. 161–87 (essays by Hedstrom and Lindell).

[37] For example, the group of Greek texts copied at Reading by the scribe Johannes Serbopoulos, including copies of Theodore Gaza's Greek grammar completed in 1489 (now Cambridge, Trinity College, MS R.9.22 (823)) and 1494 (Oxford, Corpus Christi College, 254), which predated the first, Aldine printed texts by six years.

precisely because it was unusual.[38] Here a hoard of 142 books, recorded in an Elizabethan inventory, apparently recovered from the Cluniac priory of Monk Bretton, appears an anomaly. After the suppression five of the brethren, among them the former prior, had shared a household (and possibly some form of common life) together with treasures taken from their monastery. The books appear all to have been printed editions but while it is plausible, by date of publication, etc., that some were acquired before the suppression of the house, by no means is it certain that as a whole the collection had come from the convent.[39]

The survival rate of print from mendicant networks and the nunneries is too slight to reach further than speculation on its place in their conventual collections. The anonymous auditor of Lincolnshire convents, as it were a pseudo-Leland, saw a predominance of print in four friars' libraries, of the Grimsby and Lincoln Greyfriars, the Lincoln Augustinians and the Boston Carmelites, the latter especially well supplied, 'multi sunt ibidem libri, sed tamen commune impressive'.[40] Overall, there is nothing to suggest that print was any more prominent in the mendicants' libraries than in those of the monks and canons. Of the nuns' holdings of print, David Bell has highlighted the list of twenty-nine books at (Benedictine) Barking Abbey that survives in an inventory compiled by the executors of the abbey's former steward, William Pownsett, in 1554.[41] The majority of the titles, an eclectic mix, appear to have been printed; some, such as Caxton's Aesop and Erasmus's *Enchiridion*, certainly were.[42] The inventory records the books as having been 'left in the abbey of Barking' but there is only this circumstantial reference to connect them to the sisters of Barking; a 1535 inventory of furnishings at the Augustinian priory at Kilburn in Middlesex shows that a printed Golden Legend was placed alongside a manuscript copy of the same in the women's day-room adjoining the church.[43] No other documentary record of print connected with a convent of women is known to survive.

The subordinate presence of print in conventual collections contrasted, almost certainly, with its place in the personal libraries of the religious. Here, whether we are speaking of monks or regular canons, the mendicant orders or women religious, there can be no doubt that print grew rapidly in profile; by the turn of the century printed books appear in many of the individual collections for which there is a record; by 1534, it was the mainstay of what were,

[38] BL, Royal MS Appendix 69, fol. 4r: 'sunt ibidem quamplures libri communes tamen arteque impressoria litteris dediti'. For the Premonstratensian context (where the authority is given as 'Leland'), see Gribbin, *Premonstratensian Canons*, p. 134.
[39] For the list and contents of the Monk Bretton collection, see *EBL*, pp. 266–87 (B55). For the story of the former monks that collected and perhaps conserved them, see C. Cross, 'A Medieval Yorkshire Library', *Northern History* 25 (1989), 281–90 and 'The Reconstitution of Northern Monastic Communities in the Reign of Mary Tudor', *Northern History* 29 (1993), 200–04.
[40] BL, Royal MS Appendix 69, fols 3v, 6r, 7v. See also references, represented as 'Leland', in *The Friars' Libraries*, ed. K.W. Humphreys, CBMLC 1 (1990), p. 159.
[41] D.N. Bell, *What Nuns Read. Books and Libraries in Medieval English Nunneries*, Cistercian Studies Series 158 (Kalamazoo, MI, 1995), pp. 116–20 (117); Erler, *Women, Reading and Piety*, pp. 36, 108.
[42] Bell, *What Nuns Read*, pp. 118–20. See also Erler, *Women, Reading and Piety*, p. 108. Erler observes that, since English translations of the *Enchiridion* were printed with the Latin title, the language of the Erasmus cannot be confirmed.
[43] [W. Dugdale], *Monasticon Anglicanum*, ed. R. Dodsworth et al., 6 vols (London, 1817–30), 3.424–25.

increasingly, holdings of high value and volume. Within the monasteries and the canon houses, certainly, the superiors accrued substantial collections: there are clusters of survivors connected with the penultimate, and the last, generation of abbots and priors (whose years of office cover the period between 1509 and 1536) which, if they are in any way indicative, hint at holdings that may have numbered at least in the dozens. It may be that superiors of the greater abbeys were still assigned books *ex officio*, although the *ex libris* inscription 'de studio abbatis' appears to have passed out of use.[44] Like any senior prelate, the superiors maintained their own households both within the precinct of their house and at a number of satellite manors, and each of these residences may have held book collections.

Perhaps the collection which the former Benedictine abbot of Pershore kept at his manor of Longdon in Staffordshire had originated as one such recreational library.[45] These circumstances, and the income that secured them, facilitated the formation of personal libraries on a scale unprecedented in the monastic past: when he died in 1557, Philip Hawford, the former abbot of (Benedictine) Evesham, bequeathed a collection of more than 100 books, perhaps most of which were printed; even allowing for likely acquisitions after the suppression of his house in 1540, this would point to a pattern of acquisition quite out of pace with conventual collections.[46] While there is no doubt that personal collections of such a scale were most common among the superiors of the independent Benedictine abbeys, they were not their exclusive preserve. The five printed books bearing the personal *ex libris* of the Augustinian Abbot John Ramsey of Merton are suggestive at least of a continued pattern of purchases over several decades, perhaps beginning during his years at Oxford (1513–14), as well as some distinctly contemporary tastes.[47]

The printed collections of the superiors were founded on acquisitions made before they held office, almost invariably during the period of their academic training at one, other (or, in some cases, both) of the universities. In fact, whether or not they progressed into the hierarchy, generally the graduate monks and canons of the period also amassed large personal collections of printed books. The academic context of their encounters is frequently recorded in their *ex libris* inscriptions: John Darley identified himself as 'scoller of Cambriche'; Thomas Knyghton of (Benedictine) Coventry was more self-conscious in his purchase (Maffeo Vegio (Paris, 1511)): 'scolaris reverendiisimi pastoris ecclesiae ...

---

[44] For an instance of such an *ex officio* collection in the preceding period, see books surviving from the Benedictine abbey of St Albans, eleven of which bear the inscription, 'de studio abbatis': *MLGB* (1), p. 165.

[45] See the first of his wills (5 July 1553): PRO, PCC, PROB 11/36, fols 110–11r at 110v.

[46] For Philip Hawford, see E.A.B. Barnard, 'Philip Hawford: Pseudo-abbot of Evesham (1539) and Dean of Worcester (1553–57), His Will and Inventory', *Transactions of the Worcestershire Archaeological Society* (1929), pp. 52–69. See also D. Knowles, *The Religious Orders in England*, 3 vols (Cambridge, 1949–59), 3.339–40, 429.

[47] The books in question are: Stephanus Brulefer (Basel, 1507: London, Lambeth Palace Library, **H890.B6, B7), Dionysius Carthusianus, *Opera* (Cologne, 1532: Oxford, St John's College, φ 1. 32); Erasmus (Basel, 1519: BodL 4o Z 33 Th.), Athanasius (Paris, 1519: Ampleforth Cv23a), G Odonis (Venice, 1500: Glasgow, University Library, Eg. 6 aq. 9). For Ramsey, see *BRUO 1500–1540*, pp. 473–74. See also *MLGB* (1), p. 282.

Coventrie studendi grace opibus literis exhibitus'.[48] Presumably, it was the strength of their custom that caused the booksellers of Oxford to become the dinner companions of the brethren of Canterbury and Gloucester Colleges.[49] It should be emphasised, this was not a pattern of behaviour caused by the coming of print: from the first quarter of the fourteenth century, the quota of religious sent to pursue academic studies at a *studium generale* had been supported by conventual stipends and although they went armed with books from their home library, they had been permitted, if not overtly encouraged, also to purchase the texts which they (and the brethren that came after them) might require.[50] The availability of print certainly assisted them in their efforts to provide for themselves and their colleagues, and perhaps its comparative cost allowed them to increase their supply even at an early stage: as early as the 1470s and 1480s scholar monks were returning to Durham Priory with a wide variety of printed editions of the staple syllabus authorities.[51] John Avington of (Benedictine) Winchester Cathedral Priory was perhaps affirming a greater capacity to secure books in print when he added to his Oxford purchases 'ex emptione et salario'.[52]

If survivors serve as any guide, for the generation of scholars that followed in the years either side of 1500, it was possible to acquire multiple copies of printed texts, anything between two and eight bound books, during the period of study away from the home community. Of the eight printed books now preserved from the personal collection of William Edys, monk (and later abbot) of (Benedictine) Burton-upon-Trent, two are recorded as Oxford purchases, and three others, by their date, are likely to have been (Figure 10.1).[53] Purchases were so much a part of their academic experience, these regulars were known personally to the city's booksellers: Henry Reading of (Cistercian) Thame recorded in his *ex libris* books secured from Balthazar 'bibliopola Oxonia'.[54] The next and last generation of monks and canons to pass through the universities before 1535 may have known

---

[48] Darley's book, a copy of the *Gesta Romanorum* (*c.* 1475 [1473?]), is now Oxford, BodL Auct. 2. Q. 2. 3. Darley's clerical status remains unclear. Knyghton's book is now BodL 4o V. 16 (2) Th. For Knyghton, see *BRUO 1500–1540*, p. 332; *MLGB* (2), p. 83.

[49] PRO, SP 1/146, fol. 252r (*LP Henry VIII*, 14/1.684:3).

[50] For a recent study of the development of these arrangements, in respect of the Benedictine cathedral priories, see J. Greatrex, *The English Benedictine Cathedral Priories. Rule and Practice, c. 1270–c. 1420* (Oxford, 2011), pp. 131–40, 143–59.

[51] See, for example, such staple academic *auctores* as Alexander of Hales (Durham Cathedral, Inc. 61: Oxford, 1481), Peter Comestor (Durham Cathedral, Inc. 2: Strasbourg, 1483), Nicholas of Lyra (Durham Cathedral Inc. 1a–d, Strasbourg, *c.*1474–77; 1f: Nuremberg, 1481), Scotus (Durham Cathedral, Inc. 4a: Strasbourg, 1474). The Comestor was acquired by Robert Strother, whose Durham career may only have begun *c.*1490.

[52] For this formula, see Avington's copy of Nicholas de Tudeschis (Lyons, 1516), now Edinburgh University Library, *E. 15. 24. See also *MLGB* (1), p. 315.

[53] Edys was certainly buying books at Oxford between 1514 and 1517, given the dated inscriptions preserved in several of his books. For his career, see *BRUO 1500–1540*, p. 187. His surviving printed books are CUL, Inc. 3057 (*Libellulus secundarum intentionum logicalium*: Paris, s. a.); Cambridge, St John's College, A. 2. 1 (*ps.*-Theodolus, *Ecloga*: London, 1497), Norwich City Library (Johannes de Sacro Bosco: Cologne, 1508); Oxford, All Souls College, i. 12. 15 (John of Wales: Lyons, 1511); v. 2. 13 (Sermones thesauri novi: Paris, 1497); v. 4. 12 (Guilellmus Pepin: Paris, 1534); LR 4. e. 10 (Nicholas de Orbellis: Paris, 1498); SR 62. a. 2 (Johannes Trithemius: Paris, 1512). See also *MLGB* (1), pp. 16, 232.

[54] The purchase is dated 1528: Cambridge, St Catharine's College, 25 [Bilderick]: Euclid, Venice, 1517. See also *MLGB* (1), p. 311.

Figure 10.1 'Edys': a binding inscription of William Edys, abbot of Burton upon Trent on his copy of [John of Wales] *Summa Iohannis Valensis de regimine vite humane seu margarita doctorum* [Lyons, 1511]. All Souls College, i. 12. 15.

more-or-less unregulated acquisition. In his well-known correspondence, the Evesham scholar-monk Robert Joseph regarded Oxford as his principal source of books, indeed of reading material of any serious kind.[55] A fragment of the account book of the Cambridge bookseller and binder, Garrett Godfrey, dating from c.1527–33, records as many as eight canons and monks among his clients, almost all of whom had purchased multiple volumes.[56]

This generation of graduate monks and canons were also the beneficiaries of the printed collections accrued by their predecessors. In principle, the personal possessions of individual religious passed into conventual ownership at their death. Survivors shows that the obligation continued with print: the owner-ship inscription of the Kirkstall (Cistercian) monk, Anthony Adell, found in a copy of Albertus Magnus's *Secreta mulierum* (Cologne, c.1475), is followed by its (later) conventual *ex libris*.[57] Yet it does appear that a greater number of personal printed acquisitions were assigned, or bequeathed, to named brethren. The patterns of transmission which can be recovered from *ex dono* inscriptions suggest there was a deliberate effort to provide for the next generation of university men. Some of these gifts suggest special favour, patronage conferred upon a particular youngster. It would appear that Abbot Robert Hobs of (Cistercian) Woburn marked out a certain Ralph who received two books, printed editions

---

[55] *The Letter-Book of Robert Joseph*, ed. W.A. Pantin and H. Aveling, Oxford Historical Society, New Series, 19 (Oxford, 1967), notably Letter 131, p. 201.
[56] *Garrett Godfrey's Accounts, c.1527–1533*, ed. E. Leedham-Green, D.E. Rhodes and F.H. Stubbings, Cambridge Bibliographical Society, Monograph 12 (1992), pp. 21, 42, 53, 66–68. The religious were 'Bantrop', house unknown, Hobbs of Crowland, an unidentified monk perhaps of Ely, Nicholas and Sennock of Lewes, Simpson, Spensely and Swift, perhaps Gilbertine canons, the second of them perhaps of Watton.
[57] Oxford, MS Laud Misc. 722, fols 142r–87r (Albertus); fol. 102v (personal *ex libris*), fol. 126r, 'liber for Kirstall'.

of Boethius and Cicero.[58] Such internal transmission was not the special property of print, and examples of the exchange of manuscripts are known, but surviving inscriptions give the impression that monks and canons were more inclined to pass their printed books directly to their colleagues.[59] This may not reflect any priority attached to print other than practicality: widely understood to be ephemeral, indeed perishable, print was an ideal, low-cost source of syllabus texts. Nonetheless, the generation of religious that made their profession after 1509 entered into an inheritance of a residual collection of print even before they made acquisitions of their own: the case of Thomas Swalwell (d. 1539), of Durham Priory, who has left his mark in dozens of printed books, may not have been wholly untypical.[60]

Perhaps inevitably, personal holdings of print within the convents of mendicants and women religious were not on the scale of the monks and canons. While the population of the principal friaries, at Cambridge and Oxford, London, York and Bristol, remained sizeable in the seventy-five years before 1540, there was a marked disparity between their condition and the chain of provincial convents, many of which appear to have been weakened by falling recruitment and faltering income a decade or more before the Dissolution.[61] Indeed, the traces of their reception of print may be a measure of their overall condition: there is no sign of a regular pattern of acquisition on the part of any provincial warden. The majority of provenanced survivors are connected with friars who passed through the *studia* at Cambridge, London and Oxford; these books did not form the basis of a personal library, but were circulated within the network in what was surely a conscious effort to ensure that limited resources reached as wide a constituency as possible.[62] An *ex libris* inscription added to a copy of Boethius (Lyons, not after 1489) by John Grene of the Bedford Greyfriars may be an expression of the material obstacles to the mendicants' consumption of print, 'ex elemosinis amicorum suorum'.[63] Profession gifts of print are not unknown, perhaps for the same reason.[64]

The survival of printed volumes connected with women religious suggests

[58] Boethius (no date, no place: Cambridge, St John's College, Bb. 6. 17); Cicero (Mainz, 1466: BL, IB 118). See also *MLGB* (1), p. 205.

[59] The rate of survival of the printed books of Durham Priory provides particularly clear evidence of this trend. See under such names as Aukland, Castell, Manbe and Marley: *MLGB* (2), pp. 84–100.

[60] A.J. Piper, 'Dr Thomas Swalwell: Monk of Durham, Archivist and Bibliophile (d. 1539)', in *Books and Collectors, 1200–1700: Essays Presented to Andrew Watson*, ed. James P. Carley and C.G.C. Tite, British Library Studies in the History of the Book (London, 1996), pp. 71–100. See also *BRUO* 3.1828.

[61] There remains no detailed study of the state of the smaller, provincial mendicant convents, but the reports of the visitation and, subsequently, the suppression commissioners of 1535–38, suggest a degradation of material, social and observant conditions, for example, *LP Henry VIII*, 13/1.1289 (Bangor); *LP Henry VIII*, 13/2.41 (Bridgenorth); 44 (Lichfield); PRO, SP 1/135, fol. 40r–v at r.

[62] For example, a copy of Paulus Venetus (Milan, 1476), now BL IB 26227, carries *ex libris* inscriptions from the Salisbury and Warwick Dominicans; a copy of Antonius Andreae (Venice, 1496) passed from the Newcastle Carmelites to their brethren at Coventry. See also *MLGB* (1), pp. 55, 134.

[63] Now Cambridge, Emmanuel College, 4. 1. 14. See also *MLGB* (1), p. 229.

[64] John Tyndall presented a copy of *Sermones discipuli* (Strasbourg, 1495) to his son, William, on the day of his profession at Greenwich Greyfriars in 1508. Now London, St Paul's Cathedral, 13 D.6: *MLGB* (1), pp. 93, 266.

a pattern of personal acquisition comparable to the monks and canons but perhaps in smaller proportion. Superiors certainly accrued collections of their own: Margaret Stanburne, (Benedictine) prioress of St Michael's, Stamford in Lincolnshire, owned a copy of Richard Fox's translation of the *Regula Benedicti*, *Here begynneth the rule of seynt Benet* (London, 1516, *STC* 1859), a text which was surely a popular profession gift but in Margaret's case may have been an *ex officio* acquisition; Margaret Trot, prioress of (Benedictine) Polsloe, held her own printed breviary, a text which had an obvious utility both in observance and in private devotions, but, given her status, may be the survivor of a superior's chapel or household collection.[65] While women did not share the book culture of the universities, it may be that printed book ownership passed further into the professed community, and at an earlier date, than in many monasteries and canon houses because of the widespread custom of providing books at the point of profession. A professed sister carried with her into religion a network of family and clerical connections which might yield a number of books at the inception of her career. While there are only a handful of examples of women religious identified as the holder of more than one printed book, and all of them are from Syon, it would not be unreasonable to conclude that before the Dissolution it was possible for women religious to possess multiple printed books.[66]

While it may be tempting to conclude from the evidence of survivors that print enhanced and extended the increasing individualism of pre-Reformation monastic and mendicant life, in fact by far the majority of printed books that passed into the hands of the regulars in this period did so by means of communal, conventual action. The very first encounters with print were initiated in the interests of the convent as a whole by the superior. The Canterbury commission from Werken in 1474 was made by Prior William Sellying as a part of a programme of book provisions which continued throughout his term of office; Sellyng deputed the warden of Canterbury College, Oxford to scour the city's booksellers for specific texts: between 1478/82 and 1486/90, Warden John Langdon responded that he was unable to secure a copy of Scotus on the third book of the Sentences because '[he] cannot thynke yt likely that schall come ony moo of them yn prentys as be that I her off them that sell such bokys'.[67] The earliest imprints that entered Durham in or around the same year may have come via scholar monks at Oxford, but there can be little doubt that they acted under the direction of their superiors and certainly the purchases were made from conventual resources. Here the formulae employed in *ex libris* inscriptions require careful reading: while a volume may have been held by a named individual,

---

[65] Margaret Stanburne's book is now Oxford, BodL Arch. A. d. 15, the *ex libris* at fo. G vi^v. Margaret Trot's book is now Oxford, BodL Douce BB 200. See also Bell, *What Nuns Read*, pp. 159–60 (Polsloe), 168 (Stamford).

[66] For the surviving books connected with Syon women of the pre-Reformation period, see Bell, *What Nuns Read*, pp. 173–97; M.C. Erler, *Women, Reading and Piety in Late Medieval England* (Cambridge, 2002), pp. 35–37, 118–19, 142, 146–49.

[67] For Langdon's letter to Sellyng, see *Canterbury College, Oxford*, ed. Pantin 3, 120. For Sellyng as patron of the Christ Church book collection, see R. Weiss, *Humanism in England during the Fifteenth Century*, 2nd edn (Oxford, 1957), pp. 158–59. The scale of his book collection is obscured by its destruction in a fire at Canterbury before the Dissolution. For Sellyng, see also *BRUO* 3.1666–67; *ODNB*.

not infrequently the acquisition was made on behalf of their conventual colleagues, the book was 'assignatus communi librarie per. . .', or 'emptus sumptibus. . .'. Even where there is no explicit phrase, it might be inferred that the
book had been acquired with some recognition of its wider purpose; certainly
the appearance of other names on flyleaves as subsequent custodians suggest
such books came quickly to be regarded as common property.[68] From the turn of
the century, it is possible to point to the provision of print at regular intervals for
particular conventual purposes. Perhaps only rarely did a superior, or another
officer, deploy their resources for multiple acquisitions at any one time: the
purchases of 'prynt bokes' documented during the priorate of William More of
Worcester were made over a period of fifteen years (1519–34) and may represent
nothing more programmatic than a commitment to the continued improvement
of his holdings.[69] Print was sometimes made the focus of a particular conventual
project, particularly in the years after 1500 as it became well established among
the tools of monastic labour. Marmaduke Huby's purchase and embellishment
of a printed missal for (Cistercian) Fountains did not depart from a tradition
of deluxe book patronage well established before print, but his preference for
a standard printed text was surely a self-conscious statement of intent.[70] Quite
apart from its capacity to convey a cultural statement, the pre-Reformation generation of regulars were attuned to the practical utility of print and increasingly
inclined to invest on a wider scale. Shortly before the suppression there is at least
a hint at superiors initiating the stocking, or re-stocking, of their collections with
printed authorities. In 1532 Prior John Houghton of the London Charterhouse
ordered ten copies of the *opera* of Dionysius the Carthusian and twenty volumes
of other unspecified texts, to be secured through his confrère at the Cologne
Charterhouse.[71] It would appear that Benedictine superiors responded to the
king's visitation Injunctions of 1535, which required each monastery to maintain
a daily claustral lector, with the purchase of the prescribed (printed) authorities:
at Warden (Cistercian), one of Cromwell's correspondents reported the extraordinary novelty of the authorities now expounded daily from the lectern.[72]

In all probability such provisions were never a substantial part of the
expenditure of the mendicants and the women religious. A number of surviving volumes of mendicant provenance, of comparatively early date, carry what
must be read as conventual *ex libris* inscriptions, which would suggest they were
acquired for common use and not, initially at least, for the use of a named friar.
Three volumes comprising four texts, Alexander of Hales's *Summa* (Pavia, 1489),
Angelus de Clavasio's *Summa angelica* (Venice, 1499), Bernard of Clairvaulx's
Modus bene vivendi in Christianam religionem (Venice, c.1494) and Bernardino of
Siena's *Sermones* (Basel, not after 1489), carry a general *ex libris* of the Canterbury

---

[68]   Such modes of acquisition are again especially visible among the surviving printed volumes
from Durham Priory: *MLGB* (2), pp. 84–100.
[69]   For Prior More's purchases, see *EBL*, pp. 662–74 (B117).
[70]   Abbot Huby's breviary is now Oxford, Christ Church, e. 8. 29. For an account of its acquisition, see M. Carter, 'The Breviary of Abbot Marmaduke Huby: Renaissance Design and
Religious Change in Early Sixteenth-Century Yorkshire', *Bodleian Library Record* 22, no. 1 (2009),
9–34.
[71]   Gillespie, 'Syon Abbey and the English Market', p. 121.
[72]   BL, Cotton MS Cleopatra E IV, fol. 163r (*LP Henry VIII*, 9.1167).

Greyfriars, distinct from the ownership inscription of a named individual; without a name, of course, the date of accession remains uncertain.[73] It is possible that the two-volume Bonaventure (Strasbourg, 1495) from the London Greyfriars was a conventual acquisition since it bears an inscription signed by the 'custos librarie', Andreas Bavard.[74] The purchases of small groups of books from Garrett Godfrey, made, respectively, by Gregory Dodds of the Cambridge Blackfriars and (apparently) Thomas Brygges of the Norwich Blackfriars between c.1527 and 1533 may have been for the use of their convents.[75] There is no evidence, however, that these amounted to anything more than ad hoc accessions; the resources of these houses, at any rate, allowed for nothing more. There are no such indications from the surviving books of the nuns, which, without exception, carry personal inscriptions. We might perhaps have expected to see traces of a stocking or re-stocking programme at least among the women of Winchester diocese in the wake of the publication of Bishop Richard Fox's translation of the *Regula Benedicti*, but in fact only one of the extant copies of this 1516 edition can be provenanced to a nunnery.[76] It is possible that the succession of Syon publications, not least the *Orcharde* of 1519 (*STC* 4815), stimulated the stocking of female collections but again the only surviving copies of relevant provenance appear to be personal acquisitions.

The printed books that entered the precinct as personal acquisitions may not have outnumbered conventual provisions overall but the traffic was perhaps more frequent and in its nature more diverse. Certainly the monks and canons did not confine their acquisitions to their irregular sojourns at the universities. It was not uncommon for them to buy in other markets. Abbot John Redborn of (Cistercian) Dore recorded his purchase of a copy of Athanasius (Paris, 1520) 'emptus in cimiterio sancti Pauli London, AD 1535'.[77] The monks of Christ Church, Canterbury, made personal purchases from London booksellers.[78] It is apparent from the correspondence of Robert Joseph that books were bought, exchanged or otherwise acquired also in the circles of clerks, regular and secular, in which they shared whether they were within or outside of their own house; although there is traffic in books throughout his correspondence, Joseph never once references a bookseller.[79] David Llewellyn of the Hereford Blackfriars bought as many as seven texts from Garrett Godfrey in Cambridge between c.1527 and 1533.[80] Printed books were also recovered (or removed) from other institutional collections in the same way that manuscript books had

---

[73] Respectively, BL IA 22423 (containing the first two texts), BL IB 37464, and BL IA 23301.

[74] The volumes are now in the library of the Middle Temple: *MLGB* (1), p. 123.

[75] Brygges bought two, perhaps three books, Dodds four: *Garrett Godfrey's Accounts*, ed. Leedham-Green et al., pp. 6, 68.

[76] The copy that carries a female monastic provenance bears the *ex libris* of Margaret Stanburne of Stamford Priory. See above, p. 189.

[77] The volume is now Westminster Abbey, F 4. 21. See also *MLGB* (2), p. 84.

[78] *Canterbury College, Oxford*, ed. Pantin, 1 p. 91. Thomas Anselm sold to his confrere William Wycheppe a copy of John of Turrecremata on the Regula Benedicti at a reduced sum, to take account of a debt owing. Anselm's account records 'hytt cost me at London, iii s iiii d'.

[79] *Letter Book of Robert Joseph*, ed. Pantin and Aveling pp. 24 (Letter 24), 34 (Letter 27), 50 (Letter 40), 201 (Letter 131).

[80] Llewellyn bought three works of Erasmus, a Cicero, Vergil, Theophylactus on the Epistles and an unidentified commentary: *Garrett Godfrey's Accounts*, ed. Leedham-Green, p. 82.

always been: among the printed books that bear the *ex libris* of William More of Worcester is a volume (Antonius Andreae: Venice, 1496) originally in the custody of the Newcastle Carmelites.[81] As individual owners and readers of print the monks, canons, mendicants, and nuns also engaged in the mutual exchange of books. It may have been the expressed purpose of mendicant purchases that they would be passed between convents, at least within regional circuits. Mary Erler has brought into focus the transmission of books between professed women and their devout kinswomen (and men).[82] These channels remained in place at the suppression and their continuing vigour may account for the poor survival rates: books passed out of their original monastic context, and, eventually, out of view.

Print also came into the hands of the regulars by way of patronage. The continuing role of patrons (of all ranks) in shaping monastic and mendicant book collections even in the pre-Reformation century should not be underestimated. Such benefactions brought an eclectic mix of texts into the precinct and in some consignments there is the impression of the unsold residue left to the executors after they had discharged their obligations; yet sometimes they introduced scarce or novel authorities into the precinct. The donation of a single print by Christopher Urswick, dean of York, to the Lancaster Dominicans has the impression of an off-cut or even after-thought, given the quality and value of his (principally, manuscript) donations elsewhere.[83] The copy of the clerical manual, *Fortalicium fidei*, which was passed to (Carthusian) Mount Grace by the executors of Thomas Scasby of St William's College, York, can scarcely have been unfamiliar to the Carthusians.[84] By contrast, a 1488 bequest of the *Legenda aurea* (Cologne, 1485) from William Brereton of Whittington College, London, to the Mottenden Trinitarian friars must have been amongst the first attested accessions of print to a mendicant collection in England.[85] Print became more prominent among these gifts at the same pace as its presence grew in personal libraries. An unidentified 'Magister Gerardus' gave no fewer than thirty-one books to the Crutched Friars of London in 1496, of which one printed volume survives, a copy of Lanfrancus de Oriano (Cologne, 1488).[86] It did not alter the

---

[81]   Oxford, Merton College, B.8.g.17. See also *MLGB* (1), pp. 134, 210, 283, 319.

[82]   See M. Erler, 'Widows in Retirement: Religion, Patronage, Spirituality, Reading at the Gaunt's, Bristol', *Religion and Literature* 37, no. 2 (2005), 51–75, a quasi-monastic context; *Women, Reading and Piety in Late Medieval England* (Cambridge, 2003), pp. 85–99 (Birgittine Syon), 100–15 (Franciscan (Poor Clare) Denny); 'The Exchange of Books between Nuns and Laywomen: Three Surviving Examples', in *New Science Out of Old Books: Studies in Manuscripts and Early Printed Books in Honour of A. I. Doyle*, ed. R. Beadle and A.J. Piper (Aldershot, 1995), pp. 360–73. Erler's three examples are connected with (Dominican) Dartford, (Cistercian) Marrick and (Benedictine) Barking.

[83]   Urswick is known to have presented two fine manuscripts written by the Brabantine scribe Pieter Meghen to the Cistercian abbey of Hailes in Gloucestershire in his capacity as executor of Sir John Huddelston. He may have exchanged manuscript books with Prior Thomas Goldstone of Christ Church, Canterbury. He gave a manuscript of Cicero's *De officiis*, also executed by Meghen to Henry, 2nd baron Daubeney. See also J.B. Trapp, 'Urswick, Christopher (1448?–1522)', *ODNB* [28042].

[84]   Now Oxford, BodL AA61 Th. Seld. See also *MLGB* (1), p. 283.

[85]   Cambridge, Corpus Christi College, EPD par 4. See also *MLGB* (1), pp. 132, 282.

[86]   Now Westminster Abbey CC. 18. Perhaps three of the surviving books from the house were also part of the gift: Durandus (Strasbourg, 1486: Bury St Edmunds Cathedral), Comestor (Basel, 1486: Oxford, BodL Auct. I. Q. 2. 10 and S. Baron (London, s. a.: Oxford, BodL 8o B115 Th.).

dynamics of patronage. The reach and relative cost of print do not appear to have affected the social profile of patrons; at any rate, the religious had received books from lay as well as clerical patrons long before the coming of the press. It is possible that affordable print created a new channel for modest cash donations: at (Cistercian) Pipewell, a gift funded the purchase of the *Speculum spiritualium* (Paris, 1510).[87] Nor does it appear that the religious responded differently to the donation of printed books. As in generations past, it was not the nature of the book but the status of its donor that determined its custody in the convent. It is possible that as the proportion grew, gifts of print were treated, just as manuscripts were, as of general utility and assigned to the needs of individual religious, given the number of instances where *ex dono* inscriptions are followed by marks of personal readership. The Pipewell *Speculum* was given a dual purpose from the outset, being assigned to one of the brethren but with explicit reversion to the convent as a whole: 'constat Thomas Howghton et monasterio. . .'.

It is likely that the resident clerks of the religious houses proved to be a source of print, either in life or death. Perhaps the fellows of Pembroke Hall, Cambridge, provided printed books to the Franciscan nuns of Denny, with whose spiritual direction they had been charged.[88] In the decade before the Dissolution it appears that the clergy present in, or passing through, the precinct introduced illicit imprints: the Prior of (Benedictine) Reading was caught with a cache of no fewer than sixty such erroneous books in 1528.[89]

From the outset patrons in Continental Europe had channelled print not only into their acts of general patronage but also into their governance of religious houses, particularly into their efforts to engender reform. Although an impulse for general clerical, and specifically monastic, reform was apparent in English episcopacy in the half-century before 1534, print was rarely employed in this way. Bishop John Alcock's *Spousage of a Virgin* (Wynkyn de Worde, 1496–97, STC 286–87) was presented as an 'exhortacyon made to relygyous systers'; his *Gallicantus* (Richard Pynson, 1499, STC 277) appears to have been intended to invigorate the clergy (regular and secular) of his diocese of Ely as whole, but with only fragments preserved, the extent and manner of its reception cannot be traced.[90] There can be no doubt that it was in recognition of the special properties of print that Richard Fox embarked on an English translation of the *Regula Benedicti* for the use of the women religious of Winchester diocese. It was not only the immediacy and uniformity of print which reinforced Fox's enterprise but its profile – which, when he prepared his translation, had been established for forty years – as an English medium.[91] Fox was one of a number of diocesans, monastic and mendicant governors, to pursue the reform of observance in this period and it is worth noting that none of his counterparts – Longland

[87] The volume is now Peterborough Cathedral D. 8. 17. See also *MLGB* (1), p. 294.
[88] 'Syon Abbey and its Religious Publications', p. 20; Erler, *Women, Reading and Piety*, p. 110.
[89] PRO, SP 1/47, fol. 52r (*LP Henry VIII*, 14/2.4004).
[90] For Alcock's *Spousage*, see V.M. O'Mara, 'Preaching to Nuns in Late Medieval England', in *Medieval Monastic Preaching*, ed. C. Muessig (Leiden, 1998), pp. 93–120 (102–06). See further on Alcock in *ODNB*, and Susan Powell's essay in this volume.
[91] [Richard Fox], *Here begynneth the Rule of Seynt Benet*, Richard Pynson, London, 1516? See also B. Collett, *Female Monastic Life in Tudor England: With an Edition of Richard Fox's Translation of the Benedictine Rule for Women, 1517* (Aldershot, 2001).

of Lincoln, Nix of Norwich, Redman of the White Canons – considered print as part of their plans.[92] Whether it is indicative of a continuing equivocation over print per se, or merely of practical constraints over infrastructure and cost, it is striking that the crown's own entry into the governance of the regular clergy after 1534 did not overtly exploit the printed word. Thomas Cromwell provided (via the printer under his patronage, William Marshall) twenty-four copies of Marsilio di Padua's *Defensor pacis* to the London Carthusians to persuade them of the philosophical verity of the royal supremacy, although the books may not have remained long in the house as it was reported that the president of the order compelled them to return them.[93] Yet it was an isolated intervention at a convent distinguished as much for the attention it drew from public figures. The king's Injunctions of 1535 may be represented as revolutionary, since they subjected religious observance to secular authority, but it was a revolution advanced in manuscript.[94]

It was not only texts, bound and dis-bound, that passed into the hands of the regular clergy but also a wide variety of printed ephemera. Even before the coming of the press itself, it is possible the regulars were among the audience of the single-sheet woodblock prints that circulated, at least from the first quarter of the fifteenth century, although it might be observed that they never turned to making them as did their Continental counterparts.[95] No such prints of confirmed English provenance survive, although informal illustrations of the middle and later fifteenth century at times are reminiscent of Continental examples: the crude image of the Blessed Virgin Mary and Christ Crucified added as a frontispiece to a manuscript copy of Rolle's *Incendium amoris* acquired by Robert Steward, Benedictine prior of Ely, certainly bears comparison with such block-printed sheets.[96] Without doubt, England's religious were familiar with the profusion of printed indulgences that were the commercial mainstay of the early presses. It was not uncommon for these documents to be issued under the name of a particular convent although their printed production was often at one remove from the original grant made by an ecclesiastical authority.[97] Yet not every one of these documents was so detached from the regulars they named: a Pynson indulgence of 1491 was printed for the Prior General of the Crutched Friars as part of a campaign to fund the reconstruction of their London convent;

---

[92] For the reform impulses of these bishops, see M. Bowker, *The Henrician Reformation. The Diocese of Lincoln under John Longland, 1521–47* (Cambridge, 1981), pp. 17–28; Knowles, *Religious Orders*, 3.62–86 (73–75); Gribbin, *Premonstratensian Canons in Late Medieval England*, pp. 40–100, 234–343.

[93] *The defence of peace: lately translated out of Laten in to Englysshe with the Kynges moste gracious privilege* (1535, STC 17817). See also PRO, SP 1/83, fol. 52r (*LP Henry VIII*, 7.423); BL, Cotton MS Cleopatra E IV, fols 43r–44v at 43v (*LP Henry VIII*, 9.523). See also W. Underwood, 'Thomas Cromwell and William Marshall's Protestant Books', *Historical Journal* 47, no. 3 (2004), 517–19 (523).

[94] For the king's Injunctions of 1535 and the manner of their enforcement in the religious orders, see Knowles, *Religious Orders*, 3.268–90.

[95] Scheepsma, *Medieval Women Religious*, pp. 167–68.

[96] Cambridge, St John's College, B 1 [23], fol. ivb.

[97] For the clerical and commercial dynamics of the transmission of indulgences in England, see R.N. Swanson, *Indulgences in Late Medieval England: Passports to Paradise?* (Cambridge, 2007), p. 172. See too Mary Erler's essay in this volume.

the printing of a plenary indulgence of 1494 appears to have been directed by the Augustinian friars of Cambridge, although the same order frequently acted only as intermediaries for campaigns co-ordinated from Rome. An indulgence campaign to reinvigorate the Cistercians in Wales was organised by Abbot John ap Rhys of Strata Marcella in 1528, when the printer was also Richard Pynson.[98] Certainly the last generation of religious recognised the popular appeal of printed ephemera; latterly, when the suppressions had already begun, they also turned to it as a tool. The best-known ballad of the Pilgrimage of Grace may be attributed to a monk, or monks, of (Cistercian) Sawley Abbey.[99]

While they can be counted among its first consumers, the regulars remained largely detached from the production of print, at least for the first four decades of the insular press. This stands in sharp contrast to their Continental counterparts, where monastic and mendicant convents engaged directly in early printing enterprises; here an intense interest and investment in the press in the forty years after Gutenberg had declined by the first decade of the sixteenth century. In England, there is scarcely any indication of an involvement in the activity of any press before 1525. The proximity of the early and short-lived press at St Albans to the country's premier Benedictine abbey has long raised a question over the role of the monastery. Nothing is known of the precise location of the press nor of the identity of the printer; the selection of Latin texts printed there reflects the pedagogic priorities of the academic community at Cambridge rather than the nearby monks; yet it is doubtful that a house that still dominated the commercial life of the town and its environs was wholly unaware of the press.[100] Moreover, the monks of St Albans do appear to have given assistance to Caxton at the close of his career: according to a flyleaf inscription now lost, a Latin manuscript of Mandeville's *Travels* from the abbey library was loaned to the Westminster printer shortly before his death in 1492.[101] There is the slightest hint of another monastic contact with Caxton: the pastedown of a mid-fifteenth-century copy of the *Brut* which was in the possession of the Westminster printer also carries a personal letter of the prior of (Benedictine) Spalding.[102]

In the shadow of the Dissolution there was a notable shift and for a decade and a half a number of monasteries – all of them Benedictine – became directly involved in the production of printed books. The new enterprise may be explained as the cumulative effect of an engagement with print culture which had continued, growing in breadth and depth over five decades; it is possible

[98] H. Thomas, 'An Indulgence printed by Pynson, 1491', *British Museum Quarterly* 9, no. 2 (1934), 32–33; Swanson, *Indulgences in Late Medieval England*, p. 146; David H. Williams, *The Welsh Cistercians* (Tenby, 1984), pp. 68–69, 116 [Plate].
[99] For the Sawley ballad, see M.L. Bush, *The Pilgrimage of Grace: A Study of the Rebel Armies of 1536* (Manchester, 1996), pp. 234–35.
[100] For an outline of the fitful output of the St Albans press between 1479 and 1486, see *STC* 3.211. See also *BMC XI*, pp. 301–06 and references therein.
[101] BL, Egerton MS 1982. The inscription recording the loan to Caxton appeared on the front flyleaf which was lost in post-medieval binding but is preserved in a nineteenth-century transcription. Caxton had not printed the text by the time of his death. It was subsequently printed by Wynkyn de Worde in 1499: *Here begynneth a lytell treatyse or booke named Johan Mau[n]devyll* (*STC* 17247).
[102] London, Society of Antiquaries, MS 93, fol. 97v.

it was stimulated by an awareness of the recent campaigns of a number of their Continental counterparts, who had used print to reassert the claims of their churches and shrines; perhaps it can also be connected with the dynamics of metropolitan printing: the time of the king's 'Great Matter' also saw the passing of the generation of printers which had succeeded Caxton, Julyan Notary (not active after 1520), Richard Pynson (d. 1529) and Wynkyn de Worde (d. 1534). London printing appears to have lost, at least temporarily, something of its commercial and productive force in the decade that followed and the increasing interventions of royal authority may have militated against any rapid recovery; it is quite likely that a number of them now turned towards the provinces.[103]

A press was established at (Benedictine) Tavistock Abbey by 1525 when an edition of John Walton's English translation of Boethius's *Consolatio* was printed (*STC* 3200). The edition was prepared by Thomas Richard, a graduate monk, who also added a number of additional stanzas of his own composition. Nothing further is known of Richard, and it may be that he did not live to follow the Boethius with other books, but the press remained at Tavistock to the Dissolution where it was employed on at least one further occasion (1534) to print the statutes issued by the Stannary (*STC* 6795.6), the governing body of the tin mines which originally had been established under the auspices of the abbot and convent.[104] In 1528, the abbot and convent of Abingdon invested in the production of a printed edition of their breviary (*STC* 15792). Only a single copy of the book is known to survive and it yields little evidence of the press that printed it, or the identity of its printer. It purports to have been made at Abingdon but the precise role of the monastery remains unclear.[105] There is a greater clarity surrounding presses which operated at Canterbury and St Albans during the 1530s. The printers in both instances can be identified; both had begun their trade in London and both returned there after the Dissolution. The press was not the possession of the monastery in either case, but the monastic community was its principal patron, individual monks were directly involved in the production of its editions and it may be that the press itself was set up within the precincts.[106] A last, and tantalising, glimpse of a press perhaps under the direction of a religious is provided by the survival of a printed rental from the college of Burton-upon-Trent. The document is dated on its title-page 1544; it carries royal arms which match those printed in Giles du Wes, *An introductorie for to lerne to rede* (London, 1546?: John Herford, Nicholas Hill, *STC* 7380) (Figure 10.2). Burton College was created from the dissolved Benedictine abbey

[103] The interference of London stationers in the St Alban press in 1539 might be interpreted as the expression of an impulse to recover authority after a decade of drift. On this episode, see C. Blagden, *The Stationers' Company. A History, 1403–1959* (Stanford, CA, 1977), p. 28.

[104] For the Tavistock press, see H.P.R. Finberg, *Tavistock Abbey. A Study in Social and Economic History of Devon*, Cambridge Studies in Medieval Life and Thought 2 (Cambridge, 1951), pp. 290–93. For Thomas Richard, see *BRUO 1500–1540*, p. 484.

[105] For the Abingdon portiforium, see Oxford, Exeter College, MS 15792.

[106] For the Canterbury press, see *STC* 3. 123; J. Boffey, 'John Mychell and the Printing of John Lydgate in the 1530s', *HLQ* 67 (2004), 251–60. For the St Albans press, see J.G. Clark, 'Reformation and Reaction at St Albans Abbey, c.1530–58', *EHR* 115 (2000), 297–328. See also Knowles, *Religious Orders*, 3.24–27; *STC* 3.208.

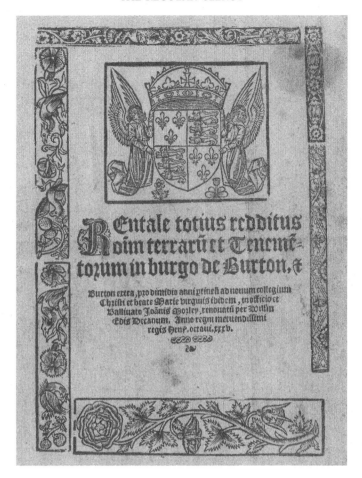

Figure 10.2 Printed rental of the College of Burton upon Trent, 1544. Staffordshire Record Office, D/W 1734/2/3/8.

of Burton, and its inaugural dean was the former abbot, William Edys. Abbot Edys's enthusiasm for print has already been noted; no other trace of printing activity at Burton is known: could the rental be evidence that Edys, the avid consumer, cultivated ties to the London presses?[107]

It was at the same moment, and among the same generation, that the regulars for the first time turned to print as a fitting medium for their own writing. The Birgittines of Syon had modelled this turn to the new medium as early as the turn of the century with a sequence of original publications, Clement Maidstone's *Directorium sacerdotum* (1487–1508, STC 17720), Simon Wynter's *Life of Jerome* (1499, STC 14508), and, the most successful of this early group, the *Ryght Profitable Treatyse* (c.1500, STC 1978) of the librarian, Thomas Betson. Their

[107] Staffordshire Record Office, D/W 1734/2/3/8. I am grateful to Dr Ian Atherton for drawing my attention to the existence of the Burton rental and for providing photographs of it.

enterprise was renewed, and extended, by the brethren that entered in the next decade.[108] For John Fewterer and, in particular, William Bonde and Richard Whitford, print was not only a means of transmission but also a mode of discourse through which the efficacy of their monastic devotions might be amplified; in the shadow of the Dissolution the discourse sharpened into polemic.[109] There can be little doubt that there was a degree of editorial engagement with the printing house, although it is rarely documented. Whitford wrote elusively in 1537 of publishing, 'whereunto I was rather moued, as I perceyeved, by the printers. . .'.[110] It has been suggested that there was a careful and co-ordinated fashioning of the corporate identity of the convent, 'the active promotion of a Syon author and identification with Syon as part of marketing the texts', although the origin of the celebrated *Orcharde of Syon* image remains obscure, and the re-use of other woodcuts would suggest a generalised mode of production. As so often with the printing of mendicant and monastic indulgences and confraternity letters, the agency of the printers appears to lie at one remove from the professed community itself.[111]

Beyond Syon, there were only sporadic signs of a comparable creative enterprise. A verse-life of Werburgh, patronal saint of the Benedictines of Chester, *The Holy Lyfe and History*, was composed by one of the brethren, Henry Bradshaw, and passed to Richard Pynson for printing in 1521 (*STC* 3506). Two further hagiographical productions ensued in the following decade from St Albans (1534, *STC* 256) and Canterbury, but both were revised editions of earlier works (in both cases, by John Lydgate); the identity of the editors is not recorded but their textual interventions appear to have been confined to a handful of stanzas. Indeed the oldest monastic order's late entry into the business of printing yielded only one wholly original author, Robert Saltwood of Canterbury, whose *Comparyson bytwene iiii byrdes, the larke, the nyghtyngale, ye thrusshe and the cucko* (*STC* 21647), a vernacular verse allegory, stands in marked contrast not only to their other imprints but also to the generality of printed texts which attracted their interest as readers.[112] It is possible that a number of original publications no

[108] C.A. Grisé, '"Moche profitable unto religious persones gathered by a brother of Syon"': Syon Abbey and English Books', in *Syon Abbey and its Books*, pp. 129–54 (131). For a fresh survey of Syon's printed output, see S. Powell, 'Syon Abbey as a Centre for Text Production', in *Saint Birgitta, Syon and Vadstena*, ed. Gejrot, pp. 50–67, and the useful appendix listing 'publications' in script and print, pp. 68–70.

[109] The Bodleian copy of Richard Whitford's *Pype or Tonne of the Lyfe of Perfecyon* carries glosses, perhaps by the author, reinforcing his assault on 'heretikes': A.M. Hutchinson, 'Richard Whitford's *Pype or Tonne of the Lyfe of Perfection*. Pastoral Care or Political Manifesto', in *Saint Birgitta, Syon and Vadstena*, ed. Gejrot, pp. 89–103.

[110] Grisé, "Moche profitable", p. 149. For the brethren's pastoral enterprise in print, see also Alexandra da Costa, 'The Brethren of Syon Abbey and Pastoral Care', in *A Companion to Pastoral Care in the Late Middle Ages*, ed. R.J. Stansbury, Brill's Companions to the Christian Tradition 22 (Leiden, 2010), pp. 235–60.

[111] Grisé, "Moche profitable", p. 138. See also M.W. Driver, 'Nuns as Patrons, Artists and Readers: Bridgettine Woodcuts in Printed Books Produced for the English Market', in *Art into Life: Collected Papers from the Kresge Art Museum Medieval Symposia*, ed. C.G. Fisher and K.L. Scott (East Lansing, MI, 1995), pp. 237–67.

[112] For Bradshaw, see *ODNB*, and for his text *The Life of Saint Werburge of Chester*, ed. C. Horstmann, EETS OS 88 (1887). For the editions of Lydgate's English life of Alban at St Albans, and his *Legend of St Austin at Compton* at Canterbury, see J.G. Clark, 'Print and Pre-Reformation Religion: the Benedictines and the Press, c.1470–c.1540', in *The Uses of Script and Print, 1300–1700*,

longer survive. The refutation of Luther which King Henry commissioned from Abbot Richard Kidderminster of Winchcombe in 1521 was surely intended for publication, although it remains unclear whether it ever appeared; there is no trace in manuscript or print of his exposition of the *Regula Benedicti* which was commended by Bishop Longland as a tool of reform.[113]

A space also emerged between patronage and production in which religious were preferred as the dedicatees of printed publications. Bishop Fisher presented both his *Spirituall Consolation* and *Wayes to Perfect Religion* to his half-sister Elizabeth White, a professed woman of (Dominican) Dartford.[114] While already attracting suspicion for his heretical sympathies, the scholar Leonard Coxe prepared an English rhetoric, *The Arte or Crafte of Rhetoryke* (*STC* 5947), for presentation to his patron, Abbot Hugh Cook of Reading.[115] The distinctly reformist drift of Abbot John Ramsey of Merton drew the attention of Thomas Paynell who honoured the Augustinian on the eve of the Dissolution with the dedication of his translation of Erasmus, *The comparation of a vyrgin and a martyr* (*STC* 10465.5).[116]

The traffic of print through the convents of the regular clergy can be more easily recovered than its effects on their conventual life. As the institutional and individual catalogues and inventories indicate, print was integrated into the textual environment of the convent as a supplement to its manuscript collections; in other words, there is little to suggest that it significantly shifted the doctrinal reference-points of the professed community. Rather, its role was to amplify them, and perhaps, as new editions of old authorities became available, to refine them; rarely, if ever, did it replace them.

Certainly print served to convey contemporary academic tastes into the convents, at least of the greater abbeys and cathedral priories and principal mendicant *studia*, and more comprehensively, perhaps, than had been the case in earlier times. For the final generation of graduates – the generation of Robert Joseph of Evesham – print secured for conventual readers the titles current in the colleges and halls, Erasmus (of the *Enchiridion*, especially, and the New Testament), Jacques Lefèvre d'Étaples, Melancthon and even Martin Luther.[117] Indeed, their exposure may have extended beyond approved novelties to the

---

ed. J.C. Crick and A. Walsham (Cambridge, 2004), pp. 71–92. For the St Albans edition, see also John Lydgate, *The Life of Saint Alban and Saint Amphibal*, ed. J.E. van der Westhuizen (Leiden, 1974), especially pp. 11–12, 286–95. For the Canterbury edition, see also Boffey, 'John Mychell and the Printing of John Lydgate', pp. 251–60. For Saltwood, see *ODNB*.

[113] For Kidderminster's lost writings and their reputation, see Knowles, *Religious Orders*, 3.91–95 (94). See also *ODNB*.

[114] Lee, *Nuns, Learning and Spirituality*, p. 170.

[115] Coxe also prepared translations of Erasmus's paraphrases on the Pauline epistles to Timothy and his *De pueris instituendis*, both intended for the patronage of Thomas Cromwell. Neither was published. See also *ODNB*.

[116] *BRUO 1500–1540*, p. 474.

[117] For the familiarity of these current authorities to the correspondents of Robert Joseph, see *Letter Book of Robert Joseph*, ed. Pantin and Aveling Letter 15: Erasmus (21–22), Letter 18: Lefèvre d'Étaples (26–27), Letter 20: Portius (27–28), Letter 35: Josse Clichtove (43–45), Letter 46: Mantuanus (55). See also the recurrence of (especially) Erasmus and Melancthon among the titles purchased by the monastic and mendicant clients of the Cambridge binder and seller Garrett Godfrey: *Garrett Godfrey's Accounts*, ed. Leedham-Green, pp. 21, 53, 68, 82, 64–67, 81–83.

new radicals: in March 1528, when the prior of Reading was reported to have received more than sixty 'erroneous books' (see above), it was through the network of Thomas Garrett.[118]

Books attested in inventories also indicate a general interest in the texts now established as the standard points of reference for humanist Latinity. Valla's *Elegantiae* was a common purchase from Garrett Godfrey in Cambridge, sometimes accompanied by an edition of Cicero's *De officiis* and works of Virgil.[119] The poor survival rate perhaps obscures the extent to which print enabled the religious' full immersion in humanist literary values.

It appears that print also widened the exposure to vernacular literature which previously had been limited, at least in the older monasteries of the unreformed orders. After 1500, the personal collections of monks and canons often include books both in Latin and English. Printed English grammars appear as early as the turn of the fifteenth century. In fact, the survival of several examples whose monastic provenance can be confirmed before 1525 would suggest that the regulars' consumption of schoolbooks printed in England was some way in advance of their secular counterparts.[120] They also acquired some of the chronicles with which the first generation of English printers had found such a ready readership.[121] There is the hint of an interest in some of the best known of recent vernacular voices – Capgrave, Lydgate – which had been largely absent from their manuscript tradition over the preceding century.[122] Only the profusion of devotional and pastoral manuals still failed to rouse a readership among the wide spread of religious, although there is an indication that they found a following at Syon, where the women cultivated a modish pattern of private devotion.[123] It may have been the English of these texts, and neither their popularity nor their printing, which deterred monks and canons, given their evident interest in the Latin alternatives, such as the *Pupilla oculi*, first printed in 1510 (*STC* 4115).[124] It was surely a measure of their increasing interest in the vernacular voice that the printing at Tavistock, Canterbury and St Albans which was directed by the monks themselves was of works written in English.

---

[118] Report from Bishop John Longland to Wolsey, 3 March 1528: PRO, SP 1/47, fols 52r–53r (*LP Henry VIII*, 4.4004).

[119] *Garrett Godfrey's Accounts*, ed. Leedham-Green, pp. 68, 80–82.

[120] On the early dominance of Continental schoolbooks, and the later adoption of texts of English origin, see N. Orme, *Medieval Schools. From Roman Britain to Renaissance England* (New Haven, CT and London, 2005), p. 126.

[121] For example, an apparent copy of Caxton's *Chronicle of England* (Westminster, 1480) among the acquisitions of Prior More of Worcester: *EBL*, B117. 20 (666).

[122] An English Capgrave, *Noua Legenda Anglie* (Westminster, 1516, *STC* 4601), passed into the conventual collection of the Hull Charterhouse, apparently in 1536. Thomas Butler, monk of Shrewsbury, owned copies of Lydgate's *Life of Our Lady* and Caxton's *Epilogue* bound together in the same volume, now Oxford, BodL, Seld. d. 10. See also *MLGB* (1), pp. 106, 271.

[123] The Lambeth Palace copy of the 1494 de Worde primer may have a Birgittine provenance since it contains a loose leaf bearing an engraving of Katherine of Sweden, Birgitta's daughter; the Bodleian copy of the same primer was thought by Neil Ker to have possible Syon connections because he considered the book's parchment fore-edge tabs to be characteristic of Syon's library.

[124] For example, the copy (Paris, 1510: St John's Cambridge S 5 24) procured ('ex provisione') for Winchester Cathedral Priory by the precentor, John Morton, in 1518. See also a copy, 'impressus', attested in the 1521 inventory of Canterbury College: *Canterbury College, Oxford*, ed. Pantin 1, p. 61.

Print enriched the literary culture of the religious orders long before it made any measurable difference to their observant life. The women of Syon were perhaps the first to follow their observances in a printed text: it is likely that the first (although not the only) intended readers for Pynson's *Myroure of Our Ladye* (*STC* 17542) were the professed ladies themselves.[125] Perhaps it was to unite monastic observance with the Minster church that Martyn Colyns, treasurer of York, presented the Byland Cistercians with a missal of the York Use in 1509.[126] A 1519 inventory of the books of the Carthusian Thomas Golwyne underlines the still gradual transition from a devotional life in manuscript to one that might be served by print: in the bundle he carried with him from London to Mount Grace were no fewer than nine 'bokes wrytten' including a calendar, primer, 'sawter', 'a large fayer boke wrytten with the lessons of dirige and the psalmys of the burying and letany and the response', a book 'conteynynge certeyn masses with the canon of the masse and a kalendar', a 'lytell penaunce boke' and 'a wrytten boke of prayers of diverse seyntes' and a 'wrytten' *Ars moriendi*, supplemented by 'a printed Portews' (i.e. a breviary), *Legenda aurea*, perhaps by Julyan Notary (London, 1504, *STC* 24877), *Directorium aureum* (i.e. Hendrik Herp, *Directorium aureum contemplativorum* (Cologne, 1509)), and *Shepherd's Kalendar* by Wynkyn de Worde (London, 1511, *STC* 22409.5).[127] Among the unreformed religious, there was lingering attachment to the aesthetic of the deluxe manuscript liturgy.[128] Only in the last decade before the Dissolution is there any indication of the adoption of print for either the daily or the festive office. Abingdon printed its breviary in 1528 and St Albans its breviary in 1534, although no other domestic use is known to have passed into print before 1539.[129] A printed breviary (Salisbury Use: Paris 1519) had entered the collection at Polsloe before its suppression, apparently for communal, conventual use, since it preserves a list of the nuns on its last leaf.[130] An eleventh-hour benefaction to the women of Easebourne in Sussex from Sir David Owen in 1535 provided a missal 'prynted in paper' for the use of the priest that celebrated his obit at the altar adjoining his tomb.[131] Perhaps the 'new psalter' which the Observant Franciscan Father

---

[125] For the text of the *Myroure of our Ladye*, see *Myroure of oure Ladye*, ed. J.H. Blunt EETS ES 19 (1873). For its reception, see N.B. Warren, *Spiritual Economies: Female Monasticism in Later Medieval England* (Philadelphia, PA, 2001), pp. 49–59; C.A. Grisé, '"In the Blessid Vyneȝerd of Oure Holy Saveour": Female Religious Readers and Textual Reception in the *Myroure of Oure Ladye* and the *Orcherd of Syon*', in *The Medieval Mystical Tradition in England, Ireland and Wales*, ed. M. Glasscoe (Cambridge, 1999), pp. 193–212.

[126] Colyn's gift is now CUL, Res. B 162. See also *MLGB* (1), p. 235.

[127] PRO, SP 1/19, pp. 168–69 (*LP Henry VIII*, 3.606). See also E.M. Thompson, *The Carthusians in England* (London, 1931), pp. 327–28; Doyle in *Syon Abbey*.

[128] Among his purchases of printed book, Prior More of Worcester invested in the 'wrytyng' of a new mass book: *EBL*, B117. 2 (664). The deluxe missal commissioned by the (Augustinian) canons of St Augustine's Abbey, Bristol (now Bristol Public Library) also belongs to this period. The monks of Hailes Abbey received a manuscript Psalter, the work of the accomplished scribe Peter Meghan, from their patron, Christopher Urswick, one of two deluxe codices he donated to the convent, now Wells Cathedral, MS 5.

[129] For the role of print in pre-Reformation liturgical practice, see R.W. Pfaff, *The Liturgy in Medieval England* (Cambridge, 2009), pp. 545–52.

[130] Oxford, BodL, BB 200.

[131] West Sussex Record Office, Cowdray/12. See also *The Victoria History of the County of Sussex*, ed. W. Page (London, 1907), 2.84–85 (85).

Abraham had left behind when he was removed to the Stamford Greyfriars was printed.[132] Printed missals may have been more widespread: a mix of manuscript and print was found when the Dissolution commissioners compiled inventories of service-books between 1536 and 1540.[133] The 'masse bokes' and missals sold by the agents of John Scudamore from the surrendered churches of the Lichfield and Stafford friars in September 1538 may also have been recent imprints given their modest sale prices (between four pence and twelve pence).[134]

The king's Injunctions of 1535 may have encouraged, if not compelled, monastic superiors to replace the repertory of 'readers' for the daily chapter with prescribed printed authorities. Witnesses to the new regime of biblical instruction required by the reformers attest to the presence of new authorities available only in printed editions. John Alcestur of Evesham went so far as to secure an English Bible (printed at Antwerp) in 1537.[135] It is possible that the English Bible which the former abbot William Edys bequeathed in 1545 had been acquired before the secularisation of his house.[136] It may have been in response to the injunctions that Abbot Stephen Sagar (alias Whalley) of (Cistercian) Hailes Abbey in Gloucestershire purchased a new imprint of the monastic fathers explicitly for use in the chapterhouse as late as 1538, scarcely nine months before he was forced to surrender the monastery.[137] A printed *Vitas patrum* was procured for the Premonstratensians of Langley, perhaps for the same purpose of communal, or indeed capitular reading.[138] At the same time, the king's commissioners complained of conspicuous non-conformity: 'they have greate pleasure in reding of suche erronyus doctours & lyttyll or none in reding of the Newe Testamente or in other good books'.[139]

The interplay between script and print in this period is focused clearly in accounts of the investigations that preceded the Dissolution. The most provocative comments on the king's Reformation were committed to (and circulated in) manuscript, the febrile climate apparently encouraging a return to personal compilations.[140] Print provided access to the leading authorities of traditional

[132] PRO, SP 1/86, fol. 91r–v at r (*LP Henry VIII*, 7.1307).
[133] For example, the inventory (?early July 1537) of the convent of the Chester Dominicans, recording in the choir, 'a print mass book of our use' together with other unspecified service-books: PRO, SP 1/133, fol. 247r–v at r (*LP Henry VIII*, 13/1.1298 (2)); at the Ipswich Franciscans the choir books were said to be '20 . . . good and ill': PRO, SP 1/141, fols 225r–226r at 225r (*LP Henry VIII*, 13/1. 699); at the Augustinian friars of Stafford there were, '2 poor mass books, one printed, one written': *LP Henry VIII*, 13/2.56 (2); at the Llanvais Franciscans in August 1538 'two print mass books': *LP Henry VIII*, 13/2.138.
[134] BL, Add. MS 11041, fols 87r–v, 89r.
[135] The book is now in the custody of the Evesham Almonry Museum. See *MLGB* (2), p. 100.
[136] PRO, PCC, PROB 11/30, fol. 75v.
[137] A copy of Bede (Paris, 1521) was in the library at Balliol College but is now untraced. A copy of Dionysius (Cologne, 1533) is now in the library of St George's Chapel, Windsor (IH. C); both books bore the remains of a common inscription giving date and purpose of the acquisition.
[138] Gribbin, *Premonstratensian Order in Late Medieval England*, p. 148.
[139] BL, Cotton MS Cleopatra E IV, fols 43r–44v at 43v (*LP Henry VIII*, 9.523). Note also the 'parchment' and 'written' bibles recorded in the inventories of the priors' and monks' chambers at Dover Priory at its surrender: *LP Henry VIII*, 9.717.
[140] For example, Dr Gwynborne of the Beverley Greyfriars was reported to have written 'divers libels against the king' and 'given copies about': PRO, SP1/85, fol. 35r (*LP Henry VIII*, 7.953); of the London Carthusians Fox and Chauncey it was said 'eche of them hathe a boke wherin be suche authorities as they do leane unto': BL, Cotton MS Cleopatra E IV, fol. 298r (*LP Henry VIII*,

ecclesiology, and, it would appear, carried them even into the convents of provincial England. The king's agents found 'the statutes of Bruno' and 'other lyke doctors' in every cell at the Charterhouse:

> Hit ys no grete mervyle thogh many of these monks have heretofore offendid God & the Kyng by theyre fowle errours, for I have fownde in the prior's and proctour's cells iii or iiii sondrye printyde books from byonde the sees of as fowle errours & heresyes as may be, and one or ii books be never printed alone, but hundreds of them, wherefore by your maisterships favour hit semyth moche necessarye that theyr cells be better serchide.[141]

From the Stamford Greyfriars, the Observant, Francis Lybert, wrote of his *Enchiridion Ecki*, from which he had been separated when placed in custody; it was a copy of the same work from which the Cistercians of Warden in Bedfordshire were reported to be reading, provocatively, in place of the lecture from scripture prescribed under the visitors' injunctions.[142] It was a printed edition of the life of Becket with which Abbot Richard Whiting was implicated when the commissioners confronted him at Glastonbury.[143] Pressure to submit to the new dispensation (the supremacy, the injunctions) also came by way of print. Thomas Bedyll left books 'bothe of myne owne and others against the primacy of the bishop of rome and also of saint Peter' with the monks of the London Charterhouse with a view (more in hope than expectation) to shifting their stance.[144] The same community was given a consignment of twenty-four copies of William Marshall's translated, expurgated *Defence of Peace*, although a similar pessimism attended the gift and one of the monks, John Rochester, retained his copy for only four or five days before burning it.[145]

It is generally argued that the advent of print transformed approaches to reading. This may be tenable in terms of lay society and the development of a domestic culture of the book, but among the religious orders patterns of communal and private reading had evolved over centuries and were perhaps too well formed to be susceptible to any sudden shift. Print may have enabled the private reading of the religious in a practical sense, since, in time at least, it ensured that books were affordable and portable, and perhaps easier to procure independent

---

7.1105); writings passed from Fisher to his supporters at Syon: BL, Cotton MS Cleopatra E VI, fol. 164r-v (*LP Henry VIII*, 8.1125).

[141] PRO, SP 1/92, fol. 188r (*LP Henry VIII*, 8.778); BL, Cotton MS Cleopatra E IV, fols 43r–44v at 43v (*LP Henry VIII*, 9.523).

[142] Lybert's book was presumably *Enchiridion locorum communium aduersus Lutheranos*, pr. 1525 &c.: PRO, SP1/86, fol. 91r-v at r (*LP Henry VIII*, 7.1307). The abbot of Warden is reported to have assigned one Thomas London to read the prescribed daily divinity lecture, and he indiscreetly read from 'Eccius's Homilies' (i.e. *Homiliarum siue sermonum doctissimi viri Johannis Eckii*, pr. 1537) which 'entreat of many things clean against the determination of the Church of England': BL, Cotton MS Cleopatra E IV, fol. 163r (*LP Henry VIII*, 9.1167).

[143] '[The visitors] searched his study and found . . . the counterfeit life of Thos. Bequet in print': Oxford, BodL, Tanner MS 343, fol. 32r (*LP Henry VIII*, 14/2.206). Presumably the text in question was either Pynson or Rastell's printing of *Here begynneth the lyfe of the blessed martyr saynte Thomas* (London, *c*.1520, STC 23954/23954.3).

[144] BL, Cotton MS Cleopatra E VI, fol. 259r-v at r (*LP Henry VIII*, 8.675).

[145] BL, Cotton MS Cleopatra E IV, fols 43r–44v at 44r (*LP Henry VIII*, 9.523). For Marshall, see W. Underwood, 'Thomas Cromwell and William Marshall's Protestant Books', *Historical Journal* 47, no. 3 (2004), 517–39 (519).

of conventual authority, but it did not change the way they were read. The books of both single and multiple owners carry varied marks of their readers' responses, none of which diverge from the repertory of nota benes, paraphs, pointing fingers and elaborate underlines found in manuscript. Indeed, the religious were perhaps more inclined to subject their printed texts to the schemes of annotations with which their predecessors had filled conventual manuscripts, recognising the continuing limitations of the critical apparatus, foliation or pagination of many editions. The venerable Benedictine scholar, Richard Kidderminster, filled the leaves of his 1502 Lyons edition of *Vitas patrum* with notes for his own use, in Latin and employing a distinctive floral siglum to signal passages of the text, and in English for, perhaps, his junior charges: 'Pallium: a mantell such as knights of ye garter do were a longe robe, a cope, a cloke.'[146] The regular and sometimes wider margins of printed leaves offered opportunities for the scribble of unrelated notes, just as they had in manuscript: William Edys found his copy of Petrus de Palude's (attrib.) Lenten sermons on the New Testament convenient to record medical recipes and the epitaph of Henry de Ferrers (d. 1093x1100), founder of Tutbury Priory in Staffordshire.[147] Printed volumes provided a canvas for the professed to articulate a personal identity but for the most part in forms that had been found in the individual manuscript anthologies of earlier generations. The elaborate *ex libris* pages of female professed owners of print have been brought into focus but it is perhaps only the poor(er) preservation of their manuscript counterparts that sets them in relief.[148]

In fact, the place of some examples of monastic provenance is indicative of an impulse to impress print into the service of manuscript. From its first appearance, print was recognised, by religious accustomed to the singular luxury of a working library with few lacunae, as a source of text exemplars from which manuscripts of greater aesthetic, personal and perhaps scholarly value might be made. Even seventy years after the advent of print, Anne Bulkeley required a transcription of William Bonde's allegory of the Mass which had first been published by Pynson.[149] Print was sometimes subordinate, a supplement to anthologies already formed from manuscript selections: Abbot Thomas Cleobury of Dore integrated three printed texts, Lichtenberger's *Prognosticatio*, the pseudo-Aristotle's *Problemata* and Sextus Aurelius Victor's *De viris illustribus* (attributed to Pliny the Younger), into a cohesive collection of medical and more broadly scientific texts already collected in manuscript.[150] John Portar alias Smythe of Durham formed a volume of diverse pastoral and theological authorities which frame a contemporary handwritten 'ballet of ye deth of ye cardynall'.[151] There

---

[146] Oxford, BodL, Rawlinson, Q. d. 12., fol. 40v. Kidderminster's *ex libris* is on the title page.

[147] Oxford, All Souls College, v. 2. 13: the notes are on the flyleaf.

[148] See, for example, Mary Erler's focus on the *ex libris* of Joanna Sewell in her copy of *Scala perfectionis*: Erler, *Women, Reading and Piety*, p. 123 & plate.

[149] 'Syon Abbey and its Religious Publications', p. 22. The manuscript is now BL, Harley MS 494 and has been edited with critical commentary by Alexandra Barrett, *Anne Bulkeley and Her Book: Fashioning Female Piety in Early Tudor England. A Study of British Library, Harley MS 494* (Turnhout, 2009).

[150] Cleobury's book is now BL, Harley MS 218. The printed texts are at fols 1r–49r, 122r–146r.

[151] Portar alias Smythe's book is now BL, Add. MS 50856. The printed texts are at fols 1r–19r, 49r–104r.

were times when it would appear that print served only as an adornment of a precious manuscript: the readers of Syon were known to paste woodblock decorations into their handwritten books.[152]

The authority of the religious orders, their observant, pedagogic and spiritual traditions, had been raised on a manuscript culture, but they proved an early and engaged audience for the printed book. Certainly the surviving traces of their consumption of print are meagre but it would be wrong to infer from the evidence that 'it took time for [print] to become accepted . . . by a group of people . . . of conservative tastes'.[153] In fact, monks and regular canons were among the avant garde of print in England; their consumption of the new medium was constrained perhaps only by a provincial supply chain that was unable to satisfy the demand. Personal collections of print were accrued first, and perhaps more quickly than conventual holdings but perhaps for no other reason than the pragmatic fact that manuscript libraries remained in situ, comprehensive in coverage and subject to continued investment. Print did not replace manuscript, although there is at least anecdotal evidence that it had become the dominant medium in some houses; more often it was held as a percentage (greater than ten per cent) proportion of the total.[154]

In spite of their early profile as consumers, England's regulars were slow to enter into the business of printing. Indeed, it was only after their Continental brethren had for the most part ended their own printing enterprise that a handful of English houses invested in productions of their own. Birgittine Syon has been, and should be the focus of this brief episode, but the productions of the presses under Benedictine patronage between 1525 and 1539 merit attention since they also served to convey a monastic voice in print. It was not print itself that projected the last generation of regulars into public discourse; rather it was a convenient and current medium for an authorial agency already reawakened by the stimulus of reform from within the orders and the rising threat of Reformation from without.

The response of the regulars serves to moderate the reputation of print as a force for cultural change. The advent of the printed book did not dissolve the old communal, conventual bonds of the professed life. Print assisted and in time augmented the private ownership of books but this was a mode of monastic behaviour which had become fixed long before the later fifteenth century. Nor was it incompatible with communality. Indeed, the repertory of procurement inscriptions preserved in surviving printed books conveys the unchallenged authority, and priority, of conventual need. Print did perhaps diversify reading tastes, at least in the somewhat mono-cultural climate of unreformed monastic orders, but it did not significantly alter approaches to reading. The potential

---

[152] Gillespie, 'Syon and the English Market', p. 111. See also M.C. Erler, 'Pasted-in Embellishments in English Manuscripts and Printed Books, c. 1480–1533', *The Library*, 6th ser., 14, no. 3 (1992), 185–206.

[153] D.N. Bell, 'Monastic Libraries', in *CHBB III*, pp. 229–54 (250).

[154] Of course, any judgment rests on the insecure testimony of the survivors and any extant book list, but the investment in, and attachment to, print which can be attested, inter alia, at Benedictine Durham and Worcester, Cluniac Monk Bretton and the Lincolnshire convents whose holdings were given summary notice in Royal Appendix 69, does perhaps underline a distinct preference, at least for working texts, among the last generation before the Dissolution.

of print to refashion the observant life was explored in the shadow of the Dissolution, but the prospect of Benedictine (or Cistercian) religion formed from common printed liturgies or re-edited patristic lore was eclipsed by a greater cultural transformation over which they had little control.

Further Reading

Armstrong, E.A., 'English Purchases of Printed Books from the Continent 1465–1526', *English Historical Review* 94 (1979), 268–90.

Barrett, Alexandra, *Anne Bulkeley and Her Book: Fashioning Female Piety in Early Tudor England. A Study of British Library, Harley MS 494* (Turnhout, 2009).

Bell, D.N., *What Nuns Read: Books and Libraries in Medieval English Nunneries*, Cistercian Studies Series 158 (Kalamazoo, MI, 1995).

da Costa, Alexandra, *Reforming Printing: Syon Abbey's Defence of Orthodoxy*, 1525–1534 (Oxford, 2012).

Cross, C., 'A Medieval Yorkshire Library', *Northern History* 25 (1989), 281–90.

Erler, M., *Women, Reading and Piety in Late Medieval England* (Cambridge, 2003).

_____, *Reading and Writing during the Dissolution: Monks, Friars and Nuns, 1530–1558* (Cambridge, 2013).

Gejrot, Claes, Sara Risberg and Mia Åkestam, eds, *Saint Birgitta, Syon and Vadstena: Papers from a Symposium in Stockholm 4–6 October 2007*, Konferenser 73 (Stockholm, 2010).

Jones, E.A. and A. Walsham, eds, *Syon Abbey and its Books. Reading, Writing and Religion, c. 1400–1700* (Woodbridge, 2010).

Rhodes, J.T. 'Syon Abbey and its Religious Publications in the Sixteenth Century', *Journal of Ecclesiastical History* 44 (1993), 11–25.

Pantin, W.A. and H. Aveling, eds, *The Letter-Book of Robert Joseph*, Oxford Historical Society, New Series, 19 (Oxford, 1967).

11

Universities, Colleges and Chantries

JAMES WILLOUGHBY

In 1517 work was begun on a new library-room at Eton College, a grander building for an expanding collection. Chains for the books were bought in three different lengths and the windows were stained with vignettes to signify the various suits of study that were laid out on the shelves below. The provost, Roger Lupton, is credited with the building, and he also gave books to the college, a mixed collection in manuscript and print. Eton has been fortunate: the building, now Election Hall, still stands; Lupton's books are still on College shelves. As such, they serve to remind us that when we come to draw our conclusions on the early circulation and impact of print we should be aware of a slant in the evidence, in that conclusions respective to one constituency or another are easier to make from surviving copies, and survival has favoured the higher secular clergy. The libraries of their colleges at Oxford and Cambridge, at Eton and Winchester, and chapter libraries at the secular cathedrals, more or less stable across the breach of the Reformation, have kept good numbers of books on their shelves, unlike the houses of regular clergy where losses were comprehensive.[1] Where there are not the physical books there is often a substantial archive that can hold catalogues or inventories of the pre-Reformation collection, or there may be testamentary evidence concerning bequests of books to the library, or registers of benefactors. Of course, not every class of secular institution was so fortunate. The houses that did not survive into the second half of the sixteenth century were the collegiate churches beyond the universities, the chantries and some of the hospitals, which all went down in two waves of suppressions in 1545 and 1547. Surviving books from such places are few but, as we shall see, there is sometimes documentary evidence that allows a statement about book provision there to be formulated.

The libraries of the collegiate universities have received very much more attention from scholars than those of these other clerical institutions, even though foundations in this latter category were greatly more numerous. The reading needs of their personnel were different and the composition of their libraries reflect that. What all these clerical libraries had in common was that books in English took no place; Latin was the currency of the clerical classes,

---

[1] Only those monastic cathedral priories that became cathedrals of the New Foundation at the Reformation, chiefly Worcester and Durham, have kept portions of their medieval libraries in situ. See James Clark's essay in this volume.

and in the main it was the Latin of the Fathers and the schoolmen rather than
of the silver or golden age. So firmly did this constituency dominate the market
for printed books that the publication of works in English in the fifteenth and
early sixteenth centuries was insignificant when set against the Latin trade. The
Latin trade itself was a Continental affair, and the native market was too imma-
ture to allow publishers in England to break into it; stationers relied instead on
importation.[2] Only a bare handful of books for this scholarly market would be
printed before 1500 on English presses, and it was small numbers thereafter.

In the first few decades of European printing until about the 1470s there was
no great difference in price between printed books and manuscripts. At the
end of the fifteenth century and after 1500 the variety of titles increased very
sharply and prices fell.[3] By the end of the sixteenth century print had utterly
transformed the hopes of private collectors, and with them expectations for
the libraries of the institutions of the secular clergy. Such libraries did not have
their own income for acquiring books. Collegiate resources might be directed
towards the acquisition of particular texts in answer to a royal or episcopal
injunction, and this was particularly the case around the mid sixteenth century
when university colleges tried to fill gaps on their shelves with the latest editions of *patristica* in Latin and Greek. Some colleges, it is true, made small purchases from corporate revenues, as New College in Oxford was doing from the
early sixteenth century onwards. But in general, libraries tended to accumulate
not by planned acquisition but in an ad hoc way by gift and, especially, by
bequest. For this reason, a lag of a generation is generally perceptible between
the time in the earlier sixteenth century when private buyers were building their
collections of printed books, to the point later when libraries received them.
In 1557, the university library at Cambridge, admittedly depleted, could show
only 163 books, whereas it was not unusual for an individual scholar of the day
to own one hundred books or more. By 1559, John Bateman, a senior scholar
and founding fellow of Gonville and Caius College, died possessed of nearly
500 volumes, a far greater resource than an average college library could have
shown a century earlier.[4]

The first two decades of the sixteenth century are barren ones for gifts to
college libraries, as if the stupendous growth of printing had called into question the continuance of a common stock. In the late fifteenth century, libraries
in the university colleges were still organised into two collections, a reference
collection chained in a dedicated room, usually called a 'libraria', and a separate

[2] 'Importation', pp. 179–201; Lotte Hellinga, 'Importation of Books Printed on the Continent
into England and Scotland before *c.* 1520', in *Printing and the Written Word*, ed. Sandra Hindman
(London, 1991), pp. 205–24; Kristian Jensen, 'Text-books in the Universities: the Evidence from
the Books', in *CHBB III*, pp. 354–79.
[3] Uwe Neddermeyer, *Von der Handschrift zum gedruckten Buch: Schriftlichkeit und Leseinteresse
im Mittelalter und in der frühen Neuzeit: Quantitative und qualitative Aspekte* (Wiesbaden, 1998);
Edward L. Meek, 'Printing and the English Parish Clergy in the Later Middle Ages', *TCBS* 11
(1997), 112–26.
[4] For the University library, see Peter D. Clarke, *The University and College Libraries of
Cambridge*, CBMLC 10 (London, 2002), pp. 72–102 (UC7); for Bateman, *Books in Cambridge
Inventories: Book-lists from Vice-Chancellor's Court Probate Inventories in the Tudor and Stuart
Periods*, ed. E.S. Leedham-Green, 2 vols (Cambridge, 1986), 1.234–44 (no. 105).

stock for circulation among the fellows, 'in electione sociorum'. Over the course of the sixteenth century, a chained collection of expensive core textbooks maintained its status and usefulness (in a room now more often called the 'bibliotheca'), but the *electio* stock came to be abandoned as fellows were able to acquire for themselves the books they wanted to read. Where evidence exists for the continuance of the *electio*, as for example from Lincoln College, Oxford, it is clear that the old stock of manuscripts had been thoroughly interpenetrated by printed books; we might imagine that such books had been given to the college and found to be unsuitable for the chained collection. Institutional booklists of the sixteenth century refer to the *bibliotheca*, and we need to be aware that such lists show not the totality of what was available to be read in a college but rather what could be fitted into the room. Library rooms and arrangements for shelving and chaining were still medieval, so it is no wonder if priority was given to the large-scale sets, since these books were the most expensive to buy, beyond the reach of many. The development of the stall system for the shelving of books as generally adopted at the end of the sixteenth century was a means of coping with new accessions now coming at flood.

Another slant of the evidence affects our conception of the subject-profile of these communal libraries. The key works were most often in folio, and large books have a better chance of survival than smaller books. Larger books could be chained, the best way of ensuring their safety in a stable setting – at least until chaining became unfashionable in the eighteenth century. Octavos seem rarely to have been chained, which would also explain the relative absence of classical Latin in the profile, these books in the sixteenth century most normally being printed in octavo and taken up enthusiastically by the private market rather than the institutional. The importance to the market of books printed in smaller formats is made clear by the declining numbers of folio imprints. In the first decade of printing some forty-five per cent of editions were folio; by the last decade of the fifteenth century the number had fallen to about thirty per cent, and that figure had more or less halved by the first half of the sixteenth century. Other categories of textbook routinely printed in folio also slid from the record after the 1535 ban on public lectures on canon law and on the Sentences and its commentators at the universities, two centres of traditional curricula.[5] Thereafter, books in these classes gradually disappeared from collegiate libraries, and bookmen who owned copies left them to friends and colleagues instead, for the private study of canon law was still permitted. A generation or two further on, books from these redundant branches of learning were frequently favoured for use as binding scrap in newer books. (The same fate befell liturgical manuscripts of the old Latin rite, another redundant class.) It is the case that Oxford libraries, so rich in early editions of civil law, have far less to show for canon law. It is a fair guess that such books, heavily abbreviated in dense gothic type, already seemed old-fashioned long before the coup de grâce was administered by royal proclamation. On the other hand, as Neil Ker pointed out, the books which would have been welcome in collegiate libraries – for example, the great 1516 edition of Jerome's *Opera* – were probably not bought by many

[5]   *LP Henry VIII*, 9.208 (no. 615).

people in a position to pass them on quickly: 'the older men died, but had not bought them; the younger men bought them but did not die'.[6]

One early purchaser who did embrace print and soon passed on his treasures was James Goldwell (d. 1499), bishop of Norwich from 1472 and the first Englishman known to have bought a printed book, a copy from the *editio princeps* of Willelmus Durandus's *Rationale diuinorum officiorum*, printed by Fust and Schoeffer at Mainz in 1459 (*GW* 9101), which he purchased in Hamburg in September 1465 when at the head of a diplomatic mission. He was an enthusiastic bibliophile, apparently buying books in Rome in the 1470s as they came off the press, and his taste and achievement as a collector are witnessed by the books he bequeathed to his old college of All Souls in Oxford, of which thirty are still on the shelves.[7] It is now known that it was through his sponsorship that printing first took place at Oxford. In 1478 he employed an anonymous jobbing printer, who used a Cologne type, to produce an edition of the *Expositio in symbolum apostolorum* by Rufinus. Goldwell owned a manuscript of the text, copied by Vespasiano da Bisticci in Florence, to which he had his arms added. These arms and the style of the miniature were both copied in the printed edition, proving that Goldwell's manuscript was the exemplar and that publication in this instance was not market-driven, but 'could stem from the enthusiasm or convictions of a book-lover, who had found a way to share a treasure with others'.[8] Oxford was a chief English market for the Latin trade, but it was probably local interest rather than demand that drove the publishing that took place there between this start in 1478 and its end in 1486 or 1487.

Goldwell's jobbing printer brought out two more quarto books, the larger one being Aristotle's Ethics in the translation of Leonardo Bruni in 1479 (*STC* 752), which was a popular text in the Oxford of the day and was no doubt once again a commission. This press was not active for long; another attempt was made after an interval of two years when another Cologne printer, Theodoric Rood, named himself in dated editions in 1481 and 1482.[9] The choice of texts printed is significant: works that were central to the curriculum of the university, such as the Lombard's Sentences and its associated commentaries or the large-scale works of canon or civil law, were not attempted. Rood's two most ambitious productions were locally particular: William Lyndwood's *Prouinciale* (*STC* 17102), which was a digest of the constitutions of the province of Canterbury, printed in Royal folio one page at a time (and glossed, a book of scholastic appearance when set against the smaller formats of both manuscript and later editions), and the Commentary on Lamentations by the English Franciscan John

[6]   N.R. Ker, 'Oxford College Libraries in the Sixteenth Century', *Bodleian Library Record* 6 (1959), 459–515 (474); repr. in his *Books, Collectors and Libraries: Studies in the Medieval Heritage*, ed. Andrew G. Watson (London, 1985), pp. 379–435 (394).
[7]   Listed by Emden in *BRUO* 2.785. On Goldwell (and Russell, Rotherham, Fox and Shirwood below), see too Susan Powell's and Alan Coates's essays in this volume.
[8]   Lotte Hellinga in *BMC XI*, p. 51. For the humanistic interest in printed books shown by Englishmen of similar rank, see Martin Lowry, 'The Arrival and Use of Continental Printed Books in Yorkist England', in *Le Livre dans L'Europe de la Renaissance*, ed. Pierre Aquilon and Henri-Jean Martin (Paris, 1988), pp. 449–59.
[9]   On Theodoric Rood, see most accessibly Hellinga in *BMC XI*, pp. 13–15; the argument for Rufinus's priority is summarised at p. 13.

Lathbury (*STC* 15297) – the only incunable edition, of which six surviving fragments are on vellum. Both the Lyndwood and the Lathbury are well represented – indeed chiefly represented – by copies in Oxford and Cambridge libraries. The copy of the Lathbury at All Souls, one of the vellum copies, carries the signatures of four fellows of the college, who, it has been argued, probably stood as financial backers for the project.[10]

The fellows of Magdalen College may have stood behind the publication of Rood's first Oxford imprint, Alexander of Hales's *Expositio super tres libros Aristotelis de anima*, published in 240 folio leaves on 11 October 1481 (*STC* 314); according to the accounts, five copies were purchased by the college almost as soon as they left the press, two of which survive at Magdalen.[11] While these may have been intended to be a lending stock, it is also possible that the fellows had undertaken to buy a portion of the print-run. That a collegiate *ex sumptibus* could lie behind an Oxford imprint need not surprise; to a college, publication was a simple business proposition offering the promise of a return, and the fellowship might expect itself to have had a reasonable eye for the market. But the venture was premature: the handful of other texts printed by Rood could be run off very much more cheaply than these others and were selected because there was no competing Continental edition. It is clear that Rood relied on different clients at different times, and he was also able to market his two scholarly titles, the Lathbury and the Alexander of Hales, in Cambridge, where there have been copies from early times. There is no trace of Rood in Oxford after 1484 at the latest, and it is probable that he returned to Cologne to continue business in the family firm of Arnold ther Hoernen.

At Cambridge a press was set up by another German denizen, Johann Siberch (*c.*1476–1554), of whom a similar story can be told as for the printers of Oxford. With an opening loan of twenty pounds from the university he began printing in 1520 or 1521 and showed a brief burst of activity before shutting up shop and returning to the Continent, probably Antwerp, probably by the end of 1523.[12] In this brief *floruit* he published a number of works likely to appeal to a humanist audience, including an unauthorised edition of *De conscribendis epistolis* by his friend Erasmus, and works or translations by Thomas Linacre, John Fisher and Sir Thomas Elyot. At the same time, between 1517 and 1528, the printer John Scolar was publishing in Oxford, specialising in grammar and elementary university textbooks. But the local market was not strong enough for large-scale production, and entrepreneurs saw no way to compete with the Continental presses that were producing university books for the whole of Europe. The market relied instead on importation from the Continent, and Continental printers seem to have sought out trade agreements with stationers at the universities.

---

[10] N.R. Ker, 'The Vellum Copies of the Oxford Edition (1482) of Lathbury on Lamentations', *Bodleian Library Record* 2 (1947), 185–88; summarised by Hellinga in *BMC XI*, pp. 35–36, 52.
[11] C.Y. Ferdinand, 'Library Administration (c. 1475 to 1640)', in *The Cambridge History of Libraries in Britain and Ireland. Volume 1, To 1640*, ed. Elisabeth Leedham-Green and Teresa Webber (Cambridge, 2006), pp. 565–91 (577–78).
[12] Otto Treptow, *Johann Lair von Siegburg (John Siberch), der Erstdrucker von Cambridge, und seine Welt* (Siegburg, 1964); abridged trans. John Morris and Trevor Jones, *John Siberch: Johann Lair von Siegburg* (Cambridge, 1970).

The extent of the dealings of one Oxford stationer, Thomas Hunt, can be told thanks to the survival of two lists of books he received around 1480–83 from Peter Actors, a London stationer, and John of Aachen, or Iohannes de Westfalia, printer to the University of Louvain.[13]

A few of these early customers were mindful of their collegiate libraries. In 1482, the time when Thomas Hunt was selling his books wholesale on the Oxford market, John Russell (c.1430–94), bishop of Lincoln, made a gift of 105 books to his alma mater, New College. Russell was another enthusiastic patron of the new technology, and his was a mixed collection, from which ten manuscripts and five printed books can be identified today.[14] Among the printed books are some reflecting his humanistic interests: a Vergil printed in Strassburg by Johann Mentelin c.1470 (one of the first editions of Vergil), Plutarch's Lives in the Jenson edition of 1478, and Albertus de Eyb's *Margarita poetica* printed at Strassburg by Georg Husner, not after 1479. Russell also had a copy of the Mainz Cicero of 1466, one of the first printed editions of any classical Latin text, which he had bought in Bruges on 17 April 1467 (Oates 28).

Magdalen College's first significant collection of printed books came by the gift of John Neele (d. 1498), master of the college of Holy Trinity at Arundel and an associate of Magdalen's founder, Bishop William Waynflete. His forty-two books in manuscript and print are known from a booklist that can stand as an exemplar of the sort of texts that filled college libraries. In part the collection was conventional but it shows also some hints of humanistic interest, represented by a Lactantius (Venice, 1478), an author prized for his rhetorical style, Niccolò Perotti's grammar *Rudimenta grammaticae*, and Leonardo Bruni's translation of Aristotle's Ethics in the edition printed at Oxford in 1479 (*STC* 752) and discussed above. Neele was also a purchaser of another Oxford edition from 'Goldwell's' press, a copy of the Rufinus already mentioned (*STC* 21443). Otherwise there was a manuscript bible and one volume (Genesis to Job) from Nicholas of Lyre's *Postilla moralis* (Strassburg, 1472), an unusual discovery in a university where the *Postilla litteralis* was the normal textbook (schoolmen favouring the literal meaning of the text derived from Hebrew over allegorical or anagogical interpretations); its interest chimes with another book in the list, a manuscript *Flores Bernardi*. There were also printed copies of Durandus's *Rationale diuinorum officium* (Paris, 1475) and Ludolf of Saxony's *Meditationes uitae Iesu Christi* (printed, but unidentified), two texts that seem to have been particularly popular among the English secular clergy. Duns Scotus was represented by a manuscript copy of the Quodlibets and by two printed parts of the Sentence commentary (Book I, Venice, 1476, and Book II, Paris, 1473). There were sermon collections, the ubiquitous Roberto Caracciolo (Rome, 1472) and *Sermones Parati* among them, Augustine's *De ciuitate Dei* (Mainz, 1473), and a manuscript Boethius. Neele's booklist uses an idiolect to distinguish between books 'in papiro' (print) and books 'in pergameno' (manuscript), which is an early example of a distinction that was regularly drawn in the 1520s, when 'prynted' books were more

---

[13] Paul Needham, 'Continental Printed Books Sold in Oxford, c. 1480–3: Two Trade Records', in *Incunabula*, pp. 243–70.
[14] The identified books are listed by Emden in *BRUO* 3.1610–11.

commonly found in libraries. His gift also demonstrates a common perception among testators of the relative needs of university and non-university colleges. While Magdalen benefited handsomely by this gift, the only books which Neele left his college of Holy Trinity at Arundel were a bible and a breviary.[15]

The great contemporary patron of books in Cambridge was Thomas Rotherham (1423–1500), archbishop of York and chancellor of England, who, as chancellor of the university, stood patron to a new library-room built above the schools and completed by 1475. He equipped it with numerous books both at foundation and thereafter, sufficient to be honoured by the university as one of its principal benefactors. The number of books in the original donation is stated, in the Donors' Book drawn up retrospectively around 1658, to have been 255; the number is disputed, at least in respect of the manuscripts; the incunabula, however, may prove to have been reported more realistically. The only books positively identifiable are those that were given labels on receipt identifying them as his donation or were otherwise marked 'My lord Chawnceler' on leaves at the beginning or end in a hand of about 1500. Among these survivors only six are in manuscript; the rest are incunabula, thirty-five separate items bound into thirty-two physical volumes. In 1484 he gave some of the earliest editions of Aristotle with the commentary of Averroes, all printed at Pavia by Laurentius Canozius in the early 1470s: *De anima*, the Metaphysics, *De caelo et mundo*, *De generatione et corruptione*, *Meteorologica*, *Parua naturalia*, and the Physics (Oates 2542–48).[16]

The gift of John Nobbys to Corpus Christi College, Cambridge, of some 240 books, most apparently in printed volumes, was also exceptionally large. The gift, or bequest, may have come around 1525, which is the date of Nobbys's last known appearance in the record; but doubts are raised by the dates of some of the editions themselves, the latest being a copy of Pius II, *Commentarii de gestis concilii Basiliensis* printed at Basel *c*.1542 and still in the library. There are also doubts as to whether this whole gift, recorded in a benefactors' register, really represented Nobbys's own property, or whether it also included college books that were in his custody as master or else had been provided in some way at his expense. Over two-thirds of the collection consists of patristics, scholastic theology and sermon collections, and it was almost entirely a collection of printed books. The other major gift to a Cambridge library at this time was that received by the university in 1528/9 from Cuthbert Tunstall, a collection of Greek printed books. The extent of the original gift is unknown, but at least seventeen survive with his donor inscription or are otherwise known to have been of his gift: these include copies of the *editiones principes* of Herodotus, Homer, Thucydides and Xenophon, as well as the Complutensian Polyglot Bible, one of the first copies of this work to reach England, and a volume of the Aldine Aristotle, as well as other folio Aldines. It is probably significant that Tunstall, like Nobbys, was a religious conservative, and both men seem to have placed some importance on communal collections of books as bulwarks against the more advanced

[15] R.M. Thomson et al., *The University and College Libraries of Oxford*, CBMLC (London, forthcoming), UO44; Neele's testament is PRO, PCC Will Registers, PROB 11/11 (19 Horne), fol. 152v.
[16] Clarke, *Cambridge*, pp. lxv–lxvi, 2–3, 728–29, and UC7; *BRUO* 3.1595, lists the books conveniently.

positions in Cambridge's increasingly agitated reformist atmosphere: Nobbys's was an orthodox collection; Tunstall's symbolic of the Erasmian humanism he was famed for, and indeed, as a friend of Erasmus, personally associated.[17]

The library of early books at Corpus Christi College, Oxford, reflects most vividly of any university college the achievement of its founder, Richard Fox (1447/8–1528), bishop of Durham and then Winchester, his 'trilingual' college embodying the values of the reformed university with the largest collection of Greek books anywhere in pre-Reformation Oxford. Many survive; most of the printed books are Aldines. Significant numbers came from the Greek scholar William Grocyn (d. 1519) and from John Claymond, president of the college from 1517 until his death in 1537 and a man deeply interested in the revival of classical learning. But the largest cache came from the founder himself, and within his gift were Latin books formerly owned by John Shirwood (d. 1493), Fox's predecessor as bishop of Durham who from 1474 had been royal proctor in Rome. Shirwood passed his spare time at the curia in building his library of Greek manuscripts and Latin editions (imprints ranging between 1461 and 1487), which Fox found at Durham after Shirwood's death.[18] Roman editions accounted for eighteen of Shirwood's thirty-three printed books, twelve of them from the bankrupt press of Sweynheim and Pannartz that had glutted the Roman market and which Shirwood must have scooped up with delight. Together with the books given by Goldwell to All Souls, they account for most of the early Roman editions in Oxford collegiate libraries, reminding us that Roman printers did not use export channels in the way of the Venetians but relied on a clientele of high-ranking ecclesiastics and diplomats drawn inevitably to the curia.

For colleges beyond the universities, the evidence allows a separation between distinguished establishments whose canons or fellows were often graduates and less visible colleges whose chaplain-fellows had followed quieter careers. The colleges had different roles and the character of their common libraries differed accordingly.[19] The internal ordering of a collegiate church left considerable latitude to the founder, but in general the older type of foundation was arranged according to a constitution imitative of the secular cathedrals, where canons lived on the income of their prebends and had a stall in choir and a voice in chapter. These canons were usually men of ministerial rank, freed by their prebends for work in public service, with the result that they were largely non-resident. In the absence of any real collegiate life above the rank of the deputising vicars there was little need for communal libraries. All that is known of a common collection at All Saints Derby is a list of a few priestly texts chained in

---

[17] For Nobbys's benefaction, see discussion by Clarke, *Cambridge*, pp. 211–14, with the books listed at pp. 214–39 (UC22); for Tunstall, pp. 74, 98–102, 741.

[18] R.J. Schoeck, 'The Humanistic Books of Bishop Richard Fox Given to Corpus Christi College in 1528', in *Acta Conventus Neo-Latini Bariensis*, ed. Rhoda Schnur et al. (Tempe, AZ, 1998), pp. 533–39.

[19] Unless otherwise stated, the following discussion derives from my forthcoming book, *Libraries of Collegiate Churches*, for CBMLC. It is the case that non-university secular colleges have been little studied. For orientation there is *The Late Medieval English College and its Context*, ed. Clive Burgess and Martin Heale (York, 2008), and on collegiate libraries, see therein Willoughby, 'The Provision of Books in the English Secular College', pp. 154–79.

the Lady chapel, precisely so that they could be available to the vicars. The collection at St Mary's Warwick was small enough to be held by a chest until 1465; sometime after that the antiquary John Rous (d. 1492) gave books and fitted out a library room above the south porch, but it might never have been large. These were colleges of the old foundation. Different collegiate structures fostered fuller libraries. The chantry college, an enormously popular type of foundation in the fifteenth century, imposed sterner conditions of residency on the fellows, who were bound to sing and pray for the souls of the founder and his kin – and these institutions seem to have been able to show rather more in the way of books. The sort of esprit de corps that could be fostered in a country college emerges nicely in the way that bequests to fellows of certain objects, sometimes books, run like a filigree through strings of related testaments. Usually the college at large was also a beneficiary, as for example St Gregory's College, Sudbury, whose library received over sixty books from different fellows in the course of the fifteenth century; from the 1480s these bequests included printed books. The libraries at Eton and Winchester, sisters to university colleges, were apparently best served of all, but caution is needed in weighing the evidence as their archives and, in part, their libraries have survived – the gift of institutional continuity.

What all these libraries had in common is the character of the texts that were gathered in. They were intended primarily to be a practical resource for the fellowship, stocked with textbooks to support the priest in his duties of preaching and teaching and his work of litigating. There is little in these libraries of the speculative theology or moral philosophy or science, of the works of Aristotle, Avicenna or Galen, that characterise university collections. There will often be canon law but only the principal repertories, rarely the commentaries with which the libraries of university colleges were replete; of Aquinas, one meets the *Catena aurea* on the Gospels or the *Secunda secundae* of his *Summa*, the part that deals with the seven virtues as applied to the clerical life (and a part that, significantly, was separately printed twice as often as any of the other parts).

Although donation remained the chief way in which older collections absorbed printed books, patrons wishing to build up a library de novo had recourse to the printed-book market before all else. Archbishop Rotherham's patronage of the university library at Cambridge has already been mentioned. The preoccupation of his later years was his foundation of Jesus College in his eponymous home town, a chantry college of three priest-chaplains who were to teach grammar, music, and the mechanical arts of writing and reckoning, with a provost set over them who was, for preference, to be a Cambridge doctor of divinity enjoined to preach the 'shortest and most certain way to Heaven'. To support the clergy in this mission, Rotherham left the college a very complete theological and pastoral collection in 107 books. The books are reported in a short-title inventory which cites a *secundo folio* for each, a form of reference that serves to identify the edition.[20] The library held many recently printed editions, albeit the proportion of printed volumes to manuscripts was of a rather different

---

[20] For the device of the *secundo folio* and what it can reveal for incunabulists, see James M.W. Willoughby, 'The *Secundo folio* and its Uses, Medieval and Modern', *The Library*, 7th ser., 12 (2011), 237–58.

order to the books the archbishop gave to Cambridge, where printed books greatly outnumbered manuscripts. At Cambridge, most of Rotherham's books are Venetian editions of the 1470s, published mainly between 1472 and 1476, with no edition that belonged to the 1480s. Instead, Jesus College had many books of the 1480s, the latest identified imprint being a four-volume Venetian Nicholas of Lyre of 1489. Naturally, Jesus College being the preoccupation of the Founder's declining years, building the collection there remained a concern after his work at Cambridge was done; and he or his agents used more manuscripts because the college did not need a library replete with curriculum texts, for which the latest editions were conveniently available, only access to a lower-level working collection, for which a principle of availability was doubtless invoked, choosing copies regardless of whether the book was in manuscript or print.

In similar manner, Richard Fox, when bishop of Durham, made a significant gift of books to the collegiate church of St Andrew at Bishop Auckland in Co. Durham – not a new foundation, but one that was clearly thought to be in want of a decent institutional library. The indenture that records his gift is dated 1499. There are thirty-seven titles in the list and together they present a comprehensive collection, as might suggest that the house was in intellectual low waters and that steps had been taken to put matters in hand. Theology and law preponderate and there is an impression that an effort had been made to gather together some basic textbooks in important subject areas: a Bible with the *Postilla litteralis* of Nicholas of Lyre, a copy of the Decretals and the Decrees, Cicero, Boethius, grammars and pastoral handbooks. By *secundo folio*, nearly three-quarters of the Bishop Auckland collection consisted of printed books, which reinforces a suspicion that they had been sourced and purchased at one time to supply a lack. The list shows a profile suggestive of the Oxford market, containing three Louvain editions by Iohannes de Westfalia, who, as we have seen, was exporting books to the Oxford stationer Thomas Hunt in 1483; and also a copy of the second book ever printed in Oxford, Giles of Rome's *De originali peccato* of 1479 (*STC* 158). It is worth noting that the inventory from Bishop Auckland again discriminates between books 'in papiro' (print) and books 'in pergameno' (manuscript).

Another episcopal endeavour, the last great collegiate foundation of the middle ages, saw Thomas Wolsey establish sister houses in Oxford and Ipswich, both glorying in the name of Cardinal's College. The college at Ipswich housed a school whose scholars would continue to the Oxford house for the completion of their education, and Wolsey wanted them to have a modern education – his schoolmaster wrote proudly that the boys were learning to speak Latin in the 'Italian' manner. Wolsey would have provided the school with a modern library. In September 1528 he sent the master a grammar from his own collection, no doubt an up-to-date humanist work in print.[21] There is no witness to either the library of the school or the fellows' library, but a list does survive from 1529 of the liturgical books belonging to this substantial choral foundation. The document reports whether these books are 'wrettyn' or 'printed' and gives *secundo folio* references for each. Forty-four of the books were in manuscript and are

[21] *LP Henry VIII*, 4/3.2269 (no. 5159); 4/2. 2037 (no. 4691).

stated to have belonged to the church as of old, or else had been brought from Bromhill priory in Norfolk, one of the lesser houses Wolsey had suppressed to enrich his college. Their number was not sufficient for the new foundation and other books were needed: these were supplied in print, a total of thirty-two volumes. Twenty-one of them were Sarum processionals, twenty printed on paper with the other one printed on vellum; the *secundo folio* establishes that the paper copies came from the edition printed at Antwerp by Christopher Ruremond in 1528 (*STC* 16237) and the vellum copy from Ruremond's edition of 1525 (*STC* 16236.7). Twenty was the number of priest-fellows (twelve) and clerks (eight), and so we can presume that the vellum copy was intended for the dean.[22]

The 'feeling' for manuscript over print – where textual accuracy was not at issue – still won out at the top end of the market. Richard Fox as bishop of Winchester translated the Benedictine Rule into English for the nuns of his diocese and had it printed in 1517 by Richard Pynson (*STC* 1859), but to each of the four convents in his diocese he gave a manuscript presentation copy, clearly judged the finer thing to have.[23] The wealthy bibliophile Christopher Urswick (d. 1522), dean of St George's Chapel at Windsor, commissioned at least nine books from the scribe Pieter Meghen. He also owned printed books, but these tended to resemble manuscripts, such as the *de luxe* copy of Augustine's *De ciuitate Dei* printed on vellum by Gabriele di Pietro at Venice in 1475 and given by Urswick to St George's (now Cambridge, Corpus Christi College, MS 346). The wealthy pluralist William Morland (d. 1492) left a clutch of fine manuscripts to his former college of St Stephen at Westminster: a two-volume legendary ('scriptam') and his book 'vocatum Henry Harpe'. This latter survives as London, BL, MS Add. 63787, a fine copy of Heinrich Herpf's *Speculum aureum decem praeceptorum Dei* by an expert professional scribe, taken from the *editio princeps* by Peter Schoeffer of Mainz, 1474 (*GW* 12226). It was copied very precisely, even to the extent of reproducing the printer's closing colophon (which was subsequently crossed out). Robert Mason (d. 1493), fellow of New College, Oxford, from 1438 to 1454 and a prodigious pluralist thereafter, gave the college in 1480 a manuscript copy of Albertus de Eyb's *Margarita poetica* (MS 307), copied from the edition printed at Rome in December 1475 by Ulrich Han (*GW* 9530). Like Morland's book, this copy includes the printer's colophon; the scribe, who had had a notarial training, was presumably a professional. While Mason might have been asserting his preference for manuscript over print for such presentation purposes, the more probable scenario in this case is that he did not have access to a printed copy to purchase; his livings were all north-country ones and opportunities for buying printed books would have been much the less.

The problem of access to the market was not felt at the English hospital of the Holy Trinity and St Thomas the Martyr in Rome, where a modest library had accumulated by the end of the fifteenth century to cater for the needs of the

---

[22] The *secundo folio* of the latter example is also a match for the edition printed at Paris by Wolfgang Hopyl for Francis Birckmann in 1519 (*STC* 16235), but there is a presumption in favour of the house of Christopher Ruremond.

[23] M.C. Erler, 'Bishop Richard Fox's Manuscript Gifts to his Winchester Nuns: a Second Surviving Example', *Journal of Ecclesiastical History* 52 (2001), 334–37.

confraternity of resident clergy, generally high-ranking English clerics involved in legal representation at the curia. After a period of corporate stagnation, in 1496 a new dispensation initiated a reform of the hospital, which included the construction of a new library-room, and impressive efforts were then made to fill the shelves – an act of policy for which equivalents elsewhere are not easy to find. In 1496 there were eighty-one books in the collection, mostly manuscript and more than half were service books; by May 1503 the number had more than doubled to one hundred and seventy-seven, and these new acquisitions were almost exclusively library books. The suits covered were those familiar desiderata of clerical libraries: sermon literature, canon law, pastoral handbooks, dogmatic theology – but with one of Europe's most vibrant markets for printed books on its doorstep, it is no surprise to find that these newcomers should have been in print. Chiefly they were Venetian imprints (for Venetian production had thoroughly interpenetrated the Roman market by this date) but Roman imprints also featured strongly, these two centres of production outnumbering all others by a factor almost of five – a profile that still hardly does justice to their dominance in the Italian market. Although the books were lost during the Sack of Rome in 1527 when imperial troops overran the hospital, they were listed in a string of household inventories between the years 1496 and 1503 in which a *secundo folio* for each entry is routinely cited.[24] Whilst unsurprising, it is nonetheless an unusual profile of imprints when compared to contemporary clerical libraries in England, which absorbed far more from German and Parisian presses.

Among the very few German editions at the hospital were two from the chaplain and confrater Thomas Bowdon, DCnL, who gave a bible in octavo size printed by Johann Froben at Basel in 1491 (*GW* 4269) and a printed copy of the Lombard's Sentences, which was from the edition printed at Basel by Nicolaus Kessler in 1492 (Goff P495) or else from the reprint of 1498 (Goff P496). Given the circumstances of Bowdon's expatriate life, in Rome as well as Bologna where he was pursuing legal studies, the octavo bible may have been deliberately acquired to be portable, and such a book could have been carried in the owner's baggage from England. The same advantage probably governed the choice by Clement Colyns, DCnL, of portable quarto editions of three legal text-books: the Decrees, the Decretals, and the Sext with Clementines. He left them all to the hospital at his death in 1498, and they were described in the inventory of that year as being 'in thre lytyll volumys in prynt'.[25] The quarto format is most unusual, at least for the Decrees and Decretals, normally published as stout folios, and one can hardly doubt that their portability as much as their cost made them an attractive purchase. Iohannes de Westphalia, in an introduction to his quarto edition of the New Testament printed after 1476 (Bod-inc B-313), justified his choice of format to his clerical clientele, stating that 'it is the case that few possess sufficient means to buy a whole bible, and some, even among the well-off, enjoy portable books' (sig. [a]2r).

---

[24] Nigel Ramsay and James M.W. Willoughby, *Hospitals, Towns, and the Professions*, CBMLC 14 (London, 2009), pp. 235–367 (SH62–87).
[25] Ramsay and Willoughby, *Hospitals*, pp. 254–55 and 275–77 (SH63.1–3, SH64. 115–122).

Portability was no longer a virtue when a book reached its institutional home, and the desirability for it to be chained to a desk was universally acknowledged – by the donor so as to safeguard his act of charity and by the recipient as an act of custodial policy. Legally, donation to an undying clerical or regular institution was the only means to incorporate a collection of books to ensure its stability. Four related libraries of common resort in medieval England, at London, Worcester, Bristol and Norwich, were settled on pre-existing chantry colleges.[26] The three large-scale law books that Bishop James Goldwell left to this library at Norwich in the Carnary chapel – copies of the *Decretales*, the *Lectura in Decretales* by Nicholaus de Tudeschis, and Henry Bohic's *Distinctiones in libros V Decretalium* – were probably in print; his enthusiasm for print has been discussed already. At All Saints' church in Bristol, where the common library was supervised by the clergy serving the Guild of Kalendars, a clutch of five printed books survives that have been together since the early sixteenth century (when the same hand wrote titles on their fore-edges). The books are editions of the *Summa* of Antoninus Florentinus (Nuremberg, 1486), the Sentence commentary of Guillermus Vorrillong (Venice, 1496, the *editio princeps*), Iohannes de Turrecremata, *Quaestiones Euangeliorum de tempore et de sanctis*, printed with Nicolaus de Byard, *Flos theologiae* (*Dictionarius pauperum*) (Deventer, 1484), a *Catholicon* (Lyons, 1503), and an edition of Aquinas's commentary on the Pauline epistles (Bologna, 1481). They are of a type that such a library might be expected to have possessed and they belong to the right period, encouraging the thought that they are part of the pre-Reformation collection still in situ.

Books were commonly chained in churches as helpmeets for the lower clergy, but occasionally something rather more ambitious might be attempted. Walter Smyth, fellow of Eton, bequeathed most of his books, into which he had written 'not to be sold', to the church of All Saints at Saltfleetby in Lincolnshire, to be a lending library supervised by the churchwardens; the books were to be available for a year's lease to the learned of the district. A survivor from this cache is a printed book, a copy of Alexander Carpenter's *Destructorium uitiorum* printed at Cologne by Heinrich Quentell in 1480 (*GW* 865) and now back in the Fellows' Library at Eton. It carries the confident inscription 'Saltfletby, Omnium Sanctorum', so quite how it should now be back at Eton is an interesting question, but may owe something to the hand of a successor rector, Richard Lylly (d. by April 1572), at least one of whose books made its way to Eton upon his death, a volume of tracts and homilies by John Chrysostom, all printed at Basel by Froben between 1525 and 1526, and containing Lylly's *ex libris* and notes in his own hand.

Contact between college men and the press was sometimes more intimate. A good example is provided by the fellows of Whittington College in London, an institution with a long tradition for learned, eloquent rectors. The most notable author was the religious controversialist John Standish (*c*.1509–70), admitted to

---

[26] Ramsay and Willoughby, *Hospitals*, pp. 23–27, 156–64, 215–20, 447–52. On the political inter-relation of these libraries, see James Willoughby, 'Common Libraries in Fifteenth-century England: an Episcopal Benefaction', in *After Arundel: Religious Writing in Fifteenth-Century England*, ed. Vincent Gillespie and Kantik Ghosh (Turnhout, 2011), pp. 209–22.

his fellowship in 1538. But collegiate contact with the press had begun earlier: in 1505 a London printer, probably William Faques, published a little book of suppositious homilies of Origen, stated in the colophon to have been done at the request of Master William Menyman, fellow of the college (*STC* 18846). Another book published shortly afterwards had been elicited by Stephen Dowce, master from 1496 until 1509, who stood as co-dedicatee with John Yonge, rector of All Hallows Honey Lane, of a Latin translation by Bartolomeo Gallo of Savonarola's *Sermo ... in vigilia natiuitatis domini*, published by Richard Pynson in October 1509 (*STC* 21800).[27] Dowce and Yonge were both Wykehamists and had been contemporaries at New College, which had no doubt set them on the path of friendship that becomes visible in this joint dedication. In December of that same year, Pynson put out another work that owed its composition to a college man from elsewhere, Alexander Barclay, lately chaplain of the Lady chapel at the college of Ottery St Mary in Devon. It was there that he penned *The shyp of folys*, his translation into English of Jakob Locher's Latin versification of *Das Narrenschiff*, a German satire by Sebastian Brant, which Barclay enlarged in several places with his own, not always good-natured, invective against local figures. The eight secondaries at Ottery were declared worthy to take first place in the ship of fools because they knew nothing and would learn nothing, even though they received their tuition free of charge and lived in a building next to the school itself. It may be that Ottery was also intended in the poet's vignette of the disorders of a contemporary church: in choir the clergy gossip about the latest battle in France or Flanders 'in myddes of Matyns in stede of the Legende', and others recount 'fables and iestis of Robyn Hode'. It seemed to the poet that 'no thynge can bynde theyr tunges to sylence'.[28]

There is very little evidence of any kind for books held at chantries in parish churches. The only real need for books at a chantry altar was for those that would support the cantarist in his duty of prayer, generally a missal and a breviary; if two priests served one altar, then two breviaries might be supplied. Such books do not survive and nor is there very much by way of descriptive value in the chantry certificates, which normally report sum totals for classes of goods and ornaments and do not describe individual items. Thanks to transcripts made by the Canterbury antiquary William Somner (1598–1669), there survive for Kent the brief declarations that were made in answer to the commissioners' questions, showing that it was in those primary returns that the varieties of service books might be mentioned.[29] The draft returns for churches in Wiltshire survive and some of these are descriptive of books, such as the return

---

[27]   See Susan Powell's essay in this volume.
[28]   *STC* 3545, fols 74r, 193v; *The Ship of Fools*, ed. T.H. Jamieson, 2 vols (Edinburgh, 1874), 1. 179; 2. 155; see further Nicholas Orme, 'Alexander Barclay at Ottery St Mary', *Devon and Cornwall Notes and Queries* 35 (1982–6), 184–89; and David Carlson, 'Alexander Barclay and Richard Pynson: a Tudor Printer and His Writer', *Anglia* 113 (1995), 283–302. Pynson's production of this edition is discussed in Daniel Wakelin's essay in this volume.
[29]   Somner's transcripts are in Canterbury Cathedral Library, MS Lit. C. 16, fols 17r–53r, *The Canterbury Charities and Hospitals, together with some others in the Neighbourhood, in 1546*, ed. Edward Lancelot Holland and Charles Cotton, Kent Archaeological Soc., Records Branch 12, Supplement (1934). The chantry certificates were printed by Arthur Hussey, *Kent Chantries*, Kent Archaeological Soc., Records Branch 12 (1936).

for Bishop Edmund Audley's chantry in Salisbury cathedral, where there were three missals, 'ij wrytten and one pryntid'. At Calne there was 'one masse booke prynted' valued at eight pence.[30] But it is only rarely that we can distinguish the books' format, manuscript or print. An exception is the arrangements for the Somerset Chantry at the Chapel of St George at Windsor, sealed on 30 July 1506. Charles Somerset KG, Lord Herbert, first earl of Worcester, did not die until 1526; his deed of foundation specifies the equipment that had been already assembled for his chantry, which included a *de luxe* manuscript psalter, two missals, one 'of paper in prent', and one breviary 'in two volumes of fyne velome in prynte with chanynes'.[31] At St Botolph's church in Boston, Lincolnshire, the records of the guild of St Mary make mention, 1523–24, of the books that the guild had supplied, and these included a small reference collection for the use of the priests that was kept in the 'parlour' off the chantry chapel. Two of these were in print: the 'first part of the half bybyll' and the popular *Sermones Discipuli* by Iohannes Herolt. In the church itself there were four missals of folio size printed on vellum.[32]

Where obits and chantries were already well established in a church then the patron would not have needed to provide additional books. One of the rare cases is the chantry of two priests that the Cambridge schoolman Geoffrey Downes founded at Pott Shrigley in Cheshire, which he supplied with a small collection of devotional reading material. The inventory, taken probably shortly after the foundation in 1492, is the only evidence for the contents of this library of ten volumes, of which perhaps as many as eight were in printed editions by William Caxton. It is an interesting collection for having been assembled for a particular purpose at one time and perhaps even in one place, and that place might conceivably have been Caxton's shop in Westminster.[33] Such detail is normally lacking for chantries and hospitals, but testamentary evidence can sometimes help. In 1511 Dan William Garnare left to the hospital of St John the Baptist in Canterbury his printed missal ('my masse boke in prynt') along with other liturgical equipment.[34] Another example, and potentially another Westminster purchase, was a missal bequeathed in 1504 by Henry Bost, provost of Eton, to the chaplains of the hospital of St James in Westminster – the hospital was a possession of Eton College and the place where the provost kept a townhouse. He left two books, a porteous in manuscript ('de materia pergameni vitulini') and a missal in print ('impressum'), whose *secundo folio* allows it to be identified as the Sarum missal printed at Westminster by Julian Notary and Jean Barbier for Wynkyn de Worde in 1498 (*STC* 16172).[35] Conceivably,

---

[30] PRO, Exchequer, Records of the King's Remembrancer, Church Goods Inventories and Miscellanea, E 117/12/9, rott. 7 and 10.
[31] Windsor, Dean and Chapter Archives, IV.B.3, fol. 236r–v.
[32] Ramsay and Willoughby, *Hospitals*, pp. 10–14 (SH4).
[33] There was indeed a personal connexion to Caxton through the brother of the co-founder of the chantry, Lady Jane Ingoldisthorpe. Her brother was John Tiptoft, earl of Worcester, whose translations of Cicero's *De amicitia* and Buonaccorso de Montemagno's *Controuersia de nobilitate* were printed by Caxton in 1481. See further in Willoughby, *Collegiate Churches*.
[34] Ramsay and Willoughby, *Hospitals*, p. 34 (SH10. 1).
[35] His testament is dated 25 November 1503; Ramsay and Willoughby, *Hospitals*, p. 427 (SH115).

Bost had bought the book locally. In 1514 the hospital of St Mary at Sherburn, Co. Durham, received a rare bequest of school-books by Lionel Jackson, fellow of Balliol College, Oxford. Along with two popular reference works, John of Genoa's popular *Catholicon* and the *Cornucopiae linguae latinae* of Niccolò Perotti, both source-books of vocabularies, there were *opera* of Terence and Vergil, both with commentaries (as was usual in printed editions), and these were to be chained in the choir where they would have been accessible to all the clergy. His remaining books, which were left to Balliol, seem to have been printed editions. Only one book in his inventory of goods is described as being 'in pergameno' (a 'Liber vocabularius' that went to Balliol), the word being intended to distinguish a manuscript among printed books.[36]

The concern for good letters is unusual outside the universities. The more familiar profile of books destined for the non-academic institutions of the secular clergy is exemplified by the probate inventory of Michael Clive, dated 1501 (an early example of this type of document). Clive had been warden of Winchester, and the college was his major beneficiary. There were thirty books in his possession, a mixed collection of manuscript and print, rich in texts of canon and civil law and in sermon collections, the staple fare of any graduate cleric of his standing. One of the highest valuations for a book was eight shillings set against a copy of William Lyndwood's *Prouinciale*, in the scholastic Oxford edition of Theodoricus Rood mentioned above (*STC* 17102) – a sum three shillings more than a printed copy of the Decrees (identifiable as either the Venetian edition of Nicolas Jenson, 1477 or of Iohannes de Colonia and Iohannes Manthen, 1480, both handsome books) and only two shillings less than three volumes of the *Lectura in Decretales* by Nicholaus de Tudeschis (Basel, 1477). Among the other printed books were copies of the *Sermones Parati* (Cologne, *c*.1480), Magninus de Maineriis, *Regimen sanitatis* (Louvain, 1486), and Michael of Hungary's *Sermones praedicabiles* from one of the five closely related Louvain editions of Iohannes de Westfalia, between 1477–83 and *c*.1484–85. A cleric of similar standing, John Parmenter, commissary-general of the diocese of Canterbury and canon of St Gregory's college, Wingham, Kent, drew up a testament on 17 August 1479 making bequests of a wide range of books, including a *Catholicon* in print (*in prende*). It is an early witness to the ownership of a printed copy of this popular work, whose printed tradition begins definitively with the edition printed at Augsburg in 1469.[37] He also owned 'unum librum vocatum *Canterbury Talis*', but there is no statement that this was also printed, although Caxton's first edition of the *Canterbury Tales* (*STC* 5082) was two or three years old by this date and could conceivably have been intended. It is one of the rare instances where a member of the higher clergy can be seen to have owned a book for which English was the text-language.

The process of building a collection by donated books worked tolerably well in the middle ages but it did not work in the new conditions of the sixteenth century, for it was not a system that could produce everything a college might

[36] Ramsay and Willoughby, *Hospitals*, pp. 386–88 (SH98).
[37] *GW* 3183, although an *editio princeps* is attested, probably from Mainz and perhaps from 1460, *GW* 3182. The testament is PRO, PCC Will Registers, PROB 11/7 (19 Logge), fols 142r–43v.

want. At Winchester, a very handsome gift of books came in 1543 from the Wykehamist William Moryn, a donation from which the college received almost all the medical texts as well as most of the scientific and philosophical works that it could show in its inventory of 1565. But only four titles were deemed fit to be chained in the new library: Jean Gerson's *Opera* (Strassburg, 1494–1502), the Lombard's Sentences (Basel, 1507), Aquinas's *Catena aurea* (Venice, 1506 or Paris, 1540), and two copies of Ptolemy's *Cosmographia*, shelved together (Vicenza, 1475 and Ulm, 1482). The other books were absorbed into the miscellaneous remnant kept in another part of the college and indifferently inventoried in 1566 with the repeated slighting comment, 'cum aliis multis veteribus libris tam impressis quam scriptis'.

The sort of private use a fellow might make of a common collection is suggested by a list of library books found in the chamber of a deceased fellow of Eton College, John Belfeld, in 1558 and returned to the bursars. Belfeld may have received the books through *electio*, a statutory custom at Eton, or else taken them from a miscellaneous collection of loose supervision as at Winchester. Probably four books were in manuscript and the rest were in print – a good number of them are still at Eton. It is an interesting list, twenty-three titles in thirty volumes, half supplying traditional clerical reading, such as Aquinas's *Catena aurea* (Venice, 1493) and Ludolf of Saxony's *Meditationes uitae Iesu Christi* (Cologne, 1487), with the other half supplying good letters. Of note are the *Thesaurus linguae sanctae* by Sante Pagnini (Lyons, 1529), *Punica* by Silius Italicus (Venice, 1483), *Decades rerum Venetarum* by Marcus Antonius Coccius Sabellicus (Venice, 1487), and a Quintilian (Venice, 1494). The first two titles in this list had been given to the college by Provost Lupton, mentioned above, the last three by the fellow William Horman (d. 1535), the humanist pedagogue. More exceptionally, there are also several works of canon law in the list, evidence that they were still valued in private study after the abolition in 1535 of the canon law faculties in the universities had made books belonging to that category vulnerable to weeding – although admittedly only one of those books, a *Repertorium quaestionum super Nicolaum de Tudeschis* by Alonso Díaz de Montalvo (Louvain, 1486), is still at Eton today.

Eton and Winchester, along with the university colleges and the royal free chapel of St George at Windsor, were exempted from the provisions of the 1547 Chantries Act. Elsewhere the dissolutions were thorough. Books were only occasionally noticed by the commissioners for the suppression of the colleges or chantries, and then only in bulk valuation. At St Mary's College, Fotheringhay, Northamptonshire, there were reported to be ninety-three books chained to the desks. At St John the Baptist's College at Stoke-by-Clare, Suffolk, five pounds was the valuation for 'the bokes in the library, with ther chenes, stalles, yrons, and waynscott'. In this case, it is possible to write a postscript, for the last master of St John's was Matthew Parker (1504–75), also master of Corpus Christi College, Cambridge, and renowned as one of England's great preservers of historical manuscripts, which he left to the library at Corpus Christi; but he was also a great donor to the library of incunabula and early printed books. Some of these show *ex libris* inscriptions for St John's at Stoke-by-Clare: a copy from the *editio princeps* of Boccaccio's *De montibus, siluis, fontibus*, printed at Venice in

1473, a *Legenda aurea* printed at Cologne by Ulrich Zel in 1483, and a handsome set of Nicholas of Lyre's *Postilla litteralis* printed in Nuremberg in four volumes in 1493. It was doubtless Parker who extracted these overlooked books from the defunct library at Stoke, and it is a nice question as to how many other, unmarked books at Corpus Christi came from the same source.[38]

The image of Parker setting these Suffolk books up on Cambridge shelves strikes an appropriately valedictory note. The libraries of the university colleges had collections of wider range than their country cousins and were used more intensively by young fellows jostling for promotion; but we must be careful not to formulate our picture of clerical libraries solely on the basis of those collegiate libraries that have survived. A thriving appetite for print among the clerical classes has left countless traces in the wide landscape that lay beyond the universities.

Further Reading

Clarke, Peter D., *The University and College Libraries of Cambridge*, CBMLC 10 (London, 2002).

Hellinga, Lotte et al., *Catalogue of Books Printed in the XVth Century Now in the British Museum*, vol. 11 ('t Goy-Houten, 2007).

Jensen, Kristian, 'Universities and Colleges', in *The Cambridge History of Libraries in Britain and Ireland*, 3 vols, 1: *To 1640*, ed. Elisabeth Leedham-Green and Teresa Webber (Cambridge, 2006), pp. 345–62.

Ker, N.R., 'Oxford College Libraries in the Sixteenth Century', *Bodleian Library Record* 6 (1959), 459–515; repr. in his *Books, Collectors and Libraries: Studies in the Medieval Heritage*, ed. Andrew G. Watson (London, 1985), pp. 379–436.

_____, 'The Provision of Books', in *The History of the University of Oxford* 3: *The Collegiate University*, ed. James McConica (Oxford, 1986), pp. 441–519.

Leedham-Green, Elisabeth, 'University Libraries and Book-sellers', in *The Cambridge History of the Book in Britain* 3: *1400–1557*, ed. Lotte Hellinga and J.B. Trapp (Cambridge, 1999), pp. 316–53.

Morgan, Nigel, '"Ligging in the choer, every of hem tied by hymself with a cheyne of iron". Chained Books in Churches in Late Medieval England', in *The Medieval Book: Glosses from Friends and Colleagues of Christopher De Hamel* ('t Goy-Houten, 2010), pp. 336–43.

Thomson, R.M. et al., *The University and College Libraries of Oxford*, CBMLC (London, forthcoming).

Ramsay, Nigel and James M.W. Willoughby, *Hospitals, Towns, and the Professions*, CBMLC 14 (London, 2009).

Willoughby, James M.W., *The Libraries of Collegiate Churches*, CBMLC 15 (London, forthcoming).

_____, 'The Provision of Books in the English Secular College', in *The Late Medieval English College and its Context*, ed. Clive Burgess and Martin Heale (York, 2008), pp. 154–79.

[38] On Parker's library in general, see R.I. Page, *Matthew Parker and His Books* (Cambridge, 1993). On the subject of ex-religious evacuating books from suppressed houses, see James P. Carley, 'The Dispersal of the Monastic Libraries and the Salvaging of the Spoils', in Leedham-Green and Webber, *Cambridge History of Libraries*, pp. 265–91.

THE CULTURAL CAPITAL OF PRINT

12

Humanism and Printing

DANIEL WAKELIN

After the death in 1521 of a Cambridge scholar, Bryan Rowe, his associates drew up an inventory of his hundred-odd books. Those books identify Rowe as a follower of the *studia humanitatis*, the studies least deceivingly translated as *the humanities* but usually translated now as *humanism*. Rowe read about classical literature and history, about grammar and rhetoric modelled on classical standards, and about the new ideas of people such as Erasmus who were inspired by a changing understanding of classical texts. Rowe's inventory tells us a lot about the use of humanist printed books in England. First, most of the works on it had not been printed in England by 1521, so Rowe's collection typifies the predominance of imported books for the *studia humanitatis* in England (the subject of the first section of this chapter). And the relative coherence of Rowe's collection also suggests that receiving imports was not a passive process; the activities of commissioning, collecting and annotating might make the usefulness and character of such books clear – and clearer to us than a mere booklist makes them.

Yet the sketchy evidence of Rowe's inventory makes it uncertain whether all his books were imports: for example, he owned grammars by the humanists Niccolò Perotti and Giovanni Sulpizio, which could have been imports but could equally have been one of eight editions printed in London (*STC* 19767.3, 23425–23427a, 23427a.7).[1] Moreover, imports involved interchange as well as one-way dissemination: so Perotti's grammar was printed in the Low Countries, but in one edition a quarter of the pages had translations of verbs and phrases into English – a book to import but with language which was an export (*STC* 19767.7).[2] Moreover, importing need not be passive but could sometimes be creative, for printers in England also contributed to overseas production by commissioning it, in energetic capitalist speculation. For although Rowe owned an edition of Terence's plays from the Parisian press of Josse Bade, who had printed thirty-three editions by 1520, there is a slim chance that Rowe owned the one which Wynkyn de Worde (d. 1534/5), a printer in London, had commissioned from Josse Bade.[3] The edition,

---

[1] F.J. Norton, 'The Library of Bryan Rowe, Vice-provost of King's College (†1521)', *TCBS* 2, no. 5 (1958), 339–51 (347).
[2] Constance Blackwell, 'Niccolò Perotti in England: John Anwykyll, Bernard André, John Colet and Luis Vives', *Studi umanisti Piceni* 2 (1982), 13–28 (15).
[3] Norton, 'The Library of Bryan Rowe', p. 345; Ph. Renouard, *Bibliographie des impressions et des œuvres de Josse Badius Ascensius, imprimeur et humaniste, 1462–1535*, 3 vols (Paris, 1908), 3.279–93.

with Josse Bade's commentary, was printed in 1504 in Paris but advertised itself to be 'sold' by de Worde in London for the 'studious youth' of England ('venundantur', 'studiosam [. . .] iuuentutem').[4] Such curios invite us to consider also (as this chapter then does) the hybrid nationalities of imported books.

Moreover, Rowe's books highlight the development of humanist printing in England too, for Rowe owned a manual for learning Greek by the Englishman Richard Croke (1489–1558), which was printed abroad by the German printer John Siberch (c.1476–1554) for sale in England.[5] But by 1521 Siberch had himself arrived in Cambridge, where he acted, in fact, as one of the witnesses to Rowe's inventory.[6] The presence of Siberch's name suggests how people in England – seldom ethnically English people – could follow closely Continental printing in serving the *studia humanitatis* (the topic of the larger section of this chapter). Most printers in England until the 1530s were themselves 'imports' – new immigrants from France and the Rhineland, from Theodoric Rood to de Worde and beyond. In Cambridge, Siberch set up a press to print books, including grammars, translations of Lucian, humanist orations and defences of learning in Latin, in fine editions in a large roman type imported from the Rhineland.[7] By comparing such books printed in England with imported books, it is easier to see what was borrowed from abroad, and what, if anything, was distinctive or local. For instance, Siberch also printed part of *De Miseriis curialium* by the Italian humanist Aeneas Sylvius Piccolomini (Pope Pius II) but in the black letter or gothic type typical of English vernacular books and rendered into English couplets by Alexander Barclay (c.1484–1552), a monk of nearby Ely.[8] Is the use of English 'unhumanist'? No, for Barclay also translates the genre of the work into eclogues, which continues the humanist influence, perhaps from the eclogues of Virgil and Mantuan recently printed in England for schools (as noted below). Yet this edition of Barclay's first eclogue offers no Latin for schoolboys to study but does offer – even in the few fragments surviving – political comment on the woes of courtly life, the virtuous princes of antiquity, the Commons and tyranny.[9] That is, while many of the books printed in England served the schoolroom, as imported books did, some books made in England did something else – something which the inventories of university-educated clerics such as Rowe often hide, and which the study of humanism often, therefore, misses. English-made books advanced the use of the English vernacular in humanist studies and offered non-academic comment on social, political and ethical questions. In such developments, humanist printing in England grew out of, and then away from,

---

[4] *P. Terentij Aphri comicorum elegantissimi Comedie a Guidone Iuuenale Uiro perquam litterato familiariter explanate* (Paris: Josse Bade, 15 July 1504; STC 23885.3), sig. a1r–v, discussed by Renouard, *Bibliographie*, 3.284–85. The copy in CUL, shelfmark Syn.4.50.7, has notes by various owners, including one who sounds like a studious youth: 'Mathew driland ys a good sun' (sig. C6v).
[5] Otto Treptow, *John Siberch: Johann Lair von Siegburg*, trans. Trevor Jones, ed. and abridged John Morris and Trevor Jones, Cambridge Bibliographical Society Monographs 6 (Cambridge, 1970), pp. 18–19.
[6] Norton, 'The Library of Bryan Rowe', 340–41.
[7] Treptow, *John Siberch*, pp. 27–28.
[8] Treptow, *John Siberch*, pp. 29–30.
[9] Treptow, *John Siberch*, p. 59; Alexander Barclay, *Eclogues*, ed. Beatrice White, EETS OS 175 (London, 1928), pp. 20–23, 26–29 (Eclogue I, ll. 631–59, 664–86, 754–830).

Continental printing; and humanist books moved from the international and yet circumscribed and marginal world of the schoolroom to the centre of England's culture.

Using Humanist Imports

The fact that England imported humanist books might seem an accidental by-product of the scale of the imports in general (described by Alan Coates in his chapter in this volume) and of the fact that most imports were learned works which, being usually in Latin, were marketable internationally; classical editions and other humanist texts formed a good proportion of imports.[10] As a result, printers in England were soon squeezed out of the market for books in Latin, and especially the lucrative trade in schoolbooks, the genre most likely to be influenced by humanism.[11] A few imports represented cunning efforts to capitalise on a specifically English market. For example, printers in Oxford and London issued at least six editions of a successful textbook of phrases from Terence with English translations, John Anwykyll's *Vulgaria quedam abs Terencio* (*STC* 23904–06, 23907.3–08); but the printer Gheraert Leeu in Antwerp also reprinted it, from one of the editions of William de Machlinia (*STC* 23907), presumably in order to import this English text back into England.[12]

Often, though, the notion of an import needs refining. The textbook imported from Leeu's press was, of course, by an English author, as possibly was the (aforementioned) edition of Perotti's grammar with English translations. England not only imported books; it exported texts. Many of England's humanists sent their works, and themselves, overseas in service of politics, careerism or scholarship. So when Archbishop Thomas Rotherham (1423–1500) was given a Latin poem in praise of the humanist Pope Sixtus IV, printed in Rome in 1477, what he was given was a poem by an English churchman, Robert Flemming (1416–83), who had spent much time in Rome himself.[13] Later, Thomas Linacre (*c*.1460–1524) went to the Italian cities to study, and it was in Venice that his Latin translations from Proclus's *De Sphaera* were printed, at the press of Aldus Manutius in 1499 in fine roman type and in companion with the original Greek, things no printer in England yet had the equipment for.[14] Even when English printers could do better, English writers still exported texts: among the most famous, Thomas More's *Utopia* was in part devised in Bruges and first printed in Louvain in 1516, and not in England for another four decades; Richard Pace's curious allegorical dialogue on

---

[10] *William Caxton*, p. 174; 'Importation', pp. 179–201 (181–83, 190).
[11] Andrew Pettegree, 'Centre and Periphery in the European Book World', *TRHS* 18 (2008), 101–28 (114–15, 118).
[12] Alexander H. Brodie, 'The *Vulgaria Terentii*', *The Library*, 5th ser., 27 (1972), 320–25 (323); *Humanism*, pp. 134–40.
[13] Francis Cairns, 'The *Lucubratiunculae Tiburtinae* of Robert Flemming (1477)', *Humanistica Lovaniensia* 39 (1990), 54–66; Bod-inc. 3.1045.
[14] Giles Barber, 'Thomas Linacre: A Bibliographical Survey of his Works', in *Linacre Studies: Essays on the Life and Work of Thomas Linacre c.1460–1524*, ed. Francis Maddison, Margaret Pelling and Charles Webster (Oxford, 1977), pp. 290–336 (290–92).

education, *De Fructu*, was devised in Constance and printed at Basel in 1517.[15] Yet these exported books reflected English concerns: Linacre addressed *De Sphaera* to Arthur Tudor, prince of Wales; More spoke in *Utopia* of his embassy in the service of Henry VIII and portrayed the household of Cardinal Thomas Morton with some affection; and Pace perhaps wrote *De Fructu* for the boys of St Paul's School in London, if also for 'an audience beyond England'.[16] The idea of an 'imported' humanist book conceals this English internationalism in contributing to their production.

Moreover, importing need not be passive but could sometimes be creative, and importing books could reflect the demand from customers and their intellectual interests. It has been well established that the interest of scholars, who often travelled abroad on embassies or ecclesiastical business, prompted many imports in the late fifteenth century.[17] Even when scholars less often had to import for themselves, because imported books became more ubiquitous objects for sale, we can deduce the deliberateness of scholars' acquisitions by examining their use of their books.

What most commonly reveals the humanist taste of owners is the joining of disparate editions in *Sammelbände* or 'bindings together', a very common way of storing early printed books. Some gatherings reflect practicality rather than intellectual coherence; even when they do have a humanist coherence, this could reflect the pragmatic ease in binding three volumes in the same format or bought in one imported batch from one press. Sometimes, however, coherence could suggest that the owner did not unwittingly receive just one humanist book but collected several consistently. One such *Sammelband* which seems to reflect not shared origins but humanist acquisition was owned after about 1521 by a Bristol schoolboy who names himself and his classmates on a flyleaf ('al thes go to schole with robart smithe the xxv day of may').[18] As well as two of Cicero's philosophical works, it includes Agostino Dati's *Elegantiolae*, a handbook of good Latin style, and Pier Paolo Vergerio's *De Ingenuis moribus*, which in the 1470s was imported in several editions and which sets out a programme for a humanist education. Though the schoolboy Smith was not the earliest owner, whoever was could well have had interests in schooling. Yet the texts here are not solely or simplistically educational, for they include *De Miseriis curialium* by Aeneas Sylvius Piccolomini – the work loosely translated by Barclay – and Poggio Bracciolini's *De Infelicitate principum*. These works too were annotated by somebody interested in their classical quotations, as a schoolboy might be, but

---

[15] *Complete Works More*, 4, *Utopia*, ed. Edward Surtz, SJ and J.H. Hexter (New Haven, CT, 1965), pp. xv–xxiii, clxxxiii–clxxxiv; Richard Pace, *De Fructu qui ex doctrina percipitur*, ed. and trans. Frank Manly and Richard S. Sylvester (New York, 1967), pp. xiii–xiv.

[16] Cathy Curtis, 'Richard Pace's *De fructu* and Early Tudor Pedagogy', in *Reassessing Tudor Humanism*, ed. Jonathan Woolfson (Basingstoke, 2002), pp. 43–77 (46).

[17] 'English Purchases', pp. 270–72; Martin Lowry, 'The Arrival and Use of Continental Printed Books in Yorkist England', in *Le Livre dans l'Europe de la Renaissance: Actes du XXVIIIe Coloque international d'Études humanistes de Tours*, ed. Pierre Aquilon and Henri-Jean Martin (Paris, 1988), pp. 449–59.

[18] CUL, shelfmark Inc. 4.E.4.1 [2915], flyleaf ii[r], described by Oates 2901, 3447, 3698, 3704, 3769, 3794.

they primarily recount the upsets of courtly life.[19] Did this book thereby offer a more nebulous political or social education?

Only a close reading of the annotations and names of owners (beyond the scope of this chapter) could strengthen this interpretation, or similar ones which could be made about other *Sammelbände*. There is a lot to learn about humanist reading from such books. But people were not obliged to read humanist works in humanist ways. After all, some *Sammelbände*, even of the same works, suggest some dilution of humanist concerns. For example, Vergerio's *De Ingenuis moribus* and Piccolomini's *De Miseriis curialium* were also bound together in another volume, now in York Minster, but there with quite different works such as *De Amicitia cristiana* by Peter of Blois and Caxton's editions of two of Lydgate's moral poems. Many of these little books came from the press of Johannes de Westfalia which had some connections with booksellers in Oxford.[20] Another copy of Vergerio's *De Ingenuis moribus* was also circulating in Oxford: it was bound with Anwykyll's textbook of phrases from Terence's plays, and owned by a John Grene studying in Oxford. Yet Grene's humanism was not exclusive, for his book also binds up Adelard of Bath's *Naturalae questiones*, a staple of scholastic learning on physics.[21] In these books, humanist education coexisted alongside other intellectual traditions, as is typical of humanism in England.

Nevertheless, English readers did pursue the *studia humanitatis* knowingly, as can be seen in annotations on imported copies of Vergerio's book; such notes often do tidily pick out humanist studies from the hybrid *Sammelbände* in which they occur. For example, the reader of Vergerio's work now in York Minster Library noted in the margin 'what fruits the study of literature offers' and so on ('quales fructus studium litterarum affert'), although he presumably already knew what they offered, as his *Sammelband* also included works by Guarino and Bruni.[22] Similarly John Grene annotated his printed copy of Vergerio's

[19] CUL, shelfmark Inc. 4.E.4.1 [2915] (Oates 3704, 3769): Aeneas Sylvius Piccolomini, *De Miseriis curialium* ([Louvain: Johannes de Westfalia/de Paderborn, 1480]), sigs a4v, a5r, c5r, Poggio Bracciolini, *De Infelicitate principum* ([Louvain: Johannes de Westfalia/de Paderborn, c.1480]), sigs b1v, b6v, c4r.
[20] *Printer and Pardoner*, p. 69; 'English Purchases', 274; *William Caxton*, p. 174. The volume is now disbound, the Latin parts being in York, Minster Library (hereafter YML), shelfmarks Inc. XVI.C.5, Inc. XVI.C.6, Inc. XVI.C.9, Inc. XVI.C.10, Inc. XVI.C.11, Inc. XVI.C.12, Inc. XVI.C.13, For mentioned items, see Aeneas Sylvius Piccolomini, *De Miseriis curialium* ([Paris: Petrus Caesaris and Johannes Stol, 1474–75]; YML, shelfmark Inc. XVI.C.6), and Peter of Blois, *De Amicitia cristiana* ([Cologne: Johann Guldenschaff or Conrad Winders, c.1472]; YML, shelfmark XVI.C.13), as well as ns 22, 24 and 25 below.
[21] BodL, shelfmark Arch G e.5; Alan Coates and Kristian Jensen, 'The Bodleian Library's Acquisition of Incunabula with English and Scottish Medieval Monastic Provenances', in *Books and Collectors 1200–1700: Essays Presented to Andrew Watson*, ed. James P. Carley and Colin G.C. Tite (London, 1997), pp. 237–59 (257, no. 27); Kristian Jensen, 'Text-books in the Universities: The Evidence from the Books', in *CHBB III*, pp. 354–79 (374–75).
[22] YML, shelfmark Inc. XVI.C.11, once item 3 (as n.20 above): Pier Paolo Vergerio, *De Ingenuis moribus* ([Louvain]: Johannes de Westfalia, [c.1477–78]), sigs a2r–v, b4r–v; Craig W. Kallendorf, ed. and trans., *Humanist Educational Treatises* (Cambridge, MA, 2002), pp. 42, 44. This is the same edition as Oates 3698 in n.18 above. For other mentioned items, see n.20 above and also Antonio Liporata, *Formule exordiorum in vnoquoque genere seorsum* (Paris: Petrus Caesaris, [1476–77]; YML, shelfmark XVI.C.12), which includes Guarino's *Regule de ornatissimo rhetorico dictamine* and *Sinonima*, and Francisco Florio, *De Amore Camilli et Emilie aretinorum* ([Paris: Petrus Caesaris and Johannes Stol, 1474–75]; YML, shelfmark XVI.C.5), which includes Leonardo Bruni's *De Duobus amantibus*, a Latin version of Boccaccio's story of Guiscardo and Ghismonda.

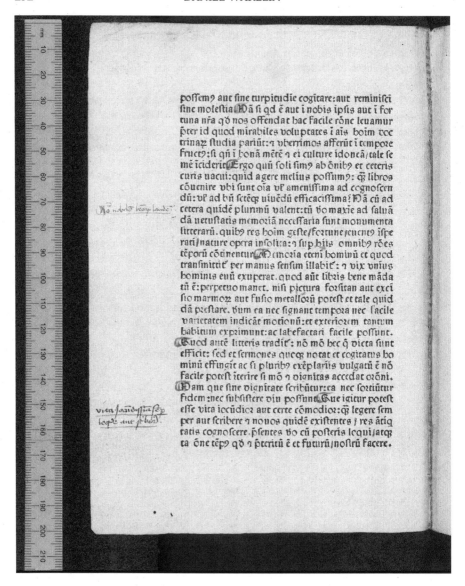

Figure 12.1 Pier Paolo Vergerio, *De ingenuis moribus [. . .]* ([Louvain]: Johannes de Westfalia, [1476–77]), sig. b3v. Oxford, Bodleian Library, Arch. G e.5.

work over 120 times, which included picking out passages on 'why the liberal arts are so called' ('quare artes liberales vocantur'), as Grene summarised it, or lines 'in praise of study', about 'how useful study is' for the commonweal and about 'the noble praise of literature' ('de laude studij', 'studium quam vtile est nota', 'nobilem litterarum laudem'; see Figure 12.1).[23] In summarising what he

[23] Pier Paolo Vergerio, *De ingenuis moribus [. . .]* ([Louvain]: Johannes de Westfalia, [1476-77]; BodL, shelfmark Arch G e.5, as in n.21 above), sigs a7r (actually the eighth leaf; the first is an

finds in this imported book, Grene is not paraphrasing passively. For example, he ignores Vergerio's references to physical exercise too, which would suit the upbringing of the noblemen or *ingenui* of Vergerio's title but not, perhaps, one of the sedentary bookworms of Oxford. Moreover, praising humanist studies becomes polemically defensive sometimes: a reader of the *Sammelband* now in York annotates Leonardo Bruni's defence 'against those who attack humanist studies' ('contra eos qui studia humanitatis vituperant').[24] That such defences needed mounting is evident in this *Sammelband*, which also included a work by Aquinas telling us to avoid secular literature – and two marks of 'nota' pick out this point too.[25]

Such annotation, then, shows how people used imported books in their studies. Indeed, the protocols for annotation were deeply influenced by humanism.[26] This annotation began even with the process of completing the book, so that it was fit to read, for in educational or academic reading one of the first tasks was to correct the printed book, which could be riddled with errors. A bilingual edition of Domenico Mancini's *De Quattuor virtutibus*, meant for 'vnlernyd chyldren', includes lists of errata and advises 'lernars' to 'first correcke them' or 'corrige : si placeat' ('correct, if it please you').[27] Learners and scholars left handwritten corrections over innumerable printed books; it has been proposed as the commonest form of annotation in scholarly books.[28] For example, a *Sammelband* of Cicero's speeches and other schoolbooks such as Aesop's fables, Anwykyll's *Vulgaria* from Terence, in an edition printed in the Low Countries, and Dati's *Elegantiolae*, in an edition printed in St Albans, looks like educational reading, and some readers of it corrected the Parisian printer's errors in Cicero's speeches. They turned 'nos' into 'vos' and f into s, where the printer had misread his exemplar or sorted his type incorrectly. They even emend errors which might not mar comprehension, but which would be harmful to good classical orthography, such as adding a macron abbreviating m to ensure that 'commemorare' has double m.[29] Such corrections are typical of the textual attention of humanists who sought to reconstruct and teach good Latin.

unsigned blank), b2r–v, b3v, and also b4r–b5r; Kallendorf, ed. and trans., *Humanist Educational Treatises*, pp. 28, 36, 38–40, 44.

[24] Vergerio, *De ingenuis moribus* (n.22 above; YML, shelfmark Inc. XVI.C.11), which includes St Basil, *Ad nepotes*, trans. Leonardo Bruni, here citing sig. d2v.

[25] Seneca, *De Remediis fortuitorum* ([Paris: Petrus Caesaris and Johannes Stol, c.1474–75]; YML, Inc. XVI.C.11), which includes St Thomas Aquinas, *Epistola de modo studendi*, here citing sig. a10r.

[26] Eugene R. Kintgen, *Reading in Tudor England* (Pittsburgh, PA, 1996), pp. 18–57.

[27] *The Englysshe of Mancyne apon the foure cardynale vertues* ([London: Richard Pynson, 1520?]; STC 17241), sigs a1v, f3r, f4v; Foster Watson, *The English Grammar Schools to 1660: Their Curriculum and Practice* (Cambridge, 1904), pp. 403–07.

[28] Ann Blair, 'Errata Lists and the Reader as Corrector', in *Agent of Change: Print Culture Studies after Elizabeth L. Eisenstein*, ed. Sabrina Alcorn Baron, Eric N. Lindquist and Eleanor F. Shevlin (Amherst, MA, 2007), pp. 21–41 (36, 41). However, Dunstan Roberts, 'Readers' Annotations in Sixteenth-Century Religious Books' (unpublished PhD thesis, University of Cambridge, 2012), p. 114, suggests otherwise for other genres.

[29] Cicero, *Orationes selectae* ([Paris: Martineau, c.1482]; CUL, shelfmark Inc. 5.D.1.10 [2429]), sigs c4r, c8v, c3v, and also sigs a3r, b12v, c4r,c8v. Somebody also frequently disambiguates similar-looking letters such as c and t. (Oates 2910, bound with 645, 749, 2978, 2798, 3442, 3479, 3486, 3542, 3889, 4209.)

After corrections, other common annotations include identifications of rhetorical or poetic tricks which might be imitated and glossed. For example, in a Venetian edition of Ovid's *Metamorphoses*, in a binding by the so-called 'Demon Binder' of Cambridge, the second of three annotators, whose handwriting is modelled on English secretary script, annotates many an extended simile as a '*comparacio*', and the third annotator, whose handwriting is modelled on anglicana, notes a poetic paraphrase ('pariphrasis') where Ovid uses a circumlocution or notes that Ovid 'speaks ironically' ('Ironice ait'). These comments evince a scholarly interest in poetic technique.[30] Other notes by readers are linguistic: for instance, these two annotators of Ovid's poem and one other in the book add glosses in Latin and twenty-three glosses in English, suggesting linguistic study, whether at school or otherwise. Glosses in English often occur in printed classical or humanist texts, as for instance in copies of Cicero's works.[31] Finally, in the annotated copy of Ovid's poem there is something much loftier than rhetoric or glossing – just once: the first annotator, who uses humanist handwriting, draws a box round one section, underlines the commentary here and recaps the point in the margin: it is Ovid's famous comment that humankind's upright form is a symbol of human dignity.[32] This idea about human dignity is often said to underpin the zeal for the humanities, as opposed to divinity, and for rationality and moral responsibility in much humanist thought.[33] However, just as they had been for centuries in manuscripts of the classics for study, such high-minded philosophies or -*isms* are rarer than schoolroom practicalities.

Humanist Printing in England

These various annotations illustrate the linguistic, rhetorical and educational assistance that readers demanded from imported books. Those demands then illuminate the choice of printers in England itself about what to supply. For humanist books printed in England extend these concerns with grammar and style. The imports also, though, ultimately highlight two other distinctive developments in home-produced books. First, whereas readers of imported books often added English glosses by hand, printers in England often printed the vernacular itself; although some books with English in them, such as Perotti's grammar or Anwykyll's *Vulgaria*, were printed abroad for import, the use of English was unsurprisingly more frequent in England itself. Second, humanist books printed in England increasingly often make explicit the broader political, social and ethical concerns which the annotations in imports reveal only intermittently.

---

[30] Ovid, *Metamorphoses* (Venice: Bonetus Locatellus, 1493), now Tokyo, collection of Prof. Toshiyuki Takamiya, printed book no. 6: sigs B1r (Ovid, *Metamorphoses*, I.533–38), B6r (II.163–64, II.184–86), B8r (II.321–22), C3r (II.623–25), C4r (wrongly labelled 'Ciii'; II.716–19), C4v (II.727–29), C5r (II.810–11), C5v (II.825–26, II.852–53), and so on at that pace. I thank Prof. Takamiya for generously letting me consult his book and his notes identifying the binder.
[31] *Humanism*, pp. 144–47.
[32] Ovid, *Metamorphoses* (as in n.30 above), sigs A2v–A3r (Ovid, *Metamorphoses*, I.74–78, 84–86).
[33] *Humanism*, pp. 184–85, 188–89.

Yet those two trends (discussed in the final section below) must not obscure the more frequent ways in which humanist printing in England is interwoven with the imported trade. The link is often evident in economics. England's first printer, William Caxton (1415x24–1492), was an importer too. The link was strong in the university towns which produced many humanist editions: one impetus for launching printing in Oxford might have been the wish to avoid import duties and undercut prices;[34] John Siberch, the witness of Bryan Rowe's inventory and the first printer in Cambridge, had previously imported books and may have set up a press in England to avoid trouble about this with the Stationers' Company.[35] The connection was spelled out in the dedicatory verses to some editions, such as the edition of the epistles ascribed to Phalaris, in a humanist Latin translation, printed at Oxford in 1485:

Hoc Teodericus rood quem collonia misit
Sanguine germanus nobile pressit opus
Atque sibi socius thomas fuit anglicus hunte .   .
Dii dent vt venetos exuperare queant
Quam ienson venetos docuit vir gallicus artem
Ingenio didicit terra britannia suo .
Celatos veneti nobis transmittem libros
Cedite nos aliis vendimus o veneti
Que fuerat vobis ars primum nota latini
Est eadem nobis ipsa reperta patres .
Quamuis remotos toto canit orbe britannos
Virgilius . placet his lingua latina tamen.

(Theodoric Rood, of German blood, whom Cologne sent, has printed this noble work, and Thomas Hunt, an Englishman, was his associate. May the Gods grant that they surpass the Venetians! That art which the Frenchman, Jensen, taught the Venetians, Britain has learned by its own wit. Venetians, stop sending us printed books; we ourselves, you Venetians, now sell them to others. The very art which was first yours, O Latin fathers, has now been discovered by us. Although Virgil sings of 'the Britons remote from the whole world', nonetheless the Latin language pleases them.)[36]

The verses spell out the national rivalry for control of trade; and they pointedly oppose the aspersion from Virgil's eclogues (I.66) that the British Isles

---

[34] *William Caxton*, p. 76.
[35] Cyprian Blagden, 'Early Cambridge Printers and the Stationers' Company', *TCBS* 2, no. 4 (1957), 275–89 (275).
[36] Francesco Accolti, trans., *Eloquentissimae Phalaridis tyranni epistolae* ([Oxford: Theodoric Rood and Thomas Hunte, 1485]; *STC* 19827), sig. m6r (my translation). Ironically, a copy in Oxford, Wadham College, shelfmark A.4.31, is bound with a Venetian import: *Nicolai Leonici Thomaei Dialogi nunc primum in lucem editi* (Venice: Gregorius de Gregoriis, 1524). That Venetian printed edition is dedicated to Reginald Pole, to whom its author, Niccolò Leonico Tomeo, was tutor, and this copy bears the signature of Arthur Pole, perhaps his brother or nephew, suggesting the circulation of books within a humanist coterie. For these people, see T.F. Mayer, 'Pole, Reginald (1500–1558)', in *ODNB* at: <http://www.oxforddnb.com/view/article/22456>, accessed 29 June 2011, and Hazel Pierce, *Margaret Pole, Countess of Salisbury, 1473–1541: Loyalty, Lineage and Leadership* (Cardiff, 2003), pp. 184–85, and n.40 below.

are a backwater. Yet the verses betray that imported books are well known in England; they assume that we will recognise the name of Nicholas Jensen, the printer in Venice. And they admit openly that printing in Oxford is, after all, imported; even Rood, the printer, is stripped of agency and made into an import by the syntax of the original Latin, in which 'Cologne' has 'sent him' ('quem colonia misit').

Moreover, as these verses hint, much humanist printing in England competed with imports by supplying books for 'the Latin language'. English printers printed and pirated the grammars and other books for teaching good Latin, which schools had a high demand for, and which were, therefore, safe bets in a competitive market. These necessary schoolbooks became staples of de Worde and Richard Pynson (c.1449–1529/30), the two most prolific London printers.[37] Some sense of the rivalry with imports emerges in Pynson's 1520 edition of the Latin translation by Gentian Hervet (1499–1584) of Aphthonius's 'creative writing' exercises for schools, his *Praeexercitamenta* or *Progymnasmata*. There were in fact several rival Latin translations of this text available on the Continent;[38] Pynson's title-page announced its fitness to rival other editions by its fine roman typeface and its proper classicising orthography – even using the æ digraph and *e-caudata* or *e* with a cedilla or tail for Latin's *ae* diphthong. It advertised its competition explicitly in declaring on the title-page its royal monopoly granted 'so that nobody else prints this book in the realm of England or sells it, printed elsewhere or imported, in the same realm of England' ('ne quis hunc in regno Angliæ imprimat / aut alibi impressum / importatumue in eodem regno Anglię vendat').[39] Pynson's announcement makes it clear that he saw his book, four decades after Rood's, still rivalling imported schoolbooks.

Yet the competition with imports could be driven by very local demand. Pynson's printing of *Praeexercitamenta* might also be driven by local influence from the translator, Hervet, who had settled in England as tutor to Arthur Pole (1531/2–70?), the scion of a powerful aristocratic dynasty.[40] In Oxford and Cambridge the demand came from the specific local needs of the universities, and perhaps in Cambridge from backers who acted more like patrons than like customers in a market.[41] Sometimes, what made grammars competitive was their usefulness for local institutions. For example, John Anwykyll who devised the phrasebook from Terence's plays, also devised a grammar, first printed in 1483 in the same format as, and with continuous quire-signatures to, his Terentian *Vulgaria*; prefatory verses by a Italian immigrant, Pietro Carmeliano (c.1451–1527), not only describe the book's influences from Italian

---

[37] *William Caxton*, pp. 119–23, 150–54.

[38] Francis R. Johnson, 'Two Renaissance Textbooks of Rhetoric: Aphthonius' *Progymnasmata* and Rainolde's *A booke called the Foundacion of Rhetorike*', *HLQ* 6 (1943), 427–44 (435–36).

[39] *STC* 699, sig: a1r. A copy in CUL, shelfmark Syn.8.52.39, has handwritten annotations, including a gloss in English ('cicadę' as 'A greshoppe': sig. a3r) and, according to a note in it, was once bound with Pynson's edition of Cicero's *Philippicae* printed a year later (*STC* 5311, discussed below).

[40] Pierce, *Margaret Pole*, p. 44, and see n.36 above.

[41] *William Caxton*, pp. 76–82; E.P. Goldschmidt, *The First Cambridge Press in its European Setting* (repr. 1955; Cambridge, 2010), p. 2.

humanist grammars but also its creation for a specific local school.[42] Similarly, when Caxton printed some papal letters as models of style and a humanist manual of rhetoric, it might have been significant that their respective editor and author were the same Carmeliano, who lived in England, and Lorenzo Traversagni (c.1425–1503) who had taught in Cambridge (STC 22588; 24188.5, 24189, 24190.3). When Traversagni's manual was reprinted at St Albans, as was a manual of style by Agostino Dati (STC 24190, 6289) otherwise often read in imported copies (as above), it might be significant that this printer was known as a schoolmaster. Grammar, style and rhetoric might, then, have been printed due to personal connections or institutional requirements. Yet these local markets were not big enough a field on which to compete with imports: across Europe printing tended to concentrate in fewer cities from the 1490s on, and in England this tendency was extreme as printing became concentrated on better capitalised presses in London and its environs – despite the obvious humanist readerships in the university towns.[43] London presses took grammars and manuals of style or conversation designed originally for use in one school and turned them into centralised bestsellers.[44]

Grammars had an obvious practical use which could drive demand. Practical uses and high demand dictated, too, the choice and presentation of classical texts. Few editions of the classics competed directly with imported ones. Up to 1535 there were only forty-seven editions of classical texts solely in Latin made in England, and over the next two decades English printers only issued one classical text on its own in Latin (STC 24810a).[45] Early on, the Oxford printers experimented with editions of Aristotle and Cicero (STC 752, 5312), but those printers failed, and thereafter presses in England produced mostly the works of late classical authors useful in rudimentary schooling such as Cato or Donatus, or of very popular authors such as Virgil and Terence and in layouts suitable for schools. For example, between 1494 and 1497, Pynson issued Terence's plays in a small quarto edition and in discrete units of separable quires (with the exception of some confusion at the join between *Adelphoe* and *Phormio*), making them portable and adaptable to different readers' requirements.[46] Moreover, he printed parts of these books with heavy leading, that is, with the lines of type spaced out to allow annotation, and to one play he added a small glossary in Latin, with one entry in English too.[47] He also used very loose paraphrases or tiny snippets of the plot summary from the ancient commentary by Donatus, which were cut up in order to annotate ('annotabimus') each act by explaining its basic plot;[48] he

[42] [John Anwykyll], *Compendium totius grammatice* (Deventer: Richard Pafraet, 4 May [1489]; STC 696.1), sig. A1v; *Humanism*, pp. 133–34.

[43] Pettegree, 'Centre and Periphery', p. 114.

[44] Hedwig Gwosdek, *A Checklist of English Grammatical Manuscripts and Early Printed Grammars c.1400–1540*, Henry Sweet Society Studies in the History of Linguistics 6 (Münster, 2000), pp. 31–32.

[45] Daniel Wakelin, 'Possibilities for Reading: Classical Translations in Parallel Texts ca. 1520–1558', *Studies in Philology* 105 (2008), 463–86 (484); the tally there of editions only in Latin needs increasing, to add STC 7016.2, 7016.5 and 7016.9.

[46] *BMC XI*, p. 278.

[47] [Terence, *Comoediae sex*] ([London]: Richard Pynson, 1495–97; STC 23885), *Andria*, sig. d5v. Each play has a separate set of signatures.

[48] [Terence, *Comoediae sex*], *Andria*, sig. a2v.

added plot summaries for *Heautontimorumenos* which Donatus had not summarised.[49] By these means, Pynson's edition serves basic comprehension, helpful for lower levels of schooling.

However, this edition could not compete with French editions of Terence which from 1492 had provided new humanist commentaries or Donatus's ancient one in full.[50] And English readers often used such commentaries: a sample of academic inventories before 1547 yields forty-six copies of Terence's plays of which nineteen are listed with commentaries, the others being unspecified.[51] From the 1510s printers in England did issue a few texts with commentaries but they too often served the schoolroom, just as the classical texts themselves did. Some of the texts commented on were school favourites, as were Aesop's and Donatus's works (*STC* 168–70, 7016–7016.9) or Virgil's eclogues in the 1510s (*STC* 24813–15). While the commentaries on Aesop's and Donatus's works are by well-known Continental scholars, the commentary on Virgil's eclogues, printed by de Worde, is similar to that of Herman van Beek (Hermannus Torrentinus), previously published in several Continental editions, but is not identical.[52] De Worde's commentary is more simplistic in its direction to schoolboys, by beginning each section with the command to them to 'Construe' or reorder the verse word-order into the word-order of English prose. It glosses difficult vocabulary into more common words; it once even glosses into English the name of the shepherd Corydon by reference to Latin *corydalis* or 'golde fynche'.[53] It also eschews the cross-references to other texts favoured by Herman van Beeck. So, fittingly, some closing verses in de Worde's book address the readers as 'iuvenes' or boys, adapting the lines which often preceded Virgil's *Aeneid* and announced that his eclogues were his apprentice work; this commentary is for apprentice scholars.[54]

Later, however, some English printing of commentaries was intellectually and visually emulative of prestigious Continental volumes: for example, Wynkyn de Worde later printed the eclogues of Mantuan (Baptista Spagnuoli) with learned commentaries taken from Continental editions by Josse Bade.[55] De Worde distinguished the neo-Latin text by setting it in roman type, leaving the northern European commentary in gothic (*STC* 22978, 22979; see also *STC* 16891 in n.71 below). Yet de Worde was borrowing the commentary second-hand, and he could only print text and commentary alternating, rather than in

[49] [Terence, *Comoediae sex*], *Heauton timorumenos*, sigs a1r, a2v, a8r, b6r, c2r, c8v.
[50] Harold Walter Lawton, *Terence en France au XVIe siècle: éditions et traductions* (Paris, 1926), pp. 294–95.
[51] E.S. Leedham-Green, *Books in Cambridge Inventories*, 2 vols (Cambridge, 1986), 2.738; R.J. Fehrenbach and others, *PLRE.Folger: Private Libraries in Renaissance England* (1992–) at: <http://plre.folger.edu>, searching for words beginning *Teren** (to gather variant spellings).
[52] Cf. e.g. Virgil, *Bucolica*, comm. by Hermannus Torrentinus (Deventer: Richard Pafraet, 1503) or (Strasburg: Joannes Knoblouch, 1512); cf. David Scott Wilson-Okamura, *Virgil in the Renaissance* (Cambridge, 2010), p. 27, n.43.
[53] *Bucolica virgilii cum commento familiari* (London: Wynkyn de Worde, 21 November 1514; *STC* 24814), sigs a2r, a6v. I cite the second edition as I have not seen the first edition (*STC* 24813) in Chetham's Library, Manchester.
[54] *Bucolica virgilii*, sig. f8v.
[55] Renouard, *Bibliographie*, 2.118–19; Lee Piepho, *Holofernes' Mantuan: Italian Humanism in Early Modern England* (New York, 2001), pp. 66–67.

parallel, unlike many Continental printers. Not until about 1535 did an English printer, Robert Redman (d. 1540), issue a new commentary on a classical text and print that commentary in parallel with the original, in a separate column twice as broad but in type half the size. That was the commentary by the humanist Florence Wilson or 'Volusenus' (d. in or after 1551) on Cicero's *Somnium Scipionis* (*STC* 5317.5). Wilson was a schoolmaster and directed his commentary to a boy, the young Gregory Cromwell, so this could again be an educational book. However, this rare printing of a more learned commentary, and in parallel, might be designed not solely for educational markets but for political positioning, as Wilson was an informer of Gregory's father, the powerful Thomas Cromwell.[56]

Printing in English

Service of the schoolroom dictated not only the reproduction of things found in imported books such as commentaries; it dictated one crucial divergence from imports: the use of English. Besides their forty-seven editions of the classics in Latin alone up to the year 1547, printers in England also issued twenty-seven editions of classical works accompanied by translations and thirty-one editions of them only in translation. The utility for schooling is evident in the bilingual excerpts offered as *vulgaria*, short phrases for learning alongside their vernacular or 'vulgar' translations, or as *flores* or 'flowers'; the picking or excerpting of flowers was a common metaphor for educational reading.[57] Terence's plays most commonly provided such excerpts: from 1483 to 1529 people printed the *Vulgaria* of Anwykyll (noted above) and from 1534 onwards they printed the *Floures* of Nicholas Udall (1504–56) from Terence's plays (*STC* 23899–903).[58] The use of such flowers might be seen in de Worde's edition of *The flores of Ouide de arte amandi* in 1513. This is a classical text packaged for the schoolroom, just as de Worde's edition of Virgil's eclogues was; indeed, *The flores of Ouide* has on its title-page a woodcut of three boys reading before their rod-wielding schoolmaster, which was also used in the eclogues (Figure 12.2).[59] There are fifty-seven couplets from Ovid's poem alternating with English translations,[60] and Ovid's Latin is quoted very selectively and sometimes slightly modified to make his amatory couplets sound more like the moral distichs of Cato. One excerpt even exhorts us to 'literal craftis' whereby we might 'lerne perfetly tway langages / latyn *and* greke' ('artes', 'linguas edidicisse duas').[61] Learning two languages was indeed furthered by these bilingual editions of *vulgaria* or *flores* for 'double

[56]   For Wilson, see *ODNB*.
[57]   Mary Thomas Crane, *Framing Authority: Sayings, Self, and Society in Sixteenth-Century England* (Princeton, NJ, 1993), pp. 58–59, 86–87.
[58]   Ágnes Juhász-Ormsby, 'Nicholas Udall's *Floures for Latine Spekynge*: An Erasmian Textbook', *Humanistica Lovaniensia* 52 (2003), 137–58.
[59]   *The flores of Ouide de arte amandi* (London: Wynkyn de Worde, 1513; *STC* 18934), sig. A1r; *Bucolica virgilii*, sig. a1r.
[60]   Frank Isaac, *English and Scottish Printing Types 1501–35, 1508–41*, Bibliographical Society Facsimiles and Illustrations 2 (Oxford, 1930), fig. 6.
[61]   *The flores of Ouide*, sig. A4v (Ovid, *De Arte amandi*, III.121–22).

The flores of Ouide de arte amandi with their en
glyſſhe afoze them: and two alphabete tablys. The
fyzſt begynneth with the englyſſhe hauyng the laten
wozdes folowynge. the other with the laten hauyng þ
englyſſhe wozdes folowynge.

Figure 12.2 Anon., *The flores of Ouide de arte amandi* (London: Wynkyn de Worde, 1513; *STC* 18934), sig. A1r. London, British Library, G.9671.

translation': they provided texts to translate in both directions, and answers for schoolboys who had tried to do so.[62]

Other schoolmasters produced *vulgaria* which they had devised themselves and which are often surprising in their contents,[63] but the inspiration of speaking like the ancients was evident. In 1520 William Horman (1457–1535) of Eton College stressed the classicism of his *vulgaria*.[64] And in Horman's book (*STC* 13811), and in the last edition of Anwykyll's *Vulgaria* in 1529 (*STC* 23908), the humanist pedigree was evident visually, too, in the use of what we now call roman type, a typeface based on a species of handwriting invented by the Italian humanists from what they thought were classical manuscripts. That the choice of typeface was not accidental is evident because there survives Horman's contract with Pynson, where he stipulates different-sized typefaces for the English and Latin and headings in 'great romayn letter' in order 'to represent goodlye and trulye the mater'.[65] The book is 'romayn' in content or 'mater' but also in typographic form. The roman typeface and, when it was used too, the italic, were associated across Europe with classical and neo-classical Latin rather than the vernacular and were popular with humanist printers and readers.[66] Some sense of their noteworthiness emerges in the records of the Oxford bookseller John Dorne in 1520 who notes twelve books as being in italic lettering ('*litera ytalica*'), all of them classical texts not yet printed in England.[67] A roman typeface was first employed in England by Horman's printer, Pynson, in 1509 for the title and closing 'LAVS DEO' of a sermon by Savonarola.[68] This was a work of piety – albeit with Florentine connections – but thereafter and more often this type was linked with classical or neoclassical learning.[69] Italic was first used in England by de Worde in 1528 for Robert Wakefield's *Oratio de Laudibus Trium Linguarum*, a speech in praise of studying Arabic, Aramaic and Hebrew (*STC* 24944).[70] In late June the same year de Worde printed in italic too Lucian's dialogues translated into Latin by Erasmus and others. In the colophon de Worde proudly announced that he had printed it 'with his very own types' ('de suis characteribus'), which slightly obscures the fact that they were copied from a set

---

[62] William E. Miller, 'Double Translation in English Humanistic Education', *Studies in the Renaissance* 10 (1963), 163–74.

[63] Paul Sullivan, 'Playing the Lord: Tudor *Vulgaria* and the Rehearsal of Ambition', *English Literary History* 75 (2008), 179–96.

[64] Juhász-Ormsby, 'Nicholas Udall's *Floures*', 140–41; William Horman, *Vulgaria*, ed. Montague Rhodes James (Oxford, 1926), p. xxii.

[65] Horman, *Vulgaria*, p. xvii; illustrated by Isaac, *English and Scottish Printing Types*, fig. 21.

[66] Rudolf Hirsch, 'Classics in the Vulgar Tongues Printed during the Initial Fifty Years, 1471–1520', *Papers of the Bibliographical Society of America* 81 (1987), 249–337 (309); Rudolf Hirsch, *Printing, Selling and Reading 1450–1550* (Wiesbaden, 1967), pp. 114–17; Harry Carter, *A View of Early Typography* (Oxford, 1969), pp. 70–71, 75–77.

[67] 'Day-Book of John Dorne, Bookseller in Oxford, A.D. 1520', ed. F. Madan, in *Collectanea*, ed. C.R.L. Fletcher, Oxford Historical Society 5 (Oxford, 1885), pp. 73–177 (nos 74–76, 90–91, 106–07, 270, 507, 516, 650–51, 731, 920, 1075, 1269, 1379–80).

[68] Girolamo [Savonarola], *Sermo Fratris Hieronymi de Ferraria In vigilia Natiuitatis domini*, trans. Bartholomaeus Mutilian ([London: Richard Pynson], 8 September 1509; *STC* 21800), sigs a1r, a4v; Carter, *A View of Early Typography*, p. 92.

[69] Carter, *A View of Early Typography*, p. 92.

[70] Isaac, *English and Scottish Printing Types*, fig. 12; Richard Rex, 'The Earliest Use of Hebrew in Books Printed in England: Dating Some Works of Richard Pace and Robert Wakefield', *TCBS* 9, no. 5 (1990), 517–25 (517–18, 523).

of types used in Antwerp for a very similar-looking edition of the same text the same month.[71]

As it happens, roman type was not in England used for a truly classical text solely in Latin until Pynson's edition of Cicero's *Philippicae* in 1521, some twelve years after he had introduced roman (*STC* 5311). But the connection of roman and italic with humanist Latin is made in contradistinction to English in bilingual books where the languages are distinguished by typeface, with the English being in black letter, by contrast. This distinction occurs from 1509 in Pynson's fabulous edition of a neo-Latin text by Jakob Locher based on a German satire by Sebastian Brant, rendered as *The Shyp of Folys* by Alexander Barclay, the monk and some-time schoolmaster (mentioned above); the two languages appear in alternation, text and translation, in roman and black letter respectively, with sidenotes in their respective types, for example, pointing out the classical allusions.[72] *The Shyp of Folys* did not need to be presented as a humanist work; another translation of it, written by Henry Watson and published the same year by de Worde, is described in its preface as a moral warning allegorically 'fygured'.[73] But Pynson presents Barclay's version as humanist scholarship by his choice of typeface. Barclay may have had some input into that, for the printer and poet seem to have worked closely together,[74] and Pynson subsequently printed other translations by Barclay from classical and humanist Latin sources – Sallust, Mantuan, Domenico Mancini – in two languages and in contrasting black letter and roman typefaces (*STC* 17241–42.5, 21626, 21627, 22992.1).[75] Other editions of classical texts with parallel English translations distinguished the languages thus from the 1520s on.[76] The first such bilingual, dual-typeface edition of the classics was of Terence's *Andria* printed in Paris for import into England (Figure 12.3; *STC* 23894). This layout might also therefore have been learned from Continental models.

English is set apart from the classical or Latin source in such books, then, and indeed English is not printed in roman type until around 1530 and not commonly for another decade.[77] But in those bilingual books English is at least admitted into proximity with the *studia humanitatis*. Nor can its use be described

[71] *COMPLVRES LVCIANI DIALOGI*, trans. Erasmus (London: Wynkyn de Worde, 27 June [5th Kalends of July] July 1528; *STC* 16891), sig. D4r, illustrated by Isaac, *English and Scottish Printing Types*, fig. 10b; *Luciani Dialogi* (Antwerp: Michiel Hillen van Hoochstraten, June 1528), illustrated by H.D.L. Vervliet, *Sixteenth-Century Printing Types of the Low Countries*, foreword by Harry Carter (Amsterdam, 1968), plate IT 14. Yet, although de Worde's book has the same collation (A–C⁸, D⁴) the types are not identical: de Worde's italic is smaller than Hillen's (respectively 20 lines = 88 mm; 20 lines = 110 mm); de Worde puts commentary in a small italic type, Hillen a small roman; de Worde puts the *tabula* in a gothic type, Hillen a small italic. More strikingly, de Worde has different preliminaries (sig. A1r–v), spaces out the *tabula* differently and, perhaps as a result, omits 31 items from it (sigs D3v–D4r).
[72] Sebastian Brant, *The Shyp of folys*, trans. Alexander Barclay (London: Richard Pynson, 14 December 1509; *STC* 3545), sig. b5r onwards.
[73] Sebastian Brant, *The shyppe of fooles*, trans. Henry Watson (London: Wynkyn de Worde, 6 July 1509; *STC* 3547), sig. A2v.
[74] David Carlson, 'Alexander Barclay and Richard Pynson: A Tudor Printer and His Writer', *Anglia* 113 (1995), 283–302 (290–93).
[75] Carlson, 'Alexander Barclay', p. 297; Greg Waite, 'Alexander Barclay, Robert [sic] Pynson, and an Unnoticed Sheet Printed by Robert Redman', *Notes and Queries* 58 (2011), 193–96 (193–94).
[76] Wakelin, 'Possibilities for Reading', pp. 485–86.
[77] Carter, *A View of Early Typography*, pp. 79–80, 91–92.

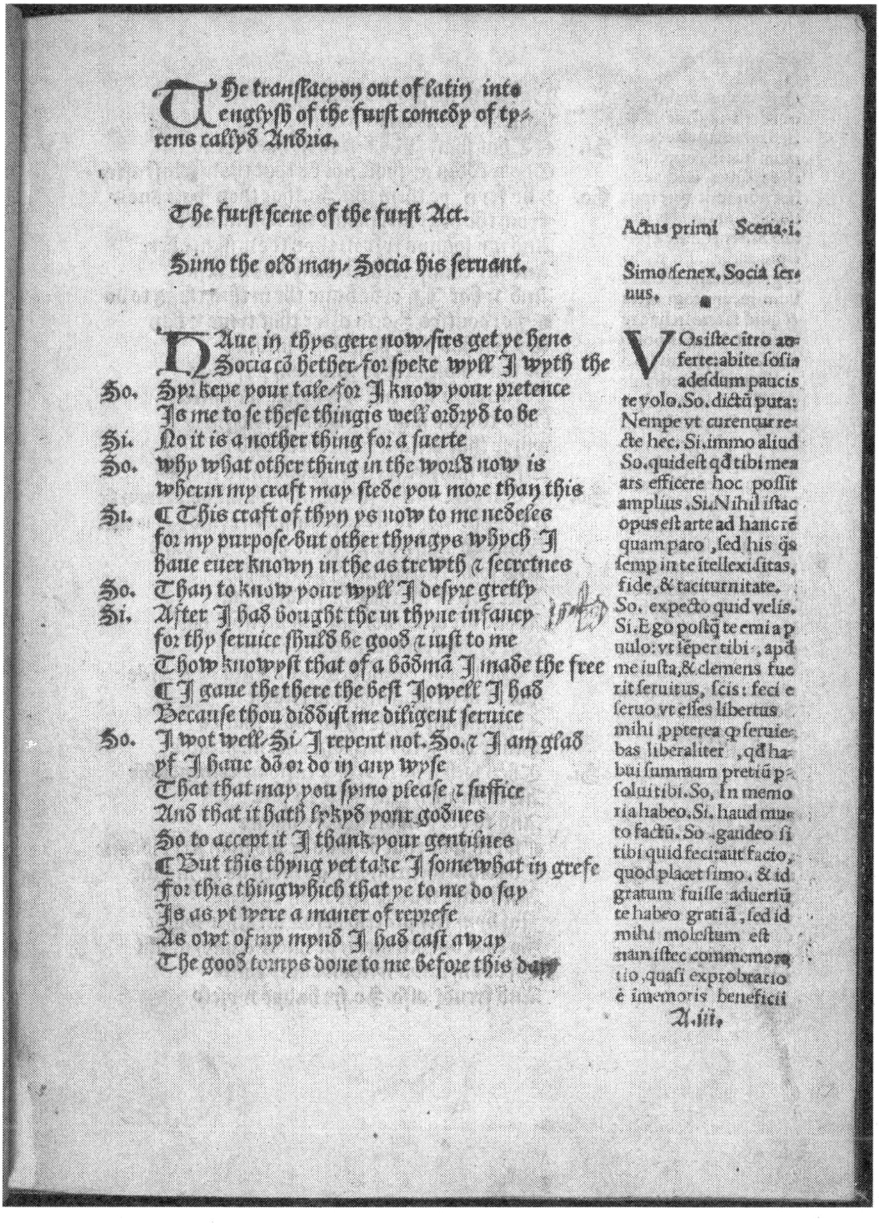
The translacyon out of latyn into englysh of the furst comedy of tyrens callyd Andria.

The furst scene of the furst Act.

Simo the old man, Socia his seruant.

Haue in thys gere now, sirs get ye hens
Socia cō hether, for speke wyll I wyth the
So. Syr kepe your tale, for I know your pretence
Is me to se these thingis well ordryd to be
Si. No it is a nother thing for a suerte
So. Why what other thing in the world now is
wherin my craft may stede you more than this
Si. ¶ This craft of thyn ys now to me nedeles
for my purpose, but other thyngys whych I
haue euer knowyn in the as trewth & secretnes
So. Than to know your wyll I desyre gretly
Si. After I had bought the in thyne infancy
for thy seruice shuld be good & iust to me
Thow knowyst that of a bōdmā I made the free
¶ I gaue the there the best Iowell I had
Because thou diddist me diligent seruice
So. I wot well. Si. I repent not. So. & I am glad
yf I haue dō or do in any wyse
That that may you symo please & suffice
And that it hath lykyd your godnes
So to accept it I thank your gentilnes
¶ But this thyng yet take I somewhat in grefe
For this thing which that ye to me do say
Is as yt were a maner of reprefe
As owt of my mynd I had cast away
The good tornys done to me before this day

Actus primi Scena .i.

Simo senex, Socia seruus.

Vos istec intro auferte: abite. Sosia adesdum paucis te volo. So. dictū puta: Nempe vt curentur recte hec. Si. immo aliud So. quid est qđ tibi mea ars efficere hoc possit amplius. Si. Nihil istac opus est arte ad hanc rē quam paro, sed his q̄s semp in te itellexi sitas, fide, & taciturnitate. So. expecto quid velis. Si. Ego postq̄ te emi a paruulo: vt sēper tibi apd me iusta, & clemens fuerit seruitus, scis: feci e seruo vt esses libertus mihi ppterea q seruiebas liberaliter, qđ habui summum pretiū psolui tibi. So. In memoria habeo. Si. haud muto factū. So. gaudeo si tibi quid feci aut facio, quod placet simo, & id gratum fuisse aduersū te habeo gratiā, sed id mihi molestum est nam istec commemoratio quasi exprobratio ē immemoris beneficii

A.iii.

Figure 12.3 Anon., *Terens in englysh* ([Paris: Philippe le Noir, *c.*1520]; *STC* 23894), sig. A3r. London, British Library, C.34.e.33.

as merely ancillary to learning Latin. Barclay and others wonder in prefaces whether we might want to read the English texts for their own sake,[78] and

[78] Wakelin, 'Possibilities for Reading', pp. 474–81; Waite, 'Alexander Barclay, Robert Pynson', p. 194.

classical and humanist works were printed in English translations alone too. Barclay's eclogues, loosely translating Aeneas Sylvius Piccolomini's *De Miseriis curialium* and two of Mantuan's eclogues, were printed in stand-alone English copies.[79] Siberch, the humanist printer at Cambridge, did this (as noted above), and other printers reproduced such editions.[80] Caxton initiated such offerings of English translations with his 1481 edition of Cicero's treatises *De Senectute* and *De Amicitia* and Buonaccorso da Montemagno's *Controversia de vera nobilitate*, a work of Florentine civic humanism.[81] Some such translations were not of the original classical texts but of French adaptations; such were those Caxton himself made of adaptations of Ovid's *Metamorphoses* and Virgil's *Aeneid*; yet they too might 'make the classical vulgar' in order to make a 'political application' of the *studia humanitatis*, as William Kuskin has termed it.[82] Aside from Barclay's efforts, there was a lull in such translations for a few decades, while English printers seem to have concentrated on rivalling the imported schoolbooks. But classical translations blossomed again from 1530, which, among others, saw a reprint of the version of Cicero's *De Amicitia* once issued by Caxton (*STC* 5275). These translations came from numerous presses but especially from the press of Thomas Berthelet (d. 1555).

These translations and loose versions represent the other important contribution of humanist printing to English culture: rather than teaching grammar or style, they offered a broader education in ethics and politics, whether seriously instructive or, as for Barclay, no less seriously satirical. Some of these works do reflect on humanist education: notably, Berthelet published twice between 1530 and about 1532 a translation by Thomas Elyot (*c*.1490–1546) of Plutarch's work on *The Education or bringinge vp of children*, the first work translated directly from Greek into English (*STC* 20056.7, 20057). In the preface, Elyot comments that his book is not useful for studying the original Greek: he has translated loosely, he warns, and so we should not seek here 'the exquisite diligence of an interpretour' or translator, and he would 'desire not to haue my boke conferred with the delectable styles of Grekes or Latines'. He avoids close comparison with the source partly because he does not want to translate some sections on pagan 'vices' but also because he is not providing a crib in a parallel text or similar which would be useful to schoolboys in training for clerical careers: 'I wryte not to clerkes', he says. Indeed, he writes for his sister Margery Puttenham as she brings up her sons, Elyot's 'litell neuewes'.[83] Given that women such as Puttenham were excluded from much formal education in this period, the sort

---

[79] Barclay, *Eclogues*, pp. lix–lxv; Piepho, *Holofernes' Mantuan*, pp. 103, 134. Greg Waite, 'Alexander Barclay's Translation of Sallust's *Jugurtha*: A Note on Sources', *Notes and Queries* 58 (2011), 196–202 (197), suggests that other bilingual editions might have been lost.

[80] Treptow, *John Siberch*, pp. 29–30; Matthew Groom, 'John Siberch (d. 1554), the First Cambridge Printer: New Findings from English Records', *TCBS* 12, no. 4 (2003), 403–13 (408–09).

[81] *Humanism*, pp. 153–59, 168–73.

[82] William Kuskin, *Symbolic Caxton: Literary Culture and Print Capitalism* (Notre Dame, IN, 2008), p. 237; *The Middle English Text of Caxton's Ovid, Book I*, ed. Diana Rumrich, Middle English Texts 43 (Heidelberg, 2011), pp. xiv–sv.

[83] Plutarch, *The Education or bringinge vp of children*, trans. Sir Thomas Elyot (London: Thomas Berthelet, [1532?]; *STC* 20057), sig. A2v–A3r. I cite the second edition as I have not seen the copy of the first edition (*STC* 20056.7) in the Newberry Library, Chicago.

of education on which he advises her is not primarily the bookish sort but is 'the trayne and rule of vertue'. This, he says, will make her children a comfort to parents and friends, a pleasure to God and – interestingly, at the end of the tricolon and the paragraph, as if trumping pleasing God – a 'commoditye and profite of theyr countray'.[84] This education is distinctively broader than mere schoolroom stuff.

There are, then, different sorts of educational book produced by humanists: those practical books for the classroom and these broader theoretical treatises. It is the broader education that is most interestingly set out in, and exemplified by, other books printed by Berthelet and his contemporaries in English. Nor are all of them translations. Original English works began to imagine this 'bringinge vp' and social service, just as new Latin works by English writers such as Pace, in *De Fructu*, had imagined formal education. This broader education is imagined in Elyot's *The boke named the gouernour*, printed by Berthelet in 1531 and reprinted by him four times: an extended treatise on the upbringing required for a 'magistrate' or person appointed to govern (*STC* 7635, 7636, 7637, 7638, 7639). It does begin with the reading to be done by him as a boy and does speak of picking the choicest flowers from the classics.[85] But it does that only in book I and contextualises it within a more general upbringing from wet-nursing to the exercise of virtue in adulthood. The goal is not only mastery of the *studia humanitatis* but mastery over oneself and over the commonweal. Elyot expresses in this and other works printed by Berthelet a deep commitment to public service and envisages humanist books preparing people for such service.[86]

Others pursued those goals too, such as Thomas More's brother-in-law John Rastell (*c.*1475–1536), lawyer, sponsor of explorers, playwright and printer, in the preceding decade or so. In several prefaces, Rastell speaks more fully than Berthelet of the purpose in disseminating 'knowlege' in print. He offers his knowledge not to the schoolroom but to 'the people of the realme' and 'the commyn welth'.[87] This service of his country works in tandem with his use of English: linguistic nationalism is a sort of civic engagement. He speaks frankly in legal books such as *The abbreuiacion of statutes* (1519) and *Exposiciones terminorum* (*c.*1524) of the need to use 'our vulgare englysh tong' for educating the citizens of England. He may be using the vernacular rather than Latin, and in the law rather than the humanities proper, but his humanist inspiration is suggested by his sense that English is fit for intellectual purposes now that it has been 'maruelously amendyd *and* augmentyd' because 'dyuers famous clerkis *and* lernid men had translate *and* made many noble workis in to our englysh tong'.[88] He explains more fully in his interlude *The .iiii. elementys* the usefulness of translation: 'The

---

[84]   Plutarch, *Education*, trans. Elyot, sig. A3r.

[85]   Crane, *Framing Authority*, pp. 58, 69–70; *Humanism*, pp. 199–207.

[86]   Cathy Shrank, 'Sir Thomas Elyot and the Bonds of Community', in *The Oxford Handbook of Tudor Literature, 1485–1603*, ed. Mike Pincombe and Cathy Shrank (Oxford, 2009), pp. 154–69 (155).

[87]   John Rastell, trans., *The abbreuiacion of statutes* (London: John Rastell, 25 October 1519; *STC* 9515.5), sig. a2v; *Exposiciones terminorum legum anglorum* (London: [John Rastell, *c.*1524]; *STC* 20701), sig. a2r; on which volumes, see E.J. Devereux, *A Bibliography of John Rastell* (Montreal and Kingston, 1999), pp. 103–04, 111–12.

[88]   Rastell, trans., *The abbreuiacion of statutes*, sig. a2r.

grek*ys* the romayns' wrote learned books in their mother tongue, and so 'clerk*ys*' could equally now 'expoun any hard sentence' in English; moreover, they could 'translate' the 'connynge laten bokys' into English in a 'correct and approbate' way to teach us in our own tongue.[89] Such comments suggest that the clerkly endeavours of translating, of correcting and of mastering the language of ancient sources – things evident in the use of imported books and in home-printed schoolbooks – might inspire effort on English too. This leads into Rastell's vision of the citizen who 'for a co*mm*yn welth bysyly | Studyeth': who is studying or desiring – the word means both things – to serve society.[90] This education in the vernacular is deliberately directed to adult life beyond the schoolroom.

Of course, printers continued to produce books for schools, and new works in English were written for schools too. By the mid century English printers even issued in English manuals of rhetoric, the art originally directed to writing and speaking good Latin; the first such, printed by Redman in 1532, was *The Art or crafte of Rhetoryke* by Leonard Cox (b. *c.*1495, d. in or after 1549), a manual partly based on Philip Melanchthon's *Institutiones rhetoricae* (STC 5947, 5947.5).[91] Cox also, in 1526, had printed in Poland, where he worked, a detailed Latin guide to humanist schooling, a sign of the continuing internationalism of humanist scholars.[92] This Latin tradition is often of tremendous intellectual quality, and the books it produced are of greater numerical quantity. They deserve to be better known. But the translations and treatises in English imagined a broader readership and a reading process of broader political and social consequence. It is arguable whether the most profound influence of humanism on English culture was ultimately in these works which did not rival the great efforts in the *studia humanitatis* of Continental printing but which, while they cut themselves off from markets abroad and from lucrative markets for schools, nevertheless contributed ideas which deeply and over the long term influenced readers and citizens in England.

Further Reading

Carlson, David R., *English Humanist Books: Writers and Patrons, Manuscript and Print, 1475–1525* (Toronto, 1993).

Carlson, David, Alexander Barclay and Richard Pynson, 'A Tudor Printer and His Writer', *Anglia* 113 (1995), 283–302.

Devereux, E.J., *A Bibliography of John Rastell* (Montreal and Kingston, 1999).

Ford, Margaret Lane, 'Importation of Printed Books into England and Scotland',

---

[89] [John Rastell], *A new iuterlude and a mery of the nature of the .iiii. elementys* ([London: John Rastell, 1520?]; STC 20722), sig. A2r–v. Richard Foster Jones, *The Triumph of the English Language* (Stanford, CA, 1953), pp. 81–89, traces humanist defences of English.

[90] [Rastell], *A new iuterlude,* sig. A3r, discussed recently by Daniel Wakelin, *'Gentleness and Nobility,* John Rastell, *c.*1525–27', in *The Oxford Handbook of Tudor Drama,* ed. Thomas Betteridge and Greg Walker (Oxford, 2012), pp. 192–206.

[91] S.F. Ryle, 'Cox, Leonard (b. *c.*1495, d. in or after 1549)', in *ODNB* at: <http://www. oxforddnb.com/view/article/6525>, accessed 29 June 2011.

[92] Andrew Breeze and Jacqueline Glomski, 'An Early British Treatise Upon Education: Leonard Cox's *De Erudienda Iuventute* (1526)', *Humanistica Lovaniensia* 40 (1991), 112–67.

in *The Cambridge History of the Book in Britain: Volume III. 1400–1557*, ed. Lotte Hellinga and J.B. Trapp (Cambridge, 1999), pp. 179–201.

Gwosdek, Hedwig, *A Checklist of English Grammatical Manuscripts and Early Printed Grammars c.1400–1540*, Henry Sweet Society Studies in the History of Linguistics 6 (Münster, 2000).

Hellinga, Lotte, *William Caxton and Early Printing in England* (London, 2010).

Hirsch, Rudolf, 'Classics in the Vulgar Tongues Printed during the Initial Fifty Years, 1471–1520', *Papers of the Bibliographical Society of America* 81 (1987), 249–337.

Lowry, Martin, 'The Arrival and Use of Continental Printed Books in Yorkist England', in *Le Livre dans l'Europe de la Renaissance: Actes du XXVIIIe Colloque international d'Études humanistes de Tours*, ed. Pierre Aquilon and Henri-Jean Martin (Paris, 1988), pp. 449–59.

Treptow, Otto, *John Siberch: Johann Lair von Siegburg*, trans. Trevor Jones, ed. and abridged John Morris and Trevor Jones, Cambridge Bibliographical Society Monographs 6 (Cambridge, 1970).

Wakelin, Daniel, *Humanism, Reading and English Literature, 1430–1530* (Oxford, 2007).

———, 'Possibilities for Reading: Classical Translations in Parallel Texts ca. 1520–1558', *Studies in Philology* 105 (2008), 463–86.

13

Women Translators and the Early Printed Book

BRENDA M. HOSINGTON[1]

Translations in the first century of printing in England played an extremely important role in a variety of fields, although the full extent of their contribution to the intellectual, social and cultural advancement of the country has not yet been fully explored. They constituted an integral part of a whole web of diverse activities, including the gradual development of a native literary tradition, the dissemination of knowledge in a wide variety of fields, the spread of social and political movements, and the exchanges involved in religious controversy. The specific relationship of translation to the early print trade is a crucial one that also remains to be studied. Yet we know enough to claim that translations do not exist in a void and that it is therefore wrong to discuss an individual translated work as an isolated production, rather than one of a range of works published at the same time on the same subject and in similar socio-historical circumstances. Nor should one ignore the ideological motivations of both translator and printer, whether these be inspired by intellectual curiosity, altruism, patriotism, faith or the marketplace.

In discussing the work of seven women translators published between 1504 and 1557, the backdrop of cultural and socio-historical events and the context of print become particularly significant, for they give the lie to the old claim that translating was a safe and silent task particularly suited to women, performed in a proscribed and private space and of little impact. The mere fact that over one thousand translations (counting all editions, re-editions, variants and issues) by men saw print in this span of fifty-three years, as compared with just over forty by women, renders absurd the claim that translation was a female activity.[2] As for the belief in the safety of translation, it is based on the now discredited assumption that translating consists merely in transferring words and meanings, with no interventions on the part of the translator. This mistaken concept of translation admits no influence of ideology, context, or audience appropriateness. Finally, the translations by Margaret Beaufort, Margaret Roper, Catherine Parr, Mary Tudor, the Princess Elizabeth, Anne Cooke and Mary Basset, as this

[1]   I should like to thank the Leverhulme Trust and the Social Sciences and Humanities Council of Canada for financial support in conducting the research necessary in the preparation of this essay.
[2]   These figures, like all those throughout this essay, have been obtained from the *Renaissance Cultural Crossroads. An Online Catalogue of Translations in Britain 1473–1640*, ed. Brenda M. Hosington et al., at: <www.hrionline.ac.uk/rcc>.

study will demonstrate, were far from being private, despite the occasional topos declaring them 'made but for my leisure'. Rather, they were intended to play a variety of roles, while their passage into print automatically brought them into the public sphere. Nor was their impact negligible.

In the early sixteenth century, as Julia Boffey says, a distinguishing feature is the appearance of women as authors, in the widest sense of the word, whose own literary productions and involvement with the whole business of books coincided with the spread of print.[3] Indeed, the translators in our study bear eloquent witness to this awakening, although, unsurprisingly, they are all learned women belonging to the aristocracy or gentry. Also, some of their translations reached print through the agency of male editors, although not, presumably, without their permission. Nevertheless, publishing remained even more difficult and controversial for women than for men, given the association of print and their fabled sexual proclivity.[4] Danielle Clarke states that the motivation for women to publish had to be strong and either personal or ideological, that their writings were sometimes printed for their 'market value as curiosities', and were often circulated by their husbands.[5] It remains to be seen whether our seven translators conform to this pattern.

Rather than assessing the value of their nine translations through close textual analysis or discussing in detail the historical and political circumstances that inspired them, I shall focus on their relationship to the print context in which they were produced, situating them within the history of the book in the period.[6] I shall also discuss the various ideological motivations of the translators, their male editors where appropriate, and their printers. These are often both spiritual and material, although all nine translations are religious.

Much has been written on the relationship of Margaret Beaufort to books and the printing trade. Her great interest in them manifested itself in her purchase of volumes from English and Continental printers, for herself, Syon Abbey with whom she was intimately connected, and Christ's College, Cambridge which she founded. Household accounts demonstrate that her books were numerous and varied, being both religious and secular, original and translated, and written in English and French.[7] This love of books also took a practical form in her patronage of the early printers, William Caxton, Wynkyn de Worde and Richard Pynson. Her involvement with all three is attested in several prologues and colophons of eleven works printed between 1488 and 1509, the year of her death.

[3]   Julia Boffey, 'Women Authors and Women's Literacy in Fourteenth- and Fifteenth-Century England', in *Women and Literature in Britain, 1150–1500*, ed. Carol M. Meale (Cambridge, 1993), pp. 159–82.
[4]   See Wendy Wall, *The Imprint of Gender. Authorship and Publication in the English Renaissance* (Ithaca, NY, 1993), pp. 1–22, for a full treatment of this subject.
[5]   Danielle Clarke, *The Politics of Early Modern Women's Writing* (Harlow, 2001), p. 9.
[6]   For a discussion of the importance of historical circumstance to some women's translations, see Brenda M. Hosington, 'Tudor Englishwomen's Translations of Continental Protestant Texts: The Interplay of Ideology and Historical Context', in *Tudor Translation*, ed. Fred Schurink (London, 2011), pp. 121–43.
[7]   See *King's Mother*, pp. 181–87, but for a far more detailed discussion, Susan Powell, 'Lady Margaret Beaufort and her Books', *The Library*, 6th ser., 20 (1998), 197–240.

Although very supportive of Caxton and de Worde, Beaufort chose Pynson for the two translations she herself authored; they represent an extraordinary accomplishment. These were the first translations into English of Book IV of one of the most important devotional works of the late Middle Ages, Thomas a Kempis's *De imitatione Christi* (The Imitation of Christ), and of another popular fifteenth-century religious manual, the *Speculum aureum animae peccatricis* (The golden mirror of the sinful soul), by either Jacobus de Gruytroede or Jacobus de Clusa. Until recently, neither translation received any real examination despite their significance. Jones and Underwood say very little about them except that they were made from French metatexts since Beaufort knew no Latin. The author of a new book on early modern translations of the *De imitatione Christi* contents himself with merely mentioning her translation in passing, not even giving its title. [8] In a recent essay I have attempted to redress this situation, claiming that the two translations stand as witnesses to Beaufort's blend of intellectual power, concern for the spiritual well-being of those unable to read Latin or French devotional works, and personal piety.[9]

The *De imitatione Christi* went through no fewer than twenty-six editions in the twenty-five years following the 1471 *editio princeps* and by 1500 was translated into Italian and German, and twice into French, in Toulouse (1488) and Paris (1493). As I have argued, Beaufort used the Paris version as her source text.[10] In 1502 she had commissioned William Atkinson to translate Books I–III from the Latin. Presumably intended for a lay audience, his translation omitted much material pertaining to the cloistered life. In the months following, Beaufort must have encountered the French translation containing four books and, given the focus of Book IV on the Eucharist, a subject particularly close to her heart, set about translating it into English.[11] She commissioned Pynson to print the whole work in two separate parts in 1504 under the title *A ful deuout gostely treatyse of the Imytacyon and folowynge the blessed lyfe of our sauyour cryste: compiled in Laten by J. Gerson: and translated into Englysshe. By W. Atkynson: at the specyalle request and commaundement of the ful excellent Princesse Margarete moder to our Souerayne lorde Kynge Henry the .vii. and Countesse of Rychemount and Derby*. However, he gave Beaufort's Book IV a separate title-page and slightly different title: *Here beginethe the forthe boke of the folowinge Jesu cryst and of the contempninge of the world. Inprynted at the comaundement of the most excellent princes Margarete . . . aud [sic] by the same prynces translated oute of frenche into Englisshe in fourme and maner ensuinge. The yere of our lord god M.D.iiii* (STC 23954.7). This set it off from

[8] *King's Mother*, pp. 184–85; Maximilian von Hapsburg, *Catholic and Protestant Translations of the 'Imitatio Christi', 1425–1650: From Late Medieval Classic to Early Modern Bestseller* (Aldershot, 2011), p. 94.
[9] Brenda M. Hosington, 'Lady Margaret Beaufort's Translations as Mirrors of Practical Piety', in *English Women, Religion, and Textual Production, 1500–1625*, ed. Micheline White (Aldershot, 2011), pp. 185–203.
[10] *Le liure tressalutaire de la ymitacion Jhesu Christ et mesprisement de ce monde* [The very profitable book of the imitation of Christ and contempt of this world] (Toulouse, 1488, *ISTC* ii0036500) and *Le livre tressalutaire de limitation de nostre seigneur jesucrist* [The very profitable book of the imitation of our Lord Jesus Christ] (Paris, 1493, *ISTC* ii00038050). See Hosington, 'Lady Margaret Beaufort's Translations', pp. 192–93.
[11] The Latin manuscripts of the *De imitatione* that circulated in England, unlike those available in France, did not contain Book IV, which is why Atkinson translated only Books I–III.

Atkinson's translation, giving Beaufort greater visibility and making it clear she was not only the patron but also the translator.

The combined volume constituted what Jones and Underwood call 'a landmark in the history of the book in England'.[12] Indeed, it proved more popular than its Paris source text, which was reissued only once, unchanged, by Lambert and Jean Treperel in 1494. Between 1504 and 1518, Beaufort's translation was printed five times. Pynson printed two issues in 1504 (STC 23954.7, 23955) and a re-edition in two parts in 1517 (STC 23957), with a variant in the same year (STC 23958), while de Worde published the two parts separately, but otherwise unchanged, probably in 1518 and 1519 (STC 23956).

The reprintings of the complete *Ful deuout and gostely treastyse of the Imytacyon* are not the only indication of its popularity and esteem. In 1531, an anonymous Syon translator, now generally thought not to be Richard Whitford, translated all four books from a Latin original. In his introduction, although disapproving of the fact that Beaufort used as her source a French metatranslation rather than the Latin original, he claims he has kept the 'substaunce and the effecte' of her version, 'though somtyme [mine] vary in wordes'.[13] Moreover, he praises her ability to achieve what he considers two essential goals of a translation: to convey as accurately as possible the content and to elicit the same response in the target readers as in the original audience. Since the purpose of Book IV of the *De Imitatione Christi* was nothing less than to make the Christian meditate on Christ's sacrifice re-enacted in the Eucharist, this was praise of the highest order.

Perhaps her success inspired Beaufort to translate another text, the *Speculum aureum animae peccatricis*, one of a group of 'mirrors' intended to direct lay Christians away from worldly matters to the pursuit of salvation through spiritual exercises. Less popular than the *De imitatione Christi*, the Latin original nevertheless went through twelve printed editions between 1476 and 1503, as well as being included in another work that went through three.[14] It, too, was translated into French twice, in 1451 by Jean Miélot and in 1484 by an anonymous translator. Beaufort used the latter as her source text.[15] Again, she commissioned Pynson as her printer. His *Mirroure of golde for the synfull soule* appeared in 1506 (STC 6894.5) and, once more, proved popular enough to be taken over later by de Worde. J. Skot printed his new edition in 1522 (STC 6895), with a variant in the same year (STC 6896), and de Worde brought out a third edition in two issues in 1526 (STC 6897, 6897.5).

Beaufort demonstrates a remarkable understanding of the nature of these two texts and the means by which their authors elicit a reader response. She adapts each text, written to encourage clerical introspection and meditation, to a lay audience, nevertheless using similar rhetorical strategies to strengthen meaning

---

[12] *King's Mother*, p. 184.
[13] *A boke newely translated out of Laten in to Englysshe, called The folowyinge of Cryste* (London, 1531?) (STC 23961).
[14] *Opusculum quod speculum aureum anime peccatricis dicitur* [A short work called the mirror of gold of the sinful soul] (Paris, 1480, 1485, 1503).
[15] *Le mirouer dor de lame pecheresse tres utile et profitable* [The very useful and beneficial mirror of gold of the sinful soul] (Bréhant-Loudéac, 1484).

and thus achieve the desired effect of turning the audience to spiritual action.[16] John Fisher, her spiritual advisor, told the congregation at the commemorative service one month after her death that she possessed many 'ryght derk' books in English and French and that 'for her exercyse *& for the prouffyte of other* she dyde translate dyvers maters of deuocyon out of Frensshe into Englysshe' (my italics).[17] The topos of the modest woman translator working in a private space and only for her own 'exercise' is somewhat contradicted by this statement. England's first woman translator to reach print in her lifetime obviously appreciated the role the new technology of book production could play in disseminating works of devotion. After all, Caxton had printed seven such translated works between 1484 and 1499, some reprinted by de Worde and Pynson between 1500 and 1506. Together with works of Christian conduct and a range of other religious works they accounted for roughly half the total output of the three earliest printers associated with Beaufort.

The fervour for religious works of all kinds continued unabated into the 1520s, many being translated from Latin or French. De Worde printed five such translations in the first two years of his career. As late as 1520–34, his religious publications still accounted for roughly 60% of his total output, although by then it included many different genres of secular writing. For Pynson in the same period, the percentage of religious texts drops to about 35 per cent, partly because he was appointed King's Printer in 1509 and partly because he turned his attention to legal publications, a field he quickly dominated. However, Thomas Berthelet, the next King's Printer, produced no fewer than eleven in the years 1520–34. One was Erasmus' *Precatio dominica in septem portiones distributa* (The Lord's Prayer divided up into seven parts) (Basel, 1523), a treatise of biblical exegesis discussing the Lord's Prayer that by 1524 had already gone through several editions. The translator was Margaret Roper, the very personification of the virtuous and learned lady so admired by many of the humanists. Her *Deuout treatise vpon the Pater noster, made first in latyn and tourned in to englisshe by a yong gentylwoman* (STC 10477) was edited and prefaced in 1524 by Richard Hyrde, a member of the More household, but published only in 1526 with a reissue in 1531 (STC 10477.5).

Roper's translation was only the second work by a sixteenth-century Englishwoman to be published during her lifetime but, unlike Beaufort's works, it appeared in print without the translator's name. Beaufort after all had financed the publication of her translation and as the king's mother wielded no small amount of power, whereas Margaret Roper, although known throughout England and on the Continent for her erudition and status as the eldest daughter of Thomas More, occupied a far more modest rank. Hyrde, her editor, explains the anonymity by resorting to the topos of the reluctant and modest female author, 'lothe to haue prayse gyuen her' (sig. biii). Yet at the same time he plants enough clues for the reader to guess the translator's identity: she is twenty years

---

[16] For a detailed discussion of these strategies, see Hosington, 'Lady Margaret Beaufort's Translations', pp. 196–202.
[17] John Fisher, 'Mornynge remembraunce', in *The English Works of John Fisher Bishop of Rochester*, ed. J.E.B. Mayor, EETS ES 27 (London, 1876), 1.289–310.

old; the preface is addressed to her cousin, Fraunces S[taverton]; it was written in Chelsea, known by everyone as the site of the More home; and Hyrde, as I have said, was employed by More.

The woodcut on the title-page of the 1526 edition, absent from the 1531 edition, was borrowed from de Worde, as indeed was the font (Figure 13.1). However, it was cropped and newly placed within an elaborate border, perhaps because it had previously been used for the satiric, bawdy and misogynist *Gospelles of dystaues*, a translation recounting the 'learning' of a group of illiterate spinners of doubtful morals, published by de Worde in 1510 (Figure 13.2). Hardly suitable for prefacing a work by a 'yong virtuous and well lerned gentyl-woman', to borrow Hyrde's description of Roper. The border, as Patricia Demers has said, suggests a cloister-like enclosing and encasing of the female subject within it;[18] on the other hand, it raises the tone of the work by its decorousness and decorativeness, thus distancing it from the *Gospelles* it originally accompanied. Similarly, the cropping of the woodcut removes the group of young men placed in the foreground whom the subject is watching and seeming to instruct – a nice touch for a satiric work dictated by uneducated female spinners but not for a translation by a studious young woman. She thus seems to be looking away from the volume on the stand, staring into space. However, her hands are actively touching the pages, while her averted gaze might well suggest she is contemplating what she has just read; the pose would later become a traditional one for depicting virtuous and learned young women. Jaime Goodrich has interpreted the woodcut as portraying a secluded female subject and purposely suggesting the private, contemplative nature of Roper's study, which in turn reflects her own personal virtue and appropriately female behaviour. Yet, as she goes on to claim convincingly, this is at odds with the publication of her work, which has a political dimension that most definitely did not confine her to a patriarchally controlled domestic space.[19]

Margaret Roper was no doubt motivated in part by personal reasons for agreeing to allow Hyrde and Berthelet to publish her *Deuout treatyse*. Erasmus had dedicated his commentary on Prudentius's hymns for Christmas and the Epiphany to her in 1523 and accompanied it by a very complimentary letter.[20] Her translation could have been a means of thanking him. He was also a friend of her father's, an eminent international scholar and sometime guest in the More household. In the 1520s that friendship was still warm and More was still defending some of Erasmus's religious views, although by 1531 when Berthelet published the second edition of Margaret's translation he had rather distanced himself from them.[21] Finally, Roper would not have been oblivious to the important role friendship played among the humanists, especially given her father's

[18] Patricia Demers, *Women's Writing in English: Early Modern England* (Toronto, 2005), p. 70.
[19] Jaime Goodrich, 'Thomas More and Margaret More Roper: A Case for Rethinking Woman's Participation in the Early Modern Public Sphere', *Sixteenth Century Journal* 39 (2008), pp. 1021–40.
[20] P.S. Allen, *Opus epistolarum Des. Erasmi Roterdami denuo recogitum et auctum per P. S. Allen* [Collected correspondence of Erasmus newly considered and augmented by P.S. Allen], 12 vols (Oxford, 1906), 10: no. 2659.
[21] L.-E. Halkin, *Erasme parmi nous* [Erasmus amongst us] (Paris, 1977), p. 260.

Figure 13.1 Title page. Desiderius Erasmus, *A deuout treatise vpon the Pater noster* (London: T. Berthelet, 1526?; *STC* 10477). London, British Library, C.37.e.6 (1).

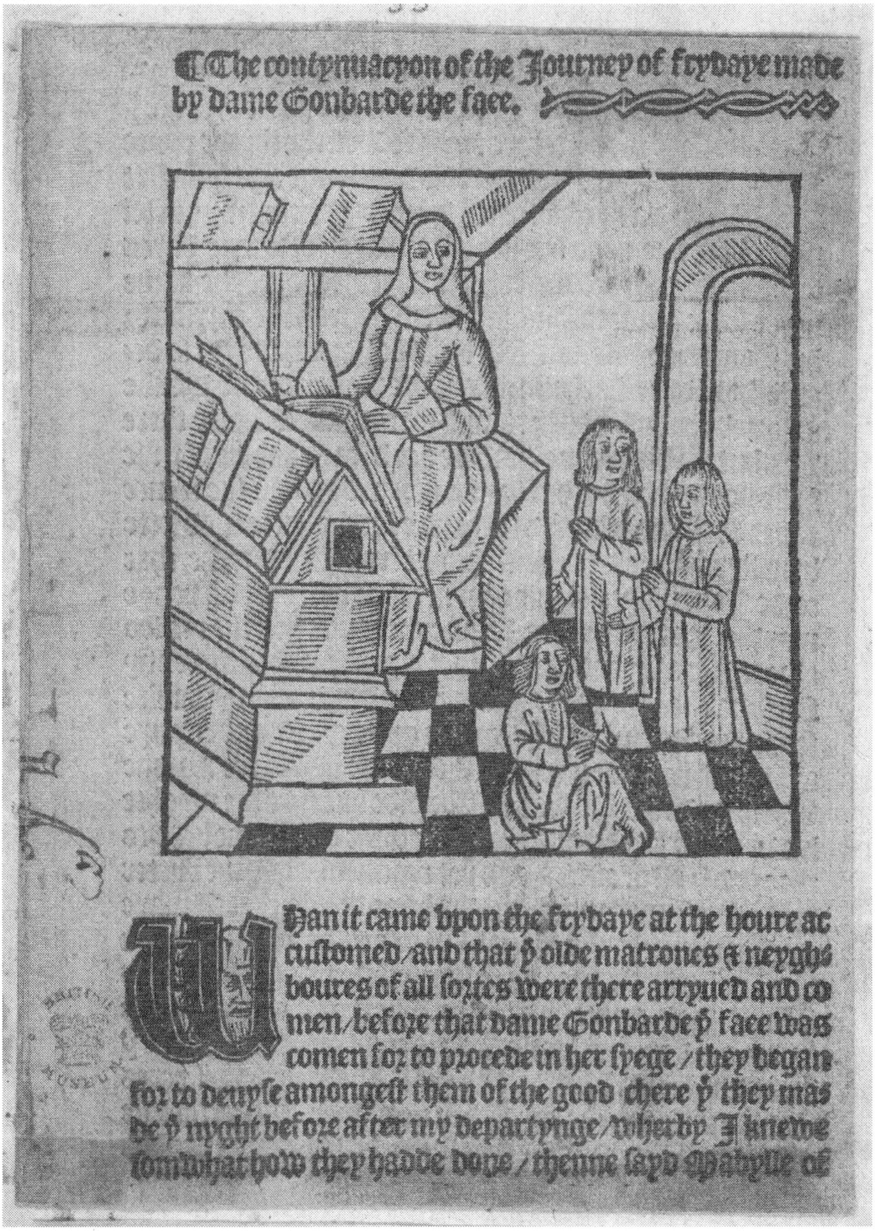

¶ The contynuacyon of the Journey of frydaye made by dame Gonbarde the face.

Whan it came vpon the frydaye at the houre accustomed/and that þ olde matrones & neyghboures of all sortes were there arryued and comen/before that dame Gonbarde þ face was comen for to procede in her syege/they began for to deuyse amongest them of the good chere þ they made þ nyght before after my departynge/wherby I knewe somwhat how they hadde done/thenne sayd Mabylle of

Figure 13.2 Anon., *The gospelles of dystaues* (London: Wynkyn de Worde, *c.*1510; *STC* 12091), sig. D2. London, British Library, Harl. 5919/35.

reputation for being, in Erasmus's words, 'a man made for friendship'. By translating the *Pater noster* and allowing it to be published she was placing herself,
however discreetly, within a humanist circle of friends.

In a larger context, Roper's translation should be seen as participating in
a movement in England to strengthen Erasmus's reputation in England. The
publication of the *Deuout treatise* and translations of Erasmus's *Dicta sapientium*
(Sayings of wise men) and *De immense dei misercordia* (on the immense mercy
of God), together with Fisher's anti-Lutheran *Sermon . . . concerning certayne
heretickes*, caused some trouble for Berthelet. Goodrich has recently suggested
that he hastily and illegally published all four works before procuring the
approval of the bishops overseeing the book trade in order to defend Erasmus
from suspicions of harbouring Lutheran sympathies, and that Roper's *Deuout
treatise* thus played a prominent role in pursuing this objective.[22] Indeed, in
December 1526, the year of the publication, her father wrote to Erasmus to try
and persuade him to take a stronger stance in print against Luther, which would
support Goodrich's view.[23] Thus the translation must be seen, not as the work of
an erudite young woman too modest to display her authorship in print, nor of a
merely obedient and dutiful daughter, but of an active agent in the religious and
political storm brewing on the English horizon.

The role played by Roper's *Devout treatise* in the religious climate of the 1520s
and 1530s can be further appreciated if placed within the context of the surprising number of Erasmian works being published, in both Latin and English.
Between 1520 and 1535, over twenty editions and translations appeared from
the presses of de Worde, Pepwell, Berthelet, Godfray, Wyer, Siberch, Byddell
and Marshall, with Berthelet heading the list. In the year 1533–34 alone, no
fewer than nine translated works were published. It is therefore no exaggera-
tion to claim that Roper's *Deuout treatise* was in the vanguard of a movement to
spread Erasmus's brand of Christian humanism by making his works available
to a wider English readership through the medium of translation.

It was also in the vanguard of another humanist-inspired movement,
to promote interest in and defend the education of women, a view strongly
defended in Hyrde's preface. One of Erasmus's colloquies presented a debate
on this very question, *The Abbot and the learned lady*, included in the 1524 publication. Magdalia, the learned lady in question, is widely thought to represent
Margaret Roper. In 1529, two years before the reprint of the Roper translation,
his *Vidua Christiana* (the Christian widow) also discussed women's education.

Two works intended for women and both with an English connection were
Vives's *De institutione foeminae Christianae* (The education of a Christian woman),
a conduct book commissioned by Catherine of Aragon in 1523, and *De ratione
studii puerilis* (On a plan of study for children), written for the education of her
daughter, the Princess Mary in 1524, the year in which Hyrde composed his
Roper preface. The former, printed by Berthelet in 1529 was translated as *A Very*

[22]   Goodrich, 'Thomas More', pp. 1030–31. For another view, see A.W. Reed, 'The Regulation
of the Book Trade before the Proclamation of 1538', *Transactions of the Bibliographical Society* 15
(1920), 157–84, reiterated by James Kelsey McConica, *English Humanists and Reformation Politics
under Henry VIII and Edward VI* (Oxford, 1965), pp. 71–72.
[23]   Allen, *Opus epistolarum*, 7: no. 1804.

frutefull and pleasant boke called the instruction of a christen woman by none other than Richard Hyrde, who says in his preface that the translation had been begun by More, who subsequently revised Hyrde's version. The same preface, like that accompanying the Roper translation, is used to promote women's education (sig. Aiii). Finally, 1529 saw the Continental publication of Henricus Cornelius Agrippa's controversial but extremely influential work on women, *Declamatio de nobilitate et precellentia foeminei sexus* (Declamation on the nobility and excellence of the female sex). The zeitgeist, then, made the publication and re-edition of a translation by Roper, an internationally known learned woman, and prefaced by a defence of women's learning, absolutely appropriate and, moreover, extremely marketable.

Berthelet was also directly involved some twenty years later in publishing another translation of a religious Latin work by a woman, this time Catherine Parr. The source text was John Fisher's *Psalmi seu precationes ex variis scripturae locis collectae. Anno 1544* (Psalms or prayers collected out of various places in Scripture) (London, 1544) (*STC* 2994), originally published in Cologne in *c.*1525 and twice re-edited by Berthelet in 1544 with some substantive variations and a slightly altered title that, significantly, omitted the name of its author, who was executed with More in 1535 for refusing to take the oath of succession. The 1544 English translation, *Psalmes or prayers taken out of holye scripture* (*STC* 3001.7) was also published anonymously but, unlike the *Deuout treatise*, contained no clues as to its authorship.[24] Rather unusually, it followed hot on the heels of the original (exactly one week later), suggesting that Berthelet was convinced of the work's commercial potential. Nor was his confidence misplaced, for it went through another edition in 1544, then five in 1545, and two before his death in 1555. Another thirteen editions published by various printers appeared between 1556 and 1613. The work certainly proved a bestseller.

However, it also owed its success to a factor other than Berthelet's commercial instinct. The full significance of Parr's translation has to be seen in the context of the need in the 1540s to publish new books of private prayer. As King's Printer, Berthelet was responsible for making such works available and the *Psalmes or prayers* constituted a valuable companion piece for Cranmer's *Litany*, used for public prayer in church, and edited four times in 1544–45. The Catholic authorship and nature of the original seems to have caused no problem. A blend of devotional and introspective meditation, scriptural paraphrasing, and quest for spiritual salvation through remorse and penance took it beyond the confines of sectarian worship. Moreover, as Janel Mueller has demonstrated, these were the very features of the work that appealed to Parr and would find an echo in her later writings.[25] Woven into the scriptural quotations and paraphrases in

---

[24]   Susan James was first to claim Parr as the translator, questioning various earlier statements that she knew but little Latin (*Kateryn Parr: The Making of a Queen* (Aldershot, 1999), pp. 200–04). More recently, Kimberly Anne Coles has offered further evidence of authorship, although recognising that no positive proof can be offered (*Religion, Reform, and Women's Writing in Early Modern England* (Cambridge, 2008), pp. 50–51). However, the very recent edition of Parr's complete writings includes the translation (*Katherine Parr: Complete Works and Correspondence*, ed. Janel Mueller (Chicago, IL, 2011), pp. 197–365).

[25]   Mueller, *Katherine Parr*, pp. 204–06. See also her following pages for a detailed and authoritative discussion of the translation itself.

the fifteen sections, each with its own title indicating the subject to be treated, are personal reflections, lamentations, and expressions of hope. The work ends with a translation of Fisher's prayer for the king, in which Parr effects significant gender-dictated changes, as Mueller demonstrates, and a second supplication, not by Fisher, entitled 'A prayer for men to saie entryng into battaile'. This was probably added to coincide with Henry's campaign in France in July 1544, when he left Parr as Regent-General of England, and has been attributed to the queen.[26]

The *Psalmes or prayers* bears witness to the fact that a printed translation by a woman was by no means an isolated event. Kimberly Anne Coles has argued with reference to both this work and Parr's 1545 *Prayers or medytacions*, re-edited six times by 1550, that their publication history demonstrates they were part of a programme to advance church reform, one in which Parr actively partici-pated.[27] Working with the king, the King's Printer, Archbishop Cranmer, and her almoner, George Day, she produced a devotional handbook that would become an enduring English reformation text, especially when bound as of July 1545 with her *Prayers or medytacions* becoming unofficially known as *The Kynges Psalmes. The Queenes Praiers* until the fourteenth edition in 1568, when this was incorporated into the official title.

These two works were not Catherine Parr's only connection with the inter-twined worlds of translation and Reformation publishing in England. In 1545–48, she became the instigator and patron of an ambitious project to translate and publish the first volume of Erasmus's 1524 *Paraphrases in Novum Testamentum* and, moreover, engaged another young woman translator in the enterprise, the Princess Mary.[28] She appointed Nicholas Udall editor, commissioned him and Thomas Key, an Oxford scholar, as translators and set Mary to translate the paraphrase to the Gospel of John. According to Udall's various prefaces, her goal was to make Erasmus's text available to all men and women who could read English, in order to improve their knowledge of the New Testament and thus encourage them to work towards their own salvation. The preface to John also highlights her own 'composing and setting forth many goodly psalms and diuerse other contemplatyue meditacions' and her choice of Mary as translator.

Parr's motives in inviting Mary to translate the 'Book of St John' were no doubt mixed. The princess had received a humanist education with a strong emphasis on Latin. However, as Parr herself demonstrated, education was an ongoing proposition; Mary could maintain her Latin by practising translation, a tried and true method of language training. Second, Parr must have known that Vives's *De ratione studii puerilis* had specifically recommended Mary read Erasmus's *Paraphrases*. Mary was also certainly aware that in his 1528 edition of the *Adagia* Erasmus had singled her out, with her parents, the Mores, and

---

[26]   All subsequent editions down to 1613 retain the two concluding prayers but the name in the prayer for the monarch changes with each succeeding reign.
[27]   Coles, *Religion, Reform, and Women's Writing*, p. 47.
[28]   Desiderius Erasmus, *The first tome or volume of the paraphrase of Erasmus vpon the newe testa-ment* (London, 1548) [*STC* 2854]. Volume 2, paraphrases on the remaining New Testament books, was financed one year later by Anne Seymour, a former member of Parr's intimate circle of court women.

the Mountjoys, as worthy examples of England's learned men and women. Another not insignificant factor was the warm friendship existing between Parr and Mary, and their shared interests in learning and religion. Perhaps most importantly, however, Parr must have hoped Mary's participation in what was a distinctly evangelical project would ensure her some protection at court, serve reformist aims, and save her soul. Her translation would be seen as being part of the whole publishing project encompassing Cranmer's *Litany* and the *Exhortacion vnto praier* (1544), the republication of the *Litany* with Parr's own translation and writings (1545), the *King's Primer* (1545), Parr's more controversial, and post-Henrician, *Lamentacion of a Sinner* (1547), and a series of new and re-edited translations of Erasmian works.[29]

It is impossible to know just how much of the translation Mary completed and how much revision was required; nor can we be certain that it really was illness, rather than qualms about the purpose of the translation, that prevented her from completing the work, although both Parr and Udall refer to her 'grievous long' sickness. Parr, writing to Mary, says that her former chaplain, Francis Mallet, whom she reappointed to Mary's household in order to supervise the translation, has 'put the finishing touch' on the work and he or someone in Mary's entourage has 'emended' the translation, which suggests that Mary did the bulk of the translation.[30] She also refers to the 'sweat' that Mary has 'laboriously put into this work'. Her comment that all these efforts have been made for the good of the commonwealth are echoed by Udall in his compliments to Parr, but patriotism as a motive was a frequent topos in translation prefaces. Parr's final comment, however, is of another order. She encourages Mary to publish the work under her own name. Perhaps this is unsurprising, given that she herself had published her first work anonymously but had allowed her name to appear on her second.[31] It would have given Mary visibility among those who did not trust her religious leanings and increased the possibility of her father's approval for the publication. Mary, however, declined the invitation to sign the translation and her name appears only in Udall's dedicatory preface to Parr, where he praises the learned women of England.

Although the English translation of the *Paraphrases* was not actually published in Henry's lifetime, it became required reading in his son's reign. Following the king's Injunctions of 1547, copies of the *Great Bible*, *Book of Common Prayer* and *Book of Homilies* were to be made available in every parish church; Volume I of the *Paraphrases* now joined their ranks. As a result, between 20,000 and 30,000 copies were sold between 1548 and 1552. Even through Mary's reign and in the context of the anti-Erasmian storm on the Continent that resulted in all of

---

[29] *Preparation to deathe* (1543, STC 10506), *De immensa dei misericordia* [On the immense mercy of God] (1547) (STC 10476), *Enchiridion* (1541 and 1544, STC 10482–84), Coverdale's abridged version of the *Enchiridion* (1545, STC 10488), and *An exhortation to the diligent studye of scripture* (1548, STC 10494.5).

[30] London, BL, MS Cotton Vespasian, F.III, art. 35, fol. 37r. The letter is reprinted, translated and discussed in Mueller, *Katherine Parr*, pp. 86–88.

[31] James (*Kateryn Parr*, pp. 228–32) has claimed Parr was also the anonymous author of the paraphrase to the Gospel of St Matthew, offering both internal and external evidence and the opinion of John Strype in *Ecclesiastical Memorials* as proof, but the identification remains controversial and the text is not included in Mueller's *Katherine Parr*.

Erasmus's works being placed on the Index in 1559, the English *Paraphrases* remained extremely popular, which probably saved it from the bonfire. Perhaps a more important factor, though, in halting Bishop Gardiner in his tracks was the potential embarrassment of banning a work in which his queen had rather publicly participated; for the same reason, she herself would have been hard put to censure it. Queen Elizabeth's 1559 Injunctions restored the work as a required text in parish churches and reprintings continued until 1583, when the patent expired. As Gregory Dodds says, it had 'undoubtedly become part of the fabric of English religious culture' and was still being referred to throughout Elizabeth's reign and into the next on account of copies being widely dispersed and well-known.[32] As the co-translator of the Gospel of St John, the Catholic Mary had rather ironically contributed to this phenomenon.

Parr's relationship with her other step-daughter would also result in a publication in the year 1548. The Princess Elizabeth had translated Marguerite de Navarre's devotional poem *Le Miroir de l'âme pécheresse* as a New Year's gift for Parr four years before, entitling it *The glasse of the synnefull soule* (Oxford, BodL, MS Cherry 36, fols 2r–63r). This was her first translation and the only one from her girlhood to be published in her lifetime.[33] It was edited and published by John Bale, an ardent Protestant and a prolific author, translator and editor, who retitled it *A godly Medytacyon of the christen sowle* and published it with a spurious colophon, Marburg. It was actually published in Wesel, where Bale had settled in exile, by D. van der Straten, who printed six of his other works before the end of 1548. To Elizabeth's text, Bale added his own 'Epistle dedicatory' and a 'Conclusion'.[34]

How Bale came to possess the manuscript translation remains a mystery, although he was obviously motivated to publish it in part for personal reasons. He says in his 'Conclusion' that Elizabeth sent her handwritten 'clauses' to him, as if she had been in direct communication with him, but no proof of this exists. Shell suggests Parr may well have sent Bale a copy of the manuscript with some emendations and additions, which he included.[35] Perhaps any one of the ladies of Catherine's court who had favoured him before his exile sent him one. Bale himself is rather coy about the matter but says specifically that he has received Elizabeth's 'golden sentences out of the sacred scriptures' written in

---

[32] Gregory Dodds, *Exploiting Erasmus: The Erasmian Legacy and Religious Change in Early Modern England* (Toronto, 2009), pp. 14–15. See also E.J. Devereux, 'The Publication of the English *Paraphrases* of Erasmus', *Bulletin of the John Rylands Library* 5 (1969), 348–53.

[33] In December 1545, Elizabeth translated Parr's *Prayers or meditacions* into Latin, French and Italian as a New Year's gift for her father (London, BL, MS Royal 7.D.X, fols 1r–117v) and Chapter 1 of Calvin's *Institution de la religion chrestienne* [Institutes of the Christian religion] into English for her step-mother (Edinburgh, National Archives of Scotland, MS RH 13/78, fols 1r–89v). Two years later, she offered her brother, the young King Edward VI, her Latin translation of Ochino's sermon, *Che cosa è Christo e per che venne al mondo* [What Christ is, and why he came into the world] (Oxford, BodL, MS Bodley 6, fols 1–36r). These are edited by Janel Mueller and Joshua Scodel in *Elizabeth I: Translations 1544–1589* (Chicago, IL and London, 2009).

[34] *A godly medytacyon of the christen sowle* (Wesel, 1548) (STC 17320). The dedication and conclusion are transcribed with modern spelling in Mark Shell, *Elizabeth's Glass: With 'The Glass of the Sinful Soul' (1544) by Elizabeth I and 'Epistle Dedicatory' and 'Conclusion' (1548) by John Bale* (Lincoln, NE, 1993), pp. 83–103.

[35] Shell, *Elizabeth's Glass*, p. 3.

Latin, Greek, French and Italian, 'most ornately, finely, & purely written with your owne hande' (fol. 7). However he procured the manuscript, in 1547 he was preparing his return to England and starting to search for patrons. Who better, then, than the young princess Elizabeth, one of a long line of noble English women whom he lavishly praised in his 'Conclusion', and the much loved sister of the young king.

Bale's other motive for publishing the translation was ideological. As David Loades has demonstrated, a move in the years 1547–49 towards a more Protestant settlement is reflected in an increase in the number of printing presses from twenty-five to thirty-nine and of titles from about 100 to about 225.[36] Printers with an evangelical bent like Day, Seres and Whitchurch took full advantage of the new situation to produce theological, doctrinal and controversial works, and Day, in particular, published similar Continental works in translation. Scoloker, an Ipswich printer also of an evangelical persuasion who in 1548 joined Seres and Day in London, printed Protestant works and even translated five himself. No fewer than 157 translations were published in the years 1547–49 (counting re-editions and re-issues), of which 64 (or 40.7%) dealt with various aspects of the reformed faith.[37] Loades mentions by name only two explicit works of Protestant theology, Bullinger's *Two epystles* and Calvin's *A faythful and most godly treatyse*, but in fact other works by these men, as well as by Melanchthon, Luther, Bucer, Zwingli and Ochino also appeared in 1548. That year, as shown by King and Rankin, was an *annus mirabilis* in the history of reformist books, over thirty of which were translations of Continental texts.[38] The time was obviously ripe for a translation of a composition by a French queen considered a female Protestant icon in England, author of a work briefly condemned by the Sorbonne theologians in 1533 for its evangelical nature. Moreover, the translation constituted a precious tool in creating Elizabeth's 'learned, pious persona – her first public identity, and an enduring one'.[39] Bale described her in his prefatory Epistle as having 'so moch virtu, faythe, scyence, & experyence of languages & letters, specyally in noble youth & femynyty' (7r–v). The translation also contributed to making her commitment to Protestantism clear, for in his 'Conclusion' Bale placed it directly after Anne Askew's 'deed of fayth', by which the Protestant martyr 'hath strongly trodden downe the head of the serpent, and achieved victory 'ouer the pestyferouse seede of that vyperouse worme of Rome' (46v).

Intertwined with Bale's Protestant zeal was a nationalistic pride in England's escape from Rome's domination and establishment of an English church closer in spirit and practices to that of primitive Christianity, which inspired several of

---

[36] David Loades, 'Books and the English Reformation Prior to 1558', in *The Reformation and the Book*, ed. Jean-François Gilmont. English version ed. and trans. Karin Maag (Aldershot, 1990), pp. 264–91.
[37] According to the *Renaissance Cultural Crossroads Catalogue*, the breakdown is as follows: in 1547 nine out of twenty-six translations were reformist, representing 31.6%; in 1548, thirty-eight out of eighty-seven, or 43%; in 1549, seventeen out of forty-four, or 38.6%.
[38] John N. King and Mark Rankin, 'Print, Patronage, and the Reception of Continental Reform: 1521–1603', *Yearbook of English Studies* 38 (2008), 49–67.
[39] Mueller, *Elizabeth I*, p. 26.

his works immediately preceding *The glasse of the synfulle sowle*.[40] The publication of Elizabeth's translation must be seen partly in this context. As Bale claims in his 'Epistle Dedicatory', she stood in a line of noble young Englishwomen, although surpassing them all because of her translations of a French godly text, scriptural aphorisms and Psalm verse (7r–v). In his 'Conclusion', in which he laments the absence of an English catalogue of learned women, he patriotically places her in a list of English noblewomen ending with Margaret Beaufort and Elizabeth of York, her great-grandmother and grandmother, but also including commoners Eleanor Cobham and Anne Askew, on account of their opposition to the hierarchy of the Roman church (42v–46v). Before this, however, he is careful to establish Elizabeth's immediate pedigree: she has inherited the blood of 'a most vyctoryouse kynge', her father, and shares it with 'a most vertueuse, & lerned kynge', her brother (40v–41r). The publication of the translation, then, responds to Bale's personal needs in re-establishing himself in England and suits his ideological agenda admirably: it compliments the new king and his sister, praises Englishwomen, amongst whom Bale most certainly hoped to find patrons, records the writings of a English author in line with his *Summarium*, reflects his vision of English history, and furthers his reformist propaganda.

Since Elizabeth must surely have approved Bale's edition, we can only presume that she accepted his rather heavy editorial interventions, which resulted in adjusting the volume to promote his own vision of establishing the reformed faith in England.[41] Already, in her dedications to her father and stepmother that prefaced her other translations, Elizabeth had begun to fashion herself as a studious and pious young woman, while already showing surprising political acumen. Now, with the accession of her brother and the appointment of the stoutly evangelical duke of Somerset as Lord Protector, she perhaps welcomed a more reformist version of her translation. There was also possibly a personal reason for her acceptance of it. In 1548, she had somewhat compromised her reputation with Thomas Seymour, her stepmother's new husband. Apparently frightened by the whole episode, she decided to return to her previous, more pious persona. Bale's edition could not have come at a better time, for it re-established her as an erudite and a virtuous young woman of evangelical sympathies. By the 1560s, and again in 1580, the work must have continued to find favour with her despite John Cancellar's similarly heavy-handed textual interventions, for as Mueller says, these 'functioned effectively to promote the mature Elizabeth's objectives'.[42]

As we have said, 1548 saw a peak in the production of published translations

---

[40] See for example, *The image of both churches* (Antwerp, 1545?); *The actes of Englysh votaryes* (Wesel [i.e. Antwerp], 1546); *Illustrium maioris Britanniae scriptorium summarium* [A list of the best British authors] (Wesel [i.e. Antwerp], 1548); *A brefe chronycle concernynge the examinacyon and death of the martyr syr J. Oldcastell* (Antwerp, 1544); *The first examinacyon of Anne Askewe* (Marpurg [i.e. Wesel], 1546) and *The lattre examinacyon of Anne Askewe* (Marpurg [i.e. Wesel], 1547).
[41] Similarly, she must have accepted John Cancellar's heavily emended edition now without a title-page (London, 1568?) (*STC* 17320.5). This was reprinted as Lamp 2 of Thomas Bentley's 1582 *Monument of matrones* (*STC* 1892) and re-edited in 1580 without Bale's dedicatory epistle (*STC* 17321). The 1590 edition restored it but omitted Cancellar's epistle (*STC* 17322.5).
[42] Mueller, *Elizabeth I*, p. 39.

of reformist texts. Within our corpus, a third translation joined Elizabeth's *Glasse of the synfulle sowle* and Mary's paraphrase to the Gospel of St John. It was Anne Cooke's translation of five sermons from Bernardino Ochino's *Prediche* entitled *Sermons of Barnardine Ochine of Sena godlye, frutfull, and very necessarye for all true Christians translated out of Italien into Englishe*, published without her name by Roger Car for William Reddell (*STC* 18764). As was the case with the princesses' works, a discussion of Cooke's translation within the interlocking contexts of religious and print activity proves fruitful in assessing motivation and impact.

The sermon was particularly associated with Protestantism, which gave it a prominent role in bringing believers to salvation and a far more prominent place in church services than in the Catholic mass.[43] As a result, translations of many Continental sermons by reformers such as Luther, Zwingli, Urbanus Regius and Calvin were published to complement printings of native ones; between 1545 and 1555 they numbered no fewer than seventeen, while in 1548 alone there were six. One was Richard Argentine's *Sermons of the ryght famous and excellent clerke master B. Ochine*, published by the Ipswich printer Anthony Scoloker, who also published five other translations of reformist texts that year.[44] While not sermons in the classic sense of the word, being written discussions of theological points rather than orations on general religious matters delivered in church, Ochino's 259 *Prediche* had been very successful on the Continent, appearing in Geneva in five instalments starting in 1543. Given this publishing success, and the fact that since arriving as a religious refugee in England in 1547 Ochino had attracted the favourable attention of the fervent Protestants surrounding the young Edward VI and had secured Cranmer's and Cheke's patronage, the publication of some of his sermons in English must have seemed both ideologically and commercially apposite.

Argentine's translation was prefaced by his dedicatory epistle to the duke of Somerset and polemical address to the reader, as well as another polemical one by Scoloker. Cooke's, however, was preceded only by her unsigned preface to the reader; unlike Hyrde's preface to Roper's translation, it contained no clues as to her identity. Yet this paratext reveals much about her beliefs and motivation. In order to describe the Christian awaiting death, watching and praying, she chooses an image associated specifically with women: the wise virgin awaiting the bridegroom, lamp trimmed (Matt. 25: 1–13) (sig. Aiir–v). She also has recourse to a traditional modesty topos, calling herself a 'begynner' and a 'learner' and begging the reader's indulgence, but then confidently promises that when more competent, she will continue to translate Ochino (sig. Aiv). Modesty, however, does not prevent her from explaining why she has translated his sermons. Christians, caught between the devil's 'busy bragging' and God's justice, must be prepared for death and final judgement; to help them, she says, 'I haue, to staye & strengthen the conscience on thes behalfes, turned into english two sermons' (the first two in her collection) (sig. Aiiiv). In concluding,

---

[43]   Ian Green, in *Print and Protestantism in Early Modern England* (Oxford, 2000), emphasises the importance of the sermon and its passage into print, listing six different types amongst which controversial sermons on doctrinal issues, pp. 194–202.
[44]   Argentine, John Foxe, Walter Lynne and an anonymous translator translated one Lutheran sermon each (*STC* 16992, 16983, 16982, 17626).

she speaks even more confidently and claims in far stronger language the importance of her future translation, to be made 'for the enformacion of all that desire
to know the truth. For they truly conteyne moch to the defacing of al papistrie,
and hipocrysie, and to the aduancement of the glorye of god' (sig. Aiv).

Scoloker never honoured the promise made in his preface to the reader to
publish more Ochino sermons; Cooke, on the other hand, did. Probably in 1551,
Day published *Fouretene sermons of Barnardine Ochyne, concernyng the predesti-
nacion and eleccion of god: very expediente to the setynge forth of hys glorye among
hys creatures. Translated out of Italian in to oure natyue tounge by A.C.* The subject
of ten of these was far more controversial and her choice of them far more
daring, although this did not prevent Day from printing her initials both in the
title and at the end of her dedication to her mother, identified as the Lady F
(Anne Fitzwilliam).[45] He also included an epistle by 'G.B.', William (Guilielmus)
Baldwin, then a corrector employed by another evangelical printer, Edward
Whitchurch, who does not name Cooke but claims he is the conduit through
whom she agreed, 'shamefastedly' and 'halfe against hyr wyll', to publish the
sermons (sig. Aii). The reluctant translator topos would ring more true and be
less grating were it not so condescending, enclosing Cooke in the domestic space
afforded by her father's house and offering this as the reason for any errors she
makes. Baldwin also calls her a 'wel occupied Jentelwoman', in an allusion to the
traditional portrait of indolent and frivolous women of court and gentry, and
with no small degree of irony describes potential male critics in sexist language
usually reserved for women.

The subject of election and predestination in the ten sermons was indeed
controversial, but it is the very one that Cooke uses to justify her translation
to her mother, who had disapproved of her study of Italian as wasting seeds
of learning in barren ground. Anne cleverly reverses the vegetation metaphor,
praising the 'excellent fruit' contained in the sermons (the doctrine of election
and predestination) and even claiming that she has but obeyed her mother in
translating them. Presumably, then, such doctrine was not unfamiliar in the
Cooke household.

Nor, presumably, did the controversial subjects of election and predestination prevent the public success of Cooke's newly translated sermons, since Day
republished them in the same year as numbers 12–25 in a collection that reprinted
Argentine's six translations (nos 1–6) and her previous five (nos 7–11). The title
owed something to Scoloker's but was greatly expanded: *Certayne sermons of
the ryghte famous and excellente clerk Barnardino Ochine. Borne within the famous
uniuersitie of Siena, Italy, now also an exile in thys lyfe, for the faithful testimony of
Jesus Christe. Faythfully translated into Englyshe* (STC 18766). By 1551, Ochino had
been appointed by Cranmer as head of the Strangers' Church in London, made a
prebendary of Canterbury and given a pension; he had dedicated an anti-papal
play to Edward VI, who owned a copy of John Ponet's 1549 English translation
of it together with one of Ochino's *Prediche*, and enjoyed the company and admi-
ration of the Princess Elizabeth, who, as we said earlier, translated his sermon

---

[45] King and Rankin repeat an earlier mistake in identifying Lady F. as Elizabeth Fane (*Print
and Patronage*, p. 60).

'Che cosa è Christo, & per che venne al mondo'.[46] Nevertheless, Day found it necessary for a wider readership to describe Ochino to his potential readers as a former student at Siena but now in exile for his religious views. Perhaps he also hoped this would elicit sympathy and thus increase sales. It is puzzling that he did not identify Cooke as the translator of the five sermons that he reprinted as numbers 7 to 11, if only by her initials, and omitted her preface to the reader; he must have known they were her work. True, he also omitted Argentine's name, but he did include his 1548 signed preface to the reader.

The 1551 joint edition must have continued to strike a popular chord, for Day reprinted it in 1570, the same year that he produced one of his greatest publications, Foxe's *Actes and Monuments*. He introduced some changes, no doubt dictated by both ideological and commercial concerns. Day was, after all, in John King's words, 'a committed ideologue' but also one of the wealthiest and most successful printers in London.[47] Interestingly, all four changes resulted in highlighting Anne Cooke and making the volume very much hers. The new title, *Sermons of Barnardine Ochyne, (to the number of .25.) concerning the predestination and election of god: very expedient to the setting forth of his glory among his creatures. Translated out of Italian into our natiue tongue, by A.C.*, explicitly turned the reader's attention to those *prediche* in her *Fouretene sermons* dealing with the controversial doctrine of the elect, although they represented only ten of the twenty-five in the joint edition. The final sentence of the new title was taken from that of the *Fouretene sermons*, identifying Cooke by her initials. Day also included Baldwin's and Cooke's epistles, but no other paratext. The omission of Argentine's name and preface, both included in the 1551 *Certayne sermons*, effectively does away with any notion of double billing. Finally, Day reversed the order of the sermons, now giving pride of place to Cooke's set of fourteen and at the same time shifting the emphasis of the collection to the subjects of election and predestination highlighted by Cooke in her dedicatory epistle. The following six by Argentine are in no way set off as being by a different translator, while Cooke's five early sermons complete the list, again not set off from Argentine's. The reader could thus assume she is the translator of all twenty-five.

The reason for promoting Cooke and eclipsing Argentine was no doubt commercial. By 1570, she was famous as the expert translator of John Jewel's *Apologia ecclesiæ anglicanæ* (Apology of the Church of England), whose 1564 English version had supplanted the 1562 anonymous one and become the official translation approved by Matthew Parker. She was also the wife of Nicholas Bacon, Queen Elizabeth's Lord Keeper of the Great Seal, and sister-in-law of William Cecil, Lord Burghley. In other words, her name, or initials, on a work would be a strong selling-point. Argentine's, on the contrary, might well be a deterrent. He had vacillated in his religious affiliations, enthusiastically embracing the new

---

[46] Ochino speaks of his discussion of predestination with Elizabeth in his preface to *Prediche ... nominate laberinti del libero o ver servo arbitrio, prescienza, predestinatione, libertá diuina & del modo per uscirne* [Sermons entitled how to find a way out of the labyrinths of free or subjugated will, prescience, predestination, and divine freedom] (Basel, 1569), sig. A3v. The subject was obviously dear to these young women's hearts.

[47] John N. King, 'John Day: Master Printer of the English Reformation', in *The Beginnings of English Protestantism*, ed. Peter Marshall and Alec Ryrie (Cambridge, 2002), pp. 180–208.

evangelism under Edward, then energetically persecuting Protestants under Mary, only to return to the Protestant fold and reap the benefits of his reconversion under Elizabeth until he angered the ecclesiastical powers. Ironically, it was Nicholas Bacon who was instructed to arraign him and Matthew Parker who reported on his misdoings in Exeter, where he had obtained a prebendary.[48] One can understand Day's reticence.

The case of Cooke's Ochino translations illustrates how the ideologies of religion and the marketplace meet and influence the production of books, although socio-historical factors are also crucial. The year 1548 saw the rise of a strongly evangelical faction led by the duke of Somerset, Lord Protector of the young king. His involvement in having reformist translations and other works published, his patronage of theologians, and his role in relaxing the censorship laws and promulgating the Royal Injunctions regarding the reading of biblical and other religious works influenced the print trade between 1548 and 1550.[49] Within the context of the court, too, another factor perhaps played in Cooke's favour. Her father was involved in tutoring Edward. Finally, 1548 saw Cranmer's publication of a collection of sermons under the title *Homilies*, which included four dealing with the evangelical belief that salvation depended on faith alone. This triggered a fierce exchange between him and Bishop Gardiner. In this climate, Cooke's 1548 translation was pertinent, for the second sermon taught that salvation was only made possible by Christ, not by works. Seeing a turn in the tide of religious events after the death of Henry VIII, both she and her publisher must have believed it opportune to make a translation of Ochino's sermons available to the public.

An even greater turn in the tide was to provide a favourable context for the publication of a translation by our final woman translator, Mary Clarke Basset, granddaughter of Thomas More and daughter of the internationally admired Margaret Roper. Her English version of More's final work, *De tristitia, tedio, pauore, et oratione Christi ante captionem eius*, 'Of the sorowe, werinesse, feare and prayer of Christ before hys taking', was included in William Rastell's 1557 *Workes of Sir Thomas More, Knyght*, and was the only translation by a woman to be published during Mary's reign.[50] Its appearance in the English *Workes* needs some explanation, for More wrote it in Latin, not English. It owed its inclusion in part to socio-historical events and the ideological motivations of the people involved in its production. Among them was Basset, who stood, not at the margins of society, translating texts in privacy for her own leisure, but at the centre of religious and political activity. In allowing her translation to be published, and in acting as patron, she was furthering a cause in which she fervently believed.

[48]   For more on Argentine, see *ODNB*.
[49]   See John N. King, *English Reformation Literature: The Tudor Origins of the Protestant Tradition* (Princeton, NJ, 1982), pp. 76–121, whose account of Somerset's involvement has nevertheless been challenged by Jennifer Loach in 'The Marian Establishment and the Printing Press', *EHR* 101 (1986), 135–48.
[50]   Thomas More, *The workes of sir Thomas More, Knyght . . . wrytten by him in the Englysh tonge* (London, 1557), sigs QQ7v–VV2v (*STC* 18076). For a fuller discussion of the background and nature of the translation, see Brenda M. Hosington, 'Translating Devotion: Mary Roper Basset's English Rendering of Thomas More's *De tristitia . . . Christi*', *Renaissance and Reformation/ Renaissance et Réforme* 35 (2012), 63–95.

At some point between 1550 and 1553, the young Mary Clarke, as she was then, offered her Latin translation of Book I and English translation of Books I–V of Eusebius's *Ecclesiastical History* to the Princess Mary.[51] This gift, together with her position as a member of the More family and the widowed daughter-in-law of a prominent Suffolk Catholic, secured Mary a place in the coronation eve procession in 1553. Two years later, she married James Basset, Bishop Gardiner's secretary, and the newlyweds were appointed to court; by 1557, they had moved up in the court hierarchy and, now extremely well connected and reasonably prosperous, were able to contribute to the costs of financing the ambitious publishing project advanced by their cousin, the printer and lawyer, William Rastell.

Historians have differed somewhat in their assessments of the importance of the printing press in Mary's reign. Indisputable evidence demonstrates that the number of London stationers decreased from eighty to forty-one, and that many presses went out of business when a good number of printers, as well as authors of religious texts, fled to the Continent. Comparisons of the years 1548–52 with 1554–58 indeed show that the number of books printed also decreased, although this is interpreted in slightly different ways, with Jennifer Loach and Andrew Pettegree, in particular, questioning previous assertions that neither Mary nor her government appreciated the power of the press.[52] Figures for the translations published in those two periods also register a decrease, from 278 to 138, with religious texts demonstrating an even greater decline, from 189 to 55, or from 67.9 per cent of the total output to 39.8 per cent.[53] Religious works, then, were not great money-makers for the Marian printers, which explains in part why the cost of producing an expensive folio volume such as *The Workes of Sir Thomas More* was borne by three printers, as well as by James and Mary Basset, Rastell and others. All were obviously driven by a greater ideological impetus than that of the marketplace, namely the return of England to the Roman fold.

Of the three printers, John Cawood was most clearly associated with Catholicism. Appointed Queen's Printer in 1553, he published key Catholic texts like Bonner's *Certaine homelyes* in 1555 and Cranmer's *Submyssyons, and recantations* in 1556.[54] Richard Totell's religious affiliations are less clear, although he was favoured by the group of Catholic exiled lawyers of whom Rastell was one, and saw his patent to print common law books renewed in 1556. He had also published More's *Dialoge of comfort against tribulacion* in November 1553, the only other religious work to come from his press, which suggests either a certain sympathy for Catholic writings or an ability to jump quickly on the bandwagon in the opening months of Mary's reign. Of John Walley we know

---

[51]   London, BL, MS Harley 1860.
[52]   See in particular, J.W. Martin, 'The Marian Regime's Failure to Understand the Importance of Printing', *HLQ* 44 (1980–81), 231–47; Loach, 'The Marian Establishment'; David Loades, 'Books and the English Reformation Prior to 1558', in *The Reformation and the Book*, pp. 264–69; and Andrew Pettegree, 'Printing and the Reformation: The English Exception', in *The Beginnings of English Protestantism*, ed. Peter Marshall and Alec Ryrie (Cambridge, 2002), pp. 157–79.
[53]   Findings provided by the *Renaissance Cultural Crossroads Catalogue*.
[54]   Cawood succeeded Richard Grafton, foolhardy publisher of a proclamation announcing the accession of Jane Grey. More prudent in terms of regime change, Cawood was able to continue as joint Royal Printer with Richard Jugge under Elizabeth. See 'Cawood, John', *ODNB*.

only that he was a prolific printer and, like Cawood and Tottell, a member of the Stationers' Company. As for Rastell himself, he was of impeccable Catholic pedigree: nephew of Thomas More, publisher of seven of his controversial works and of his son's two translations, Marian exile in Louvain, and as of 1555 protégé of Cardinal Pole. His own motivation is declared in his dedicatory epistle to Queen Mary: he wanted to make More's writings available on account of the 'eloquence and propertie of the English tongue, but also the trewe doctrine of Christes Catholike faith, the confutacion of detestable heresies, or the [work's] godly morall virtues'.[55] The print context for Rastell's *Englysh Workes* was thus decidedly Catholic.

The publication was not, however, intended solely to rehabilitate Catholicism; it was also meant to rehabilitate More. By reaching a wider audience than the Latin *De tristitia*, Basset's translation could play an important role in reinstating More as Catholic martyr. A major theme of the work is martyrdom, as exemplified by the capture of Christ in Gethsemane and his subsequent crucifixion, but the implicit parallel between Christ and More is made clear in Rastell's 'Prynter to the gentle reader'. After paraphrasing the last words of More's Latin text, 'manus iniactas in Iesum [and they laid hands upon Jesus]', Rastell says More was deprived of books, pen, ink, and paper in the Tower of London, imprisoned 'more strayghtly than before', and 'soone after also was putte to death hymselfe'.[56] The adverb 'also' and the reflexive pronoun make the parallel clear and reinforce the desire to portray More as a martyred champion of Catholicism. This most assuredly is one reason for the inclusion of this Latin work in an edition of More's English writings.

Rastell's 'Preface to the gentle reader' is revealing in another context, that of the bashful and reluctant woman translator. He tells us Basset resisted his invitation to publish the work, which she had completed some years before, saying she seemed 'nothing willing to haue it goe abrode, for that (she sayeth) it was first turned into englishe, but for her own pastyme and exercise, and so reputeth it farre to simple to come in many handes' (sig. 1350). His words echo her own in the Eusebius dedication, where she says she translated 'for myne owne onely exercyse', but of course this is a well-worn topos. Regarding her reluctance to make her private translation of the *De tristitia* public, Rastell contends that many had read it and even suggested it be printed alone because of its excellence. This rather undercuts any claims concerning its private nature, especially as Basset must have agreed to allow him to print it and, furthermore, put her name on it. As patron, she could most certainly have refused. But again, the comment echoes Basset's in the Eusebius dedication, where the claim to privacy is compromised by her saying that many had read and approved her translation.

In the same year that Basset's translation saw print, thirty-one other translations went to press. Only two religious ones were printed in England, both Catholic in nature: Elizabeth of Schőnau's *Liber viarum Dei* (Book of the ways of God), possibly printed by the Catholic Robert Caley but entered to Walley, and twelve sermons by St Augustine dedicated to Queen Mary and printed

---

[55]   Rastell, *The Workes of Sir Thomas More*, sig. Cii.
[56]   Rastell's version contains a misprint, 'Et incecerunt manus in Iesum', rather than 'iniecerunt'.

by Cawood. However, two 1557 secular reprints had a Catholic and Morean connection: Vives's *De institutione foeminae Christianae*, as we said earlier, translated first by More then by Hyrde and commissioned by Queen Mary's mother, and Erasmus's *Moriae encomium* (Praise of folly), dedicated to More. Compared with the numbers of related works published alongside the translations of the other women translators in this essay, the pickings are indeed lean. But, as we have said, Mary's reign witnessed a general decline in overall publications in England. Nor can Basset's translation compete in endurance with Beaufort's, Parr's or Cooke's, no doubt for historical reasons. Only one year after its publication, Queen Mary died and Elizabeth acceded to the throne, returning England to Protestantism. Basset lived on until 1573, but published nothing more. Rastell returned to exile in Louvain in 1563, where he died two years later. Of More's religious writings in the century following 1557 only a heavily edited *Dialogue of comfort* was published in English (1573).[57] The Catholic euphoria that had characterised Mary's accession, when Basset had been included in her triumphal procession, and the enthusiasm and hopes of the members of the More circle that had inspired the publication of the *English workes* were indeed short-lived. Basset, through her two translations, had nevertheless participated actively in both events, while her published translation remained the only English rendering of the *De tristitia* until 1976.[58]

This active participation through translation in the religious and political life of England in the first half of the sixteenth century is in fact demonstrated by all seven women in this study. As we have seen, the published translations by Beaufort, Roper, Parr, Cooke, the princesses Mary and Elizabeth and Basset all played a role in the spread and advancement of spiritual ideals, while at the same time engaging with the political context and claiming their place in the burgeoning world of print. With these compositions, the concept of the secluded learned woman, sequestered alone with her books in a domestic space and occupying her time by translating simply for her own betterment and pleasure, is put to rest. They testify to a merging of the private and public worlds that these women inhabited, to a blend of strong personal as well as ideological motivations on the part of the translators, and to a clear understanding of the various roles that translation and print could play in the religious and political arena.

It is not at all evident that these translations were published for their curiosity value, although their extremely small number compared with male-authored translations in the period, as well as their sheer novelty as works by women, might well have helped sales. The royal rank of Beaufort, Parr and the princesses is more likely to have been a factor, as of course it would have been for men. Roper's name and reputation as one of the most learned women in Europe must have spurred Berthelet to publish the Erasmus text, as did Cooke's by the time that John Day republished her translations of Ochino. While it is true that Roper's, Elizabeth's and Basset's translations reached print through the agency

---

[57] More's secular writings fared slightly better, but even his *Utopia* appeared only twice, in 1624 and 1639. His *Epigrammata* was republished in 1638 and a collection of his letters in 1633.
[58] In his *De tristitia Christi* [On the sadness of Christ] in the *Complete Works More*, 14, pt 2 (New Haven, CT and London, 1976), Clarence Miller provides a bilingual edition of the work as well as a transcribed copy of Basset's translation (Appendix C, pp. 1077–165).

of male editors, whose paratexts reveal their own personal and ideological reasons, it would be wrong to see these young women as mere pawns, subservient to male authority and ambition. Like many another translator involved in the spiritual and material issues of the sixteenth century, these women understood the power of translation as a conduit for religious and political thought and the power of the printing press as a means of putting it into action. And we must not overlook the fact that in two instances, the moving force behind the publications was exercised by women, Beaufort and Parr.

Although the number of Latin and French original texts was only nine, reprintings of the English translations ensured their continued visibility throughout the sixteenth century and for a decade or two beyond. Beaufort's *Imytacyon* and *Mirour* went through six and three respectively; Cooke's first set of sermons was reprinted twice, as was her second; Elizabeth's *Glasse* saw four editions in all; Parr's *Psalmes or prayers*, by being bound with her *Prayers or meditacions*, went through no fewer than twenty-four editions in the years 1545–1613, making the work, as Coles says, not only a bestseller within its genre, but also the most enduringly popular devotional text in that period;[59] as such, it outperformed hundreds of male-authored translations. Mary Tudor's *Paraphrases*, by being part of a work that was required reading in all English parishes, also lived on through multiple reprintings. It is perhaps no coincidence that Roper's translation saw only one reprint, while her daughter's, embedded within the *English Workes*, saw none. This spoke more to Elizabethan ideology and politics than to any reticence concerning their quality, however. Although for these reasons they were of limited impact, they enjoyed a continued reputation through the writings of More's biographers and later compilers of catalogues of learned women. All seven translators thus achieved varying degrees of visibility in print at a time when it was difficult for women to do so, while they most certainly made more impact by playing an active and a participatory role in the social and religious culture of their day than has been previously recognised.

Further Reading

Clarke, Danielle, *The Politics of Early Modern Women's Writing* (Harlow, 2001).

Coles, Kimberly Anne, *Religion, Reform, and Women's Writing in Early Modern England* (Cambridge, 2008).

Demers, Patricia, *Women's Writing in English: Early Modern England* (Toronto, 2005).

Green, Ian, *Print and Protestantism in Early Modern England* (Oxford, 2000).

Hosington, Brenda M., 'Tudor Englishwomen's Translations of Continental Protestant Texts: The Interplay of Ideology and Historical Context', in *Tudor Translation*, ed. Fred Schurink (London, 2011), pp. 121–42.

James, Susan, *Kateryn Parr: The Making of a Queen* (Aldershot, 1999).

Loades, David, 'Books and the English Reformation prior to 1558', in *The Reformation and the Book*, ed. Jean-François Gilmont. English version ed. and trans. Karin Maag (Aldershot, 1990).

---

[59] Coles, *Religion, Reform, and Women's Writing*, p. 52.

Mueller, Janel and Joshua Scodel, eds, *Elizabeth I. Translations 1544–1589* (Chicago, IL and London, 2009).

Mueller, Janel, *Katherine Parr: Complete Works and Correspondence* (Chicago, IL, 2011).

Powell, Susan, 'Lady Margaret Beaufort and her Books', *The Library*, 6th ser., 20 (1998), 197–240.

14

The Printed Book Trade in Response to Luther: English Books Printed Abroad

ANDREW HOPE

When the York publisher and bookseller Gerard Freez, who was probably of Dutch origin, died in 1510, his stock was found to include well over a thousand liturgical volumes purchased in France and brought to England.[1] Of these titles fewer than three hundred still survive anywhere from this period. This massive loss of pre-Reformation liturgical material has obscured an important aspect of late medieval Catholicism: it was a religion of the book. Sacramental grace required the use of the correct liturgical words and the new technology of printing held out the hope of imposing verbal uniformity in ways that had not been possible before.[2] Late medieval religion may have been a religion of performance, but it was words that were performative. A book trade rapidly developed to satisfy this liturgical need. Such books were often complex productions and demanded skills and experience that English printers often did not have. Liturgical texts of this type had a core of text which was common across Christendom, to which were added local variations, and it was thus possible from a single centre, say Venice or Paris, to produce books for a wide geographical market.[3]

In the two decades after Gerard Freez's death the principal publishing house for liturgical books for the English market became that run by two Dutch brothers, Franz (d. 1530) and Arnold (d. 1542) Birckmann, based in Cologne.[4] The Birckmanns had offices in London in St Paul's Churchyard, and in Paris and Antwerp.[5] Franz was exceptionally well-travelled, making journeys which brought him into close contact with the pioneers of northern humanist scholarship. The Dutch scholar Desiderius Erasmus (d. 1536) used Franz Birckmann to keep in touch with a wide range of contacts in London, Paris, the Low Countries, and Frankfurt and with the Froben press in Basel. In England mutual contacts

[1] E. Brunskill, 'Missals, Portifers, and Pyes', *The Ben Johnson Papers* 2 (1974), 20–33.
[2] Natalia Nowakowska, 'From Strassburg to Trent: Bishops, Printing and Liturgical Reform in the Fifteenth Century', *Past & Present* 213 (2011), 3–39.
[3] 'English Purchases', pp. 268–90 (278–81).
[4] Ilse Guenther and Peter G. Bietenholz, 'Arnold Birckmann of Cologne' and 'Franz Birckmann of Hinsbeck', in *Contemporaries of Erasmus: A Biographical Register of the Renaissance and Reformation*, ed. Peter G. Bietenholz, 3 vols (Toronto, 1985–87), 1.148–49 and 149–50.
[5] Henry Plomer, 'The Importation of Printed Books into England in the Fifteenth and Sixteenth Centuries: An Examination of Some Customs Rolls', *The Library*, 4th ser., 4 (1924), 146–50.

included near neighbour John Colet (d. 1519), dean of St Paul's and founder of St Paul's School, the future Lord Chancellor Thomas More (1478–1535), the bishop of Rochester John Fisher (1469–1535), and the future bishop of London Cuthbert Tunstall (1474–1559).[6] All were acquainted with Franz Birckmann and all were eager to see the fruits of Erasmus's biblical scholarship, and the scholarship inspired by him, put to the service of the renewal of the church.[7]

The watchword of humanist scholars was *ad fontes*, back to the sources, and Erasmus went to the heart of the matter in 1516 with his *Novum Instrumentum*, an edition of the original Greek text of the New Testament accompanied by a new Latin translation. The latter's departures from the traditional Latin Vulgate text, which the church had used for more than a thousand years, caused alarm— as did in England Erasmus's preface arguing that the bible should be translated into the vernacular so that it was available to all.[8] In England the association of vernacular bibles with the heresy of John Wyclif (d. 1384) resulted in their effectively being outlawed from the first decade of the fifteenth century, although Wyclif's Lollard followers continued tenaciously to circulate manuscript copies.[9] The work of Erasmus could therefore be found disquieting on a number of levels: it implied an academic re-evaluation of the texts long thought to be settled, a refocusing of Christian piety on the gospels, and text that was more accessible. Freez's stock in York did not include any bibles, the market for which was then a professional rather than a popular one.

By the early sixteenth century the changes in the English language since the days of Wyclif and Chaucer (d. 1400), the invention of printing, and the new availability of the Greek text, opened the way for a new English vernacular bible. It became the life's work of William Tyndale (*c.*1494–1536). Educated at Oxford, and after a period as a private tutor and perhaps at Cambridge, Tyndale approached Cuthbert Tunstall in 1523, now bishop of London, with a proposal for an English translation of the New Testament from the Greek. Tyndale's hope was that Tunstall's sympathy for Erasmian scholarship would lead him to override the old proscriptions. To Tunstall such a project invited the disorders he had seen in Luther's Germany. Tunstall turned Tyndale down. Tyndale concluded that not only 'was there no room in my lord of London's palace to translate the new Testament, but also that there was no place to do it in all England', and headed for Germany.[10]

[6]   Julian Roberts, 'The Latin Trade', in *The Cambridge History of the Book in Britain*, 6 vols, IV: *1557–1695*, ed. John Barnard, D.F. McKenzie and Maureen Bell (Cambridge, 2002), pp. 141–73 (153–56).
[7]   *Collected Works of Erasmus* (Toronto, 1974–), 4, *The Correspondence of Erasmus, Letters 446 to 593 (1516 to 1517)*, trans. R.A.B. Mynors and D.F.S. Thomson (1977), pp. 270–73 (letter 543). John D. Fudge, *Commerce and Print in the Early Reformation* (Leiden, 2007), p. 153, n.51. Maria Dowling, *Humanism in the Age of Henry VIII* (London, 1986).
[8]   Desiderius Erasmus, *Paraclesis*, in *Christian Humanism and The Reformation*, ed. and trans. John C. Olin (New York, 1965), pp. 92–106 (96–97).
[9]   Anne Hudson, *The Premature Reformation: Wycliffite Texts and Lollard History* (Oxford, 1988); 'The Debate on Bible Translation, Oxford 1401', in her *Lollards and their Books*, (London, 1985), pp. 67–84. See also Andrew Pettegree, *Reformation and the Culture of Persuasion* (Cambridge, 2003), pp. 174–75.
[10]   William Tyndale, *The Preface of Master William Tyndale, that he made before the Five Books of Moses, called Genesis*, pp. 392–97 (395–96), in *Doctrinal Treatises and Introductions to Different*

In the England Tyndale was leaving, there was already a trade in heretical books. In 1519 the Basel publisher Froben wrote to Luther that he was sending consignments of his books to England.[11] The accounts of the Oxford bookseller John Dorne show sales of books by Luther in Oxford during 1520.[12] Both the king and his chief minister, Cardinal Thomas Wolsey (c.1471–1530), saw the need for public demonstrations of England's orthodoxy. Wolsey mounted a spectacular book burning at St Paul's in London in 1521, and the king (or his ghost writers) refuted Luther's heresies in the *Assertio septem sacramentorum* (STC 13078, 13079), a book which earned the king the title of 'Defender of the Faith'.[13] The king's work was one among many.[14] The impact of these measures was limited however, and in October 1524 Cuthbert Tunstall felt the need to be more specific. He called London booksellers before him and warned them against selling imported books containing Lutheran heresies, and charging that all newly imported books were to be vetted by either the archbishop of Canterbury William Warham (c.1450–1532), Wolsey or Fisher before being offered for sale.[15] The exercise was repeated two years later, with the substitution of Tunstall's own name for Fisher's and with additional references to 'books in English' and 'the vulgar tongue'.[16] The addition was significant. Tyndale had completed his translation of the New Testament and copies were beginning to appear in England.[17]

In 1525 Tyndale and an apostate Jewish Franciscan Observant, William Roye (d. 1531), began printing the English New Testament at the press of Peter Quentell (d. 1546) in Cologne. Their planned edition may have been as large as 3000 copies. The printing however was discovered and stopped by the conservative Cologne authorities, although Tyndale and Roye were able to flee up the Rhine taking the half-completed print run with them (1525, STC 2823).[18] The

Portions of the Holy Scriptures, ed. Henry Walter (Cambridge, 1848). Alan Stewart, 'The Trouble with English Humanism: Tyndale, More and Darling Erasmus', in *Reassessing Tudor Humanism*, ed. Jonathan Woolfson (Basingstoke, 2002), pp. 78–98, suggests there was a closing of humanist ranks against Tyndale. On Tyndale, see J.F. Mozley, *William Tyndale* (London, 1937), and David Daniell, *William Tyndale: A Biography* (New Haven, CT and London, 1994).

[11] Heinrich Boehmer, *Martin Luther: Road to Reformation* (London, 1957), p. 266. 'English Purchases', p. 289.

[12] 'The Daily Ledger of John Dorne, 1520', ed. F. Madan, in *Collectanea: First Series*, ed. C.R.L. Fletcher (Oxford Historical Society, 1885), pp. 71–177.

[13] Carl S. Meyer, 'Henry VIII burns Luther's Books 12 May 1521', *Journal of Ecclesiastical History* 9 (1958), 173–87. 'Press, Politics and Religion'. David Loades, 'Books and the English Reformation Prior to 1558', in *Politics, Censorship and the English Reformation* (London, 1991), pp. 127–47 (128–29). David Cressy, 'Book Burning in Tudor and Stuart England', *Sixteenth Century Journal* 36 (2005), 359–74.

[14] Richard Rex, 'The English Campaign against Luther in the 1520s', *TRHS*, 5th ser., 39 (1989), 85–106.

[15] A.W. Reed, *Early Tudor Drama: Medwall, the Rastells, Heywood, and the More Circle* (London, 1926), pp. 165–66.

[16] Reed, *Early Tudor Drama*, pp. 173–74. Susan Brigden, *London and the Reformation* (Oxford, 1989), p. 159.

[17] Craig W. D'Alton, 'The Suppression of Lutheran Heretics in England, 1526–1529', *Journal of Ecclesiastical History* 54 (2003), 228–53.

[18] William Tyndale, trans., *The First Printed English New Testament*, ed. Edward Arber (London, 1871) prints many associated documents. See also Johannes Cochlaeus, *The Deeds and Writings of Dr Martin Luther from the year of the Lord 1517 to the year 1546*, in *Luther's Lives: Two Contemporary Accounts of Martin Luther*, trans. Elizabeth Vandiver, Ralph Keen and Thomas D. Frazel (Manchester, 2002), pp. 180–82. Daniell, *William Tyndale*, pp. 108–33.

first complete printing then took place at Worms at the press of Peter Schoeffer (d. 1547), probably late in 1525 or early 1526 (*STC* 2824). A reprint in Antwerp followed in 1526, about which time Tyndale also arrived in the town. The translation was almost immediately condemned in England for its vocabulary which was claimed to be anti-hierarchical and anti-sacramental, and hence pro-Lutheran.[19] It was preached against, outlawed, and publically burned. Through the 1520s and 1530s editions continued to be issued from Antwerp presses, initially that of Christopher and Hans van Ruremund.[20] The van Ruremund press at this time was also printing for Franz Birckmann. Antwerp was convenient for the English market and from 1523 to 1527 Birckmann used the van Ruremund press to print a number of traditional English service books (*STC* 16236, 15939, 16131, 15822, 16207, dated respectively 1523, 1525, 1525, 1526, and 1527).[21] Birckmann also contracted with the van Ruremunds for them to supply him with 725 English New Testaments.[22] It is likely that the arrangement was for the van Ruremunds to print an edition of 1500 copies, of which 725 would 'go to Birckmann, perhaps an equal number to the van Ruremunds from the sale of which they would derive their profits, and the balance of fifty copies would be given as payment to the author or correctors who had seen it through the press. The Birckmanns are known to have had similar relations with the Quentell press in Cologne, given which it would seem likely that Franz Birckmann was the financial backer of Tyndale's New Testament from the beginning, even though there are no known ties between Birckmann and Schoeffer at Worms.[23]

By the time of the contract with the van Ruremunds Birckmann had already been in trouble in England. In March 1527 he was summoned to appear before the King's Council at Westminster to answer questions about prohibited books coming into England. He was required to enter into a recognisance of £200 that he would not import any English books printed abroad containing scripture, or books of heresy, or of Luther's opinions, unless they were first presented to the authorities for approval. Moreover, he must 'gyve knowlege of the pryntyng of Englisshe bookes in scripture or other beyond the see yf any suche thyng from hensforth ther attempted come to his knowlege'.[24] Birckmann almost certainly did have such knowledge of the trade and kept it to himself.

Almost all long distance trade at this time required three roles to be filled, that of merchant, carrier and factor. The merchant would purchase the goods,

[19]   Morna D. Hooker, 'Tyndale's "Heretical" Translations', *Reformation* 2 (1997), 127–42; Richard C. Marius, 'Thomas More's View of the Church', in *Complete Works of More*, 8, *The Confutation of Tyndale's Answer*, ed. Louis A. Schuster, Richard C. Marius, James P. Lusardi and Richard J. Schoeck (New Haven, CT and London, 1973), part 3, pp. 1349–61.
[20]   Wim François, 'The Antwerp Printers Christoffel and Hans (I) van Ruremund, Their Dutch and English Bibles, and the Intervention of the Authorities in the 1520s and 1530s', *Archive for Reformation History / Archiv für Reformationsgeschichte* 101 (2010), 7–28.
[21]   Additionally in 1525 there was an edition of Lyndwood's *Provinciales*, the canon law collection which includes the proscription of vernacular bibles (*STC* 17111).
[22]   Antwerp, Stadtsarchief, V1236, fol. 70v. Andrew Hope, 'Suit of Jan Silverlinck vs the Heirs of Frans Birckman, Antwerp, 1530', catalogue entry 96, *Tyndale's Testament* (hereafter *TT*), ed. Paul Arblaster, Gergely Juhász and Guido Latré (Turnhout, 2002), p. 153.
[23]   Fudge, *Commerce and Print in the Early Reformation*, pp. 158–64.
[24]   PRO, C 54/395, m.26.

the carrier transport them to where they would be sold, and the factor would sell them. In practice, since most chains operated in both directions, the roles of merchant and factor were interchangeable. Each could buy and sell. The difference between them was a matter of status and whose money was being used to finance the transaction. There were often two chains in the trade in proscribed books, one from the Continent, often Antwerp, to London, and one from London to the final destination of the books. This is particularly clear in the routes established to feed the universities in the 1520s.

An early route was established to Cambridge and some of the same personnel went on to create a similar supply route to Oxford. Books would arrive at the rectory of Robert (or Thomas) Forman (d. 1528) at All Hallows Honey Lane in London.[25] They were then transported to Oxford by John Goodall, a young student, with a history of trouble-making ahead of him.[26] At Oxford they were distributed by Thomas Garrett (or Garrard, 1498–1540), nominally a curate at All Hallows. The chain was thus Forman-Goodall-Garrett. All three had probably been at Cambridge, Forman having been president of Queens'. Forman was at the end of a similar chain coming from the Low Countries. Among those supplied in Oxford were students from Cambridge who had migrated to Wolsey's new showpiece Cardinal College.[27]

The routes to the universities were principally for more academic works of heresy. Nevertheless, they give some idea of the kind of organisation and personnel necessary for the trade to operate. Hans van Ruremund brought over several hundred copies of the New Testament and offered them to Robert Necton who had a route up to his native Norwich.[28] There is one clear statement that there was an organisation specifically for the purpose of financing and distributing heretical literature. According to Sebastian Newdigate (1500–1535), a future Catholic martyr but someone with close contacts among those of very different views: 'there was made for the augmentation of christian brethren of his sort [Thomas Keyle, a London mercer] auditors and clerks within this city. And that every christian brother of their sort should pay a certain sum of money to the aforesaid clerks which should go in to all the quarters of this realm, and at certain times the auditors to take account of them.'[29] A communal approach to making religious texts more widely available was not without precedent. It lay behind the so-called 'common profit' books in fifteenth-century London.[30]

---

[25] *London Viewers and their certificates, 1508-1558: Certificates of the sworn viewers of the City of London*, ed. Janet Senderowitz Loengard (London Record Society, 1989), no. 331.

[26] T.F.T. Baker, 'John Goodale (b. c.1502) of Salisbury, Wilts)', in *The House of Commons, 1509–1558*, 3 vols, ed. S.T. Bindoff, History of Parliament Trust (London, 1982), 2.228-30.

[27] John Foxe, *Acts and Monuments*, 8 vols, ed. Josiah Pratt, The Church Historians of England (London, 1853–61), 5.421–29. TAMO, 1563 edn, 3.660–66; 1570 edn, 8.1405–09; 1576 edn, 8.1190–92; 1583 edn, 8.1218–21.

[28] Foxe, *Acts and Monuments*, 5:27; *TAMO*, 1583 edn, 8.1064. John Strype, *Ecclesiastical Memorials relating chiefly to Religion and the Reformation of It, and the Emergencies of the Church of England under King Henry VIII, King Edward VI and Queen Mary I*, 3 volumes in 6 parts (Oxford, 1822), 1, part 2, 63–65 (no. 22) [*LP Henry VIII*, 4 (no. 4030)].

[29] PRO, SP 1/237, fol.78 [*LP*, Add.1, no. 752]. Other examples of the term 'Christian brethren' may not necessarily refer to the same group.

[30] Wendy Scase, 'Reginald Pecock, John Carpenter and John Colop's "Common Profit" Books: Aspects of Book Ownership and Circulation in Fifteenth-Century London', *Medium Ævum* 6

Thus, as with Birckmann's shift from supplying Latin service books to supplying English New Testaments, it is possible to see structures of book provision remaining the same whilst the content changes.

English merchants who visited or who lived in Antwerp could of course obtain their copies at source and send them directly to friends, family or customers in England. Richard Harman, with whom Tyndale lived for a while in Antwerp in the 1520s, sent New Testaments to friends in his native Cranbrook in Kent, and William Lock (1480–1550), a major supplier of cloth to the crown, sent them to his wife.[31] Another pre-existing network along which books undoubtedly travelled was provided by Luther's own order of Augustinian friars. In the mid-1520s Essex Lollards knew to go to the London Augustinian friary where Tyndale's New Testaments could be obtained from Robert Barnes (c.1495–1540), an Augustinian friar, under house arrest there following a Lutheran sermon in Cambridge.[32]

The van Ruremund press was probably responsible for four editions of the Tyndale New Testament between 1526 and 1534, although the number is conjectural, as are the dates of specific editions. No example of the earlier editions is known to be extant and there is no evidence at all for the widespread assumption that they were pirated. By the time of Birckmann's death in 1530 he had probably been responsible for between four and six thousand copies of Tyndale's New Testament reaching England. This is just under half the probable number of missals entering the country in the same period from all sources, and under a third the number of breviaries.[33] Although these numbers are necessarily very approximate, they do suggest a penetration of the market going well beyond what might be thought of as the core constituency of Lollard heretics and those influenced by Lutheran ideas. One telling piece of evidence is the fate of Nicholas Love's *The Mirrour of the Blessed Lyf of Jesu Christ*. The work had been promoted to fill the gap left by the proscription of the English bible in 1409.[34] It was first printed by William Caxton (d. 1492) in 1484 and there followed seven further editions culminating in one by Wynkyn de Worde (d. 1534) in 1525. De Worde reprinted it in 1530, but thereafter there were no further editions until it became of antiquarian interest in the seventeenth century (*STC* 3259–69).[35] There can be little doubt that the provision of a simple English translation of the New Testament was responsible for its elimination from the market. The implication is that those who might have purchased thoroughly orthodox works of Catholic devotion were now turning to new vernacular translations.

(1992), 261–74; Anne Hudson, 'Wyclif Texts in Fifteenth-century London', in her *Studies in the Transmission of Wyclif's Writings* (Aldershot, 2008), item XV, pp. 1–18 (13–14).

[31] Andrew Hope, 'On the Smuggling of Prohibited Books from Antwerp to England in the 1520s and 1530s', in *TT*, pp. 35–38.

[32] Strype, *Ecclesiastical Memorials*, 1, part 2, pp. 54–55 (no. 17); [*LP Henry VIII*, 4 (no. 4218)].

[33] The figures for breviaries and missals are calculated editions recorded in *STC*. Since there were almost certainly editions with no surviving copies, the figures for missals and breviaries should probably be higher.

[34] Janel M. Mueller, *The Native Tongue and the Word: Developments in English Prose Style, 1380–1580* (Chicago, IL, 1984), pp. 74–85.

[35] *The Stripping of the Altars*, p. 79.

Controversial and polemical works followed.[36] In Strasbourg at the press of Johann Schott (d. c.1548), William Roye, having parted from Tyndale, printed *A Brefe Dialoge bitwene a Christen Father and his stobborne Sonne* (1527, STC 24223.3), in effect an early protestant catechism, and an anti-Wolsey satire, *Rede me and be nott wrothe* (1528, STC 21427).[37] After the publication of his New Testament, Tyndale too issued controversial works, including *The parable of the wicked mammon* (1528, STC 24454), *The obedience of a Christen man and how Christen rulers ought to governe* (1528, STC 24446), *The practyse of prelates* (1530, STC 24465), and *An answere vnto Sir Thomas Mores dialoge* (1531, STC 24437).[38] *Supplicacyon for the Beggars* (1529, STC 10883) by Simon Fish (d. 1532) was a provocative attack on purgatory. Such works, along with those of John Frith (c.1503–33) and George Joye (c.1495–1553) elicited refutations from Thomas More and others in England. They might take the form of specific rebuttals to specific works, such as More's reply to Fish, *The supplycacyon of soulys* (1529, STC 18092, 18093), or attempts to encompass and refute contemporary heresy more widely, such as his *Confutacyon of Tyndales answere* (1532–33, part one STC 18079, part two STC 18080). Since More would reprint extensive passages from Tyndale, it was possible to own Tyndale legally by purchasing More.[39]

Of works that originated from Luther or Lutheran sources, the *Epistola ad Anglos* of John Bugenhagen (1485–1558) was directly addressed to the English, to whom it rather piously commended the Lutheran cause. It was first published in Augsburg in 1525, although an English version did not appear until 1536 (STC 4021) by which time it was scarcely relevant.[40] Before 1536 there were four translations of works wholly or partly by Luther, although none was acknowledged to be such: Tyndale's *A compendious introduction, prologe or preface vn to the pistle off Paul to the Romans* (1526, STC 24438), Roye's *An exposition in to the seventh chaptre of the first pistle to the Corinthians* (1529, STC 10493),[41] Simon Fish's *The summe of holye scripture* (1529, STC 3036), and Frith's *A pistle to the Christen reader* (1529, STC 11394).[42] It may be that more were planned and failed. There were plans to set up a young English scholar Francis Denham, in Paris, where

---

[36] There is a convenient list in Anthea Hume, 'English Protestant Books Printed Abroad, 1525–1535: An Annotated Bibliography', in More, *Confutation*, part 2, pp. 1063–91.

[37] See modern editions by Douglas H. Parker, *Rede Me and Be Nott Wrothe* (Toronto, 1992) and, with Bruce Krajewski, *Brefe Dialoge* (Toronto, 1999). The identity of Jerome Barlowe is still uncertain. There is a summary of the problems in E.G. Rupp, *Studies in the Making of the English Protestant Tradition* (Cambridge, 1949), pp. 62–72. On Strasbourg printing, see Miriam Usher Chrisman, *Bibliography of Strasbourg Imprints, 1480–1599* (New Haven, CT and London, 1982), pp. 315–16.

[38] William Tyndale, *The Independent Works of William Tyndale*, vol. 3, *An Answere vnto Sir Thomas Mores Dialoge*, ed. Anne M. O'Donnell and Jared Wicks (Washington, DC, 2000).

[39] See John N. King, 'Thomas More, William Tyndale, and the Printing of Religious Propaganda', in *The Oxford Handbook of Tudor Literature*, ed. Mike Pincombe and Cathy Shrank (Oxford, 2009), pp. 105–20.

[40] *Complete Works More, 7, Letter to Bugenhagen, Supplication of Souls, Letter Against Frith*, ed. Frank Manley, Germain Marc'hadour, Richard Marius and Clarence H. Miller (New Haven, CT and London, 1990).

[41] William Roye, trans., *An exhortation to the diligent studye of scripture*, and *An exposition in to the seventh chaptre of the pistle to the Corinthians*, ed. Douglas H. Parker (Toronto, 2000).

[42] See also Pettegree, *Reformation and the Culture of Persuasion*, p. 173 and n.27. The Roye title also included an acknowledged work by Erasmus, and the Frith title an unacknowledged work by Melanchthon.

he would translate works of Continental reformers, but he was arrested in 1528 and died on his way back to London.[43] Other translations may not have survived. Geoffrey Lome, who taught at More's old school, St Antony's in London, distributed books by Luther, and translated a work by him although it is not known to have survived.[44] Lollard works were in some ways as attractive as heretical works from the Continent since they could be used to expose a continuity of clerical opposition to lay emancipation. After the book agent Thomas Hitton became the first English Reformation martyr at Maidstone in 1530, the de Keyser press in Antwerp published *The examinacion of Master William Thorpe preste accused of heresye before Thomas Arundell, Archebishop of Ca[n]terbury, the yere of ower Lord .MCCCC. and seven.* [with] *The examinacion of the honorable knight syr Jho'n Oldcastell Lorde Cobham, burnt bi the said Archebisshop, in the fyrst yere of Kynge Henry the Fyfth* (STC 24045), with an introduction by Tyndale or possibly George Constantine (*c.*1500–61) which made past parallels with Thomas Hitton clear.[45]

Most of these texts appeared under false imprints to prevent their origins being traced. Many of Tyndale's works appeared as if by Hans Luft of Marburg. Luft was a real enough printer (of Luther in Wittenberg), but Tyndale's printer was almost certainly Martin de Keyser of Antwerp (d. 1537), an identity only recently established.[46] The choice of Luft is curious since in other respects Tyndale attempted to avoid explicit association with Luther.

From 1530 Tyndale began publishing Old Testament translations, starting with the Pentateuch (STC 2350, reissued STC 2351), and a striking translation of Jonah the following year (STC 2788). A further substantial part of the Old Testament was completed but unpublished at the time of his execution in 1536. His last years were overshadowed by controversy with George Joye, another English Antwerp exile.[47] In 1530 Joye published the first primer in English, *Ortulus anime* (STC 13828.4). He was probably the author of the anonymous *The souper of the Lorde* (1533, STC 24468) which gives a remarkable picture of a reformed liturgy.[48] He published translations of the Psalms (STC 2372) and

[43]   PRO, SP 1/48, fols 101–02 [*LP Henry VIII*, 4 (no. 4327)], 103–04 [*LP Henry VIII*, 4 (no.4328)], 106–07 [*LP Henry VIII*, 4 (no. 4330)], 140–41 [*LP Henry VIII*, 4 (no. 4338)], 205–06 [*LP Henry VIII*, 4 (no. 4394)], 207–08 [*LP Henry VIII*, 4 (no. 4395)].

[44]   Foxe, *Acts and Monuments*, 5, Original Documents . . . referred to in the Foregoing Appendix, no.1: Articles and Recantations of Jeffrey Lome (unpaginated).

[45]   Anne Hudson, '"No newe thyng": The Printing of Medieval Texts in the Early Reformation Period', in her *Lollards and Their Books*, pp. 227–48, has a list of reprinted Lollard works. See also Margaret Aston, 'Lollardy and the Reformation: Survival or Revival', and 'John Wycliffe's Reformation Reputation', in *Lollards and Reformers: Images and Literacy in Late Medieval Religion* (London, 1984), pp. 219–42, and 243–72.

[46]   The pioneering work of M.E. Kronenberg ('Notes on English Printing in the Low Countries (Early Sixteenth Century)', *The Library*, 4th ser., 9 (1928), 139–63, 'Forged Addresses in Low Country Books in the Period of the Reformation', *The Library*, 5th ser., 2 (1947), 81–94, and *Verboden Boeken en Opstandige Drukkers in de Hervormingstijd* (Amsterdam, 1948)), is revised in essential respects by Paul Valkema Blouw, 'Early Protestant Publications in Antwerp, 1526–30: The Pseudonyms Adam Anonymus in Basel and Hans Luft in Marlborow', *Quaerendo* 26 (1996), 94–110.

[47]   On Joye, see Charles C. Butterworth and Allan G. Chester, *George Joye 1495?–1553: A Chapter in the History of the English Bible and English Reformation* (Philadelphia, PA, 1962).

[48]   W.D.J. Cargill Thompson, 'Who Wrote *The Supper of the Lord*?', *Harvard Theological Review* 53 (1960), 77–91. Orlaith O'Sullivan, 'The Authorship of *The Supper of the Lord*', *Reformation* 2 (1997), 207–32.

of the book of Jeremiah (*STC* 2778) at the de Keyser press in 1534. In the same year he brought out an edition of Tyndale's New Testament (*STC* 2825) having made unauthorised and unacknowledged changes to the text. Tyndale attacked Joye for the changes in his next edition of the New Testament (*STC* 2826), to which Joye replied with *An apologye made by George Ioye to satisfye (if it maye be) w. Tindale* (1535, *STC* 14820).[49] The dispute exposed theological differences and was a gift to their opponents, one line of whose attack had long been that the reformers were at heart merely quarrelsome and vainglorious.[50]

The policies of the English authorities switched from impersonal gestures of book burning and literary refutations, to a tighter control of the book trade and the apprehending and correction of individual heretics. Success was limited. Franz Birckmann was one problem. He knew far more about the book trade than those who were attempting to control it. Erasmus had long had doubts about Birckmann, and they culminated in 1523 in a colloquy, 'The Liar and the Man of Honour' which those in the know took to be an exposure of Birckmann's tricks, which included opening and reading the letters he had been entrusted with delivering.[51] A year *after* his appearance before the King's Council Birckmann managed to persuade John West, one of Wolsey's agents in the Low Countries, that he was on his side, and West became dependent on the misinformation Birckmann provided.[52]

A further problem with operations against the Antwerp printers was the low priority accorded the campaign by Wolsey. The English ambassador in the Low Countries in this period, Sir John Hackett (d. 1534), made two notable attempts to prosecute those complicit in the production and supply of heretical literature. In November 1526, on receipt of orders from the king and Wolsey, Hackett requested the van Ruremunds' prosecution for printing heretical literature. The Antwerp authorities maintained that they should be the judge of what was heretical and demanded the books be translated into Dutch. This was impractical, especially with the New Testament. They were offered certification that the books had been burned in England, but, even after it arrived, the Antwerp authorities were still disinclined to act. Eventually Hackett did secure an imperial edict against the English New Testament. Hans van Ruremund however was acquitted, and Christopher seems to have escaped with not much more than a loss of stock.[53]

Hackett again attempted to use the Antwerp courts in June 1528. Hackett had hoped to prosecute Tyndale but had to make do with Richard Harman who had been Tyndale's host. It proved difficult since, although born in England, Harman had become a burgess of Antwerp. The Antwerp authorities closed

[49] George Joye, *Apology*, ed. Edward Arber (Birmingham, 1882).
[50] Andrew Hope, 'Plagiarising the Word of God: Tyndale between More and Joye', in *Plagiarism in Early Modern England*, ed. Paulina Kewes (Basingstoke, 2003), pp. 93–105.
[51] *Collected Works of Erasmus* 39, *Colloquies*, trans. Craig R. Thompson (1997), pp. 344–50. M.E. Kronenberg, 'Notes on English Printing in the Low Countries', p. 145.
[52] *The Letters of Sir John Hackett, 1526–1534*, ed. Elizabeth Frances Rogers (Morgantown, WV, 1971), pp. 174–75, n.78.
[53] Andrew Hope, 'Ban on Possession of English New Testaments. Antwerp, 1527', catalogue entry 94, in *TT*, pp. 151–52.

ranks behind him and attempted to obstruct Hackett at every turn.[54] Hackett wrote continuously to Wolsey for evidence to back his charges but got no reply. After October, Hackett gave up writing to Wolsey. Harman was released on bail and acquitted the following Febuary.[55] Wolsey had shown little interest in either Antwerp case. He was provoked, however, to take action against Roye and Barlowe for their personal satire on him, *Rede me and be not wroth*. However, after Herman Ryngk, a Cologne senator and long-time friend of Wolsey, assured him that he had impounded all unsold copies, Wolsey again lost interest.

Hackett put the lack of co-operation in Antwerp down to popular heresy: 'the moste party of Andwerp be as good Cristen men as they be in Almany'.[56] However, constitutional sensibilities, civic pride and commercial advantage all played a part in thwarting Hackett. In addition, the diplomatic context was unfavourable. Henry VIII's attempt to annul his marriage to Catherine of Aragon dominated these years. Catherine was the aunt of the nominal ruler of the Low Countries, Charles V. The Habsburg authorities had little sympathy with heresy, but they probably thought that Tyndale, as someone who had written in support of Catherine, was worth safeguarding. Wolsey for his part was not going to expend political capital trying to persuade them otherwise.

There was also a failure to understand the economics of printed book production. To limit the circulation of a book in manuscript it may have made sense to buy up copies and burn them since a single copy required so much effort to produce. Buying up printed books to destroy them however merely gifted money to the printer and facilitated a reprint. Tunstall was the butt of a well crafted anecdote by the chronicler Edward Hall on the subject, and William Warham and Richard Nix, the bishop of Norwich, also contributed to a fund for buying up books.[57]

Purchasing books may also have been a less confrontational way of addressing the problem. In the mid 1520s a measure of restraint operated in such a way as to contain the trade without too great a damage to anybody's reputation or life. Thus in 1525 when Thomas More led a raid on the Steelyard, the London headquarters of the German Hanseatic trading league, looking for heretical books, he announced the search the day before. The four German merchants who were caught with proscribed books had only their own carelessness to blame.[58] Similarly when there was a search of lodgings at the University of Cambridge early the next year it was widely known in advance.[59] There was also a desire that actions not damage the reputations of the universities or of the church, and that they should bring erring scholars back into the fold of the

---

[54] *Letters of Sir John Hackett*, p. 161, n.70.
[55] *Letters of Sir John Hackett*, p. 200, n.95.
[56] *Letters of Sir John Hackett*, pp. 201–02, n.95.
[57] Edward Hall, *The Triumphant Reigne of Kyng Henry The VIII*, 2 vols (London, 1904), 1.160–62; *Original Letters Illustrative of English History*, ed. Sir Henry Ellis, 3rd ser., 4 vols (London, 1846), 2.86 [*LP Henry VIII*, 4 (no.3176)].
[58] A.G. Chester, 'Robert Barnes and the Burning of the Books', *HLQ* 14 (1951), 216–19; M.E. Kronenberg, 'A Printed Letter of the London Hanse Merchants (3 March 1526)', *Oxford Bibliographical Society Publications*, new ser., 1 (1947), 25–32; Rupp, *Studies in the Making of the English Protestant Tradition*, pp. 33–38.
[59] Strype, *Ecclesiastical Memorials*, 1, part 2, 64 (no. 22); [*LP Henry VIII*, 4 (no. 4030)].

church, both for their own sake and so that no credibility should be afforded to the errors and heresies they had embraced.

There was a dramatic increase in the numbers arrested after the Cambridge graduates Thomas Bilney (ex. 1531) and Thomas Arthur (d. 1532/33) were apprehended late in 1527, following preaching tours in which they were heard sympathetically by Lollards. Bilney attributed his conversion to reading Erasmus's Greek New Testament, and later evidence suggests he distributed Tyndale's English New Testament in the hope it would have the same effect.[60] The arrests spread outwards to include many in Oxford, along with those who supplied them with books, and associates of Tyndale such as Humphrey Monmouth (d. 1537) in London and Harman in Antwerp. The authorities were particularly alarmed by the extent to which books were spreading new heretical ideas among the Lollards of London and Essex. Directed by Tunstall and Warham, the approach seems to have been one of public trial and private counselling, with the hope of achieving public abjuration and private repentance. Thus would heresy be discredited and souls cleansed.[61]

Sir Thomas More, at this point under-sheriff of London, sat in on some of the trials and seems to have concluded that the methods being employed were of limited effectiveness.[62] More thought it was all too easy and typical for witnesses and defendants to be evasive in court, and dissimulating in their professions of orthodoxy.[63] Despite the appearance of a number of previously abjured heretics, who were liable to be handed over to the secular authority for burning, none was. Looking back from 1531–32, More believed 'there shold have ben mo burned by a great many then there have ben wythin this seven yere last passed. The lakke whereof I fere me will make mo burned within this seven yere next commynge then ellys sholde have neded to have ben burned in seven score.'[64]

The appointment of More as Lord Chancellor in succession to Wolsey in October 1529 marked another new phase in the campaign against heresy and heretical books.[65] More saw the prosecution of heresy as the prosecution of criminality. He was determined as chancellor both that statute law against heresy should be fully enforced, and that those prerogative powers which he exercised on behalf of the crown should be employed against heretics. Royal proclamations enabled the latter to be used, and More issued two against heretical books in his first year in office.[66] The statutory penalties of death by burning for previously abjured or obdurate heretics were now employed as they had not been

---

[60] Foxe, *Acts and Monuments*, 4:635, 642; 5:32.
[61] Craig W. D'Alton, 'The Suppression of Lutheran Heretics'; 'Cuthbert Tunstal and Heresy in Essex and London, 1528', *Albion* 35 (2003), 210–28; 'William Warham and English Heresy Policy after the Fall of Wolsey', *Historical Research* 77 (2004), 337–57.
[62] Craig W. D'Alton, 'Charity or Fire? The Argument of Thomas More's 1529 *Dyaloge*', *Sixteenth Century Journal* 33 (2002), 51–70.
[63] Louis A. Schuster, 'Thomas More's Polemical Career, 1523–1533', *Confutation*, part 3, pp. 1135–268 (1208).
[64] More, *Confutation*, pp. 320–21.
[65] D'Alton, 'William Warham', argues for the importance of Warham in policy-making in the period from the fall of Wolsey in October 1529 to mid-1531.
[66] J.A. Guy, *The Public Career of Sir Thomas More* (Brighton, 1980), pp. 103–05, 171–74. *TRP* 1.181–86, 193–97.

for nearly ten years. Two book agents who had frequented Antwerp, Thomas Hitton and Richard Bayfield were burned in 1530 and 1531. The Antwerp printer Christopher van Ruremund died in a Westminster prison.[67] Four other heretics, including Bilney, were burned in the nine months between August 1531 and April 1532.[68] More examined suspects in such a way as to build up the kind of detailed information about their activities which had been lacking before.[69] Whilst George Constantine was imprisoned in More's own house, for example, More was able to extract details of secret markings used on shipping containers. Such astute intelligence-gathering made it possible for More to intercept entire consignments of books.[70]

More's campaign was undermined in two ways. The acquittal of Harman in Antwerp early in 1529 sent out the message that Antwerp could be a safe haven for English dissidents fleeing More's enforcement campaign. John Frith, Robert Barnes and George Constantine all sheltered there. More seems to have regarded the control of the book trade as a domestic issue now, and made no attempt to mobilise his erstwhile Antwerp friends against it.

More's domestic position was also problematic. The failure, which became evident in mid-1529, to find a judicial solution to the problem of ending the king's marriage opened the way for more radical solutions. It began to dawn, as Thomas Starkey (c.1498–1538) was later to put it, that 'heretykys be not in al thyngys heretykys'.[71] They might produce arguments that were useful. Two mutually reinforcing ideas took root in Henry's mind. Henry had long felt the attractions of the Erasmian reform programme for a purified church more closely adhering to the principles of the New Testament. To this now was added a vision, derived from Luther by way of Tyndale's *Obedience of a Christen man* (1528, STC 24446, brought to his notice by Anne Boleyn), of the duties and responsibilities placed by God on the shoulders of kings. Their authority could not be gainsaid by foreign bishops. Thus, despite More's rigorous enforcement of the heresy laws, Hugh Latimer (c.1485–1555) felt able to write an open letter to Henry requesting that the bible in English should be able freely to circulate. There was no evidence, Latimer said, that vernacular bibles caused civil unrest. Its availability would mean the clergy would be subject to more exacting scrutiny.[72] Anne Boleyn used her influence in the same direction.[73] At the same time in Antwerp Martin de Keyser published an edition, probably edited by Tyndale, of what was thought to be an old Lollard work, *A compendious olde treatiyse shewynge howe that we oughte to haue ye scripture in Englysshe* (1530, STC 3021). Its purpose was presumably partly to show how long the English clergy

---

[67]   Foxe, *Acts and Monuments*, 5:37. *TAMO*, 1583 edn, 8.1069.
[68]   Guy, *The Public Career of Sir Thomas More*, p. 164.
[69]   See for example, his account of his examination of Richard Webb. More, *Confutation*, pp. 813–15.
[70]   More, *Confutation*, p. 20.
[71]   Thomas Starkey, *A Dialogue between Cardinal Pole and Thomas Lupset, Lecturer in Rhetoric at Oxford*, in *England in the Reign of King Henry the Eighth*, ed. Sidney J. Herrtage and J.M. Cowper, EETS ES 32 (London, 1878), p. 135.
[72]   Allan G. Chester, *Hugh Latimer, Apostle to the English* (Philadelphia, PA, 1954), pp. 61–65. Schuster, 'Thomas More's Polemical Career, 1523–1533', pp. 1213–14.
[73]   Eric Ives, *The Life and Death of Anne Boleyn* (Oxford, 2004), pp. 131–39, 260–63, 268–74.

had obstructed laity access to the Word of God. Parliamentary legislation was drafted in 1531 which could pave the way for an English bible.[74] In 1532 a Lollard work *The Praier and Complaynt of the Ploweman unto Christe*, which had been printed a year or two before by de Keyser in Antwerp (*STC* 20036) was reprinted by Thomas Godfrey in London (*STC* 20036.5), and became the first work previously considered to be heretical to be printed in England.[75] Lollard books had a relevance since they often appealed to royal power to reform the church.[76]

The politics of the annulment culminated in the ascendancy of Thomas Cromwell (*c*.1485–1540) in the king's counsels and the passing of the Act of Supremacy (1534), severing England from papal obedience. Books by Continental reformers which could be used to support the kind of moderate reform being pursued could now be printed in England. Nine English translations of works by Luther appeared in the years 1534–40, only one of which was printed abroad (Antwerp 1538, *STC* 20193). Caution was still necessary however. Probably in the light of Henry's personal antipathy to Luther, Luther was still not mentioned on any title-page. He was concealed behind, for example, *A boke made by a certayne great clerke* (1534, *STC* 16962), as well as *A proper treatyse of good workes* (1535?, *STC* 16988), or *An exposicion vpon the songe of the blessed virgine Mary* (1538, *STC* 16979.7). Such works could be embellished with patriotic woodcuts to ease the transition to respectability. A further ten works by other Continental reformers appeared in these years, all printed in England.[77]

In 1535 the first complete English bible was printed probably in Antwerp (*STC* 2063), edited and partially translated by Miles Coverdale (1488–1569).[78] Coverdale drew freely on the work of Tyndale, although it is unclear exactly how the translations relate to each other. Coverdale's bible circulated in England without hindrance. It was followed by a surge in reprints in Antwerp of Tyndale's New Testament, perhaps hoping to take advantage of the new freedoms (*STC* 2827, 2832, 2834).[79] In 1538 Cromwell's injunctions required all parishes to obtain a copy of the complete bible in English, and an appropriate edition was commissioned from François Regnault, a Paris printer, who had also worked for Birckmann. French authorities however became alarmed by questions of its orthodoxy. Printing was halted, just as Tyndale's at Cologne had been some thirteen years before, but this time it was completed in England (*The*

---

[74]   Guy, *The Public Career of Sir Thomas More*, pp. 151–53.
[75]   *The Praier and Complaynte of the Ploweman Vnto Christe*, ed. Douglas H. Parker (Toronto, 1997).
[76]   Loades, 'Books and the English Reformation prior to 1558', pp. 127–28.
[77]   The figures are from John N. King and Mark Rankin, 'Print, Patronage, and the Reception of Continental Reform: 1521–1603', *The Yearbook of English Studies* 38 (2008), 49–67 (54–55). As is the way with *STC*, slightly different calculations are possible. On woodcuts, see pp. 56–57.
[78]   Guido Latré, 'The 1535 Coverdale Bible and its Antwerp Origins', in *The Bible as Book: the Reformation*, ed. Orlaith O'Sullivan and Ellen N. Herron (London, 2000), pp. 89–102.
[79]   See Gwendolyn Verbraak, 'William Tyndale and the Clandestine Book Trade: A Bibliographical Quest for the Printers of Tyndale's New Testaments', in *Infant Milk or Hardy Nourishment?: The Bible for Lay People and Theologians in the Early Modern Period*, ed. Wim François and August den Hollander (Leuven, 2009), pp. 167–89.

New Testamen [*sic*], 1538, *STC* 2817; *The Byble in Englyshe*, 1539, *STC* 2068).[80] The vernacular bible had gone from proscription to prescription.[81]

Boundaries of what constituted heresy might change, but there were still lines which could not be crossed. Henry was particularly sensitive to any suggestions of sacramental heresy, that is, that the bread and the wine in the sacrament of the altar should be seen in merely commemorative or symbolic terms. After More's resignation of the chancellorship in 1532, those reformers who enjoyed promotion or royal favour, such as Thomas Cranmer (1489–1556), the new archbishop of Canterbury in succession to Warham, Hugh Latimer, who became bishop of Worcester in 1535, or Robert Barnes, were resolute in distancing themselves from this position. John Frith did not and was burned in 1533, as was John Lambert, another high-profile heretic, in 1538. Even more alarming were anabaptist heresies which questioned fundamentals of the faith as it was then understood. If baptism became an optional adult rite, church became a voluntary society. In addition, secular authority was also denied any voice in the governance of the church, and some anabaptists held beliefs about the person of Christ that ran counter to some of the oldest creeds of the church. Anabaptism was never numerically strong in England measured either by adherents or books, but it did have a presence in the Low Countries and in the early or mid-1530s there was at least one attempt to distribute in England a print run of some 500 English books of an unknown anabaptist title.[82] Anabaptist and sacramentarian works were the target of a further proclamation against heretical books in 1538.

The changes in English policy changed the nature of Antwerp dissident printing.[83] In the early 1530s Franciscan Observants William Peto (*c.*1485–1558) and Henry Elston (d. 1559), driven from England by their opposition to the king's proceedings over his marriage and the concomitant religious changes, arrived in Antwerp intent on using its presses against the king. Since both they and Tyndale opposed the king over his marriage, there was contact between them, although their relations were obviously profoundly ambiguous. When in 1533 Tyndale declined Peto's invitation to correct a book against the king's marriage he did so in a way that suggested they had co-operated before.[84] This unlikely alliance never came to much, but the fear of such a coalition of voices against the annulment of the king's marriage probably caused real anxiety to Thomas Cromwell. The problem was partially solved by the death of Catherine of Aragon early in 1536, although this may also have removed the one reason

---

[80]   J.F. Mozley, *Coverdale and His Bibles* (London, 1953), pp. 201–20; David Daniell, *The Bible in English: Its History and Influence* (New Haven, CT and London, 2003), pp. 200–01.
[81]   For sources on this process, see Alfred W. Pollard, ed., *Records of the English Bible* (Oxford, 1911).
[82]   Irvin Buckwalter Horst, *The Radical Brethren: Anabaptism and the English Reformation to 1558* (Nieuwkoop, 1972), pp. 49–51, 183–84.
[83]   G. Tournoy, 'Humanists, Rulers and Reformers: Relationships between England and the Southern Low Countries in the First Half of the Sixteenth Century', in Museum Plantin-Moretus, *Antwerp, Dissident Typographical Centre: The Role of Antwerp Printers in the Religious Conflicts in England (16th Century)* (Antwerp, 1994), pp. 20–30.
[84]   PRO, SP 1/80, fols 5–6 [*LP Henry VIII*, 6 (no. 1324)]. It is possible that it is this link which explains Sebastian Newdigate's inside knowledge of Thomas Keyle's Christian brethren.

the Habsburg authorities had for not proceeding against Tyndale. He was in custody at the time, and he was executed later in the year.

After the Act of Six Articles of 1539 and the fall and execution of Cromwell the following year, the patterns of the 1520s to some extent re-asserted themselves.[85] Ownership even of books printed in England in the 1530s could be troublesome. In 1541 John Capon (d. 1557), bishop of Salisbury, arrested John Gyrdeler, for possession of a translation of the Augsburg Confession along with the *Apologie of Melancthon*, which had been published by Robert Redman (d. 1540) in London in 1539 (*STC* 909). Capon sent the book to Cranmer, claiming it contained eucharistic heresy (which was doubtful) and with an implied rebuke that these things should have been allowed to be published. Capon also complained about 'one [blank] Sooham that hath dwelled in London who is a common messenger and also a reader of new books from town to town to such persons as be of that sect. And that there hath ben common collection of money amonges them that be of that soort, secretly gathered and sent to him towards his living and charges.'[86] Organisations for the distribution of illicit or suspicious books still existed.

A number of reformers no longer felt comfortable in England and some, such as John Bale (1495–1563), John Hooper (d. 1555) and Miles Coverdale, went into exile. Of translated works by Continental reformers published in this period for the English market, eleven of fifteen were printed abroad.[87] There were differences from the 1520s however. The trade was no longer spearheaded by a work with the immediate and wide appeal of the English bible. Works were often more obviously partisan than they had been, and their authors more ready to acknowledge the influence of Zwingli (1484–1531) and his successor in Zurich, Bullinger (1504–75).[88] Thus, for example, George Joye published *The rekening and declaracio[n] of the faith and beleif of Huldrik Zwingly* from the van Ruremund press in Antwerp in 1543 (*STC* 26138).

The accession of Edward VI in 1547, a boy under the Protectorship initially of his uncle Edward Seymour, duke of Somerset (1500–52), ushered in an unequivocally protestant regime.[89] Virtually all those who had gone into exile in the last years of Henry VIII returned. There was little reason now to publish abroad and fewer than twenty English protestant titles were imported in the course of the reign.[90] Moreover, relatively few of those who opposed the changes chose exile, and works published abroad attacking the Edwardian church were more erudite than popular. Robert Caly seems to have been the only printer who went into exile to carry on the fight against heresy by the press.[91]

[85]   King and Rankin, 'Print, Patronage, and the Reception of Continental Reform', pp. 55–56.
[86]   PRO, STAC 2/34/28, 'IV'.
[87]   King and Rankin, 'Print, Patronage, and the Reception of Continental Reform', p. 55.
[88]   Loades, 'Books and the English Reformation Prior to 1558', p. 131.
[89]   John N. King, 'Freedom of the Press, Protestant Propaganda, and Protector Somerset', *HLQ* 40 (1976), 1–9.
[90]   Loades, 'Books and the English Reformation Prior to 1558', pp. 131–32. King and Rankin, 'Print, Patronage, and the Reception of Continental Reform', pp. 58–61. On Protestant literature in Edward's reign, see Catharine Davies, *A Religion of the Word: The Defence of the Reformation in the Reign of Edward VI* (Manchester, 2002).
[91]   J.W. Martin, 'The Marian Regime's Failure to Understand the Importance of Printing', *HLQ* 44 (1981), 231–47, reprinted in his *Religious Radicals in Tudor England* (London, 1989), pp. 107–123 (113).

With Edward's death and the accession of his Catholic half-sister Mary, Caly returned to England. It was not inappropriate that one of the first works he printed was an edition of Fisher's sermon at the 1521 St Paul's book-burning (1554, *STC* 10896), since for the Marian regime print was again primarily a way in which the English church could present itself to, and position itself within, Christendom.[92] After a hesitant start Protestant printing within England was suppressed. Abroad however, Protestant books were printed in large numbers and successfully smuggled into the country. Emden was the new Antwerp, with books also coming from Wesel, Strasbourg and Geneva.[93] As in the 1520s and 1530s the printers and places of origin were often disguised with false imprints. Foreign printers, such as Steven Mierdman (d. 1559) and Nicholas van den Berghe, who had come to England in the last years of Henry VIII or the reign of Edward VI, now followed the exiles abroad. Thus they knew both their authors and their markets well, and publication could continue relatively smoothly.[94] Between 1554 and 1557 twenty-eight English titles were produced in Emden, some by authors such as Cranmer and John Philpot (1516–55) who now had the authority of martyrs.[95] Among the English exiles however, it was polemic in Latin which predominated, addressed, as the Marian literature was addressed, to a European audience.[96] One such work, printed at Strasbourg by Wendelin Rihelius in 1554 was John Foxe's *Commentarii rerum in ecclesia gestarum*. It was an early draft of what was to become one of the great publishing projects of the second half of the century, Foxe's *Acts and Monuments*, which was known popularly at the time, as later, as his *Book of Martyrs*.

Foxe had no doubt about the role which printing played in the extraordinary events of his lifetime: 'We have great cause to geeve thankes to the high providence of almighty God for the excellent arte of Printing, most happely of late found out, and now commonly practised everywhere, to the singular benefit of Christes Church.'[97] It was not merely that the new technology could not be controlled by the means which had been used to control the old – that, for example, it made no sense to buy up print runs in order to destroy them. Print changed the relationship between social networks and heretical ideas. Lollardy existed within a web of personal relations. Lollard book production, especially

---

[92] John N. King, 'The Book-trade under Edward VI and Mary I', in *CHBB III*, p. 170. Jennifer Loach, 'The Marian Establishment and the Printing Press', *EHR* 101 (1986), 135–48 (142–44). It is additionally argued that the other main religious cause served by the printing press in Marian England was the education of the clergy.
[93] Conditions in Antwerp were now much less favourable. See Andrew Johnson and Jean-François Gilmont, 'Printing and the Reformation in Antwerp', in *The Reformation and the Book*, ed. Jean-François Gilmont and Karin Maag (Aldershot, 1998), pp. 188–213 (190–91).
[94] On Mierdman, see Colin Clair, 'On the Printing of Certain Reformation Books', *The Library*, 5th ser., 18 (1963), 275–87. Andrew Pettegree, *Marian Protestantism: Six Studies* (Aldershot, 1996).
[95] See Diarmaid MacCulloch, *Thomas Cranmer: A Life* (New Haven, CT and London, 1996), pp. 607–08.
[96] For a list of books published for the English exile community at Emden, see Pettegree, *Marian Protestantism: Six Studies*, appendix 1 (168–69), and for Latin polemic published by English exiles see appendix 4 (183–96). See also Edward J. Baskerville, *A Chronological Bibliography of Propaganda and Polemic Published in English between 1553 and 1558* (Philadelphia, PA, 1979), and 'Some Lost Works of Propaganda and Polemic from the Marian Period', *The Library*, 6th ser., 8 (1986), 47–52.
[97] Quoted in Aston, 'Lollardy and the Reformation: Survival or Revival?', p. 239.

in the later fifteenth century and the early sixteenth, was very much a bespoke process.[98] Ownership of suspicious books was more often seen as a consequence of heresy than the other way around.[99] English authorities continued to pursue networks of heretics during the early Reformation, believing that this was the route to solving the problem of heretical books. Secret organisations such as the London Christian Brethren, or the group who financed Sooham, confirmed them in this view. So did the successful prosecutions of 1528 and of More's chancellorship. More wrote in 1529 that, whereas heretics might view financial loss in the production of heretical literature with equanimity, 'yet I thynke there wyll no prynter lyghtly be so hot to put any bible in prynt at his owne charge, wherof the losse sholde lye hole in his owne necke'.[100] More was wrong. Commercialisation of heresy was under way. Franz Birckmann gambled correctly that the desire to possess the New Testament in English was much wider than any heretical community. The distribution structures to meet that need were already in place, even if they had to be used surreptitiously. Even before the Reformation, illicit material seeped beyond the committed into the hands of the curious, the careless and the unaware.[101] After the Reformation production and distribution became routinised, and risks depended on definitions of heresy which changed with changing political fortunes.

Among the victims and martyrs commemorated by Foxe were Edward and Valentine Freez, nephews of Gerard Freez the York bookseller. Edward was imprisoned for heresy in such grim circumstances he was found to have lost his mind when he was released in the 1530s, and Valentine was convicted and burned with his wife in about 1540.[102] Through their connections with the print trade they had easy access to the products of the Continental presses through established routes of distribution. But so, too, would many others whose silent purchases never registered with the authorities.

Further Reading

Primary Sources
Foxe, John, *Acts and Monuments*, 8 vols, ed. Josiah Pratt, The Church Historians of England (London, 1853–61).
Pollard, Alfred W., ed., *Records of the English Bible* (Oxford, 1911).

[98] Maureen Jurkowski, 'Lollard Book Production in London in 1414', in *Text and Controversy from Wyclif to Bale: Essays in Honour of Anne Hudson*, ed. Helen Barr and Ann M. Hutchison (Turnhout, 2005), pp. 201–06. Anne Hudson, 'Some Aspects of Lollard Book Production', in *Lollards and Their Books*, pp. 181–91; and 'Lollard Book Production' in *Book Production and Publishing in Britain 1375–1475*, ed. Jeremy Griffiths and Derek Pearsall (Cambridge, 1989), pp. 125–42.
[99] Fiona Somerset, 'Censorship', in *The Production of Books in England 1350–1500*, ed. Alexandra Gillespie and Daniel Wakelin (Cambridge, 2011), pp. 239–58.
[100] *Complete Works More*, 6, *A Dialogue Concerning Heresies*, ed. Thomas M.C. Lawler, Germain Marc'hadour and Richard C. Marius (New Haven, CT and London, 1981), part 1, p. 331.
[101] Somerset, 'Censorship', pp. 244–46.
[102] A.G. Dickens, *Lollards and Protestants in the Diocese of York*, 2nd edn (London, 1982), pp. 30–33.

Secondary Sources

Arblaster, Paul, Gergely Juhász and Guido Latré, eds, *Tyndale's Testament* (Turnhout, 2002).

Blouw, Paul Valkema, 'Early Protestant Publications in Antwerp, 1526–30: The Pseudonyms Adam Anonymus in Basel and Hans Luft in Marlborow', *Quaerendo* 26 (1996), 94–110.

D'Alton, Craig W., 'The Suppression of Lutheran Heretics in England, 1526–1529', *Journal of Ecclesiastical History* 54 (2003), 228–53.

Daniell, David, *The Bible in English: Its History and Influence* (New Haven, CT and London, 2003).

François, Wim, 'The Antwerp Printers Christoffel and Hans (I) van Ruremund, Their Dutch and English Bibles, and the Intervention of the Authorities in the 1520s and 1530s', *Archive for Reformation History / Archiv für Reformationsgeschichte* 101 (2010), 7–28.

Fudge, John D., *Commerce and Print in the Early Reformation* (Leiden, 2007).

Gilmont, Jean-François and Karin Maag, eds, *The Reformation and the Book* (Aldershot, 1998).

Hudson, Anne, '"No newe thyng": The Printing of Medieval Texts in the Early Reformation Period', in *Lollards and Their Books* (London, 1985), pp. 227–48.

Hume, Anthea, 'English Protestant Books Printed Abroad, 1525–1535: An Annotated Bibliography', in Thomas More, *The Yale Edition of the Complete Works of St Thomas More*, 15 Vols, 8: *The Confutation of Tyndale's Answer*, ed. Louis A. Schuster, Richard C. Marius, James P. Lusardi and Richard J. Schoeck (New Haven, CT and London, 1973), part 2, pp. 1063–91.

King, John N., and Mark Rankin, 'Print, Patronage, and the Reception of Continental Reform: 1521–1603', *The Yearbook of English Studies* 38 (2008), 49–67.

Loades, David, 'Books and the English Reformation Prior to 1558', in *Politics, Censorship and the English Reformation* (London, 1991), pp. 127–47.

15

Thomas More, Print and the Idea of Censorship

THOMAS BETTERIDGE

In 1536 Sir Thomas Elyot wrote to Thomas Cromwell in response to a recent proclamation, 'Ordering the Surrender of Bishop Fisher's Sermon, Books'. Elyot was concerned because he did have books that fell within the scope of the proclamation, partly as a result, he told Cromwell, of his desire to read 'many books, specially concerning humanitie and morall Philosophy'.[1] Elyot went on to inform Cromwell that,

> As touching suche books as be now prohibited contayning the busshop of Romes authorite, some in deede I have: joined with diverse other warkes in one grete volume or twoo at the moste, which I never found laysor to reade. Notwithstanding if it be the kinges pleasure and yours that I shall bringe or sende theim I will do it right gladly.[2]

Elyot was worried that because he had been ill he had not had time to search all his properties for prohibited works and that he could therefore be accused of failing to carry out the duties imposed on him by the proclamation. It was perhaps this that led Elyot in his letter to ask Cromwell for more time to comply with the requirements of the proclamation.

> . . . for as moche as my books be in sondry houses of myn owne and farre sonder, I hartily pray you that I may have convenient respeyte to repayre thither after my present recovery, and as I wold that god sholde helpe me I will make diligent serche, and such as I shall finde, savering any thinge agaynst the kinges pleasure, I will putt theim in redyness either to be browght to you, or to be cutt oute of the volume wherein they be joyned with other, as you shall advyse me . . .[3]

Elyot's letter expresses a real anxiety concerning censorship. During the course of his letter Elyot offers to censor his book collection, including searching out prohibited books in all his 'sondry houses'. It is interesting to note Elyot's offer to remove the offending works from the volumes in which they are bound. This suggests an understandable desire by Elyot to protect as much of his library as possible while also appearing eager to carry out the government's policy. The

---

[1] 'The Letters of Sir Thomas Elyot', ed. K.J. Wilson, *Studies in Philology* 73, no. 5 (1976), 26.
[2] 'The Letters', p. 27.
[3] 'The Letters', p. 27.

image of Elyot that emerges from his letter to Cromwell is as an auto-didactic censor searching, inquiring and destroying material found in the possession of another person, his alter-ego, 'Thomas Elyot', the uncritical buyer of numerous diverse works. Elyot's response to Henrician censorship echoes the cultural effects of print in its emphasis on books as objects and the authoritative role that Elyot assumes in carrying out the requirement to censor works written by John Fisher. Paradoxically, print heightened the sense of books as objects *and* led to an increased emphasis on the status of authors. Manuscripts, as Kathryn Kerby-Fulton has argued, were not 'much amenable to authorial control, let alone authoritarian control'.[4] This was not the case with print which technologised the creation of books and in the process heightened cultural anxieties about the commodification of knowledge. It also, however, made the possibility of real censorship appear more practical. As Susan Powell has recently pointed out, 'the printed word was much easier to police than manuscripts (which were always subject to random, or deliberate, intrusion of error)'.[5] Print therefore had a dual potential meaning. It massively increased the number of books in circulation while at the same time, because it was a standardising and mechanising technology, it created the illusion of real control over the circulation of knowledge. These tensions were perhaps particularly strongly felt in England where, as Vincent Gillespie has pointed out, 'From very soon after the invention of commercial printing, England had been a good market for the new commodity.'[6] The sense that one gets from the works of some early Tudor writers, for example, Thomas More, of England being subjected to a tide of printed works, of all different types and quality, may be an effect of the relatively underdeveloped nature of the English print trade and the resulting reliance of booksellers on works printed abroad to satisfy their customers' desire for new exciting books to consume.

Elyot's letter to Cromwell suggests that there were times when the circulation of specific books was directly and successfully managed by government policy. The effectiveness of censorship in the early modern period is, however, a matter of scholarly dispute – some scholars have argued that, from the passing of Archbishop Arundel's Constitutions in 1409, writing in English, particularly religious, was composed within a regime of censorship, while other scholars have pointed out that in practice very few texts were censored during the fifteenth century. Thomas More appears to have had few doubts concerning the effectiveness of censorship, or at least this is suggested by his actions, for example, when he led the first of two raids on the London house of the Hanseatic merchants in December 1525 looking for heretical books. At the same time, the prefaces that More attached to a number of his works suggest an uneasiness about the symbolic implications of censorship and its relationship to the emerging world of

[4]   Kathryn Kerby-Fulton, *Books under Suspicion: Censorship and Tolerance in Revelatory Writing in Late Medieval England* (Notre Dame, IN, 2006), p. 17.
[5]   Susan Powell, 'After Arundel but before Luther: the First Half-century of Print', in *After Arundel: Religious Writing in Fifteenth Century England*, ed. Vincent Gillespie and Kantik Ghosh (Turnhout, 2011), pp. 523–541 (524).
[6]   Vincent Gillespie, 'Syon and the English Market for Continental Printed Books: The Incunable Phase', *Religion and Literature* 37 (2005), 27–49 (27).

print. The offer Elyot makes to self-censor his library, cutting out and destroying works that were distasteful to the king's pleasure, is almost certainly meant to be taken seriously; however, it does have a potentially ironic side. Elyot's letter constructs the process of censorship as relating to books as objects. He has not had the leisure to read and study the works he is about to destroy, ones that 'taste or savour' against the king. Is there a sense in which Elyot is implicitly suggesting that Tudor censorship was wrong to treat books as material objects, as things to be consumed or eaten, when what it should have been doing is engaging with the ideas that they contained? Daniel Wakelin has suggested that in his 1536 letter to Cromwell Elyot is implicitly seeking to defend himself as a humanist scholar from the emerging dictates of the Henrician regime of censorship. Wakelin argues that Elyot deploys three distinct defensive strategies in his letter – his friendship with Cromwell, the distinctiveness of *studia humanitatis* and the role of the learned reader. Wakelin goes on to comment that Elyot,

> . . . records his freedom not to read some of his books at all, as he says that he never read the popish works bound into one volume which he owns. It is the freedom of the humanist reader which he thinks will save him – and which, as he defends his life and books, he hopes to save.[7]

Elyot seeks in his letter to draw a distinction between books, which are inanimate objects, and readers, who can exercise their judgement. Such distinctions were, however, ones that the Henrician regime was not prepared to countenance.[8] More was also concerned about this distinction and in the prefaces to his anti-heretical writings he reflected upon the way that print had changed the nature of the relationship between reader, text and author.

In this chapter I am first going to examine the nature of censorship from 1409 to 1540 and then briefly comment on print as a concept, before turning to discuss in detail More's response to the question of censorship.

The Theory and Practice of Censorship 1409–1530

The Constitutions passed in 1409 by Arundel largely concern teaching and preaching; however, the seventh clause does relate directly to books:

> Item, for that a new way doth more frequently leade astray, then an old way: we wyl and commaund, that no booke or treatise made by Iohn Wycklyffe, or other whō soeuer, about that time or sithēs, or hereafter to be made: be from henceforth read in scholes, halles, hospitals, or other places whatsoeuer, within our prouince

---

[7]   *Humanism*, p. 209.

[8]   It is interesting to note that the Henrician regime was extremely exercised by a similar distinction, that between the inner and outward person in relation to oaths. The idea that, because the person being required to take an oath regarded it as unlawful, the oath could be treated as simply words that did not relate directly to the inner beliefs of the oath-taker was a source of real anxiety for Henry and his ministers. For a detailed discussion of this issue in relation to the martyrdom of John Forrest, see Peter Marshall, *Religious Identities in Henry VIII's England* (Aldershot, 2006), esp. Chapter 10.

of Canterbury aforesayd, except the same be fyrst examined by the vniuersity of Oxford or Cambrige, or at the least by. xij. persons, whom the sayd vniuersities or one of them shal appoynt to be chosen at our discretion, or the laudable discretion of our predecessors: and the same beyng examined as aforesayd, to be expressely approued and allowed by vs or our successours, and in the name and autoritye of the vniuersity, to be deliuered vnto the Stacioners to be copied out, & the same to be sold at a reasonable price, the originall thereof alwayes after, to remayne in some chest of the Vniuersity. But if anye man shall reade anye such kynde of boke in scholes or otherwyse, as aforesaid: he shal be punished as a sower of schisme, and a fauourer of heresy, as the qualitie of the fault shall require.[9]

The concerns expressed here mirror those that reappear in Tudor censorship proclamations, but with a number of notable exceptions. Arundel's main concern is focused on the circulation of new learning. The seventh clause of the Constitutions proposes a clear process by which new books (and the implication is that every book written during and after the time that John Wycliffe comes under its purview) should be assessed by scholars and approved for publication. It also requires a copy of any book that has been authorised to be kept in 'some chest of the university'. The readers of non-authorised books are condemned as 'sowers of schism' and 'favourers of heresy'. It is interesting to note that the slippage between books and readers that Elyot sought to deploy in his letter is present in this item – books are authorised and readers are condemned.

Arundel's Constitutions were issued as part of a general campaign by the Lancastrian establishment against Lollardy which was fully supported by Henry IV and V. John Lydgate's poem *Holy Church* (c.1413) celebrates the role of Henry V as a 'most worthi prince' and protector of Christ's spouse, the Church.[10] Lydgate, however, goes on to recommend to Henry the example of David:

> And thynke how Dauid ageyn Iebusse
> When that he fouht, in *Regum* as I fynde,
> How he made voide from Syon his Citee
> Unweldly, crokid, bothe lame and blynde:
> By which example always have in mynde
> To void echon, and for to do the same
> Out of thi siht, that in the faith be lame.[11]

Lydgate's argument is that Henry should model himself on David and drive the spiritually lame from his presence, the city and country. *Holy Church* was written in the aftermath of Arundel's Constitutions and it shares their precautionary but also reforming agenda. For men like Lydgate and Arundel heresy was a disease and the presence of heretics and heretical books a sign of spiritual sickness. It was their duty as responsible clergymen to work to restore their flock to health and a key element of this restoration was preventing the circulation of heretical books. The intention of Arundel's Constitutions, which was shared

---

[9]   John Foxe, *Acts and Monuments* (London: John Day, 1570; STC 11223), p. 627.
[10]   John Lydgate, 'A Defence of Holy Church', in *John Lydgate: Poems*, ed. John Norton-Smith (Oxford, 1966), pp. 30–34 (30).
[11]   *John Lydgate*, ed. Norton-Smith, pp. 32–33.

by the Tudor proclamations issued under Henry VIII, was to deny heresy the oxygen provided by the circulation of works whose orthodoxy was suspect.

Item 7 of the Constitutions is the key one in relation to the censorship of books. Although, as has been suggested, in general terms it articulates similar concerns and anxieties as the Tudor censorship proclamations, there are a number of significant differences of emphasis. Item 7 does prohibit the reading of books that sow heresy and disorder. It also, however, puts in place a regime of oversight which could in theory have authorised a work by John Wycliffe. Arundel's Constitutions combine censorship with a desire to manage the production of new works which is alien to the Tudor censorship proclamations. This is partly a product of the Constitutions' location as a part of a manuscript culture. It is not clear that, *pace* Kerby-Fulton, it is impossible to censor manuscripts effectively; however, it is undoubtedly the case that the idea of creating a 'chest' of authorised works would be meaningless in relation to a print culture. As David Scott Kastan has recently pointed out, '[T]he flood of printed books [during the reign of Henry VIII] meant that the old strategies of prohibition could no longer be effective.'[12]

Tudor proclamations dealing with censorship largely repeat the Constitutions' basic themes and tropes. In particular, there is a clear sense that heretical writing was potentially poisonous and that its circulation could cause the 'illness' of social unrest. Henry VIII, who was fond of modelling himself on Old Testament monarchs, consistently demonstrated a commitment to the religious health of his realm. The proclamation, 'Prohibiting Unlicensed Preaching, Heretical Books (1529)', attacked the sowing of 'venomous heresies, blasphemies and slanders intolerable to the clear ears of any good Christian man'.[13] It went on to require that:

> all and every person and persons having any books or writings of any such erroneous doctrine and opinion do deliver or cause to be delivered effectually and actually all and every such books and writings to the bishop of the diocese or to the ordinary of the place within 15 days after this proclamation.[14]

Not surprisingly, proclamations issued after the break with Rome condemn dramatically different books while articulating the same basic desire to prevent the spread of the disease of errors, slanders and lies. The proclamation that probably prompted Elyot to write to Cromwell, 'Ordering Surrender of Bishop Fisher's Sermon, Books (1536)', says:

> ... the King's highness straightly chargeth and commandeth all and singular justices of peace, mayors, sheriffs, bailiffs, constables, and all his loving subjects, that every of them shall put their good and effectual endeavours for the finding, espying, and bringing in of the said books and writings ... .[15]

---

[12] David Scott Kastan, 'Naughty Printed Books', in *Cultural Reformations: Medieval and Renaissance Literary History*, ed. Brian Cummings and James Simpson (Oxford, 2010), pp. 287–304 (297).
[13] *TRP*, 1.182.
[14] *TRP*, 1.183.
[15] *TRP*, 1.236.

Having imposed the duty to hunt out Fisher's works on all the king's subjects, the proclamation takes aim at a rather different danger to the realm, attacking the role of pardoners in sustaining the authority of the bishop of Rome and claiming that:

> the most part of the said pardoners, being confederate with the great errant thieves of this realm, by going about espy where the richest and most substantial man inhabit and dwell, to whose houses many times they give and bring the said thieves their confederates, to rob and spoil; and also the money, unlawfully by them exacted of the poor innocent people by colour of their indulgences, they spend in ribaldry and carnal vices, carrying about with them drabs, whores and cut-purses, to / the great slander of the realm and to the damage, deceit, and impoverishing of the King's good loving subjects.[16]

This passage evokes the literary pardoners that populate late medieval and early Tudor literature, perhaps particularly in the writing of Geoffrey Chaucer and John Heywood. It is also drawing on the anti-clerical polemical tropes developed by writers like Simon Fish. The proclamation 'Ordering Surrender of Bishop Fisher's Sermon, Books' combines specific detailed instructions in relation to the censorship of Fisher's books with a fantasy of the country being attacked by a horde of criminals and pardoners. This is a common combination in Tudor censorship proclamations. It reflects a tension between the specifics of censorship and its justification.

Recent scholarship on censorship between 1409 and 1540 has reproduced the conflicting dual focus of Tudor censorship proclamations. Nicholas Watson's important article on censorship in late-medieval England argued that:

> ... the legislation as a whole constitutes one of the most draconian pieces of censorship in English history, going far beyond its ostensible aim of destroying Lollard heresy and effectively attempting to curtail all sorts of theological thinking and writing in the vernacular that did not belong within the pragmatic bounds set by earlier legislation like Peacham's Syllabus of 1281.[17]

Watson suggests that the Constitutions had a chilling and narrowing effect not only on religious writing but also on intellectual and aesthetic texts.[18] Watson's work has been criticised by a number of scholars. Eamon Duffy has rejected the idea that the Constitutions had a profound impact on fifteenth-century English culture, arguing that:

> [i]t would be absurd to attribute what is arguably a generalised drop in cultural temperature to religious repression. England never had anything remotely like the Inquisition, and though bishops kept a weather eye open for Lollards throughout the century, there is little evidence of sustained persecution: fifteenth-century England had no thought police.[19]

---

[16] TRP, 2.236/237.
[17] Nicholas Watson, 'Censorship and Cultural Change in Late-Medieval England: Vernacular Theology, the Oxford Translation Debate, and Arundel's Constitutions of 1409', Speculum 70 (1995), 822–64 (826).
[18] Watson, 'Censorship', p. 825.
[19] Eamon Duffy, 'Religious Belief', in A Social History of England 1200–1500, ed. Rosemary Horrox and W. Mark Ormrod (Cambridge, 2006), pp. 293–339 (331).

Duffy's argument is rather sweeping but seems largely persuasive given the small number of books actually censored during the fifteenth century. Kathryn Kerby-Fulton has usefully added to the debate by pointing out that, 'the truth is that effective "censorship" as we understand it, was ultimately impossible, indeed in any absolutely sense an impractical task in the age before print'.[20] Kerby-Fulton's argument is very important since it places the focus on the relationship between the concept of censorship and the material reality. Manuscripts have writers who are invariably not their authors. At the same time, despite these criticisms, Watson's thesis is important. There was a level at which late medieval and early Tudor governments existed in order to control or 'narrow' public discussion and the circulation of texts. Early modern government regarded one of its key duties to be the protection of society from external dangers and internal conflicts.[21] Any government that did not censor during this period, as for a very short time happened under the regime of Protector Somerset, would be failing in its duties.[22] This was particularly true of kings like Henry V and Henry VIII. Indeed an aspect of Henry VIII's desire to model himself on his Lancastrian predecessor was the former monarch's status as a defender of 'Holi Church' as well as victor over the French.

In Arundel's Constitutions and the Tudor censorship proclamations there is a tension between the idea of censorship and the practice which is played out through a slippage between a metaphorical and metonymic understanding of books. David Cressy has recently pointed out that when in May 1521 Cardinal Wolsey burned a collection of Luther's works, 'What happened was a kind of metonymy, a symbolic substitution of an attribute for an entity. . .'.[23] Luther's books were burnt in place of Luther. This was a reversal of Elyot's implicit argument that the erroneous nature of the books he possessed was latent since he had not read them. All attempts at censorship between 1409 and 1540 exploit the tension between the book as an object and the metaphor of heresy/ papistry as a miasma of rumour, gossip, lies and slander. It is noticeable, however, that the Tudor proclamations are simultaneously more prescriptive and more symbolic than the Constitutions. There is no room for debate about the fact that the books being condemned are prohibited and the proclamations spend much more time conjuring up fantasy images of the dangers of heretic writers and criminal pardoners. The Tudor proclamations are more assertive and absolute in the demands they make than the Constitutions are, and more metaphoric in their descriptions of the potential dangers of heresy/papistry. This change of emphasis, and its apparent contradictory nature, is a product of print.

Print as a concept is, and was, hard to pin down. Elizabeth Eisenstein's

---

[20] Kerby-Fulton, *Books under Suspicion*, p. 17.
[21] For the continuities between medieval and Tudor attitudes to censorship, see David Loades, 'The Theory and Practice of Censorship in Sixteenth-Century England', *TRHS*, 5th ser., 24 (1974), 141–57.
[22] For the regime of Protector Somerset, see Diarmaid MacCulloch, *Tudor Church Militant: Edward VI and the Protestant Reformation* (London, 1999).
[23] David Cressy, 'Book Burning in Tudor and Stuart England', *Sixteenth Century Journal* 36 (2005), 359–74 (362).

seminal work, *The Printing Press as an Agent of Change*, argued cogently that print had a transformative effect on the circulation and control of knowledge.[24] Printing's relationship to knowledge was, however, at one level more complicated than Eisenstein suggests in her highly contested work since there is no direct relationship between 'print' as a technology and knowledge as a concept. Print does not possess knowledge. It can and may communicate it but this is a subtly different thing. Print's relationship to knowledge in early modern England was split between the metonymic and metaphoric. The tension between print as metaphor and metonym is played out through the paradox of print's simultaneous emphasis on the status of books as objects and the importance of the authorial role. At the level of metonym print was regarded as being the knowledge it articulated – Luther's works were regarded as being Luther's heresy – while at the same time Luther was seen as personally responsible for the content of the books that bore his name. Walter J. Ong has argued that 'Print suggests that words are things far more than writing did.'[25] He goes on to suggest that,

> Print encourages a sense of closure, a sense that what is found in a text has been finalized, has reached a state of completion. This sense affects literary creations and it affects analytic philosophical and scientific work. . . . Print encloses thought in thousands of copies of exactly the same visual and physical consistency.[26]

One can see the effects of the tendency of print to close down meaning in one of the key differences between Arundel's *Constitutions* and the Henrician censorship proclamations. In the former there is a possibility, however limited and partial, of the process of evaluating a work being a scholar activity. Under Henry works are simply prohibited. There is no need for any evaluation beyond the assertion that a text is papist or heretical. This certainly is partly a product of the changes to the status of knowledge that print produced.

If print suggested that words were knowledge, it also, however, had the opposite effect of undermining the relationship between the written word and what it meant. Print as a metaphor for knowledge implied a technologising of learning and wisdom which in turn suggested it could be produced by machines, circulated as a commodity and consumed by whoever bought it. The market printing created could be seen as subverting the integrity and coherence of different branches and aspects of knowledge by making them all just 'things' to be bought and consumed. Robert Copland, printer, translator and author, in the prologue to *The Seuen Sorowes that women haue when theyr husbandes be deade* (1526, *STC* 5734), produced a dialogue between himself and a consumer of print which precisely reflects the effect that print was perceived as having on the status of knowledge.

---

[24] Elizabeth Eisenstein, *The Printing Press as an Agent of Change: Communications and Cultural Transformations in Early-Modern Europe* (Cambridge, 1979).
[25] Walter J. Ong, *Orality and Literary: The Technologizing of the Word* (London, 1982), p. 118.
[26] Ong, *Orality*, p. 132.

Copland.
Why should I muse such trifles for to wryte
Of wanton toyes, but for the appetite
Of wandryng braynes, that seke for thynges new
And do not reche if they be fals or trew.
Quidam
With what newes? or here ye any tidings
Of the pope, of the Emperour, or of kynges
Of martyn Luther, or of the great Turke
Of this and that, and how the world doth worke.[27]

Copland's self-representation in this prologue is as a weary printer having to produce 'trifles' for 'wandering brains' who simply desire news. Quidam (one) is a buyer of texts whose main aim is to purchase something new. It is no accident that he has no name. Quidam is someone and everyone; the demanding buyer defined purely by their desire to buy. Copland's protestations are, of course, tongue-in-cheek. *The Seuen Sorowes* is a bawdy poem, possibly an original composition by Copland, which includes seven woodcuts illustrating the seven sorrows. As such it represents a combination of popular culture with relatively sophisticated printing. Copland's buyer sees the works he seeks to buy as objects to be consumed. The market for print imagined in the prologue to *The Seuen Sorowes* is one in which knowledge has been almost entirely hollowed out. It no longer matters if it, a work, is true or false. All that matters is that it is new and entertaining.

The Shyp of Fools (1494) was written by Sebastian Brant and translated into English by Alexander Barclay in 1509. It is a complex work of humanist scholarship, and in the prefatory material that he added to his translation Barclay explicitly locates it within a reforming tradition, telling his readers that he hopes they will reform their behaviour in order to avoid finding themselves within the ship of fools. The first fools that are discussed in Brant's work are those who collect 'inprofitable books'.

That in this shyp the chefe place I gouerne
By this wyde see with folys wanderynge
The cause is playne and easy to dyscerne
Styll am I besy boks assemblynge
For to haue plenty it is a plesaunt thynge
In my conceyt and to haue them ay in honde
But what they mene do I nat understande[28]

The Fool is happy to assemble as many books as possible but he has no idea what they mean. Indeed later in the poem the Fool explicitly states that he is happier to look at a book's 'fayre coverynge' than read it since of the few books the Fool reads the fewer he understands. There is a paradox running through *The Shyp of Fools*, of which the work is entirely conscious. One of the key definitions of foolishness in Brant's work is the collection of books simply as

---

[27] *Robert Copland Poems*, ed. Mary Carpenter Erler (Toronto, 1993), p. 85.
[28] Sebastian Brant, *The Shyp of Fools*, translated by Alexander Barclay (London, 1509, STC 3545), B.iii. (2v).

objects and, given the woodcuts and high production values of *The Shyp of Fools*, there was clearly a danger that this is precisely how it would be treated – simply as an object to be looked at but not understood. Of course, to treat *The Shyp of Fools* in this way would be to place oneself in it as a fool. Brant's work plays with the twin conflicting meanings of print, its objectification and commodification of knowledge and its ability to communicate an author's agenda, which in the case of *The Shyp of Fools* was an explicitly humanist and reforming one, effectively to a mass audience.

The proclamation 'Ordering Surrender of Bishop Fisher's Sermon, Books' embodies a metaphoric and metonymic understanding of the relationship between knowledge and print in relation to papistry. Its fantastical pardoners are parodic versions of Copland's buyers, occupying the same world. In their case what is exchanged and circulated are not bawdy tales and exciting news but treasonable rumours and criminal intelligence. At the same time, as was fully understood and mocked by Elyot, the proclamation treats Fisher's books as metonyms for the bishop of Rochester's teaching; destroy the books, even if they have not been read, and one will destroy the truth of what Fisher wrote.

Thomas More and Censorship

More's approach to censorship can be broadly divided into two parts. When he was in government as a royal councillor and later as Lord Chancellor he played an active part in the campaign against heresy including the prohibition of heretical books. He may also have been involved as High Steward of Oxford and Cambridge in the campaign to prevent the spread of heretical ideas among university scholars. It was also during his time in government that he was commissioned by Cuthbert Tunstall, bishop of London, in 1528 to read heretical works and to produce a work refuting them. The resulting work was the *Dialogue Concerning Heresies* published in 1529. The second stage to More's approach to censorship is the works he produced after resigning the Lord Chancellorship in 1532 and is articulated in the *Apology* (1533) and *Debellation of Salem and Bizance* (1533). The difference between these two stages is, however, largely institutional. It is clearly different to support censorship, as More undoubtedly did, from a position of influence and power as compared to the situation More found himself in after 1532 when it was his works that were in danger of being censored and not only those of his enemies. More's basic attitude to censorship, however, did not fundamentally alter. It is also important to note that, although More did participate in the government's campaign against heresy, the extent to which he was a leading agent is debatable. For example, the raid on the Steelyard, which was mentioned before, is often used as evidence for the role that More played in the suppressing of heretical books. Looked at in the round, however, in relation to other activities that More took part in during 1526/27 as a royal councillor, it looks less significant. John Guy comments that 'More's work at the centre turns out to have covered the full range of councilliar activity.'[29] More took part in a

---

[29] John Guy, *The Public Career of Sir Thomas More* (New Haven, CT, 1980), p. 13.

discussion of fiscal losses sustained due to evasions of the king's feudal rights, he was involved in projects to address vice and vagrancy around London and in the search for grain supplies during 1528. More's role as a councillor was to maintain the health of the commonwealth and his role in the campaign against heresy was an aspect of this, albeit one that he no doubt regarded as particularly important.

The *Dialogue Concerning Heresies* (1529, STC 18084) opens with a preface that discusses the work's genesis.[30] This is a complex piece of writing in which More plays with notions of fictionality and truth. In particular, More uses the conceit that the work is a mimetic account of a real dialogue to justify having the *Dialogue Concerning Heresies* published. More writes that having produced a written version of the dialogue he became concerned that it might fall into the wrong hands and a corrupt version be printed overseas:

> ... whan I remembred what a shrewde sorte of our apostatas are assembled / parte ronne out of relygyon / & all ronne out of [the] ryght fayth / me thought grete parell myght aryse / yf some of that company ... sholde malycyously chaunge my wordes to the worse / & so put in prynte my boke / framed after theyr fantasyes / which whan I wolde afterward reproue and shewe [the] difference. .... For eschewyng wherof I am now dryuen / as I say to this thyrde busyness of publyshynge and puttynge my boke in prynte myselfe: wherby theyr enterprise (if they sholde any suche intende) shall (I trust) be preuented and frustrate.[31]

The first two businesses that More, or rather his narrator, has been driven to are having the initial oral dialogue and then producing a written copy of it. In this passage More claims he published the *Dialogue Concerning Heresies* in order to prevent another version being printed. The joke is, however, as More himself accepts at the end of this passage, that there is no real evidence that a heretical version was going to be produced. Indeed even to talk in these terms is a misnomer since the whole of this passage is fictional. More is playing with the idea of a market for printed works. He is writing himself into a fictional dialogue and then producing through the month-piece of his alter-ego an explanation for the printing of the *Dialogue Concerning Heresies*. But of course the 'More' who provides this explanation does not, and never has, existed outside the printed text whose existence in print 'More' explains is the result of More's fear that a non-existent written version of a oral dialogue was about to appear in print. The circulatory nature of this reasoning is comic but it also has a serious side since in the *Dialogue Concerning Heresies* More reflects upon the self-regarding, self-generating nature of heresy. And he is also suggesting in this preface that print because of its commodification of knowledge has the dangerous potential to spread heretical ideas and works, since in the market for texts, as imagined by

---

[30] For the context of More's *Dialogue Concerning Heresies*, see Craig W. D'Alton, 'Charity or Fire? The Argument of Thomas More's 1529 Dyalogue', *Sixteenth Century Journal* 33 (2002), 51–70.
[31] *Complete Works More*, 6, *A Dialogue Concerning Heresies*, ed. Thomas M.C. Lawler, Germain Marc'hadour and Richard C. Marius (New Haven, CT and London, 1981), p. 22.

Copland, the 'framed fantasies' of heretics are equivalent to the truthful words of the orthodox; the market does not recognise truth or condemn lies – it is concerned only with entertainment.[32]

In the prologue to the *Dialogue Concerning Heresies* More envisages a situation in which the existence of a heretical version of the *Dialogue Concerning Heretics* leads him to having to engage in a form of parodic tautological editing – correcting in print a written version of an oral dialogue that in fact only ever existed in print. The implication of More's words is that his printed version of the dialogue with the messenger will be more authoritative than either the written or spoken versions. At the same time there is clearly a sense that the danger that More's printed version of the dialogue is designed to counter is one specifically engendered by print. The heretics' 'fantasies' are framed. This implies that they are artificial and made up since to be framed suggests composed or gathered together. It can also, however, be related directly to the frames used in weaving and printing. The danger that the *Dialogue Concerning Heresies* is intended to guard against is the spread of heresy. It uses the fixity of print as part of its strategy to counter heretical rumours and fantasies. At the same time, however, there is clearly a sense in which the way More's text imagines the spread of heresy draws on similar tropes to those deployed by other writers to represent the effects of print on the distribution and status of knowledge; it only takes a change of perspective for Copland's Quidam to become More's Messenger demanding more and more texts from Copland/More. The role of printer as imagined by Copland, constantly under pressure from a never satisfied buyer, is strangely comparable to that of the penitent defender of orthodoxy as portrayed by More in the *Dialogue Concerning Heresies* having to address the Messenger's endless doubts and questions.

The *Dialogue Concerning Heresies* presents itself to the reader as a printed version of an oral dialogue. It is therefore potentially ironic that one of the key issues addressed by More in this work is the relative weight of oral and written traditions as regards Christian teaching. Consistently in the *Dialogue Concerning Heresies* More seeks to expand the text of scripture so that it includes oral testimony and not simply the written word. R.R. McCutcheon comments that,

> The dialogue that More directs defines itself against the variety of language at large; in the course of his conversation with the messenger More progressively expands the narrow Lutheran concept of Christian discourse, confined (More maintains) to Holy Writ.[33]

More repeatedly asks the Messenger to acknowledge that Christian truth cannot be restricted to the written word of Scripture telling him, through the persona of his narrator, that,

---

[32] As Susan Powell has pointed out, 'While print allowed the faster and more accurate dissemination of a uniform and orthodox voice, it also allowed a faster dissemination of multiple voices and/or heresy than did manuscripts.' Powell, 'After Arundel but before Luther', pp. 523–41 (524).
[33] R.R. McCutcheon, 'Heresy and Dialogue: the Humanist Approaches of Erasmus and More', *Viator* 29 (1993), 375–84 (379).

And I nothynge doubte / but all had it so ben / that never gospel hadde ben written / yet sholde the substance of this faith never have fallen out of Crysten folkes hartes / but the same spyryte that planted it / sholde haue watered it / the same sholde haue kepte it / [the] same shold have encreased it.[34]

More repeats this argument a number of times referring to the history of the early Church as depicted in the New Testament to support his view:

And none Euengelyst was there nor none Appostle / that by wrytynge ever sente the faythe to any nacyon / but iff they were furste enformyd by worde . . .[35]

There are, however, a number of paradoxes at work in relation to More's valorisation of the orality in relation to the Christian teaching. The most obvious is that the *Dialogue Concerning Heresies* is itself a written text. Indeed it is a printed work designed to propagate a fictional account of an oral dialogue. It is almost as though More is deliberately and provocatively playing with the coherence of his own position, daring the reader to notice the paradoxical nature of the relationship between the form of the *Dialogue Concerning Heresies* and its argument. There is, moreover, another paradox at work here, which is that More consistently deploys the text of the Bible to support his position that Scripture should not be seen as purely textual.

More's defence of the 'unwritten verities' in the *Dialogue Concerning Heresies* is, however, coupled with an awareness of the dangers of unlimited orality. The editors of the Yale edition of the *Dialogue Concerning Heresies* comment that,

More seems to be pursuing throughout the *Dialogue* the connection between 'heresy' and 'hearsay'; for most of the Messenger's information comes from what he has heard, not from what he has seen or read.[36]

More's narrative persona in the *Dialogue Concerning Heresies* tells the Messenger that,

. . . a tale that fleeth throrowe many mouthes / catcheth many newe fethers / whych whan they be pulled away agayne / leue hym as pulled as a cote and somtyme as bare as a byrds ars.[37]

Oral words are dangerous in the *Dialogue Concerning Heresies*. In particular, they seem to circulate in a dangerous world without fixed boundaries or meanings. Heresy feeds on this proteaness in order to attack the teaching of the church through half-truths, gossip, rumours and lies. The printed version of the *Dialogue Concerning Heresies* was intended to have a fixity that would protect it against the lies of heretics partly because it was printed; it was not manuscript or oral. More clearly saw the possibility of print as a fixed and ordering technology; but there was always the possibility that works like the *Dialogue Concerning Heresies*

---

[34] More, *Dialogue Concerning Heresies*, p. 144.
[35] More, *Dialogue Concerning Heresies*, p. 144.
[36] 'Introduction', in More, *Dialogue Concerning Heresies*, p. 449.
[37] More, *Dialogue Concerning Heresies*, pp. 324–25.

would simply add to the mass of books that made up the market-place of print. The authorial role that More assumes in the *Dialogue Concerning Heresies* is that of bringing order to a world of rumour and hearsay. In the process he is exploiting the certainty and fixity produced by print's technology as a counter to the circulation of heretical texts and works that print had also enabled. The status of the authorial More is the direct counterpart to the false framed/printed versions of his conversation with the Messenger that are a metaphor for print's potential role in the spread of heresy.

When More resigned his post as Lord Chancellor in 1532, this transformed his position in relation to the campaign against heresy; no longer an agent for the government, he was now writing and printing his work as an individual writer. This change perhaps partly explains the tone of the first major work produced by More after leaving office, the *Apology*. This work is not a full-scale defence of More's actions in office but it is an attempt by More to defend his reputation in relation to his role in the campaign against heretics. As part of this the *Apology* discusses More's anti-heretical polemical writings.[38] More opens by stating that he only wrote against heresy because other people, better equipped than he was, had failed to do so:

> But like as some (I se well) there are, that can somwhat lesse than I, that yet for all that put out theyr workes in wrytynge: so am I not so blynde vpon the tother syde, but that I very well perceyue, very many so farre in wyt and erudicyon aboue me, that in such mater as I haue any thyng wryten, yf other men, as many wolde haue take yt in hand as could haue done better, yt myght myche better haue become me to let the mater alone, then by wrytyng to presume any thing to medle therwyth.[39]

Clearly More is being ironic in this passage. At the same time the *Apology* does consistently foreground a sense of the dangers of writing against heresy, as well as the labour involved. More tells the reader that, 'it is a shorter thing and soner done to wryte heresyes than to answere them'.[40] The *Apology* consistently depicts heresy through tropes that relate directly to the metaphoric understanding of print. Heretical writings are easy to consume, they entertain and amuse, they encourage the reader to indulge their sins and in the process become literally sinful writing – writing that incites sin and which is sin.

As well as being a defence of More's reputation the *Apology* is also a sustained critique of Christopher St German's *Treatise Concerning the Division between Spirituality and Temporality* (1532). Indeed these two aspects of the *Apology* are effectively the same, since a key issue in the debate between More and St German was the conduct of heresy trials and the relationship between English and canon law. In defending his actions as Lord Chancellor, More also defended the existing operation of the law against heresy which was one of St German's principal targets. More's critique of St German's arguments takes a number of

---

[38] William J. Rogers, 'Thomas More's Polemical Poetics', *English Literary Renaissance* 38 (2008), 387–407 (389).
[39] *Complete Works More, 9, The Apology*, ed. J.B. Trapp (New Haven, CT, 1979), p. 3.
[40] More, *The Apology*, p. 8.

forms. What is particularly significant for More is the use that St German made of phrases like 'some say', 'they say', 'many say', 'myche people sayth' and 'many men thynke'.[41] More's argument is partly that such phrases are used by St German as a way of denying or at least obscuring authorial responsibility for the arguments contained in *Treatise Concerning the Division between Spirituality and Temporality*. There is also, however, a poetic or generic aspect to More's critique of the way these phrases function, which is that they introduce a degree of provisionality into St German's argument that is at once effective and dishonest since it is impossible to effectively argue against. There is a sense in which what More is trying to address in the *Apology* is the tension between print and the spoken word. The phrase 'some say' invokes a collective world of spoken rumour and gossip which is solidified on the printed page of *Treatise Concerning the Division between Spirituality and Temporality* in such a way as to appear to make it authoritative. Print makes 'some say' factual or, at least, and this is of course for More the crucial point, gives it the appearance of being a fact – once something has been printed and circulated it has a status that may have no relationship to its truthfulness or value.

More consistently argues in his later works that print creates the possibility for dangerous ideas and views to circulate without control or order. He comments in relation to William Tyndale's translation of the New Testament:

> For when the thynge had ben examyned, consydered, & condempned, by suche as the iudgement and ordering of the thynge apperteyne vnto, that false poysened translacyon was forboden the people / it was an heyghnouse presumpcyon of one man, vppon the truste of his owne wyt, to geue the people corage and boldnesse to resyste theyre prynce and disobey theyr prelates, and geue them no better staffe to stand by, then suche a bald poisoned reason, that poysened bread is better than no brede at all.[42]

Given that by the time More wrote this he was no longer in the government and much of his writing could be seen as oppositional, there is clearly a potential irony here, since what is the difference between Tyndale presuming to print his New Testament and More printing his *Apology*? This is not to suggest that More was unaware of these tensions. More consistently invites his readers to indulge in the kind of self-directed censorship that Elyot offered to undertake and in the process protects himself against the charge of arrogance that he levelled against authors like William Tyndale. *The Debellation of Salem and Bizance* is a continuation of the debate started in the *Apology* with St German's legal treatises.[43] In this work, as in many of his anti-heretical writings, More is concerned to be fair to his opponents, particularly in relation to his quotations of their work. For example, he writes,

> How be it rather then I wolde geue any cause of dyuysyon agaynst me, to hym that vseth to make great dyuysyons vpon smale groundes / I shall be content to

---

[41] More, *The Apology*, p. 116.
[42] More, *The Apology*, p. 12.
[43] For the nature of this debate, see Henry Ansgar Kelly, 'Thomas More on Inquisitorial Due Process', *EHR* 123 (2008), 847–94.

geue hym his own worde agayne. And therfore I pray you good readers euery of you mende your bokis / & in the stede of prelates in that place, put in spyrytual rulers. And when you haue so done, [the] chaunge shal for the mater not be very great / & yet so myche as it shalbe, shal more serue me then hym.[44]

More's argument in this passage is that the difference between 'prelates' and 'spyrytual rulers' is not important. What is interesting about this passage is that it envisages readers correcting their copies of More's earlier work in order to make it accurate. There is, however, a sense here in which the correction of mistakes like this could go on indefinitely as though the process of printing is extended endlessly into the future as More and his opponents ask their readers to update the works they have in their possession. Indeed this is at one level precisely what happened during the course of the Henrician Reformation as Tudor censorship proclamations order different works, phrases and words to be exercised. There is, however, no sense that More, or the framers of the Tudor censorship proclamations, regarded the idea of texts as adaptable or plural as positive. The aim was always to produce the final authoritative fixed text with just one more correction, one more word cut or one more phrase changed. Ultimately, the utopian fantasy of a university chest containing fixed complete copies of all the works authorised to be read and studied that is at the heart of the Item 7 of Arundel's Constitutions remains – albeit in More's case the chest has moved out of the university into a virtual humanist study.

Conclusion

The Debellation of Salem and Bizance was one of the last polemical works that More produced. It has a rather different emphasis to the *Dialogue Concerning Heresies*, largely as a result of changes in More's own position. One was written from within the government, the other from a position of effective opposition. The attitude to heresy and its relation to print, however, remains constant. In *The Debellation of Salem and Bizance* More writes that 'in heresye the wordes be the worke. For not onely the spekyng, but also the defending therof, is in the wordes to'.[45] Elyot sought to mock the idea that an unread text or unopened book could be dangerous – how could they be heretical? For More, however, this kind of argument was simply too permissive. Words, and in particular printed ones, could articulate heretical ideas and could be heresy. More in his anti-heretical works exploited the possibilities offered by print but he was consistently aware of the potential dangers of a print's power being used to promote lies, rumours and heresy.

---

[44] *Complete Works More*, 10, *The Debellation of Salem and Bizance*, ed. John Guy, Ralph Keen, Clarence Miller and Ruth McGugan (New Haven, CT, 1988), p. 201.
[45] More, *The Debellation of Salem and Bizance*, p. 69.

Further Reading

Clegg, Candia, *Press Censorship in Elizabethan England* (Cambridge, 1997).

Cummings, Brian, *The Literary Culture of the Reformation: Grammar and Grace* (Oxford, 2002).

Gillespie, Alexandra, 'Books', in *Middle English*, ed. Paul Strohm (Oxford, 2007), pp. 86–103.

King, John N., *John Foxe's 'Book of Martyrs' and Early Modern Print Culture* (Cambridge, 2011).

Loades, David, *Politics, Censorship and the English Reformation* (London, 1991).

Logan, George M., ed., *The Cambridge Companion to Thomas More* (Cambridge, 2011).

Simpson, James, *Burning to Read: English Fundamentalism and its Reformation Opponents* (Cambridge, MA, 2007).

16

Catholicism, the Printed Book and the Marian Restoration

LUCY WOODING

'Preachers, players and printers. . . be set up of God, as a triple bulwark against the triple crown of the pope, to bring him down.'[1] John Foxe was quite sure that the invention of printing was a providential gift by which God hastened the advance of the true church. The link between printing and Protestantism has long been established in the historical imagination. Indeed, the arrival of printing has been seen as the first step in an even greater cultural transformation that incorporated Renaissance, Reformation, Scientific Revolution and Enlightenment.[2] Despite the subtleties of most historical writing on the subject, there is still a tendency towards easy contrasts: medieval against early modern, manuscript against print, Catholic obscurantism against Protestant communication. This has dovetailed with the still-lingering popular narrative which portrays the pre-Reformation church as superstitious, corrupt and unpopular and contrasts it with a Protestant movement which was reformed, biblical, popular and progressive. The still pervasive conclusion is that the printing press was the foundation of Protestantism, because Protestantism was the religion of the book.

This network of assumptions is deeply misleading. There were of course points at which the nexus between print and Protestantism was particularly influential, such as in the German states in the 1520s, or with Foxe's own magisterial work, the *Acts and Monuments*, in Elizabethan England.[3] The overall picture, however, is very different. For the first fifty years of its existence in England, the printing press served to uphold the pre-Reformation church, and as the Reformation unfolded, the Catholic use of print would prove just as versatile and influential as that of its Protestant counterparts. Loud Protestant claims about their privileged relationship with the press were made precisely because those claims were so vigorously contested by Catholics; in repeating those claims, historians have paid attention to only one half of an argument. It is

---

[1]   John Foxe, *Acts and Monuments* (*TAMO*, 1570 edn, 9. 1524).
[2]   John N. King, '"The Light of Printing": William Tyndale, John Foxe, John Day, and Early Modern Print Culture', *Renaissance Quarterly* 54 (2001), 52–85; Elizabeth L. Eisenstein, *The Printing Press as an Agent of Change: Communications and Cultural Transformations in Early Modern Europe* (Cambridge, 1980), pp. 303–04, 310, 703–04.
[3]   Andrew Pettegree, *Reformation and the Culture of Persuasion* (Cambridge, 2005), pp. 7–8; Thomas Freeman and Elizabeth E. Evenden, *Religion and the Book in Early Modern England: The Making of John Foxe's 'Book of Martyrs'* (Cambridge, 2011).

true that Protestantism tended to make proportionately more use of the printing press, but only because it relied chiefly on the printed word as a means of communication. Catholicism could make equally effective use of sacred images, devotional objects, and the ritual, music and drama of the liturgy itself. A failure to appreciate this breadth of religious media has sometimes led to criticism of Catholics for not making sufficient use of the printing press, but in fact the new technology was essential to Catholics and Protestants alike. It is also worth noting that both sides were aware of the limitations of print. Anxieties about the printing of bibles were felt on all sides, and even confirmed Protestants felt that the printed word was inferior to the spoken word. Manuscript remained the desired medium for many communications of importance, and manuscript production continued alongside printing throughout the sixteenth and seventeenth centuries.[4]

The printed book came to have an unusually dominant position within English Catholicism. From its arrival, it swiftly became a valuable instrument of religious transmission. The new technology involved no disjunction with the past, but fitted cleanly in with existing modes of religious expression. Many of the manuscript works important in late medieval libraries were given a new lease of life in print. Monasteries and colleges alike built up their print libraries. Sermons and devotional treatises appeared in print alongside the lives of saints, books of hours, primers and missals. The proliferation of print may have been slow to match the developments in Europe, but its contribution to religious life was nonetheless significant. By the time Protestant ideas began to infiltrate England from the 1520s onwards, print was the obvious medium to use to counter their effect. Luther and his followers met with immediate repudiation in print, including at the hands of the king himself.

Even as the campaign against Luther unfolded, Henry VIII found himself launching a more personal campaign of his own. The attempt to annul his first marriage expanded into his construction of the Royal Supremacy and the consequent reform of the church. Henry's religious policies and his propaganda were enforced through print. It is highly debatable whether official Henrician works should be classed as 'Catholic', yet many of them fashioned themselves as such, despite their antipapal stance. The term 'Catholic' itself remains problematic, since in its sense of 'universal' it was claimed alike by those whom history has subsequently labelled 'Catholic' and 'Protestant'. In addition, a confessionalised notion of Catholic identity was only forged as the sixteenth century unfolded, and in England in the 1530s that identity was still in flux. This essay takes the view that authors who considered themselves to be Catholic – in the sense of being opposed to the central ideas of Protestant reformers, and predominantly loyal to traditional religious belief and practice – should be understood as such, whilst emphasising the variety in religious outlook

[4]   Julia Crick and Alexandra Walsham, *The Uses of Script and Print, 1300–1700* (Cambridge, 2004), pp. 20, 24, 8 respectively; Arthur F. Marotti, 'Manuscript Transmission and the Catholic Martyrdom Account in Early Modern England', in *Print, Manuscript and Performance: The Changing Relations of the Media in Early Modern England*, ed. A.F. Marotti and Michael D. Bristol (Columbus, OH, 2000), pp. 172–99; *The Practice and Representation of Reading in England*, ed. James Raven, Helen Small and Naomi Tadmor (Cambridge, 1996), p. 7.

in the pre-Reformation church, and the fissures within Catholicism once the Reformation was underway.[5]

Henry's policies constructed an idiosyncratic form of Catholic identity based around the seven sacraments, the Latin Mass and other traditional elements, casting his attacks on the papacy and the monasteries as reform. The Henrician Reformation therefore left a legacy for English Catholicism of both reforming potential and political division. Under Edward VI, intellectual boundaries had more clarity but Catholic works had to be printed abroad and smuggled in, as in March 1551 when a 'barrel of Dr Smith's most false and detestable books from Paris' was discovered.[6] From 1553, in the reign of Mary I, Catholic print spearheaded the campaign to revive the old faith. The energetic research of the last three decades has overturned the former view of Mary's church as reactionary, moribund and unpopular, and revealed a restoration of Catholicism which built on the strengths of the past but which also used many reform ideas current at the time, making intelligent use of vernacular printed literature in its work of rebuilding. The considerable intellectual achievement of Mary's brief reign would do much to influence the work of Catholic exiles and recusants after 1558, for whom print would remain unusually important, despite Counter-Reformation trends elsewhere. Foxe's vision, in short, was largely wishful thinking. The printing press in England was not just the preserve of Protestantism; it was just as much the habitual channel for Tudor Catholicism.

The Arrival of Print

The peculiarly rich piety of the late fifteenth century found natural expression in print. Caxton's *Golden Legend*, which he translated, edited and printed, was his largest and also his most popular work. The first book to refer to Wynkyn de Worde by name as the printer was the *Speculum Vitae Christi* of 1494, and he also printed such seminal works as Walter Hilton's *Scala Perfectionis*, commissioned by Lady Margaret Beaufort, another edition of the *Golden Legend*, and *Lives of the Fathers*, which Caxton had translated before he died. This move to print was far from being a break with the past. Works which had previously circulated extensively in manuscript form were now published; indeed, of the earliest printed works, most had previously circulated as manuscripts. Mirk's *Festial* in its manuscript form was known in the Midlands, East Anglia and Wales, and Dublin, and was translated into both Welsh and an Anglo-Irish dialect. When Caxton produced two editions, Wynkyn de Worde nine editions and other printers eleven editions, they were merely continuing an established trend. The *Legenda Aurea* was hugely popular throughout Europe, as demonstrated by nearly one thousand surviving manuscripts: with the advent of

---

[5]   For discussions of terminology, see Ronnie Po-Chia Hsia, *The World of Catholic Renewal* (Cambridge, 1998), pp. 1–9; *The Counter-Reformation* (Oxford, 1999), ed. David M. Luebke, pp. 1–7; Peter Marshall, *Religious Identities in Henry VIII's England* (Aldershot, 2006), pp. 2–15, 169–97; Ethan Shagan, *Popular Politics and the English Reformation* (Cambridge, 2003), pp. 6–7.
[6]   J. Andreas Löwe, *Richard Smyth and the Language of Orthodoxy: Re-imagining Tudor Catholic Polemicism* (Leiden, 2003), p. 211.

printing, editions appeared in Latin and a range of European languages, including Caxton's English version. Early printed books were even crafted to resemble manuscripts as much as possible, with coloured initials or illumination often added by hand after printing.[7]

Printed books served to reinforce many different aspects of existing religious culture. Wynkyn de Worde established good links with monastic patrons and monastic authors alike, and the printing presses at the abbeys of St Albans, Tavistock, Canterbury and Abingdon were natural successors to the *scriptoria* of the Middle Ages.[8] Secular colleges also had libraries, and produced authors: Whittington College in London, founded 1424, had as its last master before dissolution Richard Smyth, first regius professor of divinity at Oxford and prolific Catholic author, who returned as master during the Marian restoration. Bishop Richard Foxe, who founded Corpus Christi College Oxford as an example of humanist learning, also gave books to his college at Bishop Auckland in 1499 and translated the Benedictine rule into English for the benefit of nuns in his diocese, printed by Pynson in 1517. Bishop John Alcock, who founded Jesus College Cambridge in 1496, endowed a chantry and school at Holy Trinity Hull which would in due course become Hull Grammar School; he also published sermons in both English and Latin and religious treatises in English. Bishop John Carpenter of Worcester reformed the ancient Kalendars gild in Bristol in 1464, providing a public library, which was to be open for public use, with the prior on hand to explain obscure points of Scripture; libraries on the same model were founded in Worcester and at the Guildhall in London. Lady Margaret Beaufort founded colleges, fostered the new cult of the Holy Name, and sponsored scholars; she also commissioned and translated works for publication. In these developments we see how print fitted neatly into existing patterns of religious activity.[9]

---

[7]   Lotte Hellinga, 'Prologue: The First Years of the Tudor Monarchy and the Printing Press', in *Tudor Books and Readers*, ed. John N. King (Cambridge, 2010), p. 21; Susan Powell, 'The *Festial*: The Priest and His Parish', in *The Parish in Late Medieval England*, ed. Clive Burgess and Eamon Duffy, Harlaxton Medieval Studies 14 (Donington, 2006), pp. 160–61; William G. Ryan, *The Golden Legend*, 2 vols (Princeton, NJ, 1993), 1.xiii; Martha W. Driver, *The Image in Print: Book Illustration in Late Medieval England and Its Sources* (London, 2004), pp. 5, 6.

[8]   James G. Clark, 'Print and Pre-Reformation Religion: The Benedictines and the Press, c.1470–c.1550', in *Uses of Script and Print*, ed. Crick and Walsham, pp. 71–90; Jeremy Catto, 'Franciscan Learning in England, 1450–1540', pp. 103–04, and James G. Clark, 'The Religious Orders in Pre-Reformation England', pp. 7, 20–21, both in *The Religious Orders in Pre-Reformation England*, ed. J.G. Clark (Woodbridge, 2002); David Knowles, *Religious Orders in England*, 3 vols (Cambridge, 1955), 2.15; For Syon, see Vincent Gillespie, 'Syon and the New Learning', in *Religious Orders*, ed. Clark, pp. 76–82, 93.

[9]   'Colleges: Whittington's College', in *A History of the County of London: Vol 1*, The Victoria History of the Counties of England (London, 1909), pp. 578–80; *The Register of John Morton, Archbishop of Canterbury*, ed. Christopher Harper-Bill (Woodbridge, 1987), p. 18; 'Richard Smith', *ODNB*; James Willoughby, 'The Provision of Books in the English Secular College', in *The Late Medieval English College and Its Context*, ed. Clive Burgess and Martin Heale (York, 2008), pp. 155, 160–61; Joan Greatrex, 'On Ministering to "Certayne Devoute and Religiouse Women": Bishop Fox and the Benedictine Nuns of Winchester Diocese on the Eve of the Dissolution', in *Women and the Church*, ed. William J. Sheils and Diana Wood, Studies in Church History 27 (Woodbridge, 1990), pp. 223–35; Caroline Barron, 'The Expansion of Education in Fifteenth-Century London', in *The Cloister and the World: Essays in Medieval History in Honour of Barbara Harvey*, ed. John Blair and Brian Golding (Oxford, 1996), pp. 236–37, 238–39; Nicholas Orme, 'The Guild of Kalendars, Bristol', *Transactions of the Bristol and Gloucestershire Archaeological Society* 96 (1978), 40–43; Hellinga, 'Prologue', pp. 20–21; *King's Mother*, pp. 180–87.

The use of print also facilitated and encouraged the dissemination of sermons.[10] Mirk's *Festial* provided the struggling priest with a ready-made homily for each Sunday and feast-day in the year; the author, conscious of 'myn owne symple understandynge', explained that he had written his work to help others in a similar situation, hampered by 'defaute of bokes and also by symplenes of connynge'.[11] Printed sermons underline the point that books published during the early modern era were designed not only to be read in the modern sense, but to be read *aloud*. In Margery Kempe's autobiography, from the early fifteenth century, she described the assortment of books she had heard read. The devotional habits of Cicely, duchess of York, or Lady Margaret Beaufort, show how fluid was the division between public and private reading. Popular reading, it is clear, was often a communal activity. Nearly two centuries after Margery Kempe, Lady Anne Clifford was reading two or three chapters of the Bible each day, but only if there was 'somebody to read it with me'.[12] This consideration, that books were meant to be read aloud, and often in company, suggests that the shift to printed culture was even less of a disjunction with the past.

If printing served to reinforce and enhance traditional patterns of piety, it also provided a medium for those who sought reform. Early ideas of reform, however, were given expression by humanist writers who had little thought of attacking the institutional church. Perhaps the most outspoken call for reform, John Colet's sermon to Convocation from 1512, was published in the Latin in which it had been delivered, indicating that its rhetoric was meant to admonish the higher clergy, not inflame popular anticlericalism.[13] Its publication twenty years afterwards in English would be a mark of the new and more aggressive currents stirred up by the king's 'Great Matter'. The work of Colet and other humanists, including John Fisher and Richard Whitford, aspired to greater interior piety and moral regeneration without rejecting the devotional practice and theological consensus of the time. Popular works such as Alexander Barclay's translation of *The Ship of Fools* fitted into an existing satirical tradition which attacked corruption, but not the church.[14] The arrival of print was not a challenge to the religious understanding of the past, but a new piece in a mosaic of religious media. In a culture where oral transmission remained as important as the written word, a mutually reinforcing semiotic system of images and texts had evolved in which the printed book found an immediate home.

It was a late medieval commonplace that Gregory the Great had defended

[10]   Lucy Wooding, 'From Tudor Humanism to Reformation Preaching', in *The Oxford Handbook of the Early Modern Sermon*, ed. Hugh Adlington, Peter McCullough and Emma Rhatigan (Oxford, 2011), pp. 397–420.
[11]   John Mirk, *The festyvall* (1508, STC 17971), fol. iir.
[12]   *The Book of Margery Kempe*, ed. Sanford B. Meech and Hope E. Allen EETS OS 212 (Oxford, 1940), p. 39; Andrew Taylor, 'Into his Secret Chamber: Reading and Privacy in Late Medieval England', in *Practice and Representation of Reading*, ed. Raven et al., pp. 44–61; *The Diaries of Lady Anne Clifford*, ed. David J.H. Clifford (Stroud, 2009), pp. 52–57. I am grateful to Ian Green for this last reference.
[13]   *Oratio habita a D. Ioanne Colet Decano Sancti Pauli ad Clerum in Convocatione Anno M.D.xi* (1512, STC 5545). See Wooding, 'From Tudor Humanism to Reformation Preaching', pp. 397–98.
[14]   Robert C. Evans, 'Forgotten Fools: Alexander Barclay's *Ship of Fools*', in *Fools and Folly*, ed. Clifford Davidson (Kalamazoo, MI, 1996), pp. 53–54; G.R. Owst, *Literature and Pulpit in Medieval England* (Oxford, 1933), p. 232.

images as books for the illiterate laity, but the significance of this is often over-looked. The point was that images were 'essentially textual in the way that they function': they conveyed not just form, but content, as a book might.[15] Books were understood to convey meaning in similar ways, with heavy emphasis on typological forms. John Fisher's Good Friday sermon, published 1526, under-lined this, developing an extended metaphor of the Crucifix as a book in which the believer could read the word of God. Fisher described the two wooden pieces of the cross as making the two boards of the book, Christ's limbs as the pages, his wounds the letters. Just as in the modern mind, the connection between reading and understanding is assumed, so Fisher took for granted that the act of seeing involved the comprehension of the religious message. There was no disjunction between the visual and the verbal. The image, the written and the spoken word, all worked together to transmit meaning, and the arrival of print did nothing to damage this system of understanding.[16] In other words, it was a useful addition to the tools of the past, but not a replacement.

The Onset of Reformation

In the 1520s, two developments irrevocably changed the place of print in English culture. The first was the arrival of the work of Martin Luther. It is a singular fact that Henry VIII responded to Luther's ideas by producing a book, dem-onstrating the position which print now occupied in English society. *Assertio Septem Sacramentorum* was dedicated to Pope Leo X, and its completion was marked by a Mass at St Paul's, where John Fisher preached against heresy and Luther's books were publicly burned, the start of an energetic scholarly cam-paign against Luther.[17] The second development came in 1527 when Henry VIII reached the decision to end his marriage to Catherine of Aragon, claiming it had not been valid, and justifying his stance by an appeal to Scripture. The debate which ensued gave rise to a slew of printed treatises, sermons, official statements and propaganda works. By the 1530s the use of print in England had been radicalised, polemicised and politicised. It was the beginning of a new era for the printed word, and one in which its radical potential would become more apparent.

---

[15] Mary Carruthers, *The Book of Memory: A Study of Memory in Medieval Culture* (Cambridge, 2008), pp. 275–76.

[16] Richard Rex, *The Theology of John Fisher* (Cambridge, 1991), pp. 46–48. This sermon was published as *A Sermon verie fruitfull, godly, and learned* (1526); see *The English Works of John Fisher*, ed. John E.B. Mayor, EETS ES 27 (Oxford, 1876), pp. 388–428. For discussion of semi-otic systems and the relationship between material and literary culture, see Sandra Hindman, ed., *Printing the Written Word: The Social History of Books c.1450–1520* (Ithaca, NY, 1991); Ellen M. Ross, *The Grief of God: Images of the Suffering Jesus in Late Medieval England* (Oxford, 1997); Miriam Gill, 'Preaching and Image: Sermons and Wall Paintings in Later Medieval England', in *Preacher, Sermon and Audience in the Middle Ages*, ed. Carolyn Muessig (Leiden, 2002); eadem, 'Reading Images: Church Murals and Collaboration between Media in Medieval England', in *Collaboration in the Arts from the Middle Ages to the Present*, ed. Silvia Bigliazzi and Sharon Wood (Aldershot, 2006).

[17] Lucy Wooding, *Henry VIII* (London, 2009), pp. 108–09; Richard Rex, 'The English Campaign Against Luther in the 1520s', *TRHS*, 5th ser., 39 (1989), 85–106.

It is probable that the success of the king's book against Luther helped persuade him that his assertions about his marriage could also be effectively asserted in print. Henry had already made humanist scholarship an essential part of his self-fashioning, and books as gifts, propaganda and display were central to courtly life.[18] *Assertio Septem Sacramentorum* was a collaborative work, and Henry applied the same technique to the campaign for the divorce. Initially he used manuscript works, such as the *Collectanea satis copiosa* of 1530–31, but slow progress towards resolution of the king's problems meant that in 1531 the decision was made to advance the case in print. Berthelet published *Censurae academiarum*, and an English version, *Determinations of the . . . Universities*, followed in the autumn.[19] Henry had asked the universities of Europe to decide on whether the book of Leviticus did indeed render his marriage to his brother's widow invalid. Seven universities had ruled in his favour, and their verdicts were published alongside a lengthy treatise presenting the king's case. *A Glasse of the Truth* (1532, STC 11918), published shortly afterwards, deployed the same case in more popular form, as a debate between a theologian and a canon lawyer. The targeting of both educated and popular readers, in both Latin and the vernacular, was a carefully considered strategy which set an important precedent. From henceforth, all important religious policies would be both issued and defended in different types of printed book according to the intended audience.

England's Reformation was given a unique twist by the ideological and political complications of Henry VIII's reign. There can be no easy categorisation of Henry's religious policies, but the king regarded himself as a Catholic, and many publications reflected this. Some were perhaps persuaded by the king's claims to represent a reformed version of the faith; others shaped their rhetoric to make it seem that they supported the king's views, a polemical strategy designed to heighten their chances of defending traditional doctrine in an unstable political climate.[20] Works such as Stephen Gardiner's *De Vera Obedientia* in defence of the Supremacy might thus be counted as Catholic, although it was a curious kind of Catholicism. Equally, although the first comprehensive statement of official religious doctrine in 1537, *The Institution of the Christian Man* (or 'Bishops' Book'), might be considered by some too reformed to count as Catholic, it still defended the seven sacraments and the bodily presence of Christ in the Eucharist, whilst arguing that justification through faith did not negate the need for good works. Its replacement in 1543, *A Necessary Doctrine and Erudition for any Christian Man*, was more evidently Catholic in its doctrinal formulations, although dispensing with purgatory.

These official Henrician publications are important for two reasons. They demonstrate the unstable nature of Catholic identity at this time, partly formed

---

[18] Wooding, *Henry VIII*, pp. 76–80; James P. Carley, *The Libraries of Henry VIII* (London, 2000) and *The Books of Henry VIII and His Wives* (London, 2004); Simon Thurley, 'Greenwich Palace', in *Henry VIII: A European Court in England*, ed. David Starkey (London, 1991), pp. 22–23.

[19] *The Divorce Tracts of Henry VIII*, ed. Edward Surtz and Virginia Murphy (Angers, 1988).

[20] George W. Bernard, *The King's Reformation: Henry VIII and the Remaking of the English Church* (New Haven, CT and London, 2005), pp. 228–43, 475–505; Lucy Wooding, *Rethinking Catholicism in Reformation England* (Oxford, 2000), pp. 49–113; Lowe, *Richard Smyth and the Language of Orthodoxy*; Marshall, *Religious Identities in Henry VIII's England*, pp. 2–15, 169–97.

by the ideas of the humanists which Henry liked to endorse, but also shaped
by the emphasis on vernacular Scripture and the reform of superstition which
were key parts of his justification for the Royal Supremacy. Marsilius of Padua's
Defence of Peace, published for propaganda purposes in 1535, argued that 'The
despysinge and settynge at nought of godes word: is the cause of all the present
euylles in the worlde.'[21] With this attitude underpinning every ideological
expression of the Henrician regime, it was necessary for Catholics to adapt,
and thus works which defended key points of Catholic doctrine during Henry's
reign had at the same time to deny the pope, uphold biblical authority and
deplore superstition. The second reason why these Henrician publications are
important is that they demonstrate the importance of print in shaping, explaining and defending religious policy. Henry's reforms guaranteed that even if
Catholicism did return to England in something closer to its pre-Reformation
type, it was bound to return in a more literate, vernacular, polemical and self-
conscious form than before.

Henry's emphasis on vernacular Scripture, which he viewed as the divine
authority which had dispensed him from his first marriage, was given official formulation with the Great Bible of 1539. Henry's intentions were far from
Protestant here; the restrictions on Bible reading imposed in 1543 made this clear.
An English Bible could be many things to many men, however. To Henry it represented divine sanction of the Royal Supremacy; to those evangelical reformers
who would in due course become Protestants it offered a priceless opportunity
to spread the Word of God to the people. It is not always appreciated that to
many Catholics it also offered the opportunity to evangelise. Many Henrician
Catholics became emphatic and sincere supporters of vernacular Scripture. This
reflected the views of many European Catholics at this point: one reason why
the Council of Trent never ruled on the issue of vernacular Scripture, unable to
reconcile strongly opposing views at the Council.[22]

In England the genuine commitment of Catholics to vernacular Scripture
explains why the emphasis on the English Bible in Henrician works was sustained by Catholics even after Henry's death. The *Paraphrases on the Gospels* by
Erasmus were translated in Henry's last years by a group of people, including Princess Mary, the future Mary I, who translated the paraphrase on John.
This book of paraphrases, a guide to interpreting the gospels, was placed in
every parish church by the Edwardian regime. The Catholic authors who
praised Mary's evangelical credentials had some basis for their panegyric. In
the Lambeth Synod of 1555–56, arrangements were made for the translation
of the New Testament into English by the Catholic clergy. Mary's death meant
that these plans never came to fruition, but the publication of the Rheims New
Testament in 1582 and the Douay Bible of 1609–10 was a fulfilment of that vision.
Gregory Martin, who was chiefly responsible for the Rheims translation, was one

---

[21] Marsilius of Padua, *The defence of peace* (1535, *STC* 17817), fol. 2ᵛ; Shelley Lockwood,
'Marsilius of Padua and the Case for the Royal Ecclesiastical Supremacy', *TRHS*, 6th ser., 1
(1991), 89–119.
[22] Dominique Julia, 'Reading and the Counter-Reformation', in *A History of Reading in the West*,
ed. Guglielmo Cavallo and Roger Chartier, trans. Lydia G. Cochrane (Oxford, 1999), pp. 239–40;
Hubert Jedin, *A History of the Council of Trent*, 2 vols (St Louis, MO and London, 1961), 2.70–92.

of the founding scholars of St John's College Oxford, established during Mary's reign for the defence of Catholicism. English Catholic attachment to vernacular Scripture would endure throughout the sixteenth century and beyond.[23]

Henry's policies were supported by some Catholics, with varying degrees of reluctance or cautious enthusiasm; they were fiercely opposed by others. This opposition was not easily expressed in print, unless published abroad, like Reginald Pole's *De Unitate* (published in Rome in 1536) over which he claimed to have wept as he wrote, lamenting the deaths of More and Fisher. More's own works written in the Tower would not be published until Mary's reign. It was possible, however, to print works which lambasted Protestant ideas, and defended Catholic doctrine, as long as this was done within the boundaries of Henry's idiosyncratic notions of orthodoxy. Richard Smyth, Stephen Gardiner and Cuthbert Tunstall all published works in the 1530s and 1540s which vigorously defended Catholic sacramental and soteriological doctrine even whilst upholding the Supremacy. Gardiner's work in particular, in both this reign and that of Edward VI, when he published *An explication and assertion of the true Catholique fayth* (1551, STC 11592), came to define the Catholic viewpoint. Cranmer's last words to the assembled crowd in the University Church in Oxford, before he was carried away to the stake, were 'as for the sacrament, I believe as I have taught in my book against the Bishop of Winchester'.[24]

In terms of popular devotion, the Catholic works of Henry's reign showed far more continuity with the past than enthusiasm for a reformed future. Sermon collections such as Mirk's *Festial* went on being used, as is clear from the marginalia in some copies, and other copies with references to pope and purgatory scored through. Richard Whitford's career arguably peaked in the 1530s, with multiple editions of *A Werke for Housholders*. Whitford, a Birgittine monk, had published a translation of the Augustinian rule in 1526; his popularity as an author seemed undiminished by the dissolution. His *Dyuers holy instrucyons and teachynges very necessarye for the helth of mannes soule*, published in 1541, was briskly described as 'set forth by a late brother of Syon', and his (attributed) translation of Thomas a Kempis's *Imitatio Christi* was an influential version of this important late medieval work (Figure 16.1), which would be reissued during the reign of Mary I. Primers showed signs of reform, but only gradually moved away from traditional forms.[25] By the middle of the century, English Catholic

[23] Aysha Pollnitz, 'Religion and Translation at the Court of Henry VIII: Princess Mary, Katherine Parr and the *Paraphrases* of Erasmus', in *Mary Tudor: Old and New Perspectives*, ed. Susan Doran and Thomas Freeman (Basingstoke, 2011), pp. 123–36. On Catholic evangelism, see Wooding, *Rethinking Catholicism*, pp. 117–20. On Marian plans for an English Bible, see Thomas F. Mayer, *Reginald Pole: Prince and Prophet* (Cambridge, 2000), p. 242. For Gregory Martin, see *ODNB*.
[24] Mayer, *Reginald Pole*, p. 26; Diarmaid MacCulloch, *Thomas Cranmer: A Life* (New Haven, CT and London, 1996), p. 603. See Stephen Gardiner, *A Detection of the Devils Sophistrie* (1546, STC 11591) and *A declaration of such true articles as George Ioye hath gone about to confute as false* (1546, STC 11588); Richard Smyth, *A defence of the sacrifice of the masse* (1546, STC 22821), *The assertion and defence of the sacramente of the aulter* (1546, STC 22815), *A brief treatyse* (1547, STC 22818); Cuthbert Tunstall, *A sermon.. made upon Palme sondaye* (1539, STC 24322).
[25] Susan Powell, *John Mirk's Festial*, 2 vols, EETS 334 and 335 (Oxford, 2009–2011), 1.lvii–lviii; Jan T. Rhodes, 'Syon Abbey and its Religious Publications in the Sixteenth Century', *Journal of Ecclesiastical History* 44 (1993), 11–25; Eamon Duffy, *Stripping of the Altars*, pp. 444–47.

Figure 16.1 Title page. Richard Whitford, (attributed), *A boke newly translated out of Latyn in to Englisshe, called The folowing of Christe with the Golden epistel of saynt Barnard* (London: R. Redman, 1535?; *STC* 23964.7).

print set out a variety of political and theological opinion, with an underlying conservatism in the realm of popular devotion, reflecting the conflicted, partial and politicised nature of the English Reformation.

The Reign of Mary I

The reign of Mary I was short, but influential. Once remembered as an era of religious persecution, it is now seen in a more positive light as an era of rapid and intelligent religious restoration. Even the wisdom of the executions for heresy of nearly 300 Protestants has recently been defended, and it is clear that it was only under the circumstances of Elizabeth I's reign that the heretics of Mary's reign turned into the glorious martyrs – and propaganda coup – of Foxe's *Acts and Monuments*. With regard to parish provision, religious reconstruction and moral reform, Mary's religious policies were much more vigorous, focused and balanced than once was thought, and it is clear that the printing press was a key element in the campaign for Catholic renewal.[26]

---

[26] For recent work on the Marian Restoration, see Doran and Freeman, *Mary Tudor: Old Perspectives and New*; Eamon Duffy, *Fires of Faith: Catholic England under Mary Tudor* (New

Once again, it needs to be remembered that Catholicism conveyed its message through a broader range of media than its Protestant equivalent. Much of the work of restoration involved restoring the imagery within the parish churches, the 'laymen's books' which could be read even by the illiterate. The Marian regime required the restoration of the rood screen, with its image of the Crucifixion, in every parish church. In addition, each parish was required to restore an altar, holy-water stoup, altar vessels, altar cloths, processional crucifix, censer and incense boat, sacring bell, pyx, veil, banners, handbells, holy-water vessel, paschal candlestick and chrismatory. This demanded a great deal of effort and expenditure, but evidence suggests that much of this refurbishment was achieved relatively swiftly, with the hope of reaching those whom print could not touch.[27] As Cardinal Pole said in his sermon to the citizens of London, the reading of Scripture:

> bryngeth a great knowledge, yf yt be well understode. But this I dare saye, where-unto Scrypture alsoe doeth agree, that the observatyon of ceremonyes, for obedyence sake, wyll gyve more light than all the readynge of Scrypture can doe, yf the reader have never so good a wytt to understand what he readythe.[28]

From a Catholic perspective, however reformed, printed matter was only one among several channels through which religious inspiration might flow. The revival of church music, using the talents of Tallis, Sheppard, Mundy and others, is one important though often neglected example. Even within the category of print, the scope of Catholic publications was wider than their Protestant equivalent, since it included missals and breviaries on which to base the liturgy, as well as psalters, Books of Hours and other publications unique to Catholicism, in addition to the primers, collections of sermons, devotional treatises and works of polemic with which Protestant authors were also well acquainted. The rate of production of Marian primers in particular 'swamps that of any earlier period'; at least thirty-nine editions were published, compared with seventeen for Edward VI's reign.[29]

Marian Catholicism in part drew on pre-Reformation print for inspiration.

Haven, CT and London, 2009); Judith M. Richards, *Mary Tudor* (London, 2008); *The Church of Mary Tudor*, ed. Eamonn Duffy and David Loades (Aldershot, 2006); Wooding, *Rethinking Catholicism*, pp. 114–80; Jennifer Loach, 'Mary Tudor and the Recatholicization of England', *History Today* (Nov. 1994), 16–22; Christopher Haigh, *English Reformations: Religion, Politics and Society under the Tudors* (Oxford, 1993), 203–18; *Stripping of the Altars*, pp. 524–64; Elizabeth Russell, 'Mary Tudor and Mr Jorkins', *Bulletin of the Institute of Historical Research* 63 (1990), 263–76; Stephen Thompson, 'The Pastoral Work of the English and Welsh Bishops, 1500–1558' (unpublished DPhil thesis, Oxford, 1984). For the debate on Mary's use of the printing press, see Jennifer Loach, 'The Marian Establishment and the Printing Press', *EHR* 101 (1986), 138–51; compare with her earlier 'Pamphlets and Politics 1553–8', *Bulletin of the Institute of Historical Research* 48 (1975), 31–45; see also William Wizeman, SJ, *The Theology and Spirituality of Mary Tudor's Church* (Aldershot, 2006), pp. 47–48.

[27] Duffy, *Stripping of the Altars*, pp. 546–64; see also *Archdeacon Harpsfield's Visitation 1557, together with Visitations of 1556 and 1558*, ed. Leonard E. Whatmore, Catholic Record Society 45–56 (London, 1950–51), pp. xlv–xlvi.

[28] 'Cardinal Pole's Speech to the Citizens of London', in John Strype, *Ecclesiastical Memorials*, 3 vols (London, 1733), 3: part ii, 503.

[29] Wizeman, *Theology and Spirituality*, p. 21. On primers, see *Stripping of the Altars*, p. 526.

The preface to the reprint of Thomas à Kempis's *Imitation of Christ* in 1556 noted the 'many treatyse whych have ben put out both in latyn and Englyshe, in this perylous worlde to seduce the symple people', but also observed that:

> there hath bene also in tyme past before made by dyvers lerned and vertuous men, many good treatyse whyche yf men woulde have ben so diligent to loke upon, as they were curious to loke on the other, they shuld not have fallen so sone from the true knowledge of Chrystes doctryne...[30]

This was written by the Observant Franciscan William Peto, an outspoken critic of Henry VIII and former exile. He returned to the restored Franciscan community at Greenwich, a living link with the pre-Reformation church. William Peryn, a Dominican in exile since 1534, returned to become prior of the new Dominican community at St Bartholomew's in Smithfield; he published the 1557 *Spirituall exercyses* which drew on the example of the Society of Jesus. The Benedictine monk John Feckenham published a book of two homilies, and his funeral sermon for Queen Joanna of Castile.[31] In 1556 he became abbot of the restored Benedictine community at Westminster Abbey, which Mary intended as the *exemplum* for the restoration of monasticism in England.

The Marian restoration was not merely a revival of past glories, however; it had a strong sense of its contemporary mission. Leonard Pollard wrote in the dedication to his *Fyve Homilies* of 1556:

> it is not unknowen... the number of bookes and sermons that were made to deface the churche, and the number and the diligentnes of them that wold have destroyed the churche, the which diligence of them or rather continuall ragynge yf it shulde not be matched or with like diligence of our parte overcome and outmatched, it shulde be much to the reproche of us all.[32]

Pollard, a prebendary of Worcester cathedral, wrote that he offered his book 'towardes the buylding ageyne of his blessed Temple (the Church, I meane) defaced and almost destroyde by heretickes'. Richard Smyth, returned from exile and reinstated at Oxford, explained that his *Bouclier of the Catholike fayth*, published 1554, was meant to compete with Protestant authors on their own ground,

> not to enstruct the learned in Divinitie, whiche nede not much my teachyng, but to teach the unlearned, to stay and establish the waveryng, to assure and certify the doubtfull of the trouth, to bryng them agayne unto the trouth of the catholike churche, which were disceaved through ignoraunce...

Marian authors were prepared to deploy both the wisdom of the past and the rhetorical techniques of their own time to achieve their ends.[33]

[30] *The folowinge of Chryste* (1556, STC 23966), Sig. Aii[v].
[31] William Peryn, *Spirituall exercyses and goostly meditacions* (1557, STC 19784); John Feckenham, *Two homilies upon the first, second and third articles of the Crede* (1555, STC 10745); *A notable sermon* (1555, STC 10744).
[32] Leonard Pollard, *Fyve Homilies* (1556, STC 20091), Sig. A ii[r-v].
[33] Richard Smyth, *A Bouclier of the Catholike fayth* (1554, STC 22816), Sig. €vii[r].

In consequence, the publications of Mary's reign ranged widely. Patristic works were represented by a translation of the work of St Vincent of Lerins, *The waie home to Christ* (1554, STC 24754), and *Twelve sermons of Saynte Augustine* (mistakenly attributed) which were published in 1553 and again in an augmented version in 1557. John Angel's work of 1555, *The agrement of the holye Fathers, and Doctours of the churche* (STC 634) used patristic testimony to defend the chief disputed features of the Catholic faith. More modern testimony, which would prove of great importance for English Catholic identity, came from the editions of the works of John Fisher and Thomas More. *The workes of Sir T. More… wrytten by him in the Englysh tonge* (1557) was a huge work, and one which did much to consolidate the emerging cult of More as martyr. Two editions were published of Fisher's 1521 sermon against Luther, as well as his seven sermons on the penitential psalms.[34]

Sermons were particularly strongly represented in Marian print, filling the gaps left in parish provision by the deprivation of clergy who had married during Edward's reign, or were otherwise obdurate Protestants. As well as those already mentioned, there was a large volume of sermons by Roger Edgeworth, which he described in the preface as the fruit of over forty years as a preacher during 'the mooste troubleous time, and moste cumbarde with errours and heresies, chaunge of mindes and scismes that euer was in this realme for so longe time together'. Bonner's *Profitable and necessarye doctryne* (1555, STC 3283.3/5) was accompanied by a book of homilies. Thomas Watson's book, *Holsome and Catholyke doctryne concerninge the seven sacramentes* (1558, STC 25114), was probably a response to the call for homilies made by the legatine synod of Cardinal Pole in 1556. The publication of sermons highlights the fact that print was still closely involved with aural religious culture; Roger Edgeworth had gone back to a lifetime's store of sermon notes: he recalled how distrust of his memory had caused him 'to pen my sermons much like as I entended to utter them to the audience: others I scribled up not so perfitlie, yet sufficientlie for me to perceive my matter and my processe. And of these two sortes I have kept (as grace was) a greate multitude, whiche nowe helpeth me in this my enterprise of imprintinge a boke of my saide exhortations.'[35] Print could still be subservient to other more direct forms of religious communication, and, particularly in the case of sermons, the likelihood is that the printed word was intended to be read aloud.

Print was the primary medium, however, for religious polemic, which the Marian presses also produced. The anonymous tract *A plaine and godlye treatise, concernynge the Masse* employed some strong populist argument only matched by the lively and outspoken work of Miles Huggarde, who published six works between 1554 and 1557. In particular, his work *The displaying of the protestantes* gave a vivid account of England's recent past. He described how the Protestants,

---

[34] *Twelve sermons of Saynte Augustine* (1553, STC 923; second edition, *Certaine sermons*, 1557, STC 923.5); *The workes of Sir Thomas More Knyght, sometyme Lorde Chauncellour of England, wrytten by him in the Englysh tonge*, ed. William Rastell (1557, STC 18076); John Fisher, *A sermon very notable, fruicteful, and Godlie, made at Paules Crosse in London. Anno domini 1521* (1554, STC 10896; second edition 1556, STC 10897) and *This Treatyse concernynge the fruytfull saynges of Davyd the kynge and prophete in the seven penytencyall psalms* (1555, STC 10908).
[35] Roger Edgeworth, *Sermons very fruitfull, godly and learned* (1557, STC 7482), Sig.✠ii^v; Sig .✠iii^r.

'perceiuing the cheif magistrates prone to sondrie alteracions & nouelties, beganne by litle and litle also to corrupt the consciences of the vulgare people, infecting the same with the poyson of heretical doctrin'. Huggarde described how this rose to a climax:

> then ruled they the rooste, then began they to swarme in routes, then clustered they like humble bees to deuoure the honye combes from the hiues of the poore bees, then like common souldiors after the battell began they to fall to spoyle. . . And in this sorte with heresie and spoile feding the common peoples simplicitee with a counterfait zeale, they murdred mens consciences, & distroied the realme and the common welth thereof.[36]

Huggarde's work was earthy, eloquent, populist, some of it written in doggerel verse. He was undoubtedly a propaganda asset, and Bonner made the most of him. More educated polemic came from Richard Smith, returned from exile, whilst John Churchson's *Brefe treatyse declaryng what and where the churche is* (1556, STC 5219) and John Standish's *The triall of the supremacy wherein is set fourth the unitie of christes church* (1556, STC 23211) both dealt with the issue of papal supremacy. Relatively little attention was paid to the papacy, however, by a church which had spent twenty years apart from Rome, and was loathe to rekindle anti-papal feeling.[37]

In general, the works of Mary's reign tended to avoid polemic in favour of works of instruction. Mary's policies used to be thought reactionary, but in reality the printed books of her reign were remarkably broad-minded and showed distinct signs of humanist influence and a clear intellectual debt to the reforms of Henry VIII's reign. The Wayland primer of 1555, which went into over ten editions during Mary's reign, had shed the promises of indulgences and miraculous legends of the pre-Reformation primers, and even included some Protestant prayers. Bishop Bonner's definitive work of Catholic doctrine, *A profitable and necessarye doctryne*, was based on the King's Book of 1543, even retaining such features as the reformed numbering of the Ten Commandments which Henry VIII had introduced. The *Homilies* which accompanied it also owed a substantial amount to the Edwardian Homilies of 1547, which Bonner had also helped to author.[38]

The inclusion of such material indicates the varied intellectual influences at work within Tudor Catholicism. Catholic identity had been inescapably broadened by Henry VIII's reign, and Marian authors deployed every possible text that could be of use in their work of rebuilding, from the works of Thomas More who had died a martyr resisting the Royal Supremacy to the works of Stephen Gardiner, Edmund Bonner and Cuthbert Tunstall who as bishops of Winchester,

---

[36] Miles Huggarde, *Displaying of the Protestantes* (1556, STC 13558), fol. 7[r-v]. See also Joseph W. Martin, 'Miles Hogarde: Artisan and Aspiring Author in Sixteenth-Century England', in Joseph W. Martin, *Religious Radicals in Tudor England* (London, 1989), pp. 83–105.

[37] See Wooding, *Rethinking Catholicism*, pp. 127–35, but also Wizeman, *Theology and Spirituality*, pp. 127–36.

[38] On avoiding polemic, see Wizeman, *Theology and Spirituality*, pp. 19, 34. On primers, see Duffy, *Stripping of the Altars*, pp. 538–43; Wizeman, *Theology and Spirituality*, pp. 19, 225–26. For Henrician and Edwardian influences, see Wooding, *Rethinking Catholicism*, pp. 117–37, 161–66.

London and Durham had helped to put the Supremacy in place. Paul Bush, bishop of Bristol since 1542, was deprived of his bishopric in 1554, having married during Edward's reign, but he still published *A brefe exhortation* (1556, STC 4184) which defended Christ's corporeal presence in the Eucharist relying entirely on Scripture. In Bonner's 1556 catechism for children, and Carranza's catechism intended for England, the catechetical approach of future Protestants was anticipated, just as the decree of the Lambeth Synod for the provision of seminaries anticipated the Council of Trent.[39] It was an eloquent and inventive campaign.

The more reformed features of Marian publications indicate the extent to which English Catholicism in the sixteenth century was also undergoing reformation. It is significant that the legatine synod convened at Lambeth in 1556 envisaged the future publication of an English New Testament. As the forces of Counter-Reformation abroad became increasingly hostile to religious use of the vernacular, English Catholics would hold out against the trend, and insist on their need for works in English. In 1567 Thomas Harding and Nicholas Sanders, both products of Marian Oxford, wrote a formal plea to Cardinal Morone. They asked for a special exemption from the ban on vernacular literature for the English Catholics, and requested an English translation of at least some of the Bible. Both writers went on to produce a series of important works in the vernacular defending the Catholic faith. This emphasis on printed vernacular works was a direct legacy of the Marian restoration.[40]

Mary's death in 1558 was in one sense a catastrophe for English Catholics. Yet many of the men who had sought to rebuild her church were able to make a new life in exile, joining the academic communities at Douai and Louvain. A formidable quantity of printed books resulted, starting with the response to the 'Challenge Sermon' given by John Jewel, bishop of Salisbury in November 1559. This challenged Catholics to prove their doctrine from Scripture and the works of the early church fathers. It elicited a vigorous response from Catholics well-versed in biblical exegesis and patristic scholarship. Henry Cole (deposed Dean of St Paul's), John Feckenham (former abbot of Westminster), John Rastell (fellow of New College Oxford), and Thomas Harding (formerly regius professor of Hebrew at Oxford, and fellow of New College) all responded swiftly, initiating an exchange of books which would last into the 1570s and beyond. Thomas Harding alone produced six books between 1564 and 1568. Jewel worked hard to caricature his opponents as reactionary, obfuscating, ultramontane Catholics who ascribed all to tradition and papal authority. In reality, they were of a generation of English Catholics who were as enthusiastic as their Protestant contemporaries about biblical authority and the example of the early church, locating their reformed scholarship within a view of Catholic tradition which emphasised consensus and universality. Their response to the taunts of the early Elizabethan church was forceful, intelligent and convincing, and clearly

---

[39] For Bush, see Wizeman, *Theology and Spirituality*, pp. 36, 46–47; Wooding, *Rethinking Catholicism*, pp. 123, 138–39, 155. On catechisms, see Wizeman, pp. 26–27 and Ian M. Green, *The Christian's ABC: Catechisms and Catechizing in England c.1530–1740* (Oxford, 1996). On seminaries, see *Stripping of the Altars*, p. 525.

[40] Wooding, *Rethinking Catholicism*, pp. 183–86.

had an impact; Foxe made alterations to his *Acts and Monuments* in response to their criticisms. The Elizabethan exiles were able to draw on nearly a century of Catholic printed books for their inspiration, demonstrating how reliant English Catholicism had become on the printed word. In the years ahead, deprived of holy places, priests and sacraments, Catholics would become more reliant on books than ever before. The entrenchment of the Reformation in England had brought about a new emphasis on the importance of print for Catholic and Protestant alike.[41]

Conclusion

The printed book was central to English Catholicism in the late fifteenth and sixteenth centuries. It helped to facilitate a variety of elements, from liturgy and devotion, to propaganda and polemic, preaching and instruction. It proved a valuable asset to the pre-Reformation church, amplifying and enhancing many different aspects of religious belief and practice, and, as the Reformation unfolded, it gave Catholicism a medium through which resistance, reform and revival could all be channelled. After 1558, it would spearhead the Catholic challenge to the emergent Church of England, and at the same time prove itself a capable surrogate for the clerical provision which English Catholics were largely denied.

Catholic print would also continue to exert influence over Protestant publications on several levels. Pre-Reformation works such as the *Imitation of Christ* took on a new lease of life in Protestant editions.[42] Richard Day's *A booke of Christian prayers, collected out of the auncient writers* was first published in 1578, and went through three more editions, the last one in 1608. It contained the popular medieval prayers called 'The Fifteen Oes of St Bridget', illustrated with medieval images such as the Fifteen Last Days and the Dance of Death. The work was modified to suit a Protestant audience, omitting saints, including anti-papal references, but its Catholic influences were unmistakeable. Contemporary Catholic print also made an impact, as Edmund Bunny's appropriation of the work of the Jesuit Robert Persons showed: his *First Booke of the Christian exercise* of 1582 was recast by Bunny in 1584 as the Protestant work, *A Booke of Christian exercise*. Even those books printed in refutation of Catholic works by Protestant authors could be twisted to a Catholic purpose, as readers focused on the passages quoted from Catholic works rather than the passages which refuted them. Bishop Parkhurst of Norwich worried that placing Jewel's *Replie unto M. Hardinges Answeare* (1565,

---

[41] Elizabeth Russell, 'Marian Oxford and the Counter-Reformation', in *The Church in Pre-Reformation Society*, ed. Caroline M. Barron and Christopher Harper-Bill (Woodbridge, 1985), pp. 212–27; Anne Dillon, *The Construction of Martyrdom in the English Catholic Community, 1535–1603* (Aldershot, 2005); Alexandra Walsham, '"Domme Preachers?" Post-Reformation English Catholicism and the Culture of Print', *Past and Present* 168 (2000), 72–123. On Foxe's response to Catholic criticism, see Evenden and Freeman, *Religion and the Book*, pp. 133, 137–38, 140, 147, 169.

[42] Ian M. Green, *Print and Protestantism* (Oxford, 2000), pp. 305–06, 322–25; David Crane, 'English Translations of the *Imitatio Christi* in the Sixteenth and Seventeenth Centuries', *Recusant History* 13 (1975–76), 79–100.

STC 14606) in every parish church (as Archbishop Parker had ordered in 1572) would only encourage Catholics to read the passages from Thomas Harding's work, and ignore the rest.[43]

Catholic print continued to exert these kinds of influence even as Protestantism became established in Elizabethan England. It sustained the recusant tradition through devotional treatises, the Rheims-Douay Bible, and the martyrologies which had become a dominant feature of the print landscape on both sides of the confessional divide. It challenged Protestant doctrine, policy and polemic at every turn. It also had a more subtle influence upon the shaping of Protestant print, requiring Protestant authors to emulate its tried and tested modes of religious transmission. The martyrologies of the sixteenth century were in many ways just the contemporary equivalent of the saints' lives of the pre-Reformation era. Foxe, in his preface to the 1563 edition of the *Acts and Monuments*, wrote 'I hear that there is also muttering by some who say that they are seized by long expection until this – our *Golden Legend* as they call it – is set forth.'[44] Even Foxe and his readers could dimly perceive that the crowning glories of Reformation print had only been achieved by standing on the shoulders of giants.

Further Reading

Crick, Julia and Alexandra Walsham, *The Uses of Script and Print, 1300–1700* (Cambridge, 2004).

Doran, Susan and Thomas Freeman, eds, *Mary Tudor: Old and New Perspectives* (Basingstoke, 2011).

Duffy, Eamon and David Loades, eds, *The Church of Mary Tudor* (Aldershot, 2006).

Julia, Dominique, 'Reading and the Counter-Reformation', in *A History of Reading in the West*, ed. Guglielmo Cavallo and Roger Chartier, trans. Lydia G. Cochrane (Oxford, 1999), pp. 239–40.

King, John N., ed., *Tudor Books and Readers* (Cambridge, 2010).

Loach, Jennifer, 'The Marian Establishment and the Printing Press', *English Historical Review* 100 (1986), 138–51.

Martin, Joseph W., 'Miles Hogarde: Artisan and Aspiring Author in Sixteenth-Century England', in Joseph W. Martin, *Religious Radicals in Tudor England* (London, 1989).

Russell, Elizabeth, 'Marian Oxford and the Counter-Reformation', in *The Church in Pre-Reformation Society*, ed. Caroline M. Barron and Christopher Harper-Bill (Woodbridge, 1985), pp. 212–27.

Walsham, Alexandra, '"Domme Preachers?" Post-Reformation English Catholicism and the Culture of Print', *Past and Present* 168 (2000), 72–123.

---

[43] On Day, see Helen C. White, *Tudor Books of Private Devotion* (Madison, WI, 1951), pp. 221–29; Eamon Duffy, *Marking the Hours: English People and their Prayers 1240–1570* (New Haven, CT and London, 2006), pp. 171–74. On Persons and Bunny, see Brad E. Gregory, '"The true and zealous service of God": Robert Persons, Edmund Bunny and the First *Booke of Christian exercise*', *Journal of Ecclesiastical History* 45 (1994), 238–68; Victor Houliston, 'Why Robert Persons Would Not Be Pacified: Edmund Bunny's Theft of the *Book of resolution*', in *The Reckoned Expense: Edmund Campion and the Early English Jesuits*, ed. Thomas M. McCoog (Woodbridge, 1996). On Catholic readings of Protestant works, see Alexandra M. Walsham, 'The Spider and the Bee: The Perils of Printing for Refutation in Tudor England', in *Tudor Books and Readers*, ed. King, pp. 163–90.
[44] Freeman and Evenden, *Religion and the Book*, p. 114.

Wizeman, William, S.J., *The Theology and Spirituality of Mary Tudor's Church* (Aldershot, 2006).

Wooding, Lucy, *Rethinking Catholicism in Reformation England* (Oxford, 2000).

_____, 'From Tudor Humanism to Reformation Preaching', in *The Oxford Handbook of the Early Modern Sermon*, ed. Hugh Adlington, Peter McCullough and Emma Rhatigan (Oxford, 2011), pp. 397–420.

Index of Manuscripts

Sammelbände are prefixed by #. See too the General Index.

Index of Printed Books

The material below is organised alphabetically according to country and then town. Authors, where cited, appear first, in alphabetical order of surname and Christian name, unless the author is generally known by his/her Christian name (often with place of origin); otherwise, titles appear first, normally in alphabetical order according to first significant word (contractions are silently expanded). Where more than one entry occurs for an author, the arrangement of their works is chronological. Successive editions of a work which are cited but not discussed in this volume are normally listed only briefly in the entry to the first cited edition. In accordance with *STC, USTC* and *GW* references, authors and/or titles and dates may differ from the forms used by individual contributors. Where insufficient information is recorded and/or the item has not been matched exactly, 'cf.' is used to indicate a near, but not perfect, match (see too the final section 'Unidentified')

England

Abingdon:
[Abingdon portiforium] (Abingdon Abbey: Johannes Scholarem, 1528; *STC* 15792)   196, 201

Burton-upon-Trent(?) (or London?)
Rentale totius redditus omnium terrarum et Tenementorum in burgo de Burton (no place: no printer, 1544)   196–97 and Fig. 10.2

Cambridge:
Barclay, Alexander, [The first eclogue] (Cambridge: John Siberch, 1523?; *STC* 1383); also *STC* 1384   244
Erasmus, Desiderius, [*Libellus*] *de conscribendis epistolis* (Cambridge: John Siberch, 1521; *STC* 10496)   211
Fisher, John, *Contio quam anglice habuit reuerendus pater Ioannes Roffensis Episcopus in celeberrimo nobilium conuentu Londinii, eo die, quo Martini Lutheri scripta publico apparatu in ignem coniecta sunt, uersa in Latinum per Richardum Pacaeum* (Cambridge: John Siberch, 1521; *STC* 10898)   160

Ipswich:
Luther, Martin, *A ryght notable sermon, made vponn the twenteth chapter of Johan*, trans. Richard Argentine (Ipswich: Antony Scoloker, 1548; *STC* 16992)   263 n.44
Ochino, Bernardino, *Sermons of the ryght famous and excellent clerke master B. Ochine*, trans. Richard Argentine (Ipswich: Anthony Scoloker, 1548; *STC* 18765)   263
Scoloker, Anthony, trans., *The ordenarye for all faythfull chrystians* (Ipswich: A. Scoloker, 1548; *STC* 5199.7)   64

France

Germany

Fossombrone:

Paulus de Middelburgo, *De recta Paschae celebratione* (Fossombrone: Octavianum Petrutium, 1513)   90

Milan:

Venetus, Paulus, *Expositio librorum naturalium Aristotelis* (Milan: Christophorus Valdarfer, 1476; *GW* 30374)   188 n.62

Padua:

Aristotle, *De anima* (Padua: Laurentius Canozius for Johannes Philippus Aurelianus et Fratres, 22 November 1472; *USTC* 997541)   213

Physica (Padua: Laurentius Canozius, 1472–75; *USTC* 997515)   213

Metaphysica (Padua: Laurentius Canozius for Johannes Philippus Aurelianus et Fratres, 30 January 1473; *USTC* 997527)   213

De caelo et mundo (Padua: Laurentius Canozius for Johannes Philippus Aurelianus et Fratres, 4 March 1473; *USTC* 997535)   213

Parva naturalia (Padua: Laurentius Canozius, 1473–74; *USTC* 997518)   213

De generatione et corruptione (Padua: Laurentius Canozius for Johannes Philippus Aurelianus et Fratres, 18 June 1474; *USTC* 997528)   213

Meteorologica (Padua: Laurentius Canozius for Johannes Philippus Aurelianus et Fratres, 24 June 1474; *USTC* 997526)   213

Pavia:

Alexander of Hales, *Summa* (Pavia: Franciscus Girardengus and Johannes Antonius Birreta, 1489; *GW* 872)   190

Rome:

Albertus de Eyb, *Margarita poetica* (Rome: Ulrich Han (Udalricus Gallus), 1475; *GW* 9530)   217

Caracciolo, Roberto, *Sermones quadragesimales de poenitentia* (Rome: Conradus Sweynheym and Arnoldus Pannartz, 1472; *GW* 6065)   212

Cicero, Marcus Tullius, *Orationes* (Rome: Conrad Sweynheym and Arnold Pannartz, 1471; *GW* 6761)   50

Chrysostom, Johannes, *Homiliae super Iohannem* (Rome: Georgius Lauer, 1470; *GW* M13300)   21, 51, 179–80

Flemming, Robert, *Lucubratiunculae Tiburtinae* (Rome: Printer of Flemming, 1477; *GW* 9990)   153, 229

Pole, Reginald, *Ad Henricum Octauum Britanniae regem, pro ecclesiasticae unitatis defensione, libri quatuor* (Rome: Antonio Blado, 1536; *USTC* 850087)   315

Venice:

Albertus de Padua, *Expositio evangeliorum* (Venice: Adam de Rottweil and Andreas Corvus, 1476; *GW* 784)   52

Angelus de Clavasio, *Summa angelica de casibus conscientiae* (Venice: Paganinus de Paganinis, 1499; *GW* 01945)   190

Andreae, Antonius, *Scriptum in artem veterem Aristotelis et in divisiones Boethii* (Venice: Otinus de Luna, 1496; *GW* 1672)   181 n.27, 188 n.62, 192

Aquinas, Thomas, *Catena aurea* (Venice: Bonetus Locatellus, for Octavianus Scotus, 1493; *GW* M46098)   223

Opus aureum sancti Thome de Aquino super quattuor Euangelia (Venice: Bonetus Locatellus at the cost of Octavianus Scotus, 1506; *USTC* 859387)   223

Jacobus Pentius, de Leuco, for Lazarus de Suardis, de Saviliano, 1496; *GW* M51346) 219

Vicenza:

Ptolemaeus, Claudius, *Cosmographia* (Vicenza: Hermannus Liechtenstein, 1475; *GW* M36388) 223

The Low Countries

Antwerp:

Agrippa, Henricus Cornelius, *Declamatio de nobilitate et precellentia foeminei sexus* (Antwerp, 1529) 257

'Arnold's Chronicle' (Antwerp: A van Berghen, 1503?; *STC* 782) 22

Bale, John, *A brefe chronycle concernynge the examinacyon and death of the martyr syr J. Oldcastell* (Antwerp: publisher unknown, 1544; *STC* 1276) 262 n.40

The image of both churches, after the reuelacion of saynt Johan the euangelist, 2 pts. (Antwerp: S. Mierdman?, 1545?; *STC* 1296.5) 262 n.40

The actes of Englysh votaryes, comprehendynge their vnchast practises and examples by all ages (Wesel [i.e. Antwerp]: S. Mierdman, 1546; *STC* 1270) 262 n.40

Illustrium maioris Britanniae scriptorium summarium (Wesel [i.e. Antwerp]: [D. van der Straten for] Ioannem Ouerton, 1548; *STC* 1295) 262 n.40

[Bible] *Biblia the bible, that is the holy scripture . . .* ([Coverdale's Bible], [Cologne?] [probably Antwerp]: [E. Cervicornus a. J. Soter?], 1535; *STC* 2063) 164 n.88, 284

The byble which is all the holy scripture ['Matthew's Bible'] (Antwerp: Mattheus Crom for Richard Grafton and Edward Whitchurch, 1537; *STC* 2066) 38, 164, 167, 202

Bullinger, Heinrich, *Two epystles one of Henry Bullynger another of Jhon Calvyn* (Antwerp: M. Crom?, 1544?; *STC* 4079.5) 261

Carranza de Miranda, Bartolomé, *Instruction y doctrina de como todo christiano deue oyr missa y assistir à la celebracion y santo sacrificio* (Antwerp: Christophe Plantin, 1555; *USTC* 440079) 321

Certeine prayers and godly meditacyons very nedefull for euery Christen (Malborow: J. Philoponon [i.e. Antwerp: H. Peetersen van Middelburch?, 1538; *STC* 20193) 284

Chronicles of England (Antwerp: Gerard Leeu, 1493; *STC* 9994) 49

Colet, John, [*The Aeditio*] (Antwerp: Christopher Ruremund for G. van der Haghen (London), 1527; *STC* 5542); also *STC* 5542.1–5550.5 170

A compendious olde treatyse, shewynge, howe we ought to haue ye scripture in Englysshe (Malborow: Hans Luft [i.e. Antwerp: J. Hoochstraten], 1530; *STC* 3021) 283

[*La premiere et la seconde partie des*] *dialogues francois pour les jeunes enfans* (Antwerp: Christophe Plantin, 1567) 64

Erasmus, Desiderius, *An exhortation to the diligent studye of scripture, made by Erasmus Roterodamus . . . An exposition in to the seventh chaptre of the first pistle to the Corinthians* [Martin Luther], both trans. William Roye? (Malborow: Hans Luft [i.e. Antwerp: J. Hoochstraten], 1529; *STC* 10493) 278

A shorte recapitulacion or abridgement of Erasmus Enchiridion. Drawne out by M. Couerdale (Antwerp: Adam Anonimus [i.e. S. Mierdman], 1545; *STC* 10488) 259 n.29

Fish, Simon, *A supplicacyon for the beggers* (Antwerp?: J. Grapheus?, ([1529?]; *STC* 10883) 131, 171, 278

The prophete Jonas, with an introduccion before a teachinge to vnderstonde him
(Antwerp: M. de Keyser, 1531?; *STC* 2788) 279

The souper of the Lorde ... wheryn incidently M. Moris agenst J. Fryth is confuted
(Nornburg: N. Twonson [i.e. Antwerp?], 5 April, 1533 [or London: N. Hill?,
1546?]; *STC* 24468) 279

The new testament as it was written, and caused to be written, by them that herde yt
[alt. George Joye] (Antwerp: widow of Christopher Ruremund, August 1534; *STC*
2825) 277, 280

The newe testament dylygently corrected and compared with the Greke by W. Tindale
(Antwerp: Maryne Emperowr, 1534; *STC* 2826); also *STC* 2827, 2832, 2834 280

Zwingli, Ulrich, The *rekening and declaracion of the faith and belief of Huldrik Zwingly*,
trans. George Joye (Zijryk [i.e. Antwerp: widow of Christopher Ruremund, March
1543; *STC* 26138) 286

Bruges:

Cordiale quattuor novissimorum, trans. Jean Miélot (Bruges: Colard Mansion? for
William Caxton, 1475–76; *GW* 7530) 15

Horae ad vsum Sarum (Bruges: William Caxton, *c*.1475; *GW* 13407) 65

Jacobus de Cessolis, [*The Game of Chess*] (Bruges: William Caxton and Colard
Mansion, 1474; *STC* 4920) 27, 65

[*The Game of Chess*] (Westminster: William Caxton, 1483; *STC* 4921) 29

Lefevre, Raoul, [*here begynneth the volume intituled and named*] *the recuyell of the historyes of Troye*, trans. William Caxton ([Bruges: William Caxton [and Colard
Mansion?], 1473–74]; *STC* 15375) 1, 14, 18, 27, 53, 65, 81, 98, 244

Deventer:

[Anwykyll, John], *Compendium totius grammatice* (Deventer: Richard Pafraet, 4 May
[1489]; *STC* 696.1) 237 n.42

Cicero, Marcus Tullius, *De officiis. Cato maior. Somnium Scipionis. Paradoxa* (Deventer:
Richard Pafraet, *c*.1480; *GW* 06946) 230–31 and n.18

Johannes de Turrecremata, *Quaestiones Euangeliorum de tempore et de sanctis* (Deventer:
Richard Pafraet, 1484; *GW* M48239) 219

Nicolaus de Byard, *Flos theologiae* (*Dictionarius pauperum*) (Deventer: Richard Pafraet;
1484; *GW* M48239) 219

Vergilius Maro, Publius, *Bucolicorum P. Virgilii Maronis*, comm. by Hermannus
Torrentinus (Deventer: Richard Pafraet, 1503; *USTC* 420086) 238 and n.52

Gouda:

Johannes Annius, *De futuris Christianorum triumphis in Saracenos* (Gouda: Gerard
Leeu, *c.* 1482; *GW* 2019) 154 and n.24

Louvain:

Adelard Bathonensis, *Quaestiones naturales* ([Louvain: Johannes de Westfalia,
1476–77]]; *GW* 218) 52 n.32

Alonso Díaz de Montalvo, *Repertorium quaestionum super Nicolaum de Tudeschis*
(Louvain: Johannes de Westfalia, 1486; *GW* 8307) 223

*pseudo-*Augustinus, *De virtute psalmorum* (Louvain: Johannes de Westfalia, not after
August 1479; *GW* 3032) 51 n.30, 153

Biblia: Novum Testamentum (Louvain: Johannes de Westfalia, 1476; *GW* M4567410) 218

Bracciolini, Poggio, *De infelicitate principum* ([Louvain: Johannes de Westfalia, *c*.1480;
GW M34608) 230–31 ns 18 and 19

Burlaeus, Gualtherus, *De vita et moribus philosophorum* (Louvain: Johannes de Westfalia, 1477–83; *GW* 5788) 154 and n.24

Erasmus, Desiderius, *Enchiridion militis christiani*; cf. *USTC* 403366 (Louvain: Thierry Martins) 184

Junior, Johannes, *Scala coeli* (Louvain: Johannes de Westfalia, 1485; *GW* 10947) 180

Juvenal, *Satyrae* (Louvain: Johannes de Westfalia, 1475; *GW* M15685) 24

Magninus de Maineriis, *Regimen sanitatis* (Louvain: Johannes de Westfalia, 1486; *GW* M19893) 222

Michael of Hungary, *Sermones praedicabiles* (Louvain: Johannes de Westfalia; cf. *GW* M23234, M23236, M23232 (1477), M23238 (1483), M23230, 23242, 23244 (1484)) 222

Perotti, Niccolò, *Rudimenta grammaticales* (Louvain: Hermannes de Nassau and Rodolphus Loeffs de Driel, 1485; *GW* M31164) 212

Prefatio in regulas grammaticales Nicolai perotti (Louvain: E. der Herstraten, 1486; *STC* 19767.7 227

More, Sir Thomas, [*Libellus vere aureus . . . de optimo reipublicae statu, deque nova insula*] *Utopia* (Louvain: Thierry Martens, 1516; *USTC* 400360) 229–30

Piccolomini, Aeneas Sylvius (Pope Pius II), *De duobus amantibus Euryalo et Lucretia* (Louvain: Conradus Braem, 1479; *GW* M33496) 230 and n.18

De Miseriis curialium ([Louvain: Johannes de Westfalia/de Paderborn, c.1480]; *GW* M33767) 228, 230–31 ns 18 and 19

Valla, Laurentius (Lorenzo), *Elegantiae linguae Latinae* (Louvain: Johann Veldener, 1475–76; *GW* M49274) 152, 200

Vergerius, Petrus Paulus (Pier Paolo Vergerio), *De ingenuis moribus . . .* ([Louvain]: Johannes de Westfalia, [1476–77]; *GW* M49630) 52 n.32, 230–31 and ns 18 and 22, 232 (Fig. 12.1), 233 n.24

Southern Netherlands:

[Breviarium ad usum Sarum] ([Southern Netherlands: Printer of the 'Breviarium Sarum', c.1475]; *STC* 15794) 46

Poland

Krakow:

Eck, Johannes, *Enchiridion locorum communium aduersus Lutheranos* (Krakow: Hieronim Wietor, 1525; *USTC* 240363) 203 n.142

Scotland

Donatus, Aelius, [*Ars minor*] ([Scotland?: Printer of the Aberdeen Donatus, c. 1507?]; *STC* 7018) 35

Dunbar, William, [*The tua mariit wemen and the wedo*] ([Scotland?: Printer of *The tua mariit wemen*, 1507?]; *STC* 7350) 35

Edinburgh:

[*Book of good counsel to the Scots king*] ([Edinburgh: Walter Chepman and Andrew Myllar, 1508?]; *STC* 3307) 35

Chartier, Alan, [*The porteous of noblenes translatit out of [Fr]anche in Scottis be Maistir*

Spain

Switzerland

Wales

General Index

The General Index is principally an index of names and places. Authors are cited but not the titles of their works.

Gower, John 4, 16 n.14, 28, 63, 78, 145
    n.40, 146, 148
Grafton, Richard xviii, 38–39, 41, 164,
    171 n.141, 172, 173, 267 n.54
Greenhalgh, James 182
Gregory the Great, Pope 180 n.22, 311
Grene, John 52, 188, 231–33
Grene, Simon see Foderby, Simon
Grey, Lady Jane xviii, 39
Greyfriars see Franciscans sub friars and
    friaries
Griffo (Gryphus), Pietro 71
Griffolini, Francesco 180
Grocyn, William 2, 165, 214
Gruytroede, Jacobus de 250
Guarino da Verona 231
guilds
    All Angels, Syon 6
    Corpus Christi, Coventry 137
    Corpus Christi, York 136
    Our Lady, Boston 137
    St Anne, Lincoln 143
    St Mary Rounceval, Westminster 136
    Trinity, Coventry 137
Guillaume le Talleur 69
Guldenschaff, Johann 231 n.20
Gunthorpe, John, Dean of Wells 51, 153
Gutenberg, Johann 86, 195
Guy, John 299
Gwynborne, Dr 202 n.140
Gybson, T. 41
Gyrdeler, John 286

Habsburg dynasty 281, 286
Hackett, Sir John 280–81
Hadrian VI, Pope 5
Hall, Edward 281
de Hamel, Christopher 79
Han, Ulrich 217
Hans van Ruremund see van Ruremund,
    Hans
Harding, Thomas 321, 323
Harman, Richard 277, 280–83
Harry the Minstrel 35
Hartwell, John 155
Hartwell, Thomas 155
Hartwell, William 155
Hastings, William, Lord 128
Haukyns, John 33
Havy, Nowell 82, 85
Hawarden, Humphrey 130

Hawes, Stephen 32, 41
Hawford, Abbot Philip 185
Hawkes, John 128
Hawkins, John 153
'Haywarde' (scribe) 20–21
Hellinga, Lotte 3, 45, 150–51, 155
Henricus de Herpf see Herp, Hendrik
    (Heinrich)
Henry III 61
Henry IV 293
Henry V 293, 296
Henry VII xviii, 18 n.24, 31, 48, 71, 97
    n.7, 99 n.15, 129, 143, 153, 158,
    159, 168, 171
Henry VIII xii, xviii, 8, 19, 25, 30, 38,
    40, 90, 131, 141, 145, 148, 160,
    164, 165, 171, 179, 230, 266, 281,
    286, 287, 294, 296, 308, 312, 313,
    318, 320
Henry, 2nd Baron Daubeney 192 n.83
Henry de Ferrers 204
Henryson, Robert 35
Herbert, Prior John 180
Herbort, Johannes 50
Herefordshire
    Eaton Bishop 154
    Hereford 154, 173 n.152
        Cathedral 181 n.25
        printing press 34
Herman van Beek (Hermannus
    Torrentinus) 238
Herodotus 213
Herolt, Iohannes 221
Herp, Hendrik (Heinrich) 21, 201, 217
Hertfordshire 28 n.8
    Hertford 20, 62
Hervet, Gentian 236
Heywood, John 295
Higden, Ranulphus (Ranulf, Ralph)
    29, 31, 129, 181 n.28
Hilton (Hylton), Walter 96, 144, 182,
    309
Hitton, Thomas 279, 283
'Hobbs of Crowland' 187 n.56
Hobs, Abbot Robert 187
Hobson, G.D. 78
ther Hoernen, Arnold 211
Holkot, Robert 54
Holland 4, 30, 69 see also Netherlands
Holland, Richard 35
Homer 213